ANDERSON'S
Law School Publications

Administrative Law Anthology
Thomas O. Sargentich

Administrative Law: Cases and Materials
Daniel J. Gifford

An Admiralty Law Anthology
Robert M. Jarvis

Alternative Dispute Resolution: Strategies for Law and Business
E. Wendy Trachte-Huber and Stephen K. Huber

The American Constitutional Order: History, Cases, and Philosophy
Douglas W. Kmiec and Stephen B. Presser

American Legal Systems: A Resource and Reference Guide
Toni M. Fine

Analytic Jurisprudence Anthology
Anthony D'Amato

An Antitrust Anthology
Andrew I. Gavil

Appellate Advocacy: Principles and Practice, *Third Edition*
Ursula Bentele and Eve Cary

Arbitration: Cases and Materials
Stephen K. Huber and E. Wendy Trachte-Huber

Basic Accounting Principles for Lawyers: With Present Value and Expected Value
C. Steven Bradford and Gary A. Ames

A Capital Punishment Anthology (and Electronic Caselaw Appendix)
Victor L. Streib

Cases and Materials on Corporations
Thomas R. Hurst and William A. Gregory

Cases and Problems in California Criminal Law
Myron Moskovitz

Cases and Problems in Criminal Law, *Fourth Edition*
Myron Moskovitz

The Citation Workbook: How to Beat the Citation Blues, *Second Edition*
Maria L. Ciampi, Rivka Widerman, and Vicki Lutz

Civil Procedure Anthology
David I. Levine, Donald L. Doernberg, and Melissa L. Nelken

Civil Procedure: Cases, Materials, and Questions, *Second Edition*
Richard D. Freer and Wendy Collins Perdue

Clinical Anthology: Readings for Live-Client Clinics
Alex J. Hurder, Frank S. Bloch, Susan L. Brooks, and Susan L. Kay

Economic Regulation: Cases and Materials
Richard J. Pierce, Jr.

Elements of Law
Eva H. Hanks, Michael E. Herz, and Steven S. Nemerson

Ending It: Dispute Resolution in America
  Descriptions, Examples, Cases and Questions
Susan M. Leeson and Bryan M. Johnston

An Environmental Law Anthology
Robert L. Fischman, Maxine I. Lipeles, and Mark S. Squillace

Environmental Law Series

   Environmental Decisionmaking: NEPA and the Endangered Species Act, *Second Edition*
   Jackson B. Battle, Robert L. Fischman, and Mark S. Squillace

   Water Pollution, *Third Edition*
   Jackson B. Battle and Maxine I. Lipeles

   Air Pollution, *Third Edition*
   Mark S. Squillace and David R. Wooley

   Hazardous Waste, *Third Edition*
   Maxine I. Lipeles

Environmental Protection and Justice
  Readings and Commentary on Environmental Law and Practice
Kenneth A. Manaster

European Union Law Anthology
Karen V. Kole and Anthony D'Amato

An Evidence Anthology
Edward J. Imwinkelried and Glen Weissenberger

Family Law in Action: A Reader
Margaret F. Brinig, Carl E. Schneider, and Lee E. Teitelbaum

Federal Antitrust Law: Cases and Materials
Daniel J. Gifford and Leo J. Raskind

Federal Income Tax Anthology
Paul L. Caron, Karen C. Burke, and Grayson M.P. McCouch

Federal Rules of Civil Procedure
Publisher's Staff

Federal Rules of Evidence Handbook
Publisher's Staff

Federal Rules of Evidence: Rules, Legislative History, Commentary and Authority
Glen Weissenberger

Federal Wealth Transfer Tax Anthology
Paul L. Caron, Grayson M.P. McCouch, Karen C. Burke

First Amendment Anthology
Donald E. Lively, Dorothy E. Roberts, and Russell L. Weaver

The History, Philosophy, and Structure of the American Constitution
Douglas W. Kmiec and Stephen B. Presser

Problems and Simulations in Evidence, *Second Edition*
Thomas F. Guernsey

A Products Liability Anthology
Anita Bernstein

Professional Responsibility Anthology
Thomas B. Metzloff

A Property Anthology, *Second Edition*
Richard H. Chused

Public Choice and Public Law: Readings and Commentary
Maxwell L. Stearns

Readings in Criminal Law
Russell L. Weaver, John M. Burkoff, Catherine Hancock, Alan Reed, and Peter J. Seago

Science in Evidence
D.H. Kaye

A Section 1983 Civil Rights Anthology
Sheldon H. Nahmod

Sports Law: Cases and Materials, *Third Edition*
Ray L. Yasser, James R. McCurdy, and C. Peter Goplerud

A Torts Anthology, *Second Edition*
Julie A. Davies, Lawrence C. Levine, and Edward J. Kionka

Trial Practice
Lawrence A. Dubin and Thomas F. Guernsey

Unincorporated Business Entities
Larry E. Ribstein

FORTHCOMING PUBLICATIONS

Basic Themes in Law and Jurisprudence
Charles W. Collier

Cases and Materials on the Law Governing Lawyers
James E. Moliterno

Constitutional Law: Cases, History, and Dialogues, *Second Edition*
Donald E. Lively, Phoebe A. Haddon, Dorothy E. Roberts, Russell L. Weaver, and William D. Araiza

Elder Law: Readings, Cases, and Materials
Thomas P. Gallanis, A. Kimberley Dayton, and Molly M. Wood

First Amendment Law: Cases, Comparative Perspectives, and Dialogues
Donald E. Lively, Phoebe A. Haddon, John C. Knechtle, and Dorothy E. Roberts

Introduction to the Study of Law: Cases and Materials, *Second Edition*
John Makdisi

The Question Presented: Model Appellate Briefs
Maria L. Ciampi and William H. Manz

Secured Transactions Under The Uniform Commercial Code and International Commerce
Louis F. Del Duca, Egon Guttman, William H. Henning, Fred H. Miller, and Peter Winship

FAMILY LAW IN ACTION
A READER

FAMILY LAW IN ACTION
A READER

MARGARET F. BRINIG

Professor of Law
University of Iowa College of Law

CARL E. SCHNEIDER

Chouncey Stillman Professor of Ethics,
Morality, and the Practice of Law
University of Michigan Law School

LEE E. TEITELBAUM

Allan R. Tessler Dean and Professor of Law
Cornell Law School

ANDERSON PUBLISHING CO.
CINCINNATI, OHIO

FAMILY LAW IN ACTION: A READER
MARGARET F. BRINIG, CARL E. SCHNEIDER, AND LEE E. TEITELBAUM

Anderson Publishing Co.
2035 Reading Road / Cincinnati, Ohio 45202
800-582-7295 / e-mail andpubco@aol.com / Fax 513-562-5430
World Wide Web http://www.andersonpublishing.com

ISBN: 1-58360-750-1

Dedication

To all my students
M.F.B.

To Joan
C.E.S.

For Herta
L.E.T.

Acknowledgments

Margaret Brinig wishes to acknowledge Yen Kha at George Mason University School of Law.

Carl Schneider wishes to acknowledge the dedicated assistance of Laura Harlow at the University of Michigan Law School.

Lee Teitelbaum would like to thank a number of staff at the University of Utah College of Law for their help with this manuscript. They include Kathleen Morgan, Barbara McFarlane, Uta Roth, and Rebecca Riley, all of whom pitched in willingly and with good humor.

Table of Contents

Introduction

This is a volume of readings on family law and policy drawn from a variety of disciplines. We have prepared it because family law, perhaps more than almost any other course, cannot well be taught using only casebooks. The reason is that family law casebooks have so much work to do providing students with information about family law doctrine that they have no space for conveying information about how families work internally, how families function as social institutions, and how the law interacts with families. Yet it is this information that students find absorbing and teachers find essential for teaching doctrine intelligently.

Many law school readers are compilations of articles about doctrine and theory. In a course—like torts, for example—where doctrine and theory have reached a high level of complexity and sophistication, this kind of reader is surely valuable. But in family law the doctrine—while extensive—is not particularly complex, and the problems of theory are readily gleaned from the doctrinal material in a casebook. What makes teaching family law difficult is that students need to understand the elaborate and elusive ways that people behave in families and that the law interacts with families. Our volume is intended to promote that understanding by presenting readings that explore the empirical reality family law addresses. We have, that is, tried to provide insights into how American families are organized, how Americans live their lives in families, how they think about those lives, how the institutions of family law operate, and how the law affects family members, families, and society.

Professor Schneider even suggests that the case for empirical work almost makes itself.

> In brief: "It is no doubt true that you can not get from *is* to *ought*. But you ought to know what *is* is before you say what *ought* ought to be." Empirical work, to put the point rather more elaborately, needs to be done because of the problem of what I have called hyper-rationalism. "Hyper-rationalism is essentially the substitution of reason for information and analysis. It has two components: first, the belief that reason can reliably be used to infer facts where evidence is unavailable or incomplete, and second, the practice of interpreting facts through a [narrow] set of artificial analytic categories." Hyper-rationalism thus "tempts us to believe that we can understand how people think and act

merely by reasoning, and not by investigating. Hyper-rationalism seductively justifies discussing human behavior without doing the empirical work necessary to discover how people actually behave. Hyper-rationalism is the conceptualist's revenge for the world's complexity."

The legally trained mind seems specially susceptible to hyper-rationalism. The case method intrudes empirical reality only anecdotally; rights thinking generally operates primarily on the basis of ratiocination. But when legal scholarship ventures to ask empirically whether law works as it is intended to, and even whether it has much effect at all, the answers have hardly been reassuring. Stuart Macaulay reports that businesses widely do not think of themselves as using contracts and avoid settling disputes contractually. Robert Ellickson found that the ranchers and farmers of Shasta County, California, did not know the rules of liability for damage done by wandering cattle, and did not care. Despite the Patient Self-Determination Act and much state legislation, "[n]o more than 10 percent of the population has either a living will or a durable power of attorney." I could go on at some length.

When good empirical work has been done in family law, it has been revealing and even confounding. Among the generation of family law scholars who flourished when I entered the field, for example, there are several who have done crucial empirical work (as well as important theoretical work). Robert Mnookin, for example, discovered in his empirical work that not all his theoretical speculations about the bargaining of parents on divorce were fully borne out. David Chambers perhaps found that jail, whatever its other disadvantages, was a more effective tool for collecting child support than he might originally have supposed. The contributors to *In the Interest of Children* reported that people avail themselves of due-process mechanisms a good deal less than courts and scholars usually seem to contemplate.

More particularly, Michael Wald, a principal proponent of stronger parents' rights in abuse-and-neglect law, undertook a study of that law's actual effects. His study raised the possibility that the rules of law we have been considering make less difference than one might suppose *a priori*. He concluded that, considering only "what happened to the children from the time we first saw them until the end of the study, two years later, there was not a great deal of difference between home and foster care." In short, research of this kind raises the possibility that further empirical research might indicate that the range of disagreement the Scotts and I have considered may not lead to actual changes in outcomes.

Our reader is not only empirical; it is interdisciplinary. It is interdisciplinary because a familiarity with various disciplines is essential for two purposes. One of those purposes, common to all fields, is the light that perspectives from other disciplines can shed on the formation, context, and execution of legal doctrine. For example, law and economics provides one lens through which policy and, to some extent, effects can be assessed; empirical studies (whether by sociologists or psychologists) reveal information about the premises of legal doctrine and the extent to which the behavior of law-applying agencies conforms to formal expectations.

These observations are, of course, true of family law as well, and perhaps especially important in that field. Judicial and legislative categories tend to take the form of standards rather than rules. Custodial decisions should serve the child's "best interests," property at divorce should be distributed "equitably." Information about the ways in which these standards are applied, and the effects of their application, supply much of the practical meaning of family law doctrine.

It is, however, also true that family law draws on many disciplines not only at the level of policy evaluation but for "ordinary" teaching and research purposes. To take only a few examples, it is desirable, in talking about formulations of rights, to refer to philosophies of rights and to historical sources regarding the extent and manner of their recognition. Proof of paternity in any contested setting requires some understanding of both genetics and probability theory. Determinations of custody and visitation typically involve psychological evidence and, accordingly, suppose an understanding of the method and literature in that field. Economics or finance principles are relevant to the valuation of marital property such as pensions and closely held corporations, and discussions of family violence may draw on social scientific evidence regarding the incidence, distribution, and causes of such violence.

Because of the pervasive use of non-doctrinal information in family law, we believe that some understanding of the methods of the various fields is also important. There is much poor as well as some good research touching on the legal and social situation of families, and some scholars incline to draw on both bodies of work without recognizing the strengths or weaknesses of their methodologies. In editing our volume, we have tried to incorporate enough methodological discussion to allow readers to understand those methods and, to a greater or lesser extent, evaluate the research presented. We hope these methodological portions of our readings will allow our readers to begin to develop an intelligent consumer's understanding (that is, a general understanding of the theory, method, and literature in a "non-legal" discipline) of how extraordinarily difficult it is to develop the kind of understanding of social behavior that is necessary for formulating good policy.

Finally, a word about the editing of this volume. We believe it is generally best for students of a subject to be allowed to evaluate a work of scholarship and its argument in their entirety. But we also know that the space for this work and the time of its readers allow no such recklessness. We have accordingly tried to find an editorial course somewhere between brutality and laxity. To conserve space, we have used ellipses to indicate the places where we have omitted portions of a work, but we have not sought to distinguish between omissions of a few words and omissions of whole paragraphs. Finally, we have regretfully but necessarily excised without indication tables, figures, references, and footnotes.

CHAPTER I

The Sociology, Economics, and History of the Family

Truth is never pure, and rarely simple.

Oscar Wilde
The Importance of Being Earnest

Law seeks to shape the world and the way people behave in it. This means that before we can understand and evaluate the law's workings, we need to know how the world is now structured and how people currently behave in it. It means that before we can understand and evaluate family law, we need to know something about the way the American family is structured and how people behave in it. This introductory chapter is designed to provide you that kind of information. More precisely, it is intended to give you a basic sense of how people live in families, of how one can understand the economic relations between family members, of how the family came to be the way it is, and of how the American family resembles and differs from families in other parts of the world. Be warned, however: This is only a bit of basic information, and in later chapters we will provide you with much more detailed facts about the sociology and economics of many of the specific problems family law encounters.

The material in this chapter is not only intended to provide background information about the state of the family the law regulates. It also puts the family in different disciplinary perspectives. Law tends to see families as people with special relationships to each other whose worst misbehavior needs to be restrained and whose stubbornest disputes need to be resolved. But law's approach is hardly the only, or even the best, one. Sociology, for example, asks why people behave in families as they do and looks to social interactions, patterns, and norms for answers. Economics provides another way of explaining human behavior within families—by looking to the incentives and disincentives that shape the way people allocate their resources. Finally, history sees present behavior as growing out of past practices. Each of these approaches to understanding families offers valuable insights into the problems family law confronts when it seeks to influence family life. This chapter, then, introduces each of these approaches, and later chapters will recruit them regularly.

A. The Sociology of the Family

This section of Chapter I is divided into three parts. The first delivers just the facts, ma'am. It proffers some tables which furnish basic data like the number of people who marry, the number of people who divorce, and the number of people who have children. The second section moves from evidence about behavior to a description of social attitudes. In particular, it looks through the eyes of a distinguished demographer (Norval D. Glenn) at the way Americans feel about that crucial social institution, marriage. The third section tries to put all these data into patterns. It does so by examining a hypothesis that has received a good deal of attention in recent cultural and political debates: the hypothesis that the American family is "declining." Janet Z. Giele, a professor of social work at Brandeis, summarizes those debates by outlining three central viewpoints—the conservative, liberal, and feminist positions.

JUST THE FACTS: SOME TABLES

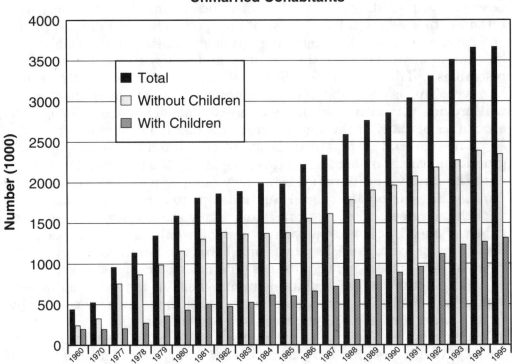

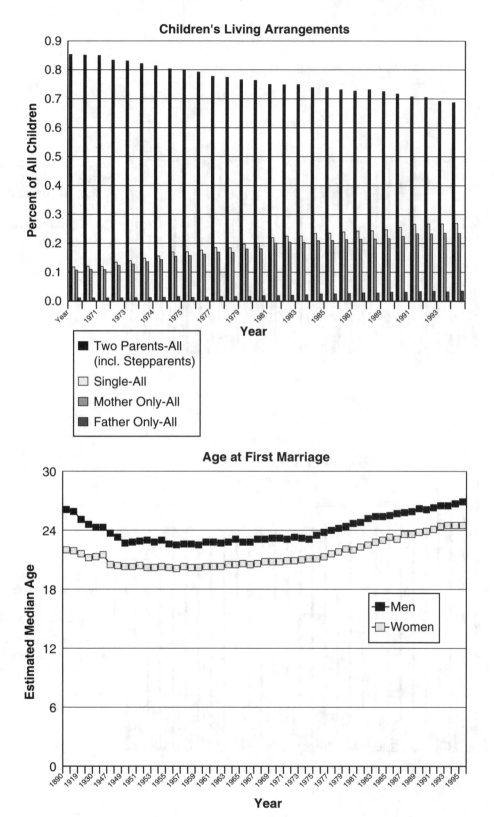

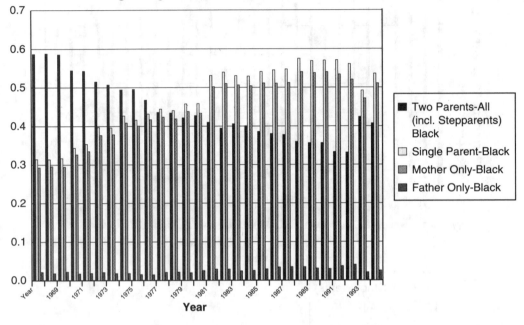

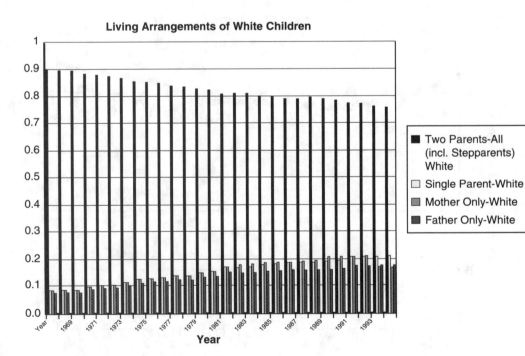

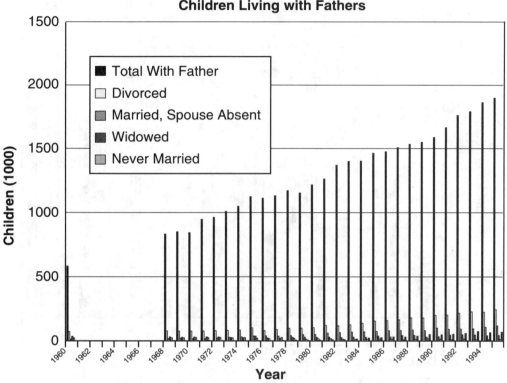

Children Living with Fathers

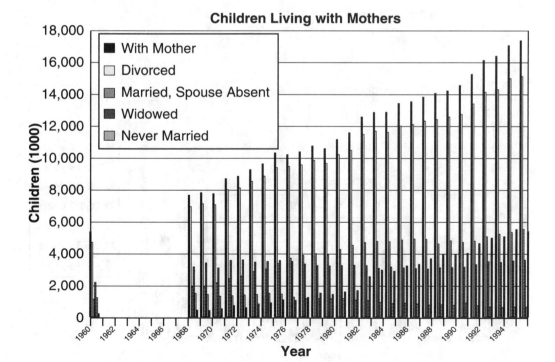

Children Living with Mothers

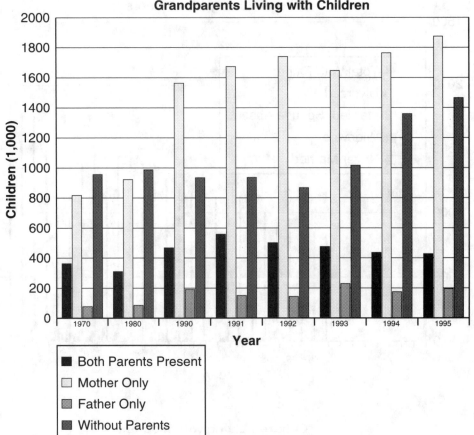

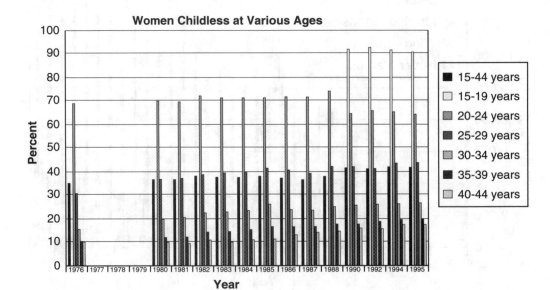

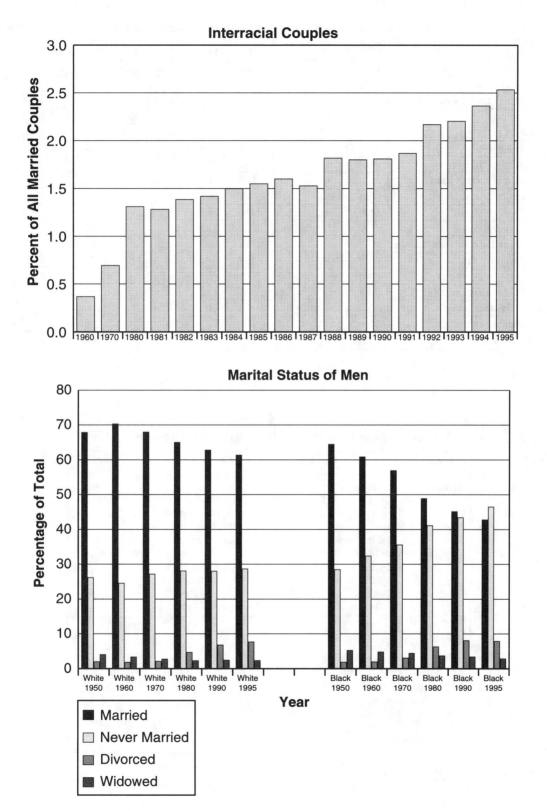

Child Care Arrangements When Mothers Are Working

Year	1977	1985	1986	1987	1988	1990	1991	1993	1994
Number of children affected	4370	8168	8849	9124	9483	9629	9854	9937	10228
Percentages:									
Care in child's home	33.9	31	28.7	29.9	28.2	29.7	35.7	30.7	33
By father	14.4	15.7	14.5	15.3	15.1	16.5	20	15.9	18.5
By grandparent	(NA)	5.7	5.2	5.1	5.7	5.2	7.2	6.5	5.9
By other relative	2/12.6	3.7	3.4	3.3	2.2	2.9	3.2	3.3	3.5
By nonrelative	7	5.9	5.5	6.2	5.3	5	5.4	5	5.1
Care in another home	40.7	37	40.7	35.6	36.8	35.1	31	32.1	31.3
By grandparent	(NA)	10.2	10.2	8.7	8.2	9.1	8.6	10	10.4
By other relative	18.3	4.5	6.5	4.6	5	5.9	4.5	5.5	5.5
By nonrelative	22.4	22.3	24	22.3	23.6	20.1	17.9	16.6	15.4
Organized child care facilities	13	23.1	22.4	24.4	25.8	27.5	23	30.1	29.4
Day/group care	(NA)	14	14.9	16.1	16.6	20.6	15.8	18.3	21.6
Nursery school/preschool	(NA)	9.1	7.5	8.3	9.2	6.9	7.3	11.6	7.8
School-based activity	(NA)	(NA)	(NA)	(NA)	0.2	0.1	0.5	0.2	0.2
Child cares for self	0.4	-	-	0.3	0.1	0.1	-	-	-
Mother cares for child at work	11.4	8.1	7.4	8.9	7.6	6.4	8.7	6.2	5.5
Other arrangements	0.6	0.8	0.8	1	1.3	1.1	1.1	0.9	0.9

Married People Claiming Extramarital Relationships, 1989

Category		Percent	Category	Percent
All		1.50%	Region	
Gender			New England	0
	Men	2.1	Mid-Atlantic	2
	Women	0.8	E. No. Central	3.2
Age			W. No. Central	1.2
	18-29	1	South Atlantic	0.8
	30-39	0	E. So. Central	0
	40-49	1.2	W. So. Central	3
	50-59	1.8	Mountain	0
	60-69	4.5	Pacific	1
	70+	1.4	Community Type	
Race			Lrg. Central Cities	0.0
	White	1.3	Oth. Central Cities	0
	Black	5.3	Sub. Lrg. Cities	5.6
	Other	0	Sub. Oth. Cities	1.7
Education			Other Urban	0.6
	Not High School	4	Other Rural	2.3
	High School	0.9		
	Jr. College	0		
	College	1		
	Post College	1.8		

Number of Sex Partners, 1989

Category	Mean	Category	Mean
All	7.15	**Education**	
Gender		Not High School	4.59
Men	12.26	High School	7.5
Women	3.32	Jr. College	6.84
Marital Status		College	8.4
Married	5.72	Post College	10.54
Widowed	3.01	**Region**	
Divorced	13.3	New England	7.48
Separated	11.75	Mid-Atlantic	5.48
Never Married	8.67	E. No. Central	6.47
Age		W. No. Central	5.88
18-29	6.08	South Atlantic	6.81
30-39	8.38	E. So. Central	5.25
40-49	9.71	W. So. Central	10.97
50-59	9.28	Mountain	6.07
60-69	4.65	Pacific	10.01
70+	3.51	**Community Type**	
Race		Lrg. Central Cities	7.98
White	7.3	Oth. CentralCities	11.37
Black	5.84	Sub. Lrg. Cities	5.94
Other	7.18	Sub. Oth. Cities	9.72
		Other Urban	5.96
		Other Rural	3.84

Employment and Unemployment

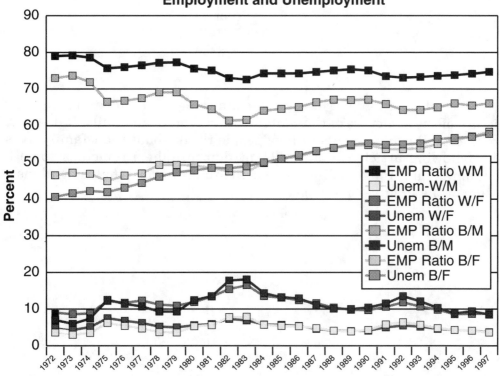

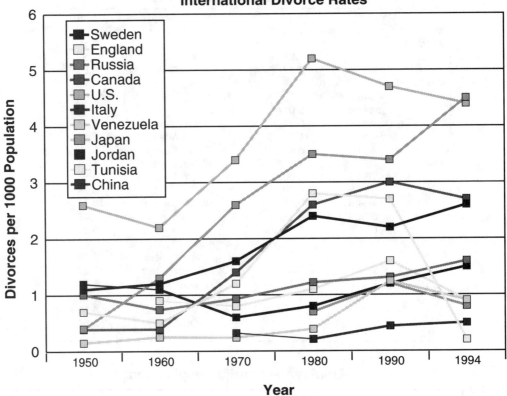

The information you have been examining is intended to give you a picture of the structure of the contemporary American family. It does not, however, tell you much about how people think about their family lives. The following article (by an eminent demographer) remedies some of that omission through a discussion of attitudes toward that central institution of the family—marriage.

Norval D. Glenn, *Values, Attitudes, and the State of American Marriage* in PROMISES TO KEEP: DECLINE AND RENEWAL OF MARRIAGE IN AMERICA, David Popenoe, Jean Bethke Elshtain, and David Blankenhorn, eds. (Rowman & Littlefield, 1996)[*]

This chapter deals with a paradox, namely, that marriage remains very important to adult Americans—probably as important as it has ever been—while the proportion of Americans married has declined and the proportion successfully married has declined even more. Most people say that having a good marriage is one of their most important goals in life, and no other variable is more predictive of the health, happiness, and general well-being of adults than whether or not they are in satisfactory marriages. The importance high school seniors say they place on marriage has increased in recent years, even though journalistic and social scientific observers of adults continue to see signs of a "retreat from marriage."

This paradox can be resolved by assuming that the decline in the probability of marital success has resulted from forces external to values, attitudes, and feelings concerning marriage. For instance, if economic and demographic changes have erected new barriers to marital success, a continued high motivation to achieve that success is unlikely to be sufficient to prevent a decline in achievement. Indeed, most authorities on American marriage rely partly on such trends as the declining earnings of young men and the increasing financial independence of women to explain the decrease in the proportion of adults who are married.

Most of these same authorities also believe, however, that changes in values, attitudes, and norms have affected American marriage. Rarely do discussions of contemporary marriage fail to mention, for instance, that spouses now expect more from marriage than they once did and that the roles of husband and wife have been redefined. A few authors refer to a decline in commitment to marriage as an institution and similar cultural and psychological changes that tend to weaken the institution and lower the probability that individual marriages will succeed.

Critics of the latter view cite national survey data on the importance of marriage to Americans as evidence that the alleged cultural undermining of marriage has not occurred. However, having a good marriage could remain a salient goal while the values and norms conducive to attainment of that goal become weaker. People could want and expect more from marriage while they become less willing to make the sacrifices and "investments" needed for marital success.

My purpose here is to consider whether or not such cultural changes have recently occurred in American society—whether or not the resolution of the paradox mentioned above is substantially within the realm of values and attitudes. For evidence I turn to data from recent national surveys of adults and adolescents, first, to review the trends in American marriage that need to be explained and then, to assess the attitudes that may help to explain them.

The State of American Marriage

The initial reaction of American family social scientists to the "divorce boom" that began in the mid-1960s and continued through the 1970s was generally positive. Most discussions of this trend emphasized that it did not indicate a corresponding increase in the tendency for marriages to go bad, since it reflected primarily, if not entirely, a decreased willingness of spouses to endure unsatisfactory marriages. And the latter change, according to the prevailing view, indicated that people were coming to place more, not less, importance on marriage.

If this view (which remained virtually unchallenged among family social scientists until I began reporting evidence inconsistent with it early in the 1990s) had been correct, the average quality of intact marriages would have increased steadily and rather sharply as the divorce rate climbed and as persons in the older and less divorce-prone cohorts became a smaller percentage of the married population—a trend that continued after the divorce rate leveled off in the early 1980s. However, the predicted increase in marital quality did not occur, as the 1973-93 data for currently married persons in Figure 2.1 show.

Rather, the proportion of married persons who reported that their marriages were "very happy" declined slightly—an indication that the probability of marital failure increased substantially. Furthermore, a downward trend in the probability of marital success is clearly indicated by the declines from 1973 to 1993 in the proportions of ever-married persons, and of all persons age thirty and older, who were in marriages they reported to be "very happy."

One might think that the lowering of legal, moral, and social barriers to divorce would at least have diminished the proportion of adults in poor marriages, but the 1973-93 data in Figure 2.2 on the percent of all persons age eighteen and older who were in marriages they reported to be less than "very happy" (labeled "unhappily married") show virtual stability. The percent in "very happy" marriages (labeled "happily married") declined substantially while the percent unmarried (never-married, divorced, separated, or widowed) increased proportionately.

A major reason for concern about the decline in marital success is its effects on children, and the trends shown in Figure 2.3 suggest that those effects have been more than trivial. Virtually everyone agrees that the best situation for children, all else being equal, is for them to live with biological (or adoptive) parents who have a good marriage. There is no agreement on the relative badness of other situations—single-parent, stepfamily, and unhappily married parent situations all being considered less than ideal. The percent of persons under age eighteen living with a less-than-happily married parent remained about the same, the percent living with a happily married parent declined, and the percent living with a single parent increased. The negative changes were even greater than the data indicate, since some of the pre-adults living with happily married parents were in stepfamilies, which is less than ideal, and the percent in such situations is known to have increased.

The percent of persons who were in successful (that is, intact and happy) first marriages at any given number of years after they first married has declined substantially in recent years, the proportion after ten years now being about one-third. When the tendency for some survey respondents to overreport the quality of their marriages is taken into account, along with the fact that some persons who report their marriages to be "very happy" have spouses who disagree, the estimate of the proportion of first marriages that are successful after ten years almost certainly should not exceed about 25 percent.

This evidence, though inconsistent with the sanguine views that have prevailed among family social scientists, is congruent with what most lay persons think has happened to American marriage. For instance, a majority of the respondents to the Virginia Slims American Women's Opinion Polls in 1974, 1979, 1985, and 1989 said they thought the institution of marriage was weaker than it was ten years earlier, although the percent was lower in 1989 (61) than in 1974 or 1979 (70).

The Importance of Marriage

An observer exposed only to the data in the preceding section might be inclined to suspect that the "retreat from marriage" has been to a large degree psychological, that Americans are marrying less and succeeding less often at marriage because alternatives have become more attractive, relative to marriage, than they once were. Such a change could have occurred because persons perceive that marriage has become less effective in meeting their needs and desires, and/or because they perceive that alternatives to marriage have become more effective. One cannot be certain that no such psychological retreat from marriage has occurred, but survey data on attitudes toward marriage gathered over the past quarter of a century provide scant evidence for it.

Unfortunately, there are no strictly comparable data gathered at regular intervals over a period of years concerning the importance that American adults place on marriage. However, all of the relevant data from the past thirty or so years show that adults of all ages say that having a "happy marriage" is one of their most important life goals. Some of the most sophisticated evidence on this topic is from the quality of American Life Study conducted in 1971 by researchers in the Institute of Social Research at the University of Michigan. Respondents were asked to rate twelve "life domains" (ranging from "an interesting job" and "a large bank account" to "having good friends" and "a happy marriage") on a five-point scale ranging from "extremely important" to "not at all important." The highest percentage of "extremely important" ratings (74) were give to "having a happy marriage," followed by "being in good health and in good physical condition" (70) and "having a good family life" (67). When the respondents were asked to pick the two most important of the twelve domains, "a happy marriage" was selected most frequently (by 55 percent of the respondents), followed by "a good family life" (36) and "being in good health and in good physical condition" (35).

More recent studies have yielded similar findings. For instance, the Massachusetts Mutual American Family Values Study in 1989 asked 1,200 respondents, who were interviewed by phone, to rate twenty-nine "values" on a five-point scale ("one of the most important," "very important," "somewhat important," "not too important," and "not at all important"). Among the "values" that could reasonably be considered life goals, "having a happy marriage" ranked first, being indicated as "one of the most important" by 39 percent of the respondents and "one of the most important" or "very important" by 93 percent. In contrast, the percent giving the "one of the most important" rating to each of the individualistic and materialistic goals was much smaller, being 18 for "earning a good living," 16 for "being financially secure," 8 for "having nice things," and 6 for "being free from obligations so I can do whatever I want to."

Each year since 1976, the Monitoring the Future Survey conducted by the Institute for Social Research at the University of Michigan has asked a sample of high school seniors to rate fourteen life goals on a four-point scale ranging from "extremely important" to "not important." In Table 2.1, I report the percent of the 1992 respondents who rated each of the goals "extremely important." "Having a good marriage and family life" ranked first, being given the highest rating by almost four-fifths of the students, although "being able to find steady work" was a close second.

The trend data from the annual Monitoring the Future Survey are generally inconsistent with the hypothesis that there has been a psychological retreat from marriage among young persons on the threshold of adulthood. For instance, the trend in the "extremely important" ratings given to "having a good marriage and family life" shown in Figure 2.4 was slightly upward for both males and females from 1976 to 1992. There were also slight upward trends in the percent who said they definitely would prefer to have a mate most of their lives and in the percent who said they most likely would choose to marry or who were already married. Of course, the period covered by these data began after most of the increase in divorce that started in the mid-1960s had already occurred, and there could have been attitudinal changes prior to 1976 opposite in direction from those shown in the figures. However, it seems unlikely that any such trends that were substantial in the 1960s and early 1970s would have completely ceased by the late 1970s.

The importance that people say they place on marriage does not necessarily mean, of course, that marriage continues to have important effects on their lives, but there is ample evidence that it does. As a whole, persons in satisfactory marriages are happier, healthier, more productive, and less inclined to engage in socially disruptive behavior than other adults, and at least among persons beyond the earliest stages of adulthood, there is no evidence of appreciable recent decline in these differences. For instance, the data in Figure 2.7 on the reported personal happiness of persons age thirty-five or older who were unmarried, happily married, and unhappily married show virtual stability from 1973 through 1993. The relationships indicated by these and similar data reflect to some degree the selection of happy, well-adjusted, and healthy persons into successful marriages, but most researchers who have studied them believe that they also result to a large extent from effects of marital situation on well-being and behavior.

Although the importance Americans say they place on marriage is consistent with the strength of the effects that marital situation seems to have on them, what survey respondents say about their attitudes and values concerning marriage should not necessarily be taken at face value. Many people may tend to give socially desirable responses or to respond in terms of what they think their values and attitudes should be rather than in terms of what they are—a topic to which I return below.

Some Evidence of Anti-marriage Influence

The evidence I have presented so far would seem to support the view that values and attitudes supportive of marriage are strong and that any "retreat from marriage" must have resulted largely from situational influences, such as changes in job opportunities and economic pressures. However, there is also evidence of attitudinal and value changes that are likely to have lessened the probability of marital success.

The trends in the attitudes of high school seniors shown in Figures 2.8, 2.9, and 2.10 can be considered anti-marriage, although the indicated changes are not large and their precise meaning is unclear. For instance, in view of the generally positive views of marriage expressed by the students in responses to other questions, it is not clear what one should make of the fact that a substantial and increasing proportion said they were inclined to question marriage as a way of life. The downward trend in the expectation of marital permanence shown in Figure 2.9 is more understandable and is not inconsistent with other trends, but the meaning of the decline in pro-marriage responses from females shown in Figure 2.10 is uncertain. It could reflect primarily a greater acceptance of being single for others, but not for oneself, or changes in views of non-marital cohabitation rather than of solitary living.

The limited trend data on adults' attitudes toward marriage suggest changes likely to have weakened the institution. For instance, the Americans View Their Mental Health Surveys, conducted in 1957 and 1976, asked respondents how a person's life is changed by being married and classified the responses into positive, neutral, or negative. The positive responses declined from 43 to 30 percent from 1957 to 1976 and the negative ones increased from 23 to 28 percent.

Probably the most important change in attitudes toward marriage has been a weakening of the ideal of marital permanence—a change that virtually all observers of American marriage agree has occurred even though there apparently are no national trend data on the topic. The best "hard" evidence on the topic is from the Study of American Families, a panel study that interviewed the same sample of mothers at four different dates. In 1962, 51 percent of the respondents said parents who do not get along should *not* stay together because there are children in the family, compared with 80 percent in 1977 and 82 percent in 1980 and 1985. Since there is no reason to think that the respondents' growing older would cause such a change, it almost certainly reflects a similar but probably larger change in the entire adult population.

Almost as important as changes in values and attitudes about marriage are changes in the strength of other values and goals, such as materialistic and achievement ones, that may detract from the pursuit of marital success. The best evidence on trends in such values is, again, for late adolescents and very young adults. Among the high school seniors who responded to the Monitoring the Future Surveys, the percent who said "having lots of money" was extremely important went from 15 in 1976 to 29 in 1992, and the percent rating "being successful in my line of work" extremely important went from 53 to 66. The Cooperative Institutional Research Program of the American Council on Education and UCLA found that only 40 percent of college freshmen in the early 1970s, compared with 70 percent in 1985, said "to be very well off financially" was a very important or essential life goal. It is not known whether these changes were part of a longer-term trend or were merely a return to the values that existed prior to an atypically anti-materialistic period in the late 1960s and early 1970s.

There are no comparable trend data for American adults, but there is evidence that many of these persons let values they say are less important interfere with their pursuit of marital success and other family values. The respondents to the 1989 Massachusetts Mutual American Family Values Study, who as a whole rated "having a happy marriage" their most important life goal and such goals as "having nice things" and "being financially secure" much lower, were asked to imagine that they were thirty-eight years old and were offered a new job in a field they liked, that the job would require more work hours and take them far away from their families more often, and that it would be more highly rewarded in certain ways than their present job. Just how the new job would be more highly rewarded differed among three versions of the question, each of which was asked of one-third of the sample (400 respondents). For two of the subsamples, the increment in reward included higher pay, but for the third subsample it was only greater prestige. The respondents were then asked how likely it would be that they would take the new job—very likely, somewhat likely, somewhat unlikely, or very unlikely.

In each of the three subsamples, around one-third or more of the respondents said it was very likely they would take the new job, and almost another third or more said it was somewhat likely they would do so. Not a single respondent said it was very unlikely that he or she would take the job. Belief that the spouse and other family members would benefit might help account for the willingness of the respondents to accept a job with higher pay, but prestige is primarily a personal reward rather than one readily shared with family members.

These data take on added meaning in light of the fact that the question about the new job came in the middle of the interview after many questions about family values and almost directly (with only one intervening question) after the following ones:

1. Do you think most people today put a higher value on family, or do most people put a higher value on material things?
2. Over the course of an average week, please tell me what percentage of your waking time you spend being with your family?
3. Would you say that you spend too much, about the right amount, or not enough time with your family?

It is well established that responses to survey questions can be influenced by the content of preceding questions, and in this case the expectation is that having responded to the earlier questions should have lowered the respondents' tendency to say "very likely" or "somewhat likely." This is especially the case in view of the fact that 85 percent said most people today put a higher value on material things, and 46 percent admitted they did not spend enough time with their families. Indeed, a "question order effect" is the only reasonable explanation for the "very likely" responses not being higher when greater pay was part of the increment in rewards associated with the new job than when the increment was only greater prestige. The earlier question about "material things" seems to have predisposed respondents not to choose greater pay over family time but apparently had less effect on their tendency to choose prestige.

These findings suggest that survey respondents are inclined to exaggerate the importance they place on marriage and the family and that many people will risk sacrificing marital success in pursuit of goals they say are less important.

Reasons for the Decline in Marriage

The survey data reviewed above provide only a very sketchy picture of what has happened to American marriage. Many of the questions that could have provided insight into changes in marriage-related values and attitudes have not been asked, and structured survey questions are inherently limited in their ability to deal with the subtleties and complexities of cultural phenomena. Furthermore, since it is impossible to demonstrate conclusively just how the trends in marital success and in attitudes toward marriage are causually interrelated, the data are amenable to differing interpretations.

To me, however, the data, when considered in light of theory and along with other kinds of evidence, suggest one major conclusion: The very importance that people place on marriage as a source of gratification has contributed to the decline of marriage as an institution. Explanation is in order.

A conjugal family system, of which the United States has an extreme form, is centered around the marriage relationship, in contrast to a consanguine family system, in which "blood" relationships are the crucial ones. In a conjugal system, spouses choose one another instead of their marriages being arranged by others, and providing for the needs and desires of the spouses is considered a primary purpose, if not *the* main purpose, of marriage. Of course, marriage in any family system performs societal functions, such as providing much of the early care and socialization of children, but in conjugal systems marital success tends to be defined in hedonistic terms and from the perspective of the spouses. The successful marriage is one that provides happiness, satisfaction, and other positive feelings to the husband and wife.

The United States has always had a conjugal family system, and by the time social scientists began writing about American marriage early in this century, hedonistic and individualistic criteria of marital success already prevailed. However, at that time persons were encouraged to pursue marital success by choosing spouses wisely and working to maintain the marriage—not, except in extraordinary circumstances, by moving from one marriage to another. Furthermore, the happiness and satisfaction pursued and attained through marriage were to a large degree through such practical benefits as economic security, social standing, and the receipt of domestic services, and these benefits were more obviously enhanced by marital stability than the less tangible ones resulting from companionship and the pleasures of associating with the spouse. Only in the past few decades has the single-minded pursuit of marital happiness through the attraction and retention of an intrinsically desirable spouse received strong and virtually unqualified social encouragement.

The greater emphasis on having an intrinsically good marriage has been accompanied by a decline in the ideal of marital permanence. To many progressive thinkers, it has seemed reasonable that lowering the legal, moral, and social barriers to divorce would enhance the average quality of intact marriages and facilitate movement from poor marriages to better ones. Although the increase in divorce that began in the mid-1960s may have come about largely for other reasons, such as the decline in economic dependence of wives on husbands, professionals interested in improving marital quality, such as social scientists and therapists, provided a strong rationale, based on the goal of enhancing personal happiness, for a greater social acceptance and even encouragement of divorce.

According to Bernard Farber, the decline in the ideal of marital permanence has taken us substantially toward a condition he calls "permanent availability." By this he means that all adults, regardless of marital status, tend to remain on the marriage market. That is, married persons as well as unmarried ones tend to assess the marital desirability of members of the opposite sex they know and meet, whether those persons are married or not, and will consider moving from their current marriage to one they anticipate will be more satisfactory. If permanent availability were to become universal, few persons would remain married for life to their first spouse.

The progressives who believed that lowering the barriers to divorce and moving toward permanent availability on the marriage market would necessarily enhance the quality of marriages and contribute to personal happiness ignored what the most astute social philosophers have always known, namely, that a completely unfettered pursuit of self-interest by individuals does not lead to the maximization of the well-being of the population as a whole. They ignored the fact that the freedom of one spouse to leave the marriage at will is the other spouse's insecurity, and that without a reasonable degree of security, it is unlikely that a spouse will commit fully to the marriage and make the sacrifices and investments needed to make it succeed.

Furthermore, marital discontent will almost certainly result when a person constantly compares his or her marriage to real or imagined alternatives to it. Persons are hardly aware of needs well served by their marriages but are acutely aware of those not very well served, and there always are some. Therefore, the grass will always tend to look greener on the other side of the marital fence; people will always tend to imagine they would be happier married to someone else or not married. It is also relevant that persons not intimately known often appear to be more desirable as prospective spouses than they really are. The person who has revealed all or most of his or her faults and weaknesses to a spouse is always at a disadvantage when competing with the well-cultivated public images of other men or women.

Although the weakening of the ideal of marital permanence is likely to be a crucial reason for the decline in marital success, I do not believe it is the only one. Increased expectations of marriage and a breakdown in consensus on the content of marital roles are almost certainly involved, and other cultural trends may have had an effect. For instance, if, as some social critics maintain, there has been a general increase in American society of a sense of entitlement—in what people believe they should receive from others—while there has been a decline in a sense of duty—of what people believe they should give to others—all institutions, including marriage, must have suffered. A related change may have been an increased tendency for people to feel they can, and deserve, to have it all—including success at marriage, parenthood, and work—and a decreased recognition that a relentless pursuit of career goals and financial success is likely to interfere with attainment of marital and parental goals.

Situational influences, such as the decline in the earning of young men, are also undeniably responsible for some of the changes in marriage, but it seems to me that the resolution of the paradox addressed by this chapter is largely in the realm of culture. As the purpose of marriage is coming to be defined more exclusively as the gratification of the married persons, and as marriage is becoming more nearly just a personal relationship, the nature of which is determined largely by the private negotiations of each married couple, the traditional institutional functions of marriage are being less well performed. The consequences of this change for children are now widely recognized, and those for adults, while less severe, also seem to be distinctly negative. An increasingly hedonistic form of marriage seems to be decreasingly able to facilitate the hedonistic strivings of those who participate in it.

The material you have so far read primarily presents data about the family. But what do those data mean? This has become one of the most passionately controverted questions in American life. In its simplest form, the question is: whither the American family? Is the family crumbling away? If so, why? Is the family simply reshaping itself to suit modern times? Attempts to answer these questions have led to three core positions which the following article explores.

Janet Z. Giele, *Decline of the Family: Conservative, Liberal, and Feminist Views* in PROMISES TO KEEP: DECLINE AND RENEWAL OF MARRIAGE IN AMERICA, David Popenoe, Jean Bethke Elshtain, and David Blankenhorn, eds. (Rowman & Littlefield, 1996)[*]

The Conservative Explanation:
Selfishness and Moral Decline

The new family advocates turn their spotlight on the breakdown in the two-parent family, saying that rising divorce, illegitimacy, and father absence have put children at greater risk of school failure, unemployment, and antisocial behavior. The remedy is to restore religious faith and family commitment as well as to cut welfare payments to unwed mothers and mother-headed families.

Conservative Model

Cultural and moral weakening	→	Family breakdown, divorce, family decline	→	Father absence, school failure, poverty, crime, drug use

Cultural and Moral Weakening

To many conservatives, the modern secularization of religious practice and the decline of religious affiliation have undermined the norms of sexual abstinence before marriage and the prohibitions of adultery or divorce thereafter. Sanctions against illegitimacy or divorce have been made to seem narrow-minded and prejudiced. In addition, daytime television and the infamous example of Murphy Brown, a single mother having a child out of wedlock, helped to obscure simple notions of right and wrong. Barbara Dafoe Whitehead's controversial article in the *Atlantic* entitled "Dan Quayle Was Right" is an example of this argument.

---

[*]   Copyright © 1996. Reprinted with permission.

Gradual changes in marriage law have also diminished the hold of tradition. Restrictions against waiting periods, race dissimilarity, and varying degrees of consanguinity were gradually disappearing all over the United States and Europe. While Mary Ann Glendon viewed the change cautiously but relativistically—as a process that waxed and waned across the centuries—others have interpreted these changes as a movement from status to contract (i.e., from attention to the particular individual's characteristics to reliance on the impersonal considerations of the marketplace). The resulting transformation lessened the family's distinctive capacity to serve as a bastion of private freedom against the leveling effect and impersonality of public bureaucracy.

Erosion of the Two-Parent Family

To conservatives, one of the most visible causes of family erosion was government welfare payments, which made fatherless families a viable option. In *Losing Ground,* Charles Murray used the rise in teenage illegitimate births as proof that government-sponsored welfare programs had actually contributed to the breakdown of marriage. Statistics on rising divorce and mother-headed families appeared to provide ample proof that the two-parent family was under siege. The proportion of all households headed by married couples fell from 77 percent in 1950 to 61 percent in 1980 and 55 percent in 1993. Rising cohabitation, divorce rates, and births out of wedlock all contributed to the trend. The rise in single-person households was also significant, from only 12 percent of all households in 1950 to 27 percent in 1980, a trend fed by rising affluence and the undoubling of living arrangements that occurred with the expansion of the housing supply after World War II.

The growth of single-parent households, however, was the most worrisome to policymakers because of their strong links to child poverty. In 1988, 50 percent of all children were found in mother-only families compared with 20 percent in 1950. The parental situation of children in poverty changed accordingly. Of all poor children in 1959, 73 percent had two parents present and 20 percent had a mother only. By 1988, only 35 percent of children in poverty lived with two parents and 57 percent lived with a mother only. These developments were fed by rising rates of divorce and out-of-wedlock births. Between 1950 and 1990, the divorce rate rose from 8.8 to 21 per thousand married women. Out-of-wedlock births exploded from 5 percent in 1960 to 26 percent in 1990.

To explain these changes, conservatives emphasize the breakdown of individual and cultural commitment to marriage and the loss of stigma for divorce and illegitimacy. They understand both trends to be the result of greater emphasis on short-term gratification and on adults' personal desires rather than on what is good for children. A young woman brings a child into the world without thinking about who will support it. A husband divorces his wife and forms another household, possibly with other children and leaves children of the earlier family behind without necessarily feeling obliged to be present in their upbringing or to provide them with financial support.

Negative Consequences for Children

To cultural conservatives there appears to be a strong connection between erosion of the two-parent family and the rise of health and social problems in children. Parental investment in children has declined—especially in the time available for supervision and companionship. Parents had roughly 10 fewer hours per week for their children in 1986 than in 1960, largely because more married women were employed (up from 24 percent in 1940 to 52 percent in 1983) and more mothers of young children (under age 6) were working (up from 12 percent in 1940 to 50 percent in 1983). By the late 1980s just over half of mothers of children under a year old were in the labor force for at least part of the year. At the same time fathers were increasingly absent from the family because of desertion, divorce, or failure to marry. In 1980, 15 percent of white children, 50 percent of black children, and 27 percent of children of Hispanic origin had no father present. Today 36 percent of children are living apart from their biological fathers compared with only 17 percent in 1960.

Without a parent to supervise children after school, keep them from watching television all day, or prevent them from playing in dangerous neighborhoods, many more children appear to be falling by the wayside, victims of drugs, obesity, violence, suicide, or failure in school. During the 1960s and 1970s the suicide rate for persons aged fifteen to nineteen more than doubled. The proportion of obese children between the ages of six and eleven rose from 18 to 27 percent. Average SAT scores fell, and 25 percent of all high school students failed to graduate. In 1995 the Council on Families in America reported, "Recent surveys have found that children from broken homes, when they become teenagers have 2 to 3 times more behavioral and psychological problems than do children from intact homes." Father absence is blamed by the fatherhood movement for the rise in violence among young males. David Blankenhorn and others reason that the lack of a positive and productive male role model has contributed to an uncertain masculine identity which then uses violence and aggression to prove itself. Every child deserves a father and "in a good society, men prove their masculinity not by killing other people, impregnating lots of women, or amassing large fortunes, but rather by being committed fathers and loving husbands."

Psychologist David Elkind, in *The Hurried Child,* suggests that parents' work and time constraints have pushed down the developmental timetable to younger ages so that small children are being expected to take care of themselves and perform at levels which are robbing them of their childhood. The consequences are depression, discouragement, and a loss of joy at learning and growing into maturity. . . .

Economic Restructuring: Liberal Analysis of Family Change

Liberals agree that there are serious problems in America's social health and condition of its children. But they pinpoint economic and structural changes that have placed new demands on the family without providing countervailing social supports. The economy has become ever more specialized with rapid technological change undercutting established occupations. More women have entered the labor force as their child-free years have increased due to a shorter childbearing period and longer lifespan. The family has lost economic functions to the urban workplace and socialization functions to the school. What is left is the intimate relationship between the marital couple, which, unbuffered by the traditional economic division of labor between men and women, is subject to even higher demands for emotional fulfillment and is thus more vulnerable to breakdown when it falls short of those demands.

Liberal Model

| Changing economic structure | → | Changing family and gender roles | → | Diverse effects: poor v. productive children |

The current family crisis thus stems from structural more than cultural change—changes in the economy, a paired-down nuclear family, and less parental time at home. Market forces have led to a new ethic of individual flexibility and autonomy. More dual-earner couples and single-parent families have broadened the variety of family forms. More single-parent families and more working mothers have decreased the time available for parenting. Loss of the father's income through separation and divorce has forced many women and children into poverty with inadequate health care, poor education, and inability to save for future economic needs. The solution that most liberals espouse is a government-sponsored safety net which will facilitate women's employment, mute the effects of poverty, and help women and children to become economically secure.

Recent Changes in the Labor Market

Liberals attribute the dramatic changes in the family to the intrusion of the money economy rather than cultural and moral decline. In a capitalist society, individual behavior follows the market. Adam Smith's "invisible hand" brings together buyers and sellers who maximize their satisfaction through an exchange of resources in the market place. Jobs are now with an employer, not with the family business or family farm as in preindustrial times. The cash economy has, in the words of Robert Bellah, "invaded" the diffuse personal relationships of trust between family and community members and transformed them into specific impersonal transactions. In an agricultural economy husbands and wives and parents and children were bound together in relationships of exchange that served each others' mutual interests. But modern society erodes this social capital of organization, trust among individuals, and mutual obligation that enhances both productivity and parenting.

The market has also eroded community by encouraging maximum mobility of goods and services. Cheaper labor in the South, lower fuel prices, and deeper tax breaks attracted first textile factories, then the shoe industry, and later automobile assembly plants which had begun in the North. Eventually, many of these jobs left the country. Loss of manufacturing jobs has had dramatic consequences for employment of young men without a college education and their capacity to support a family. In the 1970s, 68 percent of male high school graduates had a full-time, year-round job compared with only 51 percent in the 1980s. Many new jobs are located in clerical work, sales, or other service occupations traditionally associated with women. The upshot is a deteriorating employment picture for less well educated male workers at the same time that there are rising opportunities for women. Not surprisingly, ever more middle-income men and women combine forces to construct a two-paycheck family wage.

Changing Family Forms

Whereas the farm economy dictated a two-parent family and several children as the most efficient work group, the market economy gives rise to a much wider variety of family forms. A woman on the frontier in the 1800s had few other options even if she were married to a drunken, violent, or improvident husband. In today's economy this woman may have enough education to get a clerical job that will support her and her children in a small apartment where the family will be able to use public schools and other public amenities.

Despite its corrosive effect on family relations, the modern economy has also been a liberating force. Women could escape patriarchal domination; the young could seek their fortune without waiting for an inheritance from their elders—all a process that a century ago was aligned with a cultural shift that Fred Weinstein and Gerald Platt termed "the wish to be free." Dramatic improvements took place in the status of women as they gained the right to higher education, entry into the professions, and the elective franchise. Similarly, children were released from sometimes cruel and exploitive labor and became the object of deliberate parental investment and consumption. Elders gained pensions for maintenance and care that made them economically independent of their adult children. All these developments could be understood as part of what William J. Goode has referred to as the "world revolution in family patterns" which resulted in liberation and equality of formerly oppressed groups.

The current assessment of change in family forms is, however, mostly negative because of the consequences for children. More parental investment in work outside the family has meant less time for children. According to liberals, parents separate or divorce or have children outside of marriage because of the economic structure, not because they have become less moral or more selfish. Young women have children out of wedlock when the young men whom they might marry have few economic prospects and when the women themselves have little hope for their own education or employment. Change in the family thus begins with jobs. Advocates of current government programs therefore challenge the conservatives' assertion that welfare caused the breakup of two-parent families by supporting mothers with dependent children. According to William Julius Wilson, it is partly the lack of manual labor jobs for the would-be male breadwinner in inner-city Chicago—the scarcity of "marriageable males"—which drives up the illegitimacy rate.

Among educated women, it is well known that the opportunity costs of foregone income from staying home became so high during the 1950s and 1960s that ever increasing numbers of women deserted full-time homemaking to take paid employment. In the 1990s several social scientists have further noted that Richard Easterlin's prediction that women would return to the home during the 1980s never happened. Instead women continued in the labor force because of irreversible normative changes surrounding women's equality and the need for women's income to finance children's expensive college education. Moreover, in light of globalization of the economy and increasing job insecurity in the face of corporate downsizing, economists and sociologists are questioning Gary Becker's thesis that the lower waged worker in a household (typically the woman) will tend to become a full-time homemaker while the higher waged partner becomes the primary breadwinner. Data from Germany and the United States on the trend toward women's multiple roles suggests that uncertainty about the future has made women invest more strongly than ever in their own careers. They know that if they drop out for very long they will have difficulty reentering if they have to tide over the family when the main breadwinner loses his job.

Consequences for Children

The ideal family in the liberal economic model, according to political philosopher Iris Young, is one which has sufficient income to support the parents and the children and "to foster in those children the emotional and intellectual capacities to acquire such well-paid, secure jobs themselves, and also sufficient to finance a retirement." Dependent families do not have self-sufficient income but must rely on friends, relatives, charity, or the state to carry out their contribution to bringing up children and being good citizens.

Among liberals there is an emerging consensus that the current economic structure leads to two kinds of underinvestment in children that are implicated in their later dependency—material poverty, characteristic of the poor, and "time" poverty, characteristic of the middle class.

Thirty years ago Daniel Patrick Moynihan perceived that material poverty and job loss for a man put strain on the marriage, sometimes to the point that he would leave. His children also did less well in school. Rand Conger, in his studies of Iowa families who lost their farms during the 1980s, found that economic hardship not only puts strain on the marriage but leads to harsh parenting practices and poorer outcomes for children. Thus it appears possible that poverty may not just be the result of family separation, divorce, and ineffective childrearing practices; it may also be the *cause* of the irritability, quarrels, and violence which lead to marital breakdown. Material underinvestment in children is visible not just with the poor but in the changing ratio of per capita income of children and adults in U.S. society as a whole. As the proportion of households without children has doubled over the last century (from 30 to 65 percent, per capita income of children has fallen from 71 percent of adult income in 1870 to 63 percent in 1930 and 51 percent in 1983.

The problem of "time" poverty used to be almost exclusively associated with mothers' employment. Numerous studies explored whether younger children did better if their mother was a full-time homemaker rather than employed outside the home but found no clear results. Lately the lack of parental time for children has become much more acute because parents are working a total of twenty-one hours more per week than in 1970 and because there are more single-parent families. In 1965 the average child spent about thirty hours a week interacting with a parent, compared with seventeen hours in the 1980s. Moreover, parents are less dependent on their children to provide support for them during old age, and children feel less obligated to do so. As skilled craftsmanship, the trades, and the family farms have disappeared, children's upbringing can no longer be easily or cheaply combined with what parents are already doing. So adults are no longer so invested in children's futures. The result is that where the social capital of group affiliations and mutual obligations is the lowest (in the form of continuity of neighborhoods, a two-parent family, or a parent's interest in higher education for her children), children are 20 percent more likely to drop out of high school.

It is not that parents prefer their current feelings of being rushed, working too many hours, and having too little time with their families. Economist Juliet Schor reports that at least two-thirds of persons she surveyed about their desires for more family time versus more salary would take a cut in salary if it could mean more time with their families. Since this option is not realistically open to many, what parents appear to do is spend more money on their children as a substitute for spending more time with them. . . .

Interdependence: The Feminist Vision of Work and Caregiving

A feminist perspective has elements in common with both conservatives and liberals, a respect for the family as an institution (shared with the conservatives) and an appreciation of modernity (valued by the liberals). In addition, a feminist perspective grapples with the problem of women's traditionally subordinate status and how to improve it through both a "relational" and an "individualist" strategy while also sustaining family life and the healthy rearing of children. At the same time feminists are skeptical of both conservative and liberal solutions. Traditionalists have so often relied on women as the exploited and underpaid caregivers in the family to enable men's activities in the public realm. Liberals are sometimes guilty of a "male" bias in focusing on the independent individual actor in the marketplace who does not realize that his so-called "independence" is possible only because he is actually *dependent* on all kinds of relationships that made possible his education and life in a stable social order.

By articulating the value of caregiving along with the ideal of women's autonomy, feminists are in a position to examine modern capitalism critically for its effects on families and to offer alternative policies that place greater value on the quality of life and human relationships. They judge family strength not by their *form* (whether they have two-parents) but by their functioning (whether they promote human satisfaction and development) and whether both women and men are able to be family caregivers as well as productive workers. They attribute difficulties of children less to the absence of the two-parent family than to low-wage work of single mothers, inadequate child care, and inhospitable housing and neighborhoods.

Feminist Model

Lack of cooperation among community, family, and work	→	Families where adults are stressed and overburdened	→	Children lack sufficient care and attention from parents

Accordingly, feminists would work for reforms that build and maintain the social capital of volunteer groups, neighborhoods, and communities because a healthy civil society promotes the well-being of families and individuals as well as economic prosperity and a democratic state. They would also recognize greater role flexibility across the life cycle so that both men and women could engage in caregiving, and they would encourage education and employment among women as well as among men.

Disappearance of Community

From a feminist perspective, family values have become an issue because individualism has driven out the sense of collective responsibility in our national culture. American institutions and social policies have not properly implemented a concern for all citizens. Comparative research on family structure, teenage pregnancy, poverty, and child outcomes in other countries demonstrates that where support is generous to help *all* families and children, there are higher levels of health and general education and lower levels of violence and child deviance than in the United States.

Liberal thinking and the focus on the free market have made it seem that citizens make their greatest contribution when they are self-sufficient, thereby keeping themselves off the public dole. But feminist theorist Iris Young argues that many of the activities that are basic to a healthy democratic society (such as cultural production, caretaking, political organizing, and charitable activities) will never be profitable in a private market. Yet many of the recipients of welfare and Social Security such as homemakers, single mothers, and retirees are doing important volunteer work caring for children and helping others in their communities. Thus the social worth of a person's contribution is not just in earning a paycheck that shows economic independence but also in making a social contribution. Such caretaking of other dependent citizens and of the body politic should be regarded as honorable, not inferior, and worthy of society's support and subsidy.

In fact it appears that married women's rising labor force participation from 41 percent in 1970 to 58 percent in 1990 may have been associated with their withdrawal from unpaid work in the home and community. Volunteer membership in everything from the PTA to bowling leagues declined by over 25 percent between 1969 and 1993. There is now considerable concern that the very basis that Alexis de Tocqueville thought necessary to democracy is under siege. To reverse this trend, social observers suggest that it will be necessary to guard time for families and leisure that is currently being sucked into the maw of paid employment. What is needed is a reorientation of priorities to give greater value to unpaid family and community work by both men and women.

National policies should also be reoriented to give universal support to children at every economic level of society, but especially to poor children. In a comparison of countries in the Organization for Economic Cooperation and Development, the United States ranks at the top in average male wages but near the bottom in its provision for disposable income for children. In comparison with the $700 per month available to children in Norway, France, or the Netherlands in 1992, U.S. children of a single nonemployed mother received only sightly under $200. The discrepancy is explained by very unequal distribution of U.S. income, with the top quintile, the "fortunate fifth," gaining 47 percent of the national income while the bottom fifth receives only 3.6 percent. This sharp inequality is, in turn, explained by an ideology of individualism that justifies the disproportionate gains of the few for their innovation and productivity and the meager income of the poor for their low initiative or competence. Lack of access to jobs and the low pay accruing to many contingent service occupations simply worsen the picture.

Feminists are skeptical of explanations that ascribe higher productivity to the higher paid and more successful leading actors while ignoring the efforts and contribution of the supporting cast. They know that being an invisible helper is the situation of many women. This insight is congruent with new ideas about the importance of "social capital" to the health of a society that have been put forward recently by a number of social scientists. Corporations cannot be solely responsible for maintaining the web of community, although they are already being asked to serve as extended family, neighborhood support group, and national health service.

Diversity of Family Forms

Those who are concerned for strengthening the civil society immediately turn to the changing nature of the family as being a key building block. Feminists worry that seemingly sensible efforts to reverse the trend of rising divorce and single parenthood will privilege the two-parent family to the detriment of women; they propose instead that family values be understood in a broader sense of valuing the family's unique capacity for giving emotional and material support rather than implying simply a two-parent form.

The debate between conservatives, liberals, and feminists on the issue of the two-parent family has been most starkly stated by sociologist Judith Stacey and political philosopher Iris Young. They regard the requirement that all women stay in a marriage as an invitation to coercion and subordination and an assault on the principles of freedom and self-determination that are at the foundation of democracy. Moreover, as Christopher Jencks and Kathryn Edin conclude from their study of several hundred welfare families, the current welfare reform rhetoric that no couple should have a child unless they can support it, does not take into account the uncertainty of life in which people who start out married or with adequate income may not always remain so. In the face of the worldwide dethronement of the two-parent family (approximately one-quarter to one-third of all families around the globe are headed by women), marriage should not be seen as the cure for child poverty. Mothers should not be seen as less than full citizens if they are not married or not employed (in 1989 there were only 16 million males between the ages of 25 and 34 who made over $12,000 compared with 20 million females of the same age who either had a child or wanted one). National family policy should instead begin with a value on women's autonomy and self-determination that includes the right to bear children. Mother-citizens are helping to reproduce the next generation for the whole society, and in that responsibility they deserve at least partial support.

From a feminist perspective the goal of the family is not only to bring up a healthy and productive new generation; families also provide the intimate and supportive group of kin or fictive kin that foster the health and well-being of every person—young or old, male or female, heterosexual, homosexual, or celibate. Recognition as "family" should therefore not be confined to the traditional two-parent unit connected by blood, marriage, or adoption, but should be extended to include kin of a divorced spouse (as Stacey documented in her study of Silicon Valley families), same-sex partnerships, congregate households of retired persons, group living arrangements, and so on. Twenty years ago economist Nancy Barrett noted that such diversity in family and household form was already present. Among all U.S. households in 1976, none of the six major types constituted more than 15-20 percent: couples with and without children under eighteen with the wife in the labor force (15.4 and 13.3 percent respectively); couples with or without children under 18 with the wife not in the labor force (19.1 and 17.1 percent); female- or male-headed households (14.4 percent); and single persons living alone (20.6 percent).

Such diversity both describes and informs contemporary "family values" in the United States. Each family type is numerous enough to have a legitimacy of its own, yet no single form is the dominant one. As a result the larger value system has evolved to encompass beliefs and rules that legitimate each type on the spectrum. The regressive alternative is "fundamentalism" that treats the two-parent family with children as the only legitimate form, single-parent families as unworthy of support, and the non-traditional forms as illegitimate. In 1995 the general population appears to have accepted diversity of family forms as normal. A Harris poll of 1,502 women and 460 men found that only two percent of women and one percent of men defined family as "being about the traditional nuclear family." One out of ten women defined family values as loving, taking care of, and supporting each other, knowing right from wrong or having good values, and nine out of ten said society should value all types of families. It appears most Americans believe that an Aunt Polly single-parent type family for a Huck Finn that provides economic support, shelter, meals, a place to sleep and to withdraw is better than no family at all.

Amidst gradual acceptance of greater diversity in family form, the gender-role revolution is also loosening the sex-role expectations traditionally associated with breadwinning and homemaking. Feminists believe that men and women can each do both. In addition, women in advanced industrial nations have by and large converged upon a new life pattern of multiple roles by which they combine work and family life. The negative outcome is an almost universal "double burden" for working women in which they spend eighty-four hours per week on paid and family work, married men spend seventy-two hours, and single persons without children spend fifty hours. The positive consequence, however, appears to be improved physical and mental health for those women who, though stressed, combine work and family roles. In addition, where a woman's husband helps her more with the housework, she is less likely to think of getting a divorce.

The Precarious Situation of Children

The principal remedy that conservatives and liberals would apply to the problems of children is to restore the two-parent family by reducing out-of-wedlock births, increasing the presence of fathers, and encouraging couples who are having marital difficulties to avoid divorce for the sake of their children. Feminists, on the other hand, are skeptical that illegitimacy, father absence, or divorce are the principal culprits they are made out to be. Leon Eisenberg reports that *over half of all births in Sweden* and *one-quarter of births in France* are to unmarried women, but without the disastrous correlated effects observed in the United States. Arlene Skolnick and Stacey Rosencrantz cite longitudinal studies showing that most children recover from the immediate negative effects of divorce.

How then, while supporting the principle that some fraction of women should be able to head families as single parents, do feminists analyze the problem of ill health, antisocial behavior, and poverty among children? Their answer focuses on the *lack of institutional supports* for the new type of dual-earner and single-parent families that are more prevalent today. Rather than attempt to force families back into the traditional mold, feminists note that divorce, lone-mother families, and women's employment are on the rise in every industrialized nation. But other countries have not seen the same devastating decline in child well-being, teen pregnancy, suicides and violent death, school failure, and a rising population of children in poverty. These other countries have four key elements of social and family policy which protect all children and their mothers: (1) work guarantees and other economic supports; (2) child care; (3) health care; and (4) housing subsidies. In the United States these benefits are scattered and uneven; those who can pay their way do so; only those who are poor or disabled receive AFDC for economic support, some help with child care, Medicaid for health care, and government-subsidized housing.

A first line of defense is to raise women's wages through raising the minimum wage, then provide them greater access to male-dominated occupations with higher wages. One-half of working women do not earn a wage adequate to support a family of four above the poverty line. Moreover, women in low-wage occupations are subject to frequent lay-offs and lack of benefits. Training to improve their human capital, provision of child care, and broadening of benefits would help raise women's capacity to support a family. Eisenberg reports that the Human Development Index of the United Nations (HDI), which ranks countries by such indicators as life expectancy, educational levels, and per capita income, places the United States fifth and Sweden sixth in the world. But when the HDI is recalculated to take into account equity of treatment of women, Sweden rises to first place and the United States falls to ninth. Therefore, one of the obvious places to begin raising children's status is to raise the economic status and earning power of their mothers.

A second major benefit which is not assured to working mothers is child care. Among school-age children up to thirteen years of age, one-eighth lack any kind of after-school care. Children come to the factories where their mothers work and wait on the lawn or in the lobby until their mothers are finished working. If a child is sick, some mothers risk losing a job if they stay home. Others are latchkey kids or in unknown circumstances, such as sleeping in their parents' cars or loitering on the streets. Although 60 percent of mothers of the 22 million preschool children are working, there are only 10 million child care places available, a shortfall of one to three million slots. Lack of good quality care for her children not only distracts a mother, adds to her absences from work, and makes her less productive, it also exposes the child to a lack of attention and care that leads to violent and antisocial behavior and poor performance in school.

Lack of medical benefits is a third gaping hole for poor children and lone-parent families. Jencks and Edin analyze what happens to a Chicago-area working woman's income if she goes off welfare. Her total income in 1993 dollars on AFDC (with food stamps, unreported earnings, help from family and friends) adds up to $12,355, in addition to which she receives Medicaid and child care. At a $6 per hour full-time job, however, without AFDC, with less than half as much from food stamps, with an Earned

Income Tax Credit, and help from relatives, her total income would add to $20,853. But she would have to pay for her own medical care, bringing her effective income down to $14,745 if she found free child care, and $9,801 if she had to pay for child care herself.

Some housing subsidies or low-income housing are available to low-income families. But the neighborhoods and schools are frequently of poor quality and plagued by violence. To bring up children in a setting where they cannot safely play with others introduces important risk factors that cannot simply be attributed to divorce and single parenthood. Rather than being protected and being allowed to be innocent, children must learn to be competent at a very early age. The family, rather than being child-centered, must be adult-centered, not because parents are selfish or self-centered but because the institutions of the society have changed the context of family life. These demands may be too much for children, and depression, violence, teen suicide, teen pregnancy, and school failure may result. But it would be myopic to think that simply restoring the two-parent family would be enough to solve all these problems. . . .

References

Bailyn, Lotte, *Breaking the Mold: Women, Men and Time in the New Corporate World* (The Free Press, 1994).

Barnett, Rosalind C., *Home-to-Work Spillover Revisited: A Study of Full-Time Employed Women in Dual-Earner Couples*, 56 J of Marriage and the Family 647 (1994).

Barrett, Nancy Smith, *Data Needs for Evaluating the Labor Market Status of Women*, in Barbara B. Reagan, ed., *Census Bureau Conference on Federal Statistical Needs Relating to Women* (U.S. Bureau of the Census, 1979).

Bellah, Robert, *Invasion of the Money World*, in David Blankenhorn, Steven Bayme, & Jean Bethke Elshtain, eds, *Rebuilding the Nest* (Family Service America, 1990).

Bellah, Robert N., et al., *The Good Society* (Knopf, 1991).

Bellah, Robert N., et al., *Habits of the Heart* (U California Press, 1985).

Berger, Brigitte, *Block Grants: Changing the Welfare Culture from the Ground Up*, 3 Dialogue (March 1995).

Bianchi, Suzanne M., & Daphne Spain, *American Women in Transition* (Russell Sage Foundation, 1986).

Cain, Glen G., *Married Women in the Labor Force: An Economic Analysis* (U Chicago Press, 1966).

Coleman, James S., *Foundations of Social Theory* (Harvard U Press, 1990).

Conger, Rand D., Xiao-Jia Ge, & Frederick O. Lorenz, *Economic Stress and Marital Relations*, in R. D. Conger & G. H. Elder, Jr., eds, *Families in Troubled Times: Adaption to Change in Rural America* (Aldine de Gruyter, 1994).

Council on Families in America, *Marriage in America* (Institute for American Values, 1995).

Davis, Kingsley, *Wives and Work: A Theory of the Sex-Role Revolution and Its Consequences,* in S. M. Dorobasch & M. H. Strober, eds, *Feminism, Children, and the New Families* (Guilford Press, 1988).

Easterlin, Richard A., *Birth and Fortune: The Impact of Numbers on Personal Welfare* (Basic Books, 1980).

Eisenberg, Leon, *Is the Family Obsolete?,* 60 Key Reporter 1 (1995).

Elder, Glen H., Jr., *Children of the Great Depression* (U Chicago Press, 1974).

Elkind, David, *The Hurried Child: Growing Up Too Fast Too Soon* (Addison-Wesley, 1981).

Elkind, David, *Ties That Stress: The New Family in Balance* (Harvard U Press, 1994).

Ellwood, David T., *Poor Support: Poverty in the American Family* (Basic Books, 1988).

Elshtain, Jean Bethke, *Democracy on Trial* (Basic Books, 1995).

Esping-Andersen, Gosta, *The Three Worlds of Welfare Capitalism* (Princeton U Press, 1990).

Ferber, Marianne A. & Julie A. Nelson, *Beyond Economic Man: Feminist Theory and Economics* (U Chicago Press, 1993).

Fuchs, Victor, *Are Americans Underinvesting in Children?* in David Blankenhorn, Stephen Bayme, & Jean Bethke Elshtain, eds, *Rebuilding the Nest* (Family Service America, 1990).

Giele, Janet Zollinger, *Gender and Sex Roles,* in N. J. Smelser, ed, *Handbook of Sociology* (Sage Publications, 1988).

Giele, Janet Zollinger, *Two Paths to Women's Equality: Temperance, Suffrage, and the Origins of American Feminism* (Twayne Publishers, Macmillan, 1995).

Giele, Janet Z. & Rainer Pischner, *The Emergence of Multiple Role Patterns Among Women: A Comparison of Germany and the United States,* Vierteljahrshefte zur Wirtschaftsforschung (Heft 1-2, 1994).

Giele, Janet Zollinger, *Woman's Role Change and Adaptation, 1920-1990,* in K. Hulbert & D. Schuster, eds, *Women's Lives Through Time: Educated American Women of the Twentieth Century* (Jossey-Bass, 1993).

Gilbreath, Edward, *Manhood's Great Awakening,* Christianity Today 27 (February 6, 1995).

Gill, Richard T. & T. Grandon Gill, *Of Families, Children, and a Parental Bill of Rights* (Institute for American Values, 1993).

Glendon, Mary Ann, *Marriage and the State: The Withering Away of Marriage*, 62 Virginia Law Review 663 (May 1976).

Goode, William J., *World Revolution in Family Patterns* (Free Press, 1963).

Haveman, Robert, & Barbara Wolfe, *Succeeding Generations: On the Effects of Investments in Children* (Russell Sage Foundation, 1994).

Helson, Ravenna & S. Picano, *Is the Traditional Role Bad for Women?*, 59 J of Personality & Social Psychology 311 (1990).

Hernandez, Donald J., *America's Children: Resources from Family, Government, and the Economy* (Russell Sage Foundation, 1993).

Herrnstein, Richard J., & Charles A. Murray, *The Bell Curve: Intelligence and Class Structure in American Life* (The Free Press, 1994).

Hochschild, Arlie, *The Fractured Family,* The American Prospect 106 (Summer 1991).

Hoffman, Lois, *The Effects on Children of Maternal and Paternal Employment,* in Naomi Gerstel & Harriet Engel Gross, eds, *Families and Work* (Temple U Press, 1987).

Jencks, Christopher, & Kathryn Edin, *Do Poor Women Have a Right to Bear Children?*, The American Prospect 43 (Winter 1995).

Leach, Penelope, *Children First: What Our Society Must Do and Is Doing* (Random House, 1994).

Menaghan, Elizabeth G., & Toby L. Parcel, *Employed Mothers and Children's Home Environments,* 53 J of Marriage and the Family 417 (1991).

Miller, Beth M., *Private Welfare: The Distributive Equity of Family Benefits in America* (Ph.D. thesis, Brandeis University, 1992).

Mincer, Jacob, *Labor-Force Participation of Married Women: A Study of Labor Supply,* in Report of the National Bureau of Economic Research, *Aspects of Labor Economics* (Universities-National Bureau Committee of Economic Research, 1962).

Murray, Charles A., *Losing Ground: American Social Policy, 1950-1980* (Basic Books, 1984).

Offen, Karen, *Defining Feminism: A Comparative Historical Approach,* 14 Signs 119 (1988).

Oppenheimer, Valerie K., *Structural Sources of Economic Pressure for Wives to Work—Analytic Framework,* 4 J of Family History 177 (1979).

Oppenheimer, Valerie K., *Work and the Family: A Study in Social Demography* (Academic Press, 1982).

Ott, Notburga, *Intrafamily Bargaining and Household Decisions* (Springer-Verlag, 1992).

Pedersen, Susan, *Family, Dependence, and the Origins of the Welfare State: Britain and France, 1914-1945* (Cambridge U Press, 1993).

Putnam, Robert D., *Bowling Alone: America's Declining Social Capital,* 4 J of Democracy 65 (1995).

Rainwater, Lee, & William L. Yancey, *The Moynihan Report and the Politics of Controversy* (MIT Press, 1967).

Rector, Robert, *Welfare,* in American Heritage Foundation, *Issues '94: The Candidate's Briefing Book* (American Heritage Foundation, 1994).

Rodgers, Frans Sussner, & Charles Rodgers, *Business and the Facts of Family Life,* 6 Harvard Business Review 199 (1989).

Rossi, Alice S., *The Future in the Making,* 63 American J of Orthopsychiatry 166 (1993).

Scanzoni, John, *Power Politics in the America Marriage* (Prentice-Hall, 1972).

Schor, Juliet, *The Overworked American: The Unexpected Decline of Leisure* (Basic Books, 1991).

Skolnick, Arlene, & Stacey Rosencrantz, *The New Crusade for the Old Family,* The American Prospect 59 (Summer 1994).

Spalter-Roth, Roberta M., Heidi I. Hartmann, & Linda M. Andrews, *Mothers, Children, and Low-Wage Work: The Ability to Earn a Family Wage,* in W. J. Wilson, ed, *Sociology and the Public Agenda* (Sage Publications, 1993).

U.S. Bureau of the Census, *Statistical Abstract of the United States: 1994* (114th ed.) (Washington, DC: 1994).

Wallace, Ruth A., & Alison Wolf, *Contemporary Sociological Theory* (Prentice Hall, 1991).

Weinstein, Fred, & Gerald M. Platt, *The Wish to Be Free: Society, Psyche, and Value Change* (U California Press, 1969).

Wexler, Sherry, *To Work and To Mother: A Comparison of the Family Support Act and the Family and Medical Leave Act* (Ph.D. diss. draft, Brandeis University, 1995).

Whitehead, Barbara Dafoe, *Dan Quayle Was Right,* Atlantic Monthly 47 (April 1993).

Williams, Constance Willard, *Black Teenage Mothers: Pregnancy and Child Rearing from Their Perspective* (Lexington Books, 1990).

Wilson, William Julius, *The Truly Disadvantaged: The Inner City, the Underclass, and Public Policy,* (U Chicago Press, 1987).

Young, Iris Marion, *Making Single Motherhood Normal,* Dissent 88 (Winter 1994).

Young, Iris, *Mothers, Citizenship and Independence: A Critique of Pure Family Values,* 105 Ethics 535 (1995).

Zelizer, Vivianna A., *Pricing the Priceless Child. The Changing Social Value of Children* (Basic Books, 1985).

B. The Economics of the Family

Implicit in the material you have read so far is the sociological assumption that the way people behave is shaped by the people with whom they interact, the institutions in which they live, and the cultural understandings of their society. But, as we said at the beginning of this chapter, the sociological perspective is not the only one from which to approach the family. Economics provides another such perspective. Since that approach will be familiar to many of our readers and since many of them will think its viewpoint poorly suited to analyzing the family, our next reading explains the economic view of the family at some length and usefully contrasts it with the legal view. This article is important for another reason—it introduces some basic economic ideas that are relevant to family law and that will be important in some of our subsequent readings.

Ann Laquer Estin, *Love and Obligation: Family Law and the Romance of Economics,* 36 WILLIAM AND MARY LAW REVIEW 989 (Winter 1995)*

I. Law and Economics and Family Life

. . . Both economics and law traditionally have represented the household or the family as a fundamentally different sphere of human behavior than the marketplace. Economics and law have each constructed different norms to explain and govern behavior in each sphere. In law, the boundary between the family and the marketplace sometimes is described as a distinction between status and contract. In economics, the distinction is understood in terms of the difference between altruistic and self-interested motivations for behavior. Contemporary legal and economic doctrines construct different understandings of these boundaries and a new set of theories to define family life.

A.   *Traditional Approaches to the Family*

The intellectual dichotomy between family and market has encouraged an assumption that family issues are not relevant to economic and legal analysis. Economists and lawyers have not treated work in the family as comparable to work in the marketplace. Families or households are not seen as economically productive. Families do appear in the analysis of consumer behavior, but even in that analysis, economists and lawyers typically assume that the family behaves as if it were a single individual. In both disciplines, the participants in market transactions are conceived as individuals without family attachments.

1.   Work in the Household

Statistical measures of economic production, such as Gross National Product (GNP), reflect a narrow, neoclassical vision. These indicators measure only market

---

activities. The work of maintaining a family—bearing and caring for children, house-work, home maintenance, meal preparation, subsistence agriculture, and so on—is excluded unless performed for payment. Public policies reflect this confusion of market activity with economic production. Income tax laws treat only remunerated work as sufficiently productive to be taxed. Social insurance schemes, including social security payments and a whole range of unemployment, disability, and workers compensation benefits, cover only workers in the wage labor economy and their dependents. Social insurance defined to meet the particular needs of household producers without breadwinner partners—particularly the Aid to Families with Dependent Children (AFDC) program—pays much lower benefits than those available under the payroll programs.

Some economists argue that the exclusion of nonmarket work from public policy and planning creates a substantial distortion. Policy decisions based on incomplete statistics may omit important values and areas of production from the planning process. As economist Marilyn Waring has noted, the distinction between market and nonmarket production is a heavily gendered one; work done predominantly by women remains invisible to economic policy makers. Both the statistical indicators and the policies based upon these indicators privilege market production and the types of economic activity most characteristic of modern, industrialized societies over household production and more traditional economies. Reforming the treatment of household production has gained currency, in part because increasing portions of women's traditionally unpaid labor in the home has been shifting to the market. Without better information on household production, evaluating these types of changes is difficult.

Of course, it is easier to collect information on market transactions than to estimate the productive value of work in the home. Economists, however, routinely adjust their figures to include other types of nonmarket activity, such as the rental value of private home ownership.

The idea that "services" in the household are not equivalent to "work" also appears in the common law tradition. Restitution principles permit compensation only for services provided without a gratuitous intention, a rule that excludes most interactions between family members. Moreover, the law has presumed that work within a household is gratuitous. Efforts to use law to define and enforce contractual relationships between household members also have been constrained. In more recent analyses, both economic and legal theorists have come to recognize that the activities of a household are economically productive. Economic theorists began to describe the productive role of families in the 1960s. In tort law, household services are acknowledged to have "pecuniary" value, although this value remains difficult to quantify. In divorce law, rules for property division now require consideration of all contributions made by husband and wife, including "the contribution of a spouse as homemaker."

2.   Families or Individuals?

In neoclassical economics, the individual is the unit of analysis. Individuals sell their labor, receive paychecks, and purchase goods and services. Sometimes the prototypical rational economic man appears in the analysis abstracted and alone; sometimes he is understood to represent a family or a household as the breadwinner and "head" of a conventional nuclear family. "The family" exists only parenthetically, as an appendage to the individual economic actor. Many aspects of public policy reflect the assumption that families are attached to individual, usually male, workers.

Families began to appear in the economic analysis of consumer demand in the mid-1950s. Paul Samuelson is credited with providing and justifying an economic model of family behavior that treats the family as a unit with a single, unified "utility function." This model, and the absence of empirical knowledge about distributions within the family, have led economists—and government policymakers—generally to assume that a family's resources are equally distributed among its members. Although this approach has been characterized as analytically convenient, it has also been criticized for ignoring the significance of what occurs within the family.

Similarly, in the branches of economics concerned with the distribution of income and wealth, the household is the basic unit of analysis. As a result, the internal character of families or households is again largely ignored, and comparisons of the living standards of different households are distorted significantly. The problems this distortion poses are compounded by the tendency of statistical measures and public policies to ignore household production. As Edward Lazear and Robert Michael have argued, these issues pose a particular problem in analysis of family policy, especially in the context of divorce.

The law reflects a similar preoccupation with individuals. With slight differences between traditional "community property" and "title" states, the individual wage earner, not the family, has the legal right to own and control the household's money income and to determine how that income will be spent. Courts will not second-guess a wage earner's decisions regarding the allocation of income within the family. In fact, the law traditionally gave a husband and father control over the money income of his wife and children in addition to his own.

By ignoring work in the household and treating families as unitary and undifferentiated, traditional economic and legal analysis is ill-equipped to respond to contemporary policy problems. In effect, by ignoring the internal characteristics of families, economics and law define all families as the same, and many household types disappear into this theoretical void. Divorced families, single-parent families, and extended-kin families all vary significantly from the implicit legal and economic norm. Many of the intractable policy problems in property division and child support relate directly to the problem of how resources are allocated among different households in the same "family." Controversies concerning public benefits law, and the discrepancy between narrowly drawn economic policies and the wide variety of family arrangements in society, repeatedly have reached the United States Supreme Court.

B.   New Family Economic Theory

The new theory of family economics reconceptualizes family life as a process of exchange between individual family members. Marriage, divorce, and decisions concerning the household all are analyzed in terms of bargaining and rational choice. Economists recognize that exchange behavior in the family is different from exchanges in the market, and they explain the difference in terms of altruism, which serves to bond individual family members' interests.

With this theory, economists have developed a much richer understanding of the productive aspects of family life. This theory offers vocabulary and a range of models to describe interactions within families and interactions between the market and family spheres. Acknowledging these economic relationships is an important step toward correcting the oversights of traditional economic theory, and it offers important lessons for the law. The theory originated, however, when economists began to explore issues of market behavior that could not be fully explained without consideration of family behavior. For the most part, this investigation has operated within the same conceptual frameworks used to understand market production.

For these scholars, "economic analysis" means viewing family issues in terms of rational choices made by autonomous agents seeking to maximize their individual welfare or profit. Professor Becker articulates his goal as the use of "a choice-theoretic framework for analyzing many aspects of family life," based on the assumptions "that individuals maximize their utility from basic preferences that do not change rapidly over time, and that the behavior of different individuals is coordinated by explicit and implicit markets." As Becker writes, "an analysis based on rational behavior provides a powerful framework for gaining insights into family organization and structure under different laws, circumstances, and cultures." Over time, this framework has led economists to consider a widening set of family issues, and some now see their analysis as an alternative to other theories of family behavior.

This Part will sketch the framework of the new theory and note where its concepts interact with legal and policy questions. Four aspects are particularly important. First, these theorists explain the social institutions of marriage in positive economic terms as a device to facilitate specialization and division of labor. In effect, this explanation is a defense of "traditional," gender-role divided marriage. Second, the theory investigates the economic effects of this traditional type of marriage for husband and wife and develops models for valuing the nonmarket work of a homemaker in market terms. This work has potential significance for a wide range of family-related legal problems from contract and tort to the financial regulation of divorce. A third issue, which has been less neatly resolved in the theory, is the economic role of children in family life. The fourth area of concern is a pair of assumptions about family life that have been the foundation for the larger theoretical framework. One is the use of exchange as a model for family relationships, and the other is the concept of altruism as a motivation for individual choices of family members.

1.   Household Production

Household production theory treats the time and other resources of household members as inputs into the production of various goods, ranging from food and shelter to children, leisure, and love. This process occurs within a set of constraints established by the larger economic system that defines market values for the time of household members and prices the commodities that family members purchase. The theory assumes that resources available to the family are allocated efficiently in order to maximize the total satisfaction or utility of household members. Although household members realize much of this satisfaction in the form of nonmarket goods, for purposes of the theory, this satisfaction is treated as if it could be monetarized.

Economists explain the institution of marriage by the efficiencies that result from a specialization of labor. As Judge Posner notes:

> [T]he family facilitates the division of labor, yielding gains from special- ization. In the traditional family the husband specializes in some market employment (for example, engineering) that yields income that can be used to purchase the market commodities needed as inputs into the final pro- duction of the household, while the wife devotes her time to processing mar- ket commodities (for example, groceries) into household output (for example, dinner).

Because husband and wife specialize in complementary activities, both are able to max- imize the value of their time to produce a greater total output for the household.

In his book, *A Treatise on the Family*, Professor Becker demonstrates that a division of labor within the household would be efficient even without the overlay of a traditional marriage relationship, or, as he puts it, between an "intrinsically identical" husband and wife. Next, he notes that women have a "comparative advantage" when it comes to the work of bearing and rearing children and observes that even very small differences in biological advantage (or small differences caused by other factors, such as market discrimination against women) can generate much greater differences in the activities of husband and wife. This relationship suggests an explanation for highly dis- tinct gender roles—the greater the differences in the economic attributes of men and women, the greater the benefits from marriage.

In economic theory, the benefits of specialization explain marriage, divorce, and fertility behavior. Thus, Becker views the choice of a particular marriage partner as a highly significant economic event because the potential for gains from specialization is different with different potential mates. His model depicts marriage decisions as occurring in a type of market which operates to sort potential husbands and wives. Moreover, he also describes divorce as an illustration of a type of market; the decision to seek a divorce occurs when an individual compares his or her current marital satis- faction with what he or she anticipates would be available in the remarriage market or in single life.

Raising children is central to the economists' view of marriage. Judge Posner writes that specialization of labor principles do not alone explain marriage; in fact, he states that the efficient, role-divided marriage elaborated in economic theory could be replaced by a "business partnership" if it were not for the production of children. He concludes: "The key to the puzzle lies in the nature of the major 'commodity' that mar- riage produces: children. . . . [I]t is hard to believe that marriage would be a common institution if most people didn't want children." Professor Becker's conclusion is sim- ilar; he argues that the "main purpose of marriage and families is the production and rearing of own children." Posner describes rearing children as a process that demands substantial investments of the parents' resources, primarily "an enormous amount of parental (traditionally maternal) time." Traditional family structures and gender roles facilitate these investments.

The understanding of marriage as a device for efficient household production is central to the economic approach to family policy. The models define efficiency, in the sense of resource allocations that generate the maximum total level of satisfaction, as the measure of marital success. They view the economic advantages of marriage as similar to the advantages of other "organizations"; these advantages include a better flow of information between group members and various internal rewards for working for the benefit of the group.

A number of law and economics writers draw explicit analogies between marriage and various commercial relationships. From this viewpoint, marriage, a relationship "dominated by long-term repeated transactions that tie people together personally," is similar to the relationship of a landlord and tenant with a long-term lease, a parts supplier with one major client, or a car owner and his regular auto mechanic. This analysis builds on a body of economic writing developing the concept of the "firm" and legal writing discussing long-term, "relational" contracts. Likewise, the risks of marriage correlate with those of other long-term economic relationships, including the danger that one party may take advantage of the others by cheating, shirking, or other dishonest behavior. For these commentators, divorce is a problem because it may reflect "opportunism" or exploitation of the economic effects of the joint enterprise.

2.   Human Capital

In contemporary settings, many long-term benefits and risks of marriage for individuals correlate with its effects on human capital. Economic theories hold that along with the specialization of labor in households goes a differentiation, increasing over time, in the "human capital" accumulations of household members. Human capital refers to a variety of factors that increase or decrease the labor power of individuals. It may be augmented by education, training, experience, and medical care, or it can deteriorate from such causes as lack of current work experience or an addiction to heavy drinking. Empirical data suggest that human capital investments have a substantial impact on earnings. In economic theory, work in the household as well as the market can become more productive through increases in skills, experience, and good work habits.

Human capital theory has led to new methods for valuing household production. Starting from the premise that work in the home is productive, and that it involves training, experience, and a choice not to pursue work in the market, these methods focus on the opportunity cost of the homemaker's time (the price the wage labor market would pay for the time devoted to household services) as an indirect measure of the value of those services. Using this approach, economists have tied the value of time spent on household tasks to many different variables, including (1) the composition of the household, (2) the age, education, and wage rates of husband and wife, (3) the number and ages of children, and even (4) the number of rooms in the house. As the model becomes more sophisticated, some writers have added human capital considerations into the measurement of opportunity costs.

Because a homemaker's wage opportunities are limited by the fact that she has specialized in domestic rather than market labor, the opportunity costs of homemaking may be defined to "include[ ] not only current foregone earnings but also loss of [the homemaker's] market earning power, through depreciation of market skills previously acquired, and foregone opportunities to invest in market skills." As Posner describes the issue, an accurate measurement of these costs requires "estimating what her probable market earnings would have been had she entered the market at the time when instead she became a housewife."

Household production and human capital theories have become important to the analysis of damages awards in tort when a homemaker is killed or injured and to financial remedies between the parties to a divorce. The theories also help to explain the demographic changes in family life over the last half-century. Economists postulate that the dramatic changes in women's labor force participation, and the accompanying trend toward greater investments by women in their own market-oriented human capital, have had significant effects on family behavior. They note that the opportunity cost of working in the home has increased as women's real wages and labor market opportunities have increased. In economic theory, increases in the "cost" of household labor translate into an increase in the labor's value or utility to a family. One result is a shift in some aspects of housework into the market sector. Economists argue that these changes also reduce the gains from gender-role-divided marriage relationships (which may contribute to lower rates of marriage, increased rates of divorce, and significant declines in fertility rates).

Household members may devote significant resources of time, effort, and money to particular human capital investments. Several patterns of family investment in adult human capital are well recognized, including the "two person career" and the graduate school "PhT" marriage. In economic theory, many of the problems of divorce stem from the fact that a housewife's human capital is rarely valued outside a particular family. Conversely, market types of human capital improve an individual's earning potential regardless of whether a marriage continues.

Virtually all of the activities and expenses of child rearing represent investments in children's stock of capital; these parental investments are central to children's future income and satisfaction as adults. Although economic analysis views raising children as the reason for marriage and family, it is no longer so clear that parents consider the costs of raising children as an economic investment. Posner notes that although children once constituted an "income producing" investment for families, the desire to have children is now more plausibly explained by the pleasure adults receive from their children. Posner also cites an "instinct or desire to preserve the species" or to perpetuate the parents' own characteristics, name, or memory.

The decision to have children has become a question of consumer choice, a question of personal taste. Raising children is very expensive, and, in our economic system, children have no productive role. For women in particular, parenthood presents a variety of personal and financial risks that are increasingly severe. Acting rationally, a couple will choose to have children only if they perceive parenthood as more enjoyable than the other pleasures their time and money can buy.

Children also greatly complicate the economic analysis of divorce. In a family with young children, divorce dissolves the organization that was specialized to provide for their care and replaces it with a much less efficient system. Divorce significantly reduces the resources of time and money available for children. Although economic theory has been applied to issues of child support and custody after divorce, what is most revealing about the economic approach is what it suggests about a transformation of attitudes toward parenthood. Particularly in the setting of divorce, these attitudes are rooted increasingly in parental self-interest and separated from more traditional conceptions of love and obligation.

3.   Exchange and Altruism

Economic analysis of family behavior redefines family life as a process of exchange. The theory is built with models in which members of a household interact in the ways that strangers do in the marketplace: contracting around allocations of resources, using stores of wealth and power to make deals to increase each player's utility or personal happiness. In this work, however, economists have begun to investigate the role of altruism, which is described as a distinctive characteristic of family economic behavior. Altruism complicates the models of exchange within the family, but it does not displace the understanding of behavior as ultimately rational and self-interested.

According to Judge Posner, "[t]here is a substitute in marriage for the control mechanisms within a business firm. Economists naturally do not call this factor 'love,' but describe it as a form of altruism." Posner defines altruism as "the condition in which the welfare of one person is a positive function of the welfare of another."

The paradigms of exchange and altruism are especially important to questions of how resources are allocated within the family. This literature, which began with Paul Samuelson's "consensus" model, has seen the appearance of two newer models. One is based on the premise of an altruistic head of the household with power to make transfers within the family in order to achieve optimal allocations of various goods. The other model envisions explicit or implicit bargaining among family members over these questions.

Professor Becker defines an altruistic person as one whose utility function depends positively on the well-being of another. He demonstrates that in families with an altruistic head, the preferences of different family members will be maximized. In an altruistically controlled organization, each person's "happiness or utility or welfare" will be experienced by all members of the organization. As Judge Posner argues, it is a "cheap and efficacious substitute for (formal) contracting." Other economists are critical, however, of the uses to which altruism is put in this analysis. They argue that family members' interests are often in conflict and present the altruism hypothesis as a more sophisticated version of the old consensus model.

Economic models of family behavior have become part of the legal framework for understanding marriage and divorce. Increasingly, the paradigms of exchange and altruism have begun to define parenthood as well. Becker and other economists assume that parents act altruistically with respect to children. "The utility of parents depends not only on their own consumption, but also on the utility of each child and the number of children." Therefore, parents invest in the human capital of their children by spending money, time, and effort on child care, education, health care, gifts, and bequests. At the same time, economists note that expenditures on children also reduce the consumption opportunities of parents, and families (and family members) vary widely in the degree of altruism they demonstrate. Increasingly, bargaining models appear in the analysis of parent-child relationships, with children viewed either as objects of parental bargaining or participants in a process of exchanges with their parents.

C.   Limits of Economic Analysis

The new economic theories of family life present a useful remedy for many of the conceptual ills of older law and economic analysis. New theories are especially significant in their recognition of the importance of the work that occurs in households. However, constructing a legal theory of marriage and divorce on purely economic foundations would be enormously problematic. Many criticisms of law and economics appear in the literature, but these issues take on special significance in the setting of family law problems.

One issue is the very neutrality attempted by economic theorists. As James Boyd White argues, the translation of human activity into economic terms erases important values and distinctions, such as the difference between selfishness and generosity or the personal characteristics of individuals. To economists, even those interested in family life, these matters lie entirely outside their analysis, which is not concerned with the various "tastes" or "preferences" of individual economic actors. The new home economics follows this tradition, examining only certain economic implications of the choice of whether to work in the home or the market, to raise children or pets, or the preferences for either fidelity or variety in sexual partners. Although these "preferences" may be exogenous in economic theory, they remain very significant in the social and legal regulation of families. A legal theory that ignored these questions would be seriously deficient.

The problems that this limitation creates are most dramatic when it comes to parent-child relationships. Despite the fact that these analysts describe child rearing as the purpose of marriage, economic theories of the family cannot—and do not try to—explain why some couples choose to have children and some do not. Some economists have made this criticism. Zvi Griliches observes that the economic analysis of fertility begins with three premises: "[C]hildren are goods, that all goods are subject to two constraints—time and money—and that children are relatively time-intensive goods." Griliches points out that this analysis does not distinguish children from hi-fi sets, and he goes on to argue that:

> [I]f we want to study the demand for children, we have to put more content into the theory and start asking why do people want to have children; what are the returns and not just the costs of this activity? . . . If we are studying the demand for children rather than for hi-fi sets, we have to ask ourselves what it is about children that distinguishes them from other time-intensive durable goods.

For family law, it is essential to be able to distinguish children from stereo equipment.

A second problem concerns the particulars of the economic models being offered. Legal theorists need to question both the positive and normative aspects of these models. Are efficiency principles a useful normative base for family regulation? Are exchange norms adequate to represent the full range of values at stake? Can these models be extended to nonmonetary goals of families? How broadly can we assume that people live in the family types which these models describe?

Theories premised on unelaborated assumptions about family composition, opportunities, and values may be seriously deficient when applied to different types of families. Economic theory has been preoccupied with a single type of household, marked by a traditional, gender-based division of roles. We can question how accurately this model describes the reality of family circumstances. Moreover, while it may work well in theory, this model may not work as well for devising a generalized system of legal rules.

One illustration of this narrow vision is the choice of research problems. The new family economics has paid serious attention to the problems of divorce in a certain type of household, while ignoring a wide range of economic issues of desperate importance for many other types of families. For example, one of the premises of the analysis of specialization and division of labor is that the parties in fact have opportunities for paid work. In view of the extremely limited employment opportunity for men in some sectors of our society, this suggests an issue of enormous importance to poor and minority families. It has been, however, all but invisible in the economic theory of family life.

Another limitation of economic theory as a model for law results from its emphasis on individual behavior and rational choice. Rational choice theory largely ignores the social construction of "the family" and of individual choices. The analysis does not address issues of gender and issues of power. Family law doctrines have often served protective functions for women and children, both within and outside of marriage, in large part because men have tended to have more choices and greater allocations of power and resources than their female partners. Economic theories of the household have not yet incorporated these concerns.

Legal theorists must recognize that the divide between family and market still runs deep. The new household economics has had limited effect, even in those areas of family policy and law that raise the most directly economic issues. There has been no move toward broad reforms of tax and social insurance laws to recognize the value of household labor. Opportunity cost measures of the value of household services are controversial, as are rules that would treat earnings during marriage as shared resources, or human capital changes as compensable at divorce. Even when homemaking and child-rearing work are transferred to paid domestic employees, popular opinion and practice keeps this work outside the mainstream of economic life. Moreover, the controversy surrounding the inclusion of household production in the nation's GNP suggests that many dissenters continue to challenge the view that household work is economically significant.

In a previous article, I argued that maintenance law reflects a struggle to understand marriage in both economic and moral terms. I suggested that the difficulty was greatest "in those areas of family life defined by tangles of love and obligation: raising children, preparing family meals, working to be a 'good provider'—keeping groceries on the table and a roof overhead." These difficulties are expressed in the hesitation of some courts to allow compensation for one spouse's disproportionate contributions to a marriage. In law and economics, there is an opposite tendency to conceive relationships in solely economic terms and ignore the dangers of subjecting all aspects of family life to market discourse.

A vision based on exchange and altruism is not sufficient to discern the full spectrum of behavior within families. Altruism, defined as the interdependence of utility functions, is actually a type of self-interest. Economic theory fails to recognize both love, which does not assume self-interest, and obligation, which exists despite self-interest. It also ignores the wide range of less admirable motivations in family behavior such as spite, rage, and guilt.

The most difficult family law problems prove that altruism is undependable and that self-interest does not always further family and social needs. Custody disputes, marital violence, child support payments, and divorce reflect failures of altruism. The concept of altruism as defined by economic theory has not been useful in understanding these failures. Rather, it serves as a rationalization for the older economic notions that viewed the family uncritically as a single unit. Perhaps more than anything, what legal theory requires is a set of principles to employ when the power of self-interest overtakes the commitments of family life.

C. The History of the Family

Because the family in which we grew up is so much a part of ourselves, it is easy for us to believe that it is the natural form families take, the one that expresses something deep about human nature. Among the remedies for this misapprehension is to look at the family historically. The next article we excerpt does just that. In doing so, it also reveals a good deal about where many of our basic familial ideas and practices came from and about how they have been justified.

Lee E. Teitelbaum, *Family History and Family Law,* 1985 WISCONSIN LAW REVIEW 1135[*]

II. THE GENERAL THEORY OF FAMILY HISTORY

It seems to be common ground among Marxists, modernists, feminists, and the general run of historians that the family is an idealized social institution with a sort of corporate identity: a collective of husband, wife, and children. Moreover, it is now commonly agreed that this entity has changed radically between the sixteenth century when the "modern" family arises and the twentieth century. The change is not, however, primarily structural; the early hypothesis that colonial families were extended rather than nuclear has been rejected on current evidence. Rather, it is said, the function of the family in society has altered. In the seventeenth and eighteenth centuries, the household was an extension and reflection of the community at large. This notion is conventionally expressed by the preachers' description of the family as "a little commonwealth, a little church": a phrase now understood as a description of how families actually functioned as well as a declaration of expectations. John Demos suggests that the family was joined "in a relation of profound reciprocity" with the society as a whole, such that "one might almost say they are continuous with one another."

It is unclear whether the principles of family organization followed from principles generally governing social organization or the reverse. Certainly the Fifth Commandment was used to justify the sovereignty of kings and Raleigh claimed that the first governors were fathers of families, comparing the king to "the master of the household." The primary concern of political philosophy, however, is to justify the power of national rather than domestic sovereigns, and the principles of family relationships were likely developed to illustrate principles thought important for the general society. Whichever the case, the authority of colonial fathers over children clearly reflected the authoritarian views of sovereignty held by the likes of Hobbes and the Puritan Robert Bolton. While we do not know much about the affective character of Puritan home life, it is clear that sermons and advice books put affection a poor second to control as a

---

principle of parent-child relations. The words of John Robinson's *Of Children and Their Education* expressed the common view:

> For the beating, and keeping down of this stubbornness parents must provide carefully for two things: first that children's wills and wilfulness be restrained and repressed, and that, in time; lest sooner than they imagine, the tender sprigs grow to that stiffness, that they will rather break than bow. Children should not know, if it could be kept from them, that they have a will of their own, but in their parent's keeping. . . .

The principle of hierarchical order characterizing both general seventeenth century colonial society and parent-child relations extended, it is further said, to the proper place of husbands and wives. Protestants generally viewed marriage as a contract rather than a sacrament. Radical Protestants held that opinion even more strongly; the Puritans briefly but dramatically threw aside Anglican requirements of religious celebration almost upon stepping from their ships. Accordingly, the relation of husbands and wives was typically described as a union of partners, entailing mutual respect and shared responsibility.

The partnership of spouses, however, was not a partnership among equals. Although the wife was by no means a servant of her husband, her place was strictly defined by cultural understanding, and "joyful submission" to it was expected. John Robinson, whose injunction to parents regarding suppression of their children we have already seen, described the wife's role as one of "reverent subjection" to the will of her husband. Moreover, laws plainly treated wives as dependents because of the fact of their marriage. Whereas a single woman could acquire or dispose of property and make contracts on much the same basis as a male, upon marriage she lost control of her property and relinquished independent contractual power. Although a good argument can be made that the married woman's incapacity was not as great as Blackstone made it out to be, her disabilities nonetheless were genuine. When a seventeenth century New England woman became a wife, to a significant extent "she gave up everything to her husband and devoted herself exclusively to managing his household. Henceforth her duty was to 'keep at home, educating of his children, keeping and improving what is got by the industry of man.'"

The general theory identifies a radical change, occurring at least by the beginning of the nineteenth century, in the internal relationships and external functions of families. The household was fast disappearing as a unit of economic production. As family farms and cottage industries receded and cities grew, the workplace moved from home to factory or office. Although women might have followed men outside of the home, and some single women did, married women largely remained within the household. The resulting separation of women and domestic activities from the realm of economic production was clearly recognized by both contemporary culture and modern historical assessment. The world of employment was then and is now described as a jungle: competitive, impersonal, unrelenting. Men's performance was judged, not occasionally by their neighbors as had been true, but daily and systematically by remote and powerful figures. The moral implications of capitalism created immense pressure as well. Success in the workplace was a measure, and perhaps the principal measure, of individual worth. Failure in the workplace reflected a failure of character.

From such a world, it was and is agreed, refuge was necessary. Aries saw in the industrial family "*the* private domain, the only place where a person could legitimately escape the inquisitive stare of industrial society." John Demos describes the nineteenth century home as "a bastion of peace, of repose, of orderliness, of unwavering devotion to people and principles beyond the self."

These reconstructions find ample support in contemporary writings. Robert Griswold's collection of nineteenth century tributes to the family as refuge is representative enough. Extreme in its sentimentality but not in its sentiment is the following excerpt from the *Santa Clara Argus* of 1866:

> Where will our sorrows receive the same solace, as in the bosom of our family? Whose hand wipes the tear from our cheek, or the chill of death from our brow, with the same fondness as that of the wife? . . . If the raging elements are contending without, here is shelter. If war is desolating the country, here is peace and tranquility.

The separation between work and home was expressed in spousal roles. Seventeenth century families are generally viewed as a partnership of shared activities. The husband's special place was the result of explicitly patriarchal political and social principles rather than of special characteristics of his role. Nineteenth century life, in contrast, was far more sharply role-differentiated. The husband's life was in some degree polarized between job and family, but his principal obligation was discharged in the public arena. The wife's domain was the home, and most stayed there. The duty of the husband was to compete successfully in the world; that of the wife to manage the household and to rear the children.

This allocation of responsibility seemingly removed women from a sphere of activity in which they had previously engaged, but did not—again by contemporary and most current opinion—diminish the importance of what they did. Indeed, with specialization in function came, it is generally said, greater dignity and a position more nearly equal to that of husbands. In some respects, wives and mothers were more than equal to their spouses. Far from the Eve figure that haunted Puritan conceptions of women, nineteenth century wives were regarded as "guardian angels" of the home. Their positions in life were defined by a purity and altruism directly opposed to everything found in the larger world, and their functions were to "provide moral uplift for everyone else with whom they came in contact—chiefly their husbands and children."

The woman's primary responsibility for rearing children was a particularly important aspect of nineteenth century culture. Its importance lay not only in her displacement of the husband-father, in whom sole authority rested in seventeenth century law and theory, but in the heightened importance of child-rearing in the Enlightenment. Of course, mothers have in fact borne the greatest burden of child-rearing at all times, but without recognition that her responsibility for doing so was a prerogative rather than merely a duty. Even by the eighteenth century, however, sermons and advice books about child care addressed their lessons to women. Moreover, the mother's new position as primary educator and custodian of children was reflected in legal change. By steps, from virtual sole male custody to maternal custody in "exceptional cases," then to formal equality of parents and finally to a preference for maternal custody, particularly for children of tender years, the primacy of the mother's role in child-rearing emerged during the nineteenth century.

The theme of female moral superiority sounds throughout the century. It was noted by foreign observers, conceded by men, and insisted upon by women. Joined with (and reciprocally related to) recognition of women's special role in child-rearing, this theme ultimately led to places for women outside the home. Middle class women, most of whom insisted on "traditional" role assignments, were greatly responsible for creation of the juvenile court around the turn of the century and had been active in reformatory and child-saving movements even before then. Mrs. W. P. Lynde, speaking to the National Conference of Charities and Corrections in 1879, asserted that working with children offered the "truest and noblest scope for the public activities of women in time which they can spare from their primary domestic duties." A like-minded speaker several years later observed that a reformatory without a woman is "like a home without a mother—a place of desolation. In reformatory work woman is the good mother. . . . She is the one to whom all look for comfort and relief."

Nineteenth century theory and its current reconstructions specified a separate place for children as well, although with far less clarity than that created for wives. Like their mothers, minors were removed from the sphere of work and, like their mothers, a new and socially valued role was recognized for them. They would neither work nor idle but engage—for a far longer period than had previously been approved—in the "business" of educational and personal development.

Although assigning children to a special role served a number of practical ends, including constriction of the labor pool, it also flowed naturally from nineteenth century political and social theory. If infants in the seventeenth century were thought innately evil and in need of continuous repression, their nineteenth century counterparts bore in them the promise of perfection for all society. Education and training of the young took on special importance. The task of parents now was not to repress the development of children but to create an atmosphere in which correct values could be developed. The business of children was to develop their potential under the guidance of the mother and ultimately, as we will see, of professional educators.

Within the home, the place of the child significantly resembled that of the mother. Just as European travelers were struck by the equality seemingly accorded American wives by their husbands, so they were impressed (although not always favorably) by the equality seemingly accorded children. The nineteenth century household appeared, and was thought to be, a refuge for all, marked by affectionate relations among its members, a sense of shared purpose for its internal affairs, and a distance from the conditions of the world which would corrupt the young, exhaust the father, and contradict the mother's purity of instinct.

III. SEPARATION OF SPHERES IN HISTORY AND LAW

The view generally described in the preceding section is developmental, moving from an hierarchically ordered household closely integrated with the community towards an egalitarian, companionate family sharply separated from the public world. The trend is not so much towards a nuclear as an enucleated family.

A great deal of evidence has been adduced in support of this view and the story that develops seems coherent. Indeed, even those who differ greatly in their evaluations of woman's place and of family function accept the theory of separate spheres. Some historians see the separation of spheres as a substitute form of repression, relegating women to a stifling and limited domestic routine; others see it as an expression of women's equality in at least one domain and a platform from which general claims of equality could depart. Both views rely, however, upon the distinction between public and private worlds. Liberals and socialists likewise accept the distinction, although the latter consider women's roles within the home as a form of exploitation necessary to the wage labor system while the former do not.

Moreover, "privacy" for the household is often given an objective meaning. The family not only experiences itself as private but is private; and is more private in modern history than previously. The meaning given to privacy by Aries and Demos among others is the familiar one of autonomy or freedom from governmental control. A clear statement of this association has been provided by Judith Stiehm:

> In this country, intrafamily relations are a private rather than a governmental concern. The state does establish a legal basis for the family's existence, but this defining function is exercised principally when families are either being founded, as in marriage or adoption, or dissolved, as in divorce or death. Even then, the state's role is minimal unless property is involved. The government is only too happy to avoid having either to forbid or to require particular interpersonal behavior.

Both the notion of family privacy and its meaning of autonomy or freedom from governmental concern are used in legal discussions as well. Foote, Levy and Sander's casebook on family law, for example, begins with a section entitled "The Family Autonomy Tradition," using the phrases "family autonomy" and "family privacy" interchangeably. Generally, the notion of family privacy includes two situations: those in which courts decline to intervene to resolve intra-familial disputes for prudential reasons and those in which they say that law may not properly regulate certain aspects of family relationships. The most familiar illustration of the first situation is the reluctance of courts to order the financial and personal arrangements of spouses. Where the marriage is "intact," meaning that proceedings for separation or divorce have not been instituted, courts traditionally have refused to enter support decrees unless gross and dangerous neglect is proved. As the Supreme Court of Nebraska observed in *McGuire v. McGuire,* a well-known and notorious case:

> the living standards of a family are a matter of concern to the household, and not for the courts to determine. . . . As long as the home is maintained and the parties are living as husband and wife it may be said that the husband is legally supporting his wife and the marriage relationship is being carried out.

Glendon observes of such decisions that they leave spouses "to work out their roles, to make their decisions and to divide their labor by themselves so long as the marriage is functioning." The same deference to family decision-making is found in the refusal of courts generally to enforce intra-family contracts. The leading English decision, *Balfour v. Balfour,* sounds the privacy motif in this context:

> To my mind it would be the worst possible example to hold that agreements such as this resulted in legal obligations which could be enforced in the Courts. . . . The common law does not regulate the form of agreements between spouses. . . . In respect of these promises each house is a domain into which the King's writ does not run, and to which his officers do not seek to be admitted.

The notion of family privacy or family autonomy is also invoked regularly in connection with parent-child relations. Sometimes that doctrine is used to uphold the authority of a custodial parent against a non-custodial parent objecting to the former's care of the child. In *People ex rel. Sisson v. Sisson,* where Mrs. Sisson sought custody of her daughter from her former husband because of his membership in a strict religious cult, the court held that it:

> cannot regulate by its processes the internal affairs of the home. Disputes between parents when it does not involve anything immoral or harmful to the welfare of the child is beyond the reach of the law. The vast majority of matters concerning the upbringing of children must be left to the conscience, patience, and self restraint of father and mother.

On other occasions, family autonomy has been employed as a shield against state intervention. In *Pierce v. Society of Sisters,* the Supreme Court invalidated an Oregon statute prohibiting attendance at parochial schools in fulfillment of compulsory education requirements. In doing so, the Court observed that "the Act . . . unreasonably interferes with the liberty of parents and guardians to direct the upbringing and education of children under their control. . . . The child is not the mere creature of the State . . . ." And in *Wisconsin v. Yoder*, a majority of the Court emphasized "the values of parental direction of the religious upbringing and education" as it struck down a law requiring formal education through age sixteen as applied to the children of Amish parents. At its broadest, the family privacy principle has been said to mean that all or essentially all of a child's life is within the control of his parents.

Plainly, ideas such as "private sphere" and "household" exert a powerful hold over historical and legal discussion. Nevertheless, a good case can be made that the privacy of the modern family is not unequivocally supported by legal historical evidence and that, during the nineteenth and twentieth centuries, when the private sphere of the household is said to have developed (for good or ill), public concern for and involvement in child-rearing, and perhaps family relationships more generally, increased dramatically.

IV. PUBLIC INTEREST AND THE PRIVATE SPHERE

A. The Public Interest in Child-Rearing and Education

It is an integral part of current interpretations of family history that children were restricted to the home in the nineteenth century, no longer participating in family economic activities (which had by and large disappeared) and always debarred from full membership in the general community. Moreover, a special part of the wife's role in the home was that of educating her children: a role considered more important in the last centuries than previously. Thus, child-rearing is assumed to be part of the "private" sphere.

It is surely true that, by the nineteenth century, children were less likely to work in the home with their parents than had previously been the case, and it also is undeniable that child-rearing and education were considered of great importance. It is not plain, however, that a shift in child care from public to private domains can be demonstrated.

For one thing, the Puritans took child-rearing within the home very seriously. The authority of parents was matched by a duty to educate their dependents, morally and substantively. Town selectmen were required to keep a "vigilant eye" on their brethren to assure that none failed to instruct his apprentices "perfectly to read the English tongue," and we have already seen in John Robinson's advice on child-rearing the strictness with which moral education was to be conducted.

What changed from colonial times was not the importance attached to education, but views of what education meant and of the capacity of parents to discharge this function. These changes seem to have increased rather than decreased public involvement in the education and rearing of children.

The family was both the original and ultimate agency of child governance in Puritan New England. Poor laws provided for the "binding out" of children to reputable families and Massachusetts law required selectmen who found masters of families neglectful in their duties to "take such children or apprentices from them and place them with some masters . . . which will more strictly look unto, and force them to submit unto government . . . ." Thus, the remedy for an inadequate family was an adequate family.

Nineteenth century opinion required considerably more of education than learning the English tongue, the Bible, and the laws. Although Enlightenment educational theory did not suppose the innate depravity of children nor hold that education should merely serve the purposes of reproducing existing social institutions, it was hardly laissez-faire. John Locke had argued in *Some Thoughts Concerning Education* that the goal of child-rearing was a rational adult who was sufficiently disciplined to deny himself immediate pleasures in the pursuit of long-term good. "It seems plain to me," he explained, "that the Principle of all Virtue and Excellency lies in a power of denying our selves the Satisfaction of our own Desires, where Reason does not authorize them. This Power is to be got and improv'd by Custom, made familiar by an early Practice." Thus, when a child clearly wanted something, parents should make a practice of denying it in order to promote habits of obedience to parental authority and denial of appetite.

Benjamin Rush drew on Locke in proposing his educational program for the new republic. Like Locke, he hoped to develop self-discipline through early inculcation of a habit of strict obedience to authority. In this, Dr. Rush reveals the tension between revolutionary ideals and the practical necessities of government. While Republican government must recognize the sovereignty of individual wills, those wills must also be subsumed into, or at least acknowledge, the authority of the general will. It was the responsibility of education, then, to fit the wills to each other to produce "regularity and unison in government."

What Locke and Rush justified on psychological and political grounds was taken up in popular thought. Carl Degler observes that the new child-rearing literature of the 1830's and 1840's "stressed the need to subdue the child early and at almost any cost." Techniques had surely changed, as had the reasons, but in favor of greater intrusiveness in the child's development rather than less. Corporal discipline was not favored as it had been in the seventeenth century, but socialization and value formation were as important for nineteenth century as for colonial parents. The special concomitant of affectionate relationships in post-Revolutionary families was the substitution of guilt for shame and the rod as instruments for producing compliant youthful behavior.

Perhaps the special requirements for rearing the republican child would have seemed capable of fulfillment without heightened official activity in the relatively homogeneous society of colonial America. However, the vast European migration of the eighteenth century dissolved that homogeneity and, with it, confidence in the general capacity of families to raise their children appropriately. Many of the German and Scots-Irish who settled the mid-Atlantic region during this period were uneducated and poor. Benjamin Franklin, for one, doubted their capacity to adapt to American social requirements, bluntly asserting in 1753 that the German immigrants were "the most stupid of their nation," and would not take instruction from clergy or society. Even earlier German immigrants were appalled by the new arrivals; the Reverend Henry Melchior Muhlenberg worried out loud that "[s]o many rotten people are coming . . . and acting so wickedly that the name [of Palatine] has begun to stink."

The relationship of immigration to social and family disorganization was supported by environmentalist views and associationist psychology which commanded wide acceptance by the 1820's. These theories suggested that, where adults behaved badly, the reason would be found in the failures of their parents. Americans were accordingly concerned by the poverty of the newcomers, but even more by the different values and goals that immigrants were believed to carry with them and the resulting difficulty of adjusting to the "open" society of America. Not understanding the responsibilities of the society into which they moved, and not having themselves learned the values of delayed gratification and the utilitarian calculus, immigrant families could not well provide the environment in which their children could learn to become free but not licentious citizens.

The absence of informal agencies to assume responsibility for these children complicated matters. Reputable families could not be relied on to rear inadequately cared-for youth as the nineteenth century progressed. For one thing, there were simply too many such children for private households to absorb. For another, traditional forms of indenture did not work when employment moved from the home to the factory. The effect of binding out was no longer to allow children to learn a trade in the home, but to place them in industrial settings that were neither educational nor, indeed, safe.

Under these circumstances, it is not surprising to find the development of strategies for dealing with wayward or neglected children that relied on institutions other than the family. Enlightenment theory supported the intervention of educated people who would manipulate the environment so that progress might be achieved. Benjamin Rush, whose views on educating the republican child we have already encountered, strongly urged the creation of schools to correct the indulgence or ignorance of parents. These schools were intended for girls as well as boys, since the former also "should be accommodated to the state of society, manners, and government of the country in which [education] is conducted." During the early 1800's, common schools arose to educate poor children whose parents could not afford to send them to academies and could not themselves perform that function. In Boston, where concern for the capacity of families to educate their children had long existed, school attendance became compulsory during the first part of the nineteenth century, and the New York Public School Society asked for similar legislation in 1832. That this step would involve substantial intervention in parental control of children was frankly conceded and justified by Enlightenment political theory:

> Truantship [in Boston] is deemed a criminal offence in children, and those who cannot be reclaimed, are taken from their parents by the Police, and placed in an Institution called the 'School of Reformation' corresponding in many respects with our House of Refuge. . . . Every Political compact supposes a surrender of some individual rights for the general good. In a government like ours, 'founded on the principle that the only true sovereignty is the will of the people,' universal education is acknowledged by all, to be, not only of the first importance, but necessary to the permanency of our free institutions. If then persons are found so reckless of the best interests of their children, and so indifferent to the public good, as to withhold from them that instruction, without which they cannot beneficially discharge those civil and political duties which devolve on them in after life, it becomes a serious and important question, whether so much of the natural right of controlling their children may not be alienated as is necessary to qualify them for usefulness, and render them safe and consistent members of the political body.

Both the willingness of the Public School Society to intervene and its justification for doing so are important. The theory of intervention reached far more broadly than the problems created by truancy; it could and did stand for the proposition that parental control over children was generally subject to official invasion when the former were guilty of neglect.

Use of official agencies for children who were reported subject to parental cruelty and neglect did increase dramatically during the century. Almshouses were employed for the care of pauper children, and houses of refuge were established during the same period for the care of children who had been so poorly raised that they could not be reached by voluntary school programs or even by compulsory education laws. The proposal of the New York Society for the Reformation of Juvenile Delinquents in 1824 for creation of the first house of refuge indicated a broad potential clientele: vagrant and homeless youths, young criminals, boys with neglectful parents, and some delinquent girls. The readiness to assert public authority over children is most strikingly revealed, however, in *Ex parte Crouse,* which sustained the constitutionality of the commitment of a young girl to the Philadelphia House of Refuge.

The object of the charity [the house of refuge] is reformation, by training its inmates to industry; by imbuing their minds with principles of morality and religion; by furnishing them with means to earn a living; and, above all, by separating them from the corrupting influence of improper associates. To this end, may not the natural parents, when unequal to the task of education, or unworthy of it, be superseded by the parens patriae, or common guardian of the community? It is to be remembered that the public has a paramount interest in the virtue and knowledge of its members, and that, of strict right, the business of education belongs to it. . . .

By the middle of the nineteenth century, public schools, houses of refuge, state reformatories, and similar institutions were widely relied on to mold poor and wayward children "into the form and character which the peculiar nature of the edifice [of American society] demands. . . ."

As the nineteenth century wore on, this development was confirmed and expanded. Although compulsory education had been adopted in some localities before the Civil War, it gained far broader acceptance in the last third of the century. The reasons for its spread were much the same at the end of the century as at the beginning: the felt importance of education for good citizenship and social order together with the implicit conviction that parents could not routinely be trusted to discharge that function. Compulsory education laws were considered to "belong to the class of laws which are intended for the suppression of vice," and "intended to reach and bring within the influence of our schools a class who cannot be reached effectually in any other way."

During the same time, the implications of Enlightenment theory for the manner of education were also developed more fully than had been the case. The traditional method of education by mastery of bodies of knowledge was replaced by one that emphasized the individual growth and development of students. "If," as Richard Hofstadter observed of the views of Dewey, "a democratic society is truly to serve all its members, it must devise schools in which, at the germinal point in childhood, these members will be able to cultivate their capacities and, instead of simply reproducing the qualities of the larger society, will learn how to improve them." So sophisticated an approach entailed trained educators in place of parental instruction. Public schools, Dewey observed, would do "systematically and in a large, intelligent, and competent way what for various reasons can be done in most households only in a comparatively meager and haphazard manner."

Finally, urbanization came to be thought profoundly destructive of parent-child relations and a cause of corruption for youth. There is some irony in the romantic comparisons drawn by nineteenth century commentators between the raising of children in colonial times and under current conditions. Modern minded people saw in the colonial experience the "good old days . . . [when] a boy worked for his father until he was twenty-one years of age. . . . They were under the influence of home and home training, until they had passed the period of adolescence and were really young men and young women." This time had passed. "The scene has changed from the farm to the village or city. The stimulating outdoor life of the farm; filled with duties and responsibilities, has been replaced by the enervating routine of life in store, office, or factory."

Observers at the end of the century did not, however, consider the home as private refuge an adequate substitute for the home as little commonwealth. In place of close parental supervision, the reformers saw neglect; in place of rural purity, the city's immorality and vice; in place of a homogeneous, socially dedicated people, a diffuse collection of immigrant peoples. Juvenile wrongdoing was perceived as endemic to city life, and the remedy lay in public assumption of responsibility for the hordes of wayward and criminal youth spawned by urban conditions. Moreover, the need for societal intervention was laid directly to the collapse of families. Miriam Van Waters, a staunch spokesperson for the juvenile court movement and for women's roles in it, actually saw salvation for society in the creation of institutions for children. "It is significant," in her view, "that it was in America that the first juvenile court arose, for from America about the same time the civilized world received its first warning that all was not well with that ancient institution, the home." And Judge Cabot of the Boston Juvenile Court urged his readers to "[r]emember the fathers and mothers have failed, or the child has no business [in the court], and it is when they failed that the state opened this way to receive them, into the court, and said, 'This is the way in which we want you to grow up.'"

The public significance attached to proper child-rearing was expressed not only at the point of serious misconduct but at all stages of child development. Juvenile delinquency was considered simply the end product of a course of parental failure, and the public interest lay in avoiding such failure as early as possible. This interest was reflected in the juvenile court by adoption of broad jurisdictional categories intended to reach every kind of conduct by child or parent which might suggest inadequate upbringing.

The same interest can also be seen in the progress of nineteenth century child custody law. During the colonial period, of course, child custody questions rarely arose before courts. Common law doctrine assigned to fathers sole authority over their legitimate children. Mothers were entitled to respect from, but not control over, their offspring, and even after the father's death he could deny her custody by appointing a testamentary guardian.

As Michael Grossberg has clearly demonstrated, the father's paramount right to custody was replaced, in stages, by the principle of the child's best interest. As early as the 1820's, Chancellor Kent and Justice Story had indicated that the father's claim to custody was only presumptive and could be overcome by proof of special circumstances. Story made clear in *United States v. Green,* decided in 1824, that a fundamental change of policy was emerging. After observing that "in a general sense it is true" that the father has the right to custody of an infant child, he went on to caution:

> But this is not on account of any absolute right of the father, but for the benefit of the infant, the law presuming it to be for his interest to be under the nurture and care of his natural protector, both for maintenance and education. When therefore, the court is asked to lend its aid to put the infant into the custody of the father . . . it will look into all the circumstances and ascertain whether it will be for the real, permanent interests of the infant. . . . It is an entire mistake to suppose the court is at all events bound to deliver over the infant to his father, or that the latter has an absolute vested right in the custody.

This modern-sounding view was often echoed by state legislatures and courts in the first half of the nineteenth century. Moreover, even the presumption in favor of paternal custody receded from prominence. In 1840, a New York statute enabling mothers to seek custody by habeas corpus against the father was understood by the vice-chancellor to "neutralize" the common law rule and to place wives "on an equality [with husbands] as to the future custody of the children, even if it does not create a presumption in favor of the wife." A Massachusetts statute of approximately the same time relieved even the need for interpretation, declaring that the rights of parents to custody were equal and, accordingly, custodial decisions were to be governed by the "happiness and welfare of the child."

Equality was, however, only the beginning of transition from the common law rule; ultimately, it was replaced by a presumption exactly the reverse of that employed by Justice Story. An early and notorious case revealing such a reversal is the *Matter of D'Hauteville,* decided by the Pennsylvania Supreme Court in 1840. The father was a foreign nobleman who refused to live in Boston for part of the year but was otherwise blameless; the mother a native of Massachusetts who disliked living in Switzerland. Justice Story's presumption, if adopted, apparently would have required judgment for the father. The Pennsylvania justices, however, declared that "every instinct of humanity unerringly proclaims that no substitute can supply the place of her, whose watchfulness over the sleeping cradle or waking moments of her offspring is prompted by deeper and holier feelings than the most liberal allowance of a nurse's wages could possibly stimulate." As the century wore on, the "tender years" doctrine, giving mothers a presumptive claim to custody of young children, combined with a strong preference for maternal custody of all female children to destroy the last remnants of common law rules.

Modification or elimination of the common law doctrine regarding custody to some extent reflects both the enhanced position of women and the perception of separate spheres. The special moral and cultural qualifications of mothers were relied on to explain custodial preferences in their favor, and it was concomitantly assumed that fathers would rely on servants or female relatives to care for children, their own time and energy being occupied by activities in the public arena.

However, recognition of the nurturing capacities of women, and their special sphere in the home, does not mean that child care was a matter of private rather than public concern. On the contrary, changes in the law of child custody, in intent and in result, expressed a strong public interest in child rearing. Bishop's treatise on Marriage and Divorce in 1852 plainly recognized that the care of the young was a matter of state importance rather than one of parental right. "[C]hildren," he said, "are not born for the benefit of the parents alone, but for the country; and, therefore, . . . the interest of the public in their morals and education should be protected. . . ." Thus, even an agreement between parents regarding child custody was denied binding legal effect. As early as 1846, the New York Court of Chancery refused to be governed by such a contract, holding that "[t]he object of the statute in giving the court the power to direct which of the parties shall have the care and custody of minor children [upon divorce] . . . was not to gratify the wishes of the parents. It was for the protection of the children, who by the misconduct of one parent had necessarily become half orphans."

The well-being of children, then, was not confined to the private discretion of the parents. To make custody turn on the "best interests" of the child means that a court must decide what conduct and circumstances are desirable and what are not. The criteria for this decision, if not supplied by the parents themselves, must derive from the judge's views of good child rearing and good citizenship.

The state's interest in having children develop into good, sound adult members of the community which justified intervention in the careers of wayward minors found similar expression in custody cases, particularly where courts left or placed minors with a non-parent custodian. *Legate v. Legate,* an 1894 Texas decision described as typical of the time, plainly reveals the common foundation for asserting public authority in these matters. Rejecting any "property interest" in the child, the court treated the parental claim to custody as a trusteeship subject to state supervision:

> The State, as the protector and promoter of the peace and prosperity of orga-
> nized society, is interested in the proper education and maintenance of the
> child, to the end that it may become a useful instead of a vicious citizen; and
> while as a general rule it recognizes the fact that the interest of the child and
> society is best promoted by leaving its education and maintenance, during
> minority, to the promptings of parental affection, untrammelled by the sur-
> veillance of government, still it has the right in proper cases to deprive the
> parent of the custody of his child when demanded by the interests of the
> child and society.

In this case, as one might guess, the court left a two-year old girl in the custody of foster parents, with whom she had been virtually since birth.

Nineteenth century public concern with child-rearing, it seems, was pervasive, however much Americans may have considered the home a private refuge. It reached children who, at any time, would be considered public problems by reason of their criminal behavior, those who engaged in non-criminal but undisciplined conduct, children whose circumstances suggested that they might become deviant (by reason of neglect or dependency), and "normal" children whose education was nonetheless considered a governmental as well as a family responsibility. Moreover, official concern for child development was expressed daily in custody disputes. While custodial questions were resolved by categorical rules during the seventeenth century, which had the practical result of removing government from such decisions in all but the most unusual circumstances, resort in the nineteenth century to a "best interests" test made these determinations depend not on either parent's wishes or even their joint wish, but upon a court's assessment of where the public interest lay.

Of course, there have been points at which a line against "statist" intervention was drawn, but these involved genuinely exceptional situations: where the state passed laws for which no legitimate reason could be given, as with statutes effectively prohibiting parochial education or teaching the German language, or where religious freedom was unnecessarily limited, as with the Amish. What is most striking about these cases, however, is not the strong language they employ in support of values of pluralism and deference to parental authority but the narrowness of the exceptions they recognize to state authority in respect of education.

B.   The Public Interest in Other Domestic Relations

The difficulty of viewing the legal history of family relationships in terms of public and private spheres is not limited to the area of child-rearing. Other areas of domestic relations reveal a broadened public involvement, in one or another sense, during the last two centuries. An example or two may suggest why this seems to be so.

1. MARRIAGE

"Privacy," in connection with the understanding of marriage and rules concerning entrance into that relationship, would seem to be associated with the extent to which the decision to marry is left to the parties themselves. And there is, indeed, considerable evidence that at least one form of extrinsic control—that of parents—waned from the seventeenth to the nineteenth century. Paternal control over land, once widely used to control their sons' marital choices, was increasingly less common by the eighteenth century, and testamentary limitations to the same effect also became rare by the same time. Michael Grossberg argues, with considerable authority, that the first half of the nineteenth century witnessed a pervasive relaxation of formal legal restrictions on marriage as well. Common law marriages seem to have received wider recognition in the late eighteenth and early nineteenth centuries than had been true during the colonial period, and other formal conditions for marriage also diminished in importance. Nuptial fees were lowered and civil marriages were permitted where religious ceremonies had been necessary. While parental consent was still required for young persons, underage marriages were often sustained with the penalty for violation of age restriction visited upon the official who wrongly performed the ceremony rather than on the couple themselves. Decreasing state control over marriage can also be seen in the general acceptance of a conflicts of law rule by which the validity of marriages is determined by the law of the place of celebration rather than the domicile of the parties, as English and continental law had it. A choice of a marriage partner forbidden by the state of residence could nevertheless be effected simply by visiting another state.

The treatment of marriage as a matter of choice by the partners is commonly regarded as "an important stage in the evolution of woman's place in the family and in our understanding of how the family altered over time." As a matter of how spouses perceive themselves and their relationship, I have no doubt that there was and is greater freedom to marry than was the case in the seventeenth century. It is far less clear, however, that relaxation of informal and formal controls over marriage staked out a sphere of private choice, free from governmental interest.

In the first place, relaxation of restrictions on marriage did not imply that, like civil contracts, the area was now one for "private law making." Even before the Civil War, it was often said that while there was a contractual aspect to marriage, it co-existed with a public concern. A Tennessee court, perhaps atypically conservative in its views on marriage, made the following observation in 1826:

> By the English canon and ecclesiastical law, this union of marriage is of a
> nature so widely differing from ordinary contracts . . . it is a connection of
> such deep-toned and solemn character, that society has even more interest in
> preserving it than the parties themselves.

The second edition of Story's treatise on conflicts of law allowed that matrimony was a contract but also, it seemed, something more than a mere contract. It was rather an institution of society founded upon, but not controlled by, the consent of the parties. And Bishop's *Commentaries on the Laws of Marriage and Divorce,* first published in 1852, restricted the contractual aspect to the need for an agreement. Matrimony, in his view, was "the most important institution of human society." It was, once entered, a "civil status," based on the law of nature and found in "the municipal law of every civilized country."

By the 1850's, then, it was already widely believed that marriage itself was quite as much a public as a private concern. During the next one hundred years, despite the assumed separation of spheres, entrance into that condition also was subjected increasingly to restriction. The Progressive era's concern with social engineering did not leave spousal choice untouched. Most states continued to recognize informal marriage until the end of the century but, by 1915, thirteen states considered such unions void and only fifteen years later, almost one-half of the states and territories took that view. It is conventionally understood, of course, that invalidation of common law marriages rests heavily on public policy and particularly on a public interest in assuring that spouses satisfy licensing requirements.

Predictably, these regulatory requirements have also become more restrictive, beginning with the last two decades of the nineteenth century. Marital ages rose so that, by 1906, only seventeen states retained the common law ages of consent (14 for men and 12 for women). By 1935, the age had been raised in most states to 21 for males and 18 for females. These changes reflected not only changing economic circumstances but an express public concern with the soundness of youthful alliances. Early marriages were thought socially dangerous because they disregarded nineteenth and twentieth century values of sexual restraint, self-control in general, and the capacity to delay gratification.

Public concern was further expressed in regulations regarding disease. Even nineteenth century legal treatises do not mention disease, other than insanity or impotence, as an impediment to marriage, and insanity for that matter was only significant as it affected the capacity of the insane party to consent to marriage. By 1935, however, at least 19 states prohibited marriage by persons with venereal disease, 17 forbade epileptics to marry, and six denied licenses to persons with active tuberculosis or other "transmissible disease." Moreover, conventional restrictions on marriage were enforced with what seems to be special vigor, making plain the public interest in marital arrangements. In *Reynolds v. United States,* the Supreme Court turned the contract aspect of marriage on its head, using it to justify the ban on polygamy in the Utah territory. The Court observed that

> [M]arriage, while from its very nature a sacred obligation, is nevertheless, in most civilized nations, a civil contract, and usually regulated by law. Upon it society may be said to be built, and out of its fruits spring social relations and social obligations and duties, with which government is necessarily required to deal.

Plural marriage, in particular, could be prohibited because of its effect on the general social structure. "Polygamy," the Court suggested, "leads to the patriarchal principle, and which, when applied to large communities, fetters the people in stationary despotism, while that principle cannot long exist in connection with monogamy."

Finally, it should be noted that even the early nineteenth century cases upholding informal, underage, and evasionary marriages can be viewed as supporting values other than freedom of marital choice. For one thing, the result in these cases was to sustain the marriage, not only against the challenge of parents and other relatives but also against the spouses themselves. An obvious price of validating marriage, absent casual divorce laws, is to prohibit escape from marriage. Moreover, marriages were upheld when, if the relationship was viewed simply as a contract, they would have been annulled. Evasionary marriages, as we have seen, were routinely given effect although it seems clear that general contract rules would invalidate agreements in fraudulent evasion of state laws. Marriage was excepted from the general rule "on principles of policy, with a view to prevent the disastrous consequences to the issue of such marriages, as well as to avoid the public mischief, which would result" from invalidating migratory unions. Similarly, fraud in the inducement to marry was treated quite differently from other contractual misrepresentations. Whereas a civil contract can be annulled for any material misrepresentation, only fraud going to an "essential" of the marriage would suffice to dissolve that relationship. Again, the reason for special rules for marriage had to do with public policy. As Chief Justice Hosmer of the Connecticut Supreme Court of Errors explained in *Guilford v. Oxford*, decided in 1832:

> [O]rdinary contracts, which respect property only, may, with propriety and convenience, be tested, by the rule of private justice; but the marriage contract, on which so much depends for the protection, and maintenance, and education of the children, and in which the public have so essential a stake, demands a higher principle.

It is hard to see how the restrictive rules of fraud annulment served values of private choice for a spouse who had been profoundly misled into a lifetime enterprise, but easy to see their relationship to societal values of marital stability in the new republic.

D. A Comparative View of the Family

The history of the American family serves as one kind of antidote to the view that there is only one kind of family. Another such antidote is to consider the many different attitudes about familial relations that prevail in other countries. The study that follows examines sentiments about intimate relationships in a wide range of cultures. Among other things, it suggests what will seem counter-intuitive to modern Americans—that love need not be the basis for marriage. And its discussion raises some useful questions about the way people's social and economic environment shapes the way they think and act.

Robert Levine, Suguru Sato, Tsukasa Hashimoto, & Jyoti Verma, *Love and Marriage in Eleven Cultures*, 26 JOURNAL OF CROSS-CULTURAL PSYCHOLOGY 554 (September 1995)[*]

Our culture's belief in the importance of love for marriage, however, appears to be far from universally accepted. In the majority of the world's cultures, marriages are arranged by family members—not by the bride and groom. Within marriage, our conception of love also diverges sharply from those of many other cultures. In India, for example, romantic love and intense emotional attachment is typically seen as a threat to the family structure. Far from bolstering the joint family, it often disrupts it.

Virtually all empirical studies of romantic love, however, have been unicultural. The vast majority have focused on the United States, sometimes offering passing acknowledgment that their findings may be culture specific. More pertinent, there are no empirical data systematically comparing cultures or nations concerning their beliefs about the importance of love for marriage. The main purpose of the present study was to collect these data. More specifically, we compared the responses of college students from 11 developed and underdeveloped Eastern and Western countries—India, Pakistan, Thailand, Mexico, Brazil, Japan, Hong Kong, Republic of the Philippines, Australia, England, and the United States—on the questions about love and marriage posed in Simpson et al.'s U.S. surveys.

What might we predict? Theoretical discussion of romantic love has also tended to focus on the United States. In an early article, however, Goode presented a theory of love that makes predictions about the relationship of love and marriage across cultures. He argued that the importance of romantic love varies inversely with the strength of extended-family ties. In cultures with strong kinship networks and extended-family ties, romantic love relationships are viewed as irrelevant or even disastrous for marriages, because they disrupt the tradition of family-approved, often arranged, marriage

---

[*]   Robert Levine, Suguru Sato, Tsukasa Hashimoto, & Jyoti Verma, *Love and Marriage in Eleven Cultures*, JOURNAL OF CROSS-CULTURAL PSYCHOLOGY (Vol. 26, Sept. 1995) pp. 554-571, copyright © 1995 by Sage Publications, Inc. Reprinted by Permission of Sage Publications, Inc.

choices. Romantic love in these cultures must be "controlled," through social disapproval, to maintain the strength of kinship networks.

Two studies offer support for some predictions of Goode's thesis. Rosenblatt, using the Human Relations Area File, found that love was more important for marriage in cultures where economic interdependence between spouses was weak. The study by Simmons et al. also provided tangential support for the theory. They compared attitudes toward love among college students in Japan, where they assumed a priori that extended-family ties are stronger, to those of college students in the United States and in Germany. Consistent with Goode's prediction, romantic love was least highly valued in the Japanese sample.

Hofstede's massive 40-nation study of work-related values provides a database for more clearly testing Goode's theory, or at least an extension of his theory. Hofstede's study identified four main dimensions along which the dominant value systems of nations could be ordered and compared. One of these dimensions—individualism-collectivism—appears to be directly related to Goode's extended-family theory.

In societies characterized by individualism, the main concern is with one's own interests and that of one's immediate family. In collective societies, people identify with and conform to the expectations of more extended groups—their relatives, clan, or other in-group—who look after their interests in return for their loyalty.

Triandis and his colleagues, who have extended Hofstede's work, believe that individualism-collectivism is one of the most important sources of cultural differences in social behavior. In collective societies, the individual goes along with the in-group even when the demands are costly. One important feature of this process that Triandis has identified is an emphasis on social norms and duty as defined by the in-group over the pursuit of personal pleasure.

According to Goode, individual freedom of choice must be controlled in societies where the interests of the extended family predominate. Hofstede and Triandis's notion of individualism-collectivism is more general, but should lead to the same prediction: Societies where the interests of the group predominate over those of the individual should be characterized by less individual freedom of choice. Love, which is clearly associated with freedom of choice, should be viewed as less important in marriage decisions in collective cultures.

The study had two main goals: first, to examine the cross-cultural generality of the importance placed on romantic love in marriage decisions; and, second, to identify predictors and consequences of these differences. For this second goal, we extracted several social and economic characteristics of each nation from the literature. Our main hypothesis concerned collectivism, which we predicted would be negatively related to the importance placed on romantic love.

DISCUSSION

Several main findings emerged. First, as predicted, there were strong cross-cultural differences in the perceived importance of love as a prerequisite for *establishing* a marriage. Love tended to receive greatest importance in the Western and Westernized nations (the United States, followed by Brazil, England, and Australia) and least importance in the four underdeveloped Eastern nations (India, Pakistan, Thailand, and the Philippines). The two most economically developed of the Eastern nations—Japan and Hong Kong—fell between these two groups.

Second, there were also significant cross-cultural differences in beliefs about love as a prerequisite for *maintaining* a marriage. Again, the Western and Westernized nations tended to assign greatest importance, and the underdeveloped Eastern nations tended to assign least importance to love. These differences, however, were neither as strong nor as clear as the above differences pertaining to the establishment of a marriage. Cultural norms concerning the import of love for establishing a marriage, it appears, do not necessarily coincide with those regarding the maintenance and dissolution of a marriage. Future studies may need to treat these issues separately. The present data for U.S. participants provides the sharpest case in point. U.S. participants were highest in beliefs about the importance of love for establishing a marriage, but were closer to the median in their beliefs about love as a necessity for maintaining a marriage.

Third, there were few significant sex differences, either across or within countries, on any of the questions. It appears that Simpson et al.'s findings for the United States, indicating relatively few sex differences in beliefs about the necessity of romantic love for marriage, are also true for many other cultures.

Although the general lack of sex differences is consistent with Simpson et al.'s findings for U.S. participants, they are not necessarily what would be predicted in many of the countries in the current sample. There are considerable differences in sex roles within many of these countries, and the extent of these differences varies greatly from country to country. In Buss's study of human mate preferences in a similarly heterogeneous group of cultures, strong sex differences did emerge, with females more highly valuing cues to resource acquisition and males more highly valuing cues to reproductive capacity. Although neither of these two categories would necessarily imply preference for romantic love, it is certainly possible that the lack of sex differences in the current study needs further exploration. It is possible, for example, that the lack of differences may reflect sampling biases within countries. We would expect sex differences to be minimized in student samples, especially in underdeveloped countries, where women who go to college are more likely to be less restricted by traditional sex role expectations.

Fourth, our main hypothesis, concerning the relationship of individualism-collectivism to beliefs about the importance of love, was strongly supported. The high correlation (.56) between individualism and the necessity of love for the establishment of a marriage (Question 1) was particularly impressive.

Further, it should be recognized that these high correlations were based on data from different subpopulations within each country. Hofstede's collectivism sample consisted of employees in business settings, whereas our "love" sample consisted of college students. Each of our samples also came from different locations in each country. Given these differences, it would appear that the nation-level relationship between collectivism and beliefs about love for establishing a marriage is quite robust. To some degree, at least, it appears to cut across age, regional, and educational groups at the level of nations.

Fifth, economic standards of living were very strongly related to beliefs about love—particularly, again, concerning the establishment of a marriage ($r = .76$). Because the present data are correlational, it would be speculative to infer causality between economic conditions, collectivism, and beliefs about love. One possible explanation, however, is that industrial growth produces pressures toward individualism and away from collectivism. As argued earlier, the endorsement of individualism allows the freedom of choice that is inherent in marriages based on freedom of choice.

Certainly, this hypothesis is consistent with the United States' movement from collectivist values, where pragmatic marriage decisions predominated, to individualist values, where romantic love became the guiding force in marriage decisions. This change, most historians agree, coincided with the Industrial Revolution in the 19th century. Until that time, marriage in the United States was primarily an economic arrangement between two families. The Industrial Revolution, however, required that work move outside the home, eventually resulting in an escalation of individualist values, particularly those concerning marriage and the nuclear family .

Japan and Hong Kong, it has been argued, are currently undergoing this same transition. Both have achieved economic prosperity out of traditionally collectivist value systems. Both, however, now appear to be moving closer to Western style individualism. Consistent with our hypothesis, their scores on our romantic love questions tended to fall between those of the developed Western nations and the underdeveloped Eastern nations.

Sixth, it appears that beliefs about the importance of love have behavioral consequences for marital decisions. Respondents assigning greater importance to love, particularly for decisions about the formation of a marriage, tended to come from nations with higher marriage rates, lower fertility rates, and higher divorce rates. The U.S. sample, for example, which put greatest emphasis on love in decisions about getting married, had the highest marriage and divorce rates and the third lowest fertility rates in our sample.

Once again, these data are correlational. However, it is interesting to speculate about possible causative relations. It might be argued that designating romantic love as the decisive criterion for marital decisions results in less inhibition toward getting married. There may, for example, be less pressure to consider long-term consequences when potential spouses feel responsibility only toward each other, rather than knowing that their decisions will affect many others in their collective families.

After marriage, it is not surprising that fertility rates are lower in love marriages. After all, the primary reason for marriage in traditional collectivist cultures is, often, to have children, who will then take part in the larger collective.

Finally, we found that divorce rates were much higher in countries where respondents agreed with the statement that the disappearance of love warrants making a clean break from the marriage. Given that "staying in love" is a difficult proposition, it is not surprising that marriages made in cultures that place great importance on love would be less likely to endure. Also, the fact that love-marriages are less likely to produce children may reduce the pressure to remain together after love disappears.

Finally, it is important to consider Bond's distinction between "cultural-level" and "individual-level" relationships. Are a culture's norms about love and marriage, and their consequences for marital quality, more closely paralleled at the individual level in some cultures than in others? What are the consequences of marrying for love in a culture that discourages individual choice, or of marrying for pragmatic reasons in a culture that values marrying for love? Is there, as Dion and Dion have argued, an inherent conflict between individualistic values and the interdependence demanded by romantic love? These are difficult questions. Given the importance of the marital relationship, however, and the difficulties it currently faces, they warrant further study.

Table 1
Distribution of Responses to Kephart/Simpson et al. Questions in 1967, 1976, 1984, and Present Study

Question	Response	Kephart (in 1967) Male	Female	Simpson et al. (in 1976) Male	Female	Simpson et al. (in 1984) Male	Female	Present Study Male	Female
1. If a man (woman) had all the other qualities you desired, would you marry this person if you were not in love with him (her)?	No	64.6	24.3	86.2	80.0	85.6	84.9	79.2	80.0
	Yes	11.7	4.0	1.7	4.6	1.7	3.6	2.1	13.3
	Undecided	23.7	71.7	12.1	15.4	12.7	11.5	18.8	6.7
2. If love has completely disappeared from a marriage, I think it is probably best for the couple to make a clean break and start new lives.	Agree			57.0	61.9	46.2	44.3	35.4	35.4
	Disagree			26.3	24.4	26.7	33.3	27.1	38.5
	Neutral			16.7	13.7	27.2	22.4	37.5	26.0
3. In my opinion, the disappearance of love is not a sufficient reason for ending a marriage, and should not be viewed as such.	Agree			27.2	20.6	30.8	30.9	35.4	37.5
	Disagree			60.5	64.9	42.6	44.9	37.5	41.7
	Neutral			12.3	14.5	26.6	24.2	27.1	20.8

NOTE: Figures given are in percentages.

Table 2
Responses to Question 1: "If a man (woman) had all the other qualities you desired, would you marry this person if you were not in love with him (her)?"

Response	India	Pakistan	Thailand	United States	England	Japan	Philippines	Mexico	Brazil	Hong Kong	Australia
Yes	49.0	50.4	18.8	3.5	7.3	2.3	11.4	10.2	4.3	5.8	4.8
No	24.0	39.1	33.8	85.9	83.6	62.0	63.6	80.5	85.7	77.6	80.0
Undecided	26.9	10.4	47.5	10.6	9.1	35.7	25.0	9.3	10.0	16.7	15.2

NOTE: Figures given are in percentages.

Table 3
Responses to Question 2: "If love has completely disappeared from a marriage, I think it is probably best for the couple to make a clean break and start new lives."

Response	India	Pakistan	Thailand	United States	England	Japan	Philippines	Mexico	Brazil	Hong Kong	Australia
Agree	46.2	33.0	46.9	35.4	44.6	41.1	45.5	51.7	77.5	47.1	29.3
Disagree	26.0	49.6	32.1	34.7	23.2	17.1	40.9	28.0	12.7	25.5	31.1
Neutral	27.9	17.4	21.0	29.9	32.1	41.9	13.6	20.3	9.9	27.4	39.6

NOTE: Figures given are in percentages.

Table 4

Responses to Question 3: "In my opinion, the disappearance of love is not a sufficient reason for ending a marriage and should not be viewed as such."

Response	India	Pakistan	Thailand	United States	England	Japan	Philippines	Mexico	Brazil	Hong Kong	Australia
Agree	47.1	54.8	50.6	36.8	26.8	26.4	71.6	34.8	26.8	51.6	39.6
Disagree	34.6	35.7	34.2	40.3	46.4	27.9	23.9	50.9	63.4	24.8	22.6
Neutral	18.3	9.6	15.2	22.9	26.8	45.7	4.6	14.4	9.9	23.6	37.7

NOTE: Figures given are in percentages.

CHAPTER II

The Formation and Structure of the Family

Chapter II continues the approach already begun, expanding the interdisciplinary themes of the book by adding feminist thought and psychiatry to the tools available for the study of the family. We include several articles that also point out problems with empirical methodology both in data collection and analysis.

Substantively, this chapter is about the varying ways families are formed and what forms modern families take. One of the things you will notice at once is the change over time both in the ways people approach marriage and other family arrangements and in the many forms in which they live together. Another is scholarly disagreement about whether law affects behavior in families, whether family arrangements affect law, or whether there is little interaction between the two.

Historically, marriage requirements have always been occasions when the state has actively intervened in family life. Michael Grossberg, GOVERNING THE HEARTH: LAW AND THE FAMILY IN NINETEENTH-CENTURY AMERICA (1985). Although decisions about whether and who to marry are personal and private, law places some restrictions upon engaged couples—and the contracts they may wish to make—that would be "inconceivable" (in the Words of "Princess Bride's" Sicilian Count Vincini) even in very important contractual contexts.

Similarly, the decision to part with a child—necessarily made in the vast majority of adoption cases—is an intensely personal and private one. The difficulty with which parents make such decisions suggests that many problem pregnancies might be more comfortably resolved—once the expectant woman has decided to continue them—by not giving children up even if the circumstances are difficult. We present these two alternatives, and their typical consequences, in the section that follows.

Modern sociologists debate the extent to which the (1950s) icon of the "traditional family" represents reality or myth, Norval Glenn, *A Critique of Twenty Family and Marriage and the Family Textbooks,* 46 FAMILY RELATIONS 197 (1997); and Arlene Skolnick, *A Response to Glenn : The Battle of the Textbooks: Bringing in the Culture War,* 46 FAMILY RELATIONS 219 (1997). Alternatives have been actively and rigorously promoted only recently, however. The families engaged in these pluralistic forms present a series of natural experiments, and there are few who would claim to predict their outcomes with confidence. We present here some of the research done to date to measure the nature, extent and effect of these various ways of bonding together as families, realizing that effects on future generations will remain uncertain for some time to come.

A. Going Courting

Rings and Promises discusses the death of a legal rule, the suit for breach of promise to marry, not only in terms of the changing social forces involving courtship that hastened its demise but in terms of the custom that arose to replace the legal action. It is an example of empirical work in law and economics, which focuses not on people's attitudes but rather on the actions they take.

Margaret F. Brinig, *Rings and Promises,* 6 JOURNAL OF LAW, ECONOMICS AND ORGANIZATION 203 (1990)[*]

1.   INTRODUCTION

My mother had an engagement ring, but neither of my grandmothers did, although both my grandfathers were wealthy enough to afford them. Before 1930, diamond rings were certainly available. The South African diamond mines were discovered in 1880, and they soon replaced the rapidly disappearing supply of diamonds from India and Brazil. In fact, the first reported diamond engagement ring was given by the Emperor Maximilian to Mary of Burgundy in 1377. Diamonds were associated in this country with engagement beginning in the 1840s, although they were at first given to men as well as women.

However, before the Depression, diamond rings were not considered a requisite for betrothal by most Americans. What then made women rather suddenly demand diamonds on the occasion of their engagement, so that by 1945 the "typical" bride wore "a brilliant diamond engagement ring and a wedding ring to match in design?"

The diamond ring rapidly changed from a relatively obscure token of affection to what amounted to an American tradition. It is customary to explain such a shift in demand in terms of an increase in income, a change in relative prices, or a change in tastes. This assumes a stable legal setting—that contracts are enforceable. But if the enforceability of a contract is problematic, what formerly was a relatively costly (hence unused) form of private ordering may become more viable. This paper looks at the change in America's demand for diamonds during the period 1930-1985, not as a Madison Avenue success story, but rather as a natural outgrowth of economic processes. The event beginning the movement toward diamond engagement rings was the abolition, with great fanfare, of a now relatively obscure cause of action called the "breach of promise to marry."

2.   THE BREACH OF PROMISE ACTION

The breach of promise action entitled a woman whose fiancé had broken off their engagement to sue him in assumpsit for damages, including the actual expenses she had

---

incurred in reliance on the marriage. She might also recover for her embarrassment, humiliation, and loss of other marriage opportunities.

Until fairly recently, a woman's marriage was necessary to secure her social position. An "old maid" would not only be scorned because she was not attractive enough to snag a husband, but also would be disadvantaged because in later life she would not be secure financially. Marriage was, as one writer noted, the "one career open to her," and once she had made her choice of husbands, the woman's "options were suddenly, irrevocably gone."

But there was more to the doctrine than this. Many, if not most, women who brought such actions had not only lost a husband, but also their virginity. Particularly during the period between the two world wars, a woman was expected to remain chaste until the time of her engagement. Once she was betrothed, however, sexual intimacy with her fiancé reportedly occurred nearly half the time. All this was well and good, but if the marriage never came about, she was irretrievably barred from offering an unblemished self to a new suitor and suffered a loss in "market value." While a man could pretend inexperience, a woman's virginity or lack of it was a verifiable physical fact. Because of the importance of premarital chastity, damages in breach of promise actions where seduction (intercourse) had occurred were far more substantial than in cases where no sexual intimacy was alleged. The trials themselves frequently became public spectacles because of testimony regarding the woman's previous chastity (or lack of the same). By the beginning of the Depression, the breach of promise suit came to be regarded as legally sanctioned blackmail, a threat to marriage and the family.

In 1935, a legislator from Indiana sponsored a bill abolishing the heart-balm actions in that state. Almost immediately thereafter, similar statutes were passed in most of the other major urban jurisdictions, so that by 1945, sixteen states had eliminated breach of marriage promise. Today, there are only scattered reported breach of marriage promise decisions from those few jurisdictions where the action remains viable.

3.   DEMAND FOR DIAMONDS

At the same time the cause of action for breach of promise was being reconsidered, the diamond industry had faced a period of lessened demand; increased supply. For a few years following 1932, diamonds were stockpiled in Europe to prevent a glut on the market. By the mid-1930s, DeBeers, the diamond-importing institution, was holding stocks valued at four times its annual sales. New sources of diamonds had been discovered, particularly in the Soviet Union, and the price of diamonds had been in decline for some years.

There was not only a greater supply but also a reduced demand for sales during the twenty-year period prior to 1939 declined by nearly 100 percent. National advertising was thought of as "vulgar" before the Great Depression, but in 1939, four years after the first states abolished the breach of promise action, DeBeers formed an alliance with a prominent New York advertising agency, Ayers, and prepared to release a significant advertising campaign focused on the slogan that "a diamond is forever."

The advertising agency from the start aimed at a national market. One of its more successful techniques was exploitation of the burgeoning film industry: Hollywood stars were given large and conspicuous diamonds to wear off stage, and special scenes involving the presentation of engagement rings were introduced into popular movies after intervention by Ayers, a notable example of which is the Mae West-Cary Grant classic *She Done Him Wrong.*

The industry enjoyed a phenomenal success during the period following 1935, and by 1965, 80 percent of all brides chose diamond engagement rings. DeBeers attributed the changing market to the Ayers advertising campaign, but, in fact, the market for diamonds began its growth four years before national advertising when the breach of promise action was first abolished in a significant number of important states. (North Dakota had abrogated breach of marriage promise actions in the nineteenth century, but they were at least theoretically available in the other 47 states).

The selection of states that abolished the action in the ten years following 1935 itself presents an interesting study. A glance at a map shows that they appear to have little in common: both urban and farm states, with an average per capita income approximating the norm for the period. What is interesting, however, is that the marriage rate in these states before abolition of the action greatly exceeded the contemporary national rate (67 percent of the United States marriages in 1935, with only 47.7 percent of the population). This suggests that the action for damages made people marry who otherwise would not. The scanty legislative history for the statutes abolishing breach of promise indicates that one motivation, and perhaps the primary one, may have been removal of a vestige of women's historic legal inferiority to men. States especially concerned with gender equality would therefore be expected to be the leaders in this reform, and some were involved at an early stage in the abolition movement. Other states abolishing breach of promise before 1945, including Nevada, Alabama, Florida, and Indiana, had always been important sources for migratory divorces. . . .

The data show that four factors explain much of the increase in the number of diamonds demanded in the period 1935-1960. The most important explanatory variable is the abolition of the breach of promise action. The standardized coefficient of the bonding hypothesis variable is the largest, and it is statistically significant. The population of marriageable age was also significant, with the second largest coefficient. The World War II dummy was almost as important as marriageable population and was also significant, although it is negatively related to diamond demand. This suggests that the hardships and absences of the war had a greater effect on demand than the desire to purchase diamonds as investment instruments. Although there is a fourth variable with a sizable coefficient, price, it is not statistically significant. These results support the hypothesis that abolition of the breach of promise action created a need for a bonding device, a need fulfilled by the diamond engagement ring. . . .

6. CONCLUSION

Students of economics are told that demand curves shift outward because of changes in demographics or, less frequently, tastes. Becker and Stigler argued that, in fact, tastes are relatively constant: that any widespread human behavior can be explained by utility maximization. They illustrated their theory by discussing such "tastes" as those for addiction, custom and tradition, and advertising. Although they presented a sophisticated mathematical model, they did not attempt to test their hypotheses empirically. This is an empirical study that proves them as well as Kronman

right: looking at one such change in tastes with a less than obvious economic explanation, I have found some evidence that engagement rings were part of an extralegal
contract guarantee, so that the "ring is a pledge to bind the contract to marry and it is
given on the understanding that the party who breaks the contract must return it"
(*Jacobs v. Davis*, [1917] 2 K. B. 532).

The change in demand for diamond engagement rings may therefore be explained
by an increase in need for such a bond because of the abolition of a cause of action for
breach of marriage promise. My guess, having apparently found a reason for the
change in demand for diamond engagement rings, is that many other mysterious
demand changes could be accounted for as well, given some thought as to what the
commodity might mean to consumers and some exploration of the legal or other
changes of the time during which the demand change occurred.

B. What Do Couples Know When They Marry?

Baker and Emery's justly famous piece uses psychological survey data to determine what people believe about marriage and divorce law. You may want to consider, as you read about the engaged couples in particular, how the optimism reported compares with what people feel as they embark upon other major long term transactions—with college roommates or law firm partners, for example. You may also think about whether the (misguided) predictions of marital success justify increased state supervision of the decision.

Lynn A. Baker & Robert E. Emery, *When Every Relationship Is Above Average: Perceptions and Expectations of Divorce at the Time of Marriage,* 17 LAW AND HUMAN BEHAVIOR 439 (1993)[*]

Divorce has been the focus of much attention in recent years, but beliefs about the legal aspects of divorce have scarcely been studied, especially as they relate to individuals' conceptions of the marriage contract. Research on beliefs prior to divorce is needed, because some commentators have contended that spouses discover the terms of the marriage contract only upon divorce. Furthermore, it is claimed that spouses frequently view the terms imposed by the state as unfair as well as unexpected.

This article presents an empirical examination of young adults' views of the frequency, effects, and laws of divorce, all of which bear on the important question of why many spouses may be surprised by its consequences. Our survey questions addressed four major issues: (1) How do persons about to be married perceive the statutory laws governing divorce, (2) how do those individuals perceive the risk and likely consequences of divorce in the population at large, (3) how do they perceive the risk and likely consequences of divorce for themselves, and (4) how do they think the statutory laws governing divorce ought to be written? Because the consequences of divorce are systematically different for men and women, we were interested to learn whether there were significant gender differences on these four issues. In addition, we investigated whether there were significant effects of the marital history of the respondents' parents.

In Study 1, the survey was administered to a group of young adults for whom the legal terms of the marriage contract are highly personally relevant: marriage license applicants. In Study 2 [omitted here], the same questionnaire was given to a group of young adults for whom the legal terms of the marriage contract are personally and intellectually relevant: law students before and after completing a course on family law. The major question of interest was whether the sense of surprise and unfairness that may attend divorce is due to (1) ignorance about divorce law and its consequences, or (b) accurate information about the laws and consequences of divorce but a belief that this

---

information is not personally relevant. We were also interested to learn the extent to which existing laws are congruent with current social mores.

STUDY 1

Method

Participants

Surveys were mailed to 300 individuals who had recently applied for a marriage license in a major Virginia city and who had not previously been married. Each spouse was sent a separate questionnaire and was asked to complete it independently of the other spouse. Of the 300 questionnaires mailed, 9 were returned as undeliverable, 11 were discarded because one or both spouses were previously married, and 5 were largely incomplete. Of the remaining 275 questionnaires, we received 137 replies, a response rate of 49.8%.

Nearly all (94.9%) of the respondents were married when they completed the survey, and 86.9% of those had been married for less than 2 months. Twenty-seven percent of the respondents had biological or adoptive parents who had divorced. The 66 male respondents ranged in age from 18 to 57, with a median of 27. The 71 female respondents ranged in age from 15 to 38, with a median of 25. The educational level of the respondents ranged from "completed 8th grade" to "graduate/professional degree," with a median of "college degree" for the women and a median of "some college" for the men.

Measures

The survey contained three sections in addition to requested background information. The first asked a series of questions about the respondents' expectations for their own marriages. The second posed a series of questions about the risk and likely consequences of divorce "in the United States in the 1980s". The final section presented 50 statements about Virginia statutory law concerning divorce. Each statements presented either an accurate statements of a statutory provision or its opposite. For each statement, respondents were asked whether Virginia law was currently written that way and whether Virginia law *ought to be* written that way.

Results

Perceptions of the Statutory Terms of the Marriage Contract

The respondents' knowledge of the terms of the marriage contract as embodied in the divorce statutes was only slightly better than chance. In response to the 50 questions on divorce law, the marriage license applicants averaged 30.1 correct answers (60.3%). The accuracy of the responses was not significantly different for questions concerning custody (62.15), alimony (64.3%), or child support (60.9%), but it was significantly lower for property settlement questions (52.6%).

There were statistically significant gender differences in the responses to only 4 of the 50 questions. Women were more pessimistic (and, in 3 of the 4 instances, less accurate) than the men in their perceptions of the statutory law's treatment of the traditional housewife upon divorce. For example, only 48% of the women, but 78% of the men, correctly stated that when deciding the amount of an alimony award, the court is required by statute to take into account the nonmonetary contributions of each spouse to the well-being of the family. Similarly, on only 4 questions were there statistically significant differences in the responses of individuals based on their parents' marital history. In 3 of the 4 instances, respondents whose parents had been divorced had a less accurate perception of the pertinent statutes than those whose parents had remained married. For example, 50% of those whose parents remained married, but only 24% of those whose parents divorced, correctly stated that when deciding custody, the court is *not* required by statute to give a preference to whichever parent has spent more time raising the children.

Perceptions of the Frequency and Effects of Divorce

In contrast to their relatively poor knowledge of the statutory law, the respondents' median perceptions of the frequency and effects of divorce "in the United States in the 1980s" were largely accurate. For example, when asked to estimate the percent of couples in the U.S. who marry today who will get divorced at some time in their lives, the median response given by the license applicants was 50%, the closest correct approximation. . . .

Respondents' Expectations for Themselves

Respondents' predictions for the permanence of their own marriages and the consequences should they be divorced were much more optimistic than their perceptions of the likelihood and effects of divorce for others. For example, although their median response was an accurate estimate that 50% of U.S. couples who marry will divorce, the *median* response of the marriage license applicants was *0%* when assessing the likelihood that they personally would divorce.

Respondents of *both* genders were also optimistic that they would receive custody of any children in the event of divorce. The median female respondent estimated that 80% of children from divorced families live mostly with their mothers, but more than 95% of women expected to get primary custody in the event that they had children and divorced. The median male respondent estimated that approximately 20% of children from divorced families live mostly with their fathers, but more than 40% of men expected to get primary custody in the event that they had children and divorced.

Both genders were optimistic that a divorcing woman who requested alimony would be awarded it by the court. Although the median female respondent estimated (very optimistically) that 40% of divorcing women are awarded alimony, 81% of the female respondents expected that the court would award alimony to them if they requested it at divorce. Similarly, although the median male respondent estimated that 50% of divorcing women are awarded alimony, 83% of the male respondents expected that the court would award alimony to their wives if they requested it.

The greatest discrepancy between respondents' expectations for themselves and others concerned the likelihood that all alimony or child support payments would be received. When asked to estimate the proportion of all spouses who are awarded alimony who receive all the payments, the median response was 40%. Fully 100% of the respondents who expected to be awarded alimony upon divorce, however predicted that their spouse would completely comply with the court's award. Similarly, although the median response was (quite accurately) that only 40% of all parents who are awarded child support receive all of the payments, 98% of the license applicants predicted that their spouse would fully comply with the court's award.

Attitudes Toward the Statutory Terms of the Marriage Contract

On 39 of the 50 questions, a majority of the respondents expressed approval of the existing statutory laws concerning divorce. A few responses deserve highlighting, however. In regard to childrearing, 83% approved of the existing "best interests of the child" standard for custody determinations, but three changes in child custody law also received substantial support. Fifty-six percent stated that the courts should be required to give a preference to whichever parent has spent more time raising the children (a "primary caretaker" standard). Nearly 50% of respondents expressed a preference for maternal custody for children ages 6 or younger (a "tender years" presumption), and 68% stated that the court should be required to permit children above the age of 12 to choose the parent who will have custody. No significant gender differences were found for any of these items, with the exception that more women (91%) than men (75%) approved of the "best interests" standard.

A large majority of respondents favored three important changes in the alimony statutes. In making alimony determinations, 62% of respondents (71% of men; 55% of women); would require the courts to consider whether either spouse is already required to make alimony payments to another (ex-spouse). (Sixty-five percent) (75% of men; 57% of women) stated that the courts should be prohibited from making alimony awards to spouses whose adultery was the reason for the divorce. Finally, 75% of respondents (71% of men; 79% of women) stated that the size of alimony awards should be the amount necessary for the homemaker to learn a new job skill and become self-supporting. . . .

GENERAL DISCUSSION

Our major findings are readily summarized. First, those who are about to be married have largely incorrect perceptions of the legal terms of the marriage contract as embodied in divorce statutes. Second, they have relatively accurate, if sometimes optimistic, perceptions of both the likelihood and the effects of divorce in the population at large. Third, these same individuals express thoroughly idealistic expectations about both the longevity of their own marriages and the consequences should they personally be divorced. Fourth, those about to marry largely approve of the existing divorce statutes. Finally, increasing individuals' knowledge of divorce statutes does not diminish the unrealistic optimism of their expectations for their own lives.

The finding with the greatest practical and theoretical import is the discrepancy between the respondents' relatively accurate perceptions of the likelihood and effects of divorce in the population at large and their extremely idealistic expectations for themselves. This discrepancy can be understood as an example of a representativeness bias. When predicting their own futures, young adults in both of the present samples ignored population base rates. The young adults surveyed apparently considered themselves to be unrepresentative of the population of people who marry, and therefore systematically concluded that the statistical likelihood of divorce and of its various effects did not apply to them personally. Indeed, respondents of both genders [expressed unrealistically optimistic] about the likely consequences should they personally be divorced, despite expressing unrealistically pessimistic views that divorce statutes are biased against their own gender.

This systematic optimism means that young adults are unlikely to investigate the terms of the marriage contract embodied in divorce statutes until they begin having marital difficulties. In fact, although a course in family law significantly improved knowledge of divorce statutes, it had no effect on the law students' representativeness bias. It is therefore not surprising that divorce often has "unexpected and unintended consequences." Notwithstanding the high probability of divorce, young adults consider divorce laws personally irrelevant even when they gain knowledge of them.

Disregard of base rates may also explain why so few individuals formally contract around existing divorce statutes prior to marriage. Only 1.5% of the marriage license applicants expressed any interest in entering into a prenuptial agreement concerning postdivorce finances, *none* said they would enter into such an agreement concerning postdivorce childrearing, and only 4.5% indicated any interest in consulting with an attorney before marriage about *any* issues related to the marriage. A slightly larger proportion of both the Time 1 (12%) and Time 2 (11%) law students stated that they would enter into a prenuptial agreement concerning postdivorce finances.

Although prenuptial contracts may be distasteful, individuals may nonetheless benefit from accurately assessing the personal relevance of base rates. A more realistic appreciation of the risk and likely consequences of divorce, as well as of the statutory laws governing divorce, might at the margin affect various choices made during marriage. Among the most common of such decisions are whether to be a full-time homemaker or have a career in the paid workforce; how many children to have and when to have them; and how long to stay out of the paid workforce following the birth of a child. Young women may be particularly disadvantaged by their idealism since, following divorce, the typical wife suffers a substantial decline in her standard of living in comparison to her former spouse.

There may also be advantages to young adults' unrealistic optimism concerning the personal risk and consequences of divorce, however. Insofar as our society would encourage marriages, a certain amount of individual "recklessness" may advance that goal by increasing the number of marriages that are entered into. In addition, spouses' idealistic expectations about the longevity of their own marriage may increase their motivation and persistence to achieve this result.

The pervasiveness and strength of the representativeness bias suggest that legal reforms aimed at increasing rational ex ante responsiveness to divorce statutes are not likely to succeed. Individuals will rarely engage in private ordering (prenuptial contracting) at marriage, and attempts to increase public knowledge of the legal terms of the marriage contract are not likely to be effective. Proposals to minimize the demoralization costs attending divorce might take other paths, however. Because our data suggest that the statutory "default rules" governing divorce will continue to matter greatly, those rules might be a profitable focus of reform. Reducing the indeterminacy of divorce statutes, for example, might ameliorate the unpredictability of the discretionary justice that is a concomitant of attempts to accommodate pluralism in contemporary American family life. In becoming more determinate, of course, our laws concerning marriage and divorce would necessarily embody explicitly prescriptive or aspirational norms. If we cannot agree on the governing norms, this route to increased predictability would be closed, however.

In short, the difficulty both for young adults and for lawmakers is coming to terms with the non-romantic aspects of marriage in a culture that exalts romanticism in personal relationships.

C. What Kind of Family Is It? Husbands and Wives

Irwin Altman, a psychologist, has spent many years gathering information about life among modern polygamous families in the western part of the Untied States. The families he studied are so-called "fundamentalist" Mormons, who claim to follow the religious doctrine renounced by the Church of Jesus Christ of Latter Day Saints over a century ago. Altman is primarily concerned with how these families accommodate the things we take for granted in daily life—inlaws, holidays, birthdays, and proprietary feelings about the kitchen. Like Professor Altman, we think it important in our increasingly diverse society to think about a variety of family forms, whether or not we would endorse them in the end.

Bumpass and Sweet discuss one of the family forms that has become important only in the last half of the twentieth century—cohabitation without marriage. As sociologists, they use a large national data set developed from personal interviews. The statistics presented in this article are simple percentages, but tell a remarkable story both of the rise of cohabitation as a choice for young couples and of the contrast between such relationships and marriage.

Irwin Altman, *Polygamous Family Life: The Case of Contemporary Mormon Fundamentalists*, 1996 UTAH LAW REVIEW 367[*]

[There are several thousand families who, though they are not recognized by the Mormon Church, practice polygamy in various communities in the Western United States. Irwin Altman has studied how these families function.]

D.   Established Relationships in Plural Families

Of the dozen or so areas we examined concerning later phases of plural family relationships, I will discuss living arrangements, rotation of a husband among his wives and children, celebrations, budget and resource management, and place attachment. I selected these topics because they are rarely considered in research on personal relationships and because some of them reflect nicely the role of the physical environment as an aspect of the dyadic/communal dialectic. Furthermore, they all include strong temporal qualities, a central feature of the transactional perspective.

1.   Living Arrangements

Living arrangements are diverse across polygynous families and also vary within families at different times in their lives. Cultural, economic, social, and unique family needs all contribute to the variety of living arrangements.

---

[*]   Copyright © 1996. Reprinted with permission.

Many families live in primarily dyadic arrangements, where wives have separate dwellings, separate upstairs and downstairs apartments, live in a compound area with separate residences, or share a large dwelling with multiple apartments. Wives and husbands sometimes prefer a dyadic arrangement at certain times in their lives because it permits a wife to manage and control her own home and to essentially live monogamously.

Many other plural families live in primarily communal arrangements, with wives sharing a kitchen, living room, yard, entranceway, and most other parts of a home. This style of living fulfills the ideal of a communal, unified family. However, almost all communal arrangements have dyadic aspects, with wives having their own bedrooms, or sometimes occupying a separate bedroom, bathroom, and sleeping area with their children. There are also a number of mixed dyadic and communal arrangements in families. For example, in the same family some wives may live communally while other wives live in separate dwellings.

Although there are a variety of living arrangements based on economic, interpersonal, pragmatic, and other factors, the importance of both dyadic and communal factors is often raised as an explicit consideration by husbands and wives. For example, participants sometimes emphasize the need for wives to have separate and independent lives and to raise their children and be with their husband, while simultaneously acknowledging the desirability of living together and sharing a common life as a unified family. Plural families often change their living arrangements throughout the years—from primarily dyadic to primarily communal, and vice versa—and in no particular sequence. In many families a new wife lives with one or more established wives for a period of time. Eventually there may be pressure to move to a more dyadic living arrangement, as children and families grow and as wives seek independence. For years thereafter, living arrangements often change many times—from dyadic to communal, communal to mixed dyadic and communal, and so on, in different patterns. Family economics, job requirements, interpersonal compatibilities, and complexities associated with the husband visiting his families may result in varied living arrangements over the years. Our data suggest, however, that when families stop growing, and as children leave home to marry, families tend to settle down into primarily dyadic living arrangements. At least this is the pattern in the urban community; in the rural community communal living is not unusual throughout the life cycle.

Despite variations in living arrangements within and across families, many husbands and wives consistently describe their "ideal" living arrangement as an almost perfect blend of dyadic and communal. For example, they often describe some version of individual wives and their children living in separate apartments or dwellings, but with all families clustered around a common gathering space for activities that foster the goal of a unified family. Sometimes their ideal takes the form of separate dwellings around a central plaza area; sometimes it involves separate apartments organized around a central room. Such idealistic living arrangements reflect nicely the dyadic/communal dialectic that characterizes other aspects of the life of plural families and with which they struggle on a regular basis. The issue of living arrangements also highlights the importance of tracking the temporal flow of residential activity as a mirror of evolving family life and of changes in the dyadic/communal dialectic.

2.   Rotation

In polygynous Mormon fundamentalist families, a husband and each wife ideally spend some time alone with each other and with their children, doing what any monogamous couple does—eating, talking, solving family problems, interacting with children, sleeping together, and having sexual relationships. How does a husband "rotate" among wives and children to acknowledge the uniqueness of each dyad in a plural family and simultaneously preserve the family's communal unity?

We discovered that modern fundamentalists use three types of rotation systems: rigid, laissez faire, and flexible. In *rigid* rotation systems a husband visits each wife and her children according to a fixed routine, theoretically with exactly equivalent time spent with each family and in a known and predictable sequence of visits. Rigid rotation systems are used only rarely in the families we studied because the system does not take into consideration birthdays and anniversaries, travel and work schedules, or emergencies, all of which require the husband's attention out of rotational sequence. In addition, rigid rotation patterns become very mechanical for some participants, resulting in "required" and nonspontaneous visits by a husband.

In a second approach, laissez faire rotation systems, there is no particular order or predictability of when and how long a husband spends time with each wife; it is up to the husband's discretion. In some instances he might inform a wife about when he plans to be with her; in other cases he simply arrives at a wife's home unannounced and/or stays for an indefinite time. Unlike a rigid rotation scheme, the laissez faire system usually places full authority in the husband's hands, at least theoretically. He goes where he deems it appropriate or convenient, with or without advance notice, and stays as long as he wishes. Laissez faire systems are not very popular because of their unpredictability and the potential for wives to feel that they are not having equitable time.

Most families with whom we worked usually adopted some form of *flexible* rotation system. Similar to laissez faire systems, in flexible rotation schemes it is the husband who "officially" decides where he will spend his time. However, he and his wives operate under a cultural norm that he should be fair and equitable to all wives and children. Moreover, husbands and wives often discuss their rotation strategy and change it when they feel that an adjustment is warranted. Most important, flexibility is built in to accommodate special family occasions, such as birthdays and anniversaries, or to address important family problems and emergencies. Flexible rotation systems have the greatest potential for a viable interplay of dyadic and communal processes in modern plural families. Although they often place primary responsibility in a husband's hands, flexible systems include wives' participation in changing particular visits because of personal or family needs. Thus a flexible system is "owned" by everyone and can function as an agreed upon communal process. Naturally, whether or not communality is achieved depends on how fair and equitable a system is in practice.

A flexible system also has the best potential for strengthening dyadic bonds between a husband and each wife in a plural family. With flexibility, a wife's birthday or a husband's and wife's anniversary can be celebrated outside a regular rotation sequence, thereby making each dyadic relationship salient and special. Similarly, breaking a rotation to address a wife's personal problem, a husband-wife problem, or a family matter testifies to the importance of each dyadic relationship in a plural family.

Rotation processes sometimes generate stress and tension in plural families, especially when wives feel they are not being treated fairly by the husband, are jealous about the amount of time a husband spends with other wives, or feel the quality of their interaction is poor when he does visit. Once again, contemporary plural families must struggle to achieve an acceptable interplay of dyadic and communal processes in this most crucial aspect of their lives.

3.   Celebrations

Celebrations of birthdays, anniversaries, holidays, and other events in plural families also reflect dyadic and communal features. Some celebrations are primarily dyadic, such as wives' birthdays and the wedding anniversary of a husband and particular wife. These events are usually celebrated by a husband and wife alone. For example, they may see a movie, have dinner at a restaurant, spend an extra day together, or go away alone for a short period. Although other wives occasionally participate, birthdays and wedding anniversaries highlight the individuality of a wife and/or the uniqueness of a particular husband-wife pair.

A number of other events are celebrated communally, including Sunday meals, Thanksgiving, and the Fourth of July. The husband/father's birthday is often celebrated communally, perhaps symbolizing his status as husband, father, and religious and social leader of the communal family.

Many families also celebrate Christmas communally, with everyone sleeping and/or gathering in one home. In some families the communal nature of the holiday is also reflected in gift giving, whereby everyone draws a name out of a hat before the holiday, across wives and their children, to identify the family member for whom they will make or purchase a gift. In some families wives give gifts to all children of all wives. Such practices reinforce the idea that everyone is a member of a unified family. In other cases, this custom is supplemented by mothers giving special gifts to their own children, reflecting a dyadic aspect to the celebration. In one family, each of four wives and their children separately gave gifts to the one wife's ill father on different nights of Christmas. Then, on the last night the whole family sang carols to him, illustrating a blend of dyadic and communal processes.

4.   Budget and Resource Management

Another aspect of everyday life in plural families concerns budget and resource management. Polygynous families often operate in marginal or difficult financial circumstances because of many children and households to support, people working in low-paying or seasonal occupations, and other factors. As a result, wives often work, children may contribute to family income, expenses are sometimes unpredictable, and managing limited financial resources can be quite complex. Similar to other aspects of their lives, families use various budget systems, experimenting over time and trying out new approaches as income and family circumstances warrant.

In several cases, budget systems are dyadic, with wives supporting themselves and/or husbands separately supplementing each wife's income as necessary. In such systems, wives are not involved in one another's budgetary deliberations with the husband. Such purely dyadic practices are relatively rare; most dyadic systems also have communal aspects. For example, in several families all of the husband's and wives' incomes are pooled and then distributed by the husband. In other families the husband provides each wife with basic funds and wives keep their own earnings as a surplus pool. In other cases wives keep some basic amount of their own earnings and turn over any surplus to the husband for distribution to other wives. These systems are primarily dyadic because the husband negotiates the distribution of funds with each wife separately, even if the funds originate from a common pool.

Other budget and resource systems are more communal. A prototype arrangement is for everyone to pool their earnings, with the distribution to each wife made at a meeting of the husband and wives. Dyadic aspects of this strategy involve taking each wife's unique needs into account, e.g., special medical bills, and also allowing each wife to manage her own money as she sees fit. Stronger communal approaches occur when wives live in a single dwelling and share home management responsibilities. Here, money may be allocated to the wives as a communal group for collective food shopping, although direct negotiations between a wife and husband may occur for other needs, thereby adding a dyadic component to resource management.

In most families, different systems are used at different times as a result of changes in family status, tensions regarding fairness of the system, overall income, and other factors. Changes seem to shift from dyadic to communal approaches, and vice versa, in whole or in part, as families attempt to cope with their evolving circumstances and as they struggle to achieve a satisfactory dialectic balance and manage a lifestyle for which there are few cultural and personal guidelines.

6.   Place Attachment

The last area of plural-family life that I will describe concerns "place attachment" or the emotional bonds that husbands and wives have to their homes. A home is important to a plural wife because she is responsible for managing it, for raising and teaching her children in it, and for maintaining the home for herself, her husband, and her children. The home is a tangible symbol of her role as wife, mother, and religious observant and is also a place in which she may display her personality, values, and lifestyle preferences. In many ways the attachment of a polygynous wife to her home is similar to that of many women in mainstream American culture.

One aspect of attachment to homes is reflected in decorations. Homes contain decorations that symbolize four aspects of a wife's attachment: personal identity items, such as personal trophies, collections, art, or handiwork that reflect a wife's preferences, interests, and talents; personal family attachments, such as photos, memorabilia, and gifts linking a wife to her natal family and relatives; religious and cultural attachments, including photos of church leaders and church buildings, and religious objects and pictures; and dyadic attachments, or decorations symbolizing a wife's unique relationship with her husband and their children. These include photographs of the husband and wife, wedding and engagement memorabilia, gifts from the husband, photos of events in the life of the couple, genealogy charts tracing the husband and wife's lineage, and pictures and objects associated with their children. Interestingly, homes rarely display photographs of other wives or decorations reflecting the communal nature of the whole family. Wives adorn their homes to make salient their unique bond to the husband and their children. The home is not a vehicle to mirror the religious and cultural ideal of a harmonious communal family.

At the same time, and perhaps reflecting an indirect communal counterpart, husbands do not display strong attachments to homes. They seem to be neutral or uninterested in home furnishings, play no role in decorating, rarely have a place of their own in homes, are willing to move from home to home, do not display personal items in homes, and seem to act as "visitors" to the wives' dwellings. It may be that their roles as family leaders, the ideal of husbands being "fair" to all wives, and the cultural value of the home as a wife's place result in little commitment to any home. In addition, a husband's lack of attachment to any particular wife's home may avoid conflict and jealously between wives and function as an indirect mechanism for ensuring family unity and communality. In any case, attachments to homes exhibit a picture of the dyadic/communal dialectic that does not follow the straightforward pattern I discussed in other aspects of life in plural families.

IV. CONCLUSION

The study of contemporary American polygynous families is fascinating in and of itself. Polygynous relationships are an anomaly in American society and reflect an attempt by fundamentalist Mormons to engage in plural marriages on religious grounds in the face of enormous internal and external pressures. Studying coping and viability and tensions and complexities in plural families is intrinsically instructive. In addition, present-day American culture already has a variety of marital and family forms alongside the traditional nuclear family. Blended families, foster families, adoptive families, single-parent families, gay and lesbian families, and different combinations of elderly relationships are now commonplace in American society. Living in such relationships may be quite complex because participants have had little prior experience in them, and the culture at large has little guidance to offer. Furthermore, there is also relatively little research on these social structures. Polygynous families add to the mix and offer an opportunity to better understand the nature and dynamics of personal and close relationships. Studying and understanding this array of relationships is essential for practical reasons. These relationships and family forms are here to stay on the American scene for the foreseeable future. In addition to questioning our well-established cultural stereotypes about the "proper" family structure, these new relationship forms will surely challenge our legal system and its precedents regarding the nature of marriage, parental and children's rights, kinship relationships, custody issues, inheritance, and many others. . . .

Larry L. Bumpass & James A. Sweet, *National Estimates of Cohabitation,* 26 DEMOGRAPHY 615 (1989)[*]

The rapid increase in cohabitation among unmarried couples is crucial to our understanding of changing marriage patterns. Conventional measures based on the registration of marriages decreasingly represent both the timing and the occurrence of union formation. We have long recognized that the date of separation measures the end of a marriage better than the divorce date. So too, the beginning of cohabitation may be a more apt marker of union formation than the marriage date.

There is no single answer to whether cohabitation is a late stage of courtship or an early stage of marriage. It is the former for couples who are uncertain about their relationship but are considering marriage, the latter for those who would marry immediately were it not for some practical constraint, and neither for couples who do not want to marry each other. In any event, marriage decreasingly indexes the significant transitions normatively associated with it: sexual relationships, a shared household, and often even childbearing are likely to have occurred before marriage. While marriage may declare and reinforce a higher level of commitment, through both ritual and law, its actual timing may be a matter of convenience rather than a marker of a changed commitment. Hence cohabitation may represent a clearer transition in intimate relationships than marriage—at least it marks the establishment of a joint household.

Just as cohabitation may have multiple meanings for the couples involved, the cohabitation revolution is likely to have had multiple causes. Willis and Michael argue that in the context of the high divorce rate, cohabiting has increasingly been seen as an opportunity for screening out a risky marriage. They may be correct that reasons for cohabitation have gained in strength, but it also seems likely that normative barriers have weakened greatly. As we have noted earlier, the roots of the increase in cohabitation could well lie in the growth of premarital sexual intimacy more generally. Marriage is being delayed, but sexual relationships begin at increasingly earlier ages. Unmarried couples living together once faced strong social disapproval, in no small part because their living arrangements flaunted their sexual intimacy. That issue has become largely irrelevant now that sexual relationships are common regardless of living arrangements.

Two issues stand out in considering the consequences of cohabitation: the extent to which cohabitation has offset the declines in marriage and the relationship between cohabitation and marital stability. First, marriage rates have fallen during the same period that cohabitation has become common. Reports from both France and Australia indicate that couples in those countries have been forming unions at a rather constant rate despite a decline in marriage rates, with the difference being made up by cohabitation. This may also be the case for the United States. Second, because of the improved opportunity for unsatisfactory matches to dissolve before, rather than after, marriage, we might expect that the growth in cohabitation would reduce the divorce rate and that couples who cohabit before marriage would have more stable marriages. Although the

---

[*]   Copyright © 1989. Reprinted with permission.

divorce rate in the United States has plateaued since 1980, data from both Sweden and Canada suggest that marriages preceded by cohabitation are more, rather than less, likely to end in divorce.

It is clear that analyses of the formation and dissolution of unions must struggle with the changing meaning of marriage that cohabitation signals. It is because of these issues that the 1987-1988 National Survey of Families and Households (NSFH) collected unique data on cohabitation for the United States. Analyses are under way comparing cohabiting persons with other unmarried persons, on the one hand, and with married couples, on the other. The purpose of this article, however, is the more limited objective of providing the first national estimates of cohabitation trends and levels, union formation including both marriage and cohabitation, and the stability of unions preceded by cohabitation. The article concludes with a multivariate examination of the correlates of cohabitation before first marriage.

The National Survey of Families and Households

The NSFH is a national sample survey of 13,017 people interviewed between March 1987 and May 1988. In addition to a main sample of 9,643 persons aged 19 and over, we oversampled certain population subgroups. Cohabiting couples were over-sampled, as were single-parent families, stepfamilies, recently married couples, blacks, Chicanos, and Puerto Ricans. In each selected household, a randomly selected adult was interviewed and (when appropriate) a self-administered questionnaire was completed by the spouse or cohabiting partner. Interviews averaged about 100 minutes, though interview length varied considerably with the complexity of the respondent's family history.

The NSFH was designed to provide information on many aspects of family life; however, we devoted particular attention to cohabitation and the relationships between cohabitation and marriage, including the following:

1. Detailed measurement of cohabitation data in the context of marriage and separation histories.
2. A sequence on attitudes relating to marriage and cohabitation asked of never-married and previously married respondents under 35 years of age.
3. A series of questions concerning the nature and quality of the relationship between partners in both married and cohabiting couples.
4. A self-enumerated interview for the spouse or partner of the main respondent.
5. Questions relating to attitudes toward marriage and cohabitation asked of all respondents.

The final data file includes 6,881 married couples and 682 cohabiting couples. Of these, we have 5,648 spouse questionnaires and 519 partner questionnaires.

We were concerned that cohabiting relationships would tend to be underreported, so we adopted a strategy to maximize the completeness of reporting. For all respondents (except those already identified as currently cohabiting), we introduced the sequence with the phrase: "Nowadays, many unmarried couples live together: sometimes they eventually get married and sometimes they don't." Rather than offer respondents an easy out with a screener question about whether they had ever cohabited, we keyed the sequence to each spouse for ever-married respondents. Thus the question continued with respect to the first marriage: "Did you and your (first) (husband/wife) live together before you were married?" We then obtained the date on which they began living together, whether they lived together continuously until marriage, whether they cohabited with anyone else before their first marriage, how many partners they cohabited with altogether before their first marriage, when they first began to cohabit, and if the first partner was other than their first spouse, when the first cohabitation ended.

These questions were repeated for the interval before second marriage and, in reduced form, for the interval before third marriage; similar items were collected for the interval since last marriage and for never-married persons. Thus even though we do not have a complete event history of cohabitation, we have probed for each intermarital interval, have the beginning and end of the first cohabitation in each intermarital interval, and have a count of the total number of partners.

In some cases, the date on which a couple begins cohabiting may be ambiguous: for example, when living together increases gradually from several days a week to full time or when a second separate residence is maintained. The ambiguity raised by this is similar to the dating of separation in analyses of marital dissolution. In both cases, we rely on the respondents' assessment of the most appropriate date in what may have been a more gradual transition. In neither case is this likely to result in systematic or serious bias. Although there was no minimum length of cohabitation required, only about 5 percent of the cohabitations reported lasted less than 1 month.

Trends and Levels

Cohabitation Experience

We know that the prevalence of current cohabitation has increased rapidly over the last two decades and that many more persons have lived with a partner of the opposite sex than are doing so at any point in time. For example, Thornton found that although about 10 percent in the Study of American Families were currently cohabiting (at about 23 years of age), 30 percent had ever done so. The NSFH provides the first opportunity to examine national data on cohabitation patterns across cohorts.

Table 1 provides estimates by age at survey of three measures of cohabitation experience: current cohabitation, cohabitation before first marriage, and any cohabitation. The latter measure includes cohabitation after marital disruption as well as before first marriage.

Looking first at the estimates for the population aged 19 and over as a whole, we see that 4 percent are currently cohabiting, about one-sixth cohabited before marriage, and about one-quarter have cohabited at some time. Obviously, these figures include older cohorts and the levels are much higher among persons under 40 years of age. Current cohabitation peaks at one-sixth among never-married persons aged 25-34 and at slightly more than one-quarter among the separated or divorced aged less than 30. Almost none of the elderly are currently cohabiting, contrary to occasional assertions concerning such cohabitation for tax or Social Security reasons. The high level of cumulative experience over the life course is illustrated in the measures of having ever cohabited. By their early 30s, almost half of the population has cohabited at some time, and the proportion is two-thirds among separated or divorced persons under the age of 35.

Table 2 looks at this changing experience from the perspective of successive marriage cohorts. The proportion of persons who cohabited before first marriage quadrupled from 11 percent for marriages in 1965-1974, to 44 percent for marriages in 1980-1984. If this trend has continued, the proportion is most likely well over half for marriages in the late 1980s. Unnoticed at the time, remarriages led the trend toward cohabitation as early as the late 1960s and early 1970s. One-third of persons remarrying around 1970 had cohabited, and the proportion has reached two-thirds in the 1980s.

In most marriages preceded by cohabitation, cohabitation was followed by the couple's marriage. Among persons who had recently married for the first time and who had cohabited before marriage, almost all had lived with their spouse before marriage (39 of 44), and most of those who had lived with their spouse had not lived with anyone else (34 of 39). At the same time, almost one-fifth of all cohabitants had lived with someone other than their spouse.

The Formation of Unions

Cohabitation has increased markedly while marriage rates have been declining. Hence as noted in the Introduction, it is likely that the formation of coresidential unions has not declined as rapidly as we might infer from marriage trends. Table 3 presents estimates of the proportion of successive birth cohorts who, before the age of 25, had cohabited, had married, and had either cohabited or married. A comparison of marriage and any union formation (marriage or cohabitation) speaks directly to the extent to which the marked delay in first marriage has been offset by increasing cohabitation. For midcentury birth cohorts, age at first coresidential union was synonymous with first marriage, but it clearly is no longer so.

We can see both the sharp increases in cohabitation and the sharp declines in marriage. For example, among females, the proportion who had cohabited before 25 years of age increased from 3 to 37 percent over these cohorts, whereas the proportion who had married by this age declined from 82 to 61 percent. In contrast to this 21-point decline in the proportion ever married by 25 years of age, there was only a 7-point decline in the proportion ever in a union. Among males, there was a 30-point decline in marriage before the age of 25, compared with a 13-point decline in the formation of unions by that age. For the United States as well as other countries, such as France and Australia, much of the decline in marital unions has been offset by the increase in cohabiting unions.

The Stability of Unions

A critical starting point for evaluating the relationships between cohabitation and marriage is the comparative stability of the different union types. How long does cohabitation last before either marriage or disruption occurs? To what extent do cohabiting couples marry each other? What is the relative stability of unions begun by cohabitation compared with marriages with and without preceding cohabitation? These are the issues addressed in the successive rows of Table 4.

Despite the high levels of lifetime experience, cohabiting couples are a small proportion of all couples because cohabitation is a short-lived state. As we see in the first row of Table 4, most cohabiting couples either marry or stop living together within a few years. Two-fifths of cohabiting unions do not continue as cohabitations for more than 1 year, only one-third lasts 2 years, and only 1 in 10 are still cohabiting after 5 years. The median duration of cohabitation is 1.3 years. These are life table estimates based on the experience of first unions beginning between 1975 and 1984.

Table 4. Life Table Estimates of Cohabitation and Marriage Experience by Age: First Unions, 1975-1984 (cumulative %)

Experience	Duration	(years)					
	1	2	3	4	5	10	N
Cohabitations surviving	59	33	21	14	9	2	1,504
Cohabitations married	25	41	48	52	56	59	1,504
Split							
First cohabitations	17	29	35	40	45	57	1,504
First marriages	5	9	13	17	20	30	2,680
Cohabited							
With any partner	7	12	17	22	25	38	1,017
With first spouse	6	11	16	21	24	36	487
Did not cohabit	4	8	11	14	18	27	1,663
First unions	10	17	22	26	30	40	3,167

As noted earlier, cohabiting couples are likely very heterogeneous with respect to how they view their living together. For some, marriage is definitely planned and all that is at issue is the timing of a ceremony. For others, marriage is a serious possibility and living together is an opportunity to test the relationship before reaching a decision. Still others may have no interest in marrying. We are exploring attitudinal items in other analyses, but the second row in Table 4 demonstrates both that marriage is the most likely outcome and that many cohabiting couples do not marry each other. Sixty percent of first cohabitation unions between 1975 and 1984 are likely to end in marriage. If marriage is going to occur, it does so rather quickly: One-quarter marry within a year, and half have married within 3 years, representing 42 and 80 percent, respectively, of those who eventually marry.

Cohabitation raises a number of issues with respect to union stability. If our concern is with union formation and dissolution, then we should focus on all unions irrespective of whether they were begun by marriage or the individuals were ever married. At the same time, we would like to know whether marriages preceded by cohabitation are more or less stable than those that were not. We examine a number of such different definitions of union stability in the remaining rows of Table 4.

Comparing the rows for first cohabitations and for first marriages, we see that unions begun by cohabitation are almost twice as likely to dissolve within 10 years, compared with all first marriages: 57 percent compared with 30 percent. As we would expect from the breakup of unions that do not result in marriage, the difference is greatest over the first 2 years (29 percent and 9 percent, respectively).

Although some of this high level of disruption reflects the tentative, or even intentionally temporary, nature of many cohabitations, high disruption persists among cohabitors who marry. We might expect that the termination of less propitious matches before marriage and the later age at marriage associated with cohabitation would lead to greater marital stability for those who cohabit and marry. On the contrary, the proportion separating or divorcing within 10 years is a third higher among those who lived together before marriage than among those who did not (36 vs. 27 percent). This difference is similar to the results reported by Balakrishnan et al., based on Canadian data, and most recently by Booth and Johnson for the United States.

The last row of Table 4 shows that 40 percent of all first unions are dissolved within 10 years. That the dissolution rate for all first unions is higher than that of first marriages suggests that the dissolution of cohabitations before marriage is masking some of the instability of marriage-like relationships. Thus it seems plausible that part of the plateau in divorce rates since 1980 may be attributable to the screening function provided by cohabitation. Put differently, if it were not for the high prevalence of cohabitation, the marital disruption rate might well be higher than it is. This interpretation depends on the extent to which the higher dissolution rate of marriages preceded by cohabitation represents a selection into cohabitation of more tentative relationships and/or more liberal attitudes, rather than an effect of premarital cohabitation on subsequent marital success. Of course, some proportion of cohabitors also would never have married under the earlier regime.

Differentials in Cohabitation Before First Marriage

Cohabitation has become a common aspect of marriage and union formation in the United States, but is it more likely in some groups than others? To what extent is the likelihood of cohabiting affected by circumstances in one's family of origin? It is to these issues that we now turn. (This analysis is restricted to persons under the age of 45.)

The first column in Table 5 is simply the observed proportions in each category who have cohabited prior to a first marriage. These figures obviously reflect differences in exposure associated with different ages at marriage and do not represent lifetime experience because of truncation at interview. Nonetheless, they do represent the experience in the population as of 1987-1988 and provide a sense of scale when interpreting the multivariate results.

The effect parameters reported are the percentage change in risk associated with a category of a variable compared with the omitted category. These estimates are drawn from a proportional-hazard model in which exposure was censored by marriage as well as interview; that is, they represent the relative risk of cohabiting given that a person has never married. Two sets of effects are presented: those with the variable considered by itself (unadjusted) and those from a model including all of the other variables.

Despite the fact that at interview more men than women had cohabited before marriage, the rate of premarital cohabitation is 14 percent lower among men. The difference, of course, reflects women's earlier age at marriage, which reduces the amount of time they are at risk of cohabiting. Thornton also reported a higher net cohabitation rate for women. This effect very likely arises through the typically older ages of men in unions, because never-married women are more likely to cohabit with previously married men than the reverse.

A similar difference between observed proportions in cross section and relative risks is observed between blacks and non-Hispanic whites. Although blacks are more likely to have cohabited, the rate of cohabiting among never-married persons is 26 percent lower among blacks than among non-Hispanic whites. This time, however, the difference between prevalence and rates is not a consequence of nonmarital exposure, since a positive (though nonsignificant) effect is seen in the second column. It is only after education and aspects of family background (intactness and welfare receipt) are controlled that the lower cohabitation rate of blacks is seen. Hence in the context of much lower marriage rates among blacks, the formation rate of cohabiting unions is also lower among blacks. Mexican Americans are somewhat less likely to cohabit than non-Hispanic whites, but the difference is not significant.

The sharp increase in cohabitation rates over cohorts requires no further comment; age was included primarily as a control for the examination of the effects of the other variables.

Contrary to a common view of cohabitation as college student behavior, education is strongly and negatively related to rates of cohabitation before first marriage. The highest rates of cohabitation are found among the least educated. Unmarried persons who have completed college are 64 percent less likely to cohabit than those who did not complete high school. It is possible that these differences reflect associated differences in the economic resources available for marrying rather than cohabiting as well as population differences in attitudes toward the acceptability of cohabitation. We are pursuing both of these issues in ongoing analyses.

The next six measures in Table 5 were included to tap relevant aspects of the family of orientation that may affect cohabitation. Such effects could occur either through attitudes toward the acceptability of cohabitation, through push factors that might make setting up one's own household seem attractive even when marriage was either untimely or undesired, or through differences in economic resources that might affect marriage rates.

Some credibility is given the economic resources argument by the effects of the parental education variables. Both mother's and father's education are positively related to cohabitation rates, and the effect for college-educated fathers is significant. That persons with college-educated fathers are more likely to cohabit is consistent with the expectation that more liberal attitudes on this matter may be positively associated with education and that the observed negative effect of own education on cohabitation behavior reflects differential ability to marry.

Because of strong church positions with respect to marriage, we might expect those raised as Catholics to be less likely to cohabit. Surprisingly, however, we find no significant effect of having been raised a Catholic, either before or after other variables are controlled.

Mother's work during adolescence has been cited as being relevant to adolescent sexual behavior because of the concomitant reduced supervision; it may also encourage more independence in general. Although the effect is in the expected direction, we find only a weak association between mother's employment and cohabitation rates.

In sharp contrast, however, are strong and significant effects of having received welfare while growing up and of not having lived with both parents all of the time while growing up. Net of other factors, growing up in a family that received welfare is associated with a 40 percent higher rate of cohabitation before first marriage. This may reflect a greater push from the parental household when that household is poor, but it may also reflect the consequences of lower financial resources on the ability to marry. In addition, with family welfare receipt controlled along with the other variables, having experienced a broken family as a child is associated with a 62 percent higher rate of cohabitation. Parental family contexts are thus clearly relevant for the likelihood of cohabiting as a young adult.

Conclusions

In sum, this initial analysis of data from the National Survey of Families and Households documents very high levels of cohabitation for recent cohorts. In fact, the prevalence of cohabitation has substantially offset declining marriage rates. Cohabiting living arrangements do not last long: within a few years most cohabiting couples have either married or separated. More will end in marriage than in separation. Unions formed by cohabitation are also less likely to stay together than unions formed by marriage. This is particularly so while the cohabiting couple is not married, but it is also true when cohabitation is followed by marriage. Thus we have the apparent paradox that although marriages preceded by cohabitation are less stable than others, the increase in cohabitation has very likely kept the divorce rate from continuing its pre-1980 increase. Surely many relationships that in the early 1970s would have resulted in marriage followed by divorce are now resulting in cohabitation followed by disruption before the marriage occurs.

A number of background variables affect the propensity to cohabit. Cohabitation is most likely among those who did not complete high school, those whose family received welfare while they were growing up, and those who did not grow up in an intact family. Nonetheless, cohabitation before marriage has become common throughout society. For example, in spite of the large negative effect of education, more than a quarter of college graduates have cohabited before marriage.

Cohabitation has become an aspect of union formations and dissolutions that we simply cannot ignore. Measures based solely on marriage and marital stability, such as official vital statistics, are increasingly misrepresenting both the timing and incidence of actual behavior patterns.

Stephen O. Murray, AMERICAN GAY, 169 (University of Chicago Press, 1996)[*]

DECISION-MAKING

Although reports of enduring same-sex pairs come from many locales, there is a dearth of systematic data on same-sex couples even in North American cities, so that it is not possible to estimate whether the age and status disparities of some of the examples listed at the beginning of this chapter typify same-sex relationships. Many gay writers assert that gay male relationships cross racial, class, and age discrepancies more

---

[*]   Copyright © 1996. Reprinted by permission.

often than do heterosexual or lesbian relationships. "Opposites attract" is a predominant folk wisdom—except, of course when "birds of a feather flock together." What "everyone knows," thus, provides little resolution. The number of long-term lesbian and gay relationships that cross social discrepancies remains a question for systematic research. The extent to which the ideology of egalitarian relations is realized in gay and lesbian couples also remains unclear.

In what little empirical evidence exists, choice of long-term partners in same-sex relationships is based on similarity of social characteristics *(homophily)* and on opportunities for contact *(propinquity)*, just as in the usual choice of heterosexual marriage partners and of lesbian and gay "best friends"—many of whom are former sexual partners. Undoubtedly, racial and cultural differences often enhance sexual attraction. The same differences that initially intrigue and attract may become problematic for transforming a sexual affair into an enduring relationship, however. Long-term gay and lesbian relationships in which there is not the friction between male expectations and female expectations may thrive relatively better than heterosexual relationships with conflicting cultural expectations, but there remains the tendency to marry one's "own kind" despite being attracted to and even sexually involved with persons of other classes, races, and/or ethnicities. The attributes of those with whom one wants to have sex and those with whom one would consider settling down (marrying) are often quite distinct. Moreover, the kinds of relationships someone wants and seeks are not necessarily the kinds he or she has.

Most self-identified lesbians and gay men have some experience of living in a relationship. In a study conducted in San Francisco during the late 1960s, A.P. Bell and Weinberg found 51 percent of white homosexual men, 58 percent of black homosexual men, 72 percent of white homosexual women, and 70 percent of black homosexual women were in a relationship. As in most surveys of lesbigay populations, most of the rest reported having been in a relationship at some time in their lives. In a national survey of 530 black lesbians, Mays and Cochran reported 66 percent currently in committed relationships. Of these, 53 percent lived together. The median length of the longest (lifetime-to-date) relationship was 42 months, and the median number of serious/committed lesbian relationships was three. In my own 1988 nonrandom sample of gay male San Franciscans, 40 percent were coupled.

In the Bell and Weinberg study, there were no age discrepancies in 5 percent of the couples including a white male respondent, in 10 percent of the couples including a black male or white female respondent, and in 3 percent of the couples involving a black female. There were differences of more than five years in 51, 40, 35, and 47 percent of the couples, respectively. Sixty-four percent of white gay male respondents judged their social position to be similar to their partner's, compared to 39 percent of black males, 56 percent of black lesbians, and 72 percent of white lesbians. Three percent of black homosexual couples reported equal income, in contrast to 17 and 18 percent of white female and male couples, although negative effects of income disparity were reported by only 2 percent of the gay white men, 4 percent of black gay men and women, and 6 percent of white lesbians. Blacks in the sample were substantially younger than whites when they began their relationship (just as black gay men tend to have initiated homosexual sex at earlier ages than white or Asian American gay men).

In a large-scale survey of contemporary American couples, Blumstein and Schwartz found that couples in which both people felt they were genuine partners with equal control over economic assets were more tranquil. Harry found age to predict power in decision-making within gay male relationships, especially among those couples living together, but also suggested that "in gay relationships it is more likely that partners will be more similar to each other in the possession of bases of power than in heterosexual relationships."

Other studies with smaller samples of lesbians and gay men also found perceived equality in making important decisions to be central to their successful relationships. Perceived equality in decision-making is not necessarily lacking in couples who differ substantially in age, status, or income; but the older and/or more affluent partner tends to dominate decision-making in such relationships. Greater sexual marketability may also be a factor. That is, the partner who is more desirable by conventional standards of beauty may use this ("You can't do as well as me, so you'd better do what I want!"). Yet another complication, related to the immediately previous one, in predicting power within relationships is "the power of the least interest": the partner who seems to the other to be least concerned about preserving the relationship can deter opposition to his or her choices by threatening, implicitly or explicitly, to leave the relationship.

These same factors operate in heterosexual relationships. The person who brings more resources to a relationship tends to make decisions when the two disagree. In heterosexual relationships, the man typically (historically) has higher status and more economic resources and also often claims to have less interest in the relationship. Moreover, in many cultures, including North America, women are raised to support relationships and to be defined by their relationship, while men are socialized to and defined by what they do outside the domestic sphere. Despite recent social changes, North American women often continue to defer to male partners' career contingencies while men pursue their careers, either ignoring a partner's preferences or jettisoning partners unwilling to go along with their choices.

Blumstein and Schwartz's discussion of the negative consequences of perceived "failure" in the work world for couples of all kinds, and the relatively great instability of the lesbian relationships (fewer of which endured then any of the other kinds of relationships they tracked over time), suggest that success in the work world is important to the duration of a relationship. Moreover, they found that "lesbians in established relationships who have unequal income or unequal influence over spending are more likely to break up." Rather than supporting the contention by Parsons and Bales of role complementarity, these data seem to indicate that durable relationships require roughly equivalent success in the outside world on the part of partners who are not work-centered. Neither lesbian rhetoric about not letting income differences affect their relationship, nor gay men's greater tendency to pool incomes, necessarily preserves same-sex couples. Moreover, the problems of two-career relationships which same-sex couples have long faced (e.g., competition, allocation of housework, resolving the pulls of uncoordinated careers) are increasingly problematic for heterosexual couples as well. This historical drift should enhance the theoretical interest of studying same-sex couples even beyond the opportunity to sort out what can be attributed to gender, what to the legal institution of marriage, and what to heterosexuality in the marriage and family literature.

McWhirter and Mattison outlined a natural history of predictable stages within committed relationships: blending, nesting, maintaining, collaborating, trusting, and renewal. The stages are labels for recurrent patterns, not casual models of what every relationship must pass through in what order. Moreover, their model does not take any account of different kinds of love. Despite its limitations, a model of stages does draw attention to the changes that affect relationships over time. In particular, a period of initial romance and mutual discovery tends to give way to everyday coexistence and reduced frequency of sex in relationships that endure.

The gay, white, Southern California males they studied did not merge money and possessions until the trusting stage—which McWhirter and Mattison estimate as ten or more years into the relationship—after some questions about individual autonomy have been resolved to both partners' satisfaction. Whether or not it usually takes so long, if the relationship endures, lesbian couples, and even more so gay male couples, tend to pool assets. Such pooling reinforces decision-making equality among those making differing economic contributions to the relationship and maintains the stability of the relationship. Very few same-sex couples (5%) believe that one partner should support a non-working partner. Fewer still do so: Harry and Weston each reported 1 percent. Yet, even in same-sex couples in which both members work, income inequality often remains an underlying stress. Male socialization to competitiveness, a tendency to assess success in monetary terms, and a devaluation of domestic labor make economic inequality particularly problematic in male-male couples. Blumstein and Schwartz suggest that the egalitarian ideology of two strong women fighting together may also become an unconscious solvent of relationships between women of unequal income, propelling the more economically successful partner out of the relationship thinking, "If you were really strong, really my match, you'd do as well as I do!"

Blumstein and Schwartz reaffirmed that being poor and happy in a consumer society is difficult. Whether or not one can buy happiness, relative wealth generally establishes power within relationships for gay and lesbian couples, as for heterosexual couples. Monetary comparisons are less predictive of relative power in lesbian couples (in part because large income differences between women are less common). The more affluent partner has more control over the couple's recreational activities for lesbian and gay male couples. Sharing more activities outside work than heterosexual couples do may account for greater satisfaction within the couple for lesbian and gay men in relationships. Much of the social life of heterosexual men and women is homosocial in most cultures. To the extent that primary and secondary socialization shapes interests differentially depending on the sex of the child, same-sex couples are likely to have more compatible interests than mixed-sex couples.

Various studies have found lesbian couples more likely to live together than gay male couples. The extent to which this is a result of temperament or a difference of economic resources is not clear from the available data. Partners who have lesbigay friends are also more likely to cohabit. Probably integration into gay/lesbian circles cannot be separated from self-acceptance as lesbigay, and both individual and social acceptance of homosexuality make living together more conceivable.

SEX

Blumstein and Schwartz found that relationships with at least one partner more concerned with the relationship than with his/her career are more likely to endure. They also found that the relationship-centered partner usually initiated sex, whereas the more powerful one, who was more likely to be career-oriented and to have higher income, was more likely to refuse sex. The frequency of sex decreased with the duration of all types of relationships, but especially in homosexual ones. Forty-five percent of married heterosexual couples had sex three times a week or more often, compared to 67 percent of gay male couples, and 33 percent of lesbian couples. For couples who had been together ten or more years, the percentages fell to 18 for married couples, 11 for gay may couples, and 1 percent for lesbian couples.

At least prior to the devastation of AIDS, many men in gay couples were relatively casual about extramarital sex. For some, outside sex often replaced sex between partners—without being conceived as a threat to the relationship. In contrast, lesbian lovers associated non-monogamous sex with dissatisfaction and lack of commitment to their relationship. Given cultural prohibitions against females engaging in casual sex, women, including lesbians, have tended to have protracted affairs more than the one-time "tricks" with little emotional investment sought by men (gay or not). Affairs represent a greater threat to a relationship than casual encounters, so that lesbian non-monogamy is more serious for primary relationships than gay male sexual encounters outside relationships. That is, the character of the non-monogamy, not its frequency, matters. Of course, gay men sometimes have affairs as well as or instead of tricks, and possessiveness is not a monopoly of women. (Moreover, all these differences are statistical, not absolute.)

Blumstein and Schwartz also found that lesbians (along with gay men and straight men) are happier both with their sex lives and with their relationships the more they engage in oral sex. Roles in both oral and anal sex raise sensitive issues of dominance and reciprocity in gay male couples. Traditionally, anxieties were settled and sexual incompatibilities compensated for outside the relationship. Reciprocity also mutes anxieties about seeming to "submit." Blumstein and Schwartz found that "the partner who performs anal sex is not more 'masculine' or powerful than the partner who receives it." and that "for both partners, anal intercourse is associated with being masculine: in couples where both partners are forceful, outgoing, and aggressive, there is more anal sex." The gay ideology that it's not who does what to whom (in particular, who penetrates whom), but getting what one wants, that matters also undercuts the dominant culture's equation of sexual receptivity with "womanliness" and powerlessness.

D. What Kind of Family Is It? Parents and Children

The previous section examined several variations of the traditional family relations among partners. This section explores variations in the formation and structure of parent-child relations.

The first variation examined is the family headed by a single mother. The number of such families has grown dramatically because of two factors. One is the increased divorce rate. Virtually every divorce in a family with children creates, for at least some time, a single-parent and usually a mother-headed family. The other factor is a very great increase in childbearing by women who have never married. Modern family and welfare policy frequently turns on how such families are viewed: whether they are to be desired, tolerated, or discouraged. In this piece, the authors tackle part of this problem, analyzing whether families headed by single mothers are likely to constitute an urban underclass.

The second variation is the family created through adoption. Although adoption is a relatively recent method of family formation, first created by statute in the 19th century, it is now a common device. Approximately 100,000 adoptions occur each year in the United States. Adoption transforms two families. Under traditional adoption doctrine, the family of the child's origin is transformed by the loss of any legal or social relation to the child, and the family into which the child is adopted is transformed by the addition of a child who is treated for most if not all purposes as a full legal member of the household. How these important transformations are and should be managed is an important question of family policy.

We begin our examination with a statistical review of adoptions in the United States, which reveal dramatic changes over the last twenty-five years. Kathy Stolley's article reflects both the difficulties of collecting good data on adoption practices and some of the elements of change in the adoption system.

The Economics of the Baby Shortage, by Elisabeth Landes and Judge Richard Posner, is one of the most controversial pieces ever written or co-authored by this quite controversial federal judge. Although this article first appeared more than 20 years ago, it is still cited as an example of the extreme—some say, silly—positions taken by law and economics scholars. Even if one does not find deregulation of the adoption "market" plausible, the authors have laid out many of the problems caused by the paucity of children available for adoption. The "shortage" they wrote about in 1976 has grown since that time.

Maureen Sweeney's narrative presents an opposite picture of adoption and a very different methodology from that presented by Landes and Posner. The author is herself a birth mother, and the beginning of the article, like a number of feminist pieces, is a narrative of her own experience. Like Landes and Posner, she discusses the limitations of the current adoption system, though her concerns lie not so much with the number of children available for adoption as with the way all the parties—birth parents, adoptive parents and the child in question—experience the adoption process and its aftermath. You will notice that her "adoption triangle" is not the same as the "players" described in Landes and Posner.

Finally, this section takes up a third variation in family formation: the "blended" family created by the remarriage of a custodial parent. Recent work on this form by Mavis Hetherington and her coauthors suggests that some of the optimism popularized in "The Brady Bunch" may be misplaced. While stepfamilies are frequently more financially successful than single-parent families, the psychological challenges of blended families are worth considering.

Sara McLanahan & Irwin Garfinkel, *Single Mothers, The Underclass, and Social Policy,* 501 ANNALS OF THE AMERICAN ACADEMY OF POLITICAL & SOCIAL SCIENCE 92 (1989)[*]

Families headed by nonmarried women have increased dramatically during the past three decades. Whereas in 1960 about 7 percent of all children were living with a single mother, in 1987 the proportion was more than 21 percent. Over half of all children born today will spend some time in a mother-only family before reaching age 18; about 45 percent of all white children will do so, and about 85 percent of black children will. Clearly, the mother-only family will have a profound effect on the next generation of Americans.

Increases in marital disruption and single parenthood have stimulated considerable debate during the past few years and there is much disagreement over whether recent trends are a sign of progress or decline. On the one hand, the growth of mother-only families is viewed as evidence of women's increasing economic independence and greater freedom of choice with respect to marriage. On the other, it is often treated as a proxy for social disorganization. With respect to the latter, three aspects of divorce and single motherhood are seen as especially problematic: (1) the high rate of poverty among families headed by women, variously referred to as the "feminization of poverty" and the "pauperization of women"; (2) the lower rates of socioeconomic attainment among children from mother-only families as compared with children from intact families; and (3) the potential role of mother-only families in the growth and perpetuation of an urban underclass in American cities.

In our book, *Single Mothers and Their Children*, we describe in detail the first two problems: poverty and intergenerational dependence. In this article, we focus on

---

the last question, whether mother-only families represent the crystallization of an urban underclass. We begin by discussing various definitions of the underclass and by presenting our own views on the subject. Next we ask whether there are mother-only families who fit the description of an underclass, and, if so, what proportion might belong in this group. Finally, we review domestic social policy from the perspective of whether the current system and recent proposals for reform serve to perpetuate or break down the boundaries that isolate mother-only families from the rest of society.

DEFINITIONAL ISSUES

The underclass has been the focus of considerable discussion during recent years, beginning with the publication of a series of articles in the *New Yorker* magazine in the early 1980s. While there is no general consensus on whether the underclass is a place or a group of people, most analysts agree that it is more than just another name for those at the bottom of the income distribution. Auletta defines the underclass as a group of people who suffer from "behavioral as well as income deficiencies" and who "operate outside the mainstream of commonly accepted values." He includes street criminals, hustlers and drug addicts, welfare mothers, and the chronically mentally ill in his characterization of the underclass.

Whereas Auletta bases his definition of the underclass on individual behavior, others have used the word to describe particular geographical or residential areas. Sawhill and her colleagues at the Urban Institute speak of "people who live in neighborhoods where welfare dependency, female-headed families, male joblessness, and dropping out of high school are all common occurrences."

Finally, Wilson speaks of the underclass as poor people, mostly black, who live in urban ghettos in the north-central and northeastern regions of the country and who are "outside the mainstream of the American occupational system." He contends that changes in these communities during the 1970s, including deindustrialization and the exodus of middleclass blacks, greatly altered the conditions of families left behind. Ghetto residents are worse off today than they were in the 1960s, not only because their environment is more dangerous but also because they have fewer opportunities for social mobility and fewer positive role models.

Weak attachment to the labor force. A common thread running through all of these definitions is an emphasis on weak labor force attachment. Underclass people are generally described either as living in neighborhoods with high rates of unemployment or nonemployment, or as marginally attached to the labor force themselves. Weak attachment is viewed as problematic for several reasons. First, nonemployment clearly has costs for the individual, given that in a market society such as ours wages are the primary source of income for all nonelderly adults. Those who are not attached to the labor force, either directly or indirectly, are very likely to be poor or to be involved in some form of criminal activity. Moreover, their chances of gaining access to valued resources and/or power in the future are significantly lower than are the labor force.

Weak attachment to the labor force also has costs for the rest of society, whose members ultimately must pay for high levels of nonemployment either through direct income transfers such as Aid to Families with Dependent Children (AFDC) or indirectly through the crime and social disorganization that accompany unemployment and a large underground economy. In addition, conservatives and liberals express concern that weak attachment undermines the work ethic and thereby reduces productivity, whereas Marxists worry that it undermines the solidarity of the work force and thereby reduces the likelihood of successful collective action.

Disabled workers, widows, and married homemakers may be indirectly attached to the labor force either through their personal work history or through the current or past employment history of their spouse. In the case of disabled workers and widows, the primary source of household income comes from social insurance, which is linked to the past work history of the individual and the individual's spouse, respectively. In the case of married homemakers, the primary source of income is the partner's current earnings.

Persistence of weak attachment. Weak attachment to the labor force is a necessary but not sufficient condition for defining an underclass. Individuals who are temporarily out of work or ill or dependent on welfare are usually not viewed as part of the underclass, even though they may be living below the poverty line. Rather, it is the persistence of weak attachment that distinguishes underclass behavior and underclass neighborhoods from poverty areas and the poor in general. Persistence may occur either over time, as when a person is unemployed and/or dependent on welfare for a long period, or it may occurs across generations, as when a child of a welfare recipient also becomes dependent on welfare. We argue that persistence across generations is a necessary condition for establishing the existence of an underclass.

The emphasis on persistence for individuals and across generations highlights the fact that the underclass does not simply signify a particular structural position or group at the bottom of the income distribution. Rather, it means that certain individuals and their offspring occupy this position over a period of time. Thus the problem is not merely inequality—the fact that some locations or statuses in society carry with them fewer rewards than others—but an absence of social mobility—the fact that some persons do not have the chance to improve their situation. When Wilson and his colleagues talk about those left behind in the ghettos of the central cities, they are expressing concern for what they view as declining opportunity and increasing immobility.

Concern about the persistence of weak attachment to the labor force has resurfaced recently. The predominant view among poverty researchers during the 1970s was that nonemployment and dependence on public assistance were relatively short-term phenomena. According to researchers at the University of Michigan, nearly 25 percent of the population was poor at least 1 year during the 1970s whereas less than 3 percent were poor for at least 8 of 10 years. This perspective, which emphasized the fluidity of the poverty population, was seriously challenged in the early 1980s by Bane and Ellwood, who noted that a nontrivial proportion of those who became dependent on welfare were dependent for 10 or more years. Bane and Ellwood's findings coincided with a new interest in the underclass and fueled concern that certain forms of poverty, especially those associated with weak labor force attachment, might be self-perpetuating. Mother-only families have been a particular concern, because they appear to experience longer periods of economic dependence than other poor groups and because the intergenerational implications of their prolonged dependence may be of greater consequence.

Social isolation. A final characteristic essential to our definition and common to most discussions of the underclass is the notion that its members are isolated from the rest of society interims of both their connection to mainstream social institutions and their values. Isolation, be it in urban ghettos or rural areas of the South, is of concern because it reduces knowledge of opportunities. Isolation combined with spatial concentration, as occurs in urban ghettos, is especially worrisome in that it may lead to the development of a deviant subculture. Isolation is a mechanism by which weak labor force attachment persists over time and across generations.

Not all analysis agree that the underclass has a unique culture, that is, its own set of norms and values. In fact, since the late 1960s, liberal scholars have tended to avoid discussions that attribute a different set of attitudes to those at the bottom of the income distribution. Most recall that in the 1960s scholars who expressed concern over the so-called culture of poverty, even those who cited unemployment as the fundamental cause of deviant attitudes and behavior, were accused of blaming the victim. Thus recent discussions of social isolation have tended to emphasize macroeconomic conditions and the institutional aspects of isolation as opposed to its norms and culture. For example, Wilson and his colleagues describe urban ghettos as communities with few employment opportunities and lacking in the leadership and interorganizational networks that facilitate job search and sustain community morale during times of high unemployment. Weak institutions are viewed as the driving force behind cultural differences.

THE SPECIAL CASE OF SINGLE MOTHERS

Some would argue that single mothers are engaged in household production and therefore cannot be part of an underclass, even if they are not working in the paid labor force. Certainly, raising children is a valued activity that contributes to the public good by producing the next generation of young workers. A large proportion of married women devote full time to child care, at least while their children are very young, and many experts believe that this is the best use of their time. Furthermore, most industrialized countries provide children's allowances and various forms of parental leave, which make explicit the social value of children as well as the value of parental time spent on infant care. Yet in the United States, only those single mothers who are widows are provided sufficient public benefits to allow them to invest in full-time child care without paying the penalty of stigma and poverty. The fact that widowed mothers are treated differently from other single mothers suggests that something other than the mother's lack of paid employment and the cost of public transfers underlies the recent concern over welfare mothers.

One explanation for the negative attitudes toward welfare mothers is that they serve as proxies for nonemployed men, who are the primary concern of many analysts. According to this view, for every welfare mother, there is potentially a nonworking father who is part of the underclass. For critics of the welfare system, such as Murray, the AFDC mother is not only a proxy for the nonemployed father; she and the system that supports her are a cause of his unemployment. According to Murray, single motherhood encourages male irresponsibility, which in turn undermines the work ethic and social productivity. In stark contrast, Wilson argues that the welfare mother is an indicator of a failing economic system in which low-skilled men can no longer support their families. According to this view, unemployment and low-paying jobs lead to family dissolution and nonmarriage, which give rise to single motherhood.

Although the causal relationship between single motherhood and male employment is opposite in these two views, both Murray and Wilson focus on male employment as the primary problem. Concern for male employment also explain why widowed mothers are treated differently from other single mothers, even though they work fewer hours and receive higher public benefits. First, widowhood is caused by the death of a spouse and therefore is not a voluntary event. Providing for widows does not encourage male irresponsibility or reduce the motivation to work. Second, Survivors Insurance (SI), like all aspects of social insurance, is closely tied to the previous work attachment of the spouse—in the case of widows, the deceased spouse—and thus it enhances rather than undermines the work ethic. In sum, widowed mothers who are eligible for SI are indirectly attached to the labor force even though they not currently employed.

Quite apart from what it suggests about male employment, nonemployment among single mothers appears to be a growing concern in and of itself. The issue is not simply whether weak attachment to the labor force increase welfare costs, although for some this is the major problem, but whether full-time mothering has personal costs for women and children and social costs for the rest of society beyond the immediate transfer payments. Recent trends in the labor force participation of married mothers suggest that social norms about women's employment are changing, and this in turn affects how policy makers and the general public view nonemployment among single mothers. When Mothers' Pensions programs were instituted in the beginning of the century and when SI and AFDC were instituted in the 1930s, the prevailing view was that mothers should stay home and care for their children. Today, this view is changing to reflect the fact that a majority of married mothers spend at least part of their time working in the paid labor force. The fact that over half of married mothers with young children work outside the home suggests that policies that encourage long-term economic dependency are not likely to be tolerated by the public. The welfare mother is increasingly isolated from mainstream society by virtue of the fact that she is not in the labor force.

EXTENT OF PERSISTENT WEAK ATTACHMENT

Are single mothers weakly attached to the labor force, and if so does weak attachment persist over time and across generations? Both the absence of earnings and the presence of welfare are indicators of weak attachment directly; research on the duration of welfare dependence is more readily available. In 1987, 69 percent of single mothers reported earning whereas 33 percent reported receipt of some welfare. Both the earnings and welfare figures suggest that about one-third of single mothers could be classified as weakly attached to the labor force. Of this group, 56 percent will be dependent on welfare for 10 years or more. Multiplying the 33 percent of single mothers who report weak attachment by the 56 percent who are destined for long-term dependence yields an estimate of 18 percent of current single mothers who are potentially at risk for being in the underclass.

As discussed previously, nonemployment and economic dependency alone do not constitute sufficient evidence for classifying single mothers as part of the underclass, because these women are engaged in socially productive activity—taking care of children. Hence the more important question is, what happens to the children in these families? If the offspring of nonemployed single mothers become productive, independent citizens, the underclass characterization is inappropriate. Thus although some people may complain that the cost of supporting these families is too high or unfairly imposed on the rest of society, their concern is different from that of whether welfare mothers are socially productive

To address the question of intergenerational welfare dependence, detailed family histories over at least two generations are required. Such data are only how becoming available from longitudinal studies such as the Panel Study of Income Dynamics and the National Longitudinal Survey of Youth, both of which follow families and their offspring over a long period of time. Based on research by Gottschalk, we estimate that about 60 percent of the daughters from families who experience long-term welfare dependence will receive welfare themselves for at least 1 year. Based on Ellwood's research, we estimate that about 40 percent of these daughters will receive welfare for 10 or more years.

To combine and summarize these crude estimates: about 18 percent of single mothers in 1987 were dependent on welfare for a long period of time, and about 24 percent of their daughters will be dependent for welfare for 10 more years. We conclude, therefore, that about 4 percent (0.24 x 0.18) of single mothers can be classified as members of an emerging underclass.

On the one hand, the figure of 4 percent is an overestimate of the association between single motherhood and underclass status, given that only a portion of those women who ever experience single motherhood are single mothers in any particular year. Half of all women who divorce remarry within five years, and presumably most of these are not at risk for being part of an underclass.

On the other hand, 4 percent is an underestimate for some groups. Persistence of welfare dependence among single mothers varies substantially. Ellwood finds, for example, that whereas 20 percent of whites who ever receive welfare will be dependent for 10 or more years, the figure for blacks is 32 percent. Similarly, Gottschalk finds that whereas half of white daughters of welfare-dependent mothers become recipients themselves, the figure for blacks is 70 percent. Even more striking, whereas only 14 percent of divorced mothers who ever receive welfare will be dependent for 10 or more years, the figure for unmarried mothers is nearly 40 percent. Thus among some subgroups of single mothers—in particular, young unwed black mothers—the risk of being in the underclass is high.

EXTENT OF SOCIAL ISOLATION

Are mother-only families more socially isolated than other families, and does their isolation lower their mobility? As noted earlier, social isolation may occur because the community no longer functions as a resource base for its members, as when a neighborhood has no jobs, no networks for helping to locate jobs, poor schools, and a youth culture that is subject to minimal social control. Cultural isolation, on the other hand, refers to deviations from normative standards, such as the absence of a work ethic or a devaluation of family commitments.

One way to measure social isolation is to ask what proportion of mother-only families live in urban neighborhoods with high proportions of poor people. Table I presents information on the proportion of different types of families in the United States who live in neighborhoods in which 20 percent or more of the population is poor or in which 40 percent or more is poor. Poverty areas are restricted to neighborhoods in the 100 largest cities.

Several findings in Table I merit attention. First, families headed by single mothers are more likely to live in poor urban neighborhoods than other families. Second, only a small proportion—about 5.6 percent—of mother-only families live in extremely poor neighborhoods. Finally, there are huge racial differences in the degree of isolation of mother-only families. Whereas less than 5 percent of white mother-only families live in areas in which 20 percent of the residents are poor, over 34 percent of black mother-only families live in such areas. About 10 percent of black mother-only families and less than 1 percent of white mother-only families live in areas of extreme poverty.

To what extent did black mother-only families become more socially isolated during the 1970s? Our research suggests that the proportion of black mother-only families who reside in neighborhoods in which at least 20 percent of the residents are poor declined. Yet the proportion of those who reside in neighborhoods that are at least 40 percent poor increased dramatically—by about 30 percent. In other words, in the face of general economic progress for black families in the last 25 years, the proportion of poor mother-only families who are isolated increased. Finally, these extremely poor neighborhoods became more desolate with respect to the proportion of males employed and the proportion of families on welfare.

In addition to residential characteristics, offspring from mother-only families also differ with respect to certain community resources and parental values. Research based on data from High School and Beyond, a survey of 50,000 high school sophomores and seniors, shows that black adolescents in mother-only families attend lower-quality high schools and are more accepting of nonmarital births than their counterparts in two-parent families, even after controlling for socioeconomic status. In contrast, the educational aspirations of their mothers are no different from those in two-parent families.

In sum, whereas only a small proportion of mother-only families live in extremely poor—or what might be called underclass—neighborhoods, there is evidence that this group is growing. Moreover, there is some evidence that children from mother-only families are more accepting of the single-parent status than children from two-parent families. The issue of intergenerational female headship and its consequences is especially important for blacks, given their higher concentration in urban poverty areas and their high prevalence of mother-only families. An important question, which we have not attempted to answer here, is whether an increasing proportion of new birth cohorts are being born to single mothers in extremely poor neighborhoods, and, if so, how this will affect the gains in socioeconomic status made by blacks during the past three decades. . . .

Kathy S. Stolley, *Statistics on Adoption in the United States,* ADOPTION, 3 THE FUTURE OF CHILDREN 25 (1993)*

Adoption is an issue of vital importance for all persons involved in the adoption triangle: the child, the adoptive parents, and the birthparents. According to national estimates, one million children in the United States live with adoptive parents, and from 2% to 4% of American families include an adopted child. . . .

Limitations of Available Data

Despite the importance of adoption to many groups, it remains an under-researched area and a topic on which the data are incomplete. Indeed, at this writing, no comprehensive national data on adoption are collected by the federal government. Through the Children's Bureau and later the National Center for Social Statistics (NCSS), the federal government collected adoption data periodically between 1944 and 1957, then annually from 1957 to 1975. States voluntarily reported summary statistics on all types of finalized adoptions using data primarily drawn from court records. The number of states and territories participating in this reporting system varied from year to year, ranging from a low of 22 in 1944 to a high of 52 during the early 1960s. This data collection effort ended in 1975 with the dissolution of the NCSS. . . .

As these recent data collection efforts suggest, the source of adoption statistics affects the inclusiveness and the completeness of the data. This may be especially apparent in the case of independent adoptions. If adoption agencies must be relied upon as a major source of adoption statistics, an underrepresentation of independent adoptions may result because these arrangements do not fall under the auspices of the reporting agencies.

Other information regarding adoption must be drawn from a variety of research studies targeting or including adoption issues as part of their focus. Small samples, which are not representative of the American population as a whole, are informative in providing information on various aspects of the adoption process. However, they do not allow national estimates to be made regarding statistics on various aspects of adoption. Also, research findings from these studies can be misleading if inappropriate generalizations are made about the larger population not represented by the study at hand.

Other data come from national surveys, such as the National Survey of Family Growth (NSFG), the National Survey of Families and Households (NSFH), and the National Health Interview Survey (NHIS), which focus on various aspects of fertility-related behaviors, health, or family life. The recent addition of adoption questions in such large-scale surveys is a useful step in the data collection process; however, these surveys are primarily targeted at gathering a variety of information rather than focusing specifically on adoption. Additionally, they permit only estimates of statistical

---

*   Source: Stolley, Kathy S., Statistics on Adoption in the United States. *The Future of Children* (Spring 1993) 3,1:26-42. Reprinted with permission of the David and Lucile Packard Foundation. *The Future of Children* journals and executive summaries are available free of charge by faxing mailing information to: Circulation Department (650) 948-6498.

information regarding adoption. This may be problematic in that adoption, like abortion, may be underreported in such self-report surveys. Also, because adoption is a relatively rare event, the number of adoptions included even in these national surveys is so small that some statistical analyses cannot be performed reliably.

In light of this lack of comprehensive statistical information, there has been a movement toward the reinstatement of a national data collection system which will eventually replace the VCIS. Section 9943 of the Omnibus Budget Reconciliation Act (OBRA) of 1986 (Public Law 99-509) added section 479 to Title IV-E of the Social Security Act requiring the federal government to develop a national reporting system on adoption and foster care. An Advisory Committee on Adoption and Foster Care Information was established, and its recommendations, as well as those of the Secretary of the Department of Health and Human Services (DHHS) and information provided by the AIIP, resulted in DHHS-proposed regulations for program implementation as published in the *Federal Register* on September 27, 1990. This data collection system was to be implemented by October 1991 but, as of this writing, is still not functioning.

An Overview of Adoption in the United States . . .

An examination of national estimates of the number of formal adoptions reveals that there were 50,000 total adoptions in 1944. The number of adoptions steadily increased, hitting a peak of 175,000 in 1970, then declining to 104,088 domestic adoptions in 1986, according to NCFA data. Based on AIIP data, there were an estimated 118,529 total adoptions in the United States in 1990.

For a more complete picture of adoption in the United States, the number of total formal adoptions must be divided into two categories: related adoptions and unrelated adoptions. Related adoptions include stepparent adoptions and those cases in which a child is adopted by a nonparent relative. Such adoptions may often formalize a preexisting parenting arrangement for the child. Unrelated adoptions are those in which a nonrelative child is adopted. Therefore, unrelated adoptions are more likely to involve a real change in parenting for the child with the establishment of new parenting and sibling relationships for the child and the adoptive family.

The number of related adoptions increased from 38,200 in 1951 to 91,141 in 1982. However, according to NCFA data, this number dropped markedly to 52,931 in 1986. Because the majority of related adoptions involve stepparents (primarily stepfathers) adopting a stepchild, this drop may be a reflection of the decreasing rates of remarriage in the United States or may indicate that fewer stepparent families are undertaking formal adoption.

During that same time period, the number of unrelated adoptions increased from 33,800 in 1951 to a high of 89,200 in 1971. That number then declined to 49,700 in 1974 and has remained close to the 50,000 mark since that time. In 1986, the number of unrelated domestic adoptions occurring in the United States was 51,157. Thus, these latest estimates reveal a rather even division between related and unrelated adoptions. . . .

Disrupted Arrangements

Disrupted adoptions are those in which the child is removed from the home before the adoption is legalized. This is contrasted to adoptive dissolution, or the breaking of already legalized adoptions. There are no national estimates available on the numbers or percentages of disrupted or dissolved adoptions. Instead, information on adoption disruption comes from a variety of studies. Thus, estimates of the number of disrupted adoptions vary widely based on the population sampled and the calculation techniques used; however, research indicates that disruption rates are increasing.

One review of the literature on adoption disruption suggests that this is a reflection of the concentration in the pre-1970 research on placements of very young, non-handicapped, white children. Of such adoptions, only 1.9% disrupted. More recently, with the emphasis on placement of children with special needs (as discussed below), higher rates of disruption are reported, ranging widely from 3% to 53% depending on the group being studied and the calculating techniques being used. Current estimates indicate that approximately 10% to 13% of all adoptive placements disrupt. Placements of older children and children with records of more previous placements and longer stays in the foster system are more likely to disrupt.

Although accurate figures are also not available on what happens to children after adoptive disruption, it does appear that many do go on to a successful adoptive placement. This implies that it is crucial that children be moved through the placement system as quickly as possible, rather than kept in the system for extended periods. These figures also suggest that a disrupted adoption does not mean that the child is "not adoptable." Rather, it implies that adoptive parents should be fully informed and prepared for the challenges that adoptions of such children might pose.

Relinquishment of Children for Adoption

Data on women who voluntarily relinquish their children for adoption are rather limited, and our knowledge of relinquishment must be pieced together from a variety of sources. Demographic research indicates that women who choose to make an adoption plan are often from backgrounds of higher socioeconomic status and express higher educational aspirations than their counterparts who choose to parent their child. Additionally, women who relinquish their babies tend to come from intact families which are supportive of the placement decision and have not experienced teenage pregnancies of other women in the family. The child's father also has a strong influence on the young woman's decision.

Infants (particularly healthy white infants) are more in demand than older children in the adoption "market." The majority of children placed for adoption are placed before age one (81%), and 86% are under two years of age. Data gathered by the NCFA show that almost half (24,589 or 48.1%) of the unrelated domestic adoptions completed in 1986 involved children under the age of two.

The vast majority of children placed for adoption are, and traditionally have been, premarital births. According to the 1982 National Survey of Family Growth (NSFG), 88% of all babies placed for adoption are born to never-married mothers. Six percent of placements are by previously married mothers, and 6% are placed by currently married women.

Nonetheless, most unmarried mothers choose to parent their child. Indeed, the percentage of premarital births being placed for adoption has declined over the past two decades. Before 1973, almost 9% of all premarital births were placed for adoption. For premarital births occurring from 1973 through 1981, this percentage decreased to 4%; for births from 1982 through 1988, it decreased even further to 2%. . . .

Transracial Adoption

Federally published estimates on transracial adoption were last available in 1975. Yet, in that year, fewer than half the states even reported data on transracial adoptions. A more recent estimate of transracial adoption is derived from the 1987 National Health Interview Survey (NHIS). These data are limited to adoptions in which the child was still living in the adoptive mother's household at the time the information was gathered.

According to these data, 92% of all adoptions involve an adoptive mother and child of the same race. Of all adoptions, 85% involve white mothers and children, 6% involve black mothers and children, and 1% involve mothers and children of other racial/ethnic backgrounds.

In only 8% of all adoptions are the parents and children of different races. An analysis of these transracial adoptions reveals that most instances involve white women adopting children of other races. White women adopting black children accounted for 1% of all adoptions, and white adoption of children of races other than white or black accounted for 5% of all adoptions. Mothers of other races adopting white children accounted for only 2% of all adoptions. Because these estimates no doubt include foreign-born children, the actual incidence of transracial adoption among children born in the United States may be very low indeed.

International Adoption

Agency-sponsored adoption of children from foreign countries began after World War II with the adoption by U.S. citizens of European end Japanese children. During the mid-1950s, in response to the number of children orphaned in the Korean War, the Republic of Korea (South Korea) became, and has remained, the major source of foreign adoptions in the United States. However, under pressure from Korean officials, the number of adoptions of children from Korea declined during the late 1980s. In recent years, other countries such as Colombia, Peru, India, the Philippines, and Romania have provided many children for adoption by American parents.

According to NCFA data, there were 10,019 foreign adoptions in calendar year 1986, accounting for 16.4% of all unrelated adoptions occurring in that year. More than 60% of these children were infants under one year of age. The availability of infants makes foreign adoptions especially attractive to many adopters.

During FY 1991, there were 9,008 foreign adoptions in the United States. More than 60% (or 5,409) of these adoptions were also of children under one year of age. However, in 1991, the number of children from Romania skyrocketed with Romania providing 2,552 children for adoption by U.S. parents, a number far exceeding the 1,817 Korean children adopted by Americans during that year.

Special Needs Children

During the past decade, the federal government has placed a particular emphasis on finding adoptive homes for all children awaiting adoption in the United States. Through the Adoption Assistance and Child Welfare Act of 1970 (Public Law 96-272), the federal government has attempted to encourage the adoption of children tradition-ally considered hard to place through subsidies for persons who adopt these children with "special needs." Such programs include in this category older children (with age specified by each state), minority children, members of a sibling group, and children with medical problems, as well as children with physical, mental, or emotional dis-abilities.

In 1986, some 13,568 children with special needs were adopted. These special needs adoptions accounted for 26.5% of all unrelated domestic adoptions. Although some infants may be included in this category, emphasis on children with special needs is especially important in light of the general decline in the availability of infants for adoption. It calls attention to the needs and availability of other children and to the incentives which might make the option available to more adoption seekers. Also, some evidence suggests that preferential adopters (those with no fertility problems who adopt for religious, social, or humanitarian reasons) may be more likely to select chil-dren with special needs. . . .

Elisabeth M. Landes & Richard A. Posner, *The Economics of the Baby Shortage,* 7 JOURNAL OF LEGAL STUDIES 323 (1978)[*]

Introduction

Although economists have studied extensively the efforts of government to reg-ulate the economy, public regulation of social and personal life has largely escaped eco-nomic attention. With the rapid development of the economic analysis of nonmarket behavior, the conceptual tools necessary for the economic student of social (as distinct from narrowly economic) regulation are now at hand. Nor is there any basis for a pre-sumption that government does a good job of regulating nonmarket behavior; if any-thing, the negative presumption created by numerous studies of economic regulation should carry over to the nonmarket sphere. An example of nonmarket regulation that may be no less perverse than the widely criticized governmental efforts to regulate imports, transportation, new drugs, bank entry, and other market activities is the reg-ulation of child adoptions—the subject of this paper.

Sometimes natural parents do not want to raise their child; the typical case is where the birth is illegitimate. And in some cases where the natural parents do raise the child initially, their custody is later terminated for one reason or another—death or other incapacity, abuse, or extreme indigence. In either case—the unwanted infant or the abused, neglected, or abandoned child—there are potential gains from trade from transferring the custody of the child to a new set of parents. Where the new parents assume full parental rights and obligations over the child, one speaks of adoption; where they obtain simply a temporary custody (usually being partially compensated for their custodial services by the state), one speaks of foster care. An alternative to fos-ter care in a home is foster care in an institution.

---

    *   Published by the University of Chicago. Copyright © 1978. Reprinted with per-mission.

Ordinarily, potential gains from trade are realized by a process of voluntary transacting—by a sale, in other words. Adoptions could in principle be handled through the market and in practice, as we shall see, there is a considerable amount of baby selling. But because public policy is opposed to the sale of babies, such sales as do occur constitute a "black market." Recent hearings before the Senate Subcommittee on Children and Youth as well as a well-publicized indictment of baby sellers, have brought into renewed focus the existence of the black market in babies. The hearings in particular constitute a rich if unsystematic source of data and opinions on the adoption problem, facilitating appraisal of a major, and, we shall argue, probably misguided example of public regulation of nonmarket behavior.

Part I of this paper develops a model of the supply and demand for babies for adoption under the existing pattern of regulation and shows (1) how that regulation has created a baby shortage (and, as a result, a black market) by preventing a free market from equilibrating the demand for and supply of babies for adoption, and (2) how it has contributed to a glut of unadopted children maintained in foster homes at public expense. Part II explores the objections to allowing the price system to equilibrate the adoption market and argues that the objections do not justify the existing regulations though they might justify a more limited regulation of the baby market. In Part III we consider, in the spirit of the new economic analysis of the political process, some of the reasons why the government has curtailed the operation of the market in this area. Part IV proposes a method of practical experimentation with introducing a market in adoptions. Parts III and IV are highly tentative. In the course of the analysis we attempt to sketch how the world would look if a free market in babies were permitted to come into existence. We also discuss, though much more briefly, the problem of foster care. . . .

C.   The Effects of the Baby Shortage

The baby shortage generates social costs in excess of the traditional welfare loss of monopoly. The counterpart to that loss would be the lost consumer surplus from sales not made at all because of the artificial unavailability of the product . . . . To be sure, some of this loss is offset by the availability of children in the independent market, but the search costs in the independent market also represent a substantial social cost.

No effort will be made in this paper to quantify the social cost of the baby shortage (and hence of the governmental regulations that have generated it) or to measure its impact on the number of children adopted. However, the potential magnitude of the problem will be explored briefly.

A crude estimate of the potential size of the baby market can be obtained from a comparison of the fraction of married women who are childless throughout their married lives with the (much smaller) fraction of women who report, early in their marriage, that they do not intend to have any children. In 1975, 10.8 percent of white American women aged 50 or over who had ever been married were childless. Many of these were childless by choice, but another statistic suggests that many were not: in 1975 only 4.4 percent of white American wives aged 18-24 expected to have no children. The difference between these figures is some clue to the potential demand for babies that cannot be satisfied by natural means. Still another clue is the high cost (nominal, time, and risk) that childless couples incur in order to increase the probability of giving birth.

Of course, adopted children may not be a perfect substitute for natural children. The genetic characteristics of natural children are highly correlated with their parents' genetic characteristics, and this correlation could conceivably increase harmony within the family compared to what it would be with an adopted child. Nevertheless, there is considerably substitutability between natural and adopted children and it might be much greater if better genetic matching of adopted children with their adoptive parents were feasible—as might occur, as we shall see, under free market conditions.

Given that the number of white marriages has averaged close to two million a year over the past decade, about 130,000 married couples might be potential "buyers" in the baby market every year. And this is probably an underestimate. Couples who have adopted children are not counted among the 10.8 of couples who are childless. More important, most natural parents want more than one child, and presumably the same is true of adoptive parents. This alone might double the 130,000 figure for potential demand. Offsetting this to some extent is the fact that some childless couples may not consider an adopted child a substitute for a natural child. But on balance it seems clear that the 37,000 white nonrelative adoptions a year fall far short of satisfying the potential demand. . . .

Maureen A. Sweeney, *Between Sorry and Happy Endings: A New Paradigm of Adoption*, 2 YALE JOURNAL OF LAW AND FEMINISM 329 (1990)[*]

PROLOGUE

My interest in the subject of adoption and in the position of the birth mother who surrenders a child is a personal one: I am a birth mother. In the interest of explaining my perspective on these questions, and also in the belief that as a society we suffer from an enormous lack of insight into the position of the birth mother, I will begin with the story of my own experience of the adoption process. It was not a particularly bad experience; in fact my impression is that it was more positive than is the average. Nevertheless I will go into some detail because I believe it is important to articulate and understand the complexities of a birth mother's motivations and the pressures she may be facing. Only then will we be able to see clearly how the law can best respond to the needs of all the parties to an adoption proceeding.

I also believe that it is crucial for legal scholarship to take into account the experience of the individuals interacting with the legal system. Law is not a game of spinning out theories and arguments; it is arguably the principal means for allocating and sanctioning power in our society. It guides and constrains our actions, while greatly influencing the way that we think about ourselves and our world. For this reason, responsible legal scholarship must begin with some knowledge of the way in which

---

    *   Reprinted by permission of the Yale Journal of Law & Feminism, Inc. from the *Yale Journal of Law and Feminism,* Vol. 2 No. 2, pp. 329-335.

the law interacts with people, particularly in an area such as family law, which involves some of the most personal, and the most formative, moments of a person's life.

When I was nineteen years old and a sophomore in college, I got pregnant and my world came crashing down around me. The future I had always imagined suddenly looked very different, and my dreams for myself seemed to have been snatched beyond my reach. Even my self-image, of one who was in control of her life, was shattered.

I had been dating the baby's father for about six months when I got pregnant. He was several years older than I and our relationship was one in which, for the most part, he led and I followed. Shortly after we began dating, he started pressuring me to have intercourse. I resisted, but not very well and not for long. As with most things in that relationship, I soon found myself seeing his side of things and losing my own frame of reference.

When I first discovered that I was pregnant, I wanted to get married. The baby's father preferred to deny that anything had happened; he certainly did not want to get married. After several months, I realized that he was not going to save me, and I began to look within myself for strength. Somewhat to my surprise, I began to find it. Through the course of my pregnancy, the terror I felt at my body's betrayal and my lack of control over it gave way to a sense of excitement and wonder at the power I possessed to nurture this new life. This sense of power in turn helped to give me the strength to make some very difficult decisions.

When I was about four months pregnant, a friend suggested that I might want to place the baby with an agency for adoption. Until she brought it up, the idea had never occurred to me. For the next five months I struggled with the question of whether to keep my baby or to surrender him or her for adoption.

I worked all through those months with a social worker from the adoption agency who was genuinely concerned that I make the best decision for myself, whether that meant keeping the baby or surrendering him or her for adoption. By the time I was ready to give birth, I was fairly confident of my decision to surrender the baby. I had thought long and hard about the gift that I would give him (I had a boy), wanting to give him something of myself. In the end I made a baby quilt for him and wrote a short letter attempting to explain how much I loved him and why I was giving him up. His father also prepared a gift for the baby.

In this time of waiting and preparation, I was asked what sort of a family I wanted my child to have. Unconsciously, I asked the agency to replicate my own: a close extended family, active in some religious tradition, for whom education was important. I was assured that a family would be chosen that came as close as possible to this description. And so I waited to give birth, feeling ready to give my baby to this family I constantly tried to imagine.

To my surprise, however, by the time my son was born I was more than ready to keep him. The desire for me to take my son in my arms and keep him with me was tremendously strong. I saw him and touched him right after I'd given birth to him, but I didn't hold him then. For the first twenty-four hours in the hospital I was afraid to go down to the nursery and even look at him. I could feel him pulling me even from the other end of the hall, demanding with his little cries that I change my mind and continue to care for and nurture him as I had for the previous nine months. Eventually I did go down and see him. I went into the nursery and looked at him and touched his tiny hands. Then he started to cry and I reached out to hold him and quiet him. But then I pulled back my bands and quickly left the room, terrified that I would impulsively make a decision to keep him, a decision I was afraid would lead him, his father, and me into years of bitterness. My last morning in the hospital I did hold my son. I held him with tears streaming down my face.

The baby's father and I spent the weekend I was released from the hospital wrestling with the question of what we should do. We went back and forth; there was a moment when I had my hand on the phone to call a taxi to take us back to the hospital and pick up our son (who stayed there until Monday when someone from the adoption agency would take him to a foster home). In the end we decided to go through with the adoption.

On Tuesday morning we gathered together the letter and gifts and went down to the agency. We were ushered into a room where we talked for a while with my social worker. She showed us pictures of the family they had chosen for our son and told us a little about his future parents.

Then she brought out the relinquishment papers. THIS IS FINAL AND IRREV-OCABLE was emblazoned in big, bold letters three times on the one-page form. I don't remember anything else about the papers I signed, except for that ominous warning against later doubts. Illinois adoption law required that the father of a newborn, if known and identified, also relinquish his parental rights, and as we were about to sign the papers the baby's father wanted to change his mind. But after the struggle we had gone through, I was confident in the end that adoption would be best for our son. I was not going to change my mind at that point. Perhaps he realized that as the one who would have taken care of the baby, I was the one whose life would have been most radically affected by this decision. For whatever reason he went along with my insistence. Panic gave way to relief that he chose not to exercise the power he had at that moment to determine the direction of my life.

When I signed the papers relinquishing my parental rights to my son, I framed my principal reasons for the decision in terms of his best interests. Although I thought about financial issues, my main consideration was whether or not I could provide a stable family for him. After time and reflection, I believe that within that genuine desire for my son was also a desire for myself. I knew that if I kept him I would probably marry his father (who had in the weeks before the birth become the one pushing for marriage), and my instincts were clamoring that this would be a disastrous move for me. My sense of self had become lost in that relationship; in it, I had little control over my own direction. At the time of my son's birth I could not have articulated this understanding, but I believe now that I knew it subconsciously, and that it was one source of my feeling that I would not be able to provide the kind of family I wanted my son to have.

My son is now seven years old, and my love for him now is no less than it was when he was born. There are times when the pain of his absence is so intense that it is almost incapacitating. His birthday is always particularly difficult. And yet I am convinced that adoption was the best, most empowering option for him and for me, given the circumstances of my life. It allowed me to follow my conscience and to honor the sanctity of human life by carrying through my pregnancy and giving birth, at the same time allowing me to avoid being forced by circumstances into an oppressive situation. It gave my son a good chance at life in a stable, loving home. It is from the joy and pain and freedom of being a birth mother that I address the subject of adoption.

The surrender of babies for adoption has roots deep in our history. Nevertheless, the actual surrendering experience has received relatively little attention. Despite wide acceptance in our society of the practice of adoption as seen from the point of view of the adoptive family, there remains little acknowledgment of the birth mother's side of the process. This reluctance to think and speak of birth mothers perhaps stems from the stigma society has attached to the situation of most birthmothers—having an unexpected and unplanned baby outside of marriage. There is also discomfort with the idea that women give away their babies. However much this part of the process is necessary to enable adoption, we find it easier to simply avoid thinking too much about what we see as a voluntary repudiation of motherhood. Perhaps it challenges too deeply our concept of motherhood as something basically biological. Perhaps we recognize on some level the deep pain that it involves, and simply find it easier not to think about it. It is thus not entirely surprising that society has failed to focus much attention on birth mothers.

What is at first glance more surprising is the silence of the women's movement on the subject of adoption and on the concerns of birth mothers, women who tend to be in very vulnerable positions and who pose challenging questions on reproductive decisions, the nature of motherhood, and the ideal of the family. Yet feminist literature has been silent. I believe that this is largely due to the intensity of the feminist battle for the legalization of abortion. Adoption has been proposed by opponents of abortion as an alternative to abortion, and has thus been seen as opposing abortion. I believe that the women's movement has too quickly accepted this dichotomy and has too firmly embraced abortion as the solution to unexpected pregnancies. Recognizing that the feminist position on abortion developed in response to very severe opposition, it is not surprising that this position is weighted heavily to one side, emphasizing exclusively the inalienable right of the mother to control her reproduction. Nevertheless, given the current deadlock in the societal dialogue on abortion, I believe that it is time that we in the women's movement attempt to articulate a more subtle and nuanced position on reproductive choice, a position that acknowledges the terrible price that is paid in abortion, even where the choice to abort represents the lesser of evils in a woman's particular circumstances.

Women's lives unfold within a context of the injustice and oppression of sexism, a context that for many women also includes racism and economic injustice. Within this context, childbearing and childrearing often become opportunities for intensified oppression of women and, directly or indirectly, of their children. For many women, the birth of a child ensures the continuation of a cycle of poverty, because the responsibilities and financial burdens of child care cut off opportunities for employment, education and training. Women with children are often discriminated against and not taken seriously as workers because they are mothers, and many women stay in low-paying jobs because higher-paying jobs would not allow the flexibility necessary to the primary caretaker of a child.

In addition, a child can be a very effective source of power for a man over the child's mother. A child's father can use his rights to the child and the mother's desire to protect the child to control the mother. This control can be based on physical violence, on economic dependence, on the threat of taking the child away from the mother, or on a sense of moral obligation. In the same way, a woman's desire to provide for and protect her child, given her limited opportunities to do so by herself, makes her more vulnerable to becoming and staying economically or otherwise dependent on any man. This dynamic of power is of course even further accentuated when a pregnancy is the result of rape or incest, situations in which the act of intercourse itself is a clear act of domination. The birth of a child in such a situation can serve to solidify and extend that domination over a lifetime.

It is this culture of injustice and oppression of women, especially of poor women and women of color, that necessitates abortion in our world today. There are times when abortion is necessary literally to save the mother's life. In the same way, there are times when abortion is necessary to save the mother from a life of abuse and despair. Furthermore, given the imbeddedness of sexism and the failure of the dominant culture to recognize and acknowledge it, we must have the power to control our reproduction ourselves, and to recognize for ourselves the situations in which the difficult choice to abort is a matter of such pressing need as to override other considerations.

I would certainly not be the first to point out the difficulty with which most women decide to abort a pregnancy. Despite a woman's recognition of other very important considerations and of her right to make her own decisions, it is almost always difficult for her to decide to end a pregnancy with abortion. This, I believe, is due to the recognition of the life potential of the fetus and of her connection with it. To deny that life goes contrary to the experience of anyone who has been pregnant and felt her child move within her, or even of anyone who has seen someone go through pregnancy and give birth.

We must not allow the anti-abortion movement to usurp our connection, our concern, our valuation of this life. If we oversimplify the abortion issue on a theoretical level and talk only of a woman's rights, we objectify and separate ourselves from a life to which we are in fact intimately connected. We deny our own pain in making the decision to abort, and we fall to our society's pressure to use things and people only in ways that serve our own needs, and then to discard them. Women have known historically, and continue to know, the degradation and the injustice of being used as objects to satisfy the needs and whims of the more powerful. We must not allow our own empowerment to simply move us into the more powerful position. We must strive for a new model of human interaction based on responsibility and respect for ourselves and for others.

As feminists, we should be willing and able to support the legal right to an abortion and at the same time deplore the loss of human life involved and work for the day when abortion will no longer be necessary. One way of doing this is to develop alternatives to abortion that empower women. These alternatives often will not be easy, and may in fact be very difficult and painful. Fighting to affirm and value all human life (including both women and children) will not be painless, but we must not compromise our vision by succumbing to the urge of an oppressive, consumerist society to acknowl-

edge the value of only that life that we can accommodate without inconveniencing ourselves. Our ethic must encompass care and responsibility for one another, as well as a
demand for justice for the individual. We must fight for a world where no life is disposable, and where a woman's decision about reproduction is not narrowed down to a
choice between a decent life for herself and life for her fetus.

This paper looks at ways that we can develop adoption into an empowering
option for pregnant women who feel that they cannot raise the child they are carrying.
In it I seek to present a new vision of adoption—a vision that arises from within an ethic
of care for and responsibility to all those whose lives are indelibly changed by the adoption experience. . . .

E. Mavis Hetherington, Margaret Bridges, & Glendessa M. Insabella, *What Matters? What Does Not? Five Perspectives On the Association Between Marital Transitions and Children's Adjustment,* 53(2) AMERICAN PSYCHOLOGIST 167 (1998)[*]

In the past 30 years, there has been a significant decline in the proportion of two-
parent families in first marriages and a complementary increase in the number of single-parent households and stepfamilies. These changes are the result of a rapid rise in
the divorce rate that began during the 1960s and also, to a lesser extent, of an increase
in births to single mothers. Although there has been a modest decrease in the divorce
rate since the late 1970s, almost one half of marriages end in divorce in the United
States, and one million children experience their parents' divorce each year. It is projected that between 50% and 60% of children born in the 1990s will live, at some point,
in single-parent families, typically headed by mothers. Currently, stepfamilies make up
approximately 17% of all two-parent families with children under 18 years of age.

Although the high divorce rate has been interpreted as a rejection of the institution of marriage, 75% of men and 66% of women eventually will remarry, suggesting
that although people are rejecting specific marital partners, most are not rejecting marriage. Since the 1960s, however, the annual rate of remarriage has actually declined as
the divorce rate has increased. Moreover, divorces are more frequent in remarriages and
occur at a rate 10% higher than that in first marriages. Couples with remarried wives
are almost twice as likely to divorce as are couples with remarried husbands. This association may be attributable to the 50% higher rate of dissolution in remarriages in which
children from previous marriages are present, although the presence of children appears
to be less relevant to the marital quality of African American couples. As a result of
their parents' successive marital transitions, about half of all children whose parents
divorce will have a stepfather within four years of parental separation, and 1 out of
every 10 children will experience at least two divorces of their residential parent
before turning 16 years of age. These numbers underestimate the actual number of

---

household reorganizations to which children are exposed because many couples cohabit before remarriage or cohabit as an alternative to remarriage.

The national figures for marital transitions and family structure mask very different patterns among racial and ethnic groups because the social context of marriage varies across communities. African American children are twice as likely as White children to experience at least one parental divorce and also are more likely to bear children out of wedlock in adolescence and adulthood. In addition, African Americans and Hispanic Whites are less likely to divorce after separation and to remarry than are non-Hispanic Whites. Thus, in comparison with White children, more African American children spend longer periods of time in single-parent households, which often include kin and cohabiting partners.

As marriage has become a more optional, less permanent institution in contemporary American society, children in all ethnic groups are encountering stresses and adaptive challenges associated with their parents' marital transitions. Children from divorced and remarried families, in contrast to those from never-divorced families, exhibit more problem behaviors and lower psychological well-being. Little agreement exists, however, about the extent, severity, and duration of these problems because there is great diversity in children's responses to parental marital transitions. Furthermore, although it is clear that marital dissension and dissolution, life in single-parent households, and remarriage present families and children with new experiences, risks, and resources, there is some disagreement on how these factors undermine or enhance the well-being of children.

Theoretical Perspectives on Marital Transitions and the Adjustment of Children

Five main theoretical perspectives have been proposed to explain the links between divorce and remarriage and children's adjustment. These perspectives are those emphasizing (a) individual risk and vulnerability; (b) family composition; (c) stress, including socioeconomic disadvantage; (d) parental distress; and (e) family process.

Individual Risk and Vulnerability

It has been proposed that some characteristics of parents and children may influence their exposure and vulnerability to adversity. Some adults possess characteristics (e.g., antisocial behavior) that place them at increased risk for marital discord, multiple marital transitions, and other adverse life experiences. Adults with psychological problems such as depression or antisocial behavior often select partners who also experience psychological difficulties, thereby increasing their risk for marital problems and dissolution. This is called the marital selectivity hypothesis. In addition, some children have attributes that increase their vulnerability or protect them from deleterious consequences of stresses associated with their parents' marital transitions.

Family Composition

It is commonly assumed that two biological parents provide the optimal family environment for healthy child development and that any deviation from this family structure, such as single-parent families or stepfamilies, is problematic for children.

Much of the early theorizing about divorce and family structure focused on father absence.

Stress and Socioeconomic Disadvantage

This perspective emphasizes that marital transitions trigger a series of negative social and economic changes, stresses, and practical problems that can interfere with the well-being of parents and children. For custodial mothers and their children, divorce is related to a notable economic decline that is associated with living conditions that make raising children more difficult, whereas remarriage is associated with an increase in household income for single mothers. Although much of the research on stress has focused on economic stresses, both divorced and remarried families encounter other stresses related to changing family roles and relationships.

Parental Distress

This perspective suggests that stressful life experiences, including economic decline and adaptive challenges associated with divorce and remarriage, lead to parental strain, distress, and diminished well-being, which are reflected in psychological problems such as depression, anxiety, irritability, and antisocial behaviors, as well as stress-related health problems. There is great individual variability in response to negative life changes; some parents cope with such changes with apparent equanimity, whereas others exhibit marked affective disruption and distress.

Family Process

Finally, many researchers have emphasized that differences between nondivorced families and divorced and remarried families on process variables such as conflict, control, expression of positive and negative affect, and problem solving largely explain the effects of divorce and remarriage. It is argued that more proximal variables, such as discipline and child-rearing practices, are most important in affecting children's adjustment.

Although these perspectives often are presented as competing with each other, empirical support can be found for each, suggesting that they may best be considered as complementary hypotheses. In this article, research on the five perspectives is reviewed, and the direct and indirect effects of the five factors on the adjustment of children and parents in divorced and remarried families are examined. Finally, a transactional model of marital transitions involving relationships among the factors is presented.

Adjustment of Children in Divorced and Remarried Families

There is general agreement among researchers that children, adolescents, and adults from divorced and remarried families, in comparison with those from two-parent, nondivorced families, are at increased risk for developing problems in adjustment, and that those who have undergone multiple divorces are at a greater risk. For the most part, the adjustment of children from divorced and remarried families is similar. Children from divorced and remarried families are more likely than children from nondivorced families to have academic problems, to exhibit externalizing behaviors and internalizing disorders, to be less socially responsible and competent, and to have lower self-esteem. They have problems in their relationships with parents, siblings, and peers.

Normative developmental tasks of adolescence and young adulthood, such as attaining intimate relationships and increasing social and economic autonomy, seem to be especially difficult for youths from divorced and remarried families. Adolescents from divorced and remarried families exhibit some of the same behavior problems found in childhood and, in addition, are more likely to drop out of school, to be unemployed, to become sexually active at an earlier age, to have children out of wedlock, to be involved in delinquent activities and substance abuse, and to associate with antisocial peers. Increased rates of dropping out of high school and of low socioeconomic attainment in the offspring of divorced and remarried families extend across diverse ethnic groups; however, the effect is stronger for females than for males.

Adult offspring from divorced and remarried families continue to have more adjustment problems, are less satisfied with their lives, experience lower socioeconomic attainment, and are more likely to be on welfare. Marital instability also is higher for adults from divorced and remarried families, in part because of the presence of a set of risk factors for divorce, including early sexual activity, adolescent childbearing and marriage, and cohabitation. In addition, in comparison with young adults from nondivorced families, young adults from divorced and remarried families exhibit more reciprocated, escalating, negative exchanges, including denial, belligerence, criticism, and contempt, and less effective problem solving during their marital interactions. This pattern is probably related to the intergenerational transmission of divorce, which is reported to be 70% higher in the first five years of marriage for adult women from divorced families than for those whose parents have remained married.

Although there is considerable consensus that, on average, offspring from divorced and remarried families exhibit more problems in adjustment than do those in nondivorced, two-parent families, there is less agreement on the size of these effects. Some researchers report that these effects are relatively modest, have become smaller as marital transitions have become more common, and are considerably reduced when the adjustment of children preceding the marital transition is controlled. However, others note that approximately 20%-25% of children in divorced and remarried families, in contrast to 10% of children in nondivorced families, have these problems, which is a notable twofold increase. Because these difficulties in adjustment tend to co-occur and appear as a single behavior-problem, the vast majority of children from divorced families and stepfamilies do not have these problems and eventually develop into reasonably competent individuals functioning within the normal range of adjustment. This argument is not intended to minimize the importance of the increase in adjustment problems associated with divorce and remarriage nor to belittle the fact that children often report their parents' marital transitions to be their most painful life experience. It is intended to underscore the research evidence supporting the ability of most children to cope with their parents' divorce and remarriage and to counter the position that children are permanently blighted by their parents' marital transitions.

We turn now to an examination of some of the individual, social, economic, and family factors that contribute to the diversity in children's adjustment in divorced and remarried families. Each factor is discussed as it relates to the five perspectives on marital transitions.

Individual Risk and Vulnerability of Parents Associated With Divorce and Remarriage

Some adults have attributes that increase their probability not only of having dysfunctional marital relationships but also for having other problematic social relationships within and outside of the family, displaying inept parenting behaviors, encountering stressful life events, and having decreased psychological well-being. Longitudinal studies have found that, in adults as well as in children, many of the problems attributed to divorce and remarriage and their concomitant life changes were present before these transitions occurred.

Although psychological distress and disorders may increase after divorce, parents who later divorce are more likely preceding divorce to be neurotic, depressed, antisocial, or alcoholic; to have economic problems; and to have dysfunctional beliefs about relationships. In their marital interactions, they exhibit poor problem-solving and conflict resolution skills, thus escalating reciprocation of negative affect, contempt, denial, withdrawal, and stable, negative attributions about their spouses' behavior, which in turn significantly increase their risk for marital dissolution and multiple divorces. Sometimes these patterns are later found in the marital relationships of their adult offspring. In relationships with their children, parents whose marriages will later be disrupted are more irritable, erratic, and nonauthoritative as much as 8 -12 years prior to divorce. These factors contribute to problems in children's adjustment and family relations in nondivorced families, single-parent families, and stepfamilies.

Children's Individual Risk, Vulnerability, and Resiliency Associated With Adjustment to Divorce and Remarriage

In accord with the individual risk perspective, characteristics of children may make them vulnerable or protect them from the adverse consequences or risks associated with their parents' divorce or remarriage. Some of these attributes influence the experiences and adjustment of children long before marital transitions occur.

Children's Adjustment Preceding Divorce and Remarriage

Children whose parents later divorce exhibit poorer adjustment before the breakup. When antecedent levels of problem behaviors are controlled, differences in problem behaviors between children from divorced and nondivorced families are greatly reduced. Several alternative interpretations of these findings can be made. First, it is likely that maladapted parents, dysfunctional family relationships, and inept parenting already have taken their toll on children's adjustment before a divorce occurs. Second, divorce may be, in part, a result of having to deal with a difficult child. Third, personality problems in a parent, such as emotionality and lack of self-regulation, that lead to both divorce and inept socialization practices also may be genetically linked to behavior problems in children.

Children in stepfamilies also exhibit more behavior problems before remarriage occurs, and some researchers have speculated that the adaptive difficulties of stepchildren may be largely the result of experiences in divorced families. This seems unlikely, because there is an increase in adjustment problems immediately after a marital transition, and because children in newly remarried families show more problems than those in stabilized, divorced, one-parent households or than those in longer remarried, stabilized stepfamilies.

Personality and Temperament

Children who have easy temperaments; who are intelligent, socially mature, and responsible; and who exhibit few behavior problems are better able to cope with their parents' marital transitions. Stresses associated with divorce and remarriage are likely to exacerbate existing problems in children. In particular, children with difficult temperaments or behavior problems may elicit negative responses from their parents who are stressed in coping with their marital transitions. These children also may be less able to adapt to parental negativity when it occurs and may be less adept at gaining the support of people around them. Competent, adaptable children with social skills and attractive personal characteristics, such as an easy temperament and a sense of humor, are more likely to evoke positive responses and support and to maximize the use of available resources that help them negotiate stressful experiences.

Developmental Status

Developmental status and gender are the child characteristics most extensively researched in relation to adaptation to divorce and remarriage; however, the results of these studies have been inconsistent. Investigations of children's age at divorce must consider both age at the time of the marital transition and age at the time of assessment. In most studies, these variables are confounded with the length of time since the divorce or remarriage occurred. Some researchers have found that preschool age children whose parents divorce are at greater risk for long-term problems in social and emotional development than are older children. It has been suggested that younger children may be less able to appraise realistically the causes and consequences of divorce, may be more anxious about the possibility of total abandonment, may be more likely to blame themselves for the divorce, and may be less able to utilize extrafamilial protective resources. This greater vulnerability of young children to divorce has not been reported by other investigators.

In contrast, early adolescence seems to be an especially difficult time in which to have a remarriage occur. Early adolescents are less able to adapt to parental remarriage than are younger children or late adolescents, perhaps because the presence of a stepparent exacerbates normal early adolescent concerns about autonomy and sexuality. In addition, adolescence and young adulthood are periods in which problems in adjustment may emerge or increase, even when divorce or remarriage has occurred much earlier.

Gender

Although earlier studies frequently reported gender differences in response to divorce and remarriage, with divorce being more deleterious for boys and remarriage for girls, more recent studies have found that gender differences in response to divorce are less pronounced and consistent than was previously believed. Some of the inconsistencies may be attributable to the fact that fathers' custody, joint custody, and the involvement of noncustodial fathers are increasing and that involvement of fathers may be more important for boys than for girls.

Some research has shown that boys respond to divorce with increases in conduct disorders and girls with increases in depression; however, both male and female adolescents from divorced and remarried families show higher rates of conduct disorders and depression than do those from nondivorced families. Female adolescents and young adults from divorced and remarried families are more likely than their male counterparts to drop out of high school and college. Male and female adolescents are similarly affected in the likelihood of becoming teenage parents; however, single parenthood has more adverse effects on the lives of female adolescents. Female young adults from divorced and remarried families are vulnerable to declining socioeconomic status because of the sequelae of adolescent childbearing and school dropout. These sequelae are compounded in stepdaughters by early home leaving, which they attribute to family conflict.

Some girls in divorced, mother-headed families emerge as exceptionally resilient individuals, enhanced by confronting the increases in challenges and responsibilities that follow divorce. Such enhancement is not found for boys following marital transitions or for girls in stepfamilies. Boys, especially preadolescent boys, are more likely than girls to benefit from being in stepfather families. Close relationships with supportive stepfathers are more likely to reduce antisocial behavior and to enhance the achievement of stepsons than of stepdaughters. Girls are at greater increased risk than are boys for poor adjustment and low achievement when they are in either stepfather or stepmother families rather than in nondivorced families.

Some research suggests that living in stepfamilies is more beneficial to Black adolescents than to White adolescents, although these effects vary by gender. In contrast to the findings for White youths, young Black women in stepfamilies have the same rate of teenage parenthood as do those in two-parent, nondivorced families, and young Black men in stepfamilies are at no greater risk to drop out of high school than are those in two-parent families. McLanahan and Sandefur proposed that the income, supervision, and role models provided by stepfathers may be more advantageous for Black children because they are more likely than White children to live in more disorganized neighborhoods with fewer resources and social controls.

Family Composition, Parental Absence and the Adjustment of Children

The family composition or parental absence perspective proposes that a deviation in structure from a family with two first-married parents, biologically related to their children, is associated with increases in problem behavior in children. Two parents can provide support to each other, especially in their child rearing, as well as multiple role models and increased resources, supervision, and involvement for their children. If father unavailability or absence is a critical factor in divorce, father custody or contact with a noncustodial parent, stepfather, or father surrogate should enhance children's adjustment. Furthermore, children who experience loss of their fathers through divorce or death should exhibit similar adjustment problems. Less theorizing has focused on mother absence, although similar hypotheses might be proposed for mothers.

Children and adults from homes with an absent parent due to either divorce or death have more problems in adjustment than do those in nondivorced families; however, significantly more problems are found in academic achievement, socioeconomic attainment, and conduct disorders for offspring from divorced families. Although children of both divorced and widowed women suffer the loss of their fathers and economic declines, the finding suggests that other factors moderate the differences in their outcomes. One of these factors may be greater support and involvement with the extended family, especially that of the lost parent's family, following death but not divorce. Another may be the greater conflict in families preceding divorce but not the death of a parent.

The parental absence hypothesis also suggests that contact with noncustodial parents or joint custody should promote children's well-being; however, contact with both noncustodial mothers and fathers diminishes rapidly following divorce. More than 20% of children have no contact with their noncustodial fathers or see them only a few times a year, and only about one quarter of children have weekly visits with their divorced fathers. Black noncustodial fathers have higher rates of both regular contact and no contact with their children than do non-Hispanic White fathers. Decreased paternal involvement is related to residential distance, low socioeconomic status, and parental remarriage. Seltzer and Brandreth noted that custodial mothers serve as "gatekeepers," controlling noncustodial fathers' access to and the conditions of visits with their children. When conflict, resentment, and anger are high, the "gate" may be closed, and fathers may be discouraged or shut out. In contrast, when there is low conflict between divorced spouses, when mediation is used, or when noncustodial fathers feel they have some control over decisions in their children's lives, paternal contact and child support payments are more likely to be maintained.

In contrast, noncustodial mothers are more likely than noncustodial fathers to sustain contact with their children and to rearrange their living situations to facilitate children's visits. They maintain approximately twice as much contact with their children as noncustodial fathers do and are less likely to completely drop out of their children's lives or to diminish contact when either parent remarries. In addition, there is some evidence that noncustodial mothers, like noncustodial fathers, are more likely to maintain contact with sons than with daughters, although the preferential contact of fathers with sons is larger and more consistently obtained than that of mothers.

There is little support for the position that sheer frequency of contact facilitates positive adjustment in children. However, as we discuss at greater length in the Family Process and the Adjustment to Divorce and Remarriage section, under conditions of low interparental conflict, contact with competent, supportive, authoritative noncustodial parents can have beneficial effects for children, and these effects are most marked for noncustodial parents and children of the same sex. Thus, it is the quality of contact, rather than the frequency, that is important.

Research on custodial arrangements also has found few advantages of joint custody over sole residential custody. In a large study of custody in California, Maccoby and Mnookin found adolescents in the custody of their fathers had higher rates of delinquency, perhaps because of poorer monitoring by fathers. A meta-analysis of divorce by Amato and Keith, however, did not support the findings of poorer adjustment in children in families in which fathers have custody.

A corollary to the parental absence hypothesis would suggest that the addition of a stepparent might compensate for the loss of a parent. However, the family composition perspective implies that it is not only the presence of two parents but also biological relatedness to the parents that matter. Although divorce involves the exit of a family member, remarriage involves the restructuring of the family constellation with the entrance of stepparent and sometimes stepsiblings. Predictions made about stepfamilies on the basis of the family composition hypothesis are unclear. On the one hand, the presence of a stepparent might compensate for the loss of the noncustodial parent by restoring a two-parent household. On the other hand, the child must confront an additional transition to another family with a nontraditional composition involving the addition of nonbiologically related family members to the household. In a family in which both divorced parents remarry, much more complex kin networks are created within and outside the household in a linked family system or a binuclear family. A child's expanded kin network may include stepsiblings, half siblings, and stepgrandparents, as well as stepparents and biologically related kin and represent a marked deviation from the composition of the nondivorced nuclear family.

Stress, Socioeconomic Disadvantage, and the Adjustment to Divorce and Remarriage

The stress perspective attributes problems in the adjustment of children from divorced and remarried families to the increased stresses experienced in these families. Parents and children living in divorced families encounter a diverse array of stressful life events. Both custodial mothers and fathers complain of task overload and social isolation as they juggle household, child-care, and financial responsibilities that are usually dealt with by two parents. Noncustodial parents express concerns associated with the establishment of new residences, social networks, and intimate relationships; loss of children; problems with visitation arrangements; and continued difficulties in relations with their ex-spouses.

In spite of the diversity in stresses associated with divorce, most attention by sociologists and economists has focused on the marked decrement in the income of custodial mothers following marital dissolution and its accompanying risk factors. Those investigators who support a socioeconomic disadvantage perspective suggest that controlling for income will eliminate or greatly diminish the association between family structure and children's well-being. In addition, because custodial fathers do not encounter the financial decrements experienced by custodial mothers and because remarriage is the fastest way out of poverty for single mothers, it might be expected that children in father-custody families and stepfamilies will exhibit fewer behavior problems than those in divorced mother-custody households.

Because of increased enforcement of noncustodial fathers' child support payments and changes in the labor force for women, it has been speculated that custodial mothers and their children may no longer experience such drastic economic declines following divorce. A recent review suggests, however, that custodial mothers still experience the loss of approximately one quarter to one half of their predivorce income in comparison to only 10% by custodial fathers following divorce. For custodial mothers, this loss in income is accompanied by increased workloads; high rates of job instability; and residential moves to less desirable neighborhoods with poor schools, inadequate services, often high crime rates, and deviant peer populations.

Although father-only families have substantially higher incomes than do families with divorced custodial mothers, a significant number of father-only families (18%) live in poverty, and fathers rarely receive child support. However, most father-custody families have financial, housing, child-care, and educational resources not available to divorced custodial mothers. Custodial fathers report less child-rearing stress than do custodial mothers, and their children show fewer problems. This could be attributed to economic advantages in father-custody families; however, even with income controlled, children in father-custody families—especially boys—show greater well-being than those in mother-custody families.

Newly repartnered parents and their children report higher levels of both positive and negative life changes than do those in never-divorced families. Although there is a marked increase in income for divorced mothers following remarriage, conflicts over finances, child rearing, and family relations remain potent problems in stepfamilies. The economic improvement conferred by remarriage is not reflected in the improved adjustment of children in stepfamilies, and the new stresses associated with remarriage often counter the benefits associated with increased income.

Parental Distress and the Adjustment to Divorce and Remarriage

Investigators taking the parental distress perspective propose that stressors affect children's adjustment through parental distress and diminished well-being. In this view, it is the parents' response to stress, rather than the stress itself, that is most salient for children's adjustment.

Signs of diminished parental well-being and distress, including anger, anxiety, depression, loneliness, impulsivity, feelings of being externally controlled, and emotional liability, may emerge or increase in the immediate aftermath of divorce. In addition, newly remarried parents are often depressed or preoccupied as they cope with the challenges of their new family life. The mental health of parents in divorced and remarried families is related to children's adjustment through diminished competence in their parenting.

The stresses associated with marital transitions place both residential and nonresidential parents at risk not only for psychological disorders but also for disruption in immune system functioning and concomitant increased rates of illness and morbidity, which are notable in divorced adults, especially in men. Nonresidential fathers engage in more health-compromising and impulsive behaviors, such as alcohol consumption, than do fathers in any other family type and are overrepresented among suicides and homicides.

Although depression remains higher in divorced women than in nondivorced women, by two years after divorce, women show less depression and more psychological well-being than do those who remain in conflict-ridden marriages with husbands who undermine their discipline and feelings of competence. The well-being of both men and women increases after the formation of a mutually caring, intimate relationship, such as a remarriage. Most parents do adapt to their new marital situation, with concomitant decreases in psychological and physical problems. In support of the parental distress perspective, even temporary disruptions in parents' health, social, and psychological functioning may make it difficult to be competent in parenting children who may be confused, angry, and apprehensive about a divorce or remarriage, and this inept parenting adversely affects children's adjustment.

Family Process and the Adjustment to Divorce and Remarriage

Divorce and remarriage confront families with changes and challenges associated with pervasive alterations in family roles and functioning. The changes in family relationships can support or undermine the efforts of children to adapt to their new family situations. Proponents of the family process perspective argue that the impact of parental attributes, changes in family structure, socioeconomic disadvantage, and parental distress on children's adjustment is largely mediated by disruptions in family relationships and interactions, such as those involved in discipline and child-rearing practices. Without disruptions in family functioning, the former risk factors are less likely to compromise children's adjustment.

Relationships Between Divorced Couples

Marital conflict is associated with a wide range of deleterious outcomes for children, including depression, poor social competence and academic performance, and conduct disorders. Conflict, contempt, anger, and acrimony often antecede divorce, and in the immediate aftermath of marital disruption, conflict may escalate. Consequently, one of the most frequently asked questions about divorce is whether parents should stay together in an unhappy, conflict-ridden marriage for the sake of the children.

The hypothesis that conflict is a major contributor to problems in divorced families is substantiated by evidence that children in high-conflict, nondivorced families have more problems in psychological adjustment and self-esteem than do those in divorced families or in low-conflict, nondivorced families. In addition, longitudinal prospective studies of divorce indicate that divorce improves the adjustment of children removed from contentious marriages but is deleterious for children whose parents had less overtly conflictual relationships preceding divorce. When measures of marital dissatisfaction rather than conflict are used, the advantages of divorce over unhappy marital situations are less marked because many couples in unsatisfying marriages may not exhibit overt conflict.

Although contact and conflict between divorced couples diminish over time, they remain higher for couples with children as they attempt to negotiate coparenting relationships and economic responsibilities. Despite the fact that cooperative, mutually supportive, and nonconfrontational. coparenting relationships are advantageous to parents and children, only about one quarter of divorced parents attain such relationships and an approximately equal number maintain acrimonious relationships. Most coparenting relationships after divorce evolve into parallel coparenting relationships not only with little communication or coordination of parenting but also with lessened conflict because of the disengaged relationships. Cooperative coparenting is most likely to occur when family size is small and when there was little conflict at the time of divorce. With little conflict and cooperative coparenting, children adapt better not only to their parents' divorce but also to their parents' remarriages, and they tend to have more positive relations with their stepparents.

The sheer frequency of conflict may not be as detrimental as the type of conflict. Conflicts in which children are caught in the middle while parents denigrate each other, precipitate loyalty conflicts, communicate through the children, or fight about the children are most destructive to children's well-being. Children in highly conflicted families not only are more distressed but also may learn to exploit and mislead their parents and to escape monitoring of their activities when they are older. Even when children are not directly involved in their parents' conflicts, the adverse effects of conflicts may be experienced through increased parental irritability and diminished monitoring, support, and involvement.

Relationships of Custodial Mothers and Children

Children in both mother- and father-custody families show more problems than do children in nondivorced families; however, most offspring in both types of divorced families eventually are reasonably well-adjusted. Because approximately 84% of children reside with their mothers following divorce, most studies of parent-child relations following marital dissolution have involved custodial mothers. Close relationships with supportive, authoritative mothers who are warm but exert firm, consistent control and supervision are generally associated with positive adjustment in children and adolescents. In the immediate aftermath of divorce, there is a period of disrupted parenting characterized by irritability and coercion and diminished communication, affection, consistency, control, and monitoring.

The parenting of divorced mothers improves over the course of the two years following divorce but remains less authoritative than that of nondivorced mothers, and problems in control and coercive exchanges between divorced mothers and sons may remain high. Even in adulthood, relationships between sons and divorced mothers are less close than those in nondivorced families, whereas differences in closeness are not found for daughters. Preadolescent girls and their divorced mothers often have close, companionate, confiding relationships; however, in adolescence, there is a notable increase in conflict in these relationships. In comparison with adolescents in nondivorced, two-parent families, adolescents in divorced families and in stepfamilies experience the highest levels of mother-adolescent disagreements and the lowest levels of parental supervision. Both conflictive, negative parent-adolescent relationships and lack of monitoring are associated with involvement with antisocial peers—one of the most potent pathways to the development of delinquency, alcoholism, substance abuse, and teenage sexual activity and childbearing.

About one quarter to one third of adolescents in divorced and remarried families, in comparison with 10% of adolescents in nondivorced families, become disengaged from their families, spending as little time at home as possible and avoiding interactions, activities, and communication with family members. This incidence is greater for boys in divorced families and for girls in stepfamilies. If disengagement is associated with lack of adult support and supervision and with involvement in a delinquent peer group, it leads to both antisocial behavior and academic problems in adolescents.

However, if there is a caring adult involved with the adolescent outside of the home, such as the parent of a friend, a teacher, a neighbor, or a coach, disengagement may be a positive solution to a disrupted, conflictual family situation.

It has been noted that children in divorced families grow up faster, in part, because of early assignment of responsibilities, more autonomous decision making, and lack of adult supervision. Assignment of responsibility may be associated with resilience and unusual social competence in girls from divorced families; yet, if the task demands are beyond the children's capabilities, they also may be associated with low self-esteem, anxiety, and depression. Furthermore, if adolescents perceive themselves as being unfairly burdened with responsibilities that interfere with their other activities, they may respond with resentment, rebellion, and noncompliance.

The restabilizing of family relations following a remarriage takes considerably longer than that following a divorce. Whereas a new homeostasis is established in about two to three years following divorce, it has been estimated that the adjustment to remarriage may take as long as five to seven years. Because more than one quarter of remarriages are terminated within five years, with higher rates for families with children, restabilization never occurs in many stepfamilies.

In the first year following a remarriage, custodial mothers engage in less affective involvement, less behavior control and monitoring, and more negativity than nondivorced mothers. Negative mother-child interactions are related to more disengagement, dysfunctional family roles, poorer communication, and less cohesion in stepfamilies. However, in long-established remarriages, the parenting of custodial mothers with their biological offspring becomes increasingly similar to that in nondivorced families.

Relationships of Custodial Fathers and Children

Although children usually live with their mothers following the dissolution of their parents' marriage, father-headed families have tripled since 1974, making them the fastest growing family type in the United States. Arrangements about physical custody are often made on the basis of personal decisions by parents and not on judicial decree, and the preponderance of maternal physical custody, even when joint legal custody has been granted, may reflect concerns fathers have about assuming full-time parenting. Boys and older children are more likely to be placed in father-only custody, but some girls and young children do live with their fathers. In contrast to custodial mothers, custodial fathers are a very select group of fathers who may be more child-oriented than most fathers. Fathers who seek custody of their children are more involved and capable than those fathers who have custody thrust on them because the mothers were unwilling or incompetent to parent. Once their families have restabilized, custodial fathers report less child-rearing stress, better parent-child relations, and fewer behavior problems in their children than do custodial mothers.

There are different strengths and weaknesses in the parenting of custodial mothers and fathers. Although custodial mothers and custodial fathers are perceived to be similarly warm and nurturing with younger children, mothers have more problems with control and with assignment of household tasks, whereas fathers have more problems with communication, self-disclosure, and monitoring of their children's activities.

Moreover, fathers have special difficulties with monitoring adolescents' behavior, especially that of daughters.

Recent evidence indicates that adolescent adjustment is more predictable from the parenting of a custodial parent of the same sex than one of the opposite sex. This evidence parallels findings of the greater salience of same-sex parents in the adjustment of adolescents in nondivorced families. In spite of this greater influence of same-sex custodial parents, both sons and daughters report feeling closer to their custodial parent than their noncustodial parent, regardless of whether the parent is a mother or a father.

As has been found with mothers, when custodial fathers remarry, there are disruptions in father-child relationships, especially with daughters. Fathers may alter their caretaking relationships more radically than mothers do because fathers are more likely to expect a stepmother to play a major role in household tasks and parenting. However, in long-established stepfamilies, there are few differences in parent-child relations between remarried fathers and their residential biological children and those fathers and children in nondivorced families.

Relationships of Noncustodial Mothers and Children

Although less is known about noncustodial mothers than noncustodial fathers, nonresidential mothers maintain more contact with their children than do nonresidential fathers. It is not only in the quantity but also in the quality of parent-child relationships that these mothers and fathers differ. Noncustodial mothers are less adept than custodial mothers in controlling and monitoring their children's behavior, but they are more effective in these parenting behaviors than are noncustodial fathers. Children report that noncustodial mothers are more interested in and informed about their activities; are more supportive, sensitive, and responsive to their needs; and are more communicative than noncustodial fathers. Therefore, it is not surprising that children report talking more about their problems and activities and feeling closer to noncustodial mothers than to noncustodial fathers, nor that noncustodial mothers have more influence over their children's development, especially their daughters' adjustment, than do noncustodial fathers. Noncustodial mothers' warmth, support, and monitoring enhance their children's scholastic achievement and diminish antisocial, externalizing problems. In appraising some research findings that children have fewer problems in the custody of fathers than in the custody of mothers, it must be considered that part of this effect may be attributable to the more active involvement of noncustodial mothers.

When a custodial father remarries, closeness to the noncustodial mother can have some disadvantages because it is related to children's lack of acceptance of a stepmother. In contrast, there is no association between the relationship with a noncustodial father and building a close relationship with a stepfather.

Relationships of Noncustodial Fathers and Children

In contrast to mothers' behavior, the postdivorce parenting behavior of fathers is less predictable from their predivorce behavior. Some previously attached and involved fathers find the enforced marginality and intermittent contact in being noncustodial fathers to be painful, and they drift away from their children. Other fathers, especially custodial fathers, rise to the occasion and increase their involvement and parenting competence. However, most nonresidential fathers have a friendly, egalitarian, (companionate) relationship rather than a traditional parental relationship with their children. They want their visits to be pleasant and entertaining and are hesitant to assume the role of disciplinarian or teacher. They are less likely than nondivorced fathers to criticize, control, and monitor their children's behavior or to help them with tasks such as homework.

Frequency of contact with noncustodial fathers and the adjustment of children are usually found to be unrelated. Although obviously some degree of contact is essential, it seems to be the quality of the relationship and the circumstances of contact rather than frequency of visits that are most important. When noncustodial fathers are not just "tour guide" fathers but maintain more parent-like contact, participate in a variety of activities with their children, and spend holidays together, the well-being of children is promoted. Under conditions of low conflict, the involvement of authoritative noncustodial fathers can enhance children's adjustment, especially that of boys. It can even, to some extent, protect the children from the adverse consequences of rejecting or incompetent noncustodial mothers. In contrast, under conditions of high conflict, frequent contact with noncustodial parents may exacerbate children's problems.

Relationships Between Stepparents and Stepchildren

Papernow commented that the typical starting point for a stepfamily involving "a weak couple subsystem, a tightly bonded parent-child alliance, and potential interference in family functioning from an outsider" would be considered problematic in a traditional nondivorced family. Clinicians have remarked that any stepfamily that uses a traditional nuclear family as its ideal is bound for disappointment. Similar patterns of relationships in traditional families and stepfamilies may lead to different outcomes. Patterns of functioning and family processes that undermine or promote positive adjustment may differ in the two types of families. The complex relationships between families following remarriage may require less rigid family boundaries and more open, less integrated relations among the family subsystems.

Although both stepfathers and stepmothers feel less close to stepchildren than do nondivorced parents to their children, they, if not the stepchildren, want the new marriage to be successful. In the early stages of a remarriage, stepfathers have been reported to be like polite strangers, trying to ingratiate themselves with their stepchildren by showing less negativity but also less control, monitoring, and affection than do fathers in nondivorced families. In longer established stepfamilies, a distant, disengaged parenting style remains the predominant one for stepfathers, but conflict and negativity, especially between stepparents and stepdaughters, can remain high or increase, especially with adolescents. Some of the conflict in stepfamilies is due to the negative rejecting behavior of stepchildren toward stepparents. Even stepparents with the best intentions may give up in the face of persistent hostile behavior by stepchildren.

Conflict between stepfathers and stepchildren is not necessarily precipitated by the children. In fact, rates of physical abuse perpetrated by stepfathers on their stepchildren are 7 times higher than those by fathers on their biological children, and homicide rates for stepfathers are 100 times higher than those for biological fathers. These differential rates are most marked with infants and preschool-age children.

Stepmothers have a more difficult time integrating themselves into stepfamilies than do stepfathers. Remarried fathers often expect that the stepmothers will participate in child rearing, forcing the stepmothers into more active, less distant, and more confrontational roles than those required of stepfathers. Support by the fathers for the stepmothers' parenting and parental agreement on child rearing are especially important in promoting effective parenting in stepmothers. The assumption of the dominant disciplinarian role is fraught with problems for stepparents, and although authoritative parenting can have salutary effects on stepchildren's adjustment, especially with stepfathers and stepsons, authoritative parenting is not always a feasible option in stepfamilies. When custodial parents are authoritative and when stepparents are warm and involved and support the custodial parents' discipline rather than making independent control attempts, children can be responsive and adjust well.

It is not only parent-child relationships but also relationships between siblings that are more conflictual and less supportive in divorced families and stepfamilies than in nondivorced families. These effects are more marked for biologically related siblings than for stepsiblings. Less involved, harsher parenting is associated with rivalrous, aggressive, and unsupportive sibling relationships in divorced and remarried families, and, in turn, these negative sibling relations lead to low social competence and responsibility and to more behavior problems in children.

Conclusion: What Matters? What Doesn't?

In reviewing the five perspectives, it is clear that each may influence children's adjustment. The first perspective, the individual risk and vulnerability hypothesis, is supported by evidence suggesting that children and their parents have attributes that directly contribute to their experiencing marital transitions and to having more difficulties in adjusting to them. These problems may be transmitted genetically from parents to children, or the effect on children's adjustment may be indirect, due to parents' ineffective child-rearing strategies. However, individual vulnerability to the adverse outcomes of divorce and remarriage seems to involve a complex interaction among an array of individual attributes, including personality, age, gender, and ethnicity, and the effects of these interactions have been difficult to differentiate.

The family composition-parental absence hypothesis is not as well supported by the evidence. Generally, children in never-divorced families with two parents are more competent than children whose parents have divorced. However, this theory would suggest that children's adjustment should benefit from the addition of a stepparent, yet there are few indications of lower levels of problems in children in stepfamilies as compared with children in divorced families. Furthermore, some studies indicate that especially in the early stages of a remarriage, stepchildren exhibit more difficulties than do children in stabilized, divorced, single-parent families.

These comments must be qualified by findings indicating that the presence of a stepfather, especially with preadolescent boys, can attenuate problems in adjustment for stepsons, whereas the presence of either a stepmother or a stepfather may be associated with higher levels of problem behaviors for girls. These results, in conjunction with the somewhat inconsistent evidence that boys may also fare better in a father-custody family than in a mother-custody family, indicate that the presence of a father may have positive effects on the well-being of boys. Rather than rejecting the family composition-parental absence perspective, it should be concluded that there is not a simple main effect of family composition or parental absence but that it is modified by the reason for parental unavailability, the quality of family relationships, and the child's gender.

The findings thus far yield only modest support for marked direct effects of life stress and economic deprivation on children's adjustment. Even when income is controlled, children in divorced families show more problems than do those in nondivorced families. In addition, although the income in stepfamilies is only slightly lower than that in nondivorced families, children in these families show a similar level of problem behavior to that in divorced mother-custody families. Thus, the effects of income do not seem to be primary and are largely indirect.

Some investigators using large-scale survey data report that as much as half of the effects of divorce on children's adjustment is attributable to economic factors; others find no direct effects of income but a major effect of the quality of family relationships that may alter children's adjustment. Furthermore, in studies in which income has been controlled, differences between offspring in divorced and nondivorced families remain. Some of the inconsistencies in findings are due to methodological differences in studies. Surveys often have large representative samples but inadequate measures, sometimes involving only two or three items and single informants, to assess parental and family characteristics and family process variables. Studies using smaller, less representative samples but more reliable multi-method, multi-informant assessment, including observations, have found that much of the effects of family structure and economic stress are mediated by inept parenting. Furthermore, there is some support in the research on stress, economic deprivation, and marital transitions for the individual risk position. As stated earlier, antisocial individuals are at greater risk not only for job instability, economic problems, and stressful life events but also for divorce, problems in successive marital relationships, and incompetent parenting.

Although it is true that parental distress increases in the aftermath of a divorce, research indicates that the effect of parents' well-being is largely mediated through their parenting. Even temporary disruptions in parents' physical and psychological functioning due to a marital transition interfere with their ability to offer support and supervision at a time when children need them most.

Although attributes of parents and children, family composition, stress and socioeconomic disadvantage, and parental distress impact children's adjustment, their effects may be mediated through the more proximal mechanism of family process. Dysfunctional family relationships, such as conflict, negativity, lack of support, and nonauthoritative parenting, exacerbate the effects of divorce and remarriage on children's adjustment. Certainly if divorced or remarried parents are authoritative and their families are harmonious, warm, and cohesive, the differences between the adjustment of children in these families and those in nondivorced families are reduced. However, marital transitions increase the probability that children will not find themselves in families with such functioning. Research on the relationships between family members in nondivorced families and stepfamilies supports the family process hypothesis, suggesting that, in large part, it is negative, conflictual, dysfunctional family relationships between parents, parents and children, and siblings that account for differences in children's adjustment.

It has become fashionable to attempt to estimate the relative contributions of individual attributes, family structure, stresses, parental distress, and family process to the adjustment of children in divorced and remarried families. These attempts have led to conflicting results, futile controversies, and misleading conclusions because the amount of variance explained by the factors differs from sample to sample and varies with the methods and the data analytic strategies used. Moreover, different risk and vulnerability factors are likely to come into play and to vary in salience at different points in the transitions from an unhappy marriage to divorce, to life in a single parent household, through remarriage, and into subsequent marital transitions. These risk factors will be modified by shifting protective factors and resources.

A transactional model of risks associated with marital transitions is perhaps most appropriate. Divorce and remarriage increase the probability of parents and children encountering a set of interrelated risks. These risks are linked, interact, and are mediated and moderated in complex ways. These effects are illustrated in the model in different ways. For example, parental distress (e.g., maternal depression) does not have a direct effect on children's adjustment, which is not to say it does not have an impact. Instead, its influence is mediated through its link to family process, specifically the depressed mothers' diminished ability to effectively parent. In contrast, some variables moderate the relationship between other variables, such that the relationship depends on the level of the moderator. For example, children with difficult temperaments are expected to be more adversely affected by disruptions in family functioning than are children with easy temperaments. Thus, individual variables such as temperament can moderate the effect of family process on children's adjustment.

All family members encounter stresses associated with marital transitions, and it may be the balance between risks and resources that determines the impact of stresses on divorced and remarried parents and their children. All five of the factors described at the beginning of this article are associated with divorce and remarriage and with adverse outcomes for children. Studies using path analyses have helped illuminate the patterns of linkages among these risks and have suggested that many of the risk factors are mediated by proximal experiences such as disruptions in parent-child or sibling relationships. However, the fact that a path is indirect does not reduce its importance. Figure 1 presents the theoretical model describing the linkages among these factors. A set of individual attributes, such as antisocial behavior, is associated with an increased risk of divorce and an unsuccessful remarriage; problems in social relationships, including parent-child relationships; and stressful life events. All family members encounter stresses as they deal with the changes, challenges, and restructuring of the family associated with marital transitions, but these vary for different family members and for divorce and remarriage. Divorce usually leads to the loss or the diminished availability of a father and the economic, social, and emotional resources he can provide, which increases the probability of poverty and its concomitant environmental and experiential adversities for divorced custodial mothers and their children. Although some of the effects of stresses, such as living in neighborhoods with high crime rates, poor schools, antisocial peers, and few job opportunities or resources, may impact directly on children's adjustment and attainment, other effects of stress in divorced families may be indirect and mediated through parental psychological distress, inept or altered parenting, and disrupted family processes. Stresses associated with the changes and complexities in stepfamilies may also lead to distress and dysfunctional family functioning. Children, because of individual characteristics such as gender, temperament, personality, age, and intelligence, vary in their influence on family process and their vulnerability or resilience in dealing with their parents' divorce and remarriage and concomitant changes in family roles, relationships, and process. Thus, effects of the earlier risk factors on children's adjustment are mediated or moderated by associated transactional risk factors and often eventually by disruptions in family functioning. These indirect or mediated effects do not negate the importance of the earlier risk factors as a link in the transactional path of adversity leading to problems in child adjustment.

Static, cross-sectional slices out of the lives of parents and children in divorced or remarried families give a misleading picture of how risk and protective factors combine to influence the adjustment of children. An examination of the dynamic trajectories of interacting risk and protective factors associated with divorce and remarriage will yield a more valid and fruitful view of the multiple pathways associated with resiliency or adverse outcomes for children who have experienced their parents' marital transitions.

CHAPTER III
Decisions in the Family

A. Economic Decisions

When couples marry, and to a lesser extent when they cohabit for lengthy periods, they set up economic as well as social units. These relationships have been described as miniature firms (Gary Becker, A TREATISE ON THE FAMILY (1981)), and are often treated, at least by outsiders as well as such government entities as the Internal Revenue Service, as single units. In this section, we wish to explore two ways in which couples behave within these economic units: how they actually divide their work and how theoretically they tend to bargain around such routine matters as who handles the checkbook and who takes out the trash.

Many disputes of married couples revolve around such issues, which necessarily relate as well to the wider feminist concerns such as women's labor force participation, particularly, again in Joan Williams' terminology, the ability to be an "ideal worker" and equality between husband and wife. Joan Williams, *Gender Wars, Selfless Women in the Republic of Choice,* 66 N.Y.U. L. REV. 1551 (1991)*; Dissolving the Sameness/Difference Debate: A Post-Modern Path Beyond Essentialism in Feminist and Critical Race Theory,* 1991 DUKE L.J. 296. The feminist agenda of the 1960s and 70s presupposed a home where husband and wife would equally share household duties and particularly child care. But the question remains whether such sharing behavior can ever be realized. From an economic perspective, it is critical to know whether equality is efficient or whether individual married people's preferences will result in quite different—and perhaps more "traditional"—arrangements of daily affairs.

Here we include articles that illustrate the various ways couples make economic (in a broad sense) decisions in the family. To this end, we have included two pieces written from an economic perspective. Couples are like others in long-term relationships who have tremendous incentives both to share and to keep the relationship intact. At the same time, they remain individuals with their own agendas and interests.

Cathleen Zick's piece shows how time studies can be used to answer a question that has been critical to many feminists (and many married couples): which spouse does the housework, and how does this allocation change if both spouses are employed or if children are present. Zick's study considers similar couples surveyed ten years apart.

We also include the discursive portion of an article by Lundberg and Pollak. Unlike the other economists whose work we've included, Lundberg and Pollak use the technique of game theory to model behavior in marriages. Part of the usefulness of this article comes from its discussion (and rejection) of the more simple modeling done by Gary Becker and others, who assume that household decisionmaking is done by a single adult. A further interesting feature of the piece is its discussion of the way women, as compared to men, allocate money to children. The fact that when women have the power to spend money, children tend to benefit, has ramifications not only for marriage but also for public assistance policy.

Cathleen D. Zick & Jane L. McCullough, *Trends in Married Couples' Time Use: Evidence from 1977-78 and 1987-88,* 24 SEX ROLES 459 (1991)[*]

DISCUSSION AND CONCLUSIONS

Many different approaches have been used to assess time-use trends. Often times the conclusions of these studies have been at odds with one another. It was suggested in this paper that variations in data quality and methodological approaches may be responsible for some of the observed differences. If the goal is to gain insights about how household time use has changed, then it is important that the researcher (1) have data that accurately measure time use (i.e., time diary data) for similar groups of households at different points in time, and (2) use methods of analysis that allow one to test causal hypotheses generated by the underlying theoretical framework in an appropriate fashion given the inherent structure of the data. The empirical work presented in this paper is guided by these insights.

The implications of the results presented here are circumscribed by two important limitations. First, the study findings are illustrative of how time-use patterns of a particular household type in a particular geographical location changed over a ten-year period. The results should not be generalized beyond two-parent, two-child households living in Utah between 1977-78 and 1987-88. One way that individuals may change their time use is by changing their household composition (i.e., divorcing, marrying, having an additional child). Yet, the analyses done here cannot provide insights into how recent changes in the demographic composition of American households have altered individuals' time use.

Second, while this work presents insights about how and why spouses' time use in two-parent, two-child households changed between 1977-78 and 1987-88, projections about future trends, based on these results, should be made with caution. To gain a more confident picture of the age, period, and cohort-specific time-use relationships, one needs data from more than two points in time. While the research presented here

---

is illustrative of the types of analyses that can be done with two comparable cross-sections of time diary data, analyses conducted with other data from different historical periods might show the current results to be quite period and/or cohort specific.

The limitations described above help to place the study results in context. On a descriptive level, this research adds to the growing body of work that shows married women's housework time to be declining while the household work time of married men is rising. Yet, contrary to others, the analyses conducted here showed little support for the contention that the leisure time of men and women is growing. If leisure time grew between 1977-78 and 1987-88, then it grew primarily in other household types or because individuals elected to change their household composition.

Indeed, the descriptive picture of the time-use changes experienced by spouses in two-parent, two-child households during this ten-year period is a somewhat disquieting one. For the married women in these households, time devoted to paid work rose by an average of almost eleven hours per week. Yet, their housework time only declined an average of three and one half hours per week. The remaining seven and one-half hours increase in market work appears to have come at the expense of their discretionary and maintenance time.

The decline in the wives' household work time appears to be offset almost one-to-one by an increase in husbands' household work time. If the possibility of any sex-related productivity differences are assumed away, this implies that the total production in these homes remained constant, on average. Yet, because everyone has a fixed amount of time, the increase in married men's housework time also had to come at the expense of something. As with the wives, it appears that what the husbands gave up was a portion of their maintenance time. Thus, for both spouses, productive time (i.e., paid work plus housework) rose during the ten-year period at the expense of the time economists generally refer to as "leisure."

What factors were responsible for the observed shifts? The multivariate analyses revealed that husband's education and wife's age (i.e., family life-cycle stage) had significant effects on spouses' relative time allocation shares that remained relatively constant across the ten years. The descriptive statistics showed that both the average education level of husbands and the average age of the wives increased marginally over that ten-year period. Thus, some of the observed changes in time use may be the result of the general rise in education levels and the general aging of this household type.

The analyses also revealed that the nature of the relationships between spouses' time use and some household characteristics changed during the ten-year period. For example, a change in the wife's value of time and unearned income affected husbands' and wives' relative time use differently in 1987-88 than it did in 1977-78. Whereas the time use of spouses in two-parent, two- child households was fairly unresponsive to changes in the family's economic constraints during the late 1970s, their time use appears to be somewhat responsive to changes in their budget constraint by the late 1980s.

These time varying relationships suggest that some of what is observed about spouses' time use during that ten-year period may be attributable to birth cohort differences. On average, the spouses interviewed in 1977-78 would have been born in the pre-baby-boom era of the mid 1940s. In contrast, the spouses participating in the 1987-88 study were generally born during the peak baby-boom of the early to mid 1960s.

Easterlin hypothesizes that the size of one's birth cohort affects an individual's overall life course. For example, he argues that compared to the baby-bust generation of the late 1930s and early 1940s, the baby boom generation (1) faces greater competition for jobs, (2) experiences slower rates of growth in their income (causing more married women to enter the labor force), and: (3) marries later and has fewer children—all because the size of the baby-boom's birth cohort is so large. While Easterlin does not speak directly to the relationship between birth cohort and time use, the findings presented here are consistent with his theory. That is, if the baby-boom parents interviewed in 1987-88 have faced greater competition all of their lives, then it may not be surprising that their time-use patterns were observed to be more sensitive to changes in their economic environment than were the time-use patterns of their baby-bust counterparts.

The two cohorts of parents interviewed for this study also entered adulthood during very different historical periods. The parents interviewed in 1977-78, generally entered their 20s during the mid 1960s. In contrast, the parents interviewed in 1987-88, generally entered their 20s during the early-to-mid 1970s. During the 1960s and 1970s, the women's movement pressured for changes in societal attitudes about women's and men's roles. To the extent that these pressures translated into an increased awareness of the economic value of women's contributions (both in the market place and in the home) for the parents interviewed in 1987-88, this too may explain the changing relationship between the economic environment and spouses' time use that were found in this study.

To what extent does the research reported here inform the on-going scholarly debate about household time use? If anything, the empirical evidence provides partial confirmation to both camps. In support of the optimistic view, the findings show that the housework time of wives in two-parent, two-child households did decline during the ten-year period. Furthermore, there was a commensurate increase in the household work time of their husbands. Real increases in the value of wives' time, the rising education level of husbands, and growth in the ownership of home appliances, all appear to have fueled these changes.

Consistent with the more pessimistic views, the findings also show that the rise in wives' paid work time has not been offset by a one-to-one tradeoff with time spent in housework. Instead, the overall time the wives spent in productive activities rose. Yet, the substantial increase in wives' paid work time did not translate into higher household income for these families. The average household income was just over $35,000 (measured in 1987 dollars) in both years.

In 1987-88 the spouses in two-parent, two-child households in Utah simply had to work longer hours to maintain their standard of living. Their increases in productive work time came at the expense of time they had previously spent in more leisure-oriented activities. For these couples then, the "good news" regarding the more equitable distribution of paid work and household work between husbands and wives must be weighed against the "bad news" that their leisure time is shrinking.

Shelly Lundberg & Robert A. Pollak, *Bargaining and Distribution in Marriage,* 10 JOURNAL OF ECONOMIC PERSPECTIVES 139 (1996)[*]

In the 1970s, a proposed change in social welfare policy in the United Kingdom excited considerable debate. The universal child allowance, which had consisted primarily of a reduction in the amount withheld for taxes from the father's paycheck, was to be replaced by a cash payment to the mother. An excerpt from the parliamentary debate in the *House of Commons Hansard* (May 13, 1975) expresses a popular sentiment "[F]ar from a new deal for families, it will take money out of the husband's pocket on the Friday and put it into the wife's purse on the following Tuesday. Far from being a child benefit scheme, it looks like being a father disbenefit scheme."

Popular discussions of family policies such as the U.K child benefit often concern their presumed effects on distribution within the family—on the relative well-being of husbands, wives and children. The economist armed only with traditional models of the family must view these discussions as naive. Until very recently, the standard of the profession for both theoretical and empirical analysis was a "common preference" model of the family, which assumes that family members act as though they are maximizing a single utility function. A family's common preference ordering may be the outcome of consensus among family members or the dominance of a single family member, but all such models imply that family expenditures are independent of which individuals in the family receive income or control resources. Common preference models imply that all income is "pooled" and then allocated to maximize a single objective function, so that family demand behavior depends on total family income and not the incomes of individual members. This pooling of resources within the family implies that a change from child allowances paid to fathers to child allowances paid to mothers should arouse neither the ire of affected fathers nor the opposition of their parliamentary representatives. . . .

To this end, the theoretical challenge facing family economics is to develop models in which joint family decisions are derived from the sometimes divergent interests of husbands and wives and in which the formation and dissolution of marriages provide a beginning and an end to the family allocation process. In recent years, a large number of game-theoretic models of marriage and the family have been developed, building on the seminal contributions of Manser and Brown and McElroy and Horney. In general, these models impose fewer restrictions on observed family behavior than do common preference models, and recent theoretical contributions have been prompted, and supported, by a growing body of empirical evidence inconsistent with common preference models. The most provocative of this empirical work demonstrates a strong positive association between child well-being and the mother's relative control over family resources and has raised new questions about the potential effectiveness of policies "targeted" at specific family members.

A current snapshot of family economics would show the traditional framework under siege on both theoretical and empirical fronts. The political potency of gender

---

issues has given a certain urgency to the development of alternatives to common preference models. However, no new theoretical framework has gained general acceptance as a replacement for common preference models, and empirical studies have concentrated on debunking old models rather than on discriminating among new ones. In this paper, we review a number of simple bargaining models that permit independent agency of men and women in marriage, discuss their implications for distribution within marriage and for observed family behavior, and present a sampling of the relevant empirical evidence.

Models of Family Behavior

Economic models of consumer demand and labor supply begin with an individual economic agent choosing actions that maximize his or her utility function subject to a budget constraint. How can we reconcile this individualistic theory of the consumer with the reality that people tend to live, eat, work and play in families? Application of a single-agent model to the household or family raises two distinct issues—the identity of the consumer and the identity of the decision maker.

The identity of the consumer is an issue because micro-data on consumption usually report expenditures at the household level, seldom consumption at the individual level. The household purchases bread and refrigerators, ballet lessons and haircuts, but in general the data do not assign the consumption of these goods and services to individual household members. If the problem were fundamentally data-based, however, we could solve it by collecting better data on individual consumption, time allocation and income. There are two reasons why better data would be only a partial solution and, thus, no solution at all. First, goods whose consumption is inherently joint are an important component of household consumption. With household public goods, better data cannot solve the assignment problem and, hence, cannot restore the integrity of the simple single-agent consumer model. Second, family members who are linked by love and duty have an interest in each other s consumption. Even if we could assign direct consumption to individual family members, interdependent preferences would invalidate the single-consumer assumption.

Economists have dealt with the multiplicity of decision makers in the family in two ways. The first approach, in ascendancy from the 1950s until the 1980s, was the common preference approach—treating the family as though it were a single decision-making agent, with a single pooled budget constraint and a single utility function that included the consumption and leisure time of every family member. The second approach, pioneered by Manser-Brown and McElroy-Horney in the early 1980s, was to model family demands as the solution to a bargaining game. Most bargaining models of family behavior allow two decision makers—the husband and the wife. Children are customarily excluded from the set of decision making agents in the family, though they may be recognized as consumers of goods chosen and provided by loving or dutiful parents. The empirical implications of bargaining models of marriage depend upon their assumptions about the form of the bargaining game, but, in general, these models widen the range of "rational" family behavior.

Common Preference Models and the Income Pooling Assumption

Two models provide the theoretical underpinning of the common preference approach to family behavior: Samuelson's consensus model and Becker's altruist model. The consensus model was introduced by Samuelson to exhibit the conditions under which family behavior can be rationalized as the outcome of maximizing a single utility function. Consider a two member family consisting of a husband and a wife. Each has an individual utility function that depends on his or her private consumption of goods; but, by consensus, they agree to maximize a consensus social welfare function of their individual utilities subject to a joint budget constraint that pools the income received by the two family members. Then we can analyze their aggregate expenditure pattern as though the family were a single agent maximizing a utility function. This optimization problem generates family demands that depend only upon prices and total family income and that have standard properties, provided the utility functions are well-behaved. Thus, the comparative statics of traditional consumer demand theory apply directly to family behavior under the consensus model. Samuelson did not, however, purport to explain how the family achieves a consensus, the joint welfare function, nor how this consensus is maintained.

Becker's altruist model addresses these questions and also provides an account of how resources are distributed within the family. In Becker's model, the family consists of a group of purely selfish but rational "kids" and one altruistic parent whose utility function reflects a concern for the well being of other family members. Becker argues that the presence of an altruistic parent who makes positive transfers to each member of the family is sufficient to induce the selfish kids to act in an apparently unselfish way. The altruistic parent will adjust transfers so that each "rotten kid" finds it in his or her interest to choose actions that maximize family income. The resulting distribution is one that maximizes the altruist's utility function subject to the family's resource constraint, so the implications of the altruist model for family demands coincide with those of the consensus model.

Whether motivated by Samuelson's family consensus story or Becker's altruist story, the common preference framework is a simple, powerful mechanism for generating demand functions and establishing their comparative statics for use in applied problems. It remains the standard theoretical framework for analyzing consumption behavior and labor supply. Only serious deficiencies could justify replacing this approach with a more complicated alternative. In recent years, however, common preference models have been targets of an intense barrage of theoretical and empirical criticism.

Dissatisfaction with common preference models on theoretical grounds has been the product of serious study by economists of marriage and divorce. Models of marriage and divorce require a theoretical framework in which agents compare their expected utilities inside marriage with their expected utilities outside marriage. Common preference models cannot be wed to examine these decisions because the individual utilities of husband and wife cannot be recovered from the social welfare function that generates consumption, labor supply, fertility and other behavior within marriage. If the analysis of marriage and divorce is awkward, the analysis of marital decisions in the shadow of divorce is even more so. If unilateral divorce is possible, individual rationality implies that marital decisions cannot leave either husband or wife worse off than they would be outside the marriage. This individual rationality requirement, however, alters the comparative statics of the model and destroys the correspondence between the behavior of a single rational agent and the behavior of a family.

Recent empirical evidence suggests that the restrictions imposed on demand functions by common preference models are not well-supported. Rejections of the family income pooling assumption have been most influential in weakening economists' attachment to common preference models. Income pooling implies a restriction on family demand functions that appears simple to test if family members pool their income and allocate the total to maximize a single objective function, then only total income will affect demands. The fraction of income received or controlled by one family member should not influence demands, conditional on total family income. A large number of recent empirical studies have rejected pooling, finding that earned income received by the husband or wife significantly affects demand patterns when total income or expenditure is held constant. Many studies find that children appear to do better when their mothers control a larger fraction of family resources. . . .

Cooperative Bargaining Models

A viable alternative to common preference models of the family must relax the pooling assumption and must recognize, in a nontrivial fashion, the involvement of two or more agents with distinct preferences in determining family consumption. Bargaining models from cooperative game theory satisfy these conditions. A typical cooperative bargaining model of marriage begins with a family that consists of only two members: a husband and a wife. Each has a utility function that depends on his or her consumption of private goods: U^h for the husband and U^w for the wife. If agreement is not reached, then the payoff received is represented by a "threat point" (T^h, T^w)—the utilities associated with a default outcome of divorce or, alternatively, a noncooperative equilibrium within the marriage. The Nash bargaining model provides the leading solution concept in bargaining models of marriage. This solution can be illustrated by a diagram in utility space, where AB is the utility-possibility frontier.

The utility received by husband or wife in the Nash bargaining solution depends upon the threat point; the higher one's utility at the threat point, the higher one's utility in the Nash bargaining solution. This dependence is the critical empirical implication of Nash bargaining models: family demands depend not only on prices and total family income but also on determinants of the threat point.

In divorce-threat bargaining models, the threat point is the maximal level of utility attainable outside the marriage. If divorcing partners maintain ownership of income received separately within marriage, the demands emerging from marital bargaining will depend not on total family income but on the income received by the husband and the income received by the wife. The divorce threat point is also likely to depend on environmental factors . . . that do not directly affect marital utility, such as conditions in the remarriage market and the income available to divorced men and women. The family demands that result from divorce-threat marital bargaining will, therefore, depend upon these parameters as well. As McElroy points out, the absence of pooling and the presence of extrahousehold parameters in family demands yield a model that can be tested against the common preference alternative. For example, changes in the welfare payments available to divorced mothers or in laws defining marital property and regulating its division upon divorce should affect distribution between men and women in two-parent families through their effect on the threat point.

In the separate spheres bargaining model of Lundberg and Pollak, the threat point is internal to the marriage, not external as in divorce-threat bargaining models. The husband and wife settle their differences by Nash bargaining, but the alternative to agreement is an inefficient noncooperative equilibrium within marriage. In a noncooperative equilibrium, each spouse voluntarily provides household public goods, choosing actions that are utility-maximizing, given the actions of their partner. This noncooperative marriage may be better for both spouses than divorce. Divorce, the argument goes, may be the ultimate threat available to marital partners in disagreement, but a noncooperative marriage in which the spouses receive some benefits due to joint consumption of public goods may be a more plausible threat in day-to-day marital bargaining.

The introduction of this internal threat point has important implications because separate spheres bargaining generates family demands that, under some circumstances, depend not on who receives income after divorce but on who receives (or controls) income within the marriage. Control over resources within marriage need not affect the equilibrium: if both the husband and the wife make positive contributions to each public good in the noncooperative equilibrium, then household allocation will not depend upon how income is distributed between the spouses. In the separate spheres model, however, a nonpooling outcome arises when gender specialization in the provision of household public goods ensures that only one spouse makes a positive contribution. The model assumes that socially recognized and sanctioned gender roles assign primary responsibility for certain activities to husbands and others to wives. In the absence of cooperation, one household public good, q^1, will be provided by the husband out of his own resources and the other public good, q^2 by the wife out of her own resources. Lundberg and Pollak assume that this allocation of marital responsibilities reflects social norms rather than preference or productivity differences between husband and wife in a particular marriage.

In a noncooperative marriage, the husband treats the level of public good chosen by his wife as fixed and chooses quantities of his private good and the public good that he supplies so as to maximize his own utility, subject to his budget constraint. Similarly, the wife treats the quantity of the public good supplied by her husband as fixed and chooses the level of her private good and the public good that she supplies to maximize her own utility, subject to her budget constraint. These decisions lead to a pair of reaction functions that determine a Cournot-Nash equilibrium in which the public goods contributions are inefficiently low. An important characteristic of this noncooperative equilibrium, which serves as the threat point in the separate spheres model, is that the husband's utility depends upon the resources of his wife through his consumption of "her" public good and vice versa. Since the demand functions generated by cooperative bargaining depend upon the threat point, they will also be independently influenced by husband's income and wife's income. In the cooperative equilibrium, the husband's and wife's utilities will depend not on total family income but on the incomes controlled separately by each spouse.

As the divorce-threat and separate models show, cooperative bargaining does not necessarily imply income pooling. Bargained outcomes depend upon the threat point, and the income controlled by husband and wife will affect family behavior (and the relative well-being of men and women within marriage) if this control influences the threat point. This dependence implies that public policy (like taxes and transfers) need not be neutral in their effects on distribution within the family, although how they affect distribution depends upon how the alternative to agreement is specified. A divorce-threat bargaining model predicts that policies improving the status of divorced women will shift resources within marriage to wives; it also predicts that policies affecting the control of income within the marriage will have no effect on distribution within marriage if they have no effect on the incomes of divorced men and women. A separate spheres bargaining model predicts that policies reallocating income within marriage will change distribution within marriage and family demands, even if they do not affect the well-being of divorced men and women. Consider, for example, a change in child allowance policy from one that pays husbands to one that pays wives; but suppose that, in the event of divorce, the mother is always the custodial parent and receives the child allowance. Divorce-threat models predict that this change will have no effect on distribution in two-parent families, while the separate spheres model predicts redistribution towards the wife. . . .

The Marriage Market

Models that analyze bargaining within existing marriages can give only an incomplete picture of the determinants of the well-being of men and women. The marriage market, as Becker has emphasized, is an important determinant of distribution between men and women. At a minimum, the marriage market determines who marries and who marries whom. The extent to which the marriage market also determines distribution within particular marriages depends crucially on whether prospective spouses can make binding agreements in the marriage market. At one extreme, if binding, fully contingent contracts regarding marital distribution can be made prior to marriage, then there is no scope for bargaining within marriage: distribution within marriage simply implements agreements previously made in the marriage market. At the other extreme, if binding agreements cannot be made in the marriage market, then husbands and wives bargain over the surplus generated by a particular marriage.

The marriage market can also generate substantial differences between the short-run and long-run effects of tax, transfer and other redistributive policies. In Lundberg and Pollak, we consider a model in which prospective spouses can agree on a transfer payment from, for example, husbands to wives that is uncontingent on the realized values of income later in the marriage. If policymakers attempt to redistribute income by transferring the ownership of a child allowance payment from husbands to wives, some redistribution is likely to occur within marriages in existence at the time of the policy change. For the next generation of marriages, however, there will be a new equilibrium with the same pairing of men and women, but with the agreed transfer to wives reduced by the amount of the child allowance. With binding marital agreements, therefore, targeted policies that have redistributive effects in existing marriages may be "undone" by subsequent generations in the marriage market—a pure Ricardian equivalence result.

Even without binding agreements, however, the long-run effects of a redistributive policy are likely to differ from the short-run effects on existing marriages. Prospective spouses understand that marriage commits them to playing a particular bargaining game with a particular partner. A policy that transfers income from husbands to wives will make marriage relatively more attractive to women and less attractive to men. Such a change in transfer policy can alter the equilibrium number of marriages contracted in subsequent marriage markets as well as the equilibrium matching and distribution of marital surpluses.

The scope for bargaining within marriage also depends upon the alternatives available to the marital partners. In the marriage market, if there are close substitutes for each individual, then the next best marriage is nearly as good as the proposed one, and the surplus to be divided by bargaining is small. Over time, however, a sizeable surplus may develop in an ongoing marriage, perhaps because of investments in marriage-specific human capital. In this situation, the possibility of divorce (perhaps followed by remarriage) defines the scope for bargaining within an ongoing marriage by placing bounds on the distributions that can emerge as eqilibria. These "divorce bounds" depend upon the costs of divorce, including psychic costs, the resources available to divorced individuals and conditions in the remarriage market. Individual rationality ensures that no individual will accept less than he or she would receive in the next best alternative and implies that the divorce bounds apply to all bargaining models, both cooperative and noncooperative. As there is little scope for bargaining in the Marriage market when the next best marriage is almost as good as the proposed marriage, there is little scope for bargaining within marriage when the divorce bounds are tight. Bargaining models of marriage are motivated by the assumption that, in at least some marriages, surpluses are large enough that their distribution is worth modeling.

The role of marriage markets in determining distribution within marriage provides another example of the importance of social norms and institutions. When matching models have multiple equilibria, as they often do, which equilibrium is selected or realized may depend upon institutions and practices not specified in the formal model. For example, it is well-known that in a marital matching model, the equilibrium realized when men propose to women is more favorable to men and less favorable to women than the equilibrium realized when women propose to men. Pollak argues that when the selection of one equilibrium rather than another has important distributional implications, institutions and practices (for example, courting conventions) should be explicitly modeled.

Contributions of Bargaining Approaches to Marriage

Common preference models of the family have proven to be too limited a framework for the analysis of family behavior. Though the models provide a rigorous and powerful tool for analyzing family expenditure patterns and labor supply its assumption of a single family utility function and its implication of family income pooling are problematic. Furthermore, common preference models rule out analysis of intrafamily distribution or of the connection between marriage markets and marital behavior. Game-theoretic approaches to family behavior provide new models yield new results and provoke new questions. Novel questions and areas of inquiry are numerous, but three that seem particularly interesting to us are the effect of control of resources by husbands and wives on the well-being of children, the effect of social norms on marital bargaining and the relationship between marital distribution and marriage markets.

Policies that empower women have been supported not only by claims that they will increase the well-being of women and reduce birth rates, but also by claims that they will increase the well-being of children. The belief that "kids do better" when their mothers control a larger fraction of family resources, which was presumably part of the rationale for changing the U.K child benefit program in the late 1970s, has now attained the status of conventional wisdom among development agencies. This belief entails two distinct propositions, both confidently maintained in a recent World Bank monograph on gender equality. First, we must reject income pooling in favor of some alternative in which control over resources influences distribution within the family. As the World Bank puts it, "policies that specifically target women or girls can address the needs of this group more efficiently and with greater cost-effectiveness than general policy measures." Second, we must accept the additional hypothesis that "[f]emale household members tend to allocate resources more directly to children, while men tend to allocate more resources to adults."

The kids-do-better hypothesis is widely accepted and has received extensive empirical support: Bruce, Lloyd and Leonard and Blumberg cite and summarize many of the relevant studies. Economists, many of whom have been skeptical on theoretical grounds that the kids-do-better results were caused by mothers' control over resources, have found the possible endogeneity of income sources discussed earlier to be sufficient econometric grounds for discounting the empirical evidence that supports it. Though the evidence on this point is not conclusive, we think that the burden of proof has shifted to those who doubt that children benefit when their mothers control a larger fraction of family resources.

The notion that control over resources matters focuses attention on the difficult issue of the meaning and measurement of "control." Does the individual family member whose name is on the check maintain control over its disbursement? Are in-kind transfers more controllable by individual recipients than cash? To what extent are one's own earnings "owned" by the worker rather than pooled for household use? Work by sociologists on family budgeting suggests considerable heterogeneity among families in money management practices. Economists, however, are unlikely to find money management practices especially interesting as outcome variables or appropriate as explanatory variables. A more interesting focus for economists is the relationship between control over resources and the extramarital environment, on the one hand, and outcomes such as expenditure patterns, labor supply, and observable indicators of individual well-being such as morbidity and mortality, on the other. In particular, empirical studies that examine the effects of differences in tax and transfer policies that appear to establish different claims on resources within the household are likely to improve our understanding of intrahousehold allocation.

Bargaining models of marriage suggest a number of mechanisms through which social norms and institutions can affect distribution between men and women. Most directly, social norms may affect the preferences of marital partners. In bargaining models, social norms affect outcomes indirectly, often through their effect on the threat point. In the divorce-threat bargaining model, custody and child-support standards and the social position of divorced men and women will be among the extramarital environmental parameters that determine the threat point. In the context of this model, an increase in welfare "stigma" will be associated with a decline in the relative well-being of women and children in low-income families, as will reductions in the real value of welfare payments. If the threat point reflects the possibility of domestic violence, marital distribution may depend upon the expected reaction of neighbors and the behavior of police on domestic violence calls. Noncooperative outcomes may be influenced by social norms in a different way; in models with multiple equilibria, social conventions may suggest a focal point equilibrium and a way of coordinating behavior without explicit bargaining norms regarding appropriate marital or parental behavior for men and women, and may be powerful in their ability to channel the behavior of marital partners to one equilibrium among many—raising the question of how such norms develop and are maintained.

Bargaining models place distribution within marriage in a theoretical framework that is consistent with existing analyses of marriage and of divorce: two decisionmakers with well-defined preferences choosing an action or strategy from a well-specified set of alternatives. Bargaining models thus provide an opportunity for integrating the analysis of distribution within marriage with a matching or search model of the marriage market. In a unified model, marital bargaining is conditional upon the match (and perhaps contract) agreed to in the marriage market and agents in the marriage market anticipate the bargaining environment within marriage. We can expect outcomes in these two arenas for male-female contracting to be closely related. A change in the bargaining environment within marriage (for example, a change in tax policy, relative wages or social norms) can not only affect distribution within existing marriages but can also alter subsequent marriage market equilibria; under some circumstances, these marriage market effects can entirely undo the effects of the initial redistribution. We are far from a unified model of marriage, divorce and marital behavior, but a model of distribution within marriage that recognizes the independent agency of men and women within marriage is a prerequisite to a unified model.

B. Medical Decisions

The purpose of this chapter is to examine the ways families make decisions and the ways the law wants them to. Medical decisions provide a particularly good context for this inquiry. The law's view of those decisions is not entirely simple. Briefly, however, it is standard doctrine that parents generally make decisions for their minor children and that adults make decisions for themselves. Legal problems arise, however, in two kinds of circumstances. First, where parents are arguably denying their children necessary medical care and where daughters seek abortions without their parents' knowledge or consent. Second, where adults have become incapacitated and someone must make decisions for them. The first set of circumstances has provoked a large literature that explores not only what rules the law ought to adopt, but what competence children have to make medical decisions for themselves.

It is, however, the second set of circumstances that we particularly want to examine. This set of circumstances raises some basic questions. Who should decide if the patient cannot? What standard for decision should we use? Should we try to encourage patients to make decisions for themselves in advance? We begin our consideration of these issues with an excerpt from an article that looks at the familial social circumstances of the adults likeliest to be unable to make their own decisions about medical care—the elderly. This article examines what its author calls the "social myth" that "old people are alienated from their families, particularly from their children."

Ethel Shanas, *Social Myth as Hypothesis: The Case of the Family Relations of Old People,* 19 GERONTOLOGIST 3 (1979)*

. . . I want now to return to the alienation myth, the belief that older people are alienated from their families, and to consider some of the hypotheses which derive from it. These are: (1) Because of the geographic mobility of population of the U.S. most old people who have children live at great distances from their children; (2) Because of the alienation of old people from their children, most older parents rarely see their children; (3) Because of the predominance of the nuclear family in the U.S., most old people rarely see their siblings or other relatives; and (4) Because of the existence and availability of large human service bureaucracies, families are no longer important as a source of care for older people.

---

*   Reprinted with permission of the Gerontological Society of America, 1030 15th Street, NW, Suite 250, Washington DC 20005. *Social Myth as Hypothesis: The Case of Family Relationships of Old People* (Excerpt), Ethel Shanas, 19 The Gerontologist 3, 1979. Reproduced by permission of the publisher via Copyright Clearance Center, Inc.

These hypotheses all seem reasonable. Everyone knows that Americans move all the time, everyone knows at least one old person whose children all live at the other end of the continent, and everyone knows of a sick old person whose adult children are trying to find a residence for him, or, more usually, her. Despite what everyone knows, each of the above hypotheses has been disproved. In the U.S. most old people with children live close to at least one of their children and see at least one child often. Most old people see their siblings and relatives often, and old people, when either bedfast or housebound because of ill health, are twice as likely to be living at home as to be resident in an institution.

About four of every five noninstitutionalized persons over 65 in the U.S. have living children. The proportion of old people with living children is unchanged over the last 20 years. The proportion of old people with children who live in the same household with one of these children has declined, however, from 36% in 1957 to 18% in 1975. At the same time that the proportion of parents and children living in the same household has declined, there has been a rise in the proportion of old people living within ten minutes' distance of a child. As a result, the proportion of old people with children who either live with one of their children or within ten minutes' distance of a child has remained fairly constant over 20 years: 59% in 1957, 61% in 1962, and 52% in 1975. The findings indicate that while old people no longer live in the same household with a child, they now live next door, down the street, or a few blocks away. Older people and their children both place a value on separate households. Many old people say they want to be independent. Their children in turn stress a desire for privacy. As the economic situation of old people and their children has improved over the last 20 years, it has become possible to implement the desire for independence and privacy of both generations.

Old people who live alone are commonly considered a particularly isolated group among the elderly. Among all old people who live alone, however, half of those with children are within ten minutes distance of a child. Many of these persons stress that they and their children share "intimacy at a distance." It is the childless elderly living alone who are the vulnerable elderly but even they . . . call upon family resources.

Whether old people in the future increasingly will live at greater distances from their children cannot be answered from the data from the years 1957 to 1975. What these data do show is that despite the geographic mobility of the population of the U.S. older people who have children live close to at least one of these children. In 1975, three of every four persons with children either lived in the same household as a child or within a half hours' distance of a child. The first hypothesis, that because of the graphic mobility of the population of the U.S. most old people who have children live at great distances from their children, must therefore be rejected.

Living near adult children is no guarantee that the older parent will see his or her children. In 1975, however, 53% of persons with children, including those with a child in the same household, saw one of their children the day they were interviewed or the day before that. The proportion of older parents who saw at least one child during the week before they were interviewed has remained stable over roughly 20 years: 83% in 1957, 77% in 1975. Perhaps even more important, the proportion of older parents who have not seen at least one of their children for a month or more has remained stable over the 20 year period, at about one in ten. What of old people with children who live alone? About half of these persons had seen at least one child the day they were interviewed or the day before that, and three of every four had seen at least one child during the week before they were interviewed. There has been no decrease in visiting between parents and at least one of their children from the first survey to the last.

Again, the data do not answer all the questions that might be raised about the relationships between older parents and their adult children. . . . What the data do show is that older parents see adult children often. The second hypothesis, that because of the alienation of older parents from their children, most older parents rarely see their children, must also be rejected.

Even though most older people live close to and see at least one of their children often they still may have lost touch with their brothers and sisters or other relatives. The data show otherwise. David Schneider, the anthropologist, in discussing the family life of old people, speaks of the "hour glass effect" in the American kin system. Persons have many contacts with siblings and other relatives in their youth, these contacts shrink in middle life, and increase in later life.

Brothers and sisters, in particular, become important to the older person. The proportion of old persons with siblings was the same in both 1962 and 1975, about eight of every ten. Even when those persons over 75 years of age are considered separately from those under 75, seven of every ten still report surviving brothers and sisters. In 1975 one-third of all old persons with living brothers and sisters saw at least one of these during the week before they were interviewed, and more than half of old people with brothers and sisters saw at least one of these during the month before they were interviewed.

Widowed persons and old persons who have never married are especially dependent on their brothers and sisters. For many widowed persons, siblings assume some of the responsibilities of a now deceased husband or wife. Many persons who have never married live in the same household with a sibling. While about one-third of all persons with siblings had seen a brother or sister the previous week, three-fourths of these who had never married saw a brother or sister during that time.

Old people not only visit with and are visited by siblings, they also visit with other relatives who are not among their direct descendants. In 1975, about three of every ten older persons said that they had seen some relative, who was neither a brother nor a sister, a child nor a grandchild, during the previous week. For the childless elderly this relative often is a niece or nephew who assumes the responsibilities of a child.

The data confirm the findings of many other studies of family and kin in the U.S. The dominant family form for old people in the U.S. is the modified extended family. This family includes not only members of the old person's immediate family and relatives of his own generation such as siblings, it also includes nephews, nieces, and other relatives by blood or marriage. The hypothesis that because of the predominance of the nuclear family in the U.S. older people rarely see their siblings or other relatives is contradicted by the evidence and must be rejected.

Finally, what of that hypothesis that postulates that because of the existence of large human service bureaucracies, families are no longer important as a source of care for older people? Data from a variety of studies are available to test this hypothesis.

Because the health system, of all contemporary bureaucracies, probably impinges most directly on the life of the elderly and their families. I shall discuss some relevant findings about families and the health care of the elderly.

In the 1962 national survey, 2% of the elderly in the community were reported as totally bedfast at home and 6% were reported as housebound. These persons were being taken care of by family members, with some minor assistance from public health nurses and other home aides. That 8% of the elderly bedfast and housebound at home was about twice the proportion of old people in institutions of all kinds whether these were institutions for the well or the sick aged.

Health insurance for the aged, Medicare, became operational in 1966. Medicare, Title XVIII of the Social Security Act, and a companion program of medical assistance, Medicaid, Title XIX, together provide payments for long-term care of the elderly in such health institutions as chronic disease hospitals, extended care facilities, and skilled nursing facilities. Many persons expected that the passage of this legislation would result in a great increase in the number of proportion of the elderly in long-term institutions. Indeed, one of the arguments used by opponents of this legislation was that it would destroy the will of the family to take care of its sick aged.

The 1975 survey, however, indicates no marked change from 1962 in the proportion of the elderly bedfast and housebound at home. Neither is there a marked change in the proportion of the elderly in institutions. In 1975, nine years after Medicare, about 3% of the elderly were bedfast at home and about 7% were housebound. That 10% of old people bedfast and housebound at home, just as in 1962, was almost twice the proportion of old people in institutions of all kinds. There is some indication in both these surveys, however, that the greatly impaired aged are more likely to be in institutions and the less impaired are more likely still to be at home. . . .

The circumstances that bring the elderly to institutions have been carefully studied. The United States General Accounting Office in a study in Cleveland, Ohio focusing on the costs of care concluded that "The importance of family and friends is evidenced by the fact that greatly or extremely impaired elderly who live with their spouses and children generally are not institutionalized, whereas those who live alone usually are." Incidentally, our own research indicates that ill health on the part of the parent is often a cause of older parents and adult children living together.

Elaine Brody, among others, has pointed out that clinical evidence reinforces gerontological research findings that adult children do not "dump" old parents into institutions. In this connection she says: "Studies of the paths leading to institutional care have shown that placing an elderly relative is the last, rather than the first, resort of families. In general, they have exhausted all other alternatives, endured severe personal, social and economic stress in the process, and made the final decision with the utmost reluctance."

The hypothesis that because of the existence of large human service bureaucracies families are no longer important as a source of care for the elderly, like the other hypotheses derived from the alienation myth, must also be rejected.

Shanas seems to bring good news. The elderly are not alienated or even isolated from their families. Furthermore, the empirical evidence is widely understood to indicate that a high proportion of the care elderly people receive comes from their families, not from institutions. But what does this mean? What, for example, happens when adult children assume responsibility for caring for their aging parents? William H. Jarrett argues[1] that Americans tend to see families in terms of two models—the relationship between husbands and wives and that between parents and children. Both these relationships are crucially motivated by affection. Relationships with aging parents are, he argues, generally characterized by intimacy at a distance. When that distance closes and children begin to take daily care of their parents, physical intimacy may grow but emotional intimacy can deteriorate under the strain. Jarrett cites evidence that the closer the degree of kinship between a caretaker and a caregiver, the less well they tend to get along. "Only one-half of the married children in [one] . . . study claimed to get along well with the recipient on a day-to-day basis."

What does this sociological information suggest about the ability of family members to make medical decisions for each other? Many judges assume that they can do so very well. As Justice O'Connor wrote in her concurring opinion in *Cruzan v. Director, Missouri Department of Health,* 497 U.S. 261 (1990):

> Delegating the authority to make medical decisions to a family member or friend is becoming a common method of planning for the future. . . . Several States have recognized the practical wisdom of such a procedure by enacting durable power of attorney statutes that specifically authorize an individual to appoint a surrogate to make medical treatment decisions. . . . Other States allow an individual to designate a proxy to carry out the intent of a living will. . . . [A]s patients are likely to select a family member as a surrogate, . . . giving effect to a proxy's decisions may also protect the "freedom of personal choice in matters of . . . family life."

In addition, a number of states have adopted legislation which designates family members to make decisions for incompetent patients. Further, dissenters in *Cruzan* believed that as a matter of constitutional law "a State generally must either repose the choice with the person whom the patient himself would most likely have chosen as proxy or leave the decision to the patient's family." As Justice Brennan wrote:

---

[1] *Caregiving Within Kinship Systems: Is Affection Really Necessary?*, 25 GERON-TOLOGIST 5 (1985).

The testimony of close friends and family members, on the other hand, may often be the best evidence available of what the patient's choice would be. It is they with whom the patient most likely will have discussed such questions and they who know the patient best. "Family members have a unique knowledge of the patient which is vital to any decision on his or her behalf."[2]

These legal views reflect what the elderly seem to want. Dallas M. High reports that 90% of the elderly people he interviewed wanted family members to make medical decisions for them when they could not do so themselves.[3] (Most of the other 10 percent did not have close family.) One study explores this preference in some detail:

Dallas M. High & Howard B. Turner, *Surrogate Decision-Making: The Elderly's Familial Expectations,* 8 THEORETICAL MEDICINE 303, 307-311 (1987)[*]

4.   CHARACTERISTICS OF THE ELDERLY'S EXPECTATIONS

In our study, 34 of the 36 respondents who had immediate family (defined as spouse, child or sibling) expressed a preference for family surrogates in the event of decisional incapacity. It is not surprising to learn that virtually all elderly persons expect surrogate health care decision-making to be carried out by family members. This parallels a substantial body of literature showing that older people expect to turn to family members during crises and coincides with a recent multiple-choice questionaire study of patient's attitudes on decisions about life-sustaining treatment. The present open-ended interview study afforded opportunity to investigate the characteristics and reasons for familial surrogate expectations. . . .

4.1. *Priority of Surrogates*

"Well of course, the first would be my spouse—my wife," responded a 73-year-old married man when asked who would make health care decisions for him if he was unable to make them. "And then if it came to the point that she was unable . . . , or if she did not survive me, then I would say my daughter." This response is typical, as was that of a 68-year-old married woman who said, "Well, of course, first it would be my husband who would be making them should he be well." There appears to be a clearly defined order of preference for surrogates. For most married older people, an able

---

[2]   497 U.S. 325 (1990) (citing Steven A. Newman, *Treatment Refusals for the Critically and Terminally Ill: Proposed Rules for the Family, the Physician, and the State,* 3 NYLS HUMAN RIGHTS ANNUAL 35, 46 (1985)).

[3]   *Standards for Surrogate Decision Making: What the Elderly Want,* 17 J. LONG-TERM ADMINISTRATION 8 (1989).

[*]   Copyright © 1987 by D. Reidel Publishing Co. Reprinted with *kind* permission from Kluwer Academic Publishers.

spouse reasonably and naturally tops this stratification scheme; however, some prefer that adult children be included along with their spouse. "My three daughters and wife. They all would have a hand in it," relates an 86-year-old married man.

Widowed or divorced elderly who have children clearly would rely on and/or expect adult children to become surrogate decision-makers whenever necessary. Married persons who have not already included their children in the decision-making view them as back-up personnel to spouses. The elderly's most common reasoning for having children make their decisions—a presumption of what one can and/or should expect from adult offspring—is that offspring are the most immediate of relatives, if not the closest blood relative. Bill, a 71-year-old whose wife is in a nursing home because of Alzheimer's disease, chose his daughter (36 years old) even though he has a sister (65 years old) and a brother-in-law living nearby. "My daughter," said Bill, "— she would be the logical one." A 76-year-old widow reflects the common response in greater detail, adding a moral imperative: "I think, really, the way I have lived with my children it would be sort of wrong to appoint somebody besides the family to do these things . . . . I am very firm about that." The choice of children for surrogate decision-making is consistent with the study by Ethel Shanas who found that older widowed women most often turned to their children for care and support.

It is very clear that children are expected to be more deeply involved than siblings and other relatives. . . . [F]riends, doctors and lawyers are on the periphery of the circle of expected decisional surrogates.

4.2 *Tacit Understandings*

Even though the elderly are quite clear about whom they expect to make surrogate decisions, often such matters have not been discussed among the principals. Nevertheless, the elderly believe they and their expected surrogates have tacit understandings about surrogate responsibility and appropriate decisions. Typical of the comments are: "It's just one of those things that's a general understanding, of course, between the spouse and myself . . . ." And those who have talked with potential surrogate decision-makers about how they would like to be cared for in the event of incapacity, often described their conversations with important qualifiers such as "only casually," "only indirectly," "to some extent," or "not in depth". Not surprisingly, only 7 (17%) of the people we interviewed had either put any instructions in writing or executed an advanced directive such as a living will.

4.3. *Procrastination of Planning*

Putting off tasks until a later time is probably most prevalent when one thinks that there is plenty of time or perceives the task to be unpleasant. This is probably no less true for the elderly. Anyone who enjoys relatively good health, as most elderly do, is less apt to discuss and plan for difficult matters such as an incapacitating or terminal illness. Twenty-one (52%) of our sample group had not talked to anyone about how they would like to be cared for if they were too sick to participate in the decisions. "It's just one of those things you are prone to put off," relates a 73-year-old married man who has two adult children. "You know, you say, well everything's all right. I'm perfectly capable of making my own decisions, so you don't do anything about it. It's like people with wills. It's the same thing with decision-making on health care." Not only might wills be a victim of things "you are prone to put off," so too are living wills, establishment of powers of attorney, or even holding explicit and direct discussions about prospective health care decisions with one's spouse, adult children, or physician.

4.4. *Geographical Proximity*

The gerontology literature regularly cites geographical proximity of family, especially children, as a central factor in the level of familial support provided to the elderly. For example, Hays points out that family resources, in part, depend on the proximity of kin, while Kivett and Atkinson note that the interaction among older parents and children may be more reliably predicted by proximity than either sex-linkages or parental health. It seems reasonable to infer that familial expectations by the elderly may have a similar association; yet our experiences suggest that geographical proximity is *not* a factor, or at least not a primary one, in the elderly's expressed preferences regarding surrogate decision-making. For example, Jenny, a 71-year-old divorcee is the mother of five adult children, all of whom live 400 or more miles away. She does, however, have a brother (a physician) and a sister who live within an hour of her residence; yet, her preference is for her children to act as her surrogate decision-makers and confidently expects that "[her] own children would get together and decide." It is possible, of course, that Jenny and her peers are merely expressing personal preferences with little hope of their realization, but we do not believe this is the case; rather, given the ease of long-distance communication and travel, older persons realistically rely on family at a geographical distance for important decision-making—especially crisis surrogate decision-making—regarding health care. Such help or assistance is categorically different from providing help with shopping or making minor household repairs. While not wanting to be dependent on family members or to burden them, older persons do expect close kin, especially children, to be called on in the event of a crisis. And the event of becoming dependent on someone else to make a health care decision can reasonably be viewed as a crisis.

4.5. *Group Decision-making*

Jenny, as already mentioned, expects her children to jointly make a surrogate decision. This is not atypical. For as a 75-year-old widow put it, "I would want them [sons] to deal with it together . . . I don't like the idea of one person's decision." Older persons appear to prefer that surrogate decisions involve consultation of more than one member of the family. Twenty-four (60%) of our respondents explicitly indicated that preference. For those that have children but no spouse, the general expectation is that the children will consult one another. Often those with a spouse expect their spouse and children jointly to decide. . . . [W]e found resistance to the idea of appointing a single individual to make surrogate health care decisions, especially if one has close relatives (i.e. spouse and/or children). This desire for group decision-making clearly runs counter to the counsel of the judiciary (e.g. *In re Conroy*) and advice of legal ethicists, and may markedly compound, rather than solve, the problem of physicians having to deal with several family members to reach a consensus.

One reason the elderly want family members to make decisions for them seems to be that they think their families know what they want and will do it. Certainly the legal reliance on family members to make decisions for their incompetent relatives rests on the belief that, as Justice Brennan wrote in his dissent in *Cruzan,* "[i]t is they with whom the patient most likely will have discussed such questions and they who know the patient best. 'Family members have a unique knowledge of the patient which is vital to any decision on his or her behalf.'" This seems eminently logical. But is it true?

A number of studies have attempted to answer this question by asking a set of patients what kind of medical treatment they would want in a set of hypothetical cases and then asking their families what the patients wanted in those cases. The results are not what one might expect. One of these studies[4] reports that "spouses and patients estimated patient functional status and health with a good level of agreement, estimated global quality of life with a moderate level of agreement, and estimated many of the factors affecting quality of life with poor agreement." (Spouses "often considered the patients to be significantly more depressed, more anxious, and with more memory problems than did the patients.")

Another study[5] finds that "although the concordance of family members' predictions achieved statistical significance, the kappas (0.27 and 0.30) did not achieve even the moderate strength of agreement (kappa > 0.4) . . . that should be required of surrogates making life-and-death decisions on behalf of patients under the substituted judgment standard." Family members did do somewhat better than physicians at predicting the patients' preferences, but doctors "did no better than chance alone." When family members and patients disagreed, the family members were more likely to want to provide resuscitation (and doctors were less likely to want to provide it).

How much does it matter that family members seem to know less about what the patient wants than judges and legislators seem to expect? For some patients, perhaps not so much. The study by Dallas High we quoted earlier asked patients whether they wanted their surrogate to make the decision they themselves would have made or the decision that was best for them. The patients split evenly. One of the patients who chose the "best interests" standard worried about placing "too many demands" on a surrogate

---

[4]   Robert A. Pearlman, Richard F. Uhlmann & Nancy S. Jecker, *Spousal Understanding of Patient Quality of Life: Implications for Surrogate Decisions,* 3 J. CLINICAL ETHICS 114 (1992).

[5]   Allison B. Seckler, Diane E. Meier, Michael Mulvihill & Barbara E. Cammer Paris, *Substituted Judgment: How Accurate Are Proxy Predictions?,* 115 ANNALS OF INTERNAL MEDICINE 92 (1991).

because you can't always tell until it [a particular medical condition] comes. I know a person right now who is utterly and totally destroying herself, trying to take care of her mother, because of a statement that was made, "Never take me to a nursing home." It's gonna kill the daughter off.

The cultural conditions under which family members participate in medical decisions may be changing. The following study suggests that increasingly patients are taught a strong duty of independence in making medical decisions.

Carl E. Schneider, *The Practice of Autonomy: Patients, Doctors, and Medical Decisions* (Oxford University Press, 1998)[*]

The logical inference from that duty—one reflected in the behavior of some patients—is that patients should base their decisions on what is best for themselves and that their intimates should do likewise. As one cancer patient put it, "In a contest between one's integrity—doing what's necessary for one's own essential well-being—and love for another, love must lose. This view might not be romantic, but I believe it's morally and psychologically sound."

The strong duty of independence such comments embody finds more formal expression in the work of an influential set of critics of contemporary medicine. They are taken by a number of patients to be counselling the ill to fight off the impositions of their families and consider themselves first. Musa Mayer, for instance, writes of her discovery that many "theorists in the field of holistic health" believe "cancer patients possess certain psychological characteristics that make them particularly vulnerable to the disease. They are the 'nicest' people, the most patient of patients. They do not stand up for themselves, these studies claim, or follow their own dreams, but instead serve the needs of others." Mayer believed that "refocusing on the self, so characteristic of cancer patients—and especially, I would venture to guess, of women who have cancer, because their traditional role as caregivers encourages them in the direction of self-lessness, anyway—has often been referred to in literature as a 'benefit' of the illness." Mayer tried to resist the threats her sense of obligation created for her and felt she had "made real progress. Surely, I was less given to caretaking than I'd been ten years ago." But if caretaking is to be avoided, who is to take care of Mayer?

Jill Ireland, a movie actor and the wife of Charles Bronson, was personally counseled by one of the avatars of this view—O. Carl Simonton. Ireland told Simonton "how for a long time before my illness I had been driving myself, giving priority to duties and other people's problems, putting off the things I really wanted to do, simply not putting aside enough time for the quiet and solitude that I craved." He admonished her, "'I'm telling you you are living a very unhealthful life-style. If you don't change it and start honoring yourself and taking care of your needs, you will die.'" In the same vein, Rachelle Breslow came to understand that "repressing my needs and feelings for so long had caused the kind of cumulative stress that made me vulnerable to disease." As she

> began to listen more and more to my intuition, I realized how little recognition I had given to my own needs, how much I had been living other people's lives and needs while neglecting my own. It had always been so much more important to please others than to please myself. In fact, it was downright mandatory to my well-being that I be needed by others. I had to live for others, no matter what the cost to myself. It took a life-threatening, catastrophic illness to force me to be attentive to my own needs, to go within and to listen to what I was all about.

In short, these patients and their advisers believe families discourage patients from considering their own interests, interfere with patients' ability to make decisions, and exploit patients' concern for the people they love. Patients must be alert to resist these impositions and preserve their independence. It is this understanding of autonomy and of personal relationships that nurtures the view, sometimes found even among physicians, that patients should make decisions uninfluenced by their families. As one doctor (apparently an oncologist) said,

> Generally speaking, we feel the patient should make the decisions. Now, obviously family members should be present and should *hear* the information, but usually I—tend to reject—a family member—making the decisions for the patient. Because, ah, after all, it is still the patient that has to go *through* the treatment, or has to bear the results of, uh, of whatever the problem is. So in a sense, ah, that's very presumptuous on her part, that she should be telling her husband what—should happen, or telling the doctors how to treat her husband. . . . And, ah, you know, in—in pediatrics it's—it's usual for the mother to answer for the child. . . . But in adults, we generally reject that.

So seriously do some doctors take this principle that they make themselves guardians of patients' autonomy. For example, a doctor and nurse proudly describe their burn unit's practice: "When the diagnosis is confirmed, the physician and other team members enter the room. Family members are not invited into the room to ensure that the decision of the patient is specifically his own."

This suspicion of the family's influence has also marked policy toward intrafamilial kidney donations. The Simmons study reports "a widespread skepticism about the ability of an individual to make the major sacrifice of a kidney willingly and without significant regret later on. The perception is that family blackmail and pressure will be pervasive and will be the major factor motivating the potential donor." Thus, "Katz and Capron . . . have suggested societal policy curtailing the use of related donors in transplantation because of relatives' basic ambivalence and the possibility the donation will have negative psychological effects." Yet the empirical evidence refutes these gloomy suspicions: "[T]he comparison of nondonors and donors shows no difference between the two groups in the proportions who seem to be 'black sheep,' no difference in the percentage subject to undue family pressure, and little difference in underlying self-esteem and happiness." And would it be bad if people felt pressure to donate a kidney to a close relative?

This concern that families threaten patients' autonomy is not confined to medical people. As the Nelsons note, when the family surfaces in the bioethical literature, it may be treated dismissively and distrustfully: "While Buchanan and Brock, for example, point out that 'the family as an intimate association is one important way in which individuals find or construct meaning in their lives,' they immediately go on to discuss mechanisms for safeguarding the patient from being exploited by his next of kin." When I ask patients who have assimilated the autonomy principle why they should make their own medical decisions, I am usually told, "Because it's my body." I am struck by how often this discourages them from consulting their friends or family.

Even strong versions of the autonomy principle recognize a moral obligation that might reduce the distance between patients and their intimates—the obligation to communicate. Today self-expression supplants stoicism as a moral good. Patients have a duty to themselves to speak freely. They have a duty to their families to explain their situations and their feelings. And they have a duty to other members of the "'brotherhood of those who bear the mark of pain,'" a duty "not just to work out their own changing identities, but also to guide others who will follow them. They seek not to provide a map that can guide others—each must create his own—but rather to witness the experience of reconstructing one's own map. Witnessing is one duty to the commonsensical and to others."

One might expect this duty to communicate to counteract the tendencies that distance patients from friends and family. It is unclear if it does, but some clues may be found by examining patients' support groups. These loom ever larger in patients' lives, and many of the ill—like many of the well—value them. They provide medical information, sympathy, and the assurance that one's experiences are not unique. Significantly, however, they intrude little on patients' independence. Robert Wuthnow, a leading student of support groups, finds they reflect an ethic that resembles the ethic undergirding the moral argument for mandatory autonomy. That ethic "suggests that we are ultimately responsible to pursue our self-interest and that each person, independently of others, must decide how best to do that. . . . It says that people should figure out their own lives, make their own choices, and suffer their own mistakes." This duty has practical as well as normative bases: "Because each individual's experience and situation is unique, there can be no right or wrong interpretations." Thus most such groups, Wuthnow found, have "explicit rules against members giving each other advice in the context of the group. Even telling a story about one's own experiences that is too obviously geared toward providing someone else in the group with a hint about what to do is frowned upon." Wuthnow believes the "secret of the small-group movement's success is thus that it provides some sense of caring and community but does so without greatly curtailing the freedom of its members." . . .

Just as patients owe themselves a duty of independence that distances them from their intimates, intimates owe themselves a duty of independence that distances them from patients. Intimates are entitled to lives of their own, to seek the same psychological health and personal fulfillment, the same freedom from hampering commitments, that patients are entitled—perhaps obliged—to seek. Observe, for instance, the sympathy a patient with metastatic melanoma expresses for his wife:

> Lynne couldn't handle the total uncertainty of what was going on . . . . I tried to be as understanding and gentle with her as I could, but it was getting more and more difficult every day. She finally broke down and told me that she was sick of it, couldn't handle it, and didn't want to hear about it anymore. In fact she implied that if the spots kept appearing, indicating to her that I would die soon, she would have to leave because she was not prepared to deal with that. . . . I not only understood what she was saying and why, but I appreciated her leveling with me.

This patient's wife was as entitled as he to find happiness, and if that led her away from him, there she should go. She had met the obligation of her relationship, since she had communicated honestly with him. As one student of contemporary culture says, "[O]ne can love most fully by deepening the honesty and communication in a relationship, even if the relationship ends as a consequence."

CHAPTER IV

A Way to Hell: Violence Within the Family

This chapter deals with the worst aspect of family life: violence in the household against spouses, partners, and children. Domestic violence is a peculiarly difficult subject, not only because of the pain that necessarily accompanies its consideration, but also because it presents hard questions of law, history, and social science. One relatively recent discussion of family violence observes, for example, that while "acts of violence and willful neglect have been occurring as long as there have been human families," it is also true that family violence has been a subject of social science research only since the early 1960s. Lloyd Ohlin & Michael Tonry, *Family Violence in Perspective, in* FAMILY VIOLENCE 1 (Lloyd Ohlin & Michael Tonry, eds. 1989).

The definition of family violence is itself sharply contested. It may be true that acts of violence and willful neglect have always occurred in human families. But does that mean that there are kinds of conduct that everyone, everywhere has always regarded as violence or neglect, or does it mean that kinds of conduct we now regard as violent and neglectful have always occurred but, in other times and places, were and are tolerated?

Even now, when we talk about family violence, that conversation often proceeds from very different definitions. While social science has entered the field in force, there are no agreed conventions for deciding what counts as violence. Some studies and authorities limit the category to accomplished or threatened physical and sexual assault; others include emotional injury, physical or emotional neglect, or (in the case of children) educational or moral neglect. Differences in the definition of neglect have much to do with substantial differences in the reported incidence of neglect and its distribution by gender.

It is tempting to regard the lack of clarity in definitions of family violence as itself demonstrating a lack of social concern with conduct of this kind. That conclusion, however, assumes that deviant conduct within the family has some universal meaning. This assumption overlooks a variety of contingencies in our understanding of crime and wrongdoing.

Some of these contingencies are associated with the meaning of legal terms. Killing is an act; murder is more than that. To call a killing "murder" may require judgments about the subjective mental state of the actor, the existence of such provocation as would lead an ordinary person to kill, the degree of dangerousness involved in the activity leading to death, and a variety of other circumstances. Crucial elements, such as what will provoke an ordinary person to lose control or what is a "reasonable" risk, may vary from place to place and time to time.

Moreover, the meaning given by courts is not the only aspect of contingency. An event occurring in real life must first be discovered, and the observer or victim must decide to bring the matter to official attention. Those who study police behavior report that "the moral standards of the citizenry have more to do with the definition of juvenile deviance than do the standards of policemen on patrol." Donald Black & Albert Reiss, *Police Control of Juveniles,* 35 AM. SOC. REV. 63, 66 (1970). That is true for adult deviance and especially for domestic deviance. Conduct between spouses rarely occurs on the streets, and official notice depends heavily on whether the victims so identify themselves or are so badly injured as to require medical treatment, on how seriously they regard the conduct they encounter, and on whether they wish to become involved in the formal processing of a complaint. Thus, the definition of spousal deviance is largely in the control of wives and husbands. And, by the same token, the definition of child abuse is largely in the control of neighbors and school personnel.

A. Spouse Abuse

The first reading reviews much of the current research on spousal violence. In doing so, Fagan and Browne examine the data and controversies concerning the definition, measurement, and explanation of this phenomenon. How, for example, does one define spousal violence? Are all acts of aggression—including threats or psychological imposition—acts of violence? Is an intent to injure required? Does it matter whether a spouse or partner initiates a violent encounter or engages in responsive violence? For what purposes might we choose one or another definition?

These definitions have something to do with the often very different reported rates of domestic violence, and the often very different estimates of the relative frequency of violence by women and men. How does one compare and assess varying reports the claim, on the one hand, that the incidence of spousal violence by men and women is about equal and, on the other hand, that women are far more likely to be assaulted by men than the converse? Other questions, about which reports vary, concern the characteristics of those who engage in, and those who are subject to, domestic violence.

Jeffrey Fagan & Angela Browne, *Violence Between Spouses and Intimates: Physical Aggression Between Women and Men in Intimate Relationships,* **in 3** UNDERSTANDING AND PREVENTING VIOLENCE **115 (Albert J. Reiss, Jr. & Jeffrey A. Roth, eds. 1994)**[*]

INTRODUCTION

In the 1960s, Americans began to ask important questions about violence. The National Commission on the Causes and Prevention of Violence, known as the Kerner Commission, concluded in 1969 that the United States was the world's leader in rates of homicide, assault, rape, and robbery. To most people, crime in general and violent crime in particular became major sources of discontent. However, this early concern with criminal victimization focused primarily on violent incidents outside the home. Like the commission, most Americans believed that the risk of personal attack or injury lay in individuals beyond one's circle of intimates. Violence in the family—if recognized at all—was rarely considered criminal unless a death occurred. The average family, it was assumed, afforded at least some measure of nurturance and protection to its members. Twenty years later, we are now aware of the extent of violence between family members in our society and the seriousness of that violence in terms of physical and nonphysical injury.

---

    *   Reprinted with permission from Understanding and Preventing Violence. Copyright 1994 by the National Academy of Sciences. Courtesy of the National Academy Press, Washington D.C.

In the past two decades, there has been an upsurge of inquiry into violence between intimates. The growth of social services in the 1960s, designed primarily to wrestle with extramarital social problems such as stranger crime or substance abuse, not only focused public policy on the economic behavior of families but also opened up the family as a social institution amenable to public scrutiny. Accordingly, family social interactions became increasingly subject to social interventions and legal sanctions. Until public policy focused attention on the private realm of family life, few people considered the home to be other than "a compassionate, egalitarian, peaceful affair in which violence played no part."

Three major trends in this era raised doubts about this tranquil view of American family life. First, the "discovery" of child abuse through medical and sociological research in the mid-1960s focused public attention on family violence. . . .

Second, political activism by feminist organizations at that time helped make visible the use of physical force as a means of intimidation or coercion within the family and elevated it to prominence as a social concern. Much of this awareness was engendered by the modern women's movement which, in the 1960s, began to examine violence against women around the issue of rape. Such discussion revealed the prevalence of women experiencing sexual assaults by intimate male partners, rather than strangers, and provided a forum for the identification of the physical assault of wives as a problem of previously unrecognized national proportions. . . .

Third, the emphasis on victimization in criminal justice research and practice in the 1970s identified family violence as an important and complex phenomenon confronting the police and courts. During the 1970s, sweeping legal and police policy changes were instituted in response to public concern and social science investigations. Victim support was an important component of political activism that sought to reorient legal institutions toward fulfilling the entitlement of the rights of victims. Feminist groups decried the secondary victimization of "special victims," including victims of rape and wife abuse.

Research on marital violence in the United States has now spanned nearly three decades. National surveys estimate that an act of physical violence is committed by a family member in nearly half of all homes during an average 12-month period in the United States. Minimum estimates from these surveys indicate that acts of physical aggression between spouses occur in one of six homes each year. Injuries and lethal injuries from partner violence fall disproportionately on women. A minimum of two million women are severely assaulted annually by their male partners and more than half the women murdered in the United States are killed by male partners or ex-partners. Rosenberg et al. (1984) estimated that more than 20,000 hospitalizations occur each year due to acts of violence in the home. These estimates have remained remarkably consistent over time, even in the face of increased awareness and intervention. . . .

MARITAL VIOLENCE DEFINED

In this paper, the discussion of research and policy on violence between intimate adult partners includes physical assault, sexual assault, and homicide, committed, threatened, or attempted by spouses, ex-spouses, common-law spouses, or cohabitants toward their partners. We also note other harmful behaviors that occur as part of the natural history of marital violence: psychological abuse, economic deprivation, threats to others in the family, and threats as a method of coercion. These behaviors co-occur with physical assault, and although we do not focus on them specifically, they are part of the "ecology of aggression" that characterizes marital violence. They may also constitute antecedents of physical aggression, part of the maintenance of a pattern of marital violence, or displacements of aggression when assaults desist.

Definitions in the study of violence between intimates have varied extensively. Bandura defined aggression as behavior that results in personal injury or property destruction. Bandura's definition is consistent with the definition of family violence offered by Gelles and Straus as "an act carried out with the intention of, or perceived intention of, physically hurting another person." Gelles and Straus distinguished violence from aggression, which includes any malevolent action, regardless of whether physical harm is involved. However, they excluded verbal aggression, marital rape, and sexual assaults from their definition of family violence.

Collins, focusing exclusively on violent behaviors, defines violence as an actual or attempted physical attack and terms this "expressive interpersonal violence." Such broad conceptual definitions require careful attention to the operational definitions and attendant measures in the studies reviewed. For example, although Straus and Gelles define violence as actions undertaken with the intent or perceived intent to harm, their measure assesses neither intent nor perceptions.

In this paper, we are concerned with aggression between adults in families or intimate cohabitating relationships that reflects the intent to harm or to create a painful condition. These behaviors include attempted or completed physical assaults, homicides, and sexual assaults. We are also concerned with property destruction that is intended to harm the partner and with the threat of force. . . .

EVOLUTION OF KNOWLEDGE AND POLICY
ON MARITAL VIOLENCE

The new social knowledge of violence between adult partners developed during an era in which social intervention in family life had gained widespread support and created a context for defining marital violence as an urgent social problem. The ensuing social and political processes shaped both the knowledge of marital violence and policy responses. The nature of the problem and its etiological roots were subjected to varying interpretations and definitions. As would be expected, definitions, research traditions, and policy development all varied according to the interests and perspectives of the definers. Thus, the perspectives that were influential in the development of knowledge and policy responses to marital violence reflect differing assumptions regarding its definition and etiology, as well as concerns with the "ownership" of marital violence as a social problem.

Cross-Cultural Perspectives

Marital violence is intrinsic to many cultures. Levinson using cross-cultural data on family violence from the Human Relations Area Files (HRAF) data base identified eight varieties of marital violence in 330 societies. Levinson (1988,1989) estimated the prevalence of wife beating in a representative sample of 90 societies from the 330 cultural groups in the HRAF data base. Wife beating occurred in 84.5 percent of the 90 cultures. It occurred "at least occasionally" in all or nearly all households in 18.8 percent of the societies, and in a majority (but not all) in 29.9 percent. Husband beating was reported in 6 percent of all societies; it was rare or unheard of in 73.1 percent and occurred in a minority of households in 20.2 percent. Other studies (cited in Levinson, 1989) report comparable data: Wife beating occurs in 71 to 92 percent of the societies studied.

Motivations for wife beating in these societies included sexual jealousy or infidelity (45.5%), insubordination or disobedience by the wife (25.5%), and the wife's failure to meet "household responsibilities" (23.3%). Societal responses to wife beating varied extensively. In 91.2 percent of the societies, intervention by outsiders occurred. These interventions included help or intercession by kin or neighbors (17.6%), shelter for the wife (14.7%), legal intervention (17.6%), marital violence as grounds for divorce 11.8%), and supernatural sanctions (e.g., casting a spell) in an unspecified proportion. In 29.4 percent of the societies, interventions are limited to beatings that exceed societal norms for the "physical discipline" of wives. Interventions were reportedly unavailable in 8.8 percent of the societies. The study gave no indication of the legal status of wife or husband assaults in the societies studied.

Such comparative studies are complicated by several methodological and design issues. Family configurations and kinship networks vary extensively across societies, and the meaning of family and the nature of marital bonds are obviously culture specific. Consensus on a universal definition of family violence is no more evident in cross-cultural research than in contemporary research in the United States. Variations in injury, motivation, and context are consistent with variations in the social organization of these societies, the meanings attached to marital violence and the unique family configurations. . . .

EMERGENCE OF MARITAL VIOLENCE AS A POLICY ISSUE

. . . As marital violence became a public issue, the criminal justice system was obliged to respond in new ways. Traditionally, marital violence was perceived as an ever-present and perhaps intractable problem, creating dangerous situations for the police and difficult-to-resolve cases for the courts. Early writings on police responses to family violence were critical, citing their refusal to get involved in family disputes, their avoidance of arrest and other criminal sanctions and their inappropriate use of nonlegal remedies such as mediation. Police viewed family disturbance calls as dangerous to responding officers, and otherwise viewed family disturbances as problematic and intractable interpersonal conflicts that were inappropriate for police attention.

Prior to the early 1970s, many police departments actually had "hands-off" policies. Police training manuals clearly specified that, in responding to domestic disputes, arrest was to be avoided whenever possible. When arrests were made, they often were classified as misdemeanors, which typed them as less serious from the outset. A wife usually could not obtain a restraining order against a violent husband unless she were willing to file for divorce at the same time. Orders of protection were typically not available on an emergency basis and often carried no provisions for enforcement or penalties for violation. In some states, a single assault was not considered sufficient grounds for a divorce action, and until the mid-1970s, women who eventually killed their mates to protect themselves or their children from harm or death found the traditional plea of self-defense unavailable.

The new social knowledge of family violence led to recognition that domestic disputes were a major problem facing law enforcement and that specific solutions needed to be framed within a legal context. Political activity by feminists exerted pressure on the criminal justice system to fulfill its mandate to treat violence toward women as a serious crime. In addition to changes in protection orders, law reform efforts also focused on statutory changes to permit or mandate arrests without corroboration in wife assault cases.

By 1980, 47 states had passed some type of domestic violence legislation. The emphasis of this legislation was on enforcing victims' rights, increasing their legal options, and protecting victims and those near them from further assault. Substantive criminal law was also challenged to recognize a history of abuse and threat as part of a legal defense in marital homicides by women in cases in which the male was not actively threatening or abusing his wife at the time of the incident. . . .

CONTROVERSIES IN DEFINITION, MEASUREMENT, AND EXPLANATION

Once marital violence rose to the status of a "social problem," several definitions emerged that varied according to the interests and perspectives of the definer. These definitions varied on several dimensions: the victim-offender relationship, the type of abusive or violent behavior, the nature of harm or injury to the victim, and the motivation or situational context of violent events. Explanatory models of marital violence also varied, particularly in the level of explanation or the locus of etiological factors. . . .

Partly because of the early influences of the medical community (child abuse) and the criminal justice system (wife abuse) disagreements arose over the importance of physical *injury* in the definition of marital violence. The importance of emotional maltreatment, and harassment, and persistent denigration or the accrual of harm from isolated and relatively inconsequential acts that nevertheless occurred in regular episodes became the subject of debate, because little or no physical injury resulted. Although important to the well-being of victims, definitions that included these dimensions were considered to have little relevance to the codified behaviors of concern to the criminal court. Instead, criminal justice policy and research relied on definitions that stressed codified behavior to inform legal policy or response. . . .

The *context* of marital violence also was the focus of disagreement in definition and research methods. Like nonphysical injuries, it was considered irrelevant to legal decision making or to epidemiological measurement. Nevertheless, because of the complex family dynamics in marital violence and its recurrent pattern in families, aggression within families is difficult to understand in isolation from the context in which it occurs. . . .

The uneven application of these methods in spouse abuse became a source of controversy and confusion about the parameters of marital violence. The Conflict Tactics Scales became the most consistent instrument for assessing the types of violence that occur between couples and their frequency. It typifies approaches that separate the context from the assaultive acts, as well as the injuries sustained, and has become the baseline for providing epidemiological estimates and comparisons across samples (see discussion in following section). The controversy surrounding the CTS symbolized the debate over how to conceptualize, define, measure, and explain violence between spouses.

For example, prevalence rates of violence by males and females were similar, yet the frequency of both general and serious violence was higher for men whereas the prevalence rate of injury was substantially higher for women. Estimates of violence also changed when the "seriousness" of an act was arbitrarily determined apart from situational factors such as the relative strength or size of the participants, the repetition of assaultive acts during an incident, the threats and menace that accompanied physical actions, or the injuries incurred.

Accordingly, conclusions about the severity of marital violence or its explanations were fundamentally different for researchers using context-specific approaches versus cross-sectional surveys. . . . Even so, context was rarely viewed as a separate dimension of marital violence, often for reasons as simple as the difficulty of measuring it.
. . .

SOCIAL EPIDEMIOLOGY OF MARITAL VIOLENCE. . .

Participation and Frequency of Marital Violence

The two primary sources of epidemiological data on marital violence—the National Family Violence Surveys and the National Crime Survey—are based on nationwide probability samples of households. In each method brief interviews with respondents are completed. Beyond that, there are fundamental differences in their methodologies that heavily influence their results. Nevertheless, these two efforts have provided baseline knowledge about national trends in family violence for nearly two decades. Our discussion of the distribution of marital violence examines primarily dimensions of participation (the prevalence rate). Yet research on criminal careers has shown that the correlates differ for the various dimensions of criminality: participation, frequency, and seriousness. Accordingly, we also examine these other dimensions of marital violence to better understand its distribution and complexity.

Surveys of Violence in the Home: National and Local Studies . . . .

The first general population study of family violence in the United States was the 1975 National Family Violence Survey (NFVS), based on interviews with a probability sample of 2,143 intact couples in households. Straus (1978) and Straus et al. (1980) reported that 16 percent of all marital couples experienced physical aggression during the year before the survey; 28 percent had experienced physical aggression at some point in their relationship. Among those reporting at least one act of violence in the past year, more than one in three involved acts such as punching, kicking, hitting with an object, beating up, and assaults with a gun or knife. These items formed the "severe violence" scale (or what Straus initially termed "wife beating"). Straus and his colleagues reported that 3.8 percent of female respondents and 4.6 percent of males were victims of at least one of these acts of "severe violence." (Unfortunately, only one spouse per couple was included in each sampled family, so comparisons of violence were based on aggregate rates of unrelated males and females.) Questions on rape or other forms of sexual aggressive acts were not included in the 1975 study but were included in the 1985 survey.

The NFVS used the Conflict Tactics Scales (Straus, 1978, 1979)—items that operationalized tactics used by couples to settle conflicts into specific acts. Rational, verbal, and physically aggressive acts were included in the scale. Aggressive acts included eight items, ranging in severity from throwing objects to using a gun or knife. An additional item on "choking" was included in the 1985 survey and two later waves with the 1985 panel. Threats of violence were considered nonviolent acts. Respondents reported whether and how often they had engaged in each of the CTS behaviors during the past year. They also reported whether each behavior had ever happened during their lifetime. Straus et al. (1980) reported "violence participation" rates for both members of the couple. . . .

National Probability Samples. Among the national probability samples, participation rates for overall violence (number of persons per 1,000 population) are consistent for the 1975 and 1985 National Family Violence Surveys. Straus and colleagues report a decrease in male participation in wife assault from 121 to 110 per 1,000 males from the 1975 to the 1985 surveys, and a slight increase in female participation in husband assault from 110 to 120 per 1,000 females. . . .

TABLE 1 Past Year Prevalence Rates of Violence Among Intimates
(per 1,000 population)[a]

Study	Sample(N)	Husband or Male Partner	Wife or Female Partner
1. National Probability Samples			
Straus and Gelles (1990)	6,002	116	124
Straus et al. (1980)	2,143 couples	121	116
Straus and Gelles (1986)	3,520 couples	110	120
Elliot et al. (1985)	1,725 (ages 18-24)	368	471
2. Local or Statewide Probability Samples			
Schulman (1979)	1,793 Kentucky women	100	–
Russell (1982)	644 San Francisco women[b]	260	–
Kennedy and Dutton (1987)	708	112	–
Nisonoff and Bitman (1979)	297 household sample	160	110
M.D. Smith (1986)[c]	315	206	–
M.D. Smith (1987)	604 Toronto women	144	–

TABLE 1 *(Continued)*
(per 1,000 population)[a]

Any Violence by Study	Sample(N)	Husband or Male Partner	Wife or Female Partner
3. Nonprobablity Local Samples			
Rouse (1984)	120 men	108	–
Makepeace (1983)[d]	244 dating couples, college students	137	93
Brutz and Ingoldsby (1984)	288 Quakers	146	152
Dutton (1986a)	75 batterers	183	–
Makepeace (1981)[c]	2338 students and dating couples	206	120
Meredith et al. (1986)	304	220	180
O'Leary and Arias (1988)	393 dating couples	340	420
Szinovacz (1983)	103	260	300
Clarke (1987)	318 women	274	102
Lockhart (1987)	307 blacks and whites	355	–
Barling et al. (1987)[d]	187	740	730
Frieze et al. (1980)	137 Pennsylvania women ever married and comparison group	340	270
Levinger (1966)	600 divorce filings	370	–
Mason and Blankenship (1987)	155 Michigan undergraduates	18	22

[a]   Rates are for acts occurring during the previous 12 months.
[b]   Currently or ever married at time of interview.
[c]   Rates only for life time prevalence.
[d]   Study did not report whether rates are for the previous year or lifetime.

SOURCES: Straus and Gelles (1990); Frieze and Browne (1989); Ellis (1989).

When CTS measures are used in face-to-face interviews with a younger sample, the prevalence rates increase substantially. Elliott et al. reported rates among a national probability sample of 1,725 young adults (ages 18-24) in 1983 that were more than three times higher than the rates obtained by Straus and colleagues in any of the iterations of the NFVS. These data were obtained from the National Youth Survey (NYS), a panel study of a national probability sample of youths in which data are obtained through in-person interviews. In the sixth wave, conducted in 1983, Elliott et al. (1985) found higher rates for violence by women than by men, for both general and serious violence, whereas Straus and colleagues found few differences by gender for either type of violence.

Yet when the 1985 NFVS rates are calculated for the 18-24 age group, the results still show important differences in prevalence estimates for the NFVS and NYS data sets. . . .

. . . [S]tudy design and methods [heavily influence] prevalence estimates. Prevalence rates were higher for respondents ages 18 to 24 in the 1985 NFVS than for the total NFVS samples (1975 and 1985). This is consistent with the high participation rates in stranger violence for general populations in this age range. In fact, Straus et al. (1980) reports the highest violence rates for families in which the respondent is under 30 years old, nearly three times the rate for those between 31 and 50 years of age. . . .

State and Local Probability Samples. [There is also] wide variation in prevalence estimates of marital violence among local probability samples. Prevalence estimates of marital violence vary from 100 to 260 per 1,000 respondents for husbands or male partners. The rates again reflect differences in study design and methodology. For example, a 1979 telephone survey with 1793 women in Kentucky found that 21 percent of the respondents had been physically attacked at least once and that 4.1 percent. were victims of severe violence, consistent with the Straus et al. reports. Similar results were obtained by Kennedy and Dutton for a Canadian sample of males and females. However, Russell's interviews with a random sample of San Francisco women who reported that they were or had been married yielded past year prevalence estimates more than two times higher than Schulman's estimates. Yet the lifetime prevalence estimates (26%) were comparable to both the Schulman and the Straus et al. estimates. Again, especially for past year prevalence estimates, face-to-face interviews seem to result in higher prevalence estimates than telephone interviews. . . .

Estimates Of Severe Violence. Among both probability and convenience samples, base rates of severe violence are lower than the rates of general violence, but differences across studies again reflect research design characteristics. Straus and Gelles (1990) report that rates of severe violence varied across several studies, from 8 to 102 per 1,000 men and from 25 to 59 per 1,000 women. Participation in severe violence by males was far higher in the Kentucky telephone survey of women than comparable reports in the NFVS data: 87 per 1,000 respondents.

Prevalence estimates decrease when both males and females report on male-to-female violence: 34 per 1,000 women in the Straus et al. (1980) study and 23 per 1,000 women in a Canadian sample were victims of severe violence, compared to the rates obtained by [others]. This trend suggests that although males and females may agree on the prevalence of marital violence, they rate its severity differently. Reports by women of rates of severe violence by males in dating, cohabitating, or engaged couples were also far higher than in studies with probability samples of only intact or married couples. . . .

Severe Marital Violence. There were fewer distinct patterns found for participation in serious marital violence and no significant differences in offending rates by sex or demographic group. Participation rates were slightly (and significantly) higher for African American males. Although males and females reported significant differences by age group, the patterns differed: females reported the highest participation for younger males (ages 18-25), but males between ages 26 and 35 reported higher participation rates. Once again, female reports of base rates of participation were higher for all age groups. There were no differences by family income.

There were significant differences by marital status for female reports but not males: serious violence by males (as reported by females) was most prevalent among married couples. Serious violence also was more prevalent among couples in shorter marriages, and significant differences were reported by males and females. Female reports showed higher base rates. According to females, serious marital violence was more prevalent in central-city households and least prevalent in rural areas. Males reported no significant difference by area size. Participation rates in serious violence were lowest (according to females) in couples where the woman had higher educational attainment. Males reported no differences and lower base rates.

There were no significant differences in the prevalence of serious marital violence in couples where the female partner was pregnant. . . .

Continuity, Discontinuity, and Desistance in Marital Violence. There is some evidence that careers in marital violence follow patterns similar to careers in stranger violence or property crime, with discernible patterns of initiation, escalation, continuity (or persistence) and then desistance. For example, marital homicide seems to follow an age distribution similar to robbery, peaking between 18 and 24 years of age. Straus et al. also found similar age peaks, with participation rates nearly three times greater among persons between 18 and 25 years of age than older persons. There also is evidence that marital violence escalates in frequency and severity over time. . . .

Whether there is a continuity of marital violence over multi-year periods may vary by research design and samples. Feld and Straus used panel data from the 1985 NFVS and a second wave in 1986 to determine whether marital violence is stable across a two-year period. They found that among 380 male and female respondents, patterns of desistance and continuity varied by severity of violence in the first year. More than half (53%) continued their participation in severe violence, 10 percent reduced the severity of their violence to minor, and 33 percent reported no violence during the second year. Minor assaults in year 1 by either spouse were associated with more serious assaults over year 2, suggesting patterns of escalation.

Recidivism studies also illustrate the discontinuity, either lasting or temporary, that may result from interventions. Sherman and Berk found a six-month desistance rate after police intervention of 81.2 percent from official records (new complaints) and 71.1 percent from victim reports. Dunford et al. (82.6%) and Hirschel et al. (76.5%) found similar desistance rates in experiments involving police intervention. Using victim reports, Fagan et al. reported a six-month desistance rate of 72 percent for women who had sought help from several types of intervention, and 90 percent among those whose cases proceeded to criminal prosecution. When injury was used as the recidivism criterion, the six-month desistance rate was 94 percent.

There are several limitations to these analyses. The brevity of the study periods (six months to two years) may not capture the developmental patterns of marital violence that seem to unfold over far longer periods and may overestimate desistance. For example, in desistance studies, marital violence was continuous or escalating over periods lasting 3 to 15 years. Also, males who are serial assailants, who move to commit assaults in one marriage after another, are not captured in either the household surveys or the criminal justice experiments. These men in particular are likely to minimize or deny their marital violence in interviews. . . .

Official Records.

Prior to the first victimization or household surveys, research on family violence relied on official data drawn from the criminal justice, mental health, social work, and clinical records of both public and private agencies. These sources of official data remain unreconciled and marked by discrepancies, due to their focus on different aspects of the problem. . . .

For severe marital violence against females, both police calls and emergency rooms provide some indicators of its incidence. Stark et at. found that few cases of marital violence treated in an emergency room were reported to police. Nevertheless, they estimated that 22.5 percent of all injuries presented by woman to an urban hospital emergency ward were caused by a male partner's assault. A later study by Stark et al. (1981) estimated that more than 1.5 million women in the United States seek medical assistance annually for injuries sustained in an assault by a male partner. The same study found very low treatment rates for male victims of female violence.

Although their limitations are well known, criminal justice records may be the most critical source among these, due to the regularity with which they are collected and reported, their wide availability, and the legal proscriptions on reporting categories and practices. However, they also produce biased samples of offenders and offenses, and are especially prone to selective underreporting of assaults and rapes. The few direct comparisons of self-report and official data reveal that official underreporting is most serious for respondents who are the most frequent assailants. Moreover, NCS data are unequivocal on the severe underreporting of marital violence to criminal justice agencies.

In general, criminal justice records are limited in providing accurate estimates of the *epidemiology* of marital violence. They focus on crime events, rather than individuals, and are problematic for developing incidence estimates. Limitations include the willingness of victims to report marital violence to the police, and variations in local arrest policies and documentation procedures. For example, Sherman et al. reported that arrests for marital violence in Milwaukee exceeded 5,000 per year during 1986-1989, but that fewer than 1,000 arrests for marital violence were made in Washington, D.C., a city of comparable size, during the same period. . . .

GENDER DIFFERENCES IN MARITAL VIOLENCE: OFFENDING AND VICTIMIZATION

Although there may be circumstances in which men and women share equal proclivities for aggressive behavior, Maccoby and Jacklin concluded that "there is a sex-linked differential readiness to respond in aggressive ways to the relevant experiences." Eron and Huesmann concluded that male aggression is more prevalent and serious, more stable over time, and attributable to different socialization experiences in our society. Outside the home, it is widely accepted that men are more likely to commit robberies or assaults. . . .

However, there is a lively and contentious debate on gender differences between men and women in physical assaults between spouses or partners. Depending on the data source and the dimension of marital violence, gender differences may point to greater injury risk for women or, conversely, higher "violence" rates for men. The two perspectives are not easily reconciled, and the disparity goes to the heart of definitional and philosophical debates in the study of family violence. Moreover, perceptions of the relative violence rates for men and women may reflect different parameters of criminal careers that are used to weigh the evidence.

Both victimization data and intervention reports suggest that more women are victimized than men. NCS data suggest that women are victimized more often by male spouses or ex-spouses than strangers, and also by the broader group of "intimates." NCS data also show that injuries sustained by women from marital violence were more frequent, more serious, and more often required medical care. Stets and Straus showed that more women than men are injured from marital assault in the home and are also injured more often. Homicide data shows that more women than men are victims of marital homicide. From the earliest origins of family violence intervention programs, women victims sought services and protection more often than men. However, these programs often directed their outreach to women, were staffed by women, oriented their services toward women, and in residential programs, could only accommodate women.

However, self-reports reveal a different and more complex pattern. Gender specific participation rates for marital violence are 10 percent in both the 1975 NFVS data and the 1985 resurvey. The participation rates of reported wife-to-husband assaults were slightly higher than husband-to-wife assault rates when data were aggregated over the two surveys, but the prevalence of severe assaults was slightly higher for males. . . . Adjusting the rates for assaults that produced injuries showed marked gender differences; however, males inflicted injury-assaults at a rate of 3.5 per 1,000, compared to 0.6 per 1,000 for women. These reports correspond more closely to the NCS rates. . . .

Methodological Problems in Interpreting Gender Differences and Mutuality.

The question of "mutual combat" goes to the heart of the debate on gender differences in marital violence. Stets and Straus, using 1985 NFVS data, show that for 49 percent of the 825 respondents who experienced one or more assaults during the past year, both parties engaged in assaultive behaviors. Similar rates were obtained in the 1975 NFVS. Despite the comparable rates of assaultive behaviors between men and women in the two NFVS data sets, it is misleading to characterize marital violence as mutual violence. Unlike the Berk et al. study, the sequencing of events in the NFVS does not address mutuality in the same incident. Events may have occurred far apart in time, yet be aggregated for the same reporting year. Mutuality is also difficult to assess because of gender differences in self-reports of assaultive behaviors. Underreporting of the incidence and severity of marital violence by men has been well established and raises questions about the "mutuality" of assaults—especially severe assaults, in which women are more likely to be injured. Correcting this bias would in fact increase the rate of mutuality. Other data suggest that men and women rate the severity of violence differently, even when they agree that it occurred.

Although published research from the NFVS data has emphasized the "equality" of violence participation rates for women and men, Straus et al. list five reasons to interpret issues of gender equality in marital violence cautiously: (1) the perpetration of "severely" violent acts is greater for men than women; (2) violence by husbands does more damage due to their greater size and physical strength; (3) the offending rate for men is higher than for women—that is, the number of times that men hit women is greater; (4) men often hit women when they are pregnant, posing dangers of miscarriage and infertility; and (5) women remain in marriages and thus at risk for injury more often than men, primarily due to their economic circumstances.

In addition, methodological problems in both the NCS and the NFVS limit comparisons of gender differences or conclusions. Perhaps most important is the infrequent reporting of offending rates . . . for both data sources. Rarely are marital violence events analyzed in which multiple acts occur, perhaps by both parties, in a complex interaction. For example, one battering event may involve several specific acts, yet either these acts are given even weight or only the most serious act is reported. . . .

CHARACTERISTICS OF PERPETRATORS, VICTIMS, AND COUPLES

There has been much research on the prevalence of assault within marriage, the damage it does, its female victims, and the dynamics of relationships in which violence occurs. There also is much knowledge about marital violence that results in self-defensive homicide by abused women, and about the characteristics of victims who seek help from shelters or other resources for women who are threatened or abused by their partners. Less is known about the characteristics of *men* who engage in marital violence or about those men who kill current or ex-wives or girlfriends. Interview studies with women victims have supplied most of the current knowledge, although research with samples of assaultive spouses has grown in recent years. . . .

Men Who Engage in Marital Violence.

Until recently, research on marital violence has relied on victim reports, mostly from women, for information on the nature of violent events and the characteristics of victims and assailants. The few studies of violent men have been limited to small samples of repeatedly assaultive participants in treatment programs, voluntary or self-selected samples, or assailants identified by the criminal justice system who also frequently are violent. Accordingly, variations in definitions, researcher effects, sampling strategies, program criteria, and measurement techniques introduce validity threats into the emerging literature on assaultive partners.

For example, clinicians working with abusive or violent men and couples note that men vastly underreport their violent behaviors, minimize the harm it does or its severity, or even deny the behavior. Even when confirming their participation in assaultive behaviors, assaultive partners may claim more involvement by the victim (provocation, mutuality) than is justified by either witness or police reports or may excuse violent behavior as the result of alcohol. . . .

Personality Characteristics and Concurrent Behaviors. A brief review of profiles of assaultive men reveals a bewildering array of findings. In general, wife abusers have been reported to have the following characteristics: low self-esteem; extreme jealousy; need for control but lacking in assertiveness; suicidal personality; abusiveness toward children; involvement in alcohol and drug abuse; wide variations in moods; hostility or anger; distortion of cognitive perceptions of social cues; strong sex-role stereotypes; and lack of verbal skills. . . .

In an effort to sort out the extensive and conflicting evidence on personality and behavioral characteristics that typify assaultive men, Hotaling and Sugarman reviewed more than 400 empirical studies of husband-to-wife violence. Their review focused on 52 studies that employed case-comparison designs assessing 97 specific variables. Hotaling and Sugarman identified three "risk markers" that showed consistently strong associations with male violence toward women in case-control or experimental studies: sexual aggression toward wives, experiencing or witnessing violence during childhood, and perpetrating violence toward their own (and/or their partners'.) children. Alcohol usage also was consistently associated with assaultive behavior by male partners in seven of nine studies reviewed.

Variables that comprise measures of socioeconomic status also were associated with assaultive partners, but the associations obtained in studies with small clinical samples were not replicated with larger general population samples. . . .

Childhood Exposure to Violence. Exposure to violence as a child—either as a witness of parental violence or as a victim of child abuse—is an important precursor of adult violence toward children or toward spouses. Most studies have cited the importance of childhood exposure to violence in later domestic violence. The strength of the link to subsequent involvement in marital violence has been revealed in a variety of reports. In general, both national and special population studies indicate the following:

- Boys and girls are more at risk to abuse their own children as adults if they were abused themselves as children or adolescents.
- Both boys and girls, but particularly boys, are at increased risk to abuse an intimate partner in later adult relationships if they were abused as children or adolescents.
- Boys are at greatly increased risk to abuse female partners in adult relationships if they *witnessed* abuse between parental figures in their childhood homes.
- Girls are at somewhat increased risk to be abused by a male partner in adulthood if they witnessed abuse in their childhood homes.
- Children who have both *experienced* child (or adolescent) abuse and *witnessed* abuse between parental figures demonstrate a sharply increased risk of being involved in an abusive relationship as adults, compared to individuals without these dual experiences. . . .

Women Victims of Marital Violence.

For many years, empirical research on marital violence focused predominantly on women, most of whom were victims who had sought services. . . . Accordingly, knowledge of victim' (sic) backgrounds was confined for some time to higher-risk groups of women whose resources limited them to public services. For example, Washburn and Frieze, in a study in southwestern Pennsylvania, reported systematic differences among groups of women in shelters, women who filed for legal assistance, and women who responded to a research solicitation. Shelter clients more often were separated from their partners, were African American, and were unemployed. They were younger, had lower incomes and were less educated, and more often had small children. They had the fewest resources and were most in need of financial support. Other women in the study commented that they preferred to seek temporary shelter with relatives or to use credit cards to pay for a motel.

Women who had filed for legal assistance comprised an intermediate group. They were separated, worked full time, had higher educational and family income levels than women in shelters, and had older children. Their racial composition was consistent with the area makeup. They experienced similar levels of violence to the women in shelters, but more often were violent toward their male partners. They less often expressed powerlessness, and they felt that they were doing something to change the situation. The third group, respondents to solicitations, most often were still married to their assailants and generally had higher socioeconomic status. Their victimizations had not occurred recently, and they had experienced the least serious violence among the three groups. . . .

The NFVS, NCS, and other general population studies indicated the diverse socioeconomic backgrounds of victims. Although these studies indicated that younger women from lower social class backgrounds more often were victims of both simple and severe marital violence, the association with social class and income was weaker but still positive.

Other than their abuse histories and socioeconomic status, there do not appear to be consistent patterns that differentiate women victims from nonvictims. . . .

EXPLANATORY FRAMEWORKS. . .

Patriarchy, Social Networks, and Social Embedment

Early theories on marital violence, particularly those describing violence by husbands toward wives, viewed this aggression as an outworking of a culture that engendered and maintained the domination of men over women in every aspect of social life. Dobash and Dobash describe patriarchal influence as culturally normative, whereas Straus refers to the marriage license as a "hitting license." These theorists contend that the beliefs that support marital violence simply express more general cultural norms and values that uphold a hierarchical, patriarchal social organization. Such norms have been linked with wife assault in empirical studies in the United Kingdom, Canada, and the United States. . . .

Power, Control, and Domination

Although power motivation theories were first developed by McClelland and colleagues regarding drinking behaviors, they follow naturally from patriarchal theories as explanations of assaults by males against their female partners. The basic premise unifying the more recent integration of these theories is that assault is used to assert or maintain power within the relationship, particularly the power to gain victories in confrontations. Straus and Browne argue that one episode of violence can permanently alter the balance of marital power toward a strongly husband-dominant pattern. However, the empirical evidence about marital power is inconclusive, because the conceptualization and measurement of power and adherence to traditional sex-role expectations vary extensively.

Other studies emphasize the importance of power *balances* in a partner relationship. . . . Coleman and Straus, using 1975 NFVS data, found that marital violence was lowest in "egalitarian" couples that shared domestic chores and decisions. However, both male and female aggression was highest in couples in which females were dominant (i.e., had the greatest influence in decision making and control over resources). Thus, in couples in which the female partner has greater access to resources and/or decision-making power, female aggression may be either a response to male aggression or an aggressive reaction to confrontations over power. . . .

Issues of intimacy and the threat of dependency also may trigger violence in partner relationships. According to Browning and Dutton, males experience anger most readily in circumstances in which they perceive an impending loss of control over either intimacy or distance. For example, using vignettes, Browning and Dutton found that men reported anger at women's attempts at autonomy in the relationship, as well as attempts by women partners to intensify levels of intimacy and commitment. Unsatisfied power needs may produce physiological arousal that is interpreted as anger and, especially for males with limited verbal skills, may be expressed through physical aggression. . . .

Finally, the gratification that men experience from marital hegemony and male domination may also reinforce aggressive behaviors. Gratification from marital violence may come from achieving/maintaining the instrumental motive of dominance, from the expressive release of anger and aggression in response to perceived power deficits, from attainment of the positive social status that domination affords, or even from the "hearts-and-flowers" aftermath of many battering incidents. . . .

Early Childhood Socialization:
Witnessing and Observing Violence

As noted earlier, an individual-level explanation of marital violence is that such behavior has been modeled for both victims and assailants. In particular, social learning analyses view aggressive habits as developing from the learning experiences of individuals and focus on the original milieus in which such habits are acquired (e.g., by observation in the family of origin), the instigators or aversive stimuli in the current environment that trigger aggression, and the maintenance of aggressive habits through the immediate consequences that reward or punish such aggression. Thus, sex-role socialization may interact with observation of instrumental violence in the family of origin to shape perceptions of aversive circumstances (such as female independence) and acceptable or socially desirable responses. Further, the salience of social and legal controls in later years may determine whether circumstances reinforce or extinguish these socially learned responses.

Fagan and Browne analyzed not only research concerning the definition, frequency, and distribution of domestic violence and the characteristics of offenders and victims, but also examined changes in criminal justice policy regarding the appropriate response to domestic violence. The following excerpt reviews this phenomenon and, in doing so, might be read as raising a cautionary note about the use and misuse of social science research in determining legal and social strategies. That story begins with an apparently successful experiment in Minneapolis in which mandatory arrest seemed to reduce subsequent domestic violence. Although there were isolated calls for caution, findings from the Minneapolis Domestic Violence experiment were seized on enthusiastically by a public seeking an effective response to domestic misconduct, and those findings influenced police and legislative policy nationally. However, attempts to replicate the Minneapolis study in a number of other jurisdictions failed and, in some cases, found that arrest produced undesirable consequences (including, in one jurisdiction, higher recidivism rates).

Jeffrey Fagan & Angela Browne, *Violence Between Spouses and Intimates: Physical Aggression Between Women and Men in Intimate Relationships* in 3 UNDERSTANDING AND PREVENTING VIOLENCE 115 (**Albert J. Reiss, Jr. & Jeffrey A. Roth, eds. 1994)**[*]

CRIMINAL JUSTICE POLICY

Significant changes have taken place in criminal justice policy toward marital violence over the past 20 years. These developments were preceded by criticisms of the police, and the criminal justice system more generally, for failing to respond effectively to spouse assault. . . .

Police Interventions. . .

In a review of criminal justice responses to marital violence, Elliott concludes that one-third of all domestic disturbance calls involve some form of domestic violence, with the majority of these involving assaults between "intimate" cohabitants or former cohabitants. Based on observational studies of police intervention in domestic disturbances, Dutton found that arrest occurs in only 21.2 percent of wife assault cases in which prima facie evidence exists for arrest. Elliott estimated that the probability of arrest varied from 12 to 50 percent, but found mixed support for the claim that arrest is less likely to occur for family than stranger violence.

Both research and litigation have led to mandatory arrest policies in some jurisdictions for incidents in which there is probable cause of wife assault. . . .

The premise is that strict and swift application of criminal sanctions in wife assault cases will better protect victims and reduce the likelihood of repeat violence. The empirical basis for these policies derives both from accumulated evidence of the ineffectiveness of nonarrest or informal police dispositions of family violence calls and from experimental evidence of the deterrent effects of arrest compared to nonarrest dispositions.

The Minneapolis Domestic Violence experiment has been the most influential study in the development of policies to increase the likelihood of arrest in misdemeanor wife assault cases. It was designed as a test of the specific deterrent effects of arrest on the recurrence of wife assault and was intended to provide a critical test of the effectiveness of legal sanctions compared to nonlegal, informal police responses. Sherman and Berk used an experimental design in two Minneapolis police precincts to randomly

---

    *   Reprinted with permission from Understanding and Preventing Violence. Copyright 1994 by the National Academy of Sciences. Courtesy of the National Academy Press, Washington D.C.

assign violent family disputes to one of three police responses: arrest, separation of victim and assailant, and advice/mediation. The study was limited to situations in which the assailant was present when the police arrived. During the six-month follow-up, biweekly interviews with victims and reviews of official reports of family violence were collected. Despite the repeated measures on subsequent violence, dichotomous measures of recidivism were used. Neither the severity, the incidence, nor the time to recurrence was reported.

Sherman and Berk concluded that arrest was more effective in reducing subsequent violence in misdemeanor wife assault cases than other police responses. Those arrested had the lowest recidivism rate based on official (10%) and victim (19%) reports. There was no evidence of differential effects across conditions based on offender characteristics, although within-group differences were found. This led to their recommendation that "police adopt arrest as the favored response to domestic assault on the basis [in the original] of its deterrence power." A subsequent reanalysis offered more qualified support for the deterrent effects of arrest. Findings from the Minneapolis experiment, together with results of nonexperimental studies comparing arrest with other police dispositions of spouse assault cases provided evidence that influenced police policy and legislation nationwide. Thus, for several years, the Minneapolis study provided critical, determining evidence in criminal justice policy development for wife assault.

However, several reviews have cited internal and external validity problems in the Minneapolis experiment that, together with contradictory results from replications in Omaha and Charlotte, North Carolina, raise serious questions about the deterrent effects of arrest on repeat spouse assault. In both the Omaha and the Charlotte replications, there were no significant differences in recidivism for any type of police response (advice, warning, citation, arrest) for several measures of recidivism. Moreover, the incidence of recidivism in Charlotte was *highest* for the arrest group, which directly contradicted the results in Minneapolis.

Results of additional replication experiments are available for experiments in Colorado Springs, Dade County, and Milwaukee. Only Dade County reported results similar to the original Minneapolis experiment: a reduction in the prevalence of recidivism for arrested suspects in both official records and interviews. Even here, the reduction reported in official records was not statistically significant. In the Charlotte, Colorado Springs, Milwaukee, and Omaha experiments, analysis of official records showed that arrest was associated with higher rates of reoffending; but results based on interview data showed that arrest was associated with lower rates of reoffending. Except for the Colorado Springs experiment, none of the results approached traditional levels of statistical significance.

Reviewing the five replications, together with the original Minneapolis experiment, Sherman reported that three experiments found that rates of spouse assault escalated among male arrestees who were unemployed or unmarried. The results suggest that arrest has variable effects on different types of people and also people in different types of neighborhoods. Sherman claims that escalation of spouse assault following arrest was evident in neighborhoods in Milwaukee and Omaha where there were concentrations of poverty and social disorganization, but escalation was not evident in economically stable areas where unemployment was lower and poverty less acute.

How could replication results diverge so sharply from the original finding? . . . Several limitations in the design of the Minneapolis experiment suggest that it was a seriously flawed effort. First, the follow-up period was relatively short (six months), given the episodic and cyclical patterns of family violence. Second, self-reports from abusers were not obtained, which left out the possibility of a "hidden" violence period toward strangers, the original victim, or other victims in the home. Third, no distinctions were made in the level and nature of violence, leaving open questions of the relative harm (e.g., injury, intimidation) that may have accrued from battering incidents.

Fourth, the biweekly interview process may have depressed recidivism rates through research effects, response effects, or task specific biases. Awareness by offenders of victim interviews may have deterred or simply postponed recidivism during the study period. The validity of victim' reports may have been compromised because assailants often were residing with them during the follow-up period. Victim attrition also was evident but not analyzed. Fifth, not all precincts in Minneapolis participated in the experiment. Finally, other forms of wife abuse, such as persistent denigration or economic reprisal, were not investigated. These forms of abuse, noted in several studies on wife battery, are emotionally harmful even if not posing threats to physical safety and often are antecedents of physical violence.

Perhaps the most significant omission from the Minneapolis experiment was the exclusion of other than ". . . simple (misdemeanor) domestic assaults. . . . Cases of life-threatening or severe injury, usually labeled as a felony . . . were excluded from the design . . ." Thus, selection biases of participating officers' processes may have been evident in the exclusion of individual cases from the randomization procedure, based on the arresting officers' judgment about the severity of violence or the risk to the victim of nonarrest. Offenders who had left the scene also were excluded from the experiment. Accordingly, incomplete randomization introduced serious sampling biases and validity threats. . . .

The Omaha, Charlotte, and other replications followed experimental designs similar to the Minneapolis study, adding refinements that addressed many of its limitations. For example, all police calls for domestic violence, during the 4:00 to 12:00 p.m. shift in the city of Omaha were randomly assigned to three treatment groups: (1) those in which the perpetrator would be arrested, (2) those in which the perpetrator would be separated from the victim, and (3) those in which police would "mediate" the dispute. Cases were sampled around the clock in Charlotte, where the use of a police-issued citation also presented a unique intervention option. Randomized treatment was conducted only for cases in which both perpetrator and victim were present at the scene when the police arrived. However, data on those cases in which the perpetrator was not present were collected and analyzed separately in Omaha.

Both studies employed official and self-report measure to judge the effectiveness of the treatments in deterring reassault and threats over a six-month period. . . .

Neither study found that arrest was an effective deterrent. In Omaha, for example, "arresting suspects had no more effect deterring future arrests or complaints than did separating or counseling them"; similarly, victim reports showed "no significant differences between the treatment groups." Moreover, analyses controlling for prior arrests, ethnicity, and other variables showed no significant differences between police response in terms of reassault and threat. Results from the other replications were inconsistent as well. . . .

Prosecution of Marital Violence

Historically, like the police, prosecutors were accused of disinterest in family violence cases. Specific criticisms suggested that they failed to file charges (i.e., dismissed charges) or to aggressively pursue convictions and sanctions against the offenders. . . . Factors influencing prosecutorial discretion included the questionable wisdom of intervening in family affairs, the motivation and potential "culpability" of the victim, and the perceived reluctance of victims to complete the court process.

Research on factors that influence prosecution of marital violence cases reflects the absence of specific decision-making criteria and the generalization of prosecutorial discretion for stranger and family violence cases. Schmidt and Steury analyzed screening decisions of 38 prosecutors in 408 domestic violence cases in Milwaukee. Logit analyses showed that the severity of injury and the defendant's prior arrest record influenced screening and filing decisions more than the evidentiary strength of the case. In fact, prosecutors were not reluctant to charge even in weak cases. Defendants who failed to attend charging conferences and who had drug or alcohol involvement were especially likely to be prosecuted.

Elliott suggests that a high dismissal rate by prosecutors in wife assault cases offers police further disincentives to make an arrest or to carefully investigate and gather evidence for a successful prosecution. Others suggest that prosecutors often find an unreceptive judicial audience for wife assault cases, especially in sentencing deliberations. With serious sanctions not forthcoming, prosecutors have little incentive to aggressively pursue a wife assault case through conviction and sentencing. Though there was consistent evidence that the majority of wife assault cases were dismissed, both Schmidt and Steury and Elliott found little evidence that different factors were involved in the decision to prosecute family violence cases compared to stranger violence crimes. Differences were attributed in part to the quality of evidence, but primarily differences in victim/witness cooperation—a complex issue in the prosecution of family violence cases. . . .

Sanction and Control of Wife Assaulters:
Treatment Interventions

Court-mandated treatment of wife assault is essential to the criminal justice system objective of reducing recidivism. Treatment options support this goal in four ways. First, treatment provides a dispositional option for judges in imposing sanctions. It is an "intermediate" sanction and form of social control that is harsher than probation but less drastic than incarceration. Whether or not incarceration is an appropriate sanction in a particular case, judges often are reluctant to invoke such "last-resort" sanctions for marital violence when the victim has not been injured severely. They may fear the consequences to victims of the removal of economic support, and they may still (inappropriately) view marital violence cases as less serious than stranger violence and

thus less serious in the allocation of scarce jail space. The availability of this dispositional option makes these cases more salient for judges and, in turn, for prosecutors and
police.

Second, treatment has been seen as a means to protect women who chose not to
dissolve their relationship, but whose violent partners would not seek treatment voluntarily. Third, treatment placements provide a form of control that strengthens the traditional probation sanction. Monthly, superficial contacts with probation officers for
misdemeanor offenses are replaced by weekly or bi-weekly therapeutic interventions
in a structured milieu. Failure to abide by probation conditions mandating treatment
participation can result in court action and possibly an escalation in sanction severity.
Fourth, treatment has specific clinical value for recidivism reduction. Treatment interventions often are specifically designed to reinforce the substantive meaning of the
arrest sanction. . . .

These programs have been widely accepted as an option for criminal justice
processing, in part because they reflect explanations of wife assault that do not challenge basic assumptions within criminal justice agencies about the causes of crime. The
philosophical base of offender treatment for marital violence—stressing individual
responsibility and behavioral control—is compatible with contemporary intervention
models in the criminal justice system. This, in turn, creates a political context in
which treatment can be linked to probation sanctions. Court-ordered treatment, under
probationary conditions, in effect is the social control component of the legal sanction.
However, evidence of its effectiveness is inconclusive due to weak evaluation designs.
Recent evaluations reported that 64 to 84 percent of treatment participants were not violent after treatment, although measurements, follow-up times, and definitions varied.

Feminist therapy calls for a more basic resocialization of men and, in lieu of anger
management, a redirection of their view of women and sex roles and of their instrumental use of violence to retain power and domination. The social and cultural supports
that reinforce the maintenance of power are critical to this model. Although there is
much evidence to support them, critical perspectives on violence have been less influential in guiding the development of sentencing options and treatment interventions for
marital violence than models based on anger management and behavior modification.
Sanction and control continue today to express perspectives that regard violence as an
act of individual deviance.

Improving the efficacy of mandated treatment interventions depends on the resolution of critical issues. First, retention rates of assailants in counseling programs vary
according to the personality characteristics and behavioral problems of participants.
Models tailored to specific types of assaultive males are necessary. Second, ineffective
treatment compromises victim safety. Accordingly, procedures are needed to audit the
effect of interventions for assailants on the safety of victims. Third, treatment experiments with credible sanctions for control conditions (that address safety issues, for
example) are required to strengthen the empirical evidence on treatment effectiveness.
Moreover, current programs reach only a small fraction of assaultive males. Research
is needed both on the long-term effectiveness of current approaches and on mechanisms
to make such programs available to a larger number of assaulters. . . .

REFERENCES

Bandura, A.
    1973   *Aggression: A Social Learning Analysis.* Englewood Cliffs, N.J.: Pren-
            tice Hall.

Berk, R.A., and P.J. Newton
    1983   The myth of mutuality in battering. In D. Finkelhor, R. Gelles, G. Hotal-
            ing, and M. Straus, eds., The *Dark Side of Families.* Beverly Hills,
            Calif.: Sage Publications.

Browne, A.
    1987   *When Battered Women Kill.* New York: Macmillan/Free Press.

Browning, J.J., and D.G. Dutton
    1986   Assessment of wife assault with the conflict tactics scale: Using couple
            data to quantify the differential reporting effect. *Journal of Marriage and
            the Family* 48:375-379.

Coleman, D.H., and M.A. Straus
    1986   Marital power, conflict, and violence in a nationally representative sam-
            ple of American couples. *Violence and Victims* 1(2) 141-157.

Collins, J.J ., Jr.
    1988   Suggested explanatory frameworks to clarify the alcohol use/violence
            relationship. *Contemporary Drug Problems* 15:107-121.

Dobash, R.E., and R.P. Dobash
    1979   *Violence Against Wives: A Case Against the Patriarchy.* New York: Free
            Press.

Dunford, F.W., D. Huizinga, and D.S. Elliott
    1989   The Omaha Domestic Violence Policy Experiment. Final Report,
            National Institute of Justice, U.S. Department of Justice, Washington,
            D.C.
    1990   The role of arrest in domestic assault: The Omaha Police Experiment.
            Criminology 28(2):183-206.

Dutton, D.G.
    1987   The criminal justice response to wife assault. *Law and Human Behavior*
            11(3):189-206.
    1988b   *The Domestic Assault of Women: Psychological and Criminal Justice
            Perspectives.* Boston: Allyn and Bacon.

Elliott, D.S.
    1989   Criminal justice procedures in family violence crimes. In L. Ohlin and
            M. Tonry, eds., *Family Violence,* Vol. 11: *Crime and Justice, An Annual
            Review of Research.* Chicago: University of Chicago Press.

Elliott, D.S., D. Huizinga, and B. Morse
   1985   The Dynamics of Delinquent Behavior: A National Survey Progress
           Report. Institute of Behavioral Sciences, University of Colorado, Boulder.

Eron, L.D., and L.R. Huesmann
   1989   The genesis of gender differences in aggression. In M.A. Luszcz and T.
           Nettelbeck, eds., *Psychological Development: Perspectives Across the
           Life Span.* The Netherlands: Elsevier Science Publishers.

Fagan, J., E. Friedman, S. Wexler, and V. Lewis
   1984   *The National Family Violence Evaluation: Final Report,* Vol. I: *Analytic
           Findings.* San Francisco: URSA Institute.

Feld, S.L., and M.A. Straus
   1989   Escalation and desistance of wife assault in marriage. *Criminology*
           27(1):141- 161.

Gelles, R.J., and M.A. Straus
   1979   Determinants of violence in the family: Toward a theoretical integration.
           In W. Burr, R. Hill, F.I. Nye, and I.L. Triss, eds., *Contemporary Theories
           About the Family.* New York: Free Press.

Hirschel, J.D., I.W. Hutchinson, III., C.W. Dean, J.J. Kelley, and C. Pesackis
   1991   Charlotte Spouse Assault Replication Project: Final Report. National
           Institute of Justice, U.S. Department of Justice, Washington, D.C.

Hirschel, J.D., I.W. Hutchison, III, and C.W. Dean
   1992.   The failure of arrest to deter spouse abuse. *Journal of Research in Crime
           and Delinquency* 29:7-33.

Hotaling, G.T., and D.B. Sugarman
   1986   An analysis of risk markers in husband to wife violence: The current state
           of knowledge. *Violence and Victims* 1(2):101-124.

Kennedy, L.W., and D.G.Dutton
   1989   The incidence of wife assault in Alberta. *Canadian Journal of Behav-
           ioural Science* 21(1): 40-54.

Levinson, D.
   1988   Family violence in cross-cultural perspective. In V.B. van Hasselt, R.L.
           Morrison, A.S. Bellack, and M. Hersen, eds., *Handbook of Family Vio-
           lence.* New York: Plenum.
   1989   *Family Violence in Cross-Cultural Perspective.* Newbury Park, Calif.:
           Sage Publications.

Macoby, E.E., and C.N. Jacklin
   1974   *The Psychology of Sex Differences.* Palo Alto, Calif.: Stanford University
           Press.

Rosenberg, M.L., R.J. Gelles, P.C. Holinger, E. Stark, M.A. Zahn, J.M. Conn, N.N. Fajman, and T.A. Karlson

    1984   Violence, Homicide, Assault, and Suicide. Unpublished manuscript, Centers for Disease Control, Atlanta.

Russell, D.E.H.

    1982   *Rape in Marriage.* New York: Macmillan

Schmidt, J., and E.H, Steury

    1989   Prosecutorial discretion in filing charges in domestic violence cases. *Criminology* 27(3):487-510.

Schulman, M.

    1979   A Survey of Spousal Violence Against Women in Kentucky. Unpublished manuscript, Law Enforcement Administration, U.S. Department of Justice, Washington, D.C.

Sherman, L.W., J.D. Schmidt, D. Rogan, and C. De Riso

    1990   Predicting domestic homicide: Prior police contact and gun threats. In M. Steinman, ed., *Redefining Crime: Responses to Women Battering.* Cincinnati, Ohio: Anderson Publishing.

Stark, E., A. Flitcraft, and W. Frazier

    1979   Medicine and patriarchical violence: The social construction of a private event. *International Journal of Health Services* 9(3):461-493.

Stark, E., A. Flitcraft, D. Zuckerman, A. Grey, J. Robinson, and W. Frazier

    1981   *Wife Abuse in the Medical Setting: An Introduction to Health Personnel.* Monograph Series #7. Washington, D.C.: National Clearinghouse on Domestic Violence.

Stets. J.E., and M.A. Straus

    1990   Gender differences in reporting marital violence and its medical and psychological consequences. In M.A. Straus And R.J. Gelles, eds., *Psychical (sic) Violence in American Families: Risk Factors and Adaptation to Violence in 8,145 Families.* New Brunswick, N.J.: Transaction Press.

Straus, M.A.

    1976   Sexual inequality, cultural norms, and wife beating. *Victimology* 1:54-76.

    1978   Wife beating: How common and why? *Victimology* 2:443-458.

    1979   Measuring family conflict and violence. The Conflict Tactics Scale. *Journal of Marriage and the Family 41:75-88.*

Straus, M.A. and R.J. Gelles, eds.

    1990   *Physical Violence in American Families: Risk Factors and Adaptations to Violence in 8,145 Families.* New Brunswick, N.J.: Transaction Press

Straus, M.A., R.J. Gelles, and S.K. Steinmetz

    1980   *Behind Closed Doors: Violence in the American Family.* Garden City, N.Y.: Anchor Press, Doubleday.

Washburn, C., and I.H. Frieze

    1980   Methodological Issues in Studying Battered Women. Paper presented at the first national conference of Family Violence Researchers, University of New Hampshire, Durham, July.

B. Child Abuse

Then I saw that there was a way to hell,
even from the gates of heaven.

John Bunyan
The Pilgrim's Progress

Few of family law's missions are more difficult or more distressing than its goal of preventing parents from injuring their children. The mission is difficult because it is so difficult for the law to identify children who are being abused—there are so many children that cannot easily be kept track of, and most abuse occurs in private, so that only the family knows about it. The mission is distressing not just because it is so painful to see children hurt by those who should be helping them, but also because it is hard to prevent child abuse without compromising other goals we value, like the principle of non-intervention in families. The difficulty and distress of the mission are further exacerbated by the fact that even when child abuse is discovered, it is not clear how it should be dealt with. When should children be removed from the abuser's home? When should parental rights be terminated? Which abusers can be reformed? How can abuse in general be deterred? For all these questions there are more controversies than answers.

Because most child abuse occurs in private, it is hard to know how common it is. Yet that knowledge should significantly affect our willingness to intrude into families to discover child abuse and the resources we divert from other pressing social needs. Child abuse, then, is an area where reliable data need to be carefully collected and soberly evaluated. Unfortunately, our impression of the extent of child abuse is affected by newspaper accounts, which provide horrifying pictures of particularly egregious incidents. This creates what social scientists call an "availability bias": "When people are required to judge the relative frequency of particular objects or the likelihood of particular events, they often may be influenced by the relative availability of the objects or events, that is, their accessibility in the processes of perception, memory, or construction from the imagination . . . ."[1] In one study, for example, people were asked to estimate the proportion of criminals in two samples. A sample was thought to have "more criminals if the nature of the individual offenses had been particularly heinous than if the offenses had been relatively slight."[2] Similarly, vivid accounts of ghastly child abuse so stir us that

---

[1]   Richard Nisbett & Lee Ross, HUMAN INFERENCE: STRATEGIES AND SHORTCOMINGS OF SOCIAL JUDGMENT 18 (Prentice-Hall, 1980).

[2]   *Id.* at 75.

they stay in our memory and come easily to mind when we try to estimate the extent of abuse generally.

The following article is one of the best descriptions of systematic attempts to measure child abuse accurately. But it is useful not only for what it says about the extent of child abuse. It also teaches lessons about how a phenomenon like child abuse might be detected and measured and—what may be of more general importance—how difficult this kind of empirical research is. Finally, the article briefly looks at governmental programs to prevent abuse.

James Garbarino, *The Incidence and Prevalence of Child Maltreatment,* **in** FAMILY VIOLENCE, **Lloyd Ohlin & Michael Tonry, eds. (University of Chicago Press, 1989)**[*]

I. Incidence and Prevalence

A. Incidence Studies

The NIS [National Incidence Study] collected data on abuse and neglect occurring in a randomly selected sample of twenty-six U.S. counties located in ten states. . . . Child protective service agencies, schools, hospitals, police, and courts were surveyed. This resulted in the identification of what would be projected nationally to be approximately 652,000 distinct cases—212,400 known to protective services, 71,400 known to other investigatory agencies (but not protective services), and 368,200 known to other professionals. The NIS provided a basis for estimating the annual incidence of various forms of maltreatment of children under eighteen in the United States.

The NIS estimates of maltreatment, though startlingly high—one child per 100 is estimated to be the victim of maltreatment—are likely to be underestimates. Many cases of child maltreatment, perhaps most, are never reported to official agencies and thus are not reflected in studies like the NIS. Other problems suggest that NIS data should be interpreted with caution. First, definitions of abuse vary from state to state, agency to agency, and professional to professional. Second, the extent of cooperation with the NIS by state agencies varied considerably. . . .

The AHA's [American Humane Association] National Study of Child Abuse and Neglect Reporting tabulates and analyzes cases reported to (and "accepted" by) official child protective service agencies, as compiled on a state-by-state basis (approximately 80 percent of the states participate). . . . The overall volume of reporting since the AHA reports began with the 1976 data has reflected growing public and professional awareness of child maltreatment. However, like the NIS data and for similar reasons, the AHA reports are likely to be substantial underestimates of the occurrence of child maltreatment. The percentage increase in reported cases has ranged from 25 percent, from 1976 to 1977, to 3 percent in the 1981-82 comparison. Overall, when

---

changes are computed on the basis of rate of reported cases per 1,000 children, the pattern is as shown in table 2. It reveals ebbs and flows in the rate of increase that appear to reflect both actual changes in reported cases *and* artifacts of state record keeping and participation in the project. As Peters, Wyatt, and Finkelhor note, "Most people consider the rise in incidence figures . . . to be primarily a product of new education, awareness, and professional attention to the problem." . . .

The AHA patterns of types of maltreatment differ significantly from the NIS finding. Both data sources, unfortunately, can offer only crude indicators of the behaviors they attempt to measure. Nonetheless, especially with regard to palpably disturbing adult behaviors like sexual exploitation and serious physical abuse of children, both studies, whatever their other weaknesses, suggest that these behaviors are distressingly common. As table 1 shows, the NIS identified physical assault as the most common form of maltreatment (3.4 cases per year per 1,000 children under eighteen), followed by educational neglect (2.9), emotional abuse (2.2), physical neglect (1.7), emotional neglect (1.0), and sexual exploitation (0.7). Table 3 shows a breakdown of the American Humane Association's data by types of maltreatment. Neglect is the largest category, followed by minor physical injury. Tables 4 and 5 show somewhat different patterns for "major physical injuries" and "sexually maltreated children" in 1984. Compared with physically abused children, sexually abused children are (at the time of report, at least) older, more likely to be female, more likely to be white, less likely to be the perpetrator's child, and less likely to be living with unemployed care givers. Sexual abuse is less likely to include other forms of abuse when it is the principal allegation.

As public attention to problems of family violence generally and child maltreatment specifically has increased, there appears to have been a trend toward greater overall involvement of the courts. Table 6 provides data over the last decade on court involvement with reported protective service cases. But the AHA analyses suggest that this is not evidence for neglect. Rather, the overall rise in court involvement appears to stem from the rising number of sexual abuse reports (which are more likely to receive court action) and the aggressive efforts of criminal justice systems (with leadership from the federal government) to criminalize child maltreatment (as compared with a pre-1980 focus on the problem in social service/child welfare/mental health terms).

This review tells us where things stand within the formal public agencies mandated to provide child protective services. To find out more about the larger community system for dealing with child maltreatment, the National Incidence Study warrants further consideration.

The NIS is notable for employing clear operational definitions of child abuse and neglect. It proceeded from the following overall description. "A child maltreatment situation is one where, through purposive acts or marked inattention to the child's basic needs, behavior of a parent/substitute or other adult caregivers caused foreseeable and avoidable injury or impairment to a child or materially contributed to unreasonable prolongation or worsening of an existing injury or impairment." The NIS notes particularly that its definition was designed to highlight an emphasis on consequences for the child, and further specified that "injury or impairment must be of 'moderate' or 'serious' severity at minimum." It also observes that the resulting operational definitions do not include some (perhaps many) situations in which "protective or other services might be appropriate" (e.g., institutional maltreatment, in-home assault by someone other than a parent or caretaker, dangerous behavior that did not cause injury or impairment, hazards the parent was not financially capable of eliminating, and lack of care resulting from the parents' unavoidable absence from the home). Table 1 presented the overall distribution of physical assault, sexual exploitation, emotional abuse, physical neglect, educational neglect, and emotional neglect. Note that, of some 470,500 maltreated children substantiated by child protective service agencies in the target communities, only 212,400 of these children meet all NIS criteria for inclusion in the study. This discrepancy has led to criticism of the NIS, as has the inclusion of so many cases of "educational neglect"—some 20 percent of the total.

Where do the reports come from that ended up as child protective services agencies cases and met NIS criteria for inclusion? Law enforcement accounted for 12 percent of all the reports to child protective services agencies and had a high substantiation rate, as did schools. However, if cases of "educational neglect" are excluded from the schools reports, then law enforcement agencies reports had the highest substantiation rates.

The reporting pattern shown in the NIS data closely parallels AHA findings. The 12 percent of reports from police in the NIS corresponds to 11 percent in AHA data. Medical sources represent 10 percent of NIS reports and 11 percent of AHA reports. Parents, friends, and neighbors are the sources of about half of the reports in both data sets.

Why did child protective services agencies substantiate some cases and not others? Table 8 data show that law enforcement's allegations were termed "invalid" by child protective services agencies less often than other sources (except the schools). Table 9 presents national estimates based on the counties sampled and the sampling of agencies within those counties. The NIS has been criticized on this point because the small number of large, urban counties in the sample and the small number of agencies sampled within each county created the possibility of serious distortion. Indeed, some critics charge that this did happen because several large hospitals did not participate, although they were appropriately included in the design. Note again the large role played by investigatory agencies.

The NIS provides some information about incidence of child maltreatment as a function of socioeconomic and demographic factors. The most striking difference is in the incidence figures for poor versus affluent families—27.3 percent versus 2.7 percent. This reflects a more general research finding linking poverty to child maltreatment.

Table 11 shows the full range of "in-scope" maltreatment and corresponding severity of effect data. Those data reveal significant, even dramatic, differences. For example, neglect cases in the study seem to be particularly serious (32 percent of the neglect cases versus 12 percent of the abuse cases are judged "serious").

Table 12 presents this same "severity" issue in a somewhat different form. Here we see that emotional and physical neglect are most serious (not counting the 1,000 fatalities). We also see that fatalities cluster among children aged birth to five and fifteen to seventeen.

In conclusion, the NIS is valuable in shedding light on the different levels of social reality that exist in child abuse as a public phenomenon. In particular, NIS reveals the important role played by law enforcement agencies in identifying cases of child maltreatment. It sheds some light on the world of child maltreatment beyond the official reports received and investigated by state child protective services (and compiled by the AHA). Nonetheless, a separate study by AHA revealed that its compilation of reports and NIS results reveal much congruity in the demographics and socioeconomics of child maltreatment.

Straus, Gelles, and Steinmetz conducted a national probability survey of families with two adults in parental roles ("two-parent families") and at least one child three years of age or older and replicated this survey in 1985. Their results are generally cited as primary data on the prevalence and incidence of family violence. Their "violence index" includes all forms of assault, while the "severe index" excludes "throwing something at another person, pushing, shoving, or grabbing, and slapping or spanking" and includes only "kicking, biting, punching, hitting with an object, beating up, threatening with a knife or a gun, and the use of a knife or gun." Data are only partially analyzed for the 1985 study. When the socioeconomic and demographic correlates of violence are examined in the Straus, Gelles, and Steinmetz data, they generally reveal the same patterns evident in the reported abuse cases, that is, poverty is a risk factor, as are "life stress" and "stressful history." Sibling-to-sibling violence is especially high. By all accounts, this is rarely dealt with as a criminal justice system issue.

B. Prevalence Estimates

The National Incidence Study on child abuse and neglect estimated that 3.4 children per thousand (or roughly 0.34 percent of all children) are known to suffer demonstrable physical harm at the hands of a parent or other in-home caretaker in this country each year. The report also estimated that 5.7 children per thousand are victims of some type of abuse—physical, sexual, and/or emotional—and 5.3 children per thousand endure physical, educational, and/or emotional neglect. Among the low-income populations, the rate of maltreatment (abuse and neglect combined) was estimated at twenty-seven children per thousand. Of course these rates are incidence figures per year. At issue in this discussion is the total *prevalence* rate—how many children experience maltreatment over the course of their childhood (until age eighteen under law).

The overall prevalence rates are, of course, higher than the yearly incidence rates. How much higher? If each case identified by the National Incidence Study was a "once-in-a-childhood" situation, and if maltreatment typically begins to occur with equal frequency across the age span from birth to age eighteen, then we might simply add up the incidence rates for each of the eighteen years involved to get a total prevalence rate. Using the NIS data this would result in figure of a 61.0 per 1,000 children (6.1 percent) overall. This figure is very unlikely, however. For example, most estimates of the proportion of adolescent victims who are the recipients of maltreatment for the first time in adolescence average around 50 percent. This alone would lower the figure to 48.2 per 1,000 (4.8 percent). Also, most cases of child maltreatment are long-term. Thus, the same children who were identified as two-year-old victims might (if undetected or if detected but not treated successfully) be picked up as four-year-old or six-year-old or eight-year-old victims in succeeding years. We can thus expect that the 6.1 percent prevalence rate is an upper limit, and that a significantly lower figure is more likely.

Several surveys of the prevalence of sexual abuse have reported a lifetime rate of approximately 25 percent for females and 10 percent for males. Of course, this includes all forms of sexual molestation and includes sexual assaults perpetrated by strangers and other adults not typically included in the definition of child abuse (i.e., acts by a parent or guardian). Nonetheless, the inclusion of sexual abuse may push up the possible upper prevalence limit.

If the child maltreatment incidence rate of 2.7 percent for low-income children is extrapolated to an upper limit prevalence rate of 55 percent, problems of estimation also arise. The link between low income and maltreatment seems to operate mostly during childhood (particularly infancy and early childhood) and to diminish dramatically in adolescence. This would mean that most low-income-related cases would occur early in childhood and tend to be chronic. A plausible estimate is an overall prevalence of 30 percent for very poor children and youth (based on an initial 2.7 percent incidence rate then declines gradually to a 1 percent incidence rate by age seventeen). All the figures reflect guesses about the relation between incidence and prevalence, of course.

In addition to the estimates provided by the NIS and the AHA reports on the incidence of child maltreatment on which the preceding extrapolations have been based, there have been many studies of the prevalence of various forms of maltreatment. The prevalence estimates are generally substantially higher than the incidence estimates. Peters, Wyatt, and Finkelhor provide a comprehensive review of the prevalence research on child sexual abuse, and Gelles and Cornell provide an overview of research on child abuse generally. Although the earliest prevalence studies involved research subjects who were either volunteers or college students, more recent studies have involved random or stratified probability samples (e.g., national surveys in Canada [Badgley et al. 1984] and the United States [Timnick 1985a, 1985b]). These studies report prevalence estimates for child sexual abuse ranging from 6 percent to 62 percent for females and from 3 percent to 31 percent for males. The lowest rates suggest that child sexual abuse is not an uncommon experience. The highest rates suggest a social problem of staggering dimensions. There are a variety of explanations for variations in estimated prevalence rates. Studies vary in the restrictiveness of their definitions of child sexual abuse, they vary in their sample selection strategies, and they vary substantially in methodology.

II. Governmental Responses to Child Maltreatment

A. Criminal Justice System

A criminal justice model for child abuse was proposed in the 1984 report of the U.S. Attorney General's Task Force Report on Family Violence. Two premises for that report were (1) that family violence (to include child abuse) was to be considered a crime, and (2) that the legal response to family violence must be guided primarily by the nature of the abusive act and not the relationship between the victim and the abuser. A Justice Department official has noted, "The rationale provided for taking what may be considered a much stronger position on child maltreatment was simple justice."

The criminal justice system currently deals with child maltreatment in three ways: it is part of the front-line system for reporting and investigating child maltreatment cases, it is called on to prosecute cases of child maltreatment, and it contends with the consequences and sequelae of child maltreatment in the form of juvenile delinquents and adult criminals (as well as runaways and other status offenders).

By the mid-1980s virtually all police forces had developed some capacity for responding to child maltreatment cases. But most police departments in the United States have twenty or fewer sworn officers; only sixteen states have "full service" state police forces. This means that the typical "law enforcement" response is likely to be in the hands of nonspecialists in many settings, but in the hands of specialist teams in others. Of course, law enforcement and the criminal justice system are involved in all the multiple-perpetrator/multiple-victim cases of sexual abuse.

A comparison by the American Humane Association of its National Study on Child Neglect and Abuse Reporting and the NIS reveals that law enforcement personnel constitute the source of reports to child protective services in 11.6 percent of the AHA's annual compilation of reports and 12.5 percent of the NIS cases known to protective services. In the NIS data, law enforcement personnel constitute 18.4 percent of the cases known but not reported to child protective services.

In a study of Arizona, Montana, North Carolina, and Rhode Island, Greeneveld and Giovannoni reported that police investigated about 6.6 percent of the child maltreatment cases. Criminal action was recommended or initiated in 17.1 percent of these cases (and more rarely still in cases investigated by child protective services). Brown, Miller, and Burke conducted an in-depth exploration of how protective services and police operate in response to reports of child maltreatment in one major metropolitan area. In Cook County, Illinois, police investigated about 20 percent of the reported child maltreatment cases (although almost all reports *eventually* reached the protective services agency). Most (75 percent) of the cases reported to the police (77 percent of which came from the general public, as opposed to professionals) involved neglect rather than abuse. Nationwide, neglect cases outnumber abuse cases by approximately this same two-to-one ratio. The role of police in neglect cases may result from their twenty-four-hour-a-day accessibility as much as anything else, since most neglect reports are for "lack of supervision." Interestingly, the reason why police were selected for identification as the recipients of reports in the earliest model reporting laws was not "ideological" but simply "practical"—the police maintained twenty-four-hour-a-day phone coverage.

If we are to understand the role of law enforcement in reporting child abuse, however, we must understand the general role of professionals in reporting. We must understand what motivates and impedes reporting if we are to be able to predict the impact of any change in the degree of "criminalization" in the process of child protective services.

B. Issues in Reporting

Advocates for battered wives seem united in their belief that the best interests of a battered woman lie in formal actions, particularly law enforcement intervention. In contrast, many child advocates are skeptical about reliance on criminal justice approaches for dealing with child maltreatment in general, and some advocates even oppose these techniques altogether. These advocates emphasize the critical importance of parent-child attachment and psychological continuity for the child's development to proceed. They fear that the punishment orientation of the criminal justice system puts it at odds with children's needs for family stability, even in cases of child maltreatment. Punishing parents separates children from their families, as does any protective removal of the child. In this view, only the most extreme risk justifies an intervention that forces parent-child separation. Even in such an eventuality, however, the child-oriented concern is for permanency in a new or reconstituted, stable family rather than punishment of the perpetrator of abuse. This must be understood in examining the behavior of child abuse reporters, for even in the non-criminalized contexts in which most reporters operate there are many concerns expressed that reporting will initiate a process that leaves children worse off than they were before intervention.

Depending on one's point of view, reporting a suspected case of child maltreatment may be interpreted as an ethically necessary act, as a violation of confidentiality, as the simple meeting of a legal responsibility, as an act of physical courage, as a threat to one's livelihood, as an act of naive faith, or even as an act of folly. Researchers must sort out how these various interpretations reflect the actions of professionals faced with instances of child maltreatment, and how they may bear on child abuse as a criminal justice issue.

Every study conducted to date of reporting by professionals validates the widespread observation that professionals do not report all—and in some cases, even most—of the cases of child maltreatment with which they come in contact. The NIS, for example, attempted to discover the degree to which professionals were aware of cases of child maltreatment but did not report them to their local child protective services agency. Overall, only about one-third of the cases known to professionals were reported to child protective services. The NIS projected that of the 652,000 cases identified by professionals across the United States, only about 212,400 were in child protective service agency records.

In the NIS, the likelihood that a case known to a community's professionals would be reported to protective services varied as a function of characteristics such as the age of the child (cases involving young children were reported more often than cases involving adolescents), and type of maltreatment (at 56 percent, sexual abuse was more likely to be reported than were other forms of abuse and neglect).

Hampton and Newberger conducted further analysis of the NIS data to explore the roles of hospitals as reporters of child maltreatment—primarily abuse. They found underreporting of white, higher income, older parents involved in emotional abuse and neglect, particularly with adolescents. In a small-scale study of the reporting practices of 307 Virginia physicians, Saulsbury and Campbell reported congruent results with respect to type of maltreatment (i.e., emotional maltreatment was underreported). They also found that 38 percent of the physicians justified nonreporting on the grounds that a report should not be filed until diagnosis was certain, and 30 percent did so on the basis that the physician believed that he could solve the problem by working with the family rather than seeking outside intervention. This reluctance may be magnified when it is based on anticipation of law enforcement intervention.

A number of small-scale surveys of professionals and their child-abuse reporting patterns bolster the probable validity of the NIS findings with respect to the existence of a reporting gap (as it applies to professionals). These studies often involve projected responses to hypothetical cases presented by the investigator. The magnitude of the reporting gap varies from study to study, however, with most being smaller than that indicated in the NIS.

Twenty years ago, Silver, Barton, and Dublin reported that more than 20 percent of the physicians they surveyed said they would not report cases of suspected physical child abuse that came to their attention. More recently, James, Womack, and Strauss found that 62 percent of a sample of pediatricians and family physicians said they would decline to report a case of sexual abuse brought to their attention unless the family agreed that such a report should be made. In this and other studies to be reviewed it is unclear what, if any, effect there would be of substituting law enforcement for protective services as "investigators." Such a study is needed.

In a study of eighteen psychiatrists and eighty-three psychologists, pediatricians, and family counselors, Attias and Goodwin found that more than half of the psychiatrists but less than a third of the other clinicians said they would *not* report a family to child protective services in the case of an 11-year-old girl who graphically describes to her school counselor fellatio and cunnilingus with her natural father, ongoing for more than two years, if the child later retracted the allegation. The authors link this in part to widespread misunderstanding of the likelihood that such retractions, rather than the original allegations, are false.

Muehleman and Kimmons found that 81 percent of the psychologists they studied said they would report the hypothetical physical child-abuse case presented by the investigators. This represented an increase from an earlier study by Swaboda et al. in which 87 percent said they would not report the same hypothetical case. In a more highly developed form of the same procedure, Williams, Osborne, and Rappaport used a four point scale (4 = certainly would report; 1 = certainly would not report) and randomly offered four different hypothetical cases to a range of professionals (varying combinations of type of abuse—psychological or physical—and "privileged vs. non-privileged communication").

Overall, most of the professionals indicated likelihood of reporting (an average score of 2.95 on the four-point scale), with the case of physical abuse in the nonprivileged communication condition being most likely to be reported (average score 3.68). Among the professional groups studied, school nurses and ministers were most likely to report (average scores of 3.35 and 3.32, respectively), and psychologists were least likely to report (with an average score of 2.42). Teachers (2.90), psychiatrists (2.87), and physicians (2.85) stood in between these extremes. Law enforcement personnel were not included in this study.

Interestingly, on a separate test of knowledge about reporting statutes, ministers scored highest and nurses lowest, suggesting that knowledge of reporting obligations under the law was not the decisive factor in differentiating among the professional groups. Whether the case involved privileged communication (i.e., information given in the context of therapy) made a significant difference in likelihood of reporting. As the investigators point out, this is particularly interesting because the child abuse reporting statute in the state in which the study was conducted specifically excludes privilege (excepting attorney-client relationship).

As in all social problems containing a "moral" dimension, the distance between the hypothetical and socially desirable "should" and the actual day-to-day "do" can be quite large. Chang et al. reported the results of a survey of 1,367 physicians in which more than 90 percent said they agreed with the statement "physicians in your community should report cases." Slightly more than half (61 percent) said physicians in their community usually report cases. About 30 percent said they had actually seen cases of abuse in the preceding year (1973), but only one-third of these cases were "referred to a community agency." This suggests that an even smaller number were actually reported to child protective services.

Using the National Incidence Study as a basis for comparison, it seems safe to say that reporting has improved since the 1960s and 1970s. Nonetheless, a recent study of professionals' reporting of sexual abuse cases suggests that the issue is still quite alive. Using a self-selected sample of professionals with special interest, responsibility, or both, for sexual abuse cases in New England, Finkelhor found that 64 percent said they reported such cases to protective services when faced with them. The range across professional groups was from 48 percent (for mental health professionals) to 76 percent (for school personnel). Who you are (at least institutionally) seems to affect what you do about reporting.

What else do we know about influences on reporting? A recent report by Morris, Johnson, and Clasen involved a study of how physicians' attitudes toward discipline affected reporting. The fifty-eight Ohio physicians in the study indicated a significant differentiation between parental action they classified as "inappropriate" and action they would report. For example, while 98 percent identified "bruising with a belt" as inappropriate discipline, only 48 percent said they would report it to protective services as child abuse. In general, the higher the physician's tolerance for physical punishment, the less likely they were to report abuse (using a common set of ten hypothetical cases as the standard for comparison). "Personal experience with the family through previous visits" was an important factor in deciding whether to report abuse for 57 percent of the physicians participating in the study, only 30 percent of whom had in fact reported more than one case of suspected abuse in the preceding year.

These results come from physicians who agreed to participate in the survey, of course. Given that they represented a little less than half (43 percent) of the physicians originally contacted, we can expect that their responses reflect a "better" than average awareness of and commitment to the issue of intervention in child maltreatment. This is true of most (virtually all) of the surveys of professionals, which usually have a participation rate of approximately 50 percent.

What can we learn from this review? Three conclusions emerge. First, the reporting gap for child maltreatment is an empirical fact of life. Every expectation is that the results of the replication of the National Incidence Study will mirror the findings from 1979-80 that a major proportion of the professionally identified child maltreatment "caseload" is being dealt with outside of the legally mandated child protective service system. Has the reporting gap changed? Results of the NIS replication should shed some light on this issue. Due principally to the dramatic increase in identified cases of sexual abuse, the total number of child maltreatment cases reported to child protective service units has increased significantly in the period since the first NIS. The most recent data from the American Humane Association's National Study of Child Abuse Reporting suggest a reduction in the rate of increase, however.

Is reporting catching up with case identification? This is an empirical question capable of being answered in the NIS replication. However, Alfaro's 1985 survey of 243 professionals mandated by New York State law to report suggests that the problem remains significant (and may even be growing as frustration with the ability of over-burdened child protective service agencies grows). In his survey of 131 school employ-ees, sixty-two hospital employees, and fifty law enforcement employees, Alfaro found that the most important impediments to reporting abuse was a fear of reprisal against the child and doubts about the efficacy of child protective services. Forty percent of the school personnel, 18 percent of the hospital personnel, and *8 percent of the police* acknowledged instances of nonreporting. Alfaro, found that "professional judgment," not the state reporting law, is the most decisive factor in reporting. Only 19 percent indi-cated "the law was the most important factor in the decision to make a report." We can speculate that law enforcement personnel are most directly affected by the law, how-ever, given their low rate of nonreporting.

Second, moving beyond the "narrow" issue of professional reporting, there is a "broader" issue of professional case identification. Child maltreatment is intrinsically a social problem. It exists, not as some objective entity, but as the result of an on-going social process of negotiation between community standards including values, beliefs, ethical principles, conceptions of the rights of children, concepts of human nature and folk wisdom, and professional expertise including research findings, theoretical deduc-tion, and clinical insight. Thus, the very existence of child maltreatment as a category of human experience is not fixed.

The definition of child maltreatment changes and develops as professional knowl-edge increases and community standards change. Acts that were once considered "accidental injuries" (such as deaths of infants in automobile accidents while riding on the laps of their parents) may become definitionally transformed as knowledge increases (and these deaths come to be defined as "preventable accidents"). As the knowledge-values negotiation proceeds, these same events may eventually be seen as culpable acts of maltreatment. And, the probability of criminal justice system inter-vention increases correspondingly.

A similar history is evident with respect to the use of violence against chil-dren—which once was generally accepted as "positive discipline" but came to be seen first as "corporal punishment," and more recently as "physical assault," en route to being defined as "physical abuse."

Gaps in reporting may exist because of gaps between case conceptualization and identification and legally mandated responses. The lower limit for criminal justice inter-vention should be set higher than the limit for mental health or social service inter-vention. A more fully resolved "negotiation" between community values and scientific evidence and expertise is needed to justify the police function than is required to autho-rize the public health function. This is particularly evident in the matter of psycho-logical maltreatment, where such a two-tiered approach is generally recommended.

The last twenty years have seen a dramatic improvement in case identification. As Alfaro's evidence suggests, however, the practical implications of this change are not clear-cut. We must differentiate between professional responses that obstruct further therapeutic and protective action (e.g., by suppressing case identification with its implied moral imperative to intervene) and responses that facilitate such intervention. This, of course, is a "higher" rendering of the commonly asserted differentiation between a criminal justice system response and a social service, or mental health system, response. This differentiation must at least be made conceptually. In legal matter of fact, of course, there is usually no such distinction.

Legal realities do not always correspond to social and psychological realities. Even a cursory look at the processes and outcomes of litigation and criminal prosecution demonstrates this. There is an important empirical question of whether child protective service involvement results in more and better intervention for children. In its extreme form, this concern underlies Goldstein, Freud, and Solnit's objection to protective intervention in all except the most dire circumstances. This provides the context for exploring the impact of further "criminalization" of child maltreatment (and correspondingly greater reliance on law enforcement for investigation).

For sexual abuse, particularly, many service providers hypothesize that involving the child protective service machinery (particularly if it invokes a law enforcement response) produces unnecessary negative consequences for the child that outweigh any benefits. Certainly, many respondents to Alfaro's survey believe this to be the case. Most respondents cited "quality of CPS intervention" as a concern that dissuaded them from meeting their legal mandate to report child maltreatment. Newberger has been outspoken in articulating the view that, when official intervention is iatrogenic in the sense that the treatment itself is harmful (as it tends to be, in his opinion, when criminal prosecution is involved), professional intervention will be pushed outside the law. Of course, it is an empirically unresolved issue as yet, whether criminal justice's reputation for *powerful* intervention is more significant in affecting reporting than the stereotype commonly held by professionals from social services and mental health that criminal justice intervention is iatrogenic.

Different solutions are required to deal with reporting that stems more from negative motivations (i.e., from a self-interested refusal to "get involved" or a tolerance for maltreatment) than from positive beliefs that the best interests of the child are served by intervention outside the context of reports to child protective service agencies or criminal justice systems. Nonreporting of the first type can and should be dealt with by education, training, and legal sanction. But such nonreporting appears to be only part, and probably, the smaller part, of the current problem.

Narrowing the reporting gap does not appear to depend principally on further training of professionals with respect to their legal obligations or further criminalization of child maltreatment. Neither does it depend on simple exhortation. And, even allowing for the motivational impact of showcase prosecutions of nonreporting professionals, it does not depend on more active implementation of current legal mandates to report.

Rather, the answer seems to lie with raising the standard of response by child protective services and their allied investigatory and enforcement agencies. Existing evidence suggests that this should work. What we need, of course, is an experimental study demonstrating that actual and perceived improvement in the quality of protective services results in a corresponding decrease in well-intentioned resistance to reporting. This study should also test the hypothesis that the increased involvement of the criminal justice system results in better child protection and in community perception of better child protection.

Even a retrospective study demonstrating a correlational link between quality of protective services and willingness to report would be a valuable contribution (and one the NIS replication currently being conducted could provide). Some case studies are consistent with the hypothesis that better child protective service performance reduces resistance to reporting.

The key to better reporting lies in a quality of official response that meets three criteria. First, it must reinforce reporting by being responsive to the reporter's need for feedback, follow-up, and participation in the process that reporting initiates. Will criminal justice intervention do this? Some fear that the more stringent rules of evidence and due process protections invoked by criminal justice system involvement will undermine such changes. Second, better reporting methods must significantly reduce iatrogenesis, go to great lengths to explain and understand such effects when they do occur, and include good faith efforts to prevent such effects where they do occur. Here too, there are grounds for concern that the greater power of the criminal justice system will lead to greater abuses of power. Third, it must assemble a convincing data set to demonstrate the comparative benefits of reporting and of intervention not accompanied by reporting, including a demonstration of any adverse consequences of intervention undertaken in the absence of reporting to child protective services.

Burnett et al. reported on a pilot program to team police and social workers to intervene in domestic disturbance calls. Data from the program's first year of operation showed that "parent/child" problems constituted 26 percent of the 577 calls answered (as opposed to 20 percent for "runaway," 17 percent for "suicide/depression," 9 percent for "marital," 8 percent for "neighborhood problems," and 20 percent for "other"). Other programs involve training police in methods of dealing with "domestic disturbances."

A study by Andrews and Cohn reported that when police investigate reports of neglect they are likely (or at least were when the study was done in the 1970s) to begin a process that results in the youth being labeled a status offender. Of 121 cases of neglect studied, 75 percent eventually were declared persons in need of supervision (PINS). Some 53 percent of the nonneglected youth studied eventually were declared PINS.

Labeling is a recurring issue associated with criminal justice system interventions. Particularly where adolescents are concerned, the "same" youth can be defined differently depending on who does the initial intake. For example, Farber and Kinast report that a comparison between a group of adolescents classified as "runaways" and a group classified as "abuse victims" revealed no significant difference in the experience of violence in the home—both groups came from violent homes as assessed using the Conflict Tactics Scale employed by Straus, Gelles, and Steinmetz in their national survey. In a similar vein, Brown, Miller, and Burke report that the action taken by police when responding to protective service cases depends to a great extent on the options open to them. For example, if they can call on emergency homemakers they are less likely to remove children who are unsupervised. This cautions against overgeneralization to speak of the law enforcement response or the criminal justice approach.

We said at the beginning of this chapter that detecting child abuse is difficult because of the privacy in which it commonly occurs. In recent years, attempts to be more vigilant for child abuse have led to questions about the extent to which children's testimony that they have been abused can be relied on. A particularly troubling version of this problem has surfaced in the last few years. This is the possibility that abused children may repress their memories of abuse but be able to recover those memories intact many years later. The following article is an examination of several books that discuss that possibility.

This article raises a number of important issues for any empirical approach to family law. First, how should the law treat the social sciences in general and expert witnesses in particular? If a school of therapists argues that recovered memory is possible, should a judge admit their evidence? Should a judge leave it to the jury to evaluate their evidence? Is a judge capable of distinguishing between "good" and "bad" psychology? Second, how should the interest in protecting people who have been falsely accused of child abuse be balanced against the interest in protecting children from abuse?

Frederick Crews, *The Revenge of the Repressed,* THE NEW YORK REVIEW OF BOOKS 54 (November 17, 1994)[*]

1.

Throughout the past decade or so, a shock wave has been sweeping across North American psychotherapy, and in the process causing major repercussions within our families, courts, and hospitals. A single diagnosis for miscellaneous complaints—that of unconsciously repressed sexual abuse in childhood—has grown in this brief span from virtual non-existence to epidemic frequency. As Mark Pendergrast shows in *Victims of Memory*, if we put together the number of licensed American psychotherapists (roughly 255,000) with survey results about their beliefs and practices, it appears that well over 50,000 of them are now willing to help their clients realize that they must have endured early molestation. Those professionals have been joined by countless untrained operators who use the yellow pages and flea market ads to solicit "incest work." It is hard to form even a rough idea of the number of persuaded clients, because most of them take no publicly recorded action against the accused, but a conservative guess would be a million persons since 1988 alone. The number *affected* is of course

---

vastly higher, since, as all parties acknowledge, virtually every case sows dissension and sorrow throughout a family.

When one explanation for mental distress rockets to prominence so quickly, we ought to ask whether we are looking at a medical breakthrough or a fad. However, the choice between those alternatives is not always simple. As its main proponents insist, "recovered memory" is by now not just a diagnosis but a formidable sociopolitical movement. In the words of one of that movement's founders, the Harvard psychiatrist Judith Lewis Herman,

> The study of trauma in sexual and domestic life becomes legitimate only in a context that challenges the subordination of women and children. Advances in the field occur only when they are supported by a political movement powerful enough to legitimate an alliance between investigators and patients and to counteract the ordinary social processes of silencing and denial.

The larger movement in question is of course, women's liberation, including what Herman calls "a collective feminist project of reinventing the basic concepts of normal development and abnormal psychology . . . ."

However uneasy one may feel about an ideologically driven "reinvention" of scientific notions, it is possible that the feminist critique of received psychological lore is substantially right. Feminists were certainly warranted, in the 1970s and 1980s, in declaring that the sexual abuse of children was being scandalously underreported. If they now go on to claim that untold millions of victims, mostly female, have *forgotten* what was done to them, their claim cannot be discredited by the mere fact that it sprang from an activist commitment. Obviously, it needs to be assessed on independent grounds.

Yet such grounds are hard to come by. How can one count authentic cases of repressed memory when the very concept of repression stands in doubt? And what, for that matter, do the champions of recovered memory mean by repressions? It is fruitless to press them very hard on this point, since most of them show an impatience with our outright ignorance of conceptual subtleties. Thus in the movement's most influential document, *The Courage to Heal,* first published in 1988, Ellen Bass and Laura Davis proclaim that "none of what is presented here is based on psychological theories." Instead, Bass and Davis appeal directly to "the experiences of survivors"—who, however, may or may not *be* survivors of abuse, depending on whether they have actually learned the previously repressed truth or succumbed to therapeutically induced delusion.

Although it is no secret that the idea of repression derives from Sigmund Freud, few of the movement's practitioners have actually studied his texts. Consequently, they are unrestrained by certain ambiguities and outright contradictions implicit in the Freudian theory of repression. Freud's uncertainty, for example, whether *events* or *fantasies* make up the typical content of the repressed gets resolved in favor of events; as Herman puts it in the opening sentence of *Trauma and Recovery* "the ordinary response to atrocities is to banish them from consciousness." Again, whereas Freud confusingly treated repression as both a conscious and unconscious mechanism, his activist successors think of it as strictly unconscious—so much so, indeed, that they can routinely regard a young incest victim as leading two parallel but wholly independent lives, one in the warm daylight of normal family affection and the other in continually repressed horror. And while Freud only occasionally portrayed the undoing of repression as yielding undisguised, accurate information about a patient's early past contemporary "retrievers" entertain no doubts on the point; with the right coaxing, their patients can allegedly reproduce the exact details of their long-repressed traumas.

By today, recovered memory has enlisted the enthusiasm of many psychotherapists who lack the explicit feminist agenda of Herman, Bass and Davis, and other advocates whose views we will examine later. But all parties do share the core tenet of repression—namely, that the mind can shield itself from ugly experiences, thoughts, or feelings by relegating them to a special "timeless" region where they indefinitely retain a symptom-producing virulence. Clinical experience, the therapists agree, has proven the cogency of this tenet in numberless successfully resolved cases.

But has it really? When arbitrary assumptions leak into "clinical experience," confirming results can be pumped out as easily as bilge water. That is why research psychologists would insist that the concept of repression be required to pass tests in which variables are controlled and rival explanations or the gathered data are ruled out. Yet while psychoanalytic loyalists have repeatedly attempted to conduct just such experiments, their positive results have at best shown a compatibility with repression, not a demonstration of its existence. As David S. Holmes recently concluded after reviewing a sixty-year history of such efforts, "there is no controlled laboratory evidence supporting the concept of repression."

Of course, repression cannot be experimentally disproved, either. Since the concept entails no agreed-upon behavioral markers, we are free to posit its operation whenever we please—just as we are free to invoke orgone energy or chakras or the life force. Indeed, as Elizabeth Loftus and Katherine Ketcham remark in their lively new book, *The Myth of Repressed Memory,* belief in repression has the same standing as belief in God. The idea may be true, but it is consistent with too many eventualities to be falsifiable—that is, amenable to scientific assessment.

It *is* possible, however, to mount experimental challenges to corollary tenets that are crucial to recovered memory therapy. That is just what Loftus, a highly regarded researcher and a professor of psychology at the University of Washington, has done in her own experimental work—and that is also why she has been pilloried by the recovery movement as an enemy to incest survivors. *The Myth of Repressed Memory* recounts some of that vilification and tries to head off more of it by taking a conciliatory tone wherever possible. But there is simply nothing to negotiate over. The burden of Loftus's argument is that memory does not function in anything like the way that the recovery movement presupposes.

Loftus offers no encouragement to the retrievers' notion that "video-taped" records of events are stored in a special part of the brain and then suddenly yielded up to near-perfect recall. Empirical science, she reports, has established that memory is inherently sketchy, reconstructive, and unlocalizable. Whether pleasant or unpleasant, it decays drastically over time, though less so if the experience in question gets periodically "rehearsed"—just the opposite of what the retrievers' theory would predict. Furthermore, memory is easily corrupted, if not with an experimenter's deliberate intervention or a therapist's unwitting one, then with a normal "retrospective bias" that accommodates one's sense of the past to one's present values. Flashbacks to an early age, then, are highly unreliable sources of information about any event. All in all, Loftus finds no basis for thinking that repression, as opposed to gradual avoidance and atrophy of painful recollections, has figured in a single molestation case to date.

Once we have recognized that a memory can disappear because of factors other than repression, even the best anecdotal evidence for that mechanism loses its punch. Consider, for example, the closely watched case of Ross Cheit, a Brown University professor who has recently proved beyond question that his suddenly recalled 1968 molestation by a music camp administrator was real. But had that abuse been repressed in the first place? In a phone conversation with me on September 7, 1994, Cheit declared that while he takes no position on the existence of repression, he is inclined to doubt that he abruptly and completely consigned his experience to oblivion. A more likely account is that the adult Cheit *refocused* his faded but unrepressed experiences after he had read a book about pedophilia (as he did) and became morally exercised about it. While this, too, is guesswork, the fact that it can't be ruled out renders Cheit's case useless as a demonstration.

Useless, that is, from the standpoint of logic. For another purpose, that of inducing popular belief in the theory of repression, anecdotes can be powerfully effective. The very idea of repression and its unraveling is an embryonic romance about a hidden mystery, an arduous journey, and a gratifyingly neat denouement that can ascribe our otherwise drab shortcomings and pains to deep necessity. When that romance is fleshed out by a gifted storyteller who also bears impressive credentials as an expert on the mind, most readers in our culture will be disinclined to put up intellectual resistance.

One such narrator, of course, was Freud, whose shifting views about the content of the repressed will prove pivotal to an understanding of the recovery movement's intellectual ancestry. But Freud's stories purportedly explaining tics, obsessions, and inhibitions among the turn-of-the-century Austrian bourgeoisie are beginning to seem not just remote but eccentric. Not so the case histories recounted by the memory retrievers' most distinguished and fluent ally, Lenore Terr, who is not only a practicing therapist but also a professor of psychiatry at the University of California at San Francisco. Terr's deftly written book, *Unchained Memories: True Stories of Traumatic Memories; Lost and Found,* has already been welcomed both by the Book-of-the-Month Club and by early reviewers who perceived it as a balanced and learned brief for repression.

The publication of *Unchained Memories* has been especially cheering to recovery advocates because Terr is not afraid to challenge their *bête noire,* Elizabeth Loftus. "[P]sychological experiments on university students," Terr writes, taking dead aim at Loftus's work,

> do not duplicate in any way the clinician's observations. What comes from the memory lab does not apply well to the perceptions, storage and retrieval of such things as childhood murders, rapes, or kidnappings. Trauma sets up new rules for memory.

From Loftus's vantage, of course, such a passage begs the question of how these new rules are to be validated without succumbing to the notorious circularity of "clinical experience." Isn't Terr simply handing herself a conceptual blank check? Nevertheless, she scores a strong rhetorical point with her animadversion against hothouse science. If Terr is right about the special character of real-world trauma, we may have to fall back on sheer stories after all.

2.

Among Terr's own stories none carries more weight then the George Franklin/Eileen Lipsker case, which occupies the first two chapters of her book. The case, in which Terr herself served as an expert witness "to explain," as she says, "'repression' and 'the return of the repressed,'" came to national attention in 1989 with the newspaper and television reports of Eileen Franklin Lipsker's long-buried but amazingly lucid recollection of the way her father, in her terrified presence in 1969, had raped her eight-year-old best friend in the back of his Volkswagen bus and then shattered the girl's skull with a rock and covered the body on a wooded hillside south of San Francisco. In Terr's rendering, this story has about it a ring of unanswerable truth, backed up by the soberest of corroborators, a jury in a murder trial.

But Terr's account is not the only one available. It was preceded by Harry N. MacLean's scrupulous book-length retelling of the murder story, *Once Upon a Time,* and now it has been scrutinized by MacLean himself, by Elizabeth Loftus and Katherine Ketcham in *The Myth of Repressed Memory,* and by Richard Ofshe, professor of sociology at the University of California, Berkeley, and Ethan Watters in an even more trenchant new book, *Making Monsters.* In view of their findings, the Franklin matter may come to serve as a very different object lesson from the one that Terr intended. If so, a man's freedom hangs in the balance—not a good man, surely, but a man who may have been wrongly convicted.

During the 1990 murder trial in Redwood City, California, it turned out that no concrete evidence implicated Franklin in Susan Nason's death. On the contrary, Franklin's junked van from 1969, located and microscopically studied by police investigators, bore no trace of the twenty-year-old crime. Until a recollection on the part of Eileen's vindictive sister Janice was conveniently revised under therapy, Franklin had a solid alibi for his whereabouts at the time of the abduction. The jury, however, determined with little difficulty that Eileen Lipsker's recovered memory too closely matched the known facts of the unsolved murder to be considered specious. As a result, Franklin is now serving a life sentence in state prison, and the theory of recovered memory has acquired an imposing trophy.

Lenore Terr appears to have assumed from the outset that Franklin was guilty as charged, and she was eager to make herself useful to the prosecution. Awkwardly, however, her research interest in actual cases of repressed memory was quite new; it seems to have postdated the writing of her 1990 book, *Too Scared to Cry,* which contains no index entry for "repression" and which reports on cases of continuously remembered rather than forgotten trauma. Terr's expertise on sudden recall, moreover, dated from her first interview with Eileen Lipsker herself—and was then swelled by a flood of highly dubious anecdotes about other women's therapeutically prompted visions of incest. But Terr is a thoroughly trained Freudian, and as such she felt qualified, after all, to offer the Franklin jury what she calls "an education" in the reality of repressed memory and its retrieval. Coordinating strategy with the prosecutor and tailoring her testimony, as she now relates, to the job of rendering Eileen Lipsker a wholly credible witness, Terr exceeded the expectations of her temporary employers.

Of course, Terr testified, an expert such as herself can verify the authenticity of a recovered memory through careful interpretation of the subject's symptoms. In some cases, she continued, the expert can even reliably infer the nature of an *unknown* trauma. Indeed, she herself had recently done exactly that, deducing from Stephen King's novels and films the certain knowledge that in his childhood King had watched a playmate die under the wheels of a railroad train.

As Terr now recounts, she mentioned that feat of detection in order to create a helpful analogy in the jurors' minds.[8] She hoped they would see that, like Stephen King in his violence-ridden fiction, Eileen Franklin, for five years after the murder, had symptomatically acted out the awful scene that she had observed but almost immediately repressed. According to prosecutors, between the ages of nine and fourteen Eileen had continually pulled out all the hair from one segment of her crown, leaving what Terr calls "a big, bleeding bald spot." That spot uncannily corresponded to the part of Susan Nason's head that had allegedly been smashed by George Franklin. Eileen, then, had apparently turned herself into a living hieroglyph of a crime that Terr could have inferred all by herself, simply by translating the language of Eileen's symptomatic behavior into its mnemonic source within her repressed unconscious.

In an ordinary trial, caught up in claims and counterclaims about the purport of submitted evidence, the mesmerizing quality of Terr's self-depiction as a Freudian Sherlock Holmes could scarcely have assumed much importance. But this was no ordinary trial. Factually impoverished, it came down to little more than a twelve-person referendum on the photographic return of the repressed. According to the later word of several jurors, and to Terr's great present satisfaction, her testimony was decisive in obtaining George Franklin's conviction.

What most impressed both Terr and the jury about Eileen Lipsker's recovered memory was its extraordinary vividness and precision. The brands of beer and cigarettes consumed by George Franklin at the murder scene; Susan Nason's raising her right hand to ward off the fatal blow; the glint of the sun in her clear blue eyes as George brought the rock down on her head; "a crushed, stoneless, silver child's ring" on the now lifeless hand—all of these details and more were as fresh to Eileen in 1989,

---

[8] Whether Terr had actually detected anything is open to doubt. The upsetting death of King's boyhood friend was already familiar to her from King's autobiography— where, however, King reports that so far as he knows, he did *not* witness the accident in question. Thus Terr's courtroom example of trustworthy clinical reasoning—proceeding from obsessive themes in King's eventual artistic productions to a "repressed" fact about one early day in his life—actually dealt with a *still uncorroborated* detail superadded to a story in the public domain. Insofar, then, as the Franklin trial hinged on Terr's testimony about Stephen King, it appears that one no-evidence case was decided on the basis of another.

Terr says, as they had allegedly been twenty years before. How, then, could they not be authentic and conclusively damning?

One answer to that question was provided at the trail by none other than Elizabeth Loftus herself, an expert witness on the other side. Tests on thousands of subjects have shown conclusively, Loftus told the court, not only that memory always fades with the passage of time but that it readily incorporates "post-event information" (whether true or false) that becomes indistinguishable from the actual event. Those two facts together suggest that the sharpness of Eileen Lipsker's "memory" must have been caused by *recent* images—and, as we will see, there was no shortage of such potential contaminants at hand.

With coaching from Terr, however, the prosecution, was ready to remove the sting from Loftus's reported findings. Did any of her experiments, she was asked in cross-examination, deal with memories that were two decades old? Wasn't it the case that her experimentally induced distortions of memory affected only some details and not loss of the brute fact that an event had occurred? And had she ever studied a repressed memory? No, she hadn't for two excellent reasons; she wasn't sure that such memories exist, and even if they do, she couldn't imagine how one could get at them for controlled study.

Regrettably, however, this answer occurred to Loftus after she had left the stand. What she replied instead was that post-event information would probably corrupt a repressed memory in just the way that it assuredly corrupts a nonrepressed one. The concept of repression was thus left unchallenged, and the befuddled jury had no recourse but to side with the rival expert witness—the one who boasted intimacy with the dark and subtle working of the unconscious.

But Lenore Terr first needed to tiptoe across a theoretical minefield of her own. Her studies of children who had lived through the notorious Chowchilla bus kidnapping and the *Challenger* explosion had shown unambiguously that such experiences do not get repressed. Why, then, should the jury believe that Eileen Lipsker had repressed her harrowing ordeal? Just in time for the trial, but too late for prior publication, Terr came up with a face-saving theory. True, she granted, one-time trauma victims always remember the event; but victims of multiple trauma like Eileen Lipsker, whose father had been a bullying drunk and a sexual abuser of two of his other daughters, turn repression into a daily routine. By the time of the murder, according to Terr, Eileen had become an old hand at stuffing bad memories into the mental freezer.

Terr's brainstorm was remarkable in several respects. For one thing, it overlooked the fact, later acknowledged in *Unchained Memories,* that Eileen had always remembered her father's violence around the house. Second, it contradicted universal human experience of protracted duress. Has anyone past the age of, say, six who has survived racial persecution, a famine, a bombing campaign, or a brutal enemy occupation ever forgotten that it occurred? Terr had evidently confused the normal fading of *individual instances* of repeated, patterned mistreatment with willed unawareness of the mistreatment. And third, Terr was refusing to grant any distinction in memorability between George Franklin's usual brutality and the witnessed rape and murder of Eileen's best girlhood friend.

Beyond the already mentioned dubieties in Terr's version of the Franklin case lie a good number of others emphasized by MacLean, Loftus and Ketcham, and Ofshe and Watters, and more briefly by Mark Pendergrast as well. The cardinal point is that Eileen Lipsker's certainty that she had attended the murder of Susan Nason did *not* overwhelm her in a single unprompted flash on what Terr calls "a quiet winter afternoon in 1989." That was the least plausible of five distinct stories that Lipsker kept changing to forestall objections. As the trial record shows, Lipsker, whom Terr characterizes as having known "nothing at all" about repression, had already been consulting two therapists who were helping her probe her childhood "memories" and her conscious, long-standing suspicions about the murder. Both practitioners employed the theory of repression and had discussed it with her. Moreover, Eileen was aided in producing increasingly bizarre visions of George Franklin committing another murder—this one not just unsolved but completely unknown to police or anyone else—with herself as a witness and of his raping or otherwise sexually abusing her, sometimes in the presence of oblivious family members, from the ages of three through fourteen. She even came to believe that George had physically assisted her godfather in raping her. Incredibly, though, none of these barbarities had left a glint of long-term memory in her conscious mind.

Terr omits any mention of George's second "murder" committed in Eileen's presence, but she does cite the equally implausible memories of incest scenes. In doing so, however, she offers no clue that all this knowledge emanated from a regimen of therapeutic dowsing and that some of it *preceded* the original murder flashback. This latter fact is important because Eileen's newly formed belief that she had spent her childhood being molested provided her with an extra motive for wanting to see George imprisoned. Terr as author is no more interested in dwelling on such motives than the prosecution was. She uses Eileen's sexual "memories" only in the partisan and highly effective way that they were used in the trial, to establish that a beast like George was just the sort of person who could have raped Susan Nason and then bludgeoned her to death.

The fact that memory therapy lay at the very heart of the Franklin case was manifested in little-noted testimony from one of Eileen's therapists, Kirk Barrett. According to Barrett, as Ofshe and Watters report,

> Barrett remembers that from June [1989], when she initially visualized the first element of what was to become the crime scene, through July, Eileen worked both in and out of the sessions trying to sort out the meaning of her feelings, visualizations, and memories. He assured Eileen at the time that it "wasn't important . . . whether her visualizations were real or not," and that they could "sort that out later." In and out of therapy the details slowly cohered into a narrative. One day she came in and reported to Barrett that she had seen a flash image of someone hitting Susan with a rock—*but that she couldn't make out who the person was.* According to Barrett it was several sessions later, in a highly emotional moment, that Eileen revealed that she was finally able to see the face of the man who killed [Susan]. It was her father's.

Eileen Lipsker originally told her brother that the murder scene had revealed itself to her *in hypnosis* during her therapy. Later, she told a sister that she had *dreamed* the crucial knowledge—an equally suggestive fact since recovered memory therapy often employs either hypnosis or dream analysis or both. Lenore Terr wants us to regard these statements as forgivable "lies" and to put our trust in the more enchanting image of Eileen's single flashback to the murder scene. It makes a good deal more sense to suppose that Eileen only belatedly learned that evidence from hypnosis had recently been deemed inadmissible in California courts.

Kirk Barrett's neglected testimony does exculpate Eileen Lipsker in one respect: she had sincerely come to believe that her father was the murderer. Once committed to having him put away, however, she allowed her "memories" to evolve as expediency required, picking up new details and dropping others as newspaper reports disclosed the content of old police records. As Ofshe and Watters remark, virtually the only correct details in her original report were "that Susan had been killed with a rock and that her ring had been crushed—facts that she had told Barrett she had known all her life."

There remains, however, the one striking detail that captivated both the jurors and, I am sure, the early readers of Terr's book: the bleeding bald spot that was said to have marred Eileen Franklin's pate for five straight years after the murder. Quite simply, it turns out to be a figment of Eileen's adult imagination. As Ofshe and Watters discovered, more than forty photographs of her in the relevant period—potential exhibits that the prosecution wrongly withheld from the defense—show no trace of missing hair. Eileen's mother, Leah, who had changed her mind about George's guilt after finding the narrative in *Unchained Memories* so erroneous, has told Ofshe and Watters that she couldn't have failed to notice any such disfiguration if it had occurred even once. An older and a younger sister have also refuted this claim. If, as Terr believes, every symptom tells a story, in this instance the story is a fairy tale.

Once understood in its true lineaments, the Franklin/Lipsker matter turns out to be highly typical of other recovered memory cases. There is, in the first place the eerily dreamlike quality of the "memories" themselves, whose floating perspective, blow-up details, and motivational anomalies point to the contribution of fantasy.[13] There is the therapist's reckless encouragement of the client to indulge her visions and worry "later"—usually never—whether or not they are true, along with his "supportive" absence of concern to check the emerging allegations against available knowledge. There is the interpretation of the "survivor's" moral frailties as further evidence that she is a "trauma victim."[14] There is also, we can infer, the therapist's false promise that

---

[13] As for anomalies, why did George Franklin take his daughter along to watch the rape and murder of her dearest friend? How could he not have expected to be found out? Why would he then make Eileen witness another killing? Why did no one in a crowded living room notice George inserting his finger in Eileen's vagina? Etc.

[14] As Loftus and Ketcham say, "With that diagnosis all the quirks and idiosyncrasies of Eileen Franklin's personality could be explained away. Yes, she lied about being hypnotized . . . but that's understandable because she is a *trauma victim.* Yes, she used drugs and was arrested for prostitution . . . but her behavior makes sense given that she is a *trauma victim.* Yes, she repressed the memory for twenty years . . . but that's a defensive reaction common to *trauma victims.* Anything the defense might say in an attempt to undermine Eileen's credibility as a witness could be turned around and presented as an ongoing symptom . . . ."

excavation of the repressed past will lead to psychic mending instead of to the actual, nearly inevitable, result—disorientation, panic, vengefulness, and the severing of family ties. And there is the flouting or overlooking of what is scientifically known about memory, leaving the field free for dubious theories exfoliating from the original dogma of repression.

One remaining feature of the Lipsker case turns out to be reproduced in nearly every controversy over therapeutically assisted recall. The Franklin jury members, like many people who must weigh the credibility of "survivors," felt that they had to accept Eileen's story because she stood to gain nothing and lose everything by accusing her own father of murder. Of course, that was an oversimplification; Eileen felt that the pedophile George was a threat to her own child, and besides, as many observers perceived, she had a distinct taste for fame.[15] In a deeper sense, however, the jury was right: Eileen had opened a Pandora's box of bitterness and recrimination that will probably trouble her for the rest of her life. Nevertheless, the cardinal point about all this self-destructiveness went completely unnoticed. Eileen Lipsker did not *decide* to send her mind into a tailspin after making rational calculations about the opposing claims of justice and filial loyalty; she was progressively *encouraged* to do so by therapists who believed that full psychic health must wait upon a vomiting up of the repressed past.

Disastrously missed at the trial, this cardinal fact slipped away once again on a subsequent Faith Daniels talk show where, for the first time, Eileen Lipsker and Elizabeth Loftus sat down together. "Why would you want to suffer if you didn't have to?" asked one member of the audience who, like nearly all the others, believed Eileen's story and considered Loftus a heartless crank. "Why would you want to put yourself through it? There's no logic behind it." As Loftus now tells us in her book, she smiled stoically as the audience continued to berate her and rally to Lipsker's cause. And then the program was over.

Reading about this episode, one experiences an extreme frustration. Couldn't Loftus have pointed out that other parties besides Eileen had "put her through it"? That, however, was four years ago, when no one yet had an explanatory handle on the burgeoning plague that still besieges us. Now at last, thanks to the inquires of Loftus and others, it is starting to make an eerie kind of sense.

3.

The Franklin/Lipsker case, so attractive to Lenore Terr as Exhibit A of validated repression, actually shows how a "memory" originating in conscious hunches and resentments can be crystallized by protracted therapeutic *suggestion*, or the subliminal contagion of ideas between a dominant and a subordinate party. That is what we regularly find when missing elements of recovered memory stories are filled in: where repression was, there shall suggestion be. Indeed, someone who reviews many such

---

[15] Lipsker quickly become a heroine in psychotherapeutic circles, appeared on *Sixty Minutes,* collaborated on an as-told-to book, and found herself flatteringly portrayed by Shelley Long in a made-for-TV movie about the case. Her book and movie contracts, negotiated by a Hollywood entertainment lawyer, were signed before the case had gone to trial.

cases will eventually realize that the salient question isn't whether or not a bona fide instance of repression can be found, but rather whether there are any limits at all to the malleability of the human mind. Therapists, it seems, are helpful but not strictly necessary to the production of wildly fantastic memories. Given a facilitating belief structure, the compliant subject can use the merest hints as triggers to delusion. . . .

Until the recovered memory movement got properly launched in the later 1980s, most Satanism charges were brought against child-care workers who were thought to have molested their little clients for the devil's sake. In such prosecutions, which continue today, a vengeful or mentally unhinged adult typically launches the accusations, which are immediately believed by police and social workers. These authorities then disconcert the toddlers with rectal and vaginal prodding, with invitations to act out naughtiness on "anatomically correct" dolls with bloated genitals, and, of course, with leading questions that persist until the child reverses an initial denial that anything happened and begins weaving the kind of tale that appears to be demanded. As many studies have shown, small children can be readily induced to believe that they have experienced just about any fictitious occurrence. In this respect, however, they do not stand fundamentally apart from their elders. The only real difference is that the grown-ups, in order to become as gullible as three-year-olds, must first subscribe to a theory such as that of demonic possession or its scientific counterpart, Freudian repression. They then become putty in the hands of their would-be-helpers.

As it happens, the most impressive controlled illustration of this fact to date came directly from the Paul Ingram case, after the prosecutors—not the defense!—had invited the social psychologist Richard Ofshe to Olympia as an expert on cults and mind control. Perhaps, they thought, Ofshe could cast some light into the murky Satanic corner of the affair. But Ofshe, immediately struck by the conditional quality of Ingram's confessions and their suggestion that a scene was taking place in the mind's eye ("I would've," "I must have," "I see it," etc.), decided to test Ingram's suggestibility by proposing a false memory for him to accept or reject.

"I was talking to one of your sons and one of your daughters . . . ," Ofshe told Ingram. "It was about a time when you made them have sex with each other while you watched." This was one charge that had *not* been levied and would never be, but one day later, Paul proudly submitted a new written confession: . . . When Ofshe then informed Ingram that this memory was specious, Ingram refused to believe him. "It's just as real to me as anything else," he protested.

In recent decades, one of the most active debates about child abuse has concerned the question whether it is better to leave abused children in their homes and provide them and their families with "services" or to remove them from their families and place them with foster parents. One of the most ambitious efforts to answer this question empirically is described in the following chapter from the book in which the investigators reported their research. That research was conducted in two counties in California which had different policies about placing abused and neglected children in foster care or keeping them in their homes. Eventually, the study was able to draw conclusions about thirty-two white children and to discuss less thoroughly thirty-five black and Hispanic children. This chapter is important for two reasons. First, for its attempt to answer the substantive question. Second, and perhaps more significantly, for its careful statement of the numerous problems any attempt to answer this kind of empirical question must confront.

Michael S. Wald, J. M. Carlsmith & P. H. Leiderman, PROTECTING ABUSED AND NEGLECTED CHILDREN 181 (Stanford University Press 1988[*])

We undertook this study because of our belief that public policy regarding the protection of abused and neglected children ought to be based on more than ideology and fiscal considerations. Although policy decisions must ultimately rest on value preferences, evidence about the costs and benefits of alternative policies are critical in making value choices. We retain the belief that research is essential. However, we have learned a great deal about the limits as well as the benefits of research in developing public policy in this area. Before addressing the policy implications of our study, we will identify some of the study's limitations.

Our study provides a substantial amount of information about a small number of children. Looking intensely at these children proved to be very revealing. We found that many children functioned well in one domain and poorly in another, and that intervention had a differing impact on each domain. Therefore, the question "Is home or foster care better?" must be refined by asking further, "In terms of which aspects of development?" and "For which children, under what conditions?"

Unfortunately, intensive evaluation usually requires sacrificing sample size. Rarely will the money be available to study large numbers of children intensively. Small samples often mean that important questions cannot be answered. The small sample size limited our ability to determine which factors were associated with the initial status of the abused and neglected children and which factors accounted for change in individual children. Moreover, we do not feel comfortable generalizing our findings to the nationwide population of children in foster care. Obviously, our findings about the impact of foster care are limited to children in the five-to-ten-years-old age group. We doubt that our findings are applicable to younger children, who might benefit more if permanently separated from inadequate parents. Even for children in the age group we studied, some of our findings might not be replicated if the study were conducted with another sample. Some of our findings may have been influenced by chance. In addition, it is likely that some of the factors that may have accounted for the outcomes in our cases would not be present in other states, or even other counties within California. For

---

[*]   Reprinted from PROTECTING ABUSED AND NEGLECTED CHILDREN, by Michael W. Wald, J.M. Carlsmith, and P.H. Leiderman, with Carole Smith and Rita deSales French, with the permission of the publishers, Stanford University Press. © 1988 by the Board of Trustees of the Leland Stanford Junior University.

example, the outcomes for both home and foster children probably were influenced by both the quality of services to the home families and the quality of the foster homes. There is substantial variation in the quality of services and foster homes in different areas of the country and within each state.

Our analysis also was complicated by the fact that the developmental status of the home and foster children differed somewhat at the time of our initial interviews, which took place after the children had been in foster care for several months. Since there was relatively little change in the overall well-being of the majority of children during the two-year period, the reasons for the initial differences are crucial for policy analysis. . . . [W]e cannot know whether they were attributable to random variation, to differences in the children prior to intervention, or to an initial positive impact of foster care. Thus our study, which required an enormous investment of time and more money than is often available for policy-oriented social science research, became more exploratory than we had hoped or envisioned. As Lee Cronbach has written, "The hope that an evaluation will provide unequivocal answers, convincing enough to extinguish controversy about the merits of a social program, is certain to be disappointed."

Despite these limitations, we were able to address several important policy issues. We began with two central research questions: (a) Should a legislature, in enacting laws regarding alternative interventions, adopt a general preference for home supervision or foster placement? (b) What factors should a social worker or judge consider in deciding whether to use foster care for an individual child? Although we cannot provide definitive answers to these questions, we are able to delineate some of the benefits, and some of the costs, of alternative placement decisions. Our findings are most relevant at the legislative level; we have less to say to those deciding individual cases. In addition, we have identified some developmental areas in which abused and neglected children seem to be at particular risk. Our findings clearly indicate that major changes are needed in the types of interventions intended to protect abused and neglected children. In the following sections we suggest some general policies that might promote the children's well-being, regardless of whether they are living with biological parents or are in foster care. Our data also raise questions about some general theories of child development. Therefore, we end by exploring several issues relevant to those interested in research in child development.

Benefits and Costs of Alternative Placements

INFERENCES FROM THE DATA

We look first at the question "Should a legislature prefer, in general, home supervision or foster care, *for the type of cases evaluated in this study?*" Our data do not provide a clear-cut answer. Rather they illustrate the complexity of the choices, or trade-offs, that must be made. We first review the data, then discuss their implications.

Looking only at what happened to the children from the time we first saw them until the end of the study, two years later, there was not a great deal of difference between home and foster care. On *average*, there was little change in the relative well-being of each group of children. However, those changes that did occur favored foster care. Initially twenty-three white children, five black children, and six Hispanic children were left at home. During the two years, four white children and one black child (15 percent) had to be removed from their parents' custody because of continued abuse and neglect. As a result of the policy favoring leaving children at home, these children were left in an inadequate home for a longer period of time than they might otherwise have been. Trying to forestall removal is clearly costly in human terms, though only one of the children we studied seemed to show deterioration as a result of this. Looked at from the other perspective, however, 85 percent of the home group of children—considered to be in high-risk situations—were able to remain at home without being abused or neglected to a degree requiring removal.

The outcomes for those children who remained at home throughout the two years were mixed, at best. Nearly half the children were subjected to some degree of reabuse or continued neglect, though none of the children suffered serious physical harm. Yet despite the fact that many of the home environments remained only marginally adequate, there was, on average, no deterioration in the well-being of the home children in most areas of development. The only clear area of decline was in social behavior at school. In fact, with regard to the children's personal satisfaction, the home children had higher self-esteem scores and reported better peer relations over the course of the two years, though they were still the least satisfied group on these measures.

The relative stability of the home group must be viewed in light of the many problems initially exhibited by the children and noted throughout the two years. The academic performance of most home children remained below what would be expected based on their IQ scores. Nearly half the children continued to miss substantial amounts of school. Their relations with their parents remained poor; approximately half the children continued to have significant emotional problems. Thus home placement, even with services to the family, did not help the children overcome their academic, emotional, and social problems.

The outcomes for the foster children were somewhat more favorable, at least for the white children. It seems clear from our data, which are consistent with the findings of Fanshel and Shinn (1978), Festinger (1983), and others, that foster care was not detrimental to most children. All but two children were protected from further abuse or physical neglect. There was no area of development (except teachers' ratings of peer relations, in which all children—home, foster, and comparison groups alike—were rated lower over time) where the white foster children, as a group, appeared worse off at the end than initially.

In most aspects of development, the white foster children were better off at the end than at the beginning. The black foster children were not. There was some improvement in both the physical health and the academic performance of the white foster children, though few children either at home or in foster care had health problems, and most children in both settings continued to experience academic difficulties. Perhaps more significant, the foster children reported increased personal satisfaction during the two years. At least with regard to the factors measured by our self-esteem scale, they consistently seemed somewhat more satisfied than the home children. There also seemed to be much less adult-child conflict in the foster setting. Thus, foster care appeared to be meeting some of the emotional needs of the children, as well as enhancing their physical and academic development.

In reaching this conclusion, we are mindful of the fact that even though the foster children were not worse off, foster care did not alleviate some of the problems that the children evidenced when they entered care. For example, almost half the foster children exhibited emotional problems throughout the two years; although some children's school performances improved, the majority were still doing poorly academically. Moreover, the majority of the foster children still seemed to retain an emotional commitment to their biological parents; half expressed a desire to return to them. Like children of divorce, they expressed a psychological need to maintain previous ties. In addition, there were individual foster children, especially among the blacks, who experienced a general decline in overall well-being. However, for both black and white children, the chances of a child's declining in overall well-being was no greater in foster care than at home. There is every reason to believe that the children who experienced problems in foster care would have experienced problems had they been left at home, based on the findings that the home children did not do well and the biological parents of the foster children also showed little ability to change their behaviors.

In sum, although there was relatively little major change among the children in either group, there is some indication that foster care was more beneficial to the children most at risk, at least with regard to improving physical health, school attendance, and academic performance and preventing deterioration in social behavior at school. Both situations—remaining at home and placement in foster care—involved emotional stress for the children, but the stress caused by the conflict and chaos in their home environments may have had a more negative impact on the home children than the stress that separation, movement, and adjustment to new "parents" had on the foster children.

The analysis, to this point, is based only on changes we noted in the children between our initial and final data-gathering points. As we have shown, the white foster children were, on average, better off initially in terms of teachers' ratings, degree of parent-child conflict, and their own reports of personal satisfaction and peer relations. The case for favoring foster care is obviously stronger if we assume that the home and foster children were exactly comparable prior to intervention. If that were true, we would have to conclude that the initial status of the foster children represented an immediate positive impact of foster care, which did not diminish over time. However, if the two groups were noncomparable because of random factors or systematic differences in the type of children considered for home and foster care in the three counties, we can conclude only that foster care was not detrimental to the children.

[T]here is no way of scientifically determining the reasons for initial differences between the home and foster groups. It is possible that foster care had an initial positive impact: the children may have been responding to the greater structure provided by the foster homes. The day-to-day stability of life in a foster home, regular school attendance, freedom from fear of abuse, all may have led the children to perform better in school and to engage in less acting-out behavior in the foster homes. The greater security, material comforts, and attention to their personal needs may have increased the children's personal satisfaction (on those issues measured by our self-esteem scale) and enabled them to develop better peer relations.

We recognize that most literature reports an association of initial trauma with foster placement, and we also found evidence of such trauma. Many foster children in our study exhibited sleep and eating problems; virtually all of them initially said that they wanted to return home. Yet they might have had these experiences and still reacted positively to the foster homes, which provided them with stability and material advantages.

An equally strong case can be made that the initial differences between the home and foster groups were the result of chance, or reflective of nonrandom factors, or both. Two factors may have "caused" the group differences. One is the difference in the proportion of abused children in each group. There were more abused children at home. Abused children tended to be more troubled than neglected children in terms of emotional problems, self-esteem, and perception of peer relations. This factor only partially explains the group differences, however, since the foster children who were in placement because of neglect generally received higher ratings on our measures than neglected children in the home group.

A second possibility is that the home sample contained an atypical group of abused and neglected children. Among the home children, there was a small group of quite disturbed children who came from families with a great deal of parent-child conflict. We cannot know whether these children's emotional problems resulted from, or led to, parental abuse or neglect. However, these children clearly seemed more disturbed than the rest of the sample. Why were there no such children in foster care? Perhaps in Alameda and Santa Clara counties such children were handled in the mental health system, not the child-abuse/-neglect system. In San Mateo County the best way to provide services to a child was through abuse-and-neglect legal proceedings, since the special legislation provided the Department of Social Services with extra funds to handle such cases. No such services were available through that department in Alameda or Santa Clara counties. Therefore, in these counties difficult cases may have been routed to the mental health system, which had its own funding.

There are many other arguments that could be made to support either hypothesis. For example, some theorists argue that the poor social skills of abused and neglected children result from major inadequacies in the mother-child relationship, which are likely to have a lasting impact on the child's development (Sroufe 1983; Erickson, Sroufe, and Egeland 1985). If a child's social development is impaired by the quality of early mother-child attachment, it seems unlikely that the child's social skills and "likability" will improve significantly just as a result of three or four months of foster care. On the other hand, a number of studies indicate that ongoing stress and conflict are particularly detrimental to children (Emery 1982). Removal from such stressful situations might have a significant impact on a child's behavior (Rutter 1980). It may also be that the foster children came to school looking more presentable and that teachers' ratings of the child's likability and social behavior are heavily influenced by the children's appearance.

After weighing and reweighing all arguments many times, we find ourselves unable to choose between the competing hypotheses. Since there is a substantial possibility that the initial differences did not result from a positive impact of foster care, we would not base new policies on the assumption that foster care can have consequential short term impact. We suggest incorporating into policy decisions only the findings that, over the two years, foster care was not detrimental to most children, that the home children seemed to remain at substantial risk in terms of social, emotional, and academic development, and that foster care may have been slightly more beneficial than home placement in terms of the children's health and academic performance.

POLICY IMPLICATIONS OF THE FINDINGS

Regardless of whether we conclude only that foster care was not detrimental, or that the higher level of overall well-being of the foster children reflected, at least to some degree, a positive impact of foster care, we are left with a value choice. Were the benefits of foster care of such a nature that legislators should direct child welfare agencies and courts to prefer foster care for the type of cases that were the focus of this study? As a general rule, our society does not transfer children from parents to nonparents just because the child might do "better," in some aspects of development, in a new home. In addition to concern over the impact of separation from the child's perspective, our society defers to biological ties because of the importance of children to parents and in order not to impose majoritarian notions about rearing children, and because as a society we value cultural, social, and political diversity.

In considering whether to adopt a preference for foster care, it must be recognized that the benefits of foster care may be dependent upon making foster placement permanent—that is, never returning a child to the biological parents. There is no evidence indicating that the type of benefits that seemed to come from foster care would continue if a child were returned home. In fact, by subjecting children to multiple separations from attachment figures, removal and return may be particularly difficult on children. In addition, there is little reason to expect that significant changes will occur in the behavior of the biological parents while the child is away from them, at least with regard to those behaviors that might negatively affect the child's academic, social, and emotional well-being. In most instances, effecting significant changes in parental behavior such that a child's academic, social, and emotional well-being will improve probably requires working with both parent and child. There are also cost considerations in the use of foster care in cases of non-serious injury. If the majority of children in these cases are returned to their biological parents, it may be a waste of resources to remove them in the first place. Unless the child cannot be protected at home, it may be less expensive and more efficacious to leave the child at home and work with the entire family.

Although the benefits of foster care may depend on not returning the child, it seems harsh to terminate parental rights without any effort at reunification in cases in which abuse or neglect did not result in serious injury. In fact, judges and social workers generally are reluctant to terminate parental rights except in compelling cases. The more marginal the grounds for removal, the less likely that judges will terminate parental rights (Wald 1976). As a result, many children may be kept in nonpermanent foster homes and subjected to multiple placements. Without permanent placement, any benefits of foster care may disappear over time.

Thus, a legislator must decide if the harm we found to be associated with leaving a child at home, or the benefit associated with foster care, justify depriving parents of custody, perhaps on a permanent basis. What would be achieved by such a policy? The reabuse or continued neglect among the home cases was not at a level that put the child in jeopardy of serious physical harm. However, many of the home parents failed to ensure their children's school attendance. In addition, half the home environments were marked by high levels of parent-child conflict, which very likely had a negative impact on the child's emotional development. In terms of social development, the greatest problems for the home children were their poor peer relations and low ratings by teachers on social skills and likability. The home children also were, on average, less satisfied with themselves, their peers, and their schools than the foster children, though by the end of the two years the home children's overall satisfaction was not substantially different from that of the foster or comparison children.

CHAPTER V

Breaking Up is Hard to Do:
Ending the Marriage

Approximately twenty-five years ago, the United States embarked on a "divorce revolution": a dramatic change in the body of law governing the dissolution of marriage, accompanied by a dramatic change in the process by which marriages were dissolved. This was, arguably, not the first such revolution, but it is the one with which we now live.

A. Patterns of Marriage and Divorce

The "divorce revolution" is now fully upon us. It would be fair to describe this development as a form of "natural experiment" conducted by legislatures and courts. Although the driving forces of this experiment included ideological commitments to individual self-realization and practical concerns that divorce had become in fact an exercise in fraudulent testimony, the reform movement and its critics usually relied on empirical assertions. On the one hand, it was claimed, adoption of no-fault divorce would create renewed respect for legal institutions, enable persons in broken marital relationships to form new and more successful relations, spare children the daily observation of unhappiness, dissension, and abusive behavior by their parents, and the like. On the other hand, it was also claimed, adoption of no-fault divorce would destabilize marital relationships not only for those who divorce but for their children, redefine the meaning of marriage, diminish the appeal of marriage itself, and produce great unhappiness for children who would necessarily find themselves in single parent homes for at least some time.

The following set of readings provides some evidence concerning the extent to which these (and other) predictions have come to pass.

The first article, by Frank F. Furstenberg, Jr., summarizes the history and current status of divorce in the United States. It provides a demographic view of changes in divorce and remarriage, racial and ethnic differences in patterns of divorce and remarriage, and the effects of divorce and non-marital child-bearing on the family experiences of children.

The second article, by Paul R. Amato, examines one particular aspect of the divorce revolution: the effect of divorce not on those who undergo that event but on their children. Most particularly, Amato is concerned with the extent to which divorce is transmitted intergenerationally and the mechanisms by which that may occur.

Frank F. Furstenberg, Jr., *History and Current Status of Divorce in the United States,* THE FUTURE OF CHILDREN, 4 CHILDREN AND DIVORCE 29 (Summer/Fall 1994)*

As far back as the nineteenth century, when divorce was still uncommon in the United States, Americans worried about the consequences of marital dissolution for children. Then as now, opinion divided between critics of liberalized divorce practices who worried that reform would undermine the capacity of parents to protect and nurture children and reformers who believed that divorce is a necessary mechanism to ensure matrimonial success. None of the participants in these debates a century or more ago, however, contemplated an era when divorce would become an intrinsic part of our marriage system or a time when close to half of all those who entered marriage would voluntarily end their unions. . . .

The first section of this article describes trends in divorce and remarriage . . . and comments on the growing pattern of informal unions that complicates our interpretation of recent patterns of marriage, divorce, and remarriage. The commonalities and differences between family patterns in the United States and those in other industrialized nations are discussed. The second section of the article identifies some important sources of the transformation in marriage practices. . . . [T]he third section provides a demographic context for this discussion by comparing the family experiences of different cohorts of children as they have encountered increasing levels of marital instability. In doing so, it highlights the very different types of family patterns that occur among whites, African Americans, and Hispanics. In the final section, some themes that emerge throughout the article are addressed, including what sorts of trends might occur in the near future and whether various policy initiatives can influence the future of the family, the patterns of parenting, and the welfare of children who face high degrees of uncertainty in their family arrangements.

Historical Changes in Divorce and Remarriage

Until the latter part of the nineteenth century, divorce was largely proscribed by law and shunned in practice much as still happens today in many nations including some European countries such as Italy and Ireland. Most marital disruptions occurred not as a result of divorce but from desertion or informal separation. Because population surveys were not available prior to the middle part of the twentieth century, it is difficult to know how often de facto divorce took place in the United States. But, it

---

    *   Source: Furstenberg, Jr., Frank F. History and Current Status of Divorce in the United States. *The Future of Children,* (Summer/Fall 1994) 4, 1:29-43. Reprinted with permission of the David and Lucile Packard Foundation. *The Future of Children* journals and executive summaries are available free of charge by faxing mailing information to: Circulation Department (650) 948-6498.

seems likely that all but a small minority of marriages survived until the death of one or another partner, an event that typically occurred much earlier than it does today. Some have argued that the rise of divorce was partly prompted by increasing survival rates, which placed a greater strain on the ability of couples to manage marital stress or maintain marital contentment. However, there is no firm evidence to support this conjecture.

Divorce rates in the United States began to rise shortly after the Civil War and continued on an (sic) steady upward course for more than a century. Over this time rates have fluctuated, often falling in poor economic times and generally surging after major wars. But these short-term variations have been far less consequential to the long-term pattern of constant growth. Nearly two decades ago, Preston and McDonald calculated the likelihood of divorce for each marriage cohort beginning in 1867 and continuing until the mid-1960s. Their results showed a continuous trend of dissolution among successive marriage cohorts. Roughly 5% of marriages ended in divorce just after the Civil War compared with an estimated 36% in 1964. Thus, the pattern of prevalent divorce was firmly in place in this country even before the divorce revolution of the 1960s.

Nonetheless, there was a sharp increase in the incidence of divorce from the mid-1960s to the late 1970s. During a span of a decade and a half, divorce rates for married women more than doubled (from 10.6 per 1,000 in 1965 to 22.8 in 1979), pushing the risk of divorce much higher for all marriage cohorts, especially those who wed after the mid-1960s. Some researchers speculated that a majority of all marriages contracted in the 1970s and after would end, especially when both informal separations and formal divorces were counted. Other researchers reached more conservative estimates but still projected that more than two in every five marriages would end in divorce when divorce rates reached their peaks in the middle 1970s.

Divorce rates began to level off in the late 1970s and actually declined by about 10% during the 1980s. As mentioned earlier, fluctuations of this sort are common historically and do not necessarily signal a reversal in divorce trends. Nonetheless, most demographers think that divorce is not likely to continue its upward pattern, at least in the near term. There are several demographic explanations for the failure of divorce rates to increase after the 1970s which do not necessarily imply that Americans today are becoming more committed to staying married than they were in the previous two decades.

The huge cohort of baby boomers, reacting to changing economic opportunities, postponed marriage. A larger proportion opted to obtain more schooling and wait to form a family. Marriage age for women rose from just above 20 in the mid-1950s to 24.4 in 1992, an increase of more than four years. It has long been known that early marriage and lower education are associated with marital instability. Thus, the pattern of delayed marriage might have had a role in curbing the rates of divorce.

Another potent source of marital disruption, associated with early marriage, is premarital pregnancy. Fewer marriages today occur as a result of a premarital pregnancy. It also seems plausible that the greater availability of contraception and abortion in the 1970s may have discouraged the formation of early unions, reducing the number of ill-considered marriages, though evidence to support this hypothesis is not available.

Furthermore, the population has been getting older as the baby boomers mature. Older couples in long-standing marriages have a lower propensity to divorce. Thus, as the baby boomers reach middle age, a larger proportion of those married have passed through the high-risk years, when their marriages are young and relatively more fragile.

Finally, growing rates of cohabitation before marriage may have brought down the rate of divorce. As more and more couples elect to live together prior to marrying, it seems likely that many unions that would have ended in divorce end before marriage occurs. That is, a growing number of Americans are divorcing without marrying, making the official divorce statistics a less reliable barometer of union stability.

For all these reasons, it is probable that the modest drop in divorce rates does not indicate a higher propensity toward marital stability. Instead, the composition of those marrying has changed in ways that only make it appear that marriages are becoming more stable.

Remarriage

Not so many years ago, it was common for family experts to reassure those who were alarmed at the steady increase in divorce rates by pointing out that divorce typically is not a terminal event but a transition from one marriage to the next. So it was said that couples who separated lost faith in a particular marriage but not in the institution of matrimony. In 1975, close to three-fourths of all women in their fifties who had experienced a divorce had remarried. For formerly married men, the occurrence of remarriage was even higher, about four in five eventually remarried, owing to the greater pool of eligible partners. (It is easier for men to attract younger partners than it is for women.) But recently, the rate of remarriage has been declining.

In part, the trend toward lower remarriage rates may reflect the greater tendency to postpone second unions as both men and women may be more willing and able to live as single persons. But recent evidence from the National Survey of Families and Households (NSFH) suggests the rate of recoupling has not declined notably. Many divorced persons have become more cautious about reentering matrimony, preferring instead to cohabit in informal and more fluid unions. This pattern, discussed below, poses particular problems for children who are, to an increasing extent, being raised by quasi-stepparents who are often transitional figures in their households.

The lower rates of remarriage may reflect a growing reluctance to formalize unions after a failed first marriage. Couples who remarry are known to have a higher risk of divorce than couples entering first marriages. And divorces from second marriages occur more quickly than from first unions. Cherlin has shown that the proportion of couples who will marry, divorce, remarry, and redivorce has risen eightfold during the course of this century, climbing from barely 2% of those who were born in the first decade of the twentieth century to 16% of those born after 1970.

Cherlin described the changing pattens of marriage, divorce, and remarriage for four birth cohorts of women. . . . For all but the most recent cohort, the proportion ever marrying remained relatively stable while the prevalence of divorce, remarriage, and redivorce progressively increased. In the youngest cohort, women born after 1970,

Cherlin projects that marriage (and remarriage) will decline significantly and divorce will remain high among women who elect to marry or remarry.

Racial/Ethnic Differences in Patterns of Divorce and Remarriage

Rising rates of marital instability have been experienced by all Americans regardless of socioeconomic status, race, religious affiliation, or region of the country. However, the extent of marital instability differs enormously among various social groups. It is beyond the scope of this article to explore in detail the patterns described above for different social classes, religious groups, or regions of the country. It is hard to ignore, however, racial/ethnic differences in patterns of marriage, divorce, and remarriage because the experiences for whites, African Americans, and some Hispanic groups are so very disparate.

African Americans have long exhibited different patterns of family formation. As far back as the nineteenth century, blacks were more likely to marry earlier, had a higher incidence of premarital pregnancy and nonmarital childbearing, formed less stable unions, and were less likely to remarry when disruption occurred. Scholars disagree on the origin of these pattens. Some believe that they are rooted in different notions of kinship brought to America; others argue that distinctive patterns of family formation emerged in slavery; and still others contend that these family differences did not really take hold until after Emancipation, when black Americans were exposed to economic discrimination and racism. Still others argue that the differences are more recent in origin.

Whatever the particular origin or combination of origins, there is convincing evidence that African Americans are much less likely to marry, more likely to divorce, and less likely to remarry when divorce occurs. More than 90% of whites will marry compared with about 75% of African Americans; of those who do wed, African Americans have a substantially higher risk of divorce. Ten years after marriage, 47% of blacks have separated or divorced compared with 28% of non-Hispanic whites. Blacks are also far less likely to remarry after separating. As a result, African Americans spend far less time in marriage than do whites.

Much less information exists on the marriage patterns of other racial and ethnic groups. Census data on Hispanics suggest that their levels of marriage, divorce, and remarriage fall somewhere between those of whites and those of blacks. However, official statistics actually conceal as much as they reveal about the behavior of different Latino groups. There is reason to suspect that as much difference exists between Cubans or Mexican Americans and Puerto Ricans as between whites and blacks in rates of marriage and marital stability. Still, such as it is, the evidence on Hispanic subgroups reveals similar trends to those described for blacks and whites in the United States.

In sum, virtually all population subgroups have experienced a postponement of marriage, a steady increase in divorce, and a decrease in remarriage after divorce. Cohabitation as a prelude, aftermath, and perhaps alternative to marriage has become more common. These patterns are more evident among African Americans.

Childbearing

The declining institution of marriage has important ramifications for patterns of childbearing. Typically, now, marriage no longer regulates the timing of sex, and to an increasing degree, it no longer regulates the timing of first birth. Nonmarital childbearing has become more prominent over the past several decades as rates of marital childbearing have declined and rates of nonmarital childbearing have held steady or increased. In 1960, only 5% of all births occurred to unmarried women; in 1990, this proportion had risen to 28%. The increase for whites has been tenfold, from 2% to 20% in this 30-year period.

Figure 1 depicts the remarkable rise in the number of first births among women between the ages of 15 and 34 which have occurred before marriage for whites, blacks, and Hispanics. Among each of the racial/ethnic subgroups, the increase has been remarkable over the past 30 years. For whites this number rose from 8.5% for births occurring in the early 1960s to 21.6% for those that took place in the late 1980s. The rise for blacks was even more spectacular, going from 42.4% in the early 1960s to 70.3% in the late 1980s. The proportion for Hispanics doubled during the same period, going from 19.2% to 37.5%. Clearly, out-of-wedlock childbearing has become a far more important source of single parenthood for all Americans and especially so for African Americans, who now have a sizable majority of first births before marriage.

Figure 1
Percentage of First Births Occurring Before First Marriage Among Women 15 to 34 Years Old: 1960-64 Through 1985-89

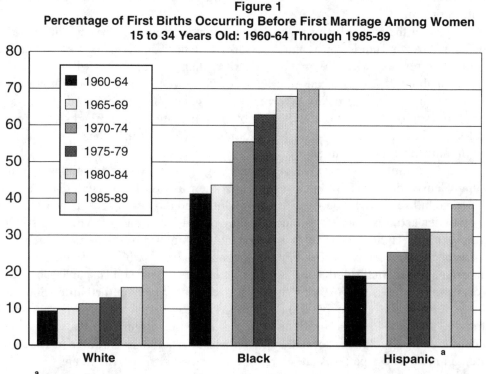

Legend:
- 1960-64
- 1965-69
- 1970-74
- 1975-79
- 1980-84
- 1985-89

[a] May be of any race.

Source: U.S. Bureau of the Census. *Households, families and children: a 30-year perspective.* Current Population Reports, Series P-23. No. 181. Washington, D.C.: U.S. Government Printing Office, 1992, Figure 6.

International Comparisons

The weakening of marriage as a social institution is not unique to the United States. Most developed countries are witnessing similar demographic trends. In some instances, the retreat from marriage is even more pronounced. For example, in Scandinavia cohabitation has become a widely accepted alternative to marriage. France and England have higher proportions of out-of-wedlock births than occur in the United States, though a higher proportion of these births occur to parents who are cohabiting than in this country.

Divorce rates have also risen sharply in a number of European nations, though none equals this country in the prevalence of divorce. Still, about a third of marriages in Northern Europe will end in divorce; in England and Scandinavia, as many as two in five marriages may dissolve. Thus, explanations for the de-institutionalization of marriage cannot reside solely in the special features of American culture or society.

Explaining Changing Marriage Patterns

Much recent scholarly activity has been devoted to accounting for the declining strength of the marriage institution. The centrality of marriage and the nuclear family in the middle part of the twentieth century makes it especially puzzling to explain what appears to be the rapid erosion of a high cultural commitment to lifelong monogamy. As we have already seen, the view that change came suddenly and only recently is certainly spurious. Many of the elements that were undermining the particular model of marriage prevalent in the 1950s have been evident for some time.

An explanation does not point to a single source of change. A configuration of many changes, some long-standing and others more recent, have shifted the balance of individual interests away from forming permanent unions to more fluid and flexible arrangements. The most important of these was undoubtedly the breakdown of the gender-based division of labor that led men to invest in work and women to specialize in domestic activity.

In the United States these changes occurred in a culture that has long trumpeted the virtues of individual choice and, more recently, personal freedom and selfactualization. Little wonder that Americans lead other nations in the divorce revolution. Our ideology of individualism may have helped to grease the main engine of change, the movement of women into the labor force which subverted the model of marriage as an exchange of goods and services between men and women.

Other simultaneous developments may have hastened the breakdown of the nuclear family. The sexual revolution in no small measure made marriage seem less attractive. As premarital sex with decreased risk of pregnancy became more accessible in the 1960s, the lure of early marriage lessened. The spread of birth control to unmarried youth and the availability of abortion played a part, but the growing visibility of sex that occurred in the post-Kinsey era was probably as influential as the availability of methods of fertility control in changing sexual practices.

Finally, the shift of public opinion favoring more liberal divorce laws may have fed the process of change. Clearly, the laws were a response to a growing demand for divorce. Increases in marital disruption preceded the legal changes or even the opinion favoring changes. However, the laws, in turn, consolidated opinion institutionalizing alternative marriage forms, replacing the permanent monogamy with conjugal succession and, of late, even more conditional arrangements.

Apart from the development of new norms, marital instability promotes more instability as individuals become more wary about the prospects of permanency. They prepare for the contingency of being alone by spending time alone, and they hedge their bets by entering temporary partnerships. As they do, they develop more resources for independence and a greater commitment to living alone unless they are highly contented in unions. Thus, the standards for what constitutes a gratifying relationship may have been rising to higher levels, some would say to unrealistically higher levels. Whether this is true or not, most Americans, perhaps women especially, are now less willing than they once were to settle for "good enough" marriages because they have the option of seeking more gratifying relationships or of living alone in the event that such relationships prove elusive.

Divorce and the Changing Family Experiences of Children

The implications of these new marriage patterns for children has been the subject of enormous attention and mounting concern. Close to a majority of children growing up today are likely to spend some time living in a single-parent family before reaching adulthood. And, at least one in five will acquire a stepparent or surrogate parent. Family instability is not novel to the latter part of the twentieth century. Uhlenberg calculated that about one quarter of all children growing up in 1900 lost a parent by death. If another 7% or 8% encountered a voluntary separation, then close to one in three spent time in a single parent household during childhood. By mid-century, families had become more stable: the rapid decline of mortality was offset to some degree by rising voluntary dissolution and slightly higher rates of nonmarital childbearing. Still, the total disruptions probably did not affect more than one quarter of all children.

Since the 1950s, when rates of stability were at their highest point, the risk of family disruption has more than doubled, owing to much higher rates of divorce and separation and, more recently, an explosion of nonmarital childbearing. Several estimates of children's probability of experiencing parental separation or divorce conclude that at least two in five children will see their parents separate before their late teens. More than one quarter of children are born to unmarried couples, generally couples who are not living together when the birth occurs. Of course, there is some overlap between these two populations, but still, close to half of all children will spend time in a single-parent household before age 18.

This staggeringly high figure does not even tell the whole story. Among African Americans, the proportion of children who live continuously with two biological parents throughout childhood is certainly less than one in five and may be as low as one in ten. Although data are unavailable on the experiences of different Latino groups during childhood, based on family composition, it is safe to assume that the difference among Hispanic populations is at least as great as the variation between Hispanics and either whites or African Americans. Puerto Rican patterns resemble those of African

Americans while Mexican Americans appear to have even higher stability than white non-Hispanics.

Marital disruption or nonmarital childbearing for many children initiates a complex family career. Most are likely to see one or both parents live with a partner for a time. Some of these partnerships eventuate in marriage; others dissolve and are succeeded by new relationships. Some remarriages persist while others end in divorce. At least one quarter of all children growing up today are likely to acquire a stepparent by marriage, and others will live with a quasi-stepparent. Beyond their household, children also may see their noncustodial parent enter new relationships. Thus, a high proportion of children growing up today will have more than two parents by the time that they reach age 18. Many more will gain additional parents in adulthood.

Paul R. Amato, *Explaining the Intergenerational Transmission of Divorce,* 58 Journal of Marriage and the Family 628 (1996)[*]

Studies based on large national samples consistently show that parental divorce increases the risk that offspring will see their own marriages end in divorce. Furthermore, this increase is large enough to be nontrivial. Using female respondents from the National Survey of Families and Households, Bumpass, Martin, and Sweet (1991), found that parental divorce increases the odds of disruption within the first 5 years of marriage by 70%. This association is present among both Whites and African Americans, although it does not appear to be as strong among the latter group. In spite of some variation across studies and populations, parental divorce is a well-documented risk factor for marital dissolution.

The explanation for the association between parental divorce and offspring divorce, however, is not clear. In this article, I assess the extent to which several mediating processes account for the transmission of divorce across generations. A few studies have assessed *some* of these factors. However, reliance on retrospective data on marital history has limited researchers' ability to examine the mediating role of variables measured *prior* to offspring divorce. In contrast, the present study draws on national longitudinal data and uses a prospective design to assess potential explanatory mechanisms.

THEORY
Model of Offspring Marital Instability

Levinger (1976) argued that the likelihood of divorce rises to the extent that various factors decrease the rewards derived from the marriage, weaken the barriers to leaving the marriage, and increase the alternatives to the marriage. Using Levinger's theory, I argue that parental divorce sets in motion a series of events and processes that affect each of these general determinants of offspring marital instability.

. . . [T]he conceptual model that guides this analysis . . . assumes that parental divorce affects three types of offspring outcomes: (a) life course and socioeconomic variables, (b) offsprings' attitudes toward divorce, and (c) offsprings' problematic interpersonal behavior. In relation to the first category, young age at marriage, cohabitation prior to marriage, low socioeconomic attainment, and wives' employment increase marital instability by affecting each of the processes identified by Levinger (1976), that is, by decreasing the rewards derived from the marriage, weakening the barriers to divorce, and increasing the alternatives to the present marriage. The model also assumes that parental divorce liberalizes offsprings' attitudes toward divorce, thus weakening a major psychological barrier to leaving marriage. Finally, the model assumes that parental divorce directly increases the likelihood that offspring exhibit interpersonal behaviors that decrease the rewards obtained from marriage.

Life Course and Socioeconomic Variables

Age at marriage. Youth with divorced parents tend to marry earlier than do those with continuously married parents. These offspring may marry at young ages because they are emotionally needy, see marriage as an escape from an economically disadvantaged household (if they are living with single mothers), or do not get along with stepparents (if their custodial parents are remarried).

Early age at marriage, in turn, is one of the best predictors of marital dissolution. People who marry early have little time to search for an appropriate partner, may be poorly prepared to assume marital roles, and often lack economic resources. These factors are likely to make the marital relationship less rewarding. Young couples also may be inclined to divorce because they have better opportunities in the (re)marriage market than do older couples, thus increasing alternatives to their present relationship. Consistent with the assumption that age at marriage plays a mediating role in the intergenerational transmission of divorce, several studies show that age at marriage accounts for some—but not all—of the association between parents' and offsprings' marital dissolutions.

Cohabitation. Although some children from divorced families marry relatively early, others marry relatively late. This may be because adult children of divorced parents are especially likely to cohabit prior to marriage. It is not clear why adult children of divorce tend to cohabit, although it may be because they are less conventional in their beliefs or more hesitant to commit to long-term relationships.

Most studies show that cohabitation prior to marriage is associated with an increased risk of marital dissolution. This may be because people who live together tend to have personal traits, such as attitudes favorable to divorce or unconventional lifestyles, that increase the likelihood of marital disruption. However, cohabitation may increase the risk of divorce if couples marry to save a failing relationship or if there are pressures from families to legitimize the relationship. Marrying under these circumstances may result in a poor match and an unrewarding marriage. Cohabitation may also liberalize people's attitudes toward life-long marriage, thus weakening the psychological barriers to marital dissolution. Consistent with the above reasoning, Bumpass et al. (1991) found that cohabitation of offspring mediated some—but not all —of the association between parental and offspring divorce.

Socioeconomic attainment. Many custodial mothers and their children experience considerable economic hardship. Single mothers are often unable to afford resources such as educational games, computers, books, and private lessons that facilitate children's educational success. Children of single mothers also may lack the economic resources to attend college. Given these disadvantages, it is not surprising that offspring from divorced families, compared with those from families that have remained continuously together, obtain less education, earn less income, and hold lower status jobs.

Low socioeconomic status, in turn, is associated with marital conflict and the risk of divorce. This may be because well-educated couples communicate more effectively than poorly educated couples, thus facilitating problem solving within the relationship. Also, the stress generated by economic hardship may increase disagreements over finances and leave spouses tense and irritable. These considerations suggest that low socioeconomic status increases the risk of divorce by lowering the rewards obtained from the marriage. Furthermore, the poor may feel relatively unconstrained by middle-class expectations of propriety, and they may hold relatively few marital assets. Consequently, the barriers to divorce may be weaker for them than for others.
. . .

Wives' employment. After marital disruption, mothers tend to become less traditional in their attitudes about family life and more oriented toward paid employment. By serving as role models, employed, divorced mothers communicate nontraditional views to their daughters. Furthermore, daughters from divorced families may value self-sufficiency because they have seen firsthand that women cannot count on the continuous economic support of men. Consistent with this logic, Goldscheider and Waite (1991) found that daughters from single-parent families, compared with those from two-parent families, had a stronger orientation to employment, planned to have fewer children, and were more likely to approve of maternal employment. The increased attachment to the labor market of adult daughters from divorced families may have consequences for their marriages. Although women's employment decreases economic hardship, it often creates tension between spouses over household chores and responsibilities, thus making the relationship less rewarding. Employment also decreases wives' economic dependence on husbands (thus weakening the barrier to leaving the marriage) and increases wives' contacts with other men (thus increasing alternatives to the marriage). Consistent with this reasoning, some studies show that women's employment increases their thoughts about divorce and the likelihood of divorce, although contradictory findings also exist.

ATTITUDES TOWARD DIVORCE

Adult children of divorce may have an elevated risk of seeing their own marriages end in divorce because they hold relatively liberal attitudes toward marital dissolution. Studies show that young adults who grew up in divorced families are more pessimistic about the chances of life-long marriage and evaluate divorce less negatively than do other young adults. Offspring from divorced families may hold these attitudes because of experiences with cohabitation or low socioeconomic status. In addition, parental divorce may have a direct effect on children's attitudes. By observing their parents' divorce, children learn firsthand that it can be a solution to a problematic marriage.

People who hold liberal attitudes toward divorce, compared with those who hold conservative attitudes, may feel less compulsion to stay in an unhappy marriage, thus weakening the barrier to divorce. Consistent with this reasoning, one longitudinal study found that people who hold favorable attitudes toward divorce are more likely to end their marriages than are those who hold unfavorable attitudes. Due to a lack of data on attitudes measured prior to marital dissolution, no studies have directly tested this explanation for the intergenerational transmission of divorce. However, . . . if parental divorce lowers children's commitment to marriage, then the effects of parental divorce should be stronger in low divorce populations (where commitment to marriage is strong) than in high divorce populations (where commitment to marriage is weak). Their results tended to support this assumption.

PROBLEMATIC INTERPERSONAL BEHAVIOR

Through the process of socialization, parental divorce (and the disturbed family relationships that often precede and accompany divorce) may increase the likelihood that offspring develop traits and interpersonal orientations that interfere with intimate relationships in adulthood. For example, children from families marked by discord or lack of affection between parents do not have the benefit of prolonged exposure to models of successful dyadic behavior. As a result, some children may not learn interpersonal skills (such as communicating effectively and compromising) that facilitate mutually satisfying, long-term ties with others. In addition, the stress associated with marital conflict may cause parents to be less affectionate and more punitive toward their children. Disturbed marital and parent-child relationships may lead children to develop personal traits (such as a lack of trust, jealousy, or an inability to commit to a particular partner) that spring from a sense of emotional insecurity. This perspective holds that adult children of divorce are more likely than other adults to exhibit behaviors that interfere with the quality of marital relationships, thus lowering the rewards associated with marriage and increasing the risk of marital dissolution. Note that this explanation focuses on poor marital quality among parents, rather than parental divorce, as the ultimate cause of offspring divorce. . . .

EXTENDING PREVIOUS RESEARCH

Previous research has been limited by the use of cross-sectional data and retrospective accounts of respondents' marital histories and other variables. Although studies based on these data sets can assess the mediating role of life course and socioeconomic variables, they can say little about the mediating role of attitudes or the interpersonal behavior problems of offspring. In contrast, the present study is based on 12-year longitudinal data from individuals in which all variables (including attitudes and behavior problems) are measured prior to divorce. In this analysis, I use parental divorce to predict the odds of offspring divorce. I then enter the explanatory variables into the equations in a series of steps, thus allowing an assessment of the extent to which these variables account for the association between parental divorce and offspring divorce.

The [theoretical] model . . . does not establish a causal ordering among the explanatory variables. Although causal linkages between these variables almost certainly exist, the direction of effects is unclear in some cases and is likely to be reciprocal in others. For example, liberal attitudes toward divorce could be a cause or a consequence of cohabitation. Similarly, the wife's full-time employment could be a cause or a consequence of interpersonal behavior problems. Rather than estimate the causal linkages among the explanatory variables, the present study has a more modest, but realistic, goal: to determine the extent to which the three types of mechanisms (life course and socioeconomic variables, attitudes, and interpersonal behavior problems) individually and collectively mediate the association between parental divorce and offspring divorce.

The present study also considers the timing of parental divorces. All of the explanations for the intergenerational transmission of divorce assume that parental divorces are problematic if they occur when offspring are young or at least adolescents. For example, parental divorces that occur when offspring are older (say, in their early 20s) are unlikely to increase the probability of early marriage or cohabitation, to lower socioeconomic attainment, or to affect daughters' attachment to the labor force. However, whether parental divorces that occur in early childhood or during adolescence have a greater impact on children is a question that has not been answered clearly. In the present study, I compare parental divorces that occur during three time periods: childhood, adolescence, and early adulthood. . . .

RESULTS
Bivariate Analyses

Table I shows the percentage of married couples who divorced between 1980 and 1992. Consistent with research reviewed above, couples in which husbands or wives experienced a parental divorce were somewhat more likely to divorce than were couples in which neither spouse experienced a parental divorce. This was true in both first and second marriages. However, the likelihood of divorce was especially high if both spouses came from divorced families of origin. Also, consistent with previous research, the likelihood of divorce was considerably higher for those in second marriages than in first marriages. However, because we lack data on the timing of first divorces among remarried couples and because the determinants of divorce differ somewhat for second marriages than for first marriages (such as the presence of stepchildren), the remainder of this article focuses on the 1,387 respondents in first marriages.

		All Marriages	First Marriage for Both	Second Marriage for One or Both
TABLE 1. PERCENTAGE OF MARRIAGES ENDING IN DIVORCE OR PERMANENT SEPARATION BETWEEN 1980 AND 1992 BY PARENTAL DIVORCE				
Neither spouse's parents divorced	%	13	11	23
	(n)	(1,271)	(1,064)	(207)
Husband's parents divorced	%	19	14	32
	(n)	(194)	(138)	(56)
Wife's parents divorced	%	19	16	28
	(n)	(192)	(146)	(46)
Both spouses' parents divorced	%	37	28	60
	(n)	(54)	(39)	(15)
Chi-square		29.22***	13.08**	10.56*

*p<.05. **p<.01. ***p<.001.

Table 2 [not included] shows the explanatory variables by the four categories of parental divorce. Consistent with previous research, age at marriage was relatively low when either the husband's or the wife's parents divorced; however, it was unexpectedly high when both spouses experienced parental divorce. Also consistent with previous studies, the likelihood that couples lived together prior to marriage was higher when parents divorced, especially when both sets of parents divorced. (The high frequency of cohabitation when both sets of parents divorced probably accounts for the relatively older age of these couples at first marriage.) Parental divorce also was associated with less education. However, it was not associated with income for either spouse. The results for the wife's employment were contrary to expectations: Parental divorce was negatively related to full-time employment, although the association was not significant. Parental divorce was associated with more positive attitudes toward divorce, although the trend only approached significance (p = .11). Finally, parental divorce was linked with more problematic interpersonal behaviors, especially when both spouses experienced parental divorce. Overall, these results suggest that age at marriage, cohabitation, education, and interpersonal behavior problems are the most likely candidates to serve as mediators of the effects of parental divorce. . . .

DISCUSSION

This study yields a number of findings that contribute to our understanding of the intergenerational transmission of divorce. First, the present study replicates previous research by showing that adult children of divorced parents have an elevated risk of seeing their own marriages end in divorce. The analysis extends this finding by showing that it holds in second marriages as well as in first marriages (see Table 1). Furthermore, most previous studies present data on the respondent's family background only, but the present study reveals that the risk of divorce is particularly high if *both* spouses experienced parental divorce. Such a finding is intuitively compelling: If one parental divorce increases the risk of offspring divorce, it makes sense that two parental divorces further increase the risk. In addition, the analysis indicates two conditions under which the effects of parental divorce are most apparent: (a) in offspring marriages of short duration, and (b) if parental divorces occur when children are 12 years of age or younger.

The present study also assessed a conceptual model of the intergenerational transmission of divorce, based on Levinger's theory of divorce and previous empirical work. The analyses show that life course variables (in particular, age at marriage and cohabitation) mediate some of the estimated effect of parental divorce. These findings support the results of several prior investigations.

More importantly, the present study was able to use prospective data to assess two additional explanations for the intergenerational transmission of divorce not addressed in prior research. These analyses reveal that people's attitudes toward divorce mediate little of the estimated impact of parental divorce. This indicates that parental divorce does not increase the risk of offspring divorce by making offspring more accepting of marital dissolution (that is, by weakening the psychological barrier to divorce).

In contrast, the impact of parental divorce appears to operate largely through spouses' interpersonal behavior. Offspring whose parents divorced, compared with those whose parents remained continuously married, are more likely to have an interpersonal style marked by problematic behavior (problems with anger, jealousy, hurt feelings, communication, infidelity, and so on), and these interpersonal problems, in turn, increase the risk of divorce. Furthermore, life course and socioeconomic variables mediate little of the association between parental divorce and interpersonal behavior problems. These findings suggest that parental divorce has a *direct* impact on these interpersonal behaviors. These findings are consistent with the notion that adult children from divorced families are exposed to poor models of dyadic behavior and may not learn the skills and attitudes that facilitate successful functioning within marital roles. Similarly, children of divorce may be predisposed to develop traits (such as a lack of trust or an inability to commit) that exacerbate relationship tension. In Levinger's terms, therefore, parental divorce increases the risk of offspring divorce, not by weakening barriers to leaving the marriage nor by increasing alternatives to marriage, but by making the relationship less rewarding.

This interpretation is consistent with several other findings. First, it is consistent with previous qualitative descriptions of adult children of divorce. Second, this explanation is consistent with the finding that offspring from divorced families have an elevated risk of divorce in second, as well as in first, marriages. If problematic dyadic skills and interpersonal orientations undermine one marriage, then these same problems are likely to recur in subsequent marriages. Third, it is consistent with the finding that the risk of divorce is maximized when both spouses come from divorced backgrounds. If one spouse exhibits problematic behavior, the relationship may still be viable if the other spouse is skillful, trusting, and committed. But if both spouses have problems maintaining relationships, the risk of marital dissolution should be particularly high. Finally, this explanation is consistent with the finding that parental divorces are especially problematic if they occurred when children were young because this gives children less time to learn appropriate dyadic behaviors.

Of course, alternative explanations exist. For example, it is possible that parents with personality problems transfer these traits to their children (either through genetic influence or child-rearing methods) and that these problems increase the risk of divorce for both generations. This explanation suggests that the apparent effects of parental conflict and divorce on offspring are spurious. This explanation cannot be ruled out with the present data and must await new research.

But if the conceptual model underlying this study is correct and if parental divorce affects offspring divorce mainly through its impact on children's interpersonal behavior, then several additional hypotheses follow. First, children whose parents are unhappily married but do not divorce should also experience an elevated risk of divorce. A second hypothesis is that offspring with divorced or unhappily married parents experience a relatively high level of instability in other intimate associations, such as cohabiting unions or dating relationships. Third, when parents remarry after divorce and when these remarriages are successful (both happy and stable), the intergenerational transmission of divorce should be weaker, especially if this occurs when children are young. Finally, if children manage to have a close relationship with one or both parents (or other adults), they may gain social skills and a sense of emotional security in spite of interparental conflict and divorce. In these cases, the intergenerational transmission of divorce should also be weaker. These hypotheses all would serve as useful starting points for future research.

References

Bumpass, L.L., Martin, T.C., & Sweet, J.A. The impact of family background and early marital factors on marital disruption. *Journal of Family Issues*, 12, 22-42 (1991).

Goldscheider, F.K., & Waite, L.J. *New Families, no families: The transformation of the American home*, Berkeley: University of California Press (1991).

Levinger, G. A socio-psychological perspective on marital dissolution. *Journal of Social Issues*, 52, 21-47 (1976).

B. The Divorce Process

One way of interpreting the divorce revolution is as part of a general decline in moral discourse in domestic relations, with a consequent transfer of responsibility "from the law to the people the law once regulated." Carl E. Schneider, *Moral Discourse and the Transformation of American Family Law,* 83 MICH. L. REV. 1803 (1985). Whereas legal policy once closely defined the occasions for ending a marriage, no-fault divorce allocates that decision to the spouses themselves. This does not, however, mean that the parties manage divorces entirely by themselves. Even the divorce itself—unlike other civil actions—must go before a judge in most jurisdictions, even if the judicial hearing is typically entirely formulary. And in many cases, much remains at stake in the divorce process, including the distribution of marital and sometimes separate property, awards of spousal support, and child custody and visitation.

The following readings explore various aspects of the divorce process. The first three excerpts deal with pre-judicial aspects of dispute resolution, of the kind now commonly described as "alternative dispute resolution." The first reading explores the relations between lawyers and clients in divorce cases, and is a useful antidote to the perception that the controversy that often attends divorce results primarily from the attitudes of attorneys. The second reading deals with the process of negotiation, through which some 90% of all divorce matters are resolved. The third excerpt examines the incorporation of mediation into the resolution of divorce processes, and the uses this strategy has for lawyers as well as clients.

Austin Sarat & William L.F. Felstiner, *Law and Strategy in the Divorce Lawyer's Office,* 20 LAW & SOCIETY REVIEW 93 (1986)[*]

I. INTRODUCTION

Traditionally, the sociology of the legal profession has portrayed lawyers as important intermediaries between clients and the legal system, many more people see lawyers than have direct contact with formal legal institutions. (sic) Lawyers serve clients as important sources of information about legal rights, help clients relate legal rules to individual problems, and introduce clients to the way the legal process works. The information provided by lawyers shapes in large measure citizens' views of the legal order and their understanding of the relevance, responsiveness, and reliability of legal institutions. What lawyers say to their clients is not necessarily derived from statutes, rules, and cases and does not involve a literal translation of legal doctrine, nor

---

[*] Reprinted by permission of the Law and Society Association.

could the legal system as it is presented in the lawyer's office be understood by clients from untutored observation.

More is at stake, however, in the interaction between lawyers and clients than a unidirectional movement of information and advice from lawyer to client. In addition, this interaction provides one important setting where law and society meet and where legal norms and folk norms come together to shape responses to grievances, injuries, and problems. In some instances those worlds may be complementary; in others there may be little fit between them.

Despite the importance of the discourse between lawyers and their clients, we know very little about what actually goes on in the lawyer's office. . . . [W]ithout direct knowledge of such communications, it is difficult to pose or answer major questions about the content, form, and effects of legal services, the nature of dispute transformation, and the transmission of legal ideology. Indeed it may be that we have ignored an important means of understanding the law itself: Perhaps social science should begin its "study of law with the proposition that law is not what judges say in the reports but what lawyers say—to one another and to clients—in their offices."

II. THE RESEARCH, THE CASE, AND THE CONFERENCE

In the research from which this paper is derived, we developed an ethnographic account of lawyer-client interaction in divorce cases. We chose to examine divorce because it is a serious and growing social problem in which the involvement of lawyers is particularly salient and controversial. . . .

We observed cases over a period of thirty-three months in two sites, one in Massachusetts and one in California. This effort consisted in following one side of forty divorce cases, ideally from the first lawyer-client interview until the divorce was final. We followed these cases by observing and tape-recording lawyer-client sessions, attending court and mediation hearings and trials, and interviewing both lawyers and clients about those events. Approximately 115 lawyer-client conferences were tape-recorded. . . .

In this paper we focus on one lawyer-client conference to provide the reader with the maximum opportunity to follow these themes and see them at work "on location." Only through such concentration are we able to convey the level of detail that we believe is necessary to convey the full social significance of the interplay between the lawyer and client.

This conference is typical of our sample of conferences. We made our choice after having reviewed the data twice, first as we observed the conferences in the lawyers' offices and then as we read the transcripts with the specific questions raised in this paper in mind. Although the behavior that we report is not, of course, universal . . . , it is the most common pattern and appeared repeatedly in our cases. . . .

The lawyer involved in this case graduated from one of the country's top-ranked law schools. He was forty years old at the time of the conference and had practiced for fourteen years. His father was a prominent physician in a neighboring city. The lawyer had spent four years as a public defender after law school and had been in private practice for ten years. He considers himself a trial lawyer and states that he was drawn to divorce work because of the opportunity it provides for trial work. He is married and has never been divorced.

The client and her husband were in their late thirties and had no children. Their marriage had been stormy, involving both substantial separations and infidelity by the husband. Both had graduate degrees and worked full-time; financial support was not an issue. They owned a house, bank stocks, several limited partnerships in real estate, his retirement benefits, and personal property. The house was their major asset. It was an unconventional building to which the husband was especially attached. Housing in the area is very expensive. This divorce was the client's second; there were no children in the first marriage either. She had received extensive psychological counseling prior to and during the case which we observed.

The parties in this divorce initially tried to dissolve their marriage by engaging a mediator and did not at that time individually consult lawyers. The mediator was an established divorce lawyer with substantial experience in divorce mediation. At the first substantive session, the mediator stated that he did not think that further progress could be made if both the spouses continued to live in the house. Although she considered it to be a major sacrifice, the wife said that she had moved out of the house to facilitate mediation after her husband absolutely refused to leave. Thereafter, she visited the house occasionally, primarily to check on plants and pets. The client reported that she was careful to warn her husband when she intended to visit.

Over time, however, this arrangement upset her husband. Rather than raise the problem at a mediation session, he hired a lawyer and secured an *ex parte* order restraining the client from entering the property at any time for any reason. The husband had previously characterized the lawyer that he hired as "the meanest son-of-a-bitch in town." The restraining order ended any prospects for mediation and the client, on the advice of the mediator and another lawyer, hired the lawyer involved in this conference.

Subsequently, a hearing about the propriety of the *ex parte* order was held by a second judge. The issues at this hearing were whether the order should be governed by a general or a divorce-specific injunction statute, what status quo the order was intended to maintain, and whether the husband's attempt to secure the order violated a moral obligation undertaken when the client agreed to move out of the house. The second judge decided against the client on the first two issues, but left consideration of the bad faith question open to further argument. The client's therapist attended the hearing and the lawyer-client conference that immediately followed. At that conference the therapist stressed that contesting the restraining order further might not be in the client's long-term interest even if it corrected the legal wrong.

The conference analyzed in this paper followed the meeting attended by the therapist and was the seventh of twelve that occurred during the course of the case. It took place in the lawyer's office five weeks after the first meeting between lawyer and client. Its two phases, interrupted for several hours at midday, lasted a total of about two hours. . . .

III. THE LEGAL PROCESS OF DIVORCE

Clients look to lawyers to explain how the legal system works and to interpret the actions and decisions of legal officials. Despite their lack of knowledge about and contact with the law, clients are likely to have some general notions that the law works as a formally rational legal order, one that is rule governed, impersonal, impartial, predictable, and relatively error free. How do lawyers respond to this picture? . . .

In this conference the lawyer presents the legal process of divorce largely in response to questions or remarks by the client. In many conferences clients ask for an explanation of some aspect of the legal system's procedures or rules. In this conference the client repeatedly inquires about both. While most of her questions concern the details of her own case, several are general. Thus, she invites her lawyer to explain the way that the legal process operates as well as to justify its operation in her case. At no point does the lawyer deliver a monologue on how it works. Instead his comments are interspersed in the discussion of major substantive issues, particularly concerning what to do about the restraining order and how to proceed with settlement negotiations. Throughout the conference the client persists in focusing on the restraining order until finally she asks:

Client: How often does a case like this come along—a restraining order of this nature?

Lawyer: Very common.

Client: It's a very common thing. So how many other people are getting the same kind of treatment I am? With what, I presume, is very sloppily handled orders that are passed out.

Lawyer: Yeah, you know, I talked, I did talk to someone in the know—I won't go any further than that—who said that this one could have been signed purely by accident. I mean, that the judge could have—if he looked at it now—said, I would not sign that, knowing what it was, and it could have been signed by accident, and I said, well, then how does that happen? And he said, well, you've got all this stuff going; you come back to your office, and there's a stack of documents that need signatures. He says, you can do one of two things: you can postpone signing them until you have time, but then it may be the end of the day; the clerk's office is closing, and people who really need this stuff aren't going to get the orders, because there's someone else that needs your attention, so you go through them, and one of the main things you look for is the law firm or lawyer who is proposing them. And you tend to rely on them.

The lawyer thus states that a legal order of immense consequence to this woman may have been handled in a way that in several respects is inconsistent with the formalist image of a rational system: It may have been signed by accident. Moreover, the lawyer claims that he has received this information from "someone in the know," someone he refuses to identify. By this refusal, he implies that the information was given improperly, in breach of confidence. Furthermore, the lawyer's description of how judges handle court orders suggests a high level of inattention and routinization.

Judges sign orders without reading them to satisfy "people who really need this stuff." While the judge is said to ignore the substance of the order, he does pay attention to the lawyer or law firm who requests it. The legal process is thereby portrayed as responding more to reputation than to substantive merit. Thus, the client is introduced to a system that is hurried, routinized, personalistic, and accident prone.

Throughout this conference, the theme of the importance of insider status and access within the local legal system is reinforced by references to the lawyer's personal situation. The conference begins with a description of his close ties to the district attorney:

Observer: You're what? You're on a jury?

Lawyer: Well, no, I'm sitting there waiting to get questioned. It's a criminal case, and I think the chances of my being selected are rather remote, because I just came back from lunch with the District Attorney. And then the next question will be: How often does this happen? And I'll say, with some degree of regularity. And they'll say, with whom? Who else do you guys eat with when you meet? And I'll say, nobody.

Shortly afterward, he reminds the client that he serves on occasion as judge *pro tem* in divorce cases . . . :

The lawyer later claims that he knows one of the judges involved in this client's case well enough to tell him off in private ("I'll tell you when this is over, I'm going to take it to John Hancock and I don't think he'll ever do it again") and that he supported the other's campaign for office. These references, suggest that a lawyer's capacity to protect his client's interests depends in part on his special access to the system's functionaries who will react to who he is rather than what he represents. We found this emphasis on insider status, reputation, and local connections repeatedly in the cases that we observed. . . .

Not only is the legal process inconsistent, but it cannot be counted on to protect fundamental rights or deal in a principled way with the important matters that come before it. Thus, the lawyer validates the client's expressed belief that her rights are neither absolute nor secure in the legal process. . . .

Moreover, as they continue to discuss how the legal system deals with property, the lawyer repeatedly uses the word "arbitrary" to describe the valuation process.

Lawyer: Okay, it's $9,500 to $10,200. So that's, once again, that would have been probably $1,000 less if the appraisal were 3 to 4 months ago, because the decline in interest rates has increased the value—the present value—of pensions on an actuarial basis. I'm not sure I truly understand why that's true, but it is. And so, in a way, that's an arbitrary value that's been placed, just like these appraisals are arbitrary.

                                    . . .

Lawyer: You may think of it in terms of $1,250, but if that's what it takes to settle this case, to give up that in an exchange for what are really illusory values on some of this other stuff—on three of the things, the values are really arbitrary: The value of the house, any real property appraisal, is arbitrary; the value on the retirement is definitely arbitrary; and the value on the limited partnerships is very definitely. . . .

In total, the lawyer's description of the legal process involves an open acknowledgment of human frailties, contradictions between appearance and reality, carelessness, incoherence, accident, and built-in limitations. The picture presented is both cynical and probably considered by the lawyer to be realistic. Whereas others claim that legal actors, particularly appellate judges, present the law in highly formalistic terms and work to curtail inconsistencies and contradictions in legal doctrine, many of the lawyers that we observed engage in no such mystification. . . .

IV. TO FIGHT OR TO SETTLE?

Given such a legal process, how should divorce disputes be managed? This concern is central in most of the cases that we observed, and it is an issue that may recur as lawyer and client discuss each of the major controversies in a divorce case. Generally, the question is whether the client should attempt to negotiate a settlement or insist on resolution before a judge. . . .

While many clients think of the legal process as an arena for a full adversarial contest, most divorce disputes are not resolved in this manner. Although not all lawyers are equally dedicated to reaching negotiated agreements, most of those we observed advised their clients to try to settle the full range of issues in the case. This is not to say that these divorces were free of conflict, for the negotiations themselves were often quite contentious. . . .

The conference we are examining revolves around two major issues: (1) whether to ignore or contest the restraining order; and (2) what position to take concerning disposition of the family residence. Much of the conference is devoted to discussing the restraining order—its origins, morality, and legality; the prospects for dissolving it; the lawyer's stake in contesting it; and the client's emotional reaction to it. Substantively the order is not as important as the house itself, which received much less attention and generated much less controversy. Both issues, however, force the lawyer and client to decide whether they will retain control of the case by engaging in negotiations or cede control to the court for hearing and decision. The lawyer definitely favors negotiations.

Lawyer: Okay. What I would like your permission to do then is to meet with Foster, see if I can come up with or negotiate a settlement with him that, before he leaves . . . I leave his office or he leaves my office, he says, we've got something here that I can recommend to my client, and I can say, I've got something here that I can recommend to my client. My feeling is, Jane, that if we reach that point, both lawyers are prepared to make a recommendation on settlement to their respective clients, if either of the clients, either you or Norb, find something terribly disagreeable with the proposal that we have, the lawyers have come to between themselves, then the case just either can't be settled or it's not ripe for settlement. But we would have given it the best shot. . . .

The client in this case is reluctant to begin settlement negotiations until some attention is paid to the restraining order. While she acknowledges that she wants a reasonable property settlement, she reminds her lawyer that is not her exclusive concern:

Client: Yes, there's no question in my mind that that [property settlement] is my first
         goal. However, that doesn't mean it's my only goal. . . .

The lawyer responds by acknowledging that he considers the restraining order to
be legally wrong and that he believes it could be litigated. Thus, he confirms his
client's position and inclination on legal grounds. Yet he dissents from her position and
opposes her inclination to fight on other grounds. First, he states that the restraining
order, although legally wrong, is "not necessarily . . . completely wrong" because it
might prevent violence between spouses. This complicated position is a clear example
of a tactic frequently used by lawyers in divorce cases—the rhetorical "yes . . . but."
The lawyers we observed often appeared to be endorsing the adversarial pursuit of one
of the client's objectives only to remind the client of a variety of negative consequences
associated with it. In this way lawyers present themselves as both an ally and an
adviser embracing the wisdom of a long-term perspective.

Second, the lawyer is worried that an effort to fight the restraining order would
interfere with the resolution of the case, that is, of the outstanding property issues.
Although the lawyer considers the restraining order to be a legal mistake, its effect
would end upon final disposition of the house. In the meantime, the client can either
live with the order or pay for additional hearings. He believes that it would be unwise
for her to fight further not only because the contest would be costly but also because
it would postpone or derail entirely negotiations about the house and other tangible
assets. . . .

. . . Time and again in our study we observed lawyers attempting to focus their
client's attention on the issues the lawyers thought to be major while the clients often
concentrated on matters that the lawyers considered secondary. While the disposition
of the house in this case will have long-term consequences for the client, the restraining order, as unjust as the lawyer understands it to be, is in his view a temporary nui-
sance. His sense of justice and of the long-term best interests of his client lead him to
try to transform this dispute from a battle over the legality and morality of the restraining order to a negotiation over the more narrow and tangible issue of the ultimate disposition of the house and other assets, which he believes can and should be settled.

In attempting this transformation, the lawyer allies himself with the therapist:

Lawyer: I agree with Irene that [fighting the restraining order] is not the best way.
         . . . It's probably the worst way. This [negotiating] hopefully is the best way.

This reliance on the therapist is noteworthy because it is often assumed that a therapeutic orientation is antithetical to the adversarial inclination of law and the legal profession. Yet in this case the lawyer uses the therapist to validate his own position. The
legal ideology and the therapeutic ideology seem to him to be compatible; both stress
settlement and disvalue legal struggles. . . .

. . . [A]s they move further into the discussion of whether to fight or settle, the
client begins to interpret settlement as a capitulation and to reiterate her own ambivalence about how to proceed.

Client: And I think I feel some level of fear about this process of negotiation and
         how much more I'm going to have to give up. . . . You know, there's a part

Lawyer: of me that does not feel very satisfied with having capitulated repeatedly, and now we're simply doing it with a property settlement.

Lawyer: That's, yea, that's a . . . .

Client: I mean, I don't want to fight and I do want to fight, right? That's exactly what it comes down to.

Lawyer: Yes, you're ambiguous.

Client: Oh, boy, am I ever. And I have to live with it.

She may have to live with her ambivalence, but her lawyer needs a resolution of this issue. The lawyer seeks this resolution by allying himself with the "don't fight" side of the struggle. Her advocate, her "knight," has thus become the enemy of adversariness. Through him the legal system becomes the champion of settlement. Ironically, the client's ambivalence serves to validate the lawyer's earlier suggestion that he might be wasting his time and her money trying to settle this case because she might refuse at the last minute to agree to a deal. . . .

V. THE LEGAL CONSTRUCTION OF THE CLIENT

To get clients in divorce cases to move toward accepting settlement as well as to carry out the terms of such agreements, lawyers may have to try to cool them out when they are at least partially inclined toward contest. In divorce as in criminal cases, the lawyer must help redefine the client's orientation toward the legal process. In the criminal case this means that lawyers must help the client come to terms with dropping the pretense of innocence; in divorce work this means that lawyers must help their clients view the emotional process of dissolving an intimate relationship in instrumental terms. In both instances, lawyers and clients struggle, although rarely explicitly, with the issue of what part of the client's personality is relevant to the legal process. . . .

The negotiation of the legal self in this case begins by focusing on the relative importance of emotions engaged by the legal process and the symbolic aspects of the divorce as opposed to its financial and material dimensions. Throughout this conference the lawyer warns his client not to confuse the realms of emotion and finance and instructs her that she can expect the legal process to work well only if emotional material is excluded from her deliberations.

This emotional material is rather complex and difficult for both lawyer and client to sort out. The client is, in the first instance, eager to let her lawyer know that she feels both anger and mistrust toward many participants in the legal process. . . .

The client continues to express her anger throughout the conference, especially when the conversation turns directly to her husband's lawyer:

Client: The other option I see could have been that Norb would have gotten different legal advice from the beginning. So the thing, I suppose, that I'm concerned about, I'm concerned about Foster. I'm concerned about the kind of person he is. I distrust him as thoroughly as I do Norb, and I think you have been very measured in your statements about him. I think he's a son-of-a-bitch, and there's nothing I've seen that he's done that changed my mind about that.

The client's mistrust is not reserved exclusively for the opposition. She is, to an extent, wary of her own lawyer as well. . . .The predicament in which client finds herself—needing to trust a stranger when trust has just been betrayed by an intimate—is one that faces and perplexes divorce clients generally. . . .

How does the lawyer respond to the client's emotional agenda, to her efforts to define those parts of herself that are legally relevant? With respect to the problem of trust and the need for a gesture, the lawyer once says, "Ouch," once, "I don't blame you," and once he changes the subject. . . .

By playing down the question of trust the lawyer is telling the client that the emotional self must be separated from the legal self. Gestures and symbolic acknowledgment of wrongs suffered belong to some realm other than law. He is, in addition, defending himself against a kind of emotional transference. Much of the emotion talk in this conference involves the lawyer himself, directly or indirectly. In the discussion of trust the client makes the lawyer into a kind of husband substitute ("a major trust relationship has ended. And then . . . I'm supposed to entrust somebody else . . ."). The client described him as her "knight in shining armor," an image of protection and romance; she acknowledges having sexual fantasies about him and she speaks of her expectation that he would protect her from "judicial abuse." These demands on her lawyer typify the kind of environment in which divorce lawyers work. . . .

By downplaying emotions and signaling the limited relevance of gestures, the lawyer defends himself against both the transference and the test. He must find a way to be on his client's side (e.g., repeatedly acknowledging the legal error of the restraining order) and, at the same time, to keep some distance from her (e.g., responding "Ouch" to the image of the knight). . . .

The need to exclude emotional issues is thus linked to a warning that emotions can jeopardize satisfactory settlements. The notion of satisfactory disposition, however, is itself problematic. The lawyer's definition of "satisfactory" tends to exclude the part of the client's personality that is angry or frustrated. Satisfactory dispositions are financial. The question of who is satisfied is left unasked. For the client, no definition of the case that ignores her emotions seems right; to the lawyer, this is the only definition that seems acceptable. Moreover, the responsibility for finding ways to keep emotions under control is assigned to the client. The lawyer offers no help in this task even as he acknowledges its relevance for this client and for the practice of divorce law. If no settlement is reached it will, at least as far as their side is concerned, be because of a failure on the part of the client.

Marygold S. Melli, Howard S. Erlanger & Elizabeth Chambliss, *The Process of Negotiation: An Exploratory Investigation in the Context of No-Fault Divorce,* 40 RUTGERS LAW REVIEW 1133 (1988)*

INTRODUCTION

This Article explores the process of negotiation in the context of no-fault divorce. Its purpose is twofold: (1) to increase understanding of the general process of negotiation by examining it in the context of divorce; and (2) to examine an important component of the divorce process, support for the children of divorcing parents, as a negotiated outcome.

Although the study which forms the basis of this report was conducted in Wisconsin, the issues which it investigates are common to all American jurisdictions. Negotiation is the mode of handling questions arising in divorce throughout the United States. Some form of no-fault divorce exists in all American states and support for children of divorcing parties is part of the divorce process in all jurisdictions. Therefore, the particular configuration of negotiating a child support award in the context of a no-fault divorce is a common occurrence.

I. BACKGROUND. . .

B. *The Setting of the Research*

The study upon which this Article is based was conducted in the Family Court Division of the Dane County (Madison), Wisconsin Circuit Court. At the time of the study four judges heard all divorce cases and other matters related to marriage. About 50% of the divorce cases involved the setting of child support. Also, at the time of the study, Wisconsin had just adopted a major reform of its divorce law, known as The Divorce Reform Act of 1978, which provided for no-fault divorce. The statute listed "irretrievable breakdown" as the sole ground for divorce.

The Divorce Reform Act of 1978 not only introduced no-fault divorce to Wisconsin but also attempted to guide the discretion of the court in making various decisions related to the divorce. Historically, the decisions about the incidents of divorce have been highly discretionary. Actions taken by the court were "in the best interest of the child" or as it "deemed just and reasonable." The statute changed the court's authority to set an amount of child support it considered "just and reasonable" by adding a list of factors and presumptions to be considered by the court in exercising its discretion in setting amounts.

The study, which was conducted in two phases, looked at divorces granted in Dane County to spouses who had one or more minor children at the time of the divorce. The first phase consisted of taking data from 349 court files of divorce actions commenced from June 1, 1978 through May 31, 1979. The second phase involved interviews with participants in 27 divorce cases which went to judgment in June or July 1982. In this phase, cases were chosen based on the parties' availability for interviews.

For each, we attempted to interview both parties and their attorneys, hoping to add a new dimension to negotiation research by looking at the same fact situation from the different perspectives of the four negotiating parties. Forty-eight parties were interviewed, and thirty-nine of the forty-two parties who had lawyers authorized interviews with them. In addition, interviews were conducted with three family court commissioners and four judges who handled divorces at the time of the study.

C. *Characteristics of the Families Involved in the Study*

The 349 files examined in the first phase of our study reveal some characteristics of divorcing families with minor children. The couples were relatively young; more than two-thirds of the women and about three-fifths of the men were under the age of 35. Yet, since they all had children, the average marriage had lasted nearly 10 years. The number of minor children ranged up to five, but 45% of the families had only one child, and 39% had two. The children were young; in half of the cases the youngest (or only) child was under six. In three-fifths of the cases, the oldest child was under thirteen.

The families appear to be slightly below the median of Dane County residents in terms of income and, in general, the financial resources of the families were limited. Of 333 families for whom we had information concerning net worth, 61 families reported debts exceeding their assets, while 62 families reported net assets of $50,000 or more. The remaining 210 families fell between those two groups. . . .

Negotiation was certainly not a "marginal peripheral aspect" of the divorce actions we studied in Dane County. The great bulk of the cases ended not as a result of litigation but due to negotiated settlements. Negotiation is not just the typical outcome; it is also the *expected* mode of dispute resolution in the minds of the parties and their lawyers. Contrary to the conventional view that the parties expect a judge to decide their case but *may* settle before trial, these parties saw settlement as the solution, and the judicial process as the alternative. . . .

II. PERSPECTIVES ON NEGOTIATION

A. *Negotiation as Alternative Dispute Resolution*

Over the past two decades, many studies, including ours, have found that the predominant mode of dispute resolution is not litigation, but negotiation. Of the 349 files examined in the first phase of our study, only 32 involved a dispute between the parties that had to be settled by a judge. Several commentators have noted that, given findings such as these, to speak of negotiations as "alternative dispute resolution" is nonsensical. Marc Galanter has argued: "On the contemporary American legal scene the negotiation of disputes is not an alternative to litigation. . . [I]t is not some marginal peripheral aspect of legal disputing in America; it is the central core." . . .

Negotiation was certainly not a "marginal peripheral aspect" of the divorce cases we studied in Dane County. The great bulk of the cases ended not as a result of litigation but due to negotiated settlements. Negotiation is not just the typical outcome; it is also the *expected* mode of dispute resolution in the minds of the parties and their lawyers. Contrary to the conventional view that the parties expect a judge to decide their case but *may* settle before trial, these parties saw settlement as the solution, and the judicial process as the alternative. . .

B. *The Shadow of the Law? Adjudication in the Shadow of Bargaining*

The literature on negotiation stresses that the influence of the courts is pervasive, even when the parties and their lawyers negotiate on their own. . . . The primary influence of the courts is said to result from their administration and enforcement of legal rules that guide and limit the parties' negotiation. If negotiation fails, the courts will decide.

In our interviews, there was evidence consistent with this conventional view of the importance of the courts. Parties who settled were clearly influenced by their lawyers' predictions of how the court would decide. One husband, who was reluctant to settle because he thought the settlement was unfair, gave in based upon his attorney's advice:

> I told [my lawyer] a number of times how I felt, but he pulls out a stack of law statutes and law books and says, "the judge is going to look at or take that into consideration." That came up a number of times . . . she had a right to ask for it or a right to collect it. . . .

However, most striking about our interviews was evidence which demonstrated the minimal role of the judge as reviewer of the substance of the parties' agreement. In divorce cases the influence of the court is believed to be more significant than in other types of civil disputes, because even fully stipulated cases must be reviewed by a judge. However, we found the role of the judge as reviewer to be extremely limited. In only one of the 349 court files examined in the first phase of our study was the stipulation of the parties not approved by the court. . . .

It is possible, of course, that the absence of numerous judicial revisions of the parties' stipulations reflects not the absence of review, but rather a situation in which clear standards result in accurate predictions by the attorneys. This does not seem to be a complete explanation, however, for several reasons.

First, it appeared that the court's main concern was not to review the substance of the parties' decision, but to establish that the parties had actually reached the particular stipulation and understood its terms.

Explained one judge:

> If they know what they're doing, even if it is out of line, then it is not my job to change their decision. I'll inquire to make sure they know what they are doing. I have to let them know what their options are. But I won't usually change it. I don't know if I have ever changed an amount set by the couple. . . .

The parties also found the review to be directed at the voluntariness, rather than the substance, of the agreement. One party's view:

> I thought maybe [the judge] would ask, "Do you think this is the right amount?" Or ask me personal type questions about the divorce. . . .

[The judge] just read through all the settlement, called us up on the stand one at a time, asked if the settlement information was true . . . and that was that . . . kind of a slam-bam thing. . . .

The result was a rubber stamp quality to the court review: "I'd heard that if things are settled when you go to the judge, then it's a relatively pro forma appearance. And that's exactly what it turned out to be." "Well, it went very quickly. You know, in fifteen minutes it was over, nothing to it." . . .

The foregoing description of the actual divorce process raises the question of who is in fact casting the shadow of the law—the judge (as is typically presumed) or the litigants themselves. The setting of child support is a decision committed to the "sound discretion of the trial court." At the time of this study, the statute directed the judge to consider certain factors but specified no monetary amounts. Therefore, the expectation of what a particular judge would set for child support had to be determined from the cases in his or her court—most of which involved settlements. The shadow of the law, therefore, was cast by the agreements of the parties. It seems that, rather than a system of bargaining in the shadow of the law, divorce may well be one of adjudication in the shadow of bargaining.

C. *The Bargaining Arena of Divorce*

Divorce negotiation takes place not only in the shadow of the court but in the context of a particular bargaining arena. . . .

In divorce, unlike other legal processes, much of the negotiating is done by the parties themselves. The close personal relationship of the parties, the intimate nature of decisions involving child custody and support, and the need for continuing relationships where children are involved are all factors in this structure. One attorney has described the bargaining process in divorce as "four party bargaining": whatever counsel negotiate is often discussed privately by the parties and, perhaps, re-negotiated. This close involvement of the parties to a divorce in the negotiation process makes their ability to participate meaningfully a vital aspect of that process. . . .

The bargaining arena of divorce is quite unlike that of any other; it is one of emotional turmoil for the parties. The partner who seeks the divorce often experiences feelings of guilt; the one who is rejected usually feels hurt and angry. Partners who are mutually interested in obtaining a divorce may experience ambivalence and doubt in facing the uncertainties and problems inherent in changing their life situation. Although the law must deal with the economic and juridical aspects of this change, the parties are grappling with their personal and emotional problems at the same time. Sometimes it is necessary for them to work through these personal adjustments to a certain point before they can face the issues with which the law deals. Sometimes they are unable to do this until after the legal proceeding.

The comments of the lawyers about their clients are instructive:

[The time frame of a divorce] depends on the emotional states of the parties . . . you try to move a case ahead on some arbitrary kind of time frame that as a lawyer I think should be followed, it doesn't coincide with their emotional state and it happens that being very efficient and moving along in a very efficient manner brings people to a position that they aren't really emotionally ready to accept and then they reject that. Then you have problems in getting them later to accept something they've already rejected which they might later realize is reasonable. . . . [Sometimes] there's an agreement to most things but then the proposal is rejected on some minor point. Just offhand, rejected. If that happens a couple of times with the same party, I become curious as to whether or not the person's agenda is really to get a divorce . . . it's coming too close to having the divorce completed . . . and the real agenda is not to get the divorce. . . . And [so you don't want to] advance a case too quickly, when one of the parties is not yet accepting.

Another lawyer says:

The pattern I see is that [clients] usually come in fairly calm and in a reasonable frame of mind, and with the desire to work things out in a way that's not destructive. And then at some point people just have to get angry to be able to make that separation you get in a divorce. [So I] sort of warn people that that is the typical part of the pattern—not to get upset if their spouse who was so reasonable suddenly goes through a period of being totally intractable. And that it could happen to them, too. . . . I regard it as fairly healthy. It doesn't alarm me any. Usually by the time the process is over, which takes a minimum of about 6 months, people are back in a frame of mind of being reasonable and wanting to negotiate.

All of this has led J. Griffiths to observe that "lawyer and client are busy with two different divorces: the lawyer with a legal divorce, the client with a social and emotional one."

D. *Why Do Parties Settle?*

. . . [A] considerable body of literature . . . has attempted to explain the prevalence of negotiated settlements, particularly in the criminal justice system. In this section we explore the relevance of these theories to divorce settlements and analyze our data to determine whether any additional explanations can be found in the divorce area.

1. Pressure from the Court

One of the most frequently cited reasons for the large percentage of negotiated pleas in criminal cases is the heavy case load of the courts. Recently this explanation has been subject to some criticism as researchers have noted that the phenomenon of settlement is not as recent as is presumed by those advancing the "work load" thesis. Nevertheless, it is clear in both the civil and criminal contexts that (1) the work load is heavy, and (2) there is pressure from the courts to "clear the calendar" through negotiated settlements. The Dane County Court is no exception; it employs a set of procedures which subtly and sometimes overtly fosters stipulation by the parties.

A case cannot be placed on the court calendar until a certificate of readiness is issued. This is a form which must be signed by a family court commissioner (FCC) and which outlines the issues still in dispute and estimates the amount of court time which will be required to handle these issues. If the parties have not reached an agreement on the issues in the divorce by the time the court requests a certificate of readiness, the case will be assigned for a pretrial conference before an FCC. The purpose of a pretrial conference is two-fold: to settle the case or, failing that, to outline clearly the issues which cannot be settled. If a case is set on the court calendar for a contest, the judge may set it for a pretrial hearing, particularly if there are several undecided issues. Alternatively, the judge may suggest that the parties try to settle the case without the court's presence.

Both lawyers and clients feel these pressures and, to the extent that they are interested in formal adjudication of the case, come to realize the difficulties involved. In some instances, the pressures become explicit. The comment of one judge was very typical of judicial treatment. "I'll say, 'Look folks, you've got three quarters of an hour left before I'm going on to something else. If you can settle, we'll go on to court and get this over with today. Otherwise, you can have a date in [a distant month]."

2. Uncertainty of Outcome

Another oft-cited reason for the settlement of cases is the concern of the parties about the uncertainty of result of a trial. "A bird in the hand is worth two in the bush," and most people are risk-averse. Therefore, it is striking that there was very little reference to the uncertainties of a judge-made decision in the considerations about negotiating a settlement. Although our common sense tells that this factor had to be present to some degree, it was clearly overshadowed by other concerns.

3. The Costs of Litigation

Another frequently given reason for the high incidence of settlement is the cost of litigation. The term "cost of litigation" covers both monetary and emotional costs. In divorce there is no shortage of either.

a. Monetary costs

For divorcing parties, the costs of trial may make that type of dispute resolution unrealistic. They are already financially strained because of the need to maintain two households instead of one and they cannot afford to pay attorney fees. In addition, the value of the property may not be sufficient to justify the cost of a trial.

One of the themes throughout the client interviews is concern about the cost of the attorney's fees. In discussing why he did not press for further negotiations on the amount of child support which he felt was too high, one father worried:

> I think my attorney fees were already up to $1700. I didn't want to drag it out anymore. . . . I didn't want to [do] something that was going to put me in such a financial bind. . . . [The attorney] did a good job [and I wanted to] be able to pay him and not run it up to a point where I couldn't pay him.

The concern with attorney fees also reflected a feeling that, given limited resources, the parties were reluctant to spend them on litigation. Said one client: "We were trying to avoid paying attorneys as much as we could and trying to avoid using up our resources . . . in litigation costs." Said another: "I don't want the money wasted on that."

The attorneys were also very concerned about costs and frequently cautioned their clients on the expense of litigating issues. For example, in explaining why he did not seek custody of his children one father pointed out: "[My lawyer] discouraged me. [He said] you will have to fight it for a couple of years—it will cost you $15,000."

Furthermore, lawyers often felt that the value of the dispute did not justify the cost of the litigation. One lawyer put it this way:

> Sometimes you get to the point where you can either accept this [or fight]. Say you want to pay $1000 less on the house and you want $15 more a month in support. Okay say we win on these . . . you are going to end up with an attorney fee from me for $4000 or $5000 for going to trial . . . do you want to spend that to get that extra bit of money?

b. Emotional costs

Under the best of circumstances, a contested trial is difficult for the parties. Add this to the fact that divorce itself is an emotionally draining experience and it becomes clear that many parties to a divorce proceeding will settle to reduce the tension and emotional strain.

A mother, discussing why she agreed to a rather small child support amount, said: "I mean 50 lawyers could tell me to go after more money and I wouldn't have. I just didn't want to buck [my husband]. . . . I just wanted it over." A father explained: "As far as I was concerned [I wanted] to get it over as quickly as possible. And as far as I was concerned if I had to give up more than I really wanted that was fine because it would end it."

Another important element is the perception of the parties that they cannot risk the additional rift and strain that a trial entails. Unlike a settlement in a tort case, where the parties probably will never see each other again, parents in a divorce must face the need to maintain a continuing relationship.

> You can't obviously cut all the ties particularly when there are kids involved. We both realized that for his interest alone we would have to maintain an open and friendly relationship. That had we fought over the finances it would have been just terrible all the way around, just a no-win situation for everybody.

Another view to the same effect: "[I]f you are sitting around fighting and stuff it's not good for the kids. You have got to put your best foot forward and talk."

E. *Why Do Parties Go to Trial?* . . .

About one-sixth (58) of the 349 cases examined in our court file study went to trial. It is striking that 26 (45% of these cases) did not involve a dispute between the parties. Thirteen of these cases required judicial determination because the court lacked personal jurisdiction over one of the parties or because one party defaulted. In 13 of the remaining 45 cases the only dispute involved an objection by the Child Support Enforcement Agency; thus, one significant reason cases go to trial is to protect the interest of the state in fair reimbursement for welfare costs.

Our interviews provided some insight into reasons that the remaining 32 cases went to trial. First, those that go to trial are not fundamentally different from those that do not. Rather, there is a continuum from cases that settle easily, through those that settle reluctantly, to those that go to trial. For example, 94 of the 349 cases in our court file study had disputed issues at the time the certificate of readiness was filed; but by the time of the final hearing, over half of these were settled, leaving only the 45 disputed cases discussed above.

Judging from the interviews, one important factor in whether a case is difficult to settle is the attitude of the parties toward the divorce. Although the issue contested in these cases is child support, child custody or property division, the underlying issue often is opposition to the divorce itself. Because the only ground for divorce in Wisconsin is irretrievable breakdown, we did not find any formal contests on the issue of whether a divorce should be granted. Obviously, this did not mean that in all cases both parties favored the divorce. However, because they lacked any substantial legal basis for litigating the fundamental issue of whether to end the marriage, they fought about other matters. An attorney in one of the cases that went to trial put it this way:

> What happens with the "no-fault" law is that because the grounds for the divorce are very easily provable that the marriage is irretrievably broken, if somebody doesn't want a divorce, they can't fight it realistically on those grounds so they contest the financial issues that the court has to decide.

Of the 27 cases in which we conducted interviews, only two went to trial; in both of these cases one of the parties had unilaterally made the decision to divorce. In one of the cases, the husband described his wife's reaction to his decision to obtain a divorce: "I moved out on a Friday night and I served the papers on the following Tuesday. . . . She couldn't believe I was going to leave. . . . She thought everything about the marriage was fine and nothing was wrong." Similarly, in the other case that went to trial, counsel for one of the parties said: "In the first place, [the husband] didn't want the divorce. That had a lot to do with it."

F. *The Nature of Divorce Settlement*

Much of the literature on negotiation has assumed that settlements represent solutions to which both parties agree. Therefore, a negotiated settlement is seen as much more acceptable to the parties than one imposed by a court. . . .

[O]ur interviews suggest that much negotiation in divorce proceedings does not involve people who want the flexibility to arrange their affairs to the best advantage of each. Divorcing couples are usually in a major life crisis and one or both are bitter; the resulting "settlement" does not represent genuine agreement but a "best I can get" solution. In other words, true agreement between the parties is much less common than the frequency of settlement might indicate. We have data on satisfaction with the settlement for 41 of the 44 parties interviewed. Twenty of these were satisfied; six said they were satisfied but nonetheless felt that the settlement was unfair to them, while 15 were very dissatisfied. The following are typical comments from the latter 21 parties, who constitute half the group for which we have data; clearly their settlements do not represent consensual agreements.

> I said to [my lawyer] "you cannot make me sign those papers . . . you're talking about 14 years of my life. . . . I'm still carrying on the responsibility for two kids . . . and if I stay [in the house] till the kids are out of school I'll owe [my husband] $26,000 . . . ."
>
> Well, I was worn down. . . . I cried through the whole thing, I could hardly say yes, I could hardly sign it. [But I did and] I walked out of there and cried for probably two weeks straight.

Another respondent says: "A lot of things I didn't like and I didn't agree with. I just sort of swallowed it, maybe foolishly . . . she came out with the lion's share there— just about everything."

This characteristic of divorce negotiation—that it often results in settlements which are not agreeable to one or both of the parties—may help explain a current problem in the divorce courts: the high volume of post-divorce litigation. . . .

G. *The Limits of "Private Ordering"*

Most students of family law would agree that the present method of dispute resolution in divorce can be characterized as one of private ordering by the parties. Our data clearly supports this view, showing the clear preference of divorcing parties for negotiation over litigation and the statistical prevalence of settlement in divorce cases. We have also shown the limited nature of court review, noting that the role of the courts, as seen by the judges, the lawyers, and the parties, is primarily one of assuring that the parties understand what they are doing and what their options are.

One could argue that the present system embodies the most appropriate method for resolving divorce disputes: it places a premium on decision-making by the parties themselves, who know their own situation best. The system allows them the flexibility to fashion a settlement to their own needs, which should insure their satisfaction and compliance with the accord reached. Less costly for the parties and more efficient for the courts, this system should replace the bitterness and emotional turmoil of litigation with negotiation.

However, our findings suggest that while the *potential* for these advantages exists in the present system of negotiated settlements, that potential is not always realized. The existence of a negotiated settlement does not necessarily imply that the advantages of private ordering have been achieved. We have found instead that the process of negotiation is complex and that a high percentage of divorce settlements do not represent consensual agreements which satisfy both parties.

Even more important than our findings that divorce settlements frequently fail to reflect the preferences of the parties are the findings reported in the next section of this Article. There we analyze the relationship between the process of negotiation and one important outcome of that negotiation, the amount of child support in the settlement. We found that:

(1)   The ability . . . to decide whether a particular agreement is in their best interests was, in some cases, considerably diminished because of emotional strain.

(2)   The outcome of negotiation (child support in this study) was often affected by legally irrelevant variables, such as the attitude of the parties toward the divorce. For example, it appears that the ability of one party to "hold out," because that party is reluctant to end the relationship or is emotionally hurt by the other party's decision to leave, has an important effect on outcome.

(3)   The child support bargain which was satisfactory to the parties might not be fair to the child, given the standard of living the supporting parent could provide, or might not be fair to the state, which must support children whose parents fail to provide adequate support.

These findings raise questions about the capability of the negotiation process to be fully responsive to public policy concerns about the support of children. . . .

III. FACTORS THAT AFFECT THE AMOUNT OF THE CHILD SUPPORT AWARD

In this section, we examine the outcome on a particular issue in divorce—the amount of child support—in an attempt to understand the relationship between negotiation and outcome. Although there have been a number of studies analyzing the factors that affect the amount of child support, they have tended to assume the decision was made by the judge. There has been little recognition that the process is primarily one of negotiation, not adjudication. . . .

A. *Parental Ability to Pay*

Our data from the court files allows us to shed some light on the debate over the relationship between parental ability to pay and the amount of the child support award. Using multiple regression analysis we found that three factors—the number of children, the income of the supporting parent, and the couple's estimated net worth—accounted for almost 50% of the variation in the amount of child support. This is an impressively high relationship by social science standards and should dispel some of the concern about the failure of child support awards to reflect parental ability to pay.

On the other hand, our review of individual awards revealed a large amount of variation which is unexplained by parental income. For example, the court files include two fathers who are assessed the same amount of child support per month, yet one earned less than $300 per month while the other earned over $2000. Similarly, for 16 fathers, all of whom had one child and earned $800-$900 per month, child support awards ranged from less than $50 per month to $349 per month. Thus, while ability to pay is a powerful influence on the amount of support, individual cases still vary widely.

B.   *Other Factors. . .*

. . . We sought to explore this phenomenon in our interviews. We began our analysis by examining the 18 cases in which the mother was the sole physical custodian and the parties had agreed to a stipulation prior to the final hearing. Examining the amounts of child support to which these parties had agreed, we found the same kinds of variations we had observed in the court file cases. The child support awards for parents with one child ranged from 7% to 18% of the supporting parent's income; those for parents with two children ranged from 13% to 34% of income.

As we analyzed the interviews, we sensed that the attitudes of the parties themselves toward the decision to divorce was a factor of some significance. In most cases, the decision to divorce was not mutual. One party wanted out of the marriage, often to pursue another relationship. Following up on this analysis, we classified the parties as "impatient" or "reluctant" based on attitude toward ending the marriage. For example, a party who sought the divorce was classified as "impatient," one who opposed the divorce and hoped for reconciliation was classified as "reluctant." Some of the parties were neither "impatient" nor "reluctant"; these we classified as "accepting.". . .

Analyzing the data from this perspective, we found that for impatient custodial mothers and reluctant supporting fathers, child support tended to comprise a lower than average percent of father's income; conversely, for impatient supporting fathers and reluctant custodial mothers, the percent of father's income paid in child support was higher than average. The highest percent of income paid occurred in a case in which the father was anxious to divorce and the mother reluctant. Concerned with the possibility of prolonged dispute or litigation, the father made a generous offer, the mother reluctantly took it and the divorce was granted.

The role of impatience and reluctance in shaping the amount of the award is illustrated most graphically by comparing mean awards, keeping in mind that because of the small size and nonrandom character of the interview phase of the study, the results presented here are offered only as tentative indications of the factors shaping child support settlement. The mean award for two children was 23% of the supporter's income. However, in the seven cases where the supporting parent was reluctant or the custodial parent impatient (or both), the mean award was 19% of father's income; in the five cases where the custodian was reluctant or the supporting parent impatient (or both), the mean award was 29% of father's income.

To the extent that this finding is representative of the dynamics of the settlement process in divorce, it is especially interesting in light of other research on legal negotiation. Studies in personal injury claims settlement, for example, indicate that delay, when used intentionally by a negotiator, can be an effective bargaining weapon. Impatient parties often fail to secure the claim they are legally entitled to, but parties who hold out and negotiate reluctantly often receive settlements in excess of what might be expected. These data indicate that the same dynamic occurs in divorce.

. . . [A]n interesting paradox exists: clients with the best settlements were among the least satisfied, whereas those with objectively poor settlements tended to evaluate them more highly. For example, the mother who received the highest percentage of the father's income (46%) said about the "agreement":

> I know I got screwed royally. I know [his business] was worth more. . . . He kept saying "my books are open, my books are open, come look at them." I can't look at them." I couldn't read them . . . I couldn't get my lawyers to look at them. . . . There was so much garbage going on it was difficult to figure out what the truth was, what his real income was, his real standard of living.

This paradox arises because for many parties satisfaction with the award is not a consequence of its size. Rather, both size and satisfaction of award may result from the attitude towards the divorce. A person who does not want to divorce will tend to get a more favorable settlement, because of his or her reluctance to settle; but he or she will be dissatisfied with the process because for this party monetary award was not the goal.

IV. SUMMARY AND IMPLICATIONS

This Article has attempted to add some new dimensions to the study of informal settlement by exploring negotiation as a process and by examining its effect on outcome.

We have emphasized the role of negotiation as the principal mode of disposition of divorce disputes both statistically and functionally. Divorce litigation does not proceed initially as a case to be presented in court. It begins as a series of bargaining episodes; only if these fail does it change direction and proceed to court.

We have raised questions about the role of judicial decision making in shaping the character of negotiations. In a system in which the overwhelming number of cases that come before the court are decided by the parties themselves without substantive court review, the benchmarks used by the judge in the few cases requiring a judicial decision may actually have been established by the parties.

We have emphasized the importance of the bargaining arena on the negotiation process and the outcome. Settling disputes by negotiation appears to be at least as complex a process as adjudication. In particular, there may be more officials involved in a negotiation context and their roles may be more ambiguous. The personal and emotional involvement of the parties appears to have a greater impact than in adjudication.

We have noted that, in a legal regime of no-fault divorce, the spouse who is reluctant to end the marriage appears to retain an important bargaining tool through his or her reluctance to enter into an agreement. Custodial parents who were reluctant to end the marriage and/or whose spouses were impatient to do so obtained significantly better child support awards than the mean of the group.

The most important public policy implications of our study concern two connected issues. The first is the relationship of child support to parental ability to pay. Current policy highly values a link between the income of the supporting parent and the amount of child support awarded. Although our findings suggest that awards are very responsive to that factor, the evidence still points to considerable variation in awards due to factors not related to income. Furthermore, the process of negotiation is controlled by parties whose agendas often include extra-legal considerations, particularly emotional factors such as impatience or reluctance to obtain the divorce itself.

Thus, the problem of linking the amount of child support to parental ability to pay may be more complex than is usually acknowledged. What is needed is not just rules to control the discretion of the judge but also—and perhaps more important—some mechanism for requiring the negotiating parties to follow similar guidelines. . . .

Craig A. McEwen, Lynn Mather & Richard J. Maiman, *Lawyers, Mediation, and the Management of Divorce Practice,* 28 LAW & SOCIETY REVIEW 149 (1994)[*]

Discussions of legal practice and dispute resolution are often dominated—and distorted—by the tendency to view the world in either-or terms. Both the popular and academic literatures are preoccupied with contrasts between formal and informal processes, competitive and cooperative attorney styles, clients' rights and needs, lawyer and client control of decision making, and so on. Whatever utility it may have for framing rhetorical questions about legal reform, such binary thinking does not accord with the more complex realities of legal practice, which are often located not at one end or another of such polarities but in the dynamic interplay between them.

The experiences and observations of divorce attorneys who participate in mediation with their clients provide a new angle of vision on some of these central realities of day-to-day law practice. They also offer fresh perspectives on the highly variable character of divorce mediation itself. In this article, we examine how lawyers in the state of Maine report understanding and participating in mandatory, court-sponsored divorce mediation. From the lawyers' descriptions of their work, we identify four central challenges of divorce practice. Although experienced attorneys may give them little conscious thought, these dimensions of practice require numerous and sometimes difficult decisions that lie at the heart of divorce lawyers' work: how to pursue both negotiation and trial preparation; how to encourage client participation in case preparation while retaining one's professional authority; how to provide clients with legal advice while addressing vitally important nonlegal issues; and how to structure and manage cases so that they can be moved predictably and expeditiously.

While viewing the practice of divorce law as organized around the decisions necessary to solve these problems, we also see—through the eyes of participating lawyers—a mediation process that is far more varied and complex than the simple models of many of its advocates and critics. This mediation, for example, permits talk about rights as well as problem-solving negotiation; encourages client involvement while providing opportunity to lawyers to advocate for and support clients; and structures negotiation at least as often as it substitutes for trial. Indeed, we believe that the wide acceptance of mediation by divorce lawyers in Maine can be understood in terms of its apparent capacity to expand the options and ease the choices for lawyers in dealing with the demands of their divorce practices. . . .

---

[*]   Reprinted by permission of the Law and Society Association.

I. Data and Methods

This examination of the integration of divorce mediation into divorce law practice draws from data gathered in a larger study of the day-to-day work of divorce attorneys in Maine and New Hampshire. Here we focus on data from Maine. . . . Our data come primarily from lengthy semi-structured interviews with 163 divorce lawyers, conducted by the authors in 1990-91. To select lawyers to interview, we sampled the 1989 divorce dockets of courts in three New Hampshire and four Maine counties that were roughly similar with regard to population size, urban concentration, and income. In each court we recorded the names of the lawyers of record, developing a frequency distribution of their appearances. Then we sampled the list, taking all the lawyers with the most frequent representations, about half of those with moderate frequencies, and a few of those with lesser frequencies. In no case did we choose from the many lawyers who represented only one or two divorce clients a year. We supplemented this list of active divorce lawyers with names identified by other attorneys and by court clerks.

Through this process we identified 178 divorce lawyers and arranged and completed interviews with 92% of them. Our interviewees included 88 lawyers in Maine and 75 in New Hampshire. Of the total interviewed, 37% were female and 63% were male. Most of the lawyers worked as solo practitioners or in small law firms.

Our interviews averaged 90 minutes each and were taped and later transcribed. Only one part of the interview focused on the relationship between mediation and divorce practice. We asked questions about the nature and frequency of lawyers' participation in mediation, the advantages and disadvantages of mediation in divorce cases, and the lawyers' perceptions of mediation in Maine. . . .

II. Divorce Mediation in Maine

Divorce mediation differs widely across the United States, and thus statements about "divorce mediation" in general should be suspect. As examples of this variation, consider that in some areas mediation is purely voluntary, while in others it is mandated by the state or by the local court; mediation may address all issues of a divorce or be limited by law to child custody and visitation; and either public or private mediators can deliver mediation services. Some mediation programs exclude the parties' lawyers, while others encourage them to participate. Mediators themselves vary in their backgrounds, credentials, and training, so that some mediators see their roles largely as nondirective and facilitative, while others seek to be more active and judgmental. . . .

Given this diversity in mediation policy and practice, our analysis of divorce mediation must be carefully contextualized. We are reporting on mediation in Maine, a state that has organized divorce mediation differently from many states. In July 1984, divorce mediation became mandatory in Maine prior to the scheduling of any contested hearing in all cases involving minor children. Unlike most divorce mediation statutes, the Maine law allowed mediation to focus on *all* issues in divorce, not just on child custody and visitation. Also, the mandate means in practice that if parties with children have reached a settlement on their own or anticipate doing so, they need not schedule mediation. Only in those cases where one or both parties want mediation or where one or both anticipate the possibility of a contested hearing is a request made—by the parties, not the court—to schedule mediation. Generally, mediation in Maine is done by nonlawyer mediators who have limited formal training and who work for very modest wages from the state. Divorce cases in Maine typically involve only one mediation session, held at the local courthouse, lasting on average between two and three hours.

As a consequence of the 1984 mandate, the number of divorce mediation sessions increased precipitously, from 350 in 1983 (when mediation was voluntary and only available in parts of the state) to 4,918 in 1985. In 1985, the first full year of mandated mediation, close to 30% of the total divorces filed in Maine went to mediation, compared to about 4% in 1983. In 1986 the state assessed a fee of $60 per couple for the mediation service. Thereafter, the percentage of divorces going to mediation declined to a rate of about 22% by 1990.

Maine lawyers have, from the start, actively assisted their clients in making strategic decisions about whether to enter mediation. Lawyers' recommendations about mediation depend, of course, on their having had prior involvement in the case. In Maine, lawyers typically represent fewer than half of divorcing parties, a figure that is consistent with other studies nationwide. In our sample of Maine divorce cases from 1979 to 1988, neither party was represented in 16% of the cases, only the plaintiff was represented in another 44%, and the defendant only in less than 2%. Both parties had legal representation in 38% of the cases.

The typical mediation case in Maine, however, usually involved two attorneys. In our sample of mediated cases since 1984 (n = 422), 80% involved two lawyers, and another 17% had one lawyer, typically for the plaintiff. In only 3% of the cases did both mediating parties proceed without any lawyer. Mediated cases also had substantially more than the average level of legal contest. Analysis of our docket data shows that, on average, mediated cases took twice as long to dispose of as nonmediated cases in the same courts (355 days vs. 184 days); had more than three times as many temporary or discovery motions (1.82 motions per case vs. 0.5) and court actions such as motion hearings and issuance of temporary orders (.48 court actions per case vs. .14). In stark contrast to the assumption that mediation substitutes for an adversarial legal process, mediated cases in Maine since 1984 appear to have been more legally contested than nonmediated cases and *more* likely to have two attorneys involved. Clearly, the requirement in Maine that contested cases be mediated produced this result.

Not only were lawyers likely to represent parties in mediation, but they also regularly attended mediation sessions. Of the Maine lawyers we interviewed, 78% reported they "always" attended mediation sessions while another 17% "usually" attended. The partial exception was one Maine county, where only 48% of the respondents reported always attending mediation. However, there was general agreement among the lawyers in that county that their local practice was moving toward attorney attendance, the norm for much of the rest of the state.

Maine divorce lawyers have not only accepted mandated mediation as a fact of life but have with a few exceptions embraced it warmly. Of our Maine lawyers, 89% expressed unambiguous support for mediation, while 8% reported finding it useful for custody but not for financial issues, and 4% said they disliked mediation. Eighty-five percent of lawyers indicated that they voluntarily sought mediation, at least occasionally, in cases where there were no minor children. However, one-third of the lawyers voiced concerns about the uneven quality of divorce mediators or about the cost and time absorbed by mediation.

We are left to question, then, how and why Maine divorce lawyers have adapted to mediation so completely? The answer lies, we believe, in the character of divorce law practice and the capacity of mediation to assist lawyers in handling some of the key challenges in their day-to-day work.

III. Adaptation: Incorporating Mediation into Divorce Law Practice . . .

. . . We have identified four dimensions of divorce practice, each involving its own particular challenges. These dimensions have been abstracted from our data, and thus they are analytic rather than "folk" categories. They are, however, firmly anchored in the literature about law practice—in empirical research, in the extensive commentary on practice, and in the normative literature prescribing codes of professional conduct. The four dimensions which we examine are (1) pursuing negotiated settlement and preparing for trial, (2) controlling clients while allowing their participation in decision making, (3) handling nonlegal issues as well as legal issues in the divorce, and (4) directing the legal process through strong case management. In the next sections, we describe these dimensions in detail and draw on our interviews to show how divorce attorneys perceive mediation as a valuable resource in dealing with the challenges they pose.

A.   Negotiation of Settlement and Preparation for Trial

Lawyers are often characterized as either adversarial or cooperative in their general approach to case resolutions. Such a juxtaposition obscures the frequent necessity in law practice of moving between and combining approaches. Flexibility in approach is made difficult, however, by the fact that the formal legal process is organized around the steps to trial. Although most cases ultimately settle through negotiation, lawyers must orchestrate negotiation largely on their own, with the occasional help of court-initiated settlement conferences on the eve of trial. . . .

The character of law practice compounds the challenges for lawyers of dealing with simultaneous demands for trial preparation and settlement activity—whether through competitive advocacy or cooperation. The press of handling many cases and clients typically prevents sustained attention to any single case until an official deadline forces it. As a consequence, lawyer-guided negotiation is likely to be episodic and drawn out, proceeding in fits and starts through exchanges of letters or phone calls, interspersed with consultation with clients. . . .

According to lawyers we interviewed, mandatory mediation changes the structure of the formal legal process, by adding an official settlement event that involves parties directly in the negotiation process. Attorneys thus report that mediation encourages a focus on settlement, in part by preparing their clients for it. The gathering of lawyers and clients together in the same place also improves the clarity and efficiency of communication. When attorneys participate in mediation, they find that the nature of communication is transformed as well, as mediators set normative restraints on overly aggressive conduct. At the same time, mediation does not preclude and may even enhance trial preparation. Lawyers especially appreciated mediation for the information it gave them about the other side and for the opportunity to test out arguments that might be used at trial. . . .

In an adversarial process, a lawyer learns to distrust the portrait of the other spouse painted by the opposing lawyer. At the same time, attorneys must remain skeptical of their own client's portrayal of the situation and of the other side. The information derived through a face-to-face meeting with both spouses and lawyers thus fills a vacuum that affects crucial assessments of the credibility of the other party and lawyer and, ultimately, of one's own client. With that information, the lawyer may feel better informed about how to approach settlement effectively as well as how to evaluate the prospects for trial.

The presence of the mediator, the relative formality of the mediation event, and the ideology of mediation can influence not only the organization and content but also the tone of discourse between parties and lawyers. Unlike lawyer-to-lawyer or party-to-party negotiation or even a four-way conference, mediation diminishes the temptation and—especially with mediators pushing each side to compromise—the ability to behave antagonistically rather than cooperatively. . . .

> The climate is there for compromise and if you get, sit in a room with two lawyers, I think, clients tend to think that they've got these two champions there and so that's the whole mode. It's just such a different dynamic when you get into the mediation room. . . .

Although permitting expressions of anger, the norms of mediation also demand civility and a sense of decorum that may be lacking in the private interchanges between lawyers or their clients. . . .

> Lawyers never talk to each other face to face. It's easy to be Tarzan over the telephone, it really is. It's real hard to pull that garbage when the client [is present] . . . you can call my client a slut or a crook over the telephone, but it's real different to have the guts to do that when they're sitting across from you. A lot of lawyers who will do that nonsense over the telephone won't do it in person. . . .

Lawyers' understandings of legal rights and predictions about likely outcomes at trials cast a strong shadow on the advice they reported giving about settlement before, during, and after mediation sessions. Maine lawyers balanced their view of mediation as an advantageous place to reach settlement with an awareness that the mediation process could pressure parties into unwise agreements.

Consistent with the concerns of critics of divorce mediation, Maine lawyers said they knew of clients who had experienced the pressure or "momentum" of mediation or "being browbeaten" by particular mediators who were too concerned with getting a settlement. But the lawyers saw themselves as playing the role of rights-oriented advocate, advising and protecting their clients during the mediation process. . . .

B. Controlling Decisionmaking

Another key dimension of legal practice lies in the complex relation between lawyer and client, in particular the balance that must be struck between lawyer and client control over decisionmaking. . . . The traditional model of lawyer-client inter-action presumes that lawyers direct decisionmaking and that clients play a fairly pas-sive role, but concerns about problems created by lawyer dominance have led scholars recently to articulate a more "client-centered" model. Rather than seeing the lawyer-client interaction as an either/or matter, Felstiner and Sarat emphasize the fluidity inher-ent in the relationship. Thus, they argue that "power in lawyer-client interactions is less stable, predictable, and clear-cut than the conventional view holds . . . [and that] it is continuously enacted and reenacted." We agree, and see the issue of lawyer-client con-trol to be one of the most central in law practice.

Precisely because the professional expertise of the lawyer may make it difficult for clients to exercise decisionmaking authority attorneys must constantly demonstrate their identification with a client's interests and needs. Lawyers thus may build client trust by accepting and supporting a client's world-view. At the same time, however, lawyers must try to act as objective and skeptical advisors. The skeptic's role often means telling clients things they do not want to hear and urging compromise, thus plac-ing in jeopardy the clients' trust in them as vigorous allies. . . .

The problems of managing the balance between lawyer and client control are at least as great in negotiation as in formal legal proceedings. When lawyers take on a major role in negotiating a divorce, clients can easily lose track of where things are because they are not privy to phone exchanges between attorneys and may find it dif-ficult to penetrate and interpret legal correspondence. Clients are distanced from set-tlement activities by the reliance on lawyers as intermediaries for exchange and interpretation of information. Frequently, in response to the sense of exclusion, clients demand the time and attention of their lawyers, wondering what has happened or, more likely, not happened and why.

Lawyers in Maine report that mandated mediation gives them new ways both to share information and decision making with clients and to influence client decisions. In the lawyers' view, mediation is particularly useful because it supports their efforts to reshape client expectations. Further, lawyers recognize that mediation involves their clients directly in the actual settlement process but at the same time permits the attorney to supervise that participation.

The fact that lawyers use mediation to reinforce selectively the advice that clients resist hearing was remarked on by over half of the Maine lawyers with whom we spoke.

> I can't force my client to do something the client is uncomfortable with. I'm not there to argue the other person's case. Whereas at mediation, it's an opportunity for my client to kind of expose his or her case to reality and the mediator many times is going to say, "Wait, is that what you really mean? Do you really think a judge is going to listen to this? Listen, I've just heard it for the first time and let me tell you what my reaction is." And you're kind of exposing . . . and many times when you say it to your attor-ney, it will be received, obviously, differently from just a completely dis-interested person.
>
> In other words, you can say [to a client], "You can't get that" and go to mediation, the mediation takes place, and this and that, and it shows that

it's not only my ideas. Then I can come out and say, well, I told you. It gives them almost a second opinion. . . .

The potential for conflicts between the lawyer's role as client advocate and as reality tester is particularly great where there are children in a divorce. . . . The heavy emotional charge attached to children makes it especially hard for lawyers to challenge their clients on these issues, particularly without strong legal grounds. Mediation, however, may provide a context to broach these issues safely. As one lawyer noted, "A mediator . . . can talk about what's in the best interest of the child in a way that an attorney can't." . . .

Although mediation may strengthen lawyer control in some ways through its reinforcement of attorney advice, it also can give parties greater opportunity to participate in what otherwise can be a fairly remote and mysterious process of seeking settlement. At the very least, it opens up the process to observation by clients.

> I think it makes them feel like they're more in control of the situation because they're involved, they're not out there in left field while the attorneys are working on it. They're right there.

> I just think it's really helpful for them to see the process, to see the give and take of both sides rather than having them always feel like, I'm giving again, I'm giving again.

Typically according to Maine divorce lawyers, clients do far more than listen in mediation; indeed, attorneys reported encouraging clients to take an active role in the process.

> I'm much more inclined to let the client talk in the mediation room . . . my experience has been that sometimes that room is the first time [since the marital breakdown] that clients have been face to face, or it's one of the few times they have the opportunity to be face to face, and they need to get some stuff off their chest, and it can be done in that setting safely and usefully.

> I want to sit back and listen, and I'm not going to interrupt unless I feel that you've misstated something or you're misinformed on an area or need some counseling.

> I tell them ahead of time that I'm there to protect them if I think things are not being run fairly, and to watch out for their interest, but primarily it's them, the mediator, and the other spouse. And most of the attorneys I deal with apparently work the same way because everybody sits there, doesn't do all the talking, sits there and lets them work it out. . . .

. . . At the same time, almost every Maine lawyer we interviewed conceded that he or she sometimes had to play the central role in mediation sessions because certain clients could not—or would not—play that role themselves. Unlike voluntary mediation, where more willing and articulate parties self-select into the process, mandatory mediation draws in quite diverse parties. For example,

It depends on the client, but I'll tell them, if you want to talk, feel free to talk. The mediator would rather have you talk, but if you prefer me to talk, that's fine. . . .

In sum, Maine lawyers valued mediation because it involves their clients directly—but under supervision—in discussing settlement, hearing the other side, and weighing the reasonableness of each party's position. Yet, lawyers also recognized that the active role of mediators in challenging parties and their positions can also reinforce the lawyer's influence over the client. Thus, Maine's mandated mediation appears to assist attorneys in increasing client participation in negotiation while simultaneously reinforcing the lawyer's professional role as guide, adviser, and advocate.

C. Handling Nonlegal and Legal Issues

. . . The turmoil of many divorces draws lawyers into the private lives of their clients, while the substantive issues of divorce often involve practical assessments of living arrangements and the children's needs. Although a primary task of lawyers is to translate personal troubles into legal issues, lawyers also face demands to offer personal advice and to situate their legal advice in a broader context. Thus, central to legal practice is a dimension that moves lawyers back and forth from dealing with technical legal issues to counseling clients about their problems of living.

These problems of living include a wide range of issues for which there is no clear-cut solution that would result from the application of legal rules. Such nonlegal issues include, for example, making future household arrangements, dividing up personal property, and arranging the details of child visitation schedules. The issues also include coping with the client's emotional distress over the broken relationship or fear of an insecure and uncertain future.

In divorce cases a failure to deal with these nonlegal issues may prevent the attorney from getting her legal work accomplished. For example, angry and upset clients can be "unreasonable" and may resist settlement or demand legal tactics that, in the lawyer's view, have no chance of success. Alternatively, a client may want to give up on some legal entitlement to speed resolution or to deal with guilt over ending a marriage. Divorce attorneys thus struggle to manage emotional clients and to find ways to work through that emotion deflecting it, suppressing it, or venting and putting it behind. . . .

Similarly, traditional legal representation and lawyer-guided negotiation do not provide a structure for direct meetings between clients to decide the "pots and pans" issues. Although many lawyers encourage clients to work through such problems on their own, not all couples can do so. . . .

In this context, mediation may provide a setting where anger and feelings about the other spouse can find an outlet. . . .

Mediation can give the parties a chance to work through or even just to voice strong emotions to one another or to some official third party. Clients' opportunity to express these feelings in mediation may also relieve the lawyer of the burden of hearing them privately; and by relying on mediation to provide outlets for their expression, the lawyer can more easily focus attention on reaching settlement.

Mediation sessions also lend themselves to pursuing those issues that lawyers may view as trivial yet crucial to divorcing parties. Lawyers generally acknowledged the value of mediation in working through property division and visitation arrangements. The potential in mediation to work out these intricate problems leads to greater detail in mediated divorce agreements, according to 10 of the lawyers we interviewed. As a result, according to one lawyer,

> You've got some real sausage-looking agreements, I'll tell you, some real strange looking beasts because of what was perceived to be a real concern of the parties, or one party even, but that they reached agreement on . . . visitation schedules . . . are often the bulk of a divorce judgment now. . . .

Thus, in mediation, Maine lawyers have an opportunity to guide their clients through the often intertwined legal and nonlegal issues of a divorce. By giving an outlet for parties to meet one another and to express their feelings, mediation can assist attorneys in moving their clients beyond these emotional issues and toward "reasonable" settlement. At the same time, mediation may unite the discussions of children, of pots and pans issues, and of financial matters, and thus pressure those lawyers who prefer to concentrate only on "legal" issues to support clients in the "nonlegal" areas of controversy as well. . . .

The introduction of mandated mediation in Maine thus has opened up new opportunities for lawyers both to establish and to lose control over the management of divorce cases. The largely favorable views of mediation among the Maine divorce bar reflect the general sense that it improves case management while, at the same time, assisting lawyers in dealing simultaneously with trial preparation and settlement, client participation and professional direction, and legal and nonlegal issues. Moreover, by examining lawyers' perceptions of mediation and its utility to them, we understand better the fluid nature of divorce law practice.

C. Handling Nonlegal and Legal Issues

The last reading in this section deals with the management of divorce by judges. The context for this discussion is the nature of the norms governing judicial decisions in domestic relations matters. It is something of a cliche that those norms take the form of standards rather than clear rules. Property distributions and alimony are to be "just and equitable"; custody and visitation orders are to serve the "best interests" of the child.

The use of norms accounts for the peculiarly "fact-intensive" nature of divorce hearings and decisions. It also suggests the importance associated with "correct" decisions, not across the board or on average, but in each case. Whereas clear rules are less sensitive to special fact situations and aim for desirable decisions across a range of circumstances, standards such as "just and equitable" seek to enable judges to make decisions that are right in each case. In doing so, they also and perhaps necessarily convey to decision-makers a broad range of discretion as they determine what is just and proper, or in a child's "best interests."

Concededly, the openness of norms for divorce cases is over-stated in some degree. Whether by judicial or legislative decision, broad standards are often qualified by intermediate rules guiding, or limiting, the exercise of judicial discretion. In many jurisdictions, custody should presumptively be given to the parent who has cared for the child prior to the divorce and property awards may presumptively begin with equal distribution of marital wealth.

Nevertheless, the operation of discretion is a peculiarly important question in family law cases. How do judges supply content to indeterminate legal standards? Do, for example, extra-legal factors explain their decisions to a considerable degree? The following empirical study of discretionary decision-making in divorce cases takes us some distance in understanding this phenomenon.

Marsha Garrison, *How Do Judges Decide Divorce Cases? An Empirical Analysis of Discretionary Decision Making,* 74 NORTH CAROLINA LAW REVIEW 401 (1996)[*]

Introduction

Divorce law has traditionally relied on judicial wisdom to achieve fair results. Instead of bright-line rules, legislatures have typically given judges in the divorce court almost unlimited discretion, bounded only by indeterminate standards or lists of fac-

---

tors that may be considered. Judicial discretion has also been enhanced by the rarity of jury trials in divorce cases; in almost all divorce actions the judge both determines the facts and interprets the law.

During the past two decades, judicial discretion in divorce cases has expanded. Title-based property division has been succeeded by discretionary distribution principles rather than new bright-line rules. The adoption of gender-neutral divorce laws has similarly enhanced the role of judicial discretion in custody and alimony decisions. In some states, judicial discretion in awarding alimony has been further expanded as a result of the removal of fault barriers to an alimony award and the development of durational alimony as an alternative to a permanent award. Only in the area of child support, as a result of directives from the federal government, has judicial discretion been curtailed.

The expansion of judicial discretion in divorce cases has met with decidedly mixed reviews. Some commentators have claimed that indeterminate standards produce decisions that are inconsistent, expensive, and biased against women. Others have argued that bright-line rules are too broad, too rigid, and too insensitive to case variation to govern divorce decision making. . . .

. . . Although there has been considerable research on divorce outcomes over the past two decades, research focusing on judicial decision making at divorce has been rare. We know almost nothing about the characteristics of the decision-makers, the cases they decide, or the impact of appellate courts. As to the outcomes produced by the judicial process, the evidence consists of a handful of reports that suggest contradictory conclusions.

In order to decide how much discretion judges should have, we need better information about the results of current discretionary decision making: Do judges rely on many factors in reaching a decision or only a few? Do judges agree on which factors are important and their relative weights? Does the pattern of decision making vary depending on factors such as the judge's age, sex, experience, or location? Does it exhibit consistent biases based on litigant characteristics such as gender or social class? Do judicial decisions differ from the results of settled cases? Do the cases judges decide differ from the typical divorce action? Only when we know how judges make decisions, and how their decisions affect the settlement process, can we decide whether and how judicial discretion should be curtailed.

One reason for the lack of evidence on these questions is that judicial divorce decisions are in fact a rarity; the vast bulk of cases are settled. Divorce researchers, in attempting to portray overall outcomes, have thus understandably given short shrift to judges. While the outcomes of settled cases might reveal the impact of indeterminate rules on the settlement process, researchers have typically described only aggregate data; my recent research on the impact of New York's 1980 Equitable Distribution Law was the first to assess the predictability and range of divorce outcomes.

In this article I describe and analyze the results of an empirical study of judicial decisions on alimony, property distribution, and child support, dating from a major statutory reform in the research state's alimony and property distribution rules in 1980 to that reform's tenth anniversary. My analysis suggests that the exercise of discretion is a complex phenomenon: Depending on which of the various discretionary decisions made by judges we focus, the research findings provide evidence to support the claims of *both* discretion's critics and champions. There is evidence of regional variation, class bias, the intrusion of private values into the decision-making process, of utter unpredictability, *and* of highly predictable decision making consistent with the statutory standard; there is evidence both to support and contradict the claim of gender bias in judicial decision making; there is evidence of settlement results that are highly consistent—and inconsistent—with the decision-making patterns of judges.

In interpreting these results, I found that what at first glance appears contradictory and chaotic in fact evidences the natural evolution of discretionary decision making. While the claims on both sides of the current debate over discretion in divorce cases typically rely on a static, "snap-shot" perspective, my research results support an alternate view of discretion as a dynamic, evolutionary phenomenon that is guided by the legislature's directives (or lack thereof), shaped by cumulative judicial experience, and set in a shifting social context. While this is not a novel view of discretion—it has been variously embraced by theorists writing from both a social science and economic perspective—it is one that is often neglected in the debate over the appropriate role of discretion in divorce. It is also a view of which we have had little empirical evidence.
. . .

II. THE DECISION MAKING BACKGROUND: THE LAW, THE RESEARCH SAMPLE, THE JUDGES AND THE LITIGANTS

* * *

B. The Research Sample

My analysis of judicial decision making under the Equitable Distribution Law is part of a larger research project aimed at determining the impact of the change in legal standards upon divorce outcomes. For analysis of the statute's overall impact, data were drawn from the court files of approximately 900 divorces filed in 1978, two years before enactment of the Equitable Distribution Law, and from the files of approximately 900 divorces filed in 1984, four years after the law's passage. In order to examine regional variation in case outcomes, cases were selected in equal numbers from three diverse counties: one from New York City, one from the suburban belt surrounding it, and one representative of the mixed urban/rural upstate region. Analysis of the case data revealed that the average property distribution varied little over the research period but that the frequency and duration of alimony awards declined markedly. Case outcomes for both time periods were also highly variable; the passage of the law thus appeared to have little effect in improving the consistency of results.

Judicial decision making under the new statute could not be analyzed through data from this sample because, as a result of the extreme infrequency of divorce trials, it contained almost no judicial decisions. A judicial case sample that represented decisions over a longer period was also desirable in order to detect shifts in decision-making patterns over time and the impact of the 1986 statutory amendments. A separate sample of judicial opinions was thus compiled.

The judicial sample was assembled from decisions published during the first ten years after the Equitable Distribution Law became effective. All published trial court decisions on alimony and property distribution in New York State were included.

Appellate decisions were utilized to expand the sample: If an unpublished trial court decision could be determined either from the appellate decision itself or from the appellate record, the case was included in the sample. This approach yielded a total of 383 decisions dating from the statute's effective date of September 1, 1980, to September 1, 1990. . . .

C. Who Decides: The Judges

As it was rare for any judge to have decided more than one or two of the sample cases, 198 different decision-makers, from all parts of New York State, are represented. While the size and geographic range of the group might suggest a fair amount of diversity among the judges, in many respects they were a remarkably homogeneous group. Overwhelmingly, they were male, "sixtyish," and the product of a local education. Only 7% of the judges were female. Only 18% were under the age of fifty-five; 48% were clustered between the ages of fifty-five and sixty-four. Eighty-five percent attended either college or law school at a school in or near the community in which they sat as a judge; more than half attended both college and law school locally.

The judges exhibited more diversity in the extent of their judicial experience . . ., and in their political party and religious affiliations. . . . In contrast to the judges' age, sex, education, and judicial experience, party and religious affiliation were strongly and significantly correlated with the location of their courtrooms. Fifty-four percent of judges for whom political party affiliation could be determined were Republican and 46% Democratic; given the dominance of the Democratic Party in New York City and of the Republican Party in upstate New York, it is not surprising that 88% of New York City judges were Democrat and 75% of upstate judges were Republican.

Religion, too, was highly correlated with geography. Overall, 53% of the judges identified themselves as Catholic, 23% as Protestant, and 24% as Jewish. Protestant judges were disproportionately concentrated in upstate counties, Jewish judges in New York City, and Catholic judges in the suburban counties. As a result, the religious composition of the judiciary from each region was quite different.

Given the lack of published data on the characteristics of the trial court judiciary in New York, the extent to which the sample judges are representative of their peers on the trial bench is not altogether clear. It was possible to obtain information on the age and sex of New York State judges active during 1992; on these bases, the judges in the sample are a fairly representative group.

Nor is it clear whether judicial characteristics typically play an important role in determining case outcomes. Despite general consensus that judges' decisions may be affected by their past experience and personal values, litigation theorists do not agree on the extent to which such influences can be detected and measured in the outcomes of litigated cases. The prevailing litigation models derived by economists typically posit no correlation between judicial characteristics and case outcomes, on the theory that litigants will take judicial predilections into account during settlement negotiations. Litigation models developed by political scientists, by contrast, assume that "the political values and orientations of the judges do affect the way they resolve judicial issues, especially when precedents are conflicting or when the court is being asked to tread in new and uncharted realms," and thus posit that judges' life experience and values will have a measurable impact on judicial decision making. Empirical researchers have reported results that support both viewpoints.

One reason for the difference in results may be an underlying difference in the type of cases examined. The economists have tended to focus on routine tort and commercial litigation, while the political scientists have typically addressed more controversial issues such as crime, civil rights, and civil liberties. Neither group has examined divorce. Nor has either group focused on outcomes, like those that characterize much of divorce litigation, where the result is best described as a "how much" rather than a "who won." The research reported here thus offers the opportunity to assess the impact of judicial characteristics on litigation outcomes in a new, and important, context.

D. The Litigation Pyramid: Characteristics of the Judicial Sample as Compared to the General Divorce Population and the Settlement Case Sample

While judges who decided sample cases are, in all probability, fairly representative of their peers on the trial court bench, the couples whose cases they heard are definitely not representative of the larger divorce population. Nationally, half of divorcing couples have been married for less than seven years, and four of ten have not had children together. Half of divorcing wives are younger than thirty-three; half of divorcing husbands are younger than thirty-six. Although national statistics on employment levels, income, education, and wealth at divorce do not exist, the available data demonstrate that divorce is more likely when the husband is poorly educated or unemployed; the poverty rate among divorcing couples is thus higher than that of married couples generally.

When compared to this general divorce population, the judicial sample was disproportionately older, longer married, and more likely to have children. The median marital duration for the sample was more than double that reported by the Census Bureau for divorced couples nationally; the median age of both husbands and wives was about a decade older. In contrast to the below-average educational attainments and incomes of the general divorce population, the median educational level, family income, and net worth of the judicial sample were markedly higher than those of married couples in the United States. . . .

These differences were marked, and statistically significant, even when the judicial group was compared to the subset of my New York divorce sample in which the divorce was initially contested (hereinafter the "settlement sample") and thus had the potential to go to trial. Couples in the settlement sample were also older, longer married, and higher income than the general divorce population. They were also far more likely to have employed attorneys than are divorcing spouses generally; while the majority of divorcing couples today employ only one attorney or none at all, 97% of the couples in the settlement group employed attorneys for both spouses. The settlement sample thus appears to be fairly representative of that segment of the divorce population for which litigation is plausible. It represents the world of divorce as seen by the divorce lawyer rather than the judge.

When compared to the settlement group, couples in the judicial sample were still older, longer married, and higher income. But the most striking difference was in asset values. Approximately one quarter of the judicial sample had net assets exceeding half a million dollars; the median value of their net assets was more than six times that of the settlement sample. . . . Although higher asset values for judicial sample are expectable given the group's higher family incomes and lengthier marriages, the magnitude of the difference is still notable.

Most of the group's assets were acquired during the marriage and therefore subject to division. Couples in the judicial sample were less likely to claim debts and no more likely to claim separate property than were their counterparts in the settlement sample. Nor did separate property comprise, on average, a larger fraction of their total assets. The median value of net marital assets in the judicial group was thus more than seven times greater than that of couples in the settlement sample. . . .

Couples in the judicial sample were also far more likely to own their own home and to possess business assets, real estate, and a pension than were couples in the settlement group . . . or married couples generally. Indeed, they were wealthy enough that they often failed even to list personal possessions or household goods among their assets. The composition of each case group's average asset pool was thus quite different.

Most of the judicial sample's wealth was owned jointly or by the husband. Property owned by the wife represented, on average, only 9% of family assets, while joint property represented 52% and husband-owned property 39%.

The wealth gap between husbands and wives in the judicial sample was matched by a large disproportion in their average incomes and occupational status. In half of the cases, the husband's income represented at least 85% of family income; 30% of husbands were in high-status jobs, as compared to only 4% of wives. On each measure, the average difference between husbands and wives was much larger in the judicial sample than in the settlement group. . . .

Whether and how the disproportionate wealth and status of judicial sample husbands might have affected the litigation process is unclear. Judicial sample cases took, on average, much longer to conclude than did those in the settlement sample, but case duration may have been enhanced by spiteful litigation tactics as well as case complexity; in 22% of the judicial sample cases, for example, some portion of the interim support payments ordered by the court were unpaid when the case went to trial. Moreover, although researchers have reported that social status influences the manner in which judges exercise discretion, researchers have not investigated intrafamilial litigation. We do not know whether judges view family members as having one uniform social status or, alternatively, view them as separate individuals. Nor do we know if the results that researchers have reported are equally applicable in the divorce context.

It is clear, however, that in comparison to the general divorce population—and even the settlement group where litigation was threatened—the judicial sample was disproportionately composed of cases involving very high stakes. In many cases, the income and occupational status gap between husband and wife was sufficiently great that divorce had the potential to cause a long-married, economically dependent wife's standard of living to plummet from the extremely comfortable to the nearly impoverished.

The overrepresentation of such cases is not surprising. Litigation to trial appears to be most likely when the stakes are high. But it serves as a reminder of the fact that the picture of divorce that judges see in the courtroom, and that is thus reflected in published opinions, is by no means representative of divorce generally; indeed, it is not even an accurate reflection of what the divorce lawyer sees in her office, a case set that likely resembles the settlement sample.

The judicial sample shows us only the tip of the litigation pyramid. Although these cases can thus tell us little about divorce as experienced by the typical American couple, we have every reason to believe that they accurately represent what judges see in their courtrooms. They can thus tell us a good deal about the reality of judicial decision making at divorce.

III. JUDICIAL DECISION MAKING UNDER NEW YORK'S EQUITABLE DISTRIBUTION LAW: PROPERTY DIVISION, ALIMONY, AND CHILD SUPPORT

A. Property Division

1. The Results of Judicial Decision Making vs. Settlement: The Judicial and Settlement Samples Compared

a. Average Outcomes

Given the significant disparities between the judicial and settlement samples in the ownership, composition, and value of marital property, it would not be surprising if the ultimate distributions of marital property were different as well. But the mean division of marital property and debt in the two case sets was in fact extremely similar: At the trial level, judges awarded wives an average of 49% of marital property, 24% of marital debt, and 49% of net marital property; in the settlement sample, wives received an average of 51% of marital property, 31% of marital debt, and 55% of net marital property. On average, then, the results of litigation do not appear significantly different from those of settlement. (See Tables 6, 7).

The composition of the typical award to wives in each group was also quite similar. In both case groups, the wife's average property award was heavily concentrated in home equity, and the value of nonliquid property substantially outweighed liquid assets. . . .

Although home equity constituted a larger percentage of the average award to wives in the judicial sample than it did in the settlement group, the difference appears to reflect the lower home ownership rate of the latter case set more than an alternate distributional pattern. Although wives in the judicial sample were significantly more likely to obtain occupancy of the home than were their counterparts in the settlement group . . . , they were not more likely to obtain ownership. Sale of the home (immediate or future), typically with a relatively equal division of the net proceeds, was also more common in the judicial sample. The average percentage of marital home equity received by wives in the two case groups was thus virtually identical. . . .

The greater importance of business assets and pensions as components of the wife's share also appears to reflect ownership rates more than distributional differences. When the distribution of individual assets is considered by type, judicial sample wives' average share of business assets and pensions was not markedly higher than that of wives in the settlement sample; nor, indeed, did the average distribution of any asset type differ significantly by case group. (See Table 5.)

TABLE 5: DISTRIBUTION OF INDIVIDUAL MARITAL ASSETS,
BY ASSET TYPE AND CASE GROUP

Asset Type	Judicial Sample		Settlement Sample	
	Wife's Mean %	Wife's Mean (n)	Wife's Mean %	Wife's Mean (n)
Automobiles	48	297	42	378
Business Interests	23	147	19	64
Household Goods	76	138	58	163
Liquid Assets: Bank Accounts	49	288	48	601
Other	40	161	40	125
Professional Licenses	18	38	**	**
Real Estate: Marital Home	64	296	63	188
Other Real Estate	29	174	27	95
Retirement Assets: Pensions	31	216	29	64
Other	40	135	40	91
Other Assets	40	244	45	339
All Assets	45	2130	44	2069
All Debts	28	249	34	1028

Although judicial decision thus was not associated with any tangible advantage to wives in terms of the percentage or types of marital assets awarded, judicial sample wives nonetheless emerged from the divorce better off than their counterparts in the settlement group. The reason is simply that, because couples in the judicial sample generally had much more valuable assets, the wife's percentage share was worth more. Indeed, the median value of the wife's net property award was approximately ten times higher in the judicial sample than in the settlement group.

b. The Tendency Toward Equal Division

Although average outcomes in the judicial and settlement case groups were not markedly different, the averages derive from significantly different distributional patterns. Settlement outcomes were highly disparate and widely distributed along a zero to one hundred percent scale. Judicial outcomes, by contrast, exhibited a strong tendency toward equality. Although marital debts were disproportionately distributed to husbands in both case groups (Table 6), judges divided marital assets (Table 7) and net marital wealth . . . relatively equally in almost half of the cases for which a distribution could be determined.

**TABLE 6: PERCENTAGE DISTRIBUTION OF NET UNSECURED
MARITAL DEBTS (COUPLES WITH MARITAL DEBTS),
BY CASE GROUP**

Debt Distribution	Judicial Sample % (n = 80)	Settlement Sample % (n = 158)
67%+ to Husband	68%	60%
56%-66% to Husband	5%	4%
Relatively Equal*	14%	8%
56%-66% to Wife	0%	3%
67%+ to Wife	14%	25%
Median % to Wife	1%	10%
Mean % to Wife	24%	34%

* Relatively Equal = Between 45% and 55%

**TABLE 7: PERCENTAGE DISTRIBUTION OF MARITAL ASSETS
(COUPLES WITH MARITAL ASSETS), BY CASE GROUP**

Asset Distribution	Judicial Sample % (n = 277)	Settlement Sample % (n = 142)
67%+ to Husband	16%	34%
56%-66% to Husband	18%	7%
Relatively Equal*	46%	12%
56%-66% to Wife	9%	8%
67%+ to Wife	13%	39%
Median % to Wife	50%	51%
Mean % to Wife	49%	51%

* Relatively Equal = Between 45% and 55%

While this is not as large a percentage of equal distributions as that reported by another researcher who reviewed a substantial number of reported judicial decisions on property division at divorce, it is approximately four times the proportion of the settlement sample with a relatively equal net asset distribution. . . . Indeed, the distributional patterns of the judicial and settlement groups are almost mirror images, with judicial outcomes clustered at the center and settlements toward the extremes.

The judicial tendency toward equal division also increased significantly after the first few years of experience with equitable property distribution. Thirty-three percent of the cases decided between 1980-83 resulted in a relatively even division of net worth, as compared to 54% of those decided between 1984-86. The tendency toward equal division appears to have levelled off at this point, however, as the percentage of cases resulting in equal division did not increase during the period from 1987 to 1990.

The judicial sample differed from the settlement group in the direction as well as the likelihood of a disproportionate outcome. In the judicial sample, 61% of disproportionate outcomes favored the husband and 39% the wife. In the settlement sample, these percentages were exactly reversed.

The tendency toward disproportion favoring the husband in the judicial sample should be read in context, however. Because judges were far more likely to divide net assets equally, judicial sample wives were somewhat more likely to be awarded an equal or larger share of net marital assets than were their counterparts in the settlement group; indeed, fewer than a third (32%) of husbands in the judicial group were awarded a disproportionate share of net marital assets. The evidence thus fails to support the claim that judges typically award wives less than half of the marital assets. It instead suggests the emergence of an equal division norm.

2. The Predictability of Equitable Property Distribution

a. Statutory Factors and Case Outcomes

Disproportionate outcomes were not only less common within the judicial sample but also more predictable. Among couples in the settlement group, property outcomes were not significantly correlated with any of the litigant characteristics specified in the statute as relevant to property distribution and for which case information was available. Neither age, marital duration, employment, health, income, occupational status, the award of custody, or the award of alimony was significantly correlated with the percentage division of net marital assets.

Judicial outcomes, by contrast, were significantly correlated with several of the statutory factors. Although marital duration, age, the award of alimony, and the award of custody again evidenced no significance as predictive variables, a cluster of variables related to the wife's relative need—her health, employment, income, occupational status, and the percentage of family income that she earned—were all significantly correlated with the percentage division of net marital assets at the .05 confidence level or better.

While a correlation between these variables and the property division outcome is not surprising given the legislative requirement that such factors be considered in marital property distribution, it is intriguing that wives' income, employment, health, and occupational status were significantly related to case outcomes while husbands' were not. Even more surprising is the direction of the correlations. Indications that the wife was particularly needy—poor health, unemployment, low income, low occupational status, and income representing a small fraction of family income—were all *negatively* correlated with the wife's percentage award. Wives in poor health, for example, were significantly less likely to receive an equal or larger share of marital assets than were wives in good health. Similarly, women earning half or more of family income were four times as likely to be awarded a disproportionate share of the net marital property as were their counterparts earning less than ten percent of family income. (See Table 9.) These data strongly support the claim by women's advocates that judges tend to give more weight to monetary contributions than to contributions as a spouse and parent.

TABLE 9: PERCENTAGE DISTRIBUTION OF NET MARITAL ASSETS (JUDICIAL SAMPLE: COUPLES WITH POSITIVE NET WORTH), BY PERCENTAGE OF FAMILY INCOME EARNED BY WIFE

Percentage Distribution of Net Marital Assets	Wife's Income/Family Income			
	0%-9% (n = 93)	10%-29% (n = 73)	30%-49% (n = 49)	50%+ (n = 25)
Disproportionate Share to Husband	41%	31%	25%	28%
Relatively Equal*	48%	53%	49%	28%
Disproportionate Share to Wife	11%	16%	26%	44%

* Relatively Equal = Between 45% and 55%

A cluster of property-related variables was also significantly linked to the net distribution, and some of these relationships again suggest a tendency to elevate monetary over other contributions. If, for example, the husband owned a business or possessed a professional license—and husbands almost invariably held these assets when they were present in the pool of marital property—he was significantly more likely to obtain a disproportionate share of the marital wealth. (See Table 10.) Wives were awarded a relatively equal or larger share of net assets in three-quarters of the cases in which the husband did not own such an asset, as compared to roughly half of the cases in which he did.

TABLE 10: PERCENTAGE DISTRIBUTION OF NET MARITAL ASSETS (JUDICIAL SAMPLE: COUPLES WITH POSITIVE NET WORTH), BY HUSBAND'S OWNERSHIP OF BUSINESS OR PROFESSIONAL LICENSE

Percentage Distribution of Marital Net Worth	Husband Did Not Own Business, Professional Degree or License (n = 231)	Husband Owned Business, Professional Degree or License (n = 91)
Disproportionate Share to Husband	25%	48%
Relatively Equal*	52%	40%
Disproportionate Share to Wife	23%	12%

* Relatively Equal = Between 45% and 55%

Although husbands owning either a business or a professional degree were disproportionately likely to obtain the lion's share of the marital wealth, husbands with professional degrees did particularly well: Fully 54% of this group obtained a
disproportionate share of net marital assets. This result is perhaps foreseeable given the
novelty of the property interest at stake, the lack of consensus on whether it should be
treated as a divisible asset at all, and appellate case law finding disproportionate division of professional assets equitable.

But the correlation between title and the percentage division of net assets is
more surprising. Although an express aim of New York's Equitable Distribution Law
was to ensure that title did not determine the distribution of assets acquired during the
marriage, the percentage of marital assets solely owned by the husband (but not the
wife) was a significant predictor of the divisional outcome. Husbands who owned at
least 60% of marital assets were more than twice as likely to receive a disproportionate share as were their counterparts owning less than 20%. . . . Title, unlike the litigant
characteristics enumerated in the statute or the other property-related factors considered, was also significantly correlated with the net property division in the settlement
group. . . .

The other property variables significantly related to the divisional outcome do not
suggest a uniform judicial preference for monetary contribution as compared to need,
however. The value of the husband's (but not the wife's) separate property was positively, and significantly, correlated with the wife's percentage award; comparatively
needy wives whose husbands had substantial separate property tended to receive a disproportionate share of marital property. The distributional outcome was also significantly correlated with the value of marital property; the smaller the value of net assets,
the greater the likelihood that the wife would receive a disproportionate share. Thus in
the handful of cases where debts exceeded assets, 80% of husbands were required to
assume disproportionate liability, and approximately 80% of wives received a relatively
equal or larger share of net marital assets when those assets were worth less than
$50,000. But when net assets were worth at least $400,000, only 55% of wives were
awarded a relatively equal or larger share. . . .

To the extent that disproportionate distribution to one spouse was predictable, it
thus tended to reflect monetary contribution to the marriage instead of need. The husband's ownership of a large percentage of marital assets, of a business or professional license, and a higher value for net marital assets were all associated with an
increased likelihood that the husband would receive a disproportionate percentage of
marital net worth. The spouse who had contributed more income to the marriage
tended to receive more property. But this apparent judicial emphasis on monetary contribution was not uniform. In cases of relative poverty, the wife—in all probability the
needier party—tended to receive the lion's share of the assets. The husband's ownership of a relatively large amount of separate property was, again, associated with disproportion in favor of the less-propertied wife.

b. The Predictability of Net Worth Distribution: More Detailed Analysis

Property division outcomes were also analyzed taking into account a variety of
judicial characteristics and other case variables unrelated to the legislative factors in

order to determine whether these extra-statutory considerations had any value in predicting divisional outcomes. They did not: Neither the judge's sex, age, religious affiliation, political party, judicial experience, nor educational status score was significantly correlated with judicial sample net worth distributions. Nor, in the judicial sample, did the case processing time, case region, the gender of the spouse against whom the divorce was granted, or the specific fault allegations upon which the divorce was based demonstrate a significant relationship to the net worth distribution.

For the settlement sample, variables that might suggest strategic bargaining behavior were also assessed. No significant predictive relationships were found. Although litigation theorists have often posited that women confronted with the possibility of a custody battle may make economic concessions to obtain custody, an unrealized custody threat by the husband was insignificantly related to the distributional outcome. Nor did case processing time, another potential conflict indicator, evidence a significant predictive relationship. . . .

B. Alimony and Child Support

1. The Award of Alimony

a. The Judicial and Settlement Samples Compared

Although litigation to trial appeared to confer no remarkable advantage on judicial sample wives with respect to property division, it was associated with a higher alimony rate. At the trial court level, 62% of wives in the judicial sample were awarded alimony, an award rate more than four times that of divorced women in both New York state and the nation, and approximately double the alimony award rate of wives in the settlement sample.

The best predictors of alimony in both the judicial and settlement groups were spousal income and marital duration; the high alimony rate for the judicial cases thus reflects, in part, the greater proportion of lengthy marriages, low-income wives, and high-income husbands in this group. For example, the alimony rate for employed women married less than ten years varied insignificantly by case group. But there were approximately twice as many women with these characteristics in the settlement group as in the judicial sample. (See Table 14.)

**TABLE 14: PERCENTAGES OF SAMPLE WIVES AWARDED ALIMONY,
BY MARITAL DURATION, WIFE'S EMPLOYMENT STATUS, AND CASE GROUP**

Marital Duration & Wife's Employment Status	Judicial Sample		Settlement Sample		Difference
	%	(n)	%	(n)	
Unemployed wives married ≥ 10 years	83%	(116)	49%	(47)	-34***
Unemployed wives married < 10 years	74%	(31)	50%	(32)	-24*
All Unemployed Wives	82%	(151)	52%	(79)	-30***
Employed wives married ≥ 10 years	53%	(170)	27%	(132)	-34***
Employed wives married < 10 years	23%	(39)	21%	(73)	-2
All Employed Wives	48%	(214)	26%	(208)	-22***

* p<.05, *** p<.001

The higher alimony award rate in the judicial group does not appear to result simply from sample composition, however. Long-married and low-income wives, who had the highest alimony award rates in both case sets, had significantly higher award rates when the case was judicially decided. Among women married twenty or more years, for example, 69% of the judicial group were awarded alimony compared to 39% in the settlement sample. (See Table 15.)

**TABLE 15: PERCENTAGES OF SAMPLE WIVES AWARDED ALIMONY,
BY MARITAL DURATION AND CASE GROUP**

Marital Duration	Judicial Sample		Settlement Sample		Difference
	%	(n)	%	(n)	
0 -4 years	50%	(14)	27%	(44)	-23
5 -9 years	46%	(59)	28%	(71)	-18*
10 -14 years	58%	(77)	29%	(68)	-29***
15 -19 years	64%	(73)	22%	(51)	-42***
20 or more years	69%	(144)	39%	(79)	-30***
All Sample Cases	62%	(377)	31%	(313)	-31***

* p<.05, *** p<.001

Similarly, 89% of wives who earned less than 10% of family income were awarded alimony by the judges, as compared to an alimony award rate of 58% for this group in the settlement sample. (See Table 16.)

**TABLE 16: PERCENTAGES OF SAMPLE WIVES AWARDED
ALIMONY, BY WIFE'S INCOME PERCENTAGE (WIFE'S
INCOME/FAMILY INCOME) AND CASE GROUP**

Wife's Income/ Family Income	Judicial Sample		Settlement Sample		Difference
	%	(n)	%	(n)	
0% -9%	89%	(113)	58%	(76)	-31***
10 -29%	76%	(86)	31%	(49)	-45***
30 -49%	39%	(56)	12%	(57)	-27**
50% or more	4%	(28)	4%	(23)	-0

**p<.01, *** p<.001

Litigation to trial was thus associated with a higher alimony award rate both because the judicial sample contained more long-married and low-income wives—the group with the best alimony prospects—and because wives with these characteristics received alimony awards more frequently from judges than through the settlement process.

b. Changes in Judicial Alimony Decision Making Over Time

The advantages of litigation were not consistent over the ten year period reviewed. The judicial alimony award rate for the period 1980-83 was fourteen percentage points higher than for the period 1987-90; a later decision year was, in fact, a significant negative predictor of an alimony award. Nor was the lower alimony rate for the later period confined to women in short marriages. Women married for twenty or more years experienced a decline in their alimony prospects identical to that experienced by women married for less than ten years. . . .

The alimony prospects of women who earned an extremely small percentage of family income were unaffected by the lower award rate in later research years, however. Wives earning less than 10% of family income were not significantly less likely to be awarded alimony in the last triennial period than they were in the first. . . . Women earning at least 30% of family income, on the other hand, saw their alimony prospects decline by almost half over the research period. The declining alimony award rate over the ten year period reviewed thus appears to reflect increased judicial emphasis on need as compared to other factors. . . .

2. The Duration of Alimony

a. The Judicial and Settlement Samples Compared

In contrast to the markedly higher judicial alimony rate, litigation to trial was not associated with significantly enhanced prospects of a permanent alimony award. Only 35% of judicial alimony awards were permanent, as compared to 31% in the settlement group.

Nor were long-married and older women more likely to be awarded permanent alimony by judges than through the settlement process. Although marital duration was a highly significant predictor of a permanent award for both case groups, permanent awards to long-married wives were no more frequent in the judicial sample than in the settlement group. (See Table 19.)

TABLE 19: PERCENTAGES OF SAMPLE ALIMONY AWARDS THAT
WERE PERMANENT, BY CASE GROUP AND MARITAL DURATION

Marital Duration	Judicial Sample %	(n)	Settlement Sample %	(n)	Difference
0 -9 years	24%	(33)	28%	(32)	+4
10 -19 years	28%	(93)	20%	(30)	-8
20 or more years	46%	(98)	45%	(31)	-1
All Sample Cases	35%	(230)	31%	(93)	-4

Age, too, was a significant predictor of a permanent award for both case sets, but the likelihood of a permanent alimony award for women over fifty was actually somewhat lower in the judicial sample than in the settlement group.

Nor, when time-limited alimony was awarded, were judicial awards likely to extend over a significantly longer period. The average length of a time-limited award was 5.0 years in the judicial sample and 4.6 years in the settlement group.

b. The Impact of Statutory Change Upon Judicial Awards

Although the 1986 amendments to the Equitable Distribution Law were intended to reverse the trend toward durational alimony, these amendments had no apparent impact. The proportion of alimony awards that were permanent was *lowest* in 1987-90, after the amendments went into effect. . . . Indeed, a later decision year was a significant negative predictor of a permanent award. The passage of the amendments was, however, associated with stabilization of the permanent alimony rate among long-married wives; although the permanent alimony rate for this group did not increase after 1986, wives married twenty or more years did not see a further decline in their prospects of a permanent alimony award. Wives married for shorter periods, on the other hand, saw the likelihood of permanent alimony continue to fall. . . .

3. The Value of Alimony and Child Support

a. The Judicial and Settlement Samples Compared

In contrast to the similarity of judicial and settlement permanence outcomes, the average value of both alimony and child support varied substantially by case group. The average value of combined alimony and child support in the judicial group was, indeed, almost double its value in the settlement sample. (See Table 21.)

**TABLE 21: MEAN ALIMONY AND CHILD SUPPORT AWARDS
(1990 DOLLARS), BY CASE GROUP**

Mean Award (1990 Dollars)	Judicial Sample $ per month (n)	Settlement Sample $ per month (n)	Difference
Alimony:			
when awarded	$1084 (233)	$ 978 (98)	-106
all cases	$ 677 (373)	$ 307 (312)	-370***
Child Support:			
per family	$ 778 (225)	$ 481 (196)	-297***
per minor child	$ 430 (225)	$ 301 (196)	-129**
Total Alimony & Child support:			
minor children	$1474 (225)	$ 709 (208)	-765***
no minor children	$ 675 (143)	$ 429 (97)	-246
all cases	$1163 (368)	$ 620 (305)	-543***

** p<.01, *** p<.001

While the higher dollar values of judicial alimony and child support awards reflect, to some extent, the higher incomes of couples in the judicial sample, judicial awards also constituted a larger percentage of obligor income. For judicial cases involving minor children, the average percentage of obligor income awarded in combined alimony and child support was 31%, as compared to 23% in the settlement sample. Although the difference between the settlement and judicial groups was not significant at all income levels . . . it was consistent over the ten-year period reviewed. . . .

Alimony and child support payments also constituted a larger fraction of the recipient's post-divorce income in the judicial sample. (See Table 23). For women with minor children, for example, the value of alimony and child support represented an average of 62% of post-divorce income, as compared to 44% in the settlement group.

TABLE 23: MEAN PERCENTAGE OF RECIPIENT'S TOTAL INCOME (INCLUDING ALIMONY AND CHILD SUPPORT) REPRESENTED BY ALIMONY AND CHILD SUPPORT, BY RECIPIENT'S INCOME (EXCLUDING ALIMONY AND CHILD SUPPORT) AND CASE GROUP

Recipient's Gross Income (1990 Dollars)	Child Support Award/Recipient's Total Income: Mean %		Child Support & Alimony Award/ Recipient's Total Income: Mean %	
	J Group (n)	S Group (n)	J Group (n)	S Group (n)
$0-$4,999	51% (66)	68%** (47)	97% (66)	94% (47)
$5,000-$19,999	32% (53)	26%* (70)	51% (53)	32%*** (70)
$20,000 +	19% (48)	12% (48)	27% (48)	14%*** (48)
All Sample Cases	36% (167)	34% (165)	62% (167)	44%*** (165)

J Group = Judicial Sample; S Group = Settlement Group
Difference between group means: * p<.05, ** p.<01, *** p<.001

4. Post-Divorce Income and Standard of Living

Even if the impact of their legal expenses is ignored, child support and alimony awards to women in the judicial sample were typically inadequate to prevent a marked drop in their post-divorce standard of living. Although women in this group suffered a slightly smaller average decline in per capita income and standard of living than did women in the settlement sample, the difference was insignificant. In both case sets, the average woman's standard of living fell markedly, while that of her husband improved. (See Table 25.) Because judicial sample wives were more likely to receive some portion of the husband's post-divorce support obligation in the form of alimony, it is indeed possible, given the prevalence of short-term alimony awards, that they would be worse off than their settlement group counterparts within a few years after the divorce.

**TABLE 25: CHANGES IN HUSBANDS' AND WIVES' PER CAPITA INCOME
AND LIVING STANDARDS POST-DIVORCE, BY CASE GROUP**

Household Category	Judicial Sample		Settlement Sample	
	Median Per Capita Income (1990 Dollars)		Median Per Capita Income (1990 Dollars)	
	Mean %	(n)	Mean %	(n)
Pre-Divorce Family	$20,544	(287)	$14,781	(205)
Husband's household after divorce:	$35,177	(296)	$27,028	(221)
Ratio of post to pre-divorce per capita income:	172%	(266)	182%	(196)
Ratio of post to pre-divorce living standard:*	126%		135%	
Wife's household after divorce:	$12,515	(292)	$9,710	(262)
Ratio of post to pre-divorce per capita income:	71%	(266)	68%	(196)
Ratio of post to pre-divorce living standard:	61%		57%	

* Measured as ratio of post to pre-divorce per capita income, adjusted by family size.

In both case sets there was also significant variation in the ratio of the wife's to husband's post-divorce standard of living. In both groups, wives in the highest income category married to husbands in the lowest actually enjoyed a higher post-divorce living standard, on average, than did their husbands, while wives in the lowest income category married to husbands in the highest experienced the largest relative decline. (See Table 26. . . .)

**TABLE 26: MEAN RATIO OF WIFE'S POST-DIVORCE STANDARD OF
LIVING/HUSBAND'S POST-DIVORCE STANDARD OF LIVING* (JUDICIAL
SAMPLE), BY HUSBAND AND WIFE PRE-DIVORCE INCOME**

Wife's Income	$0 -$34,999		Husband's Income $35,000-$59,999		$60,000+	
	mean ratio	mean (n)	mean ratio	(n)	ratio	(n)
$ 0 -$4,999	.48	(21)	.26	(32)	.23	(42)
$5,000 -$19,999	.42	(40)	.45	(31)	.33	(24)
$20,000+	1.83	(19)	.88	(29)	.44	(29)
All Samples Wives	.77	(80)	.52	(92)	.32	(95)

* Measured by post-divorce family income adjusted by size (0.73).

This pattern suggests that the prime determinant of post-divorce living standards is the pre-divorce income of each spouse, rather than income transfers in the form of alimony and child support. The ratio of the wife's and husband's post-divorce living standards was significantly and positively correlated with the percentage of family income earned by the wife and the value of her income. The award of alimony to the wife and the value of combined alimony and child support, on the other hand, were (at least for cases in the judicial sample) significant negative predictors of the ratio.

While a judicial decision was thus associated with the award of more valuable alimony and child support, in amounts representing a higher proportion of obligor and recipient income, these transfers were, in the vast majority of cases, inadequate to ensure wives and children a post-divorce living standard equal to that enjoyed by the husband. Nor was the average gap between the post-divorce living standards of wives and husbands significantly smaller in the judicial sample than the settlement group.

It is important to note, however, that the post-divorce gap in the living standards of husbands and wives produced by discretionary decision making was not demonstrably greater than that which would be produced under New York's new, determinate child support guidelines. Although these guidelines curtailed judicial discretion in order to reduce post-divorce income disparities, the average percentage of obligor income awarded as child support in both the judicial and settlement samples was fairly equivalent to what one would predict under the support guidelines. Although direct comparisons are not possible, the results of discretionary decision making do not appear to be markedly different from those mandated under these new bright-line rules.

5. The Predictability of Alimony and Child Support Decision Making

a. The Award of Alimony

In contrast to property division, where only a few of the factors enumerated in the statute had explanatory value, the award of alimony was significantly correlated with a long list of litigant characteristics deemed relevant by the legislature. In both the judicial and settlement groups, the variables most strongly correlated with the award of alimony were the wife's income, employment, and the percentage of family income that she earned. In the judicial sample, the wife's education, occupational status, health, marital duration, whether the marriage produced children, the percentage of the husband's income paid in child support, and the husband's occupational status were also significant at the .05 confidence level, as were the value of the wife's assets, net marital assets, and her net property award.

Although a number of statutory variables that demonstrated significance within the judicial sample failed to do so within the settlement group, the strength and direction of the variable correlations in the two case sets were often quite similar. Only one variable, the husband's income, was significantly related to the alimony decision in the settlement case group and failed to demonstrate significance in the judicial sample.

The relationship between various nonstatutory factors and alimony awards was also assessed. In the judicial sample, the likelihood of an alimony award varied significantly by case region; a later decision year was also significantly and negatively correlated with the alimony outcome. The only judicial characteristic that demonstrated significance at the .05 confidence level was the judge's age, although the judge's sex narrowly escaped significance at the .05 confidence level. Neither the judge's political party, length of judicial experience, educational background, or religion was significantly correlated with the alimony outcome. In the settlement sample, variables suggesting strategic bargaining—case processing time and an unrealized claim of custody by the husband— again failed to evidence a significant predictive relationship with the alimony decision; the case's fault ranking did, however.

Logistic regression analysis was employed to determine the relative impact of statutory, judicial, and other case-related variables on alimony outcomes and the extent to which these variables could be used to predict alimony awards.

Both models produced accurate predictions of alimony outcomes in more than 80% of the cases. . . .

With information on the percentage of family income earned by the wife, the value of her income, marital duration, the value of net marital property, and the husband's job status, the model accurately predicted alimony outcomes for 83% of the cases, a rate considerably better than that achievable by random assignment. Although the model achieved highly disparate results depending on whether alimony was awarded or not, the improvement over random assignment was substantial for each category. . . .

Regression analysis was also applied to alimony outcomes in the settlement sample. The relative importance of the predictive variables within the regression model for this group was fairly consistent with the results obtained for the judicial sample (the most important were the percentage of family income earned by the wife and the husband's job status) although the accuracy rate achieved was several percentage points lower. This accuracy rate still constituted a substantial improvement over random assignment overall. . . .

While regression analysis thus suggests that much of the variation in alimony outcomes can be explained by reference to the statutory factors, the number of inexplicable outcomes was still substantial, particularly in the settlement case group. Forty-five percent of settlement sample wives earning less than 20% of family income were not awarded alimony, and the case data fail to reveal why. The importance of the husband's job status as a predictive variable is also notable. The husband's status was, in both case sets, a more powerful predictive variable than his income, suggesting that socioeconomic class may play a role in alimony determination, independent of its correlation with income, that comparatively disadvantages women in low-status families.

But the analysis also suggests that the legislative scheme did play a significant role at trial and in settlement negotiations. A substantial majority of alimony outcomes could, for both case groups, be explained on the basis of the statutory factors alone. The analysis also reveals that, among all variables for which case information was available, the spouses' relative need was the dominant factor in alimony determination. Indeed, with information on the percentage of family income earned by the wife alone, it was possible to accurately predict 80% of alimony outcomes in the judicial sample and 72% of those in the settlement group. This result, coupled with the failure of any fault-related variables to contribute significantly to the predictability of alimony results, suggests that the "rehabilitative" alimony concept adopted by the New York legislature, which posits alimony as a remedy for need rather than a reward for marital virtue, now reigns as the governing principle in alimony determination. . . .

b. The Duration of Alimony

In contrast to the wealth of litigant characteristics recited in the alimony statute that were significantly correlated with judges' alimony award decisions, only three variables— the wife's age, her health, and marital duration—were significantly correlated with the decision to award alimony for an unlimited time period. A similar pattern was evident in the settlement sample, where the wife's health, marital duration, and (curiously) the husband's age were the only variables to demonstrate significance at the .05 confidence level or better.

In the judicial sample, several nonstatutory factors were also significantly correlated with the permanence of alimony. The decision year was again a significant negative predictor of a permanent award. Democratic judges were significantly less likely to award permanent alimony than were Republican judges. And the judge's educational background was significantly correlated with alimony permanence as well. Judges with high educational status scores and those who had attended both college and law school outside the region in which they served were significantly more likely to award permanent alimony than judges educated locally and those with low status scores. . . .

The length of the alimony period for nonpermanent awards was even less predictable than alimony permanence. In the judicial sample, not a single litigant characteristic enumerated in the alimony statute as relevant to the decision was significantly correlated with the length of a durational alimony award. Several nonstatutory factors— the case region, the appellate department, the judge's age, and the judge's political party—were correlated, at the .05 confidence level or better, with the length of the alimony period, but their explanatory value was slight. Several litigant characteristics were significantly related to the length of the alimony period in the settlement sample, but regression analysis, employing these variables, explained less than 1% of the variation in durational outcomes. The alimony duration decision thus presents a fairly marked contrast to the more basic decision on whether alimony should be awarded. While the alimony *award* decision appears to be fairly predictable, highly correlated with the specific factors and principles contained in the alimony statute, and largely uninfluenced by personal judicial values, the alimony *duration* decision does not. . . .

6. Alimony and Child Support Decision Making: A Summary

A review of the data on the predictability of alimony and child support reveals a striking fact: Virtually every possible claim regarding discretionary decision making finds support somewhere.

On the issue of consistency, there is evidence of regional variation (the value of alimony in cases without minor children), class bias (the award of alimony), the intrusion of private values into the decision-making process (alimony permanence), different decision-making patterns from one year to the next (alimony, alimony permanence, child support values), utter unpredictability (the duration of nonpermanent alimony awards), and of highly predictable decision making quite consistent with the statutory mandate (the award of alimony, child support values).

On the issue of gender bias, there is evidence that judicial decisions produced post-divorce income disparities, comparable to those reported in settled cases, that seriously disadvantage women and children. But the average percentage of obligor income judges awarded under discretionary standards does not appear to be smaller than the average percentage judges would presumptively award under the determinate child support guidelines now in effect in New York. Judges were less prone to award alimony, and particularly permanent alimony, over the research period. But the decline in alimony was offset, for women with minor children, by higher child support awards, a shift that, given the taxability of alimony and its loss upon remarriage, may have provided a net advantage to women with minor children.

On the issue of how discretionary decision making affects the settlement process, the picture is also mixed. No strategic bargaining effects were evident. Depending on which decision we consider, settlements were either highly consistent with judicial decision-making patterns (alimony, child support) or quite inconsistent (alimony duration).

What we do not see in the alimony and child support data is *overall* consistency. Depending on where we look, there is evidence that suggests both discretion's success and its failure. . . .

IV. JUDICIAL DECISION MAKING IN RETROSPECT: DIRECTIONS FOR DIVORCE REFORM

A. *Interpreting the Data*

1. Discretion's Diversity

If any single thing is apparent from this inquiry into judicial decision making at divorce, it is that the results of discretionary decision making are by no means uniform. Each discretionary decision judges made—property division, the award of alimony, the duration of alimony, the value of alimony and/or child support—presents its own unique features. Depending on which economic decision we take as an example, evidence can be found to support the claims of either discretion's critics or its champions.

Discretion's champions might use the alimony award data, which suggest a fair degree of consensus among judges on the litigant characteristics that determine an alimony claim and on their relative weight. That consensus not only reflects the factors specified in the legislative scheme but, as the results of settlement track those of judicial decision making tolerably well, appears to have been quite faithfully transmitted to the practicing bar. The data on alimony and child support values similarly suggest a fair degree of consensus among judges on a decision making model, a consensus that both comports with the statute and is reflected (albeit imperfectly) in the results of settled cases.

Discretion's critics, on the other hand, might point to the alimony duration data, which suggest the intrusion of private values as decision-making criteria and the lack of developed consensus within the judiciary on the relevance and weight to be accorded particular litigant characteristics. The apparent link between trial court permanence decisions and political party, for example, suggests just the sort of arbitrariness that critics have complained about; so do [sic] the apparent class bias in alimony awards, the regional variation in alimony values, and the complete unpredictability of alimony duration decisions. The property division data also lend weight to the critics' claims.

Judges seem to agree on relatively equal division as a prototypical outcome, but do not appear to have reached sufficient consensus on the factors that justify departure from equal division, to permit reliable outcome predictions. The infrequency of equal division in the settled cases also suggests that judges were not able, at least during the Equitable Distribution Law's first few years, to transmit the new norm to the divorce bar. Moreover, the judicial tendency to award the ill and relatively needy wife less than half of the net assets certainly runs counter to the equal partnership principle that underlies the statute.

Discretion thus sometimes produced outcomes that appear to rely more on private values than on public standards. Outcomes were sometimes unpredictable, and sometimes failed to reflect the factors that the legislature had specified as relevant. Judicial consensus was not necessarily reflected in the outcomes of settled cases. But discretionary decision making was at times highly predictable and highly correlated with the legislative scheme. The results of settlement sometimes mirrored, albeit imperfectly, those achieved through litigation, and no evidence of distortions in settlement outcomes due to strategic bargaining could be found.

2. Explaining Discretion's Diversity

How can we explain these disparities?

a. Discretionary Standards Differ

One relevant factor may be differences in the discretionary standards themselves. Some discretionary standards subtly curtail the exercise of discretion, while others do not. Professor Mnookin, for example, reports the "rather surprising" finding that every pregnant minor who sought judicial authorization for an abortion under a statute permitting waiver of parental consent based on a judicial finding that the minor is mature or that "an abortion would be in her best interests" ultimately obtained it. His explanation for this finding was that judges, many of whom personally opposed abortion, believed it impossible to justify finding both that a minor was insufficiently mature to choose an abortion, and that it was also in her best interests to bear a child: "The law puts judges in the ridiculous position of being rubber stamps," one judge complained. "There is no way you could substantiate such a decision."

While no provisions of the Equitable Distribution Law constrained judicial discretion this tightly, there were differences in the level of restraint imposed by specific statutory provisions. Some were premised on coherent themes or principles that tended to rein in discretion; others were not. Viewed from this perspective, the unpredictability of durational alimony awards may derive, in part, from the "rehabilitation" concept that underlies the alimony provisions of the law. Judges, in an apparent attempt to conform their decisions to the rehabilitation principle, tended to focus on when the alimony recipient would become self-supporting. But while it is easy to predict this time period when the alimony recipient plans to obtain further job training, neither the statute nor the rehabilitation concept outlines any logical method for making such a prediction in the far more typical case in which the recipient does not. The economic circumstances of an older alimony recipient with little education and a job history confined to low wage, dead-end employment cannot be expected to improve. The predictive question, in these cases, verges on incoherence and thus may have enhanced the unpredictability of judicial response.

By contrast, the "partnership of coequals," concept that underlies the property distribution rules offers a clear decision-making principle applicable to each and every case: Equal partnership implies equal treatment. Given this underlying statutory principle, it is not hard to see why judges gravitated to an equal division norm. The statute itself invites, indeed drives, judges in this direction. Nor is it surprising that appellate courts have enhanced the tendency toward equality. With a statute premised on equal partnership, this is the most logical result and the one easiest to justify.

Given the equality norm underlying the property division provisions of the statute, the extent of judicial consensus on equality is perhaps less surprising than the number of departures from that norm. Even after appeals are taken into account, slightly more than 40% of the cases resulted in unequal division. A partial explanation lies, again, in the nature of the constraints imposed by the statute: It is an underlying principle that suggests equality, rather than a literal statutory command. Moreover, the statute, by requiring a multifaceted consideration of case circumstance, implies that departure is appropriate in a variety of circumstances.

b. "Familiarity Breeds Precedent"

A second explanation for the diversity of results derives, I believe, from the relative novelty of some statutory commands as compared to others: The extent of judicial experience under a discretionary standard will, like the discretionary standard itself, affect the manner in which judges exercise their discretion. The reasons for this phenomenon are uncomplicated. Decision-makers gravitate toward routine decision-making norms when repetitively confronted with cases of a similar type. Judges, moreover, are expected to strive for like results in like cases and thus rely heavily on accumulated precedents. Routinized norms also serve a time allocation function, permitting the decision-maker to give adequate consideration to the atypical. Judges thus gravitate toward factual and legal stereotypes in order to achieve consistent and efficient results.

As a result of this tendency toward consistency, the predictability of both judicial decisions and lawyer-negotiated settlements may vary substantially based on a decision-making standard's age and case volume. The intrusion of disparate private values into the decision-making process, as indicated by the correlation of case outcomes with judicial characteristics, appears most likely when the decision-making standard is young and when the case volume is light. Clear decision-making norms that rely on a few key facts are, conversely, more likely to be encountered as the standard ages and as case volume increases.

The research results conform quite closely to this "natural history" of discretionary decision making. Standards for determining child support did not change at all as a result of the 1980 Equitable Distribution Law. Judges could thus rely on an established consensus developed over decades, and judicial decisions on the value of child support were accordingly quite predictable. By contrast, durational alimony, where judicial decisions were quite unpredictable, was newly established as a norm by the 1980 law. Judges and lawyers had only the statute to guide the decision-making process. So, too, with property division. Given the fact that New York had no marital property distribution scheme prior to the Equitable Distribution Law, judges and lawyers confronted a blank slate.

c. Consensus Does Not Hold

Yet another explanatory factor for the diverse results achieved by the Equitable Distribution Law is the dynamic nature of judicial consensus. The flexibility inherent in a discretionary standard permits dramatic shifts in judicial perceptions and decision-making patterns. Rules thus codify the consensus of a given moment; discretion embraces the consensus of yesterday, today, and tomorrow.

The shifting nature of judicial consensus is evident in the fact that the year of decision was a significant predictor of the award of alimony, the likelihood of a permanent alimony award, and the value of child support (as well as child support and alimony combined). The flexibility inherent in a discretionary standard permitted child support awards to drift upward. It permitted the percentage of cases in which alimony and permanent alimony were awarded to drift downward as well.

These shifts tracked social and public opinion trends. Over the ten-year research period, increasingly large numbers of married women with young children were in the paid labor force, a shift that decreased not only the need for both short-and long-term alimony, but public support for such transfers as well. The period also saw a genuine sea change in public sentiment regarding child support. Over the decade the low value of child support awards came under intense public and political scrutiny; during the later years of the research period, child support guidelines, which would eventually supplant discretionary decision making altogether, were being actively debated in the state legislature. By contrast, judges were not required to respond to a new public opinion climate or to the threat of major statutory change in the area of property division, and these outcomes were not significantly related to the decision year.

While it would be impossible to establish clear links between the decision-making climate and judicial decisions themselves, "[t]he great tides and currents which engulf the rest of men, do not turn aside in their course, and pass the judges by." The tides of social change do not, of course, break with equal force upon all decision-makers, a fact perhaps evidenced by the tendency of older judges to award alimony more frequently than younger ones, and of Republican judges to award permanent alimony more frequently than Democratic judges.

The variable rate and manner in which individual judges respond to changing social and legal conditions, coupled with the resulting tendency of judicial consensus to shift over time, thus ensure that the results of discretionary decision making can never be perfectly predictable. Indeed, given the rapid pace of change in public opinion and in gender and marital roles during the research period, it is perhaps surprising that the judicial decisions reviewed exhibited as much predictability as they did.

3. Evaluating Discretion's Results

a. Consistency, Gender Bias, and Settlement Patterns

The research findings, which at first glance appear chaotic and contradictory, thus reveal, in the end, some consistent themes. They show us judges struggling conscientiously to give form and content to their discretionary mandate, a process guided by legislative directives (or lack thereof), shaped by experience, and set in a shifting historical context. They show us the impact of individual values and social climate. And they also show us the channelling effect of institutional norms, appellate precedent, and legislative principle, which tend over time to produce more uniform and predictable case outcomes.

On the issue of consistency, the research findings thus suggest that if trial judges are given clear legislative and appellate guidance, discretionary divorce decision making may, over time, produce highly predictable results. Discretionary decision making will, of course, remain subject to shifting trends, but the tendency of discretion to evolve toward routinized norms should ultimately produce patterns that are more reliant on institutional values than on individual judicial predilection.

That judges have failed to achieve predictable and consistent outcomes in many areas of divorce decision making appears to derive from the novelty of the statutory provisions, coupled with the conflicting, and at times incoherent, principles upon which judges have been directed to base the decision-making process. Novelty will pass. But how fast and how well courts will evolve clear decision-making principles where legislative guidance is sparse remains to be seen. The research findings thus suggest that discretion could produce fairly consistent results, but do not reveal whether it will.

On the issue of gender bias, the research findings suggest equally ambiguous conclusions. Judicial decisions often reflected traditional gender stereotypes. For example, judges who awarded the wife a small share of business or professional assets sometimes justified that decision by noting that the wife had been awarded substantial alimony, a choice that reflects, and reinforces, a tradition of wifely dependence upon an economically dominant husband who controls the family purse strings. The tendency of judges to award husbands the lion's share of marital debts, and to require little or no child support from women who did not obtain custody, also suggest reliance on this stereotype of wifely dependence.

But as these varied examples make plain, judicial adherence to traditional gender stereotypes did not uniformly advantage either husbands or wives. The conscious and unconscious influence of gender stereotype should not be confused with consistent bias. Of the former, there is plentiful evidence. Of the latter, there is little.

It is true that the results of the discretionary decision-making process ultimately produced considerable inequality in post-divorce living standards. On average, women and children suffered a sharp decline in their standard of living, while men obtained an improvement. But we cannot attribute this result simply to judicial bias. The New York legislature, which reduced judicial discretion in awarding child support in order to improve children's post-divorce living standards, adopted guidelines that would presumptively transfer no more income to women and children than did judges acting under discretionary standards. For the typical family, where husband earns substantially more than wife, this "improvement" over discretionary decision making produces outcomes fairly comparable to those produced by judges. We are all, as Professor Regan reminds us, "both cause and effect of the gender system, which means that we may unwittingly reproduce it even as we seek its demise."

As for the impact of discretionary decision making on the settlement process, the research shows that settlements can track the results of judicial decision making tolerably well. No adverse effects due to strategic bargaining behavior could be found; custody-for-money trade-offs, thought to be common under discretionary standards, were not evident. But strategic behavior may take different forms than theorists have supposed. More importantly, the tendency of settlements to predictably track judicial decision patterns, and the lack of strategic bargaining effects, may be due to the high rate of legal representation in the settlement sample and thus unrepresentative of results in the general divorce population.

Overall, the research results suggest that discretionary decision making at divorce is not clearly inferior to rule-based decision making. It is capable of producing consistent, predictable results. It is no more prone to gender bias than recent legislative rules. At least if the settlement process is guided by lawyer intermediaries, adverse effects resulting from discretionary standards are not demonstrable.

b. Discretion and Rule: The Tendency Toward Convergence

It is also probable that, in some instances, discretion and rule will produce relatively equivalent results. The reasons for this phenomenon derive from the contrary effects of rule and discretion on the decision-making process. As noted above, discretionary standards will typically, through the development of informal rules of thumb and formal precedents, become more rule-like. An historical example of this channelling tendency of discretion can be found in child custody law. Courts, ostensibly deciding custody based on a broad examination of a child's best interests, over time adopted what might be best described as a set of presumptions: in favor of the mother for a child of "tender years;" in favor of the parent preferred by a mature child; against the parent whose conduct exposes the child to immorality.

In contrast to the channelling tendency of discretion, rules tend to produce exceptions. Indeed, the narrower the rule that constrains the decision-making process, the greater the likelihood and the number of exceptions that will occur. These exceptions may result from judicial interpretation of the rule itself, rejection of the rule in favor of a competing rule or higher principle, or even from legislative reaction to judicial rule enforcement that results in perceived injustice.

As a result of these divergent tendencies, the results of discretionary and rule-based decision making, if shaped by similar principles within the same historical context, may ultimately converge. Marital property distribution is a potential example of this phenomenon. With only a few years' experience with equitable property distribution, it appears that New York courts already view equal division as a prototypical outcome, or perhaps as an analytical starting point. Professor Reynolds, reviewing a collection of reported equitable property distribution decisions from six states with older equitable division regimes, reports that judges almost never divided marital property unequally. By contrast, in a state like California that has an established equal division rule, it has been necessary to carve out exceptions to the equality requirement to meet equitable concerns: for cases of negative net worth, for cases in which the custodial parent needs the home, and for cases of asset dissipation. Judicial decisions made under a mature equitable property distribution standard and a mature equal division rule thus may not, in the end, differ greatly.

CHAPTER VI

She Got the Goldmine and I Got The Shaft: The Economics of Marital Dissolution

A. The Economics of Husband and Wife

The divorce revolution of the last twenty-five years has now produced something of a "counter-revolution." Laura Bradford, *The Counterrevolution: A Critique of Recent Proposals to Reform No-Fault Divorce Laws,* 49 STAN. L. REV. 607 (1997). That counterrevolution has been driven by a critical assumption: that the divorce revolution has impoverished women and the children who live with them. LENORE WEITZMAN, THE DIVORCE REVOLUTION (1985). Economists such as Gary Becker and H. Elizabeth Peters predicted that changes in divorce law allowing one spouse to divorce the other unilaterally would have strongly negative effects on women's post-divorce income and, ultimately, their power in marriage. GARY BECKER, TREATISE ON THE FAMILY (1981); H. Elizabeth Peters, *Marriage and Divorce: Informational Constraints and Private Contracting,* 76 AMERICAN ECON. REV. 437 (1986). See also Amy L. Wax, *Bargaining in the Shadow of the Market,* 84 VA. L. REV. 509 (1998).

The important question of whether divorce affects men and women differently also directs the answer to questions about whether the high rate of late 20th century divorce in the United States has been affected by changes in divorce rules. Even more fundamental, perhaps, is the normative question of whether changes in marriage stability are desirable or even, to use the economists' term, efficient.

Finally, even if the outcome at divorce may be what is best for the couple involved, policy makers commonly worry about the effect of divorce on children. For example, if marital assets are divided inequitably, as Marsha Garrison's article in the last chapter suggests, the income available to children typically declines. Further, even if the court awards are adequate, the fact that many noncustodial parents do not make full payments also contributes to what has been called the "feminization of poverty," J. Thomas Oldham, *Abating the Feminization of Poverty: Changing the Rules Governing Post-Decree Modification of Child Support Obligations,* 1994 BYU L. REV. 841.

Richard Peterson, a sociologist, reconstructed the data and regressions used in one of the most famous articles on the adverse consequences of divorce for women and the children who live with them. We include this excerpt both because it reveals some of the pitfalls of those who rely on statistics and because it reviews much of the literature on this subject. We do caution the reader, as Professor Peterson does, that although he disputes the magnitude of the changes Weitzman found, no one disagrees with their direction: men economically fare slightly better after divorce than they did when married, women do significantly worse. You may wish to think about how Peterson's method was likely to reach the result he did: that men's standard of living increased only slightly, while women suffered a small decline.

Diane Galarneau & Jim Sturrock, *Family Income After Separation,* 9 PERSPECTIVES ON LABOUR AND INCOME 18 (1997)[*]

The economic situation of ex-spouses presents an often striking discrepancy between men and women. A number of studies have demonstrated a clear deterioration in the economic status of women in the year following separation, and an immediate improvement in that of men.

This article is an extract of a recent longitudinal study that looked at the income of separated persons in Canada. That analysis was based on a new version of Statistics Canada's Longitudinal Administrative Databank (LAD), which covers virtually the whole Canadian population (See Data source). It has recently become possible to subtract support payments from the income of payers, who have been required to report these separately since 1986, so the study should enrich the discussion about the setting of child support payments. New rules relating to this issue came into effect May 1, 1997, aiming to "[ensure] that Canadian children whose parents separate or divorce receive the financial support they deserve."

The study focused on married persons who became separated between 1987 and 1993 and who had children before the breakup. IT tracked changes in family composition and aftertax income. Attention was also paid to the relative situation of payers and recipients of support payments. Finally, income sources of separated persons were compared before and after separation. This article presents key findings and several tables published in the study.

---

    *   Adapted from Statistics Canada, Perspectives on Labour and Income, Catalogue No. 75-001, Summer 1997, Volume 9, Number 2, pages 18-28. Statistics Canada information is used with the permission of the Minister of Industry, as Minister responsible for Statistics Canada. Information on the availability of the wide range of data from Statistics Canada can be obtained from Statistics Canada's Regional Offices, its World Wide Web site at http://www.statcan.ca, and it's toll-free access number 1-800-263-1136.

Data source

This article is based on the Small Area and Administrative Data Division's (SAADD) Longitudinal Administrative Databank (LAD). At the time of writing, this covered a 12-year period from 1982 to 1993. It is derived from SAADD'S T1 file of families created from Revenue Canada income tax returns. The LAD represents a random sample of 10% of all taxfilers and their dependents who have social insurance numbers (SIN). This is a new version of the LAD, which formerly covered only 1% of taxfilers and persons with SIN's. The database is "longitudinal," meaning once individuals are selected for inclusion they remain in the file year after year. Some selected individuals may be missed in certain years because they did not file a tax return, or did so after the deadline. In 1993, the non-weighted LAD contained information on 2,083,590 individuals; when weighted, it covered over 96% of the Canadian population (according to post-censal estimates).

While the LAD includes only a few demographic and labour-related variables, it does contain valuable information on income.

Matching of couples in the LAD

Even though the T1 family file and the LAD contain information on families, they remain files of individual records. The family files are built up through a series of operations; spouses and children are identified using such variables as name, SIN, age, sex, mailing address, marital status and certain tax credits. Different variables are used to match couples, depending on whether they are married or living common law.

Married couples are matched primarily by their SINs, since these individuals are required to report the SIN of their partners on the tax form. Some people living common law may have been counted as married if they reported their partner's SIN. Before 1992, however, there were few ways to match couples living common law, since they were not recognized as couples by Revenue Canada. They were matched by their mailing address and such variables as age of *de facto* spouse and family name, to avoid matching a son with his mother or a brother with a sister.

All separated persons

Change in family composition

Family composition was examined the year before separation (T_{-1}) and in subsequent years (T_{+1}, T_{+2}, ... T_{+5}). The actual year of separation (T_0) was not really considered because of the many family adjustments taking place at the time. Separated persons were divided into three family types depending on whether they had become part of another couple, were the heads of single-parent families, or were single. By definition, everyone in the sample had been married in the year prior to separation (T_{-1}) and all had dependent children.

The year after separation (T_{+1}), the majority of men were single (52%), while most women headed single-parent families (68%). The great majority of women found themselves with children under 18 years (89% in T_{+1}), a less common experience for men (36%). The proportion of women with children later dropped to 76% in T_{+5} whereas that of men in the same situation grew to 42%.

A significant proportion of both men and women became part of a couple in the years following separation. Though men did so earlier, the gap between the sexes was small; one year after separation 30% of men and 26% of women had formed new unions. The gap widens with time, however; five years after separation 54% of men had a new partner, but only 45% of women did.

Five years after separation, some 35% of men were single, while a large percentage of women (46%) headed single-parent families.

Family income after separation

Post-separation income is expressed as after-tax income in 1993 dollars. This has been adjusted for the number of family members in order to make family income comparable regardless of family type. Support payments have been deducted from the total income of those paying, since they no longer have use of this money no adjustment is made for recipients, as the amount is already included in their total income. Changes in adjusted family income (AFI) are measured up to five years after separation(T_{+5}). Comparisons are always with the situation prior to separation (in T_{-1}), to show whether separated persons eventually resume their former income level and, if not, how much it changes. Results given are medians.

In the year of separation (T_0), women experienced a median loss of around 38% ($7,100) of AFI. This number must be interpreted with caution, though, because of the many changes in conjugal living arrangements taking place that year. For this reason the analysis focuses on results for succeeding years.

After separation, women lost around 23% of AFI (close to $3,000) between T_{-1} and T_{+1} (Table 2). They recovered a major portion of their losses in succeeding years, but by T_{+5} they were still 5% ($1,000) below their pre-separation AFI. These losses are attributable to two factors: first, women generally have a lower personal income than men; thus, many lose a major source of financial support on separation. Second, most women have custody of their children upon separation; this is taken into account when family income is adjusted for the number of family members.

In general, women who formed new relationships seemed to be less affected financially than those heading single-parent families or remaining single. Not only did the latter two lose a significant portion of their income after separation, but they made up a smaller proportion of it over time and did so more slowly. Consequently, five years after separation single mothers still had 21% ($3,700) less than their pre-separation income, and single women still had 19% ($3,600) to make up. Five years after separation these two groups still accounted for over 55% of separated women. Of the remaining women, those in couples experienced post-separation gains of 8% in T_{+1} and 14% in T_{+5}.

**TABLE 2: MEDIAN CHANGES * IN ADJUSTED FAMILY INCOME (AFI),
ALL SEPARATED PERSONS, 1987-1993**

	T_0	T_{+1}	T_{+2}	T_{+3}	T_{+4}	T_{+5}
Men						
All separated men	11	10	10	12	12	15
Couples	24	11	12	14	15	18
Single parents	—	1	1	3	3	5
Single persons	16	14	14	13	13	16
Women						
All separated women	-38	-23	-18	-13	-10	-5
Couples	4	8	9	11	13	14
Single parents	-41	-31	-29	-26	-24	-21
Single persons	-33	-32	-29	-25	-22	-19
			1993			
Men						
All separated men	2,000	2,000	2,000	2,200	2,400	2,800
Couples	4,500	2,100	2,300	2,700	2,900	3,200
Single parents	—	100	100	500	500	800
Single persons	3,000	2,800	2,600	2,500	2,600	2,900
Women						
All separated women	-7,100	-3,900	-3,000	-2,300	-1,600	-1,000
Couples	700	1,300	1,500	1,900	2,300	2,600
Single parents	-7,700	-5,700	-5,400	-4,800	-4,300	-3,700
Single persons	-7,300	-6,800	-6,100	-5,100	-4,700	-3,600

Source: Longitudinal Administrative Databank, 1986-1993
*The median percentage changes do not necessarily correspond to the median income changes
because medians were calculated separately.*

Men's AFI, in contrast, immediately went up about 10% ($2,000) after separation (T_{+1}). The gain eventually (T_{+5}) rose to 15% ($2,800). The size of the gain varied according to family composition. Single men had the highest increases and single fathers the lowest. With time, men living in a new relationship did somewhat better than single men. These AFI gains arose because men whose incomes were higher than women's contributed more to family income before separation (T_{-1}), and because fewer men than women lived with their children after separation.

A recent study based on an earlier version of the LAD and covering the period 1982 to 1986, found an increase in men's adjusted family income of 11%, 14% and 8%, respectively, one, two, and three years after separation. Respective figures for women were decreases of 33%, 29% and 30%.

If splitting of family assets is taken into account (homes, furniture, automobiles, pension plans and so on), different results are possible, given the considerable amounts that may be exchanged between spouses but do not show up in the LAD. In the case of a pension plan, for example, the accrued value at the time of separation must be divided between the spouses. If not, the pension paid on retirement will be reduced proportionately unless other arrangements are made. For most couples, pension plans are among the most important holdings. In couples where only the man had such a plan, the sharing of retirement funds can be a major issue. This is why some people opt for alternative arrangements, such as signing over a larger portion of the house or other family assets to the ex-partner in order to maintain full pension on retirement. At present, there are no data on such arrangements or on the total worth of family assets; therefore, it is difficult to determine how these variables might affect the results noted here.

Shared custody is also not accounted for by tax data. Some divorce statistics show that shared custody takes place in 15% to 20% of divorces, though these figures can vary over time. Not known are the costs involved in shared custody, or which partner claims the deduction for dependent children.

The following subsection shows income levels for men and women before and after adjustment for the number of family members, whose effect seems most important for women.

Adjusting family income

Family income of separated persons has been adjusted for several factors, including the number of persons dependent on that income, to take into account the economies of scale achieved when several people live together. This adjustment used an equivalence scale based on low income measures. To make it comparable to the income of a single individual, family income for a person in a couple was divided by 1.4, and that for a couple with a child by 1.7, and so on.

This calculation affects women's post-separation income more than men's, since women usually have custody of the children. Thus, in T_{+1}, family income for women overall slipped from \$23,300 to \$13,700 when adjusted, and that for men dropped from \$28,500 to \$21,900.

Payers and recipients of support payments

In the year following separation, 35% of separated women in this sample were receiving support payments, while 44% of separated men were payers. These ratios may seem low, given that everyone in the sample had children at the time of separation, but some of the men not paying support had custody; in fact, 28% of all separated men (in T_{+1}) reported dependent children and were grouped with the non-payers. For some of this group, however, the children would belong to their new partners. Other arrangements, as with shared custody, do not show up in income tax files. To be recognized as such by Revenue Canada, support payments have to be a fixed amounts paid regularly. Couples who had opted for lump-sum or irregular payments would thus not appear in the LAD. Whatever the case, it is difficult to estimate the proportion of men who should pay but do not, because of a lack of national data on the subject.

The proportion of recipients later dropped to 29% (in T_{+5}), while that for payers slipped to 39%. These drops reflect the fact that, with time, financial ties between children and non-custodial parents diminish because of reduced need or changes in the family situation of one or both ex-spouses.

Both payers and recipients of support payments tend to behave similarly with respect to new unions. Women receiving payments are much less likely than non-recipients to form new relationships. Likewise, men paying support take longer than no-payers to do so. As a consequence, a greater proportion of payers than separated men in general find themselves single (46% versus 35% in T_{+5}).

Family income after separation

When the analysis is restricted to payers and recipients of support payments, the gap in AFI between men and women widens. One year after separation, recipients have heavier losses (-29% or -$6,100) than separated women generally (-23% or -$3,900). Payers experience gains in AFI (20%, or $4,200) twice those of separated men in general (10%, or $2,000). In subsequent years, compared with all separated women, recipients recover a lower portion of their losses and do so more slowly. On the other hand, compared with separated men overall, payers see larger increases in AFI.

Recipients thus fare relatively less well than separated women in general, in spite of receiving support payments. This group consists largely of single parents (82%, as opposed to 61% of non-recipients in T_{+1}), who remain so longer (by T_{+5}, 62% of recipients were still in this category, versus 40% of non-recipients). Most of them have children under 18 to care for (in T_{+1}, 96%, compared with 85% of non-recipients), a situation that persists for at least five years (in T_{+5}, 92% of recipients and 70% of non-recipients still had children under 18 in their care).

In general, payers of support experienced a greater growth in income than separated men in general. In fact, they had a higher median family income (not adjusted for family size) than non-payers, even after allowing for support payments (in T_{+1}, payers had $29,300 and non-payers $27,700). Moreover, they maintained a slight edge throughout the observation period ($34,800 versus $32,200 in T_{+5}). This may indicate that having a higher income increases the likelihood of their making support payments. As time passed, if they kept their advantage, it was largely because more of them remained without children (in T_{+1}, 81% of payers had no children living with them, as opposed to 50% of non-payers; by T_{+5}, the proportions were 72% and 50%, respectively). Also, a relatively large proportion of non-payers headed single-parent families (23% in T_{+1} and 14% in T_{+5}, compared with 10% and 5%, respectively, for payers).

Among those receiving support payments, income differed significantly by family type. In fact, only those women who formed new relationships avoided major decline in AFI; they registered gains throughout the period, which reached 14% by T_{+5}. Women heading single-parent families and single women, in contrast, suffered sizeable losses; even after five years, they still had over 20% to make up. The situation for payers was less variable; men who were heads of single-parent families were the only ones to register smaller gains in AFI.

The importance of the definition of income

Support payments have been declared separately to Revenue Canada since 1986, hence, they could be subtracted from the payer's income. This section examines the extent to which changes in the AFI of those making support payments would have differed if support payments had not been subtracted.

The subtraction of support payments generally has a considerable effect on the AFI of payers. Had it not been subtracted, the AFI of payers would have risen by 43% in T_{+1} rather than 20%. The extent of the difference depends on family composition, with the greatest difference occurring for single men.

Conclusion

After separation, men become part of a couple again more quickly than women, though the difference is not significant (30% are part of a couple after a year, compared with 26% of women). Some 52% of men are single, while 68% of women are single parents. This difference between the sexes still exists five years after separation, although it is less pronounced because a high proportion of individuals have again become part of a couple.

One year after separation, women most often have custody of the children—89% lived with children under 18 years of age, compared with 36% of men. Five years after separation, this proportion falls to 76% for women and rises to 42% for men.

Women experience a considerable decrease in adjusted family income (taking into account the number of family members) after separation (-23%, or $3,900 one year later); men show an increase of 10% ($2,000). Five years after separation, women have recovered a large part of their loss, but still have an adjusted family income 5% ($1,000) lower than before separation. Men maintain their initial advantage, even increasing their gains to 15% ($2,800) by five years post-separation. Unlike most men, women experience a decline in adjusted family income following separation, both because their personal income is usually lower and because they most often have custody of the children.

These calculations do not take into account all factors that come into play during a separation, such as moving costs, division of family property and shared custody. It is difficult to evaluate the extent of their influence on results, since no data on them currently exist.

These changes in family income vary with family type. Women on their own and those who are heads of single-parent families experience the greatest loss. A year after separation, their adjusted family income has fallen by 32% ($6,800) and 31% ($5,700), respectively. Women who are part of a couple experience an increase of around 8% ($1,300). Men who are single have the highest increases and those who are single parents, the lowest.

Some 35% of women receive support payments the year following separation, while 44% of men make payments. Recipients experience greater losses in adjusted family income than separated women overall (-29%, or -$6,100 one year after the breakup), while payers post gains twice those of separated men in general (20% or $4,200). Five years after separation, gains would have reached 47% ($9,600), but instead were reduced to 30% ($5,900). These figures show the importance of the definition of income.

B. The Economics of Parents and Children

The following three excerpts deal directly with economic issues associated with the parent-child relationship. John Langbein's provocative article addresses the way wealth is transmitted from one generation to the next. His thesis is that, unlike earlier times, most parents now give to their children primarily through wealth transfers during life, as by providing for their education, rather than through inheritable estates. He thus develops the important topic of human capital: investments in others' earning capacity. Langbein notes that in modern American families, the children, who might in the past have supported the parents in old age, can expect the parents to take care of themselves through some combination of Social Security and private pensions. Langbein writes also of the role the government has played in this transformation.

This is followed by an excerpt taken from Beller and Graham's book discussing which custodial mothers receive child support, how much they receive, and how these trends have changed over the past quarter century. The authors find significant disparities based upon race and marital status, and suggest that child support awards have not kept pace with growing incomes or the cost of living. They offer some hope from federal guidelines, which require states to somehow match child support amounts with parental incomes.

We conclude with part of a study by Richard Lempert, who takes data compiled by law professor David Chambers on compliance with child support orders, and analyzes the various factors that caused some, but by no means all, fathers to make payments as ordered. He specifically looks for evidence that jailing some men deterred them (or others) from noncompliance. The article is also notable because it uses (and explains) the common empirical technique of regression analysis.

John N. Langbein, *The Twentieth-Century Revolution in Family Wealth Transmission*, 86 MICHIGAN LAW REVIEW 722 (1988)[*]

The ancient field of trust-and-estate law has entered upon a period of serious decline. In some law firms, even seasoned practitioners have begun to diversify away from the field. In leading circles of the trust-and-estate bar, there is now open discussion of diminishing clientele, difficulty in billing for legal services at rates comparable to the rates for other specialties, and the reluctance of new associates to enter the field.

Although it has been fashionable to attribute this decline to the dramatic 1981 revision of the federal transfer taxes, which effectively relieved the middle classes from

---

[*]   Copyright © 1988. Reprinted with permission.

entanglement with the estate tax, the theme of this article is that the phenomenon has causes far more profound. The decline of the probate bar reflects the decline of probate. The decline of probate has two quite different dimensions. One is the much-remarked rise of the nonprobate system. Financial intermediaries operate a noncourt system for transferring account balances and other property on death with little or no lawyerly participation. . . .

The decline of probate has another dimension that has not been well understood. Fundamental changes in the very nature of wealth have radically altered traditional patterns of family wealth transmission, increasing the importance of lifetime transfers and decreasing the importance of wealth transfer on death.

In this article I shall be concerned with private-sector wealth. Into the eighteenth century, land was the dominant form of wealth. The technological forces that broke up older family-centered modes of economic organization called forth two new forms of private-sector wealth. One category is what we today call financial assets—that is, stocks, bonds, back deposits, mutual fund shares, insurance contracts, and the like—which now comprise the dominant form of wealth. The other great form of modern wealth is what the economists call human capital. It is the skills and knowledge that lie at the root of advanced technological life.

The main purpose of this article is to sound a pair of themes about the ways in which these great changes in the nature of wealth have become associated with changes of perhaps comparable magnitude in the timing and in the character of family wealth transmission. My first theme, developed in Part II, concerns human capital. Whereas of old, wealth transmission from parents to children tended to center upon major items of patrimony such as the family farm or the family firm, today for the broad middle classes, wealth transmission centers on a radically different kind of asset: the investment in skills. In consequence, intergenerational wealth transmission no longer occurs primarily upon the death of the parents, but rather, when the children are growing up, hence, during the parents' lifetimes.

My other main theme, developed in Part III, arises from the awesome demographic transformation of modern life. For reasons that I shall explore, those same parents who now make their main wealth transfer to their children inter vivos are also living much longer. The need to provide for the parents in their lengthy old age has put a huge new claim on family wealth, a claim that necessarily reduces the residuum that would otherwise have passed to survivors. A new institution has arisen to help channel the process of saving and dissaving for old age: the pension fund. The wealth of the private pension system consists almost entirely of financial assets. I shall emphasize a distinctive attribute of pension wealth, namely, the bias toward annuitization. When wealth is annuitized, virtually nothing is left for transfer on death. . . .

At the outset, I must emphasize a pair of exclusions from the trends being described in this article. I shall be talking about the patterns of wealth transmission that characterize the broad generality of American wealth-holders—roughly, the upper third to upper half of the populace. I mean, in short, the middle and especially the upper-middle classes, which is to say, the mostly white-collar, technical, managerial, and professional cohort. These people propel the knowledge-based economy of our post-industrial age, and they command much of its wealth. The trends I shall be discussing have had less influence upon the wealth transmission practices at the extremes of our society—among the very rich and among the poor.

The modes of gratuitous transfer have never had much relevance to the poor or near-poor. If you lack appreciable wealth, you will face many problems in life, but one problem that you will be spared is the question of how to transmit the wealth that you do not have.

At the other end of the spectrum, among those who populate the uppermost tail of the wealth distribution—people somewhere within the top one percent of wealth-holders—the trends that I shall be discussing have also not been of great significance. I shall have more to say about why the great forces canvassed in this article are largely spent before they touch dynastic wealth.

I. PROLOGUE: FAMILY WEALTH THEN AND NOW

It is often the case that the best way to broach the subject of the new is to identify the important characteristics of the old. In this instance, I begin by flipping the calendar backward a century and more, to the days when Abraham Lincoln lived on the American prairie and when his contemporaries were building the cities of the Atlantic seaboard, the Great Lakes, and the Ohio and Mississippi Valleys. We want to remind ourselves of some central traits of wealth holding and wealth transmission in this period.

A. Family Property Relations in the Last Century.

The family was prototypically a unit of production. Nineteenth-century America was overwhelmingly a nation of small farms. In the towns and cities, the predominant economic entities were small-firm producers and small shops. Farmers, artisans, and shopkeepers had in common the tradition that the entire family worked in the enterprise. In those circumstances, contemporaries had little occasion to distinguish between what we think of as earned income (income from one's labor) and investment income (the return to property). The two income streams were merged in a single endeavor. Both the generation of the parents and the generation of the children looked to the farm or the firm for their livelihood, with scant attention to idle accounting questions about how much of their income to apportion to labor and how much to property.

In emphasizing that the returns to labor and capital were composite, I do not mean that the property component was unimportant. Property was desperately important. Ownership of a farm or a firm rescued you from a mean life of stoop labor in someone else's field, mill, or household. In former times, it was vastly harder to live by your skills alone, without patrimony. Accordingly, people of means aspired to nothing so much as to leave their children similarly advantaged. You hoped to transmit the farm or the firm, and thus in the quaint phrase of the time, to make for your children 'a provision in life.'

There was relatively little formal education. This was a low-tech age, and the transmission of skills, like so much else, could still occur within the family. You learned your trade alongside your parents and your relations, in the fields, in the firm, or at the hearth. Put differently, the family was not only the primary unit of production, it was the primary educational entity as well. Only a few crafts and learned professions required external education; and even in those pursuits, education was frequently assimilated to a domestic model through the apprenticeship system of training.

Succession to ownership rights in this multigenerational enterprise occurred upon death—that is, upon the death of the parents, typically of the father. Various familiar arrangements were made for the widow, not only the common-law life estate known as dower, but also life interests in fee or in trust that could provide a larger fraction than dower and that could extend beyond realty. But the tendency both in intestacy and for testate estates was to limit the widow to a life interest, in order to assure continuity of the enterprise in the hands of the next generation, whose members had already been long employed in the enterprise.

Notice in this connection that widowhood was materially less common than today. I do not happen to have American data on this point, but I can report some German numbers gathered by a leading German scholar, Dieter Leipold. He found that as late as 1876-1880, for each 100 marriages that ended in death, the female survived in 56.5%. By the year 1965, females were the survivor in 70% of marriages ending in death. Thus, over the century, female survivorship expanded from a modest probability to a probability that is better than two-to-one. The reasons, of course, are not hard to discern. There has been a precipitous decline in the rate of mortality associated with childbearing. Furthermore, while both sexes have benefitted from huge increases in longevity across the century, the advantage in favor of women has consistently expanded. Whereas spousal succession today is overwhelmingly a widow's business, in earlier times the wife was materially less likely to survive her husband than she is today; and when she did survive him, it was not likely to be for very long.

Accordingly, succession to the family farm or family firm typically occurred on the father's death. There was no reason for him to surrender dominion over the family patrimony inter vivos. Ownership until death reinforced parental control over the extended family and over its collective enterprise. Remember that although wealth transmission occurred on death, death occurred very much earlier than it does today. That is to say, succession on death occurred when both the parents and the children were younger than we now expect. This difference is, of course, no mystery. It results from the awesome change in life expectancy over the past century, a fascinating subject about which more is said in Part III. Thus, even though wealth transfer in the previous century tended to occur on death rather than inter vivos, decedents were less often elderly. The successors were typically young adults, as compared to the middle-aged children who typically succeed when parents die in modern circumstances.

Finally, to complete this snapshot of important traits of nineteenth-century wealth transmission patterns, I wish to say something about the diminished expectations of daughters. Perhaps the easy way to make this point is to remind you how often you have come across some family firm from earlier times in which the father associated the son or sons in the firm's name—for example, Steinway & Sons; but you have not seen firms called Steinway & Daughters. Although there were many exceptions, the wealth transmission process tended to favor the male line. The firm or the farm had to be worked. Except when a family had only a daughter or daughters, continuity within the patrimony emphasized the son.

B. Family Property Relations in Modern Times

In the late twentieth century, the family has in general ceased to be an important unit of production. To be sure, you can still find dribbles of cottage industry in America, and there is still a fair amount of Mom-and-Pop retailing, but in the main the production and sale of goods and services has forever left the home. The technological sophistication and marketing complexity of modern modes of production and distribution impose enormous capital requirements. Village blacksmiths cannot manufacture automobiles, airplanes, and oil rigs. The village entrepreneur can still sell a screwdriver or make a hamburger, but the evidence is overwhelming that the customer mostly prefers to patronize K-Mart or McDonald's. Thus, the characteristic unit of production in our age is corporate rather than domestic, it is the share company.

These trends extend to farming as well. American agriculture is ever more technology driven and capital intensive. It has become a byword that we live in an era of corporate agriculture. Family farms still exist in America, indeed, in some farming areas it would be fair to say that family farms remain characteristic. But a large fraction of them are hobby farms, secondary enterprises conducted by people whose main livelihood derives from employment outside the home. As farms have grown in size and productivity, an astonishing agricultural depopulation has occurred. In what used to be a nation of farmers, we are now fed by a mere 5% of the population, down from 44% in 1880, and it should be remembered that these people are not only feeding the rest of us, they are running our largest export industry as well.

Thus, in the main, we neither farm nor manufacture at home. The family has undergone a specialization of function. In economic terms, the family remains a unit of consumption but no longer a unit of production. Enterprise is organized outside the home, and the worker now leaves the home for his employment. Such a worker contributes his labor to his employment, but he no longer supplies the plant and equipment as he did in the bygone day of the family enterprise. The reason that most workers use external capital is, of course, closely connected to the technological and marketing forces that have magnified the size and complexity of the productive processes, the forces that drove the worker out of the home in the first place. Modern modes of enterprise are capital intensive. The blacksmith could afford his anvil, but we cannot expect the autoworker to supply his factory or the airplane pilot to bring along his own Boeing 747.

The ever-larger capital requirements of technologically advanced enterprise required modes of financing that exceeded the capabilities of the family. Ownership of a small firm or a small farm could lie within the scope of family-based capital accumulation and capital transmission, but we understand why IBM, General Electric, and AT&T cannot be family firms. The corporate form arose to facilitate the pooling and allocation of capital, as did the specialized institutions of finance. In the late twentieth century we recognize three dominant modes of financial intermediation: first, the corporation, and with it, the securities industry that makes the market in corporate shares and corporate debt; second, banking—commercial, investment, and savings and loan; and third, the insurance industry. All three were primitive in antebellum America. Not only have these financial intermediaries now displaced the family's role as the unit of capital accumulation, they have also created the new forms of wealth in financial assets—the various securities, depositary claims, and other contract rights.

These instruments of financial intermediation now absorb the savings that the family previously devoted to the family enterprise. Because family wealth is no longer retained but rather invested externally, it now takes the form of claims on outside enterprises. These financial assets have become the characteristic form of transmissible wealth. It is the stuff of the financial pages. As Roscoe Pound said in an arresting dictum, 'Wealth, in a commercial age, is made up largely of promises.' I shall have more to say about how the prevalence of financial assets has altered the patterns of family wealth transmission. For the present, however, I want to direct attention to that other species of new property that is associated with the breakup of the family as a unit of production: human capital.

II. WEALTH TRANSFERS THROUGH HUMAN CAPITAL

The same underlying technological and economic forces that caused the dissolution of family-based enterprise have also stripped the family of much of its role as an educational institution. This development, which is in a sense quite obvious to us all, has had enormous implications for family wealth transmission, implications that have not been adequately appreciated.

It is a truism that a technological age requires a technologically proficient workforce. The awesome expansion of human knowledge over the past century and more has made the family obsolete as a repository and transfer agent for this huge range of knowledge. In olden times, I have said, you learned your trade at home and hearth, or else in apprenticeship to a neighbor. Only a handful of callings required training beyond these domestic patterns. Today, by contrast, we have gone so far in the opposite direction—toward externalizing education—that we even send people outside the home to prepare for life in the home. (I refer not simply to the study of what is called home economics, but to our ever-greater reliance upon the schools for basic acculturation.)

A. Educational Expenditure

The educational demands of modern economic life have become immense, and so has the cost of providing children with this educational endowment. A central thesis of this article is that paying for education has become the characteristic mode of intergenerational wealth transmission for most American families.

Look at the statistics in order to get a sense of the underlying magnitudes. Total expenditures for formal education in the United States in 1840 have been calculated at $9.2 million. This sum increased over the nineteenth century, a period of relatively low inflation, to stand at $289.6 million in 1900. By 1959 the figure had reached $23.9 billion, which amounted to 4.8% of gross national product. Less than thirty years later, in the 1986-1987 academic year, the total expenditure on formal education stood at $282.1 billion, a figure that represented 7% of gross national product. Of these amounts, 60% went to fund primary and secondary education, 40% went to higher education.

While the official educational statistics are valuable for conveying a general sense of the magnitudes, they conceal many subtle issues of definition and measurement. Many sins pass under the label of education. Not every course in basketweaving deserves to be reckoned as investment in human capital. On the other hand, much of our financial investment in our children takes forms that, somewhat arbitrarily, fall outside the category of formal education. If you take your children to a nature preserve or on a tour of French cathedrals, that's private recreation, whereas when some educational institution takes your kid square dancing, that's education. Indeed, as my colleagues Walter Blum and the late Harry Kalven pointed out in a celebrated book some thirty years ago, the most important inheritance of all—the thing that decisively advantages middle-class children—is the cultural bequest from their parents. That parental transfer of language, of values, and of psychological well-being sets the stage for all the formal learning and achievements of later years. None of that gets captured in the educational statistics. Nevertheless, once due allowance is made for the shortcomings of what the statisticians deem to be education, the numbers are so enormous that they bespeak an enterprise of daunting importance.

In 1870 only 2% of the population was graduating from high school; by 1970 the figure was 75.6%. In 1870 institutions of higher learning in the United States conferred a total of 9,372 degrees, of which 9,371 were bachelor's degrees and exactly one was a doctorate. In 1970 the total number of degrees conferred showed an increase of more than a hundredfold over 1870. The figure stood at 1,065,000, of which almost 30,000 were Ph.D. or equivalent degrees. College enrollments as a percentage of the college age population reached 12.5% in 1946, 29.6% in 1970, and 31.3% in 1985. As recently as 1940, only 4.6% of the American population had completed four or more years of university study. By 1985, almost 20% (19.4%, to be precise) had done so.

Economists who have examined this gigantic education industry have increasingly been of the view that expenditures on education ought not to be viewed as a simple consumption expense, like money spent on corn flakes or handkerchiefs. Rather, they see educational expenditure as an investment, closely akin to conventional investment in plant, equipment, and inventory. Education produces skills, and skills are as much an input in the productive process as machines. Economists now routinely liken these skills to capital, the species of capital that they call human capital. Modern productive processes are skill-driven. Whether we speak of new fields like aeronautics or ancient ones like health care, the story is the same. While plant and equipment become increasingly sophisticated—robotics and computers and CAT scanners and all that—the skills of the workforce become still more decisive. Human capital thus substitutes for nonhuman capital. Skill embodies knowledge, and new knowledge not only displaces old knowledge, it displaces plant and equipment as well. Think of the advance in medical science that made polio a preventable disease and consigned the iron lung industry to the scrapheap: Skill displaced machines.

Human capital, being literally embodied in mortals, is distinguished from physical capital by the frailty of the human condition. Human capital dies with the holder and thus needs to be created afresh in each generation. Of course, the highly transitory quality of human capital is really more a difference of degree than of kind. Machines and structures also fall apart or become obsolete, which is why we systematically account for the artifacts of physical capital by means of depreciation schedules.

Careful econometric study has documented that human capital has steadily increased over the twentieth century as a fraction of total capital and as a fraction of gross national product. The percent of GNP spent on both education and on job training grew by 80% from 1929 to 1969, in which year it stood at 15.4% of GNP. A recent set of calculations 'implies that education costs society approximately as much as investment in nonresidential physical capital.'

There is no mystery about who has been paying the bill for this vast expansion of education. Even allowing for some scholarships, loans, and student labor, the main burden falls upon the parents. Indeed, even childless people pay substantial sums in taxes to support the public educational establishment. But for present purposes, the focus is upon propertied families who are raising children.

My thesis is quite simple, and, I hope, quite intuitive. I believe that, in striking contrast to the patterns of last century and before, in modern times the business of educating children has become the main occasion for intergenerational wealth transfer. Of old, parents were mainly concerned to transmit the patrimony—prototypically the farm or the firm, but more generally, that 'provision in life' that rescued children from the harsh fate of being a mere laborer. In today's economic order, it is education more than property, the new human capital rather than the old physical capital, that similarly advantages a child.

We know that income levels correlate powerfully with education. In 1985 the median annual income of full-time male workers aged twenty-five and over who had completed some years of high school but had not graduated was under $20,000; for those who had completed four years of college the figure was above $30,000; and for those with more than four years of college, the figure approached $40,000. The comparable earnings figures for female workers were lower, but differences in educational attainment among women produced similar disparities in favor of the well educated.

Family wealth and its corollary, family income, are crucial determinants of access to education. A sociologist of education recently summed up the data in the following way: The amount of schooling that individuals obtain and their school continuation decisions are strongly affected by characteristics of their families. Persons whose parents have more schooling, higher income, and better jobs; whose families are smaller; and who were raised in urban areas typically obtain more schooling than persons from less-advantaged backgrounds.

The process of delivering educational advantage to children begins when they are very young. There has been a huge increase in formal preschool education in recent decades. In the years of primary and secondary education, propertied parents strive to locate in suitable school districts, or to send their children to private schools. By the way, the distinction between private and public schools is far less meaningful than might appear at first glance. Many of those distinguished suburban school districts that represent the high-water mark of quality in our public school tradition are in truth better understood as private schools with tax-deductible tuition—the tuition taking the form of relatively high real estate taxes that are deductible against income taxes. Parents tend to move into these school districts when they have school-age children, and to move out when they no longer need the schools.

And then there is college. The federal government's Digest of Education Statistics 1987 reports that the average annual charge for tuition, room, and board for undergraduates in the 1985-1986 academic year was $3,640 at public colleges and $8,870 at private colleges. Because these numbers are averages, which lump low-cost local institutions with elite schools, they understate the bills that parents face when they send children to the major universities. At the premier private universities, the bill for tuition, room, and board now exceeds $15,000 a year; travel and incidentals can easily bring the figure to $20,000. In the graduate and professional schools, the price tag is higher still. This year, most of the major private law schools are charging about $13,000 in tuition alone. Tuition, fees, books, and supplies at the University of Chicago Law School this academic year are estimated to cost $13,550. At Chicago, we project total annual expenses for an unmarried law student at more than $21,000 per year, which puts the effective price tag of a three-year Chicago degree at about $65,000. By the way, it costs us a further $35,000 to deliver that degree to the student, money that comes from endowment income, a trickle of foundation and government grants, and a torrent of alumni support.

A story in Newsweek in May of 1987 used figures on the annual cost of undergraduate education at Johns Hopkins. The $15,410 that Johns Hopkins charged in 1987 for tuition, room, and board constituted 31% of a family income of $50,000 per year. By contrast, the $2,000 that Johns Hopkins charged in 1960 represented only 15% of the inflation-adjusted equivalent family income for 1960, which was $13,505.

Now it is quite obvious that very few families can afford to pay 31% of family income, or anything near it, on what we would call—in an accounting sense—a current basis. That is especially true when the family has more than one child in the educational mill at the same time. For most families, therefore, these education expenses represent capital transfers in a quite literal sense: The money comes from savings, that is, from the family's capital; or debt is assumed, meaning that the money is borrowed from the family's future capital. . . .

The same Newsweek article that discussed the education cost figures from Johns Hopkins recounted the saga of a parent named C. Y. Lu, who presently has the financial misfortune to have one son attending Princeton while the other is at the Harvard Law School. Mr. Lu is reported to have sold off investments, taken out educational loans, and refinanced his home mortgage by $60,000, in order to raise a total of $140,000. Mr. Lu is quoted as saying, 'I've told my sons, your education is going to be your inheritance.'

There in Mr. Lu's words you see my theme encapsulated. Education is displacing inheritance, lifetime transfers are displacing succession on death. Back in the nineteenth century or earlier, Mr. Lu would have husbanded his wealth and left it to his sons at his death. Today, in mid-life, he cashes out and goes into debt in order to fork over his savings to Princeton and Harvard.

Nobody forces Mr. Lu to do this. It was quite open to him to say to his two sons, 'Boys, I'll make you a deal. I'll buy you out of those admission letters from Princeton and Harvard. Stay away from those cauldrons of red ink, and content yourselves with attending the community college down the road—or better yet, go right to work in an accessible career like pumping gas at the corner filling station. Then, I'll have $140,000 more in family wealth that I can invest through Merrill Lynch. It will compound and be available for you on my death.' Well, we all know that virtually no parent behaves that way. Parents understand full well the point that the economists have been demonstrating with their studies of human capital. Those degrees from Princeton and Harvard are superior investments when compared to any class of financial assets, by virtue of a very conventional test: The degrees produce a far larger income stream. . . .

From the proposition that the main parental wealth transfer to children now takes place inter vivos, there follows a corollary: Children of propertied parents are much less likely to expect an inheritance. Whereas of old, children did expect the transfer of the farm or firm, today's children expect help with educational expenses, but they do not depend upon parental wealth transfer at death. Lengthened life expectancies mean that the life-spans of the parents overlap the life-spans of their adult children for much longer than used to be. Parents now live to see their children reaching peak earnings potential, and those earnings often exceed what the parents were able to earn. Today, children are typically middle-aged when the survivor of their two parents dies, and middle-aged children are far less likely to be financially needy. It is still the common practice within middle- and upper-middle-class families for parents to leave to their children (or grandchildren) most or all of any property that happens to remain when the parents die, but there is no longer a widespread sense of parental responsibility to abstain from consumption in order to transmit an inheritance.

B. Consequences for the Ethos of Inheritance

At the outset of this article, I cautioned that the revolution in family wealth transmission would be seen to be less significant for dynastic wealth holders. School bills make little dent in large fortunes. There are intrinsic limits to how much education an individual can absorb, and those limits are reached long before the holders of great wealth would notice.

Nevertheless, there is a deeper sense in which the forces that have transformed the patterns of wealth transmission for the broad middle classes have also touched the holders of great wealth. The new pattern has become a social norm, a norm so powerful that it has begun to chip away at the ethos of older notions of inheritance.

This is a phenomenon that I first became aware of as a result of talking with practicing estate planners. Recently, I noticed Fortune magazine running a story on it. Fortune reported on the thinking of some extremely wealthy people who planned to leave their children only token inheritances. The story led off with the views of Warren Buffett, chairman of the Berkshire Hathaway holding company, whose personal wealth is estimated at $1.5 billion. Buffett is quoted as explaining why he plans to leave each of his three children only a few hundred thousand dollars. Having put the children through college, Buffett says he expects them 'to carve out their own place in this world.' It would be 'harmful' and 'antisocial' to set up his children with 'a lifetime supply of food stamps just because they came out of the right womb.' Buffett's $1.5 billion will go to charity. So will the $50 million fortune of a New York entrepreneur named Eugene Lang, who sent his three children to college, gave each 'a nominal sum' after college, and plans to disinherit them. He explained to the Fortune reporter: 'To me inheritance dilutes the motivation that most young people have to fulfill the best that is in them. I want to give my kids the tremendous satisfaction of making it on their own.'

People like Messrs. Buffett and Lang are quite exceptional. Most people of great means prefer to leave most of their wealth to their descendants, hoping to shape the younger generations so that the wealth will be used responsibly. The hostility towards conventional succession expressed by Messrs. Buffett and Lang is noteworthy not because such hostility is prevalent, but simply because it would have been inconceivable a century or more ago. Can we imagine the twelfth Earl of Carlisle arranging for the dissipation of the family seat, in order to stimulate the thirteenth Earl to the challenge of reacquiring it?

Messrs. Buffett and Lang are voicing an attitude toward conventional wealth transmission that is not only quite exceptional, it is historically very recent and also very American. Behind it, I think, are two novel ideas. One is the assumption that wealth is largely fungible, that there is no great sentimental attachment nor any particular social significance to the family's existing patrimony. That is why Mr. Buffett could liken his fortune to a pile of food stamps, and why Mr. Lang could hope that his children would experience the satisfaction of 'making it on their own.' By it, he means, something like it, but not the identical property. This notion that wealth is fungible is an idea that fits the new forms of wealth better than the old, an idea that fits American circumstances better than English or European. You're much more likely to be sentimental about your ancestors' manor house than about the family's portfolio of marketable securities.

Further, the disdain for customary modes of wealth transfer that Messrs. Buffett and Lang are voicing presupposes that these gentlemen have already achieved for their children the characteristic wealth transfer of modern times, the investment in human capital through education. More and more, Americans expect personal wealth to take the form of earned income, that is, we expect it to be a return on human capital. Messrs. Buffett and Lang have taken that expectation to its limit; in their eyes, conventional wealth transfer has lost its legitimacy. The esteem associated with holding property really now applies only to earned income, to property that embodies the fruits of human capital. In this sense, the revolution in family wealth transmission, which is overwhelmingly an event of the broad middle classes, touches even the holders of great wealth. . . .

III. THE PENSION REVOLUTION

The other great chapter in the saga of fundamental change in family wealth transmission being told in this article concerns the phenomenon of retirement and the rise of the private pension system. Pension funds are another artifact of the new forms of wealth that arose in consequence of the breakup of older, family-centered modes of production. Neither on the prairie nor in the cities of Abraham Lincoln's day had anybody ever heard of a pension fund. Your life expectancy was such that you were unlikely to need much in the way of retirement income. If you did chance to outlive your period of productive labor, you were in general cared for within the family.

Not only is the need for a retirement income stream relatively recent, but so too is the mode of wealth that now supplies it. Pension funds are composed almost entirely of financial assets—the instruments of financial intermediation—that distinctively modern form of property that was still of peripheral importance in the last century.

As late as World War II, the private pension system was minuscule. Today, the assets of nonfederal pension plans (that is, private plans plus the pension funds of state and local government employees) total approximately two trillion dollars. As of 1984, pension funds owned 22.8% of equity securities in the United States and about half of all corporate debt. For many middle- and especially upper-middle-class families, pension wealth is their largest asset. But pension wealth has traits that mark it off sharply from traditional property, especially when we look at it from the standpoint of family wealth transmission.

A. The Enhancement of Life Expectancy

The way to begin thinking about the pension revolution is to grasp the magnitude of the underlying demographic phenomena that brought it about. Life expectancy a hundred years ago was about forty-five years. Today, it is seventy-five years and climbing.

Behind the awesome spurt in life expectancy over the last century or so is a phenomenon that has been called 'the elimination of premature disease.' In a nutshell, the insight is that diseases belong in two categories—the infectious or acute diseases that we have now largely banished from the mortality tables; and those diseases of old age that appear to set intrinsic limits on human longevity. Some researchers think that they see age eighty-five as the approximate eventual norm of the human life span. In 1980 white females were living to within seven years of that ideal. Three of those seven years of what is called 'average premature death' are accounted for by violent death—automobile accidents, bathtub falls, and so forth. Thus, from the medical viewpoint, it is being said that the 'task of eliminating premature death . . . has been largely accomplished.'

. . . I have travelled (I hope not detoured) into this demographic data, because I think that without it one cannot really grasp what the pension revolution is all about. The pension fund is a direct response to the new demographics, in the setting of the new property. That point is best made if we return for a moment to our baseline in antebellum America, in order to see how the phenomenon of aging transpired when family wealth relations centered on the common patrimony in farm or firm.

Why were there no pension funds? The most important explanation is that, on account of the lower life expectancy of the times, far fewer people outlived their period of productive employment. You were, so to speak, much more likely to die with your boots on. I do not want to exaggerate this point. The forty-five-year life expectancy that prevailed a century ago is a composite figure, greatly distorted by infant mortality. Your chances of surviving to a reasonable age were much enhanced in the last century once you had navigated the shoals of infancy. A white male who lived to age twenty in the year 1900 had an ultimate life expectancy of 62.2 years; a white female aged twenty in 1900 had a life expectancy of 63.8 years; in 1980 the projected life expectancy for whites aged twenty was 72.7 years for the male, a gain of 10.5 years; and 79.7 for the female, a gain of 15.9 years. The comparable figures for nonwhites are lower, but the rate of improvement across the twentieth century has been better, especially for women. Thus, we see that even after we correct for infant mortality, the diminished life expectancy of the last century was marked enough to explain why contemporaries so seldom had occasion to talk about what we call the retirement income problem. If you chanced to out-live your productive years, you did not in general do it for very long.

But what of the relative handful who did need retirement support? The well-known pattern was one of reverse transfer. Within the family, the children, now mature, would support superannuated parents. For propertied persons, however, this image of reverse transfer conceals an important point. In the age of family-centered economic organization, the parents still owned the farm or the firm. In a sense that defies accounting precision but that is nevertheless worth emphasizing, when the elders received support from the children, they were living from their capital in the family enterprise—that enterprise to which the children would succeed when the elders died.

Now return to the late twentieth century to see what has changed. Not only have the demographics altered so that the elders are routinely surviving for long intervals beyond their years of employment, but in consequence of the transformation in the nature of wealth, their property has taken on a radically altered character. That family farm or family firm that was the source of intrafamilial support in former times has become ever more exceptional. Most parental wealth (apart from the parents' own human capital) now takes the form of financial assets, which embody claims upon those large-scale enterprises that have replaced family enterprise.

B. Pension Wealth

In propertied families, today's elderly no longer expect much financial support from their children. The shared patrimony in farm or firm that underlay that reverse transfer system in olden times has now largely vanished. Instead, people of means are expected to foresee the need for retirement income while they are still in the workforce, and to conduct a program of saving for their retirement. Typically, these people have already undertaken one great cycle of saving and dissaving in their lives—that program by which they effected the investment in human capital for their children. Just as that former program of saving was oriented toward a distinctively modern form of wealth, human capital, so this second program centers on the other characteristic form of twentieth-century wealth, financial assets.

A priori, we might expect that individuals would be left to save for retirement without government guidance, much as they are left alone to save and spend for other purposes, but that has not been the case. Instead, the federal government has intervened by creating irresistible tax incentives to encourage people to conduct much or most of their retirement saving in a special mode, the tax-qualified pension plan.

There are three crucial advantages to conducting retirement saving through a tax-qualified pension plan. First, most contributions to the plan are tax-deferred. When my employer contributes to a qualified pension or profit-sharing plan on my behalf, or when I contribute to a defined contribution plan such as a 401(k) or, in the case of academic personnel, a 403(b), I am saving with pretax dollars. If I am in the 25-percent bracket, the Treasury is contributing to my pension savings plan 25 cents in foregone taxation for my 75 cents in foregone consumption.

The second great tax advantage is that the earnings on qualified plan investments accrue and compound on a tax-deferred basis. It is not until the employee retires and begins to receive distributions of his pension savings that he pays income tax on the sums distributed. The third major advantage associated with pension taxation is that, because most retirees have lower taxable income in their retirement years than in their peak earning years, they find that distributions from pension accounts are usually taxed at lower marginal rates. As the progressivity of the income tax has abated in recent years, however, this attribute of the system has become less significant.

As a matter of tax policy, it is open to serious question whether Congress should be granting the level of tax subsidy for pension saving that it now does, but that is a topic for another day. The present point is that the tax attractions of conducting retirement saving through the medium of a tax-qualified pension plan are simply overwhelming. These advantages explain why employers incur the regulatory costs incident to sponsoring these plans; and why employees, especially those in higher tax brackets, prefer to take compensation in the form of pension saving rather than cash wages. The private pension system—this two-trillion-dollar savings scheme—is tax driven.

C. Annuitization Eliminates Succession

From the standpoint of our interest in the patterns of family wealth transmission, what is especially important about the pension system is that it has been deliberately designed to promote lifetime exhaustion of the accumulated capital. The same body of federal law that encourages pension saving also tries to ensure that pension wealth will be consumed over the lives of the worker and his spouse. I do not mean to say that the federal policy in favor of lifetime consumption of retirement savings cannot be defeated for particular clients using appropriately designed plans; indeed, that is one of the major avenues of tax and estate planning for the carriage trade that has arisen with the pension system. My point is simply that, in the main, the federal policy achieves its goal, and only a negligible fraction of pension wealth finds its way into intergenerational transfer.

The mechanism by which pension wealth is consumed is annuitization. Just as life insurance is insurance against dying too soon, annuitization insures against living too long. Annuitization allows people to consume their capital safely, that is, without fear of running out of capital while still alive. Annuitization requires a large pool of lives, which is achieved by various methods of aggregating the pension savings of many workers. Sometimes the employer runs the pool, sometimes an intermediary such as an insurance company or (for multiemployer plans) a labor union. Annuitization requires assets that can be liquidated predictably as distribution requires. That is a trait characteristic of financial assets. Annuitization is wonderfully effective in allowing a person to consume capital without fear of outliving his capital, but the corollary is also manifest: Accounts that have been annuitized disappear on the deaths of the annuitants. Not so much as a farthing remains for the heirs.

From this brief tour of the private pension system, I hope it will be clear why I place this topic alongside my other main topic, wealth transfer by means of investment in human capital, as the two central chapters in what I have been calling the twentieth-century revolution in family wealth transmission. Both are developments of enormous magnitude, and both lead away from traditional wealth transfer on death. Propertied parents used to live from their patrimony in farm or firm and then transmit the patrimony at death. Modern parents tend to possess nontransmissible human capital more than older forms of property. Using their human capital to create lifetime income streams, modern parents now undertake two cycles of saving and dissaving, one for the children's education, the other for retirement. The investment in the children necessarily occurs in the parents' lifetimes. And especially when the retirement saving program is channelled through the enticing format of the qualified pension plan, the pressures for annuitization cause this enormous component of modern family wealth to be largely exhausted upon the parents' deaths. Transfer on death, the fundamental pattern of former times, is, therefore, ceasing to characterize the dominant wealth transmission practices of the broad middle classes. . . .

V. CONCLUSION

Increasingly, estate planning services for the middle and upper-middle classes have the quality of contingency planning. The client is motivated largely by concern to make arrangements for his family in the unlikely event that he should die prematurely. He does not expect property actually to pass under the instrument he executes. In this sense, he views his estate plan somewhat like his term life insurance policy. It is catastrophe insurance, worth having even though it is unlikely to be needed.

The modern expectation is that for middle-class wealth, the main intergenerational transfer will occur in mid-life, in the form of educational expenditures. The characteristic wealth of later years, the income streams from the public and private pension systems, do not give rise to heirship. Thus, wealth transfer on death is ever less important to the middle classes; and when it does occur, it is ever more likely to be channelled through the nonprobate system. These are the great forces that underlie the decline of the trust-and-estate bar.

So long as the carriage trade abides, the trust-and-estate bar will not go the way of the blacksmith, but the precipitous decline of the middle-class market is likely to continue. From the revolutionary changes that have affected the family property relations of the middle and upper-middle classes, only table scraps remain for the trust-and-estate lawyer. The days of routine, lawyer-guided wealth-transfer-on-death for the middle classes have largely passed.

Andrea H. Beller & John W. Graham, SMALL CHANGE: THE ECONOMICS OF CHILD SUPPORT 82 (Yale Univ. Press, 1993)[*]

The first steps toward receiving child support payments from an absent parent are to obtain an award and negotiate an adequate amount of support. As we have seen, as of April 1986, only about 60 percent of mothers with children from an absent father had taken the first step successfully, and among mothers due payments in 1985, the average amount due was only $2,500. In this chapter we shift our focus from aggregate to individual analyses of these outcomes to provide answers to some of the questions posed at the end of chapter 2.

Award Rates

We begin by attempting to answer the question: why do some mothers have an award while others do not? We find that award rates differ significantly by the mother's race, current marital status, educational attainment, age, residential location, and by the number and ages of her children. Using these results, we next examine the racial and marital status differentials averaged over the period 1979-86 in more detail. We show that somewhat more than half of the differential in award rates between black and non-black women—but less than one third of that between ever-married and never-married women—can be accounted for by racial or marital status differences in average socioeconomic characteristics. We then assess the impact of various changes over time in the population eligible for child support on the aggregate award rate, which rose 2.2 percentage points between 1979 and 1986. Among other things, we show that its rise would have been nearly twice as large had the proportion of the eligible population never married not increased.

Finally, by restricting our attention to ever-married mothers, for whom we know the year of marital disruption, we study historical trends in the likelihood that a mother who becomes newly eligible for child support will obtain an award. Extending our analysis in chapter 2, we show that new award rates have been rising at least since 1958 and have risen more quickly for blacks than nonblacks. We also show that the secular increase in new award rates, especially among nonblacks, slowed considerably after 1975, coincident with the introduction of federal child support enforcement legislation. We speculate on the causes of this apparent slowdown in the growth of new awards and offer evidence that much of it can be attributed to the stagnation in the growth of real incomes of men after 1973.

Demographic Determinants of Award Rates

In this section we examine the statistical association between certain socioeconomic characteristics of a mother and her children and the likelihood that she has a child support award. As we argued in chapter 3, whether or not a mother obtains a child support award depends in part upon her own behavior and in part upon that of the children's father. Her decision to seek an award depends upon her expected needs for support and her perceived costs of obtaining it, whereas his decision to offer one depends upon his financial ability to pay and his desire to support his children. Although we cannot observe these factors directly (in part, because the absent father could not be interviewed), the behavior of both the mother and father is likely to vary systematically with some characteristics of the mother that can be observed. The results discussed here, which are derived from multivariate probit analyses, show the effect of a one unit change in a given characteristic on the likelihood of having a child support award, all else being equal.

We present these estimates in table 4.1, for all women eligible for child support, and for ever-married and never-married mothers separately. Rather than discussing the effect of all characteristics in detail, we highlight only the most significant ones, relating them back to the underlying concepts of mother's needs for and costs of support and the father's ability and desire to pay. Our discussion focuses on all women, but we note significant differences by marital status where they occur.

Ex ante, a mother's education has an indeterminate effect on award rates since it serves as a proxy (substitute) for both her expected needs and his ability to pay. All else being equal, the greater her education the less likely she is to require financial assistance from the father, but given positive assortative mating, the more able he is to provide it. Ex post, we find a positive relation: among all mothers, each additional year of education is on average associated with a 2.8 percentage point increase in the likelihood of having a child support award. The effect of education, however, is nonlinear at the upper end: college graduates are only 4.3 percentage points (rather than 11.2 points) more likely to have an award than high school graduates. Among the never married, the only significant (and positive) association between award rates and education is whether or not the mother has graduated from high school.

Like education, the mother's age may reflect the earnings potential of both parents. Age, however, may also be a proxy for the date of the marital disruption. Older women whose disruptions occurred longer ago may be less likely to have an award if the likelihood of obtaining support has risen over time. When we do not control for the date of the marital disruption, the mother's current age has a small but significantly negative effect. All else equal, women who are ten years older than average are 2 percentage points less likely to have an award or 3 points less likely if they have never been married. But when we control for the date of marital disruption directly, age is no longer significantly related to award status, suggesting that, among ever-married mothers, age primarily captures differences in dates of disruption.

As we saw in chapter 2, the likelihood of obtaining an award differs sharply by race and ethnicity, which reflect a variety of cultural and economic factors. Holding differences other than race (or ethnicity) constant, we find that the award rate of black (Hispanic) women is 15.4 (11.5) percentage points lower than that of nonblacks (non-Hispanics). These ceteris paribus differentials are less than half the size of the aggregate differentials observed in chapter 2. This suggests, as we show in detail in the next section, that more than half of the aggregate racial differential in award rates can be explained by differences in characteristics of the mother.

Like race, current marital status reflects a variety of factors, including differences in mother's needs, father's ability to pay, and the legal environment. We find that a mother who has never married is 62.7 percentage points less likely to have an award compared with a mother with the same socioeconomic characteristics who is currently divorced. A separated (remarried) woman is 33.2 (4.3) percentage points less likely to have an award than an otherwise identical divorced women. These ceteris paribus differentials by marital status are almost as large as the aggregate differentials we reported in chapter 2. This suggests that unlike racial differentials, marital status differentials in award rates are largely unexplained by differences in the mother's socioeconomic characteristics.

The number and ages of the children affect both the mother's needs and the father's desire to pay. All else equal, we find that each additional child raises the probability of having an award by 2.2 percentage points. If one or more of the children is aged six to seventeen, the likelihood of an award is 11.2 percentage points higher than if all the children are younger or older.

Award rates also differ by geographic location. We find that women living within the boundaries of a central city of a metropolitan area (SMSA) are 3 percentage points less likely to have an award than those who live in the suburbs. Like central city residence, region may reflect cultural and cost-of-living differences, but it is also likely to capture legal differences pertaining to marital dissolution and child support. Although laws concerning divorce, paternity establishment, child custody, and child support awards differ from state to state, states that share a common boundary often have a history or tradition of similar legislation. We find that women in north central states are 5.3 percentage points more likely to have an award, while women in the Northeast are 2.4 points less likely to have an award than otherwise identical women living in the West.

Accounting for Racial and Marital Status Differentials

Some of the most striking findings to emerge from our aggregate analyses in chapter 2 were the large differentials in award rates by race and marital status. Of course, we might expect some differential by race (or marital status) because, on average, black (never-married) women differ from nonblack (ever-married) women in some important respects. For example, as we have just seen, women with more education and those living outside of the central city are more likely to have a child support award. We have also seen that on average black women have less education and are less likely to live outside of the central city than nonblacks. Thus, we might expect that, on average, blacks will have a lower award rate than nonblack women. In what follows, we attempt to divide racial and marital differentials in award rates into the portions that can be explained by observable demographic differences and the portions that remain unexplained. We identify particular factors that contribute the most to explaining the differential in award rates and speculate on why some of the differential remains unexplained.

RACIAL DIFFERENTIAL. Averaged over the period 1979-86, the aggregate award rate of black women was about half that of nonblacks. Among all women eligible for child support, 33.4 percent of blacks had an award, compared with 69.1 percent of nonblacks, for a racial differential of 35.7 percentage points. Although there are no discernible racial differentials in award rates among the never-married among the ever-married, blacks were 25.1 percentage points less likely to have an award. In table 4.2 we decompose these racial differentials in award rates for all eligible women and for ever-married mothers into the portions that can and cannot be explained by racial differences in demographic characteristics. . . .

To summarize, once we control for differences in marital status, age, education, family size, geographic location, and (for ever-married women) an estimate of the absent father's income, we can explain around 70 percent of the racial gap in award rates. Among all women, the difference in marital status is the single most important explanatory factor; among the ever-married, differences in the mother's characteristics and father's income are about equally important. Thus, we conclude that around 30 percent of the differential in award rates between black and nonblack women cannot be attributed to differences in observable socioeconomic factors other than race itself. As argued earlier, race per se represents a complex set of cultural, behavioral, and economic factors that are difficult to disentangle; however, we will try to consider some of the more important components.

In part, race may reflect economic and behavioral differences between black and nonblack absent fathers. When we do not control for male incomes directly, race certainly reflects the lower ability to pay of black fathers relative to their nonblack counterparts. When we approximate father's income by the income of full-time black and white male workers, we still may fail to control fully for racial differences in the ability to pay to the extent that black men are less likely to be full-time employees. In addition to ability, race may also represent differences in the father's desire to pay. Yoram Weiss and Robert Willis report that by 1985, 50 percent of black mothers who had graduated high school in 1972, compared with only 5 percent of similar white mothers, had borne one or more children before their first marriage. For one thing, a father is less likely to agree to a child support award if the mother has other children to support since he cannot be certain that all of his payment will go to his children. For another, if a father has children by several different women, his allegiance may be spread rather thin.

Among mothers, race may reflect differences in needs, especially if there are racial differences in access to alternative sources of support. For example, the social stigma attached to receiving public assistance may be less in predominantly black communities where large segments of the population already receive it. In addition, black women have been more likely to be in the labor force, at least historically, and more willing to turn to their own extended families (especially, the mother's own mother) for help in the support of their children. Finally, the black mother may be reluctant to try to formalize a child support agreement if her child's father is already providing support on an informal basis. This informality is consistent with patterns of marital disruptions among black women, for whom separations often do not end with a formal divorce.

Racial differences in access to the legal system may also contribute to the unexplained differential in award rates. Black women may be less knowledgeable about the types of legal assistance available or how to obtain help when fathers fail to offer support. Blacks may be less able to afford private attorneys and less willing to seek public legal assistance, owing perhaps to a historical distrust of government and the courts. The lower incidence of both marriage and divorce among blacks relative to nonblacks is consistent with the notion that black women are less likely to use the legal system to formalize family arrangements.

MARITAL STATUS DIFFERENTIALS. Averaged over the 1979-86 period, 15.7 percent of never-married mothers had an award, compared with 71.6 percent of ever-married mothers, for an overall differential of 55.9 percentage points. Among the ever married, award rates of currently separated women were 35.6 percentage points lower than those of the ever-divorced (i.e., currently divorced or remarried). In table 4.2 we decompose each of these differentials into the portions explained and unexplained; we identify important explanatory factors and speculate on why large residuals remain unexplained.

Never-married mothers have many characteristics that tend to lower award rates. Compared with the ever-married, they have almost one year less education; are only half as likely to have a child between the ages of six and seventeen; are nearly twice as likely to live within a central city; are more likely to live in the Northeast; are slightly more likely to be Hispanic; and are more than three times as likely to be black. Taken together, these differences explain one-third or 18.5 percentage points, of the overall differential. The most important explanatory factor is the higher proportion of never-married mothers who are black, followed by their lower incidence of children aged six to seventeen, fewer years of education, a higher incidence of central city residence, and higher proportion Hispanic

Within the ever-married group, differences in the mother's characteristics explain less of the award rate differential. Taken together, 11 observable differences in characteristics account for less than 20 percent, or 6.4 percentage points, of the differential between ever-divorced and separated women. Compared with ever-divorced women, currently separated women are three times as likely to be black, have fewer years of education, and are less likely to have a child aged six to seventeen. As above, race is the single most important explanatory factor, but 88 percent of the differential remains unexplained.

Some of the unexplained marital status differentials in award rates may be owing to differences in the father's ability and desire to pay. Income differences are likely to be large between the ever-married and the never-married. According to recent aggregate data, the average income of never-married males (age eighteen years and over who work year-round, full-time) was $19,959 in 1985, compared with $27,781 for those men currently divorced. Given even this admittedly crude approximation of income differences, we can account for an 8.1 percentage point differential in award rates between ever-married and never-married mothers, thereby reducing the unexplained residual from 37.4 percentage points to 27.3 points. In addition, fathers who have been married to their children's mother are likely to have a greater emotional attachment to their children (and to be more certain of paternity) than single fathers who may never even have shared the same household with their children. Since some never-married women have children with different men, the father of one child may be reluctant to provide support if he believes some of it will benefit children who are not his. Finally, fathers who are only separated from their children's mother may abstain from offering child support as a bargaining tactic to either speed a divorce settlement or a reconciliation.

Some of the unexplained marital status differentials may also be from differences in the mother's costs and benefits of obtaining a child support award. Unlike the ever-married, never-married mothers may have to locate their child's father and establish paternity before even attempting to secure an award. Thus, they incur not only higher legal expenses but also the social stigma of being labeled an unwed mother. In addition, even if an award is obtained, its expected value is likely to be very low, as we saw in chapter 2. Thus, given the high costs and meager benefits, many never-married mothers never attempt to obtain an award from their child's father, preferring instead to make other arrangements for the child's support, such as living with their own parents. Even among the ever-married, mothers may behave differently. Unlike the ever-divorced, separated women may believe their current living arrangements to be only temporary. They may not want to insist on a formal child support order if the absent father is already providing support informally, particularly if that may further destabilize already tenuous marital relations.

Accounting for Trends in Award Rates across Survey Years

To summarize, for all marital and racial subgroups, we find that between 1979 and 1986 award rates rose by more than would have been expected on the basis of observable shifts in the composition of the population eligible for child support. What might account for these unexpected increases? In what follows we show that they can be attributed to higher award rates among those women who became *newly* eligible for child support between 1979 and 1986. Higher new award rates, in turn, may be associated with improvements in the social and legal environment surrounding the child support award process per se, a topic we investigate in greater detail in chapter 6.

It may be observed that the aggregate award rate in a given survey year represents the percentage of all women currently eligible for child support (the eligible pool) who have an award. Each year this pool changes as some mothers who are no longer eligible for support exit and other mothers who are newly eligible enter. Over time, the aggregate award rate is subject to change as women who newly enter the pool find themselves more (or less) likely than those already in it to obtain an award at the time of their marital disruption. In other words, unexpected changes in the aggregate award rate allow us to make inferences about changes in the new award rates of women who have only recently become eligible for support. If we find that the aggregate rate has risen across survey years even after adjusting for demographic changes in the eligible population, we can deduce that new award rates have been rising.

It turns out that it is possible to look behind these aggregate statistics to investigate historical trends in new award rates directly from 1958 to 1985. We then use our findings from this analysis to account for the unexpected portion of the increase in the aggregate award rate between 1979 and 1986 and to predict future trends in the award rate.

Trends in New Award Rates, 1958-1985

As in chapter 2, we define the *new* award rate as the likelihood that a mother who becomes newly eligible for child support obtains an award in a given year. Since mothers were not asked to provide the date they obtained (or attempted to obtain) an award, we restrict our attention to the ever-married and use the date of the marital disruption as a proxy for the date of the award (which allows us to trace new award rates back to 1958). [N]ew award rates of ever-married mothers have generally risen over time. They rose more for blacks than nonblacks and more for separated than divorced women. As we also noted, the upward trend in new award rates, particularly among nonblacks, appears to have slowed in the mid-1970s, coincident with the introduction of federal child support legislation in August 1975.

Why might we expect new award rates to have risen over time? As we argued in chapter 3, award outcomes depend upon the prevailing economic, social, and legal environments at the time of the marital disruption. The period since 1958 has seen rapid economic, social and legal changes—especially ones favorable to increasing award rates. On the economic front, real incomes of men (working full-time) rose 44 percent between 1958 and 1986, although most of the increase occurred before 1974. On the social front, divorce rates more than doubled between 1965 and 1980 (from 10.6 to 22.6 per 1,000 women fifteen years or older), and the number of families headed by women alone rose sharply (from 5 to 8.7 million). As a result, the stigma of divorce and single parenthood diminished, family courts dealt increasingly with the problems of marital dissolution, and social scientists, the press, and government bodies paid increasing attention to the economic impoverishment of mothers and their children. On the legal front, one result of this increased attention was the introduction of many new child support enforcement laws, particularly after 1975. . . .

ACCOUNTING FOR WHAT WE FOUND. . . .To summarize, among all ever-married mothers eligible for child support, the likelihood of obtaining a child support award upon marital disruption increased at an average annual rate of 0.47 percentage points or at a rate of 0.88 points per year from 1958 to 1975 and 0.06 points per year from 1976 to 1986. We find that we are able to account for about one-fourth of the upward trend in new award rates over the entire period and all of the apparent slowdown in the trend after 1975 on the basis of changes over time in the real income of year-round, full-time male workers in the year of the award. Controlling for these changes, we conclude that new award rates grew at an average annual rate of 0.36 percentage points over the entire period 1958 to 1986 or, in other words, rose about 1 percentage point every three years. We might attribute this remaining upward trend to changes over time in the social and legal environments surrounding the award of child support. As we will see in chapter 6, however, the first state laws about awards were established only in 1975, and even after 1975 we find no significant effect of laws on award rates. . . .

Award Amounts

Securing a child support award is only part of the first step toward ultimately receiving payment; negotiating an adequate award amount is the other part. As we saw in chapter 2, the amount of child support due varies considerably by race and marital status and in real terms declined sharply between 1978 and 1985.

We begin our analysis of award amounts by estimating how the real value of support currently due (measured in 1985 dollars) varies with the socioeconomic characteristics of the mother, the year in which the award was made, and the sample year in which it is due. Then, we use these results to try to account for racial and marital status differentials in the value of child support due and to identify reasons why the real value of support due declined during the 1980s. We conclude that about two-thirds of the differential in the value of support due between ever-married black and nonblack mothers can be explained on the basis of racial differences in mother's characteristics and in male incomes. About half of the differential in awards between ever-married and never-married mothers can be explained on the basis of differences in socioeconomic characteristics alone.

We show that demographic changes over time in the population due support and the erosion from inflation in the real value of old (i.e., existing) awards account for only a small portion of the decline in the real value of child support due between 1978 and 1985. Rather, we argue that the decline stems from the failure of new awards made after 1978 to keep up with increases in consumer prices or male incomes. Looking at historical trends in new awards directly, we show that, at least since 1958, the value of new awards obtained by ever-married mothers (measured in current dollars) has been rising only half as fast as either consumer prices or average male incomes. As a result, the real value of awards has been declining at an average annual rate of about 3.5 percent. We offer several hypotheses to explain the persistence of this decline. . . .

Accounting for Racial and Marital Status Differentials

On average, black mothers are due considerably less child support than nonblacks, and never-married mothers are due much less than the ever-married. We examine to what extent we can account for these differentials on the basis of differences in average demographic characteristics by race or marital status, and we also speculate on why a part of the differentials remains unexplained.

RACIAL DIFFERENTIALS. On average, between 1978 and 1985, black women were due $2,238 in 1985 constant dollars, or $612 (21%) less than the $2,850 due nonblack women. In statistical analyses, the details of which are not reported here, we find that we can attribute as much as one-third of this overall racial differential in dollars due to the much lower percentage of black mothers who have ever married their children's father. . . .

To summarize, while among ever-married women, we expect blacks to be due less child support than nonblacks on the basis of racial differences in the father's income, we expect blacks to be due more support on the basis of their socioeconomic characteristics. Combining these two effects, we expect ever-married black women to be due, on average, $245 less child support than nonblack women. In other words, only about one-third of the total racial differential ($127/$372) cannot be accounted for by racial differences in either the mother's characteristics or the father's income.

What accounts for the lower award amounts of blacks that cannot be explained by either demographic or income differences? As we have already suggested in our discussion of racial differences in award rates, one possibility is that our income proxy based upon the earnings of full-time workers may underestimate actual racial differences in income. In addition, even when correctly measured, income may not fully capture the full racial difference in the father's ability to pay. Recent research on racial differences in wealth show that among young families in the 1970s, the assets of blacks were about one-sixth the value of those of whites and that this wealth difference is far greater than could be expected on the basis of income differences alone. Given their lower wealth, higher unemployment rates, and lower labor force participation rates, black men may offer to pay less support than nonblacks, and many court judges may expect them to be less able to pay.

The racial differences in mother's socioeconomic characteristics that we can observe may not fully control for all differences between black and nonblack mothers. Given the lower ability to pay of black fathers, many black mothers may not believe it is worth their while to press for higher awards, particularly if that means going to court. Black women may be more willing to seek alternative sources of support for their children, including their own extended families, and public assistance. Some recent work finds that race is an important factor in explaining welfare participation: black women are significantly more likely to be on AFDC than are similar nonblacks. another study by Robert Moffitt found no racial difference in a variable measuring "welfare stigma," that is, the mother's distaste for going on AFDC.

MARITAL STATUS DIFFERENTIALS. Even larger than the racial differential in award amounts is that between never-married and ever-married mothers. As we saw in table 2.4, on average between 1978 and 1985, never-married mothers were due $1,383, or $1,460 less than the $2,843 due ever-married mothers (measured in constant 1985 dollars). Our statistical analysis suggests that somewhat less than half (46%) of this differential can be accounted for by socioeconomic factors. None of the differential can be explained by differences in family size per se, since both ever-married and never married mothers have an average of 1.7 children. Compared to the ever-married, however, never-married mothers are younger, have less education, and are more likely to be black—all characteristics associated with lower-than-average child support awards. On the basis of differences in all observable socioeconomic characteristics, we can expect never-married mothers to be due $674 less support on average than the ever-married. The $786 residual unexplained by these factors may reflect unobservable differences among mothers in their cost of obtaining support (due, in part, to additional legal hurdles for the never-married) and differences between fathers in their ability and desire to support their children.

It is likely that we could account for a substantial portion of this $786 unexplained differential in award amounts if we were able to control for differences in the father's income. On average, we would expect fathers of children of never-married mothers to have much lower incomes than those of ever-married mothers. We might approximate their income by average incomes in 1985 of men by current marital status. According to these data, the income of never-married men averaged $19,959, or 72 percent of that of divorced men of $27,781. Among ever-married mothers only, we find that each $1,000 increment to the father's income raises the value of child support due by $73. Using this relation to evaluate the $7,822 income difference by marital status, we would expect a never-married mother to be due $571 less support than an otherwise identical ever-married mother. In other words, it appears that marital status differences in father's incomes alone would be able to account for about 73 percent of the $786 unexplained differential in award amounts.

Accounting for Trends in the Amount Due across Survey Years

. . .To summarize our findings to this point, changes in the socioeconomic characteristics of ever-married mothers due support and the erosion of old awards resulting from inflation account for little of the $760 decline in the average real value of child support due between 1978 and 1985. During a period of very high inflation, 1978 to 1981, they do account for more than one-third of the decline, but during the period of relatively little inflation, 1981 to 1985, they account for none of the decline, and in fact make the unexplained decline appear even larger.

Intuitively, when we hold the observable determinants of child support due constant, the unexplained decline in the real value of support due represents changes in the underlying award process or experience itself. Hence, we can attribute unexplained changes across survey years in child support due to the entry of mothers with new awards. As we now show, the real value of *new* awards declined at an average annual rate of 3.5 percent between 1958 and 1985, causing the real value of both new awards and support due to decline almost 22 percent between 1978 and 1985.

Trends in the Value of New Awards, 1958-1985

... To summarize, on average between 1958 and 1985, the current dollar value of new awards increased about half as fast as either consumer prices or male incomes, leading to a decline in the real value of new awards at an average annual rate of 3.4 percent. This finding is important for at least two reasons. First, it means that mothers newly eligible for child support increasingly find themselves bearing a greater share of the burden for the support of their children. Second, the decline in the real value of new awards is an important part of the explanation of why, among all women due support, the real value of support due declined between 1978 and 1985. It is to this topic that we now return.

Trends in the Value of Child Support Due: Policy Implications and Projections

We have argued that, largely as a result of a continuing decline in the real value of *new* awards, the average amount of child support *due* ever-married mothers declined by more than 22 percent between 1978 and 1985. In part a response to this decline, the very first provision of the Family Support Act of 1988 mandates that states make use of numerical guidelines in setting new award amounts and that they review the adequacy of existing awards on a periodic basis.

To what extent could the decline in child support due between 1978 and 1985 have been prevented had one or both of these provisions already been in force? If all child support awards were not only reviewed but fully indexed to the price level, the real value of child support due in each of our four survey years would have been substantially greater. Specifically, suppose that all women due child support in 1978 had negotiated a fully indexed child support contract at the time of their marital disruption, automatically linking changes in their award amount each year to changes in the CPI. We calculate that rather than being due on average $3,360, they would have been due $4,445.93 In other words, the real value of support due in 1978 was almost 25 percent less than it would have been had all awards established prior to 1978 included a full cost-of-living adjustment. Table 4.9 records similar calculations for each of the other three surveys. Because of the unusually high inflation rates that occurred between 1978 and 1981, the actual average value of child support due in 1981 was almost 32 percent less than it would have been with full indexation. With lower inflation rates after 1981, the value lost because of nonindexation is somewhat less—26.5 percent as of 1985. It is clear that indexation, or at a minimum periodic review, is an important reform that would raise the average amount of child support due. . . .

If, however, our analysis of trends in award amounts through 1985 is correct, then it is likely that neither compositional changes nor changes in the value of existing awards is the principal reason why the real value of support due increased. Rather, consistent with our earlier analysis, we conjecture that the 14 percent rise in average support due is largely the result of increases of similar magnitude in the value of newly made awards. To what extent these in turn are a result of the introduction of award guidelines (made advisory by federal law in 1984 and mandatory in 1988) awaits future research.

Richard Lempert, *Organizing for Deterrence: Lessons from a Study of Child Support,* 16 LAW AND SOCIETY REVIEW 513 (1981-82)[*]

11. GENERAL DETERRENCE

Enforcement of Child Support Decrees

This paper draws on and reanalyzes data from a recent study of the enforcement of child support decrees in the state of Michigan. For comparative purposes, reference is also made to data from Dane County, Wisconsin. The data bear on a number of important issues: the existence of individual deterrence, the role of severity in individual deterrence, the way in which aggregate data may confound different responses to a sanction threat, the relationship between special and general deterrence, and the importance of organizational variables in a theory of deterrence.

The process of enforcing child support orders in Michigan is nominally civil, but the ultimate threat is a sentence of up to one year in jail as determined by a court. There are, however, important differences between the enforcement of child support decrees and the enforcement of the criminal law. While these differences inescapably limit our ability to generalize, they also highlight contingencies in deterrence theory that have not been heretofore specified, and they allow a more precise and uncontaminated measure of deterrence than has been heretofore possible.

The child support enforcement process in Michigan revolves around an organization called Friend of the Court. The office of the Friend of the Court is responsible for collecting child support payments from the noncustodial parent (almost always the father) and forwarding the money collected either to the child's custodian (almost always the mother) or to the welfare department, if the child is receiving Aid to Families with Dependent Children (AFDC). If the father falls behind in his payments, the agency may remind him of his obligation and warn him of the sanction he faces, work out special payment arrangements, and, if less drastic measures do not stimulate payment, arrest the father and have him jailed for contempt of the court's support order. Because jail for nonpayment of child support is a civil sanction, the accused "carries the keys to the jail in his own pocket." If he complies with the court order by paying his entire debt, the court must order his release. In practice, few who are jailed can pay off their entire debt, but many can manage part payment.

The decision to jail is in principle a judge's, but judges in the county where the process was most closely studied almost always followed the lead of the Friend of the Court in deciding whether to impose a jail term. They also left it to the Friend of the Court to determine whether an offer to pay only part of an accrued debt was sufficient to avoid a jail sentence or to be released from one that was being served.

The enforcement of child support obligations may be distinguished in three crucial respects from the ordinary process of enforcing the criminal law. One distinction is a matter of degree. Certainty of detection, a key source of variance in deterrence research, is seldom problematic. The failure to pay child support is readily discovered,

---

and the person responsible is always known. In the county most closely studied, biweekly computer printouts alert enforcement officers to both. Apprehension for continued failure to pay is difficult only in the larger counties and unlikely only where the father has left the jurisdiction. With detection certain and apprehension easy, one would expect deterrent effects to be substantial, provided only that there is a substantial marginal group.

The two other distinctions are distinctions in kind. First, the organization of the enforcement process allows *targeted threats*. The threat inherent in the criminal law is communicated to unnamed persons who may or may not be violating or contemplating a violation of the law. In the child support setting, one who has missed a payment may be addressed and warned (threatened) by name. The targeted threat is arguably not a specific deterrent as that term has been traditionally defined, because the warned violator has not experienced punishment. He has merely received an additional threat, albeit one which is specific in a way that the threat inherent in a general statute is not. Yet, the distinction may, for certain purposes, be "without a difference." Receiving a targeted threat is like punishment in that it is a personal experience that increases the salience of the threat inherent in the general legal command. It is for that reason that one would expect the ability to target threats to enhance deterrence.

Second, the threat or imposition of a jail sentence for failure to pay child support is *coercive* in a way that the usual criminal sanction is not. Its goal is to force people to do something they would rather not do, while the goal of threatened or actual criminal punishment is usually to persuade people not to do things they would rather do. This distinction has important implications for surveillance capacity which in turn relates to the certainty of punishment. Ordinarily it is easier to determine whether someone has done something he has been ordered to do than to determine whether he has refrained from forbidden action. In the one case, showing that a specific action has been taken (e.g., making a weekly payment) is enough to prove compliance. Showing specific actions, however many and however law abiding, will not prove that the forbidden action was not also taken. The distinction may also have important implications for the kinds of treatments that will promote compliant behavior.

However, surveillance is not an end in itself. The way in which an enforcement agency uses information is crucial. In child support cases, even if there is no agency to collect and transfer money, the mother, at least, will know when the court's order has been violated and who is responsible. However, if she must mobilize officials to act, the deterrent potential of the child support laws will depend on the willingness of an agency to respond to her requests. Even if the enforcement agency routinely responds to private complaints, the implications for deterrence of a reactive system may differ substantially from the implications of a proactive system.

Andenaes, Chambliss, and others have pointed out that deterrence processes are likely to work differently in different areas of the law. The failure to pay child support may be regarded as a "specific offense" that has not heretofore received the attention of deterrence theorists. It is only by attending to a range of such offenses that we will develop a general theory of deterrence. Obviously one cannot readily generalize from deterrence in the child support context to the deterrence of murder, armed robbery, or auto theft; but the reason is because child orders are enforced civilly while index felonies are crimes. There are just as salient differences between the enforcement of traffic offenses or of drinking laws on skid row and the enforcement of major felony statutes. Only by attending to deterrence in a variety of settings can we learn which variables are crime or situation-specific and which apply across settings. . . .

TABLE 3. CRUCIAL VARIABLES IN EXPLAINING MEAN PAYMENT RATE FOR 28 MICHIGAN COUNTIES DURING 1974-75

Variable	B	Beta	T-Ratio	Sig. Level	Unique Contribution to R**	R² if Alone
High Jail/Proactive*	14.8	.64	6.36	.001	.40	.51
Log$_{10}$ Population	-10.8	-.47	-4.72	.001	.22	.27
Unemployment Rate	-2.65	-.22	-2.20	.05	.05	.09
Total R² = 76.5 (unadjusted); 73.6 (adjusted)						

* This variable has the value of 1 in the case of high jailing (above the median rate of jailing) proactive counties and the value of ")" for all other combinations.

**Increment in total R² when given variable is entered into the regression after the other two variables.

As can be seen, the jail/proactive factor is the most important. It explains the greatest proportion of the variance in mean payment rate when each variable is taken by itself or when each is entered after the other two variables. County population is the second most important variable. The unemployment rate is also statistically significant, but by itself explains little of the variance. When the jailing rate and the proactive factor are entered separately rather than in interaction with each other, the total explained variance diminishes by 13.7 percent (19.7 percent without adjustment), and the unemployment rate no longer contributes significantly. Entering the actual jail rate if the county is proactive and a zero if it is not also diminishes what can be explained.

These data suggest to me that what is crucial to the attainment of substantial deterrence is a sense of inevitability about the enforcement process. Potential violators must feel that meaningful punishment is the normal result of continued violation. In the proactive/high jailing counties (e.g., Genesee) this feeling is likely to exist. Fathers under orders who know or hear of others who have been sentenced to jail will learn that for these men skipping several payments resulted in warnings which if ignored were followed by jail. While they may know people who at some time built up large arrearages, they will know few who ceased payment entirely and "got away with it." In reactive counties like Washtenaw, or in counties where the agency does not act at all, like Dane, fathers may, if the jail rate is sufficiently high, know some men have been jailed for nonpayment of support. However, they are also likely to know men who have stopped paying and been ignored. In these circumstances, jail may seem to be a haphazard or random event. One would expect a deterrence system that appears to punish violators by chance (the unlucky) to be less effective with those at the margin than a system in which punishment appears to be a normal contingency of violation, even if both systems punish similar proportions of the relevant population. Only in the latter circumstances is a man fully responsible for his fate.

Whether or not one accepts this analysis, the findings of Chambers' 28-county study together with the results of the Dane-Genesee comparison have an important implication for deterrence studies that use aggregated measures of objective uncertainty: *the implications of a sanction rate for an offense rate may depend on how that sanction rate is generated.* The failure to attend to the way rates are generated may explain why researchers seeking to predict crime rates from sanction measures often find significant associations without ever being able to explain more than a modest proportion of the total variance. . . .

A Payment Climate?

Michigan counties have been classified proactive or reactive on the basis of how they handle nonwelfare cases. When a woman receives AFDC, all Friends of the Court in Michigan take a proactive stance. Yet the proactive factor is nearly as important in explaining variations among counties in their welfare cases as it is in their caseload as a whole. Chambers suggests that this may be because proactivity serves as a proxy for other organizational variables that make for a persistent and efficient collection system. Several aspects of the enforcement process, including thoroughness of bookkeeping, size of the enforcement staff, and dollar expenditure in relation to caseload, correlate mildly with both performance and proactivity. I would suggest another, although not mutually exclusive, explanation—namely, that county proactivity, with all it stands for (including, perhaps, a more efficient and persistent staff) when coupled with the substantial use of jail, creates a "payment climate" which affects men similarly regardless of their ex-wives' welfare status. The climate may result either directly from the existence of the threat or indirectly with community customs or normative sentiments, which would not exist at different levels of threat, serving as immediately antecedent variables.

The communication necessary to generate and sustain a "payment climate" probably exists. In Genesee, by no means the highest jailing county in Michigan, one father in four will spend at least a few hours in jail over the life of a decree. Thus many, if not most, men in the Friend of the Court's caseload will have been jailed for child support or will know someone who has been. A sense of inevitability may develop when other men within friendship or work groups are known to have been pursued and perhaps jailed for failure to pay support. Of course, communication networks may also contribute to the development of a "nonpayment climate" if some men known to be delinquent in support payments are not pursued and others are said to receive threats that are never consummated.

If what is crucial to deterrence is a sense that apprehension and punishment are the likely results of failing to pay child support, the influence of county size is explained. Fathers in less populous counties must feel, and indeed are, substantially more visible than those in the larger counties. If one is tied by a job or family connections to a county of fifty thousand, there is no place to hide. Punishment upon failing to pay child support is likely to be seen as an almost inevitable contingency if the Friend of the Court enforces the law vigorously. In a county with several million people (like Wayne County, Michigan, the home of Detroit), a change in one's place of residence and daily routine will for a period of time render one immune to capture. More importantly perhaps, it may give one the feeling he is immune. Chambers' study supports the hypothesis that effects of differences in the organization of deterrence processes are attenuated by increased size. Among counties with populations under 100,000, the differences in the mean portion of the judgments collected by proactive/high jail counties, and the mean portions collected by proactive/low jail, reactive/high jail and reactive/low jail counties are 15 percent, 25 percent, and 16 percent, respectively. For counties with more than 100,000 people, the respective differences are 7 percent, 10 percent, and 12 percent. However, there are so few counties in the different cells that these results can at most be considered suggestive. . . .

III. LESSONS FOR SPECIFIC DETERRENCE

Now let us turn to a specific concept that is important to theory but rarely treated empirically. Indeed, with the possible exception of Murray and Cox, no one working with aggregate as opposed to anecdotal data has, to this time, been able to identify a situation in which it seemed likely that the *deterrent* impact of incarceration increased subsequent law-abiding behavior. While it appears that there is at least a substantial minority of incarcerated first offenders who do not offend again, we do not know what proportion has been specifically deterred from future crimes, how many have again engaged in crime but not been caught, and how many are refraining from crime for reasons that have little to do with deterrence.

Most research on recidivism avoids the deterrence issue. Inherent in the controlled designs and multivariate methods which characterize the best investigations of recidivism is the decision to ignore those special deterrent effects that may be consistently associated with arrest and punishment. Independent variables in research on recidivism typically are limited to characteristics of the convict (e.g., age at release from prison); characteristics of the prison or parole experience (e.g., was group counseling mandatory); or characteristics of the setting that the convict reenters (e.g., availability of a full-time job). Only rarely have researchers attempted to measure the effects of factors that might be interpreted as indicators of deterrence while controlling for the likelihood that the most severe punishments are visited on the worst candidates for "rehabilitation."

The civil offense of failure to pay child support has three characteristics which facilitate the search for evidence of special deterrence. First, the extreme sanction is a jail rather than a prison sentence. Most jails, unlike many prisons, do not attempt to "treat" their inmates. It is certainly true that in the county we shall focus on, jail was a (most uncomfortable) place to spend time and not a place to be rehabilitated. Thus, behavioral changes following a jail sentence cannot plausibly be attributed to rehabilitative programs. Second, subsequent offending will always be discovered and may be measured with precision. Thus, the data are not confounded by the possibility that many of those classified as law-abiding are in fact recidivists who have not been caught. Furthermore, deterrent effects that result in only partial or temporary compliance with the legal norm may be measured. This is so because one may determine for each releasee what proportion of the amount due was paid and how long such payments continued. Finally, it is reasonable to assume that if the unpleasantness of jail or the threat of jail did not have some effect on subsequent behavior, the pattern of nonpayment that led to jail or the threat thereof would continue. Nothing is likely to occur while the father is in jail which absent jail would increase his probability of payment. Fathers are unlikely to grow closer to their children or former spouses while incarcerated, and their ability to earn the money needed to make payments can be expected to diminish rather than increase. While nonpaying fathers who are not jailed do not suffer the same disabilities as those incarcerated, too, once they lose the habit of paying child support, are unlikely to have aspects of their incentive structure apart from threat—change so as to make renewed payment likely.

The aggregate data from Dane and Washtenaw Counties are consistent with, though not proof of, the assumption that the threat and experience of punishment are for most men the only contingencies likely to change entrenched habits of nonpayment. Data from Genesee County allow a more rigorous test of the possibility of special deterrence. The data included formation on a nonjailed control group. Although post hoc attempts to control are necessarily imperfect, since entrenched bits of nonpayment are unlikely to change without official intervention, imperfections in the attempt to control do not seriously threaten our attempt to identify a deterrent effect. Whatever the behavior of the control group, payments made by those jailed during or following incarceration should be attributable in some way to the punishing experience.

Table 4 reports responses to the four principal devices used by the Genesee Friend of the Court to stimulate child support payment: the *warning,* harsh and threatening in tone but leading to no adverse consequences if heeded; the *wage assignment,* described in detail below; *the judicial appearance,* solemn threat on occasion formalized in probation or a suspended sentence and issued in a setting where the feared consequences of jail can follow immediately if nonpayment is not satisfactorily explained or future compliance promised; and the *jail sentence,* in Genesee County usually for a full year unless vacated upon payment of the debt or commuted when a payment plan is accepted by the Friend of the Court. The data presented in Table 4 are drawn from individual payment histories but are organized around specific enforcement efforts. Since most fathers are subject to more than one enforcement effort over the life of a decree, the data on two or more enforcement efforts may reflect the behavior of the same person at different points in time. . . .

When we turn to Table 4, we shall look first at the efficacy of different efforts in inducing lump sum payments, one-time responses to an actual or imminent sanction. The lump sum payment belongs to a category of behavior I call "avoidance responses." The incidence of avoidance responses is reflected in measures of general deterrence, but they occur in circumstances that give them special characteristics not heretofore attended to by students of deterrence. We must understand these circumstances and their implications for deterrence theory before we examine the data.

Avoidance Responses

The fact that a painful experience or the imminent threat of a painful experience induces compliant behavior does not mean that compliance will continue when the pain ceases or becomes less imminent. An analogy may be made to a looter who approaches a store during a riot intending to steal a television but leaves upon seeing a police officer standing guard. We can (and would) say that the police officer's presence deterred the looter from crime, but the fear which deterred is so situation-specific that the looter's decision to obey the law in this instance gives little reason to expect that he will spare the next appliance store if he finds it unguarded. This contrasts with the situation where there is a deterrent effect attributable to sanctions that are less imminent. One who refrains from breaking into a store to steal a television because he perceives a 25 percent chance that he will be punished is unlikely to break into the next appliance store he sees.

If we could know subjective perceptions, we would interpret threat-induced compliance differently depending on the perceived imminence of the threatened sanction. Where sanctions were seen as distant and problematic, law-abiding behavior in situations of temptation would predict future compliance. Where sanctions were seen as imminent and certain, law-abiding behavior would have little predictive value. In the latter situation, one might think of law-abiding behavior as an *avoidance response,* for the behavior of the would-be criminal (i.e., what deterrence has led him to do or that behavior which occurs in lieu of what he has been deterred from) is similar to the action of the psychologist's rat that must press a lever or move from a grid in order to escape actual or threatened shock.

What is crucial to an avoidance response is the existence or imminence of punishment. Imminence combines two qualities that have been treated as separate variables in classic formulations of deterrence theory: certainty and celerity. We can say that punishment is imminent when it is virtually certain to be applied in the very near future. The imminence of punishment may, of course, be contingent on the forbidden act. Since apprehension for a crime is in itself punishing, it is likely that perceptions of celerity are, as an empirical matter, consistently associated with perceptions of certainty. From this perspective we can understand why celerity has been largely ignored or found to be unimportant in the modern empirical research on deterrence. If the effect of celerity is largely to induce avoidance responses, differences in celerity from the time of apprehension to the time for formal sanctioning, such as imprisonment, should matter very little. The difference that does matter, from the time the crime is committed to the time of the first punishing response, typically apprehension, is confounded with a measure conventionally understood only as an indicator of certainty.

Indices of the effectiveness of general deterrence, such as the crime rate, may reflect the prevalence of avoidance responses in a jurisdiction. While one might expect the avoidance response component of such an index to be minimal, since persons so deterred have no general threat-induced proclivity not to commit a crime, in the case of crimes that are essentially unplanned reactions to vulnerable targets—and much juvenile crime may be of this sort—or that depend on the vulnerability of targets that can be made less vulnerable as was the case with airplane hijacking—structuring situations to elicit avoidance responses may substantially depress crime rates. To the extent that situations which can be structured to induce a substantial rate of avoidance responses are only sometimes so structured, variance in crime rates should depend far more on situational than on individual characteristics. An example that must be hypothetical for lack of variance is airplane hijacking. One would expect the presence or absence of an airport security system to more accurately predict the probabilities of hijacking than the number of radicals or mentally ill individuals who use a particular airport.

In this paper avoidance responses will be treated as an aspect of deterrence, and deterrence attributable to avoidance responses will at places be combined with deterrence attributable to fears of certain but less imminent punishment. At other places avoidance responses will be treated separately, for there will often be good theoretical reasons to distinguish between the ways that threats or punishment deter.

Lump Sum Payments

The lump sum payment tends to satisfy a legal normative requirement but it does not necessarily reflect a commitment to law-abiding behavior rooted in the fear of sanctions. Conceiving of the lump sum as an avoidance response, it is not surprising that lump sums are most commonly paid by jailed men. Men in jail are very much like the behaviorist's rat. They are actually being punished and know that the only way to cut the punishment short is to pay a substantial portion of their debt.

Nevertheless the magnitude of the payment rate differences is striking. More than half of those who are jailed make a lump sum payment, compared to less than five of those who agree to wage assignments and only a quarter of those warned by mail or by a judge in court. To some extent these differences reflect the outcome of negotiations involving fathers, enforcement officers, and on occasion, judges. The fact that lump sums are almost never paid by those who agree to wage assignments does not reflect the absence of substantial debts among this group of fathers. The median debt owed by those agreeing to wage assignments is $527, or about 17 weeks' worth of payment, and the mean debt is more than twice this amount. However, a father who agrees to enter a wage assignment is allowed to amortize his debt by, for example, paying $40 a week on a $30 a week order, the excess being credited to the accrued debt.

Acceptance of wage assignments does not explain the differences between the judge and jail groups. Although 21 percent of those fathers who appear before a judge and are not jailed are placed on a wage assignment, a similar proportion of men released early from jail are asked only to sign a wage assignment. The difference lies in the fact that about 70 percent of those released early from jail are released only after they have made a lump sum payment. About 50 percent of those who appear before a judge and are not jailed are given more time, presumably upon a promise to pay a lump sum and/or begin regular payments. Some manage to keep their promise, while others do not.

A difference in negotiating contexts cannot, however, explain the fact that the jailed are more than twice as likely to make lump sum payments as those merely warned. Such payments are demanded of the warned, and they do not negotiate alternatives. This payment pattern is also unlikely to reflect differences in ability to pay. Such differences tend to favor the warned.

The most likely explanation for the different responses to warnings and jail lies in the harshness of the latter sanction, particularly the immediacy with which pain is felt. Jail is more likely to elicit avoidance responses. Since these are responses to punishment imposed, we may think of them as an example, albeit a special kind of example, of individual deterrence.

When we look at the subset of individuals who actually made lump sum payments, we see that the largest dollar payments were made by those brought to court but not jailed. However, the difference between this group and the jailed group would not be large (median payments are the same) but for the presence of two cases involving very high payments. The median sum paid by those who responded to warnings is about half as much as that made by men responding to judicial pressure or jailing.

When payments are measured with respect to amounts owed, a different picture emerges. Those judged but not jailed pay lump sums that on the average amount to only 37 percent of what they owe, and the median payment clears only 18 percent of the debt. This contrasts with a median sum among those jailed that clears 60 percent of what is owed and a median sum among the warned that clears 63 percent of their debt. The high mean figure for the warned group reflects the fact that the figure for the proportion of the debt paid divides the amount received after the effort by the amount owed at the time of the effort. Men warned about small amounts owed might wait several weeks and then send payments that cleared the then current debt but amounted to 150 percent or more of the sum owed at the time the warning was issued. Looking only at the 186 warnings issued to men who owed more than $315 (95 percent of those jailed owed this amount or more), we find that the average person paying cleared only 44 percent of his debt. Thus, for debts closer to the size found in the jailed sample, a warning—when it has any return—returns, on the average, a third less of what is owed.

The pattern of lump sums elicited from those jailed is surprisingly high given the unemployment rate, alcoholism, arrest records within this group. However coercive a sanction, it is hard to see how it can be effective if the recipients are unable to comply. One would expect that many of those jailed, perhaps a substantial majority, would not have sufficient funds to buy their way out at the Friend of the Court's going rate.

The answer to this puzzle may lie in an interesting characteristic of the lump sum which distinguishes it, in a known number of instances, from effects commonly associated with deterrence. Threats that deter are assumed to because of their primary impact on potential violators of legal norms While no statistics are available on who pays lump sums anecdotal evidence indicates that lump sum payments often come not from the father himself but from his parents, friends, siblings, second wife, or current girlfriend. Thus, one effect of threatened punishment for nonpayment of child support is to induce fathers to seek the aid of third parties and to induct third parties to rescue the father. One wonders whether analogous effects may be attributed to other laws. When violations are made illegal, do parents and others who fear seeing their loved one punished take special steps to insure that those they care for do not violate the law. If such effects exist, it will be difficult, if not impossible, to distinguish them, at the aggregate level, from the deterrent effects of threatened sanctions on potential law breakers. . . .

These data illustrate the dangers of working with aggregate data in an area as complicated as deterrence. It is to be expected that factors associated with personality, social structure, and the actual or threatened experience of sanctions will interact. The interaction may be such that similar sanctions will in different circumstances have opposite implications for subsequent conformity. *In this situation aggregate data may make it appear as if the sanctions studied had little if any impact when behavior was, in fact, substantially changed in diverse ways.*

Measures which aggregate behavior "within" individuals may also hamper the search for deterrent effects. The chief offender is the use of recidivism after some number of years as a measure of deterrence. The measure may confound a period in which deterrence was viable with a period in which the deterrent effect ceases and in the usual case will ignore differences in the rate of offending. In Genesee County, for example, almost 60 percent of those who began periods of payment after their release from jail stopped within 24 months of their release, and most of these men did not, during the period in which they paid, fully comply with their legal obligations. Had this research been limited to measures as insensitive as recidivism within a year, deterrent effects associated with jail might not have been spotted. . . .

Returning to Table 5, we note that the most salient feature in the data is the marked difference between the collection experience in Genesee and Macomb Counties. Macomb during the year studied did substantially better than Genesee at tracing periods of regular payments among those released from jail. The socioeconomic status of men jailed in Macomb is known, but other information suggests that they were not substantially better candidates for "rehabilitation." About the same portion of men in each county were being jailed for the second (to sixth) time, and the arrearages of those jailed in each county were comparable and high. (In each county about two-thirds of the men were behind by at least half a year's payment). Furthermore, the use of wage assignments upon release, which indicate that the father had a job lined up, seems to have been substantially more common in Genesee. Macomb does jail at a somewhat higher rate than does Genesee, and to this extent may be jailing people better able to pay.

But the difference in jail rates does not seem sufficient to explain the difference in results. The most salient difference between the two counties is in time served in jail. In Macomb the median time served was 13 days, while in Genesee it was 52 days. This is in part because Genesee's judges set longer sentences than Macomb's, in part because Genesee's judges, implementing a policy by the Genesee Friend of the Court, demanded higher lump sums for release than did the judges in Macomb. In Macomb where the median lump sum paid was $360, 68 percent of those had bought their way out. In Genesee the median lump payment was $500, and 52 percent of the men bought their way out of jail.

Time served appears to be associated with subsequent payment behavior. Table 7 presents the data for Genesee and Macomb Counties. In both counties those who served the least in jail paid the most after release. The effect is particularly powerful in Genesee, where those who served three days or less (whom we shall call "short servers") paid at average rate five times higher than those who served 91 days or more ("long servers"). It is likely that those who served short sentences were, for reasons apart from their time in jail, substantially better payment risks than those serving extended terms. However, the multiple classification analysis reported in Table 8 suggests that for Genesee County, the only county for which we have detailed data, this is only a partial explanation of the difference in payment rates. After adjusting other factors that might explain post-jail payments, those jailed for three days or less are still expected to pay at twice the rate of those jailed for 91 days or more. Of the factors knowable at the time a father is released from jail, the time served before release is the single best predictor of subsequent payment rates.

The most plausible explanation for this finding is that a lengthy jail sentence may change the tenor of the lesson conveyed or the conditions under which one reenters the community. One would expect, for example, that long sentences are associated with difficulties in finding work upon release, and they might also increase a man's resentment toward his former spouse and thus increase his reluctance to pay.

The relationship between time served and payment rates may also be explained on grounds that relate to deterrence. While the general deterrent effect of the threat of jail is likely to vary directly, if at all, with the length of time likely to be served, the special deterrent effect may diminish with time served. For a brief period the contrast between jail and freedom may give a special horror to the jail experience. However, some men serving long sentences may grow accustomed to jail and come to feel that it is not that bad.

Thus, those who experience only a few days in jail may regard the prospects of a subsequent lengthy sentence with substantially more horror than would those who have already spent a long time in jail.

Overall, serving a long sentence appears more likely to induce migration from the county than to induce payments upon release. Fifty-three percent of the long servers left Genesee after they were released from jail, compared to 21 percent of the short servers. This may be because long servers found that their ties to the county were ruptured during their time in jail, or it may be that they spent so long in jail because they had few strong ties to the county to begin with. It is also possible that serving an extended period of time caused men to fear remaining in Genesee. This would not be expected if short sentences have greater special deterrent force than long ones, but it is possible, if not likely, that the reactions of some people to lengthy sentences will be quite different from the reactions of others. Whatever the reason, when leaving the county upon release from jail is added to the variables in Table 8, it becomes the single best predictor of subsequent low payments, yet it does not reduce significantly the importance of time served. . . .

In Genesee, those intimidated by the threat alone can see that those who have ignored the threat tend to be jailed, or they can ignore the threat and find that they are on the brink of being jailed. To the extent that those who would not have been intimidated by an empty threat resume payment without being arrested, their subsequent payments reflect the general deterrent impact of punishment on others. However, an implication of the comparison with Dane is that this impact would have been minimal had not a threat *with their name on it* made those receiving it particularly concerned with the fate of others who had engaged in the deviance they were contemplating. From this perspective, the targeted threat seems to combine mechanisms of specific and general deterrence. It has an effect because it changes the experience of those who receive it. One way it changes experience is by increasing the salience of the experience of others who have engaged in the contemplated deviance.

Before concluding, we should attend to one final organizational variable: the wage assignment. The above discussion suggests that the crucial difference between Genesee and Washtenaw lies in the proactivity of the Genesee Friend of the Court and the incremental fear which warnings in Genesee are likely to induce because fathers know that their failure to respond is first step on a short road to jail. Yet, it is possible that what a proactive county does and how it channels the fear it arouses is as important as the fact that it is proactive or that its policies are in some sense terrifying. In Genesee, the Friend of the Court often seeks wage assignments from men who are not paying. Chambers found that 43 percent of the Genesee random sample were, at least once in the life of their orders, placed on a wage assignment.

We have already seen that the returns from wage assignments are substantial. When wage assignments are contrasted to second warnings, they produce, on the average, 41 more weeks of payments. In comparison with jailing they produce, after taking into account the lump sums that jail elicits, the equivalent of 28 additional weeks of regular payment, and they do not cause the lapse in payment associated with incarceration. One must be cautious in comparing the group on wage assignments with groups jailed or warned because those on wage assignments are more likely to have been employed steadily and more likely to have had certain types of jobs (e.g., skilled or unskilled work in the auto industry) than those treated in other ways. However, wage assignments in Genesee almost always follow a period of nonpayment and almost never are the first treatment used. Therefore, it is likely that the returns to wage assignments are substantially higher than the returns that would have been produced by other methods. Since Genesee used at least one wage assignment in 43 percent of its cases while Washtenaw used them in only 12 percent of its cases, the use of wage assignments may account for a substantial proportion of the difference in the amounts collected by the two counties over the lives of their decrees. Indeed, it might seem that the differential use of wage assignments could explain those differences in collection rates that are associated, in the 28-county study, with the interaction of proactivity and high jailing. However, from the fragmentary evidence cited in footnote 14, it appears that this is not the case. Nevertheless, the differences between Washtenaw and Genesee counties should alert us to another organizational contingency. It may be that in coercing behavior *it is not only the degree of threat that is important but also the organizational options that exist for ensuring future compliance by those induced by threat to cooperate on at least one occasion.* It is also possible that the two interact. Wage assignments may be terminated by quitting work. Fathers in Genesee may have been more reluctant to quit their jobs than were similarly situated men in Washtenaw.

IV. CONCLUSION

Ideal types have a long and honorable history in the sciences, both physical and social. Their limitations are familiar. They are abstract constructs, in their very purity unlike any entity or situation which in fact exists. They are at the poles of continua, whereas the real is distributed between poles. They have endured not because scientists are unaware of their limitations but because of their utility in advancing theoretical discussion. The child support collection process in Genesee County, Michigan has, in its relation to deterrence theory, some of the characteristics of an ideal type. Neither the fact of offending nor the identity of the offender may be hidden from the authorities; and, except in those cases where the father leaves the jurisdiction, continued violation is almost certain to be sanctioned. But the child support enforcement process is not an abstract concept; it is an existing system. As such it is interesting in its own right. If Chambers (1979) has identified an effective way of collecting child support payments, the transfer of literally billions of dollars may be affected (New York Times, 1979). If our own inquiry into this system provided convincing evidence of general and specific deterrence, we can be satisfied, despite the ambiguity of prior research, that these forms of social control are in some circumstances viable ways of ordering human behavior.

However, there are great differences between the child support enforcement process and systems of sanctioning those felony crimes that are of most interest to deterrence theorists. The child support system we have investigated is like an ideal type in that its primary utility is to highlight certain possibilities or relationships and suggest key variables for future exploration. If the reality of the child support system gives it an advantage over an ideal type, it is that our confrontation with data forces us to ask questions which we might not have thought to pose of pure types, and it shows us relationships which might not have been visible in a mere construct.

This investigation suggests a series of propositions about deterrence and the traditional methods of looking for deterrent effects, which at this stage in theory development should be taken as hypotheses to be tested. The propositions are stated generally, because their implications are not limited to the setting which suggested them. Some are not original but have been generally ignored since they were first advanced, while others are, to my knowledge, new:

1. Certainty, celerity, and severity are often confounded in measures, such as arrest and imprisonment rates, that are conventionally assumed to measure only one aspect of deterrence. This may explain the relative unimportance of severity in most published research, and the failure to attend to celerity.

2. In some settings it is possible to target threats to those on the margin of deviation. Such threats are likely to be considerably more effective in ordering behavior than threats directed to the unnamed general population would be.

3. The way an enforcement system is organized to deter may be as important or more important in preventing crime than the apprehension or conviction rate which the system generates. What is crucial to the maximization of deterrence is that the system gives those on the margin the impression that continued violation inevitably leads to sanctions. Merely knowing a sanction rate may tell us very little unless we also know how it is generated.

4. Since sentences fail to reflect other punishing ways communities organize for deterrence, the relationship between sanction severity and subsequent behavior (whether at the individual or general level) is likely to be suppressed when sentence length is the sole index of severity. The relationship is also likely to be weak if marginal differences in patterns of sentencing are psychologically slight. Thus, research on the marginal effects of incremental changes or differences in sentence length may tell us little about the place of severity in a theory of deterrence.

5. Specific deterrence are different phenomena. They interact—in complex ways. The specific deterrent effects of a sanction may depend on the level of general deterrence in the community to which the punished person returns. Thus statistics measuring specific deterrence may reflect rates of general deterrence. Conversely, rates conventionally understood as measures of general deterrence may reflect levels of specific deterrence or other forms of specific prevention. This interpenetration can be substantial if those once punished constitute a large proportion of the relevant marginal group.

6. When situations are structured so that punishment upon offending is imminent, or so that ongoing punishment will cease only if the law is complied with, avoidance responses may be engendered. Certainty and celerity are crucial to this special form of deterrence. Rates conventionally taken as measures of general deterrence may be affected substantially by the degree to which situations are structured so as to engender avoidance responses.

7. Where specific behavior is demanded, one may refine the conception of the marginal group for purposes of evaluating the effects of threats or punishment. This group consists of those with a propensity to violate who are capable of performing the desired behavior.

8. Factors associated with personality, social structure, and actual or threatened punishment may interact so that similar sanctions may have quite different implications for subsequent behavior. Where this is the case, aggregate data may suggest that the sanctions studied had little if any impact when behavior was in fact changed substantially in diverse ways. This possibility will also exist where a sanction has different implications for general and specific deterrence.

9. Finally and most important, to understand how punishments deter, we must attend more closely to group processes and organizational variables. If I am correct in my analysis it is in this direction that significant advances in deterrence theory lie.

CHAPTER VII

An Understanding Heart:
Child Custody Decisions

Over the last twenty-five years, custody decisions have come to affect a very large number of children, and parents, annually. The following table summarizes living arrangements for children in 1994.

LIVING ARRANGEMENTS FOR ALL CHILDREN UNDER 18: 1994
(N = 69,508,000)[1]

LIVING ARRANGEMENT	NUMBER OF CHILDREN	% OF ALL CHILDREN
TWO PARENTS		
Biological Parents[2]	38,467,000	55%
Step-parents	9,617,000	14%
Total	48,084,000	69%
MOTHER ONLY		
Never Married	6,000,000	9%
Separated	3,124,000	5%
Divorced	5,799,000	8%
Widowed	696,000	1%
Other	714,000	1%
Total	16,334,000	24%
FATHER ONLY		
Divorced	1,077,000	2%
All Others	1,180,000	2%
Total	2,257,000	4%
NEITHER PARENT	2,866,000	4%

[1]   Data taken from Arlene F. Saluter, *Marital Status and Living Arrangements: March, 1994* (CURRENT POPULATION REPORTS P20-484).

[2]   The Marital Status and Living Arrangements Reports include biological, adoptive, and step parents in the category of two parents in the home. The data presented reflect other data indicating that step parent families make up approximately 20% of all two-parent families.

One measure of the potential for custodial disputes is the incidence of single-parent and remarried families with children. Twenty-five years ago, one-parent families were uncommon. Only 13% of all families with children in 1970 were headed by a single parent. In 1994, 28% of all such families were single-parent households.

Not all of these single-parent families are the result of divorce. Indeed, a child in a single-parent home in 1994 was just as likely to live with a parent who had never married as with a divorced parent. Nine percent of all children, and 36% of children in one-parent families, lived with never-married mothers, while 10% of all children and 37% of those in one-parent families lived with a divorced parent. Another 23% of the children in one-parent homes lived with a parent who was separated or living apart for some other reason. However, custodial decisions may arise in both divorced and non-marital circumstances, especially as unmarried fathers and grandparents are entitled to custodial claims.

Even the seemingly safe two-parent families are only apparently free from the risk of custodial issues. Census Bureau data include in the definition of "two parent" families all families where there are two parents, which may include step- and adoptive parents. The 69% figure for two-parent families in 1994 included a substantial number of households where the biological parent has a child from a prior relationship, whether married or not, and therefore faces a risk of custodial conflict. Only 55% of all families with children in 1994 were comprised of both of the children's natural parents and presumably free in most instances of the risk of custodial dispute.

The extent to which families face potential custody disputes differs for some subgroups from the risk for the population at large. The following table summarizes living arrangements for African-American children in 1994.

LIVING ARRANGEMENTS FOR ALL AFRICAN-AMERICAN CHILDREN UNDER 18: 1994
(N = 11,177,000)[3]

LIVING ARRANGEMENT	NUMBER OF CHILDREN	% OF ALL AFRICAN-AMERICAN CHILDREN
TWO PARENTS		
Biological Parents[4]	2,978,000	27%
Step-parents	745,000	7%
Total	3,722,000	33%
MOTHER ONLY		
Never Married	3,321,000	30%
Separated	1,126,000	10%
Divorced	1,138,000	10%
Widowed	151,000	1%
Other	230,000	2%
Total	16,334,000	53%
FATHER ONLY		
Never Married	175,000	2%
Divorced	154,000	1%
All Others	88,000	<1%
Total	417,000	4%
NEITHER PARENT	1,063,000	10%

[3]   Data taken from Arlene F. Saluter, *Marital Status and Living Arrangements: March, 1994* (Current Population Reports P20-484).

[4]   The Marital Status and Living Arrangements Reports include biological, adoptive, and step parents in the category of two parents in the home. The data presented reflect other data indicating that step parent families make up approximately 20% of all two-parent families.

It is an interesting but not, as far as we know, much explored question whether the different distribution of living arrangements increases or decreases the likelihood of custody disputes. Although the proportion of children living in two-parent families is much lower than for the overall population, African-American one-parent households are much likelier to be headed by never-married than by divorced or separated mothers. If the unmarried fathers of these children are not in a position to assert custodial claims, the incidence of custodial claims may be no greater, or even less, than the rate of such claims for all families.

The assignment of custody for children is not only a common feature of the legal and social landscape, but is generally considered the most emotionally fraught and the most difficult issue in proceedings concerning families. Courts and, to a lesser extent, legislatures have taken a variety of approaches to resolution of custodial disputes.

Until recently, domestic relations doctrine presumed that children and especially young children should be placed with their mothers (unless unfit), and that custodial authority should not be divided through joint custody arrangements. The former principle drew heavily on the empirical assumption that mothers, whether by nature or by social role, were more familiar with and better able to care for their children than were fathers. Opposition to joint custody rested on convictions that such arrangements would produce inconsistent guidance for children and reintroduce into children's lives the parental conflict that divorce sought to eliminate.

Custodial doctrine now differs considerably. The maternal preference has been widely, although not quite universally, abandoned and many jurisdictions now permit and indeed encourage joint custody. These changes were accompanied by changes in empirical assumptions. It is now assumed that it is continuity in care-giving, rather than the gender of the care-giver, that is important and that shared responsibility for children will encourage both parents to retain significant social and economic relations with them. As Franklin Zimring has observed, however, the movement toward joint custody—like that to no-fault divorce—took place with

> no public commitment or private initiative for the systematic assessment of the legal changes on patterns of custody or on child welfare. As fashions change and new interest groups emerge, family law is at risk of becoming a series of experiments that never report results in ways that can help inform the legislative process.

Franklin E. Zimring, Foreword, to Stephen D. Sugerman & Herma Hill Kay, DIVORCE REFORM AT THE CROSSROADS viii (1990).

The following three readings explore some of the questions about which one would like information in evaluating these changes in custodial policy. The first, an excerpt from an article by David Chambers, reviews the social science evidence concerning various grounds for choosing between mothers and fathers as custodians as an anodyne to reliance on ideological and political grounds. The second reading is taken from a review of the largest and best-conducted empirical study of custodial practices, Eleanor Maccoby and Robert Mnookin's DIVIDING THE CHILD: SOCIAL AND LEGAL DILEMMAS OF CUSTODY (1992). This study was conducted in California, with its commitment to gender-neutral custody rules and sympathy for joint custody, and the excerpts from Lee Teitelbaum's essay reviewing that study shed light on the character of custodial disputes, the ways in which custody is distributed between mothers and fathers, and the frequency and implications of joint custodial arrangements.

The third excerpt, from an article by Catherine Albiston, Eleanor Maccoby, and Robert Mnookin explores some further implications of joint custody, using data collected in connection with the study described immediately above. It explores the relationships that developed in joint custodial families and particularly the levels of contact between parents and their children, payment of child support, visitation, and concord between the parents.

David L. Chambers, *Rethinking the Substantive Rules for Custody Disputes in Divorce*, 83 MICHIGAN LAW REVIEW 477 (1984)[*]

III. INFORMATION BEARING ON RULES FOR SOLE CUSTODY

A. *What We Know About the Needs of Children*

A predisposition toward placing children after divorce with their mothers, with primary caretakers, or with the parent of the same sex may be justified by a belief that children in such settings will receive more nurturing, feel more loved or secure, or, in the long term, be more competent and effective as adults. In this section, I appraise whether or not existing research provides any substantial support for such beliefs. I begin with research that directly studies children of divorce in various settings and move to the more indirect evidence provided by research on the responsiveness of men and women in general to children and on the relation of children to each parent in intact families.

1. Research on the Children of Divorce

. . . Two recent studies have been particularly celebrated because the authors followed families over a period of years and sought to develop a comprehensive understanding of the lives of the children and the parents. The first, by Mavis Hetherington, Martha Cox, and Roger Cox, followed seventy-two nursery-school-age children in forty-eight families over a two-year period after divorce. The second, by Judith Wallerstein and Joan Kelly, followed 131 children of all ages from sixty families over a five-year period after separation. (For simplicity, I will refer to the studies as "Hetherington" or "Wallerstein.") Each has done further follow-ups of the same families that await publication. For our purposes, these studies are in one sense simply a more probing version of the old father-absence research, subject to the same limitation of providing no direct information on the probable consequences of placements with fathers or secondary caretakers. Moreover, neither set of researchers drew on a random sample of divorced families and the samples of both were of somewhat higher social status on average than the divorcing population in general. Wallerstein's group almost certainly included a disproportionate number of troubled families, because she obtained her sample by soliciting volunteers for short-term counseling.

Nonetheless, because the two studies drew on extensive interviews with all family members and because they offered a more detailed view of the lives of divorcing families than had been previously available, their findings have been widely discussed and their broad outlines widely accepted. Part of their acceptance probably flows from the fact that their findings are generally consistent with one another, although Wallerstein's are somewhat bleaker than Hetherington's.

What the authors report is that for most children, custodial mothers, and noncustodial fathers, the period immediately after separation is a period of stress and anx-

---

iety. Each person is affected by the absence of a person (or persons) who had been central to their lives. Each person is forced to adjust to a substantially altered living situation at a time when each is least well-armed psychologically to cope with it. Custodial mothers must cope with all the old tasks of childcare while shaping a new role as the sole decisionmaker, disciplinarian, and principal or sole breadwinner. Children's basic physical needs are met during this period, but nearly all children experience severe emotional distress and grieve for the absent father, particularly if he does not visit regularly. Many feel unhappy and disoriented for long periods after the divorce for reasons that appear to relate to the breakup of the family. According to Hetherington, young children cry more, whine more, and throw more temper tantrums than children in two-parent families. Wallerstein reports that children of all ages have problems, although the reactions and problems vary depending upon the age of the child at the time of the breakup.

During the year or so after separation, many mothers report the temporary loss of traits they most prized as personal qualities in themselves, traits that many writers associate with primary-caretaking mothers and that might incline us toward preferring placement with them. Thus, mothers report feeling less able to reach out to their children, less able to be sympathetic and compassionate or to control their own tempers, and more likely to use negative sanctions. In a large proportion of families, the worst point in mother-child relations is not reached until a full year after divorce when mothers describe their relationships with their children as "declared war," "the old Chinese water torture," and "like being bitten to death by ducks." Mothers report particular difficulties in their relationships with their sons, and more sons than daughters seemed troubled. Mothers also report less satisfaction with their own performance of many of the day-to-day household tasks. They also report experiencing severe financial distress that exacerbated the other problems they faced. According to Wallerstein and Kelly, as long as three to five years after divorce, a significant minority of the mothers still report major difficulties in their relationships with their children that they and the authors attribute at least in part to their divorce.

During the early part of this period, the noncustodial fathers report no greater satisfaction with their lives. Feeling rootless, they find painful the visitation relationship and many, though by no means all, find it difficult to maintain or build a satisfying relationship with their children.

Both studies report that within a few years after the divorce, most families appear to have restabilized and the children's problematic behavior had subsided from its peak at approximately one year after the divorce. Nevertheless, both boys and girls are reported to be functioning somewhat less well than their peers from intact homes and boys continue to be comparatively more unhappy and pose more problems of discipline.

One limit of the Wallerstein and Hetherington works, even as studies of children in maternal custody, is that, though longitudinal and thorough, they have not yet followed the children up to adulthood. No study has done so. Oddly, it is also the case that there are few retrospective studies of adults whose parents were divorced when they were young to learn whether they report suffering or appear to suffer more problems than persons whose parents remained married throughout their childhood. One study, analyzing data from two broad national surveys of the self-reported life satisfaction of

Americans, found very few differences between persons whose parents had and had not divorced, and no differences in reported current life satisfaction, but did find that more children of divorce looked back on childhood as the least happy time of their lives. Although the study did not analyze separately children raised by their fathers, the vast majority of the respondents to the study whose parents had been divorced had almost certainly lived with their mothers.

About a dozen smaller-scale studies reporting on families headed by fathers have now in fact been published. Nearly all were written within the last decade and in all the mothers of the children studied had been the primary caretakers of the children before the father assumed custody. These studies help us begin to understand both the experiences of children raised by men and the experiences of children whose care is taken over by secondary caretakers.

Sad to say, although they seem directly responsive to the questions posed in this Article, the studies of children with fathers cannot provide the answers we need. One inherent limit is that because father-custody is still relatively unusual in our society, even a study of a random sample of fathers with custody today might tell us only a limited amount about what children's experiences are likely to be if far more fathers became custodians. In fact, the studies so far conducted are not based on random samples. They nearly all rely on samples of volunteers obtained through divorce support groups or advertisements. Most mix children whose parents divorced with children whose mothers have died.

In addition, few of the children were infants and none of the studies reports at any length on fathers caring for infants. Most involve interviews conducted several years after the father had assumed custody and thus after the point at which Wallerstein and Hetherington report children living with mothers suffering the greatest difficulties. Most describe only how fathers viewed their own situations or at most how the fathers believed their children were faring; only a few include direct observations and interviews with the children comparable to those conducted by Hetherington and by Wallerstein. One would be inclined not to report their findings at all except that they share a remarkable surface similarity.

The surface similarity is the positive tone of their findings. They report an expectable difficult time of transition: like mothers, fathers with custody report loneliness, frustration, and a sense of inadequacy. They faced the difficult task of mastering new skills of caregiving while trying to handle their former jobs. Because the new tasks the father was fumbling to learn involved more intimate contact with the children than the new tasks of the mother and because the children were facing adjustment to a new primary caretaker, one might expect the immediate post-separation period to be even more stressful than that depicted for mothers by Hetherington or Wallerstein. Unfortunately, with two exceptions, none of the studies compared the situations of custodial fathers and mothers, and few report at all on the period of adjustment as experienced by the child.

In any event, all the studies report that fathers appear to attain rapidly the housetending and childtending skills they previously lacked. More basically, not one of the studies reports father-headed families in chronic disarray, with fathers unable to cope and children either physically or emotionally neglected. Interviewers found the men knowledgeable about their children and highly motivated to meet their needs. They report that the fathers believed that their children were generally in good emotional condition, though some fathers worried that they lacked a "mother's touch."

The few studies in which the researchers directly observed the children report complementary findings regarding the children's conditions. A study of thirty-three preschool children being raised by fathers, which the author himself treats as merely "exploratory," found no abnormal behavioral problems and reports that the children were generally well-adjusted and capable of a high degree of independent functioning for their age. Another small study of boys aged nine to fourteen, some raised by fathers, some by mothers, found no significant differences between the groups. One very recent study does report that children of divorcing parents seem to be better off with the parent of the same sex, but found no evidence whatever of overall inadequacies of custodial fathers who had previously been secondary caretakers in comparison with custodial mothers who had been primary caretakers all along.

That study, the results of which are still being analyzed, merits discussion at somewhat greater length because it is nearly unique in including samples of father-headed, mother-headed, and two-parent families and because its findings bear so directly on the questions posed in this Article. The authors, John Santrock and Richard Warshak of the University of Texas at Dallas, located samples of roughly twenty children each in father custody, mother custody, and intact two-parent custody and relied upon psychological tests, laboratory observations of the custodial parent with their children, and structured interviews with the children. At the time of the study, all the children were between six and eleven, and the parents in the divorced families had been separated an average of slightly over three years. The authors' principal purpose was to test whether or not the gender of the parent with whom a child lived seemed to make a difference in the child's condition or development after divorce. The authors' early findings are expressed in forceful terms: they found that, in general, the children within their sample who lived with parents of the same sex were less anxious, less demanding, and less angry; were warmer and more honest; and displayed higher levels of maturity, self-esteem, and social conformity than the children living with parents of the opposite sex. Although some of their measures may not be relevant for our purposes, the sum of their findings suggests that, within their sample, children with the same-sex parent felt on the whole happier and more secure, a relevant consideration in deciding custody under almost any test.

The Santrock and Warshak findings are provocative, especially because they suggest an easily applied rule of decision for judges, at least in cases in which the children involved are in the range of ages that the authors studied and all the children in the family are of the same sex. As the authors acknowledge in part, however, there are many reasons to be cautious about their findings, cautious to the point of waiting for further research before using them in making recommendations for rules of custody.

Santrock and Warshak's use of matched samples and a diverse range of tests and observations are exemplary and their findings were "robust" in the sense that they were consistent across many different sorts of observations. Unfortunately, however, their samples were very small—only about ten each of mother-custody sons, mother-custody daughters, father-custody sons, and father-custody daughters. They are also nonrandom.

. . . [I]n few of these father-custody cases had there been a fight over custody. It is thus possible that the comparative difficulties for many girls living with their fathers, for all of whom their mothers had been the primary caretaker before separation, derived not so much from their situation after divorce as it did from some aspect of the mother-daughter relationship before separation. It hardly follows, and the authors do not claim, that these particular girls would have been happier or more secure if placed in the custody of their mothers. It is also possible that the parents themselves were in some way affected in their voluntary decisions about placement by the gender of the children and that whatever factors guided their decision continued to affect the children's experiences.

These criticisms do not prove that Santrock and Warshak's conclusions are wrong. They simply suggest that their proposition, though tantalizing, and though consistent with some evidence from studies of intact families reviewed below, remains unproven one way or the other. . . .

In the end, the only safe conclusion to be drawn from the current research on children living with fathers who had been secondary caretakers is that substantial numbers of individual children are reported to be faring well on a day-to-day basis. That isn't much. The limits on our knowledge make clear why as much or more reliance needs to be placed on the growing body of research about men and women in general in relation to children and about mothers and fathers in relation to their children in intact families.

2. The Indirect Evidence from Intact Families and Other Sources

a. The relevance of gender.

(1) *Evidence favoring mothers because they are women.* Are women substantially more likely than men to possess traits such as patience or warmth or attentiveness to children's physical or emotional needs? Under any definition of children's best interests, such traits would probably be considered important to children's, especially young children's, well-being.

Until the recent past, most states applied formal statutory or judicially created evidentiary presumptions in favor of mothers in custody disputes involving young children, children of "tender years." Most states have now eliminated any formal preference, but even within the last decade, some state supreme courts have defended the continued use of the presumption. Even without statutory or appellate-court authorization, many trial judges believe that young children generally belong with mothers and tend to place children with them. . . .

It is not judges alone who believe that women have special gifts as caretakers of children. The sociologist Alice Rossi has, for example, argued that women have a predisposition toward childcare that is, at least in part, genetically transmitted. Erik Erikson also claimed that women have a "biological, psychological, and ethical commitment to take care of human infancy." Freud had similar beliefs. Conversely, speaking of men, Bruno Bettelheim once argued that "[M]ale physiology and that part of his psychology based on it are not geared to infant care. . . . [T]he relationship between father and child never was and cannot now be built principally around child-caring experiences. It is built around a man's function in society: moral, economic, political."

Rossi, Erikson, Freud, and Bettelheim have some obvious evidence that can be adduced in their support. Only women can bear children and only women can nurse. Over the whole history of humankind, childrearing has been a central role for women, a secondary role for men. In America today, as in all other countries of the world, it is women who perform most of the holding, feeding, and consoling of young children.

Women are also widely perceived as possessing particular character and behavioral traits that especially suit them for the care of young children. One common characterization is that women are "expressive," while men are "instrumental." Women are thought to be more open in displaying affection; to have a greater capacity for gentleness, empathy, and compassion; and to possess a greater solicitousness for the needs of others. These qualities when lavished on a young child may convert mere impersonal task-performing into true "nurturing." Men, by contrast, are perceived as finding satisfaction in activities that garner power or prestige rather than from activities that provide private satisfactions. They are viewed as more likely to be competitive, self-reliant, and aggressive and more concerned about the family's relationship to the outside world. These qualities, though probably important over time in the child's development, may be thought less central to a young child's well-being than those associated with the mothers. Whatever role biology plays in shaping these general characteristics, it is plainly the case that from early childhood on, most boys and girls in the United States are taught that certain traits are desirable for boys and different traits, including nurturing traits, are desirable for girls.

For our purposes, however, the issue is not quite so global as whether, in general, women are better suited to be childtenders than men. Custody disputes arise between two people who are each the parent of the child at issue and who have each indicated a willingness to be the child's caretaker. A review of the available research suggests, although less clearly than those who claim that there are no differences between the sexes might wish, that gender alone provides little useful information for making decisions between contending parents. A review also helps separate those issues that distinctly relate to the parents' gender from those that relate to a parent's status as primary caretaker, a difficult task in a world in which the overwhelming majority of primary caretakers are women.

The broad generalizations about the personalities and behavioral traits of men and women hold up rather poorly when individual adults are studied. While researchers do report some persistent, sex-linked differences in the psychological responses of men and women in general, they also find that large numbers of individual men display traits stereotypically associated with women. The more specific research examining males and females in their interest in children, attentiveness to them, and capacity to understand and respond to their needs—what might be collectively termed their "responsiveness" to children—is especially inconclusive. . . .

In the context of custody disputes, the issue of special nurturing traits associated with one sex is posed most purely in cases involving newborns when neither parent has become the primary caretaker for the child and in cases involving preschool children when parents have shared in roughly equal measure the caregiving responsibilities. Hence, the most relevant studies to us . . . are those seeking to compare the responsiveness of mothers and fathers of young children. Here the findings are complex and somewhat mixed. Some studies have reported that women already serving as the primary caretaker of a young child are more responsive than their husbands to the young children of others, for example, when observed in a waiting room. On the other hand, when fathers and mothers are observed with their own newborns before either has assumed differing caretaking roles, fathers are in general as likely to hold them closely, rock them, talk to them, and look directly at them. New fathers seem as skilled and gentle as mothers with their own children. Observers in the home at later stages, even after differing roles have been assumed, have found that although fathers interact with young children differently than mothers do, with more physical and less patterned, rhythmic play, there still seem to be few differences in the degree of parents' interests in their children or in their capacities to respond to their infant's signals. . . .

What then is the lesson, for our purposes, of the research on gender-related traits? The perplexing question is not whether men are able to perform various childrearing tasks. No one has doubted their physical ability to do so. The issues are whether or not fathers (1) are as capable as mothers of reading their children's signals regarding various needs, (2) have the patience and dedication to apply themselves to responding to those needs over time and, (3) have the capacity and motivation to accompany the provision of care with whatever emotional qualities are needed by a child to feel loved, respected, and secure. The studies . . . leave some doubt about whether or not, in general, men are as capable of reading children's signals as women, though the concern about men's capacities in this respect probably does not extend to children after they become old enough to verbalize most of their needs. Few studies shed much light on the second question of whether or not men are as likely as women to apply themselves adequately over time to the provision of care to young children. The impressionistic studies of children in father-custody reviewed earlier and the few American and Swedish studies of primary-caretaker fathers in intact families indicate that some fathers are doing so, but these fathers may not be representative of fathers in general or even of the sorts of fathers who will volunteer for custody. Furthermore, if men receive little reinforcement from employers and peers for serving in a caretaking role, it will be harder for them than for women to sustain their efforts, even if they begin with equal motivation to succeed.

The third question, whether or not fathers in general can infuse caregiving with the appropriate emotional qualities, is especially difficult to answer. We have seen that men, even men who are primary caretakers of children, may typically behave toward children somewhat differently than women do. From this alone, of course, it does not follow that women's behavior better serves children's needs. For our purposes, the issue is not whether "father's touch" is identical to "mother's touch" but whether "father's touch," whatever it is like, is likely to lead to a less desirable quality of life or less desirable outcome for the child in either the short or long term. In this regard, the Swedish study and American studies of primary-caretaking fathers provide no clear answers and some mixed signals.

The conclusions to be drawn on the basis of all that is now known about the differences between men and women are not obvious. It is not possible to say that there are no sex-linked differences between men and women that bear on childtending. In fact, while no evidence points toward a conclusion that men are more responsive to children than women, some evidence points in the opposite direction. Given the roles that men and women have performed over millennia and the ambiguous messages from the research on sex differences, a risk-averse legislator or judge might be inclined to retain or revive old preferences for women based simply on their gender. They might be especially inclined to do so, if they believe that judges in any given dispute will have grave difficulties determining the responsiveness and attentiveness of the men and women before them to their children. . . .

(2) *Evidence favoring matching children with the parent of the same sex.* In the section describing current research on children of divorce in various settings, I described a recent study by Santrock and Warshak that concluded that, by several different measures, children aged six to eleven placed after divorce with a parent of the same sex seemed "better adjusted" than children of the same age in the custody of a parent of the opposite sex. I also reported, however, that for many reasons, Santrock and Warshak's research should be regarded as exploratory. There is nonetheless psychological theory and some research to support a view that children have a special affinity for the parent of the same sex and special difficulties in their relations with the parent of the opposite sex.

Freudian psychological theory has long suggested an especially strong identification by children with the parent of the same sex. Social learning theory suggests much the same conclusion, focusing on the way children learn by observing and interacting with the parent of the same sex. Moreover, in a society in which men and women still are encouraged toward different activities on the basis of their sex, a child is simply more likely to enjoy participating in (and receive peer approbation for participating in) the activities of the same-sex parent. As a guide through the perils of growing up, a same-sex parent is likely to be more able to remember comparable moments in his or her own childhood and thus understand better the problems that the child encounters.

Studies of intact families provide some support for these hypotheses. In the next section I will discuss the strong bonds that seem to develop between children and both of their parents, but, as recently reviewed by Ross Thompson, some evidence points to especially strong relationships by sex, especially between boys and fathers. From infancy on, as Thompson summarizes, fathers in general take more interest in their sons than daughters. In observation-based studies, they typically touch and talk more to their infant sons, a pattern that continues through infancy. A comparable but milder preference has been found of mothers for daughters. In turn, children seem to respond preferentially to the parent of the same sex. At least after the first year, researchers find that young children, especially boys, seek out more contact with the parent of the same sex than the parent of the opposite sex.

The studies of children of divorce to which I have already alluded also suggest some special problems for children, or at least for boys, separated from parents of the same sex. Studies of boys raised by single mothers have suggested that such boys more frequently experienced problems of sex-role identification and self-control than did the boys in two-parent families. Hetherington, Cox, and Cox found that mothers, in general, reported more difficulties in handling their sons than in handling their daughters. They relate a pattern, particularly common with boys, of mothers caught in a vicious cycle with a problem child in which the relationship steadily worsened and the mother felt more and more powerless, angry, and depressed.

Similarly, Wallerstein and Kelly found that some mothers were especially harsh on their sons after separation, in part because the boys reminded them of their ex-husbands. At eighteen months after the divorce, more boys than girls longed for their fathers, more boys than girls were depressed, and only half as many boys had improved in their overall adjustment since separation. It is possible, however, that whatever problems boys face (or pose to their mothers) in mother-custody homes would be nearly as likely to arise in father-custody homes and are traceable either to problems the boys faced before divorce or to special problems for boys of living in any single-parent situation. Furthermore, the Wallerstein study was of families in which the custodial mother believed she needed help, and it may be that the problems of boys in mother-custody simply display themselves earlier than the problems of girls. Hetherington in an earlier writing suggested that the problems for girls in homes without their fathers are most likely to show up in adolescence in the form of greater difficulties in relating to boys.

In sum, the current body of research provides strong hints that many children will be happier when placed with the same-sex parent. Andrew Watson, for example, has recommended that girls be placed with their mothers. To my reading, more research is needed before recommending any sort of preference based on shared gender. Although there is an abundance of research on boys in mother-headed homes, there is very little research, apart from the work of Santrock and Warshak, comparing boys in father-headed families with boys in mother-headed families or discussing girls in single-parent homes headed by fathers. Even in Santrock and Warshak's study, the youngest of the boys and girls studied were at least six years old at the time they were observed.

b. The relevance of primary-caretaker status. Women have no attributes that so especially suit them for childrearing that they merit a preference in custody disputes simply because of their gender. On the other hand, men and women involved in custody disputes during divorce do not simply possess parenting or nurturing qualities in the abstract. They have each had a relationship with the particular child over whom they are fighting. One of them, more commonly the woman, has typically spent far more time giving care to the child than the other parent. When there is such a person within the family, I will call him or her the "primary caretaker."

Three arguments can be advanced for preferring placement with parents who have been the primary caretaker: they know more about the particular child; they have demonstrated a dedication to meeting the child's needs; and they have built an emotional bond with the child that may be more important for the child to sustain on a daily basis than whatever bond the child has with the other parent. Of the three arguments, the last is the one most commonly advanced in favor of the primary caretaker. I will focus principally on this claim of the importance of sustaining a special emotional bond between the child and the primary caretaker. The other two arguments will be taken up along the way.

Unlike the arguments in the preceding section, the arguments for the primary caretaker can be framed without reference to the gender of the parent for whom they are being advanced. On the other hand, it is extremely difficult to discuss the arguments in any detail without alluding to gender, for, with a few exceptions, all the writing about children and their primary caretakers has relied on observations of children being raised by primary caretakers who were women. Indeed, much of this writing uses the terms "mother" and "primary caretaker" interchangeably. In the section that follows, the term "primary caretaker" will be used without reference to gender in discussions of theory or general propositions but the term "primary-caretaking mothers" will be used in discussions of specific research based on observations of mothers.

Here then is an attempt to state the strongest case that can be made for placing children with primary caretakers. Remember as you read that this is the partisan's brief for primary over secondary caretakers. After the case is set forth, the several ways in which it is not fully persuasive will be examined.

One of the central tenets of modern psychoanalytic and social learning theory is that the intimate interaction of a caretaker with an infant produces a bond between them, generally referred to as an "attachment." Young children can, and typically do, form attachments to more than one adult, including secondary-caretaking fathers, but the tie between a child and a primary-caretaking mother is generally depicted as stronger and more salient to the child than the tie with the father. "[M]ost theorists," says psychologist Michael Lamb, "whatever their orientation, have assumed that the mother-infant relationship is unique and vastly more important than any contemporaneous, or indeed any subsequent, relationships."

In the early months of a child's life, a primary-caretaker mother typically touches, caresses, and holds her child many times every day and feeds her several times a day. Within a few months, the child can typically identify her, has positive feelings toward her, and can tell her apart from others. By some point between around six months and a year, the child begins to display what is commonly called "attachment behavior": seeking to be near her, becoming distressed on separation from her, showing pleasure or relief on reunion with her, and orienting herself to her even when not in physical contact (listening for her voice, checking to make certain that she is not too far away).

Before becoming fully verbal, children and their primary caretakers develop elaborate and personal rituals of communication that apply to feeding, diaper-changing, responses to small injuries, and most of a child's other repeated events. Through these rituals, a high level of communication takes place in a "language" that no one else knows fully how to "speak." The mother assumes a place in her infant's psyche that others cannot replace by performing the same services.

Many writers about child development believe that the importance to the child of the psychological bond that develops between the child and primary caretaker in this early period stretches well beyond what might be inferred from these visible small events and interactions. They consider attachment to a primary caretaker the essential cornerstone for a child's healthy emotional development. At the earliest stage, it is critical to the child's learning to place trust in others and to have confidence in her own capacities. Later, it plays a central role in the child's capacity to establish emotional bonds with other persons. The sense of trust in others and in self that the attachment provides may also affect the child's development of intellectual and social skills. The growing child passes through many developmental stages, each requiring her to acquire critical skills and capacities. At one stage, a child needs to learn how to interact successfully with other children, at another to begin to master the skills (reading, hunting, weaving, or whatever) needed to become a productive member of the larger society. The original bond of the child with the primary caretaker is believed to have an important continuing effect on the child's ability to pass through each stage with success.

What harms are likely to befall a child who is separated from her primary caretaker at divorce and placed with the other parent? The greatest concern is likely to be expressed for preschool children. Unfortunately, as related in the preceding section, there are only a few studies of children of any age placed with secondary caretakers after divorce and none focusing on preschool children placed with secondary caretakers. The research that has been conducted on children separated from their parents that provides analogies to the divorce setting is primarily of two sorts. One is studies of children raised in orphanages or other institutions who never developed strong attachments as infants to any consistent caretakers. Such children, by the time they reach school age, often become withdrawn and restless and suffer severe problems in relating to others, even when adopted by loving parents in their late preschool years. The other relevant research is on young children who have formed attachments but are separated from both parents for periods of a few days to a week. James and Joyce Robertson, for example, conducted a study and produced a series of films of young children whose mothers were briefly hospitalized and who were taken care of by strangers. Within as short a time as four days, the children suffered substantial distress and displayed withdrawal, loss of appetite, prolonged crying, and difficulty in sleeping.

On the basis of this evidence and the general theory of attachment, both short- and long-term fears might be expressed for a child placed with a secondary caretaker, at least so long as it is assumed that the child's relationship to the secondary caretaker is not nearly as central to her sense of well-being as her relationship to the primary caretaker is. If placed with a secondary caretaker, the child might thus find the period immediately following separation especially stressful. Her needs will not be met in the way she has come to expect. Whether or not objectively cared for as well as before, the young child, and perhaps even the older child, is likely to feel anxious, sad, and less secure. Over the months that follow, the child may fail to master, or even regress in mastering, developmental tasks on which she is currently working.

The expectable long-term consequences of separation from the primary caretaker are less certain. Bowlby, however, has expressed the belief that the child who is separated from a primary caretaker early in life is more likely than other children to develop into an adult less capable than others of forming and maintaining emotional ties and to be subject to sudden depressions and to periods of acute anxiety. . . .

These are the arguments for primary caretakers that derive from attachment theory. Much about them is attractive. But the foundations of the case for primary caretakers prove wobbly when subjected to close scrutiny. A small part of the weakness is that the role of attachment bonds in child development has probably been overstated by Freud, Bowlby, and their other principal proponents. In their zeal to make certain that the importance of attachment was recognized, they ignored or undervalued the significance of other factors. Some recent research outside the context of divorce suggests that, even when a child moves permanently from her parents to caretakers she has not previously known at all, her long-term adjustment to separation "will be primarily determined by the quality of the relationship with the new caretakers, not by the experience of separation" from the previous attachment figure.

For our purposes, however, the weakest part of the case for primary caretakers is not that it exaggerates the importance of attachment in general but that it exaggerates the importance of the bond to the primary-caretaker parent in comparison to the bond with the other parent. The claim for primary caretakers posits a minor position for secondary-caretaking parents in the development of children, or put more precisely, rests on observations of the mother-child relationship that have not included comparisons with any of the child's other relationships. Very few of those conducting the research with mothers have spent time observing the father-child relationship. They watched the miraculous bond that develops between primary-caretaking mothers and children and simply assumed that it was unique.

Only within the last two decades has substantial research been conducted on the ties that children develop to their fathers in two-parent families. It indicates that although children have very different relationships with their secondary-caretaker fathers than with their mothers, they typically form strong attachments to both.

An initial, uniform finding from interviews with parents is that, in general, fathers spend far less time with infants than mothers, even when mothers work outside the home. A high proportion of fathers report that they perform no regular caregiving functions at all.

On the other hand, as early as eight months of age, and quite clearly by a year and a half, children differentiate both between their mothers and strangers and between their fathers and strangers, and their behavior toward their fathers is much more like their behavior toward their mothers than it is like their behavior toward strangers. Some studies have found that at about one year, children more commonly seek out their primary-caretaking mother in preference to fathers for relief when tired or anxious and both parents are present. But, at about the same age, when both are present, children more commonly turn to the father for social interaction. Forced to choose, many people would believe that the primary caretaker's relief-giving capacity is more important; yet, there is very little evidence to suggest that when only a secondary-caretaking parent is available, that parent is not fully adequate to provide the needed reassurance.

The central message of this research is that by the time most children are toddlers, they have formed substantial emotional bonds with both parents. As children grow, primary-caretaking mothers continue to devote more time than fathers to childcare, but fewer of the tasks require intimate physical interaction with the child. The amount of time that parents actually spend in social interaction with their children typically draws closer. During these years, secondary-caretaking fathers generally perform other important functions for children that seem to affect positively the strength of children's emotional ties to them. They help to establish and enforce rules of conduct; they provide models of appropriate behavior and express expectations for the children's conduct; they concern themselves with the child's physical safety; and they engage in various sorts of reciprocal behaviors such as "buddy" or "flirt."

To be sure, many of the functions the father performs are mediated by the role of the mother: what the child derives from the father is affected in part by the child's relationship with her mother and by the child's perception of each parent's relationship to the other. Nonetheless, whatever the mediating forces, fathers in the two-parent family typically hold a central position in children's daily lives and in their sense of well-being. . . .

Despite these encouraging suggestions from the research on father-child relationships, fears about the effects of secondary-caretaker custody may nonetheless persist for the youngest children, those up to four or five years of age. To be sure, there is little basis for such a fear in any of the studies actually observing mothers and fathers with their young children. On the other hand, these studies—typically brief observations in laboratories—cannot in themselves disprove the theories of Bowlby, Freud, and others who posit a unique bond between infants and primary-caretaking mothers that develops over the early years. At most, they raise doubts. There is still no methodologically rigorous research on children placed in the custody of secondary caretakers at an early age. Thus, where one comes out in the end with regard to custody decisions involving young children will depend in large part not on empirical research but on the persuasiveness of theory. . . .

As to the next older group of children, those between roughly five and ten, theorists might still express some concerns, but their claims about the dangers that might accrue to children placed with a secondary caretaker whom they know well are almost certain to be more muted. Moreover, neither the research on single-parent fathers or single-parent mothers nor the research on single-parent families justifies a belief that secondary-caretaking parents who volunteer to care for children in this age group will perform less well because of their earlier secondary status.

In the end, developmental theory supports some sort of weight in the decisional process for primary caretakers of very young children. It also provides guidance toward a functional definition of "primary caretaker." It suggests that what is important is not simply tasks performed for the child but interactions with the child—direct contact in feeding, bathing, talking, snuggling, and so forth. If one parent performs many more of those interactions than the other parent, that parent should probably be considered the primary caretaker, even if he or she works part or full time outside the home and someone else provides the caregiving during work time. On the other hand, as the differences between the parents' roles decrease and the difference in time spent by them in these sorts of interactions becomes more nearly equal, theory and available evidence suggest little basis for drawing fine lines. . . .

B. What We Know About the Needs of the Parents.

In Part II above, I argued that judges and legislators would be acting sensibly if, in framing rules for resolving custody disputes, they accorded some weight to the interests of parents, so long as they continued to give primary weight to the interests of children. I suggested in particular that a rule creating a rebuttable presumption for primary caretakers might justifiably rest in part on a finding, if one could be made, that primary caretakers typically suffered emotionally much more than secondary caretakers on the loss of the custody of their children. In this section I ask whether such a finding can in fact be made.

Unfortunately, just as there are no longitudinal studies comparing children in the custody of mothers (or primary caretakers) with children in the custody of fathers (or secondary caretakers), so there are no longitudinal studies comparing the experience of primary caretakers who are denied custody of children with that of secondary caretakers in the same position. . . .

Despite the paucity of direct observations and comparisons, the hypothesis that primary caretakers generally will be more seriously affected emotionally by the loss of custody than secondary caretakers has substantial plausibility. Whenever one parent receives sole custody of a child, the other parent is necessarily shifted into being just a "visitor." The shift is likely to mark a much more dramatic change in the lives of most primary caretakers than it will for most secondary caretakers. For primary caretakers, shifting to "visitor" status almost certainly leads to a substantial reduction in time spent with the child. While it is true that the primary caretaker who loses custody is freed from the petty drudgery of washing school clothes and packing lunches, for many caretakers the predictable rhythm of these very tasks had given structure to their lives. They are likely to experience the sudden freedom as a loss.

In addition, primary caretakers, whether female or male, may well be more dependent than secondary caretakers on the emotional support and stimulation they receive from the small interactions with the child, especially the young child—the cuddling, the seemingly aimless chatter, and so forth. Moreover, those primary caretakers, especially those who have been full-time homemakers, often have no identity other than their identity as spouse and parent to fall back upon. Divorced and without their children, they have nothing to make them feel valued. Most secondary caretakers, at least most secondary-caretaking men, have a second identity through their job. However much the parenting role has meant to them and however much they complain about their work, it seems likely that when they lose custody, they are less frequently left without any activity from which they derive a sense of worth and a sense of place.

For all these reasons, one might suppose that, in general, primary caretakers, and especially those primary caretakers not employed outside the home, suffer emotionally more than secondary caretakers when deprived of the opportunity to live with their children. Luepnitz, in her interview study of parents after divorce, quoted one mother who, though speaking only about her own children and former husband, summarized well the case for primary caretakers: "He is an excellent parent, but they are the most important thing in my life, and I would not have survived without them. They would have been happy either way, but I wouldn't have pulled through if I had lost them."

Lee E. Teitelbaum, *Divorce, Custody, Gender, and The Limits of Law: On Dividing the Child,* **92** MICHIGAN LAW REVIEW **1808 (1994)**[*]

* * *

I. THE RESEARCH METHOD

A. *The Research Setting and Focus*

Seemingly inevitably, Maccoby and Mnookin's research was conducted in California. . . . California is fairly believed to be in the "vanguard" of divorce law reform. It adopted the first entirely no-fault divorce law in 1969, rejected the traditional preference for maternal custody in 1972, initiated a preference for joint parental custody in 1979, and mandated mediation of custody disputes in 1981. . . .

B. *The Research Design*

The difficulties of conducting reliable research in connection with domestic relations are familiar and well documented. Many studies involve small samples and often specialized populations. Well-educated white families provide the usual focus for research, and father- or joint-custody families rarely appear. Researchers have rarely conducted studies of divorced families over time, nor do they often use multiple sources of information about important questions.

Maccoby and Mnookin do not claim to provide the perfect research setting, but their design is far more sophisticated and reliable than those of most existing studies. Their choice of design follows their belief that divorce is a dynamic process, taking shape over a series of stages.

Given this assumption, it is plainly important to collect information about divorcing couples at the point of separation, when they divorce, and after divorce. Accordingly, the authors adopted a limited longitudinal design, focusing on a *cohort:* a group of persons similarly situated for relevant purposes who will be followed for the research period. The cohort for this study included families who had recently filed for divorce when the study began. Researchers first interviewed the parents making up this cohort shortly after they filed for divorce, typically about six months after separation. A second interview took place one year later, when many of the divorces had been completed. The third interview occurred after two more years had passed, or about three and one-half years after separation.

Because this study focused on the process of divorce and custody, the cohort only included families with children who would remain minors for the duration of the study. These families were chosen from court records of divorce petitions in two counties and screened for eligibility under the criteria described above. Efforts were made to reach all of the apparently eligible families: a total of about 2300. About 2000 of those ultimately fit the criteria for the cohort . . . .

Ultimately, the research sample included approximately 1100 families who filed for divorce in San Mateo or Santa Clara County between September of 1984 and April of 1985. Although there was some predictable attrition from the cohort as time went on,

---

[*]   Copyright © 1994. Reprinted with permission.

the authors—again through considerable effort—maintained a very high level of participation.

The families making up the cohort generally resembled national sample data in a number of respects. About the same proportion were white (88.4% of the research sample; 86.6% nationally); employment rates were almost identical for mothers (about 84%), as were numbers of children (1.7 in the California sample and 1.8 nationally). However, the mothers were two years younger than a national sample from the same time period. More important, their earnings were considerably higher ($18,607, compared with $10,504 in the national sample), and the marriages were of shorter duration (10.7 years compared with 12.3 years). Although comparisons with national data of divorcing fathers with minor children are not available, the California sample seems better educated and better paid than is true generally. The most common salary level for the fathers was about $35,000. Only eleven percent of the sample had not finished high school, and almost one-third had finished college, often with some graduate or professional training. . . .

II. AN OVERVIEW OF THE FINDINGS. . .

A. Conflict and Hostility in Divorce and Custody

If there is one thing about which virtually everyone interested in divorce and custody would agree, it is that this process involves, and perhaps creates, the most deeply antagonistic relations suffered by humans in modern society. Just that perception accounts for much of the current interest in alternative dispute resolution techniques for marital dissolutions, particularly custody matters.

Remarkably, Maccoby and Mnookin seem to find that the families in their sample encountered little legal conflict, or even much heartburn, over the custodial and financial terms of their divorce decrees. The authors use two sources of information in order to determine the level of conflict. As a measure of *legal* conflict, they reviewed court records to determine whether the divorce was contested and, if so, whether its resolution required judicial intervention. In addition, they asked parents during their interviews to rate the level of hostility felt in connection with divorce and its various aspects, including custody, visitation, child support, and alimony.

To nobody's great surprise, Maccoby and Mnookin report that levels of legal conflict were low. Three-quarters of the families studied experienced little if any conflict over the terms of the divorce decree. Almost exactly one-half of the 933 cases that had proceeded to final decree during the study went uncontested, and the parties settled another thirty percent through negotiation. Most of the remaining twenty percent settled after mediation, a smaller percentage required a formal custody evaluation, and less than four percent went before a judge. Only 1.5% of the total cases were finally resolved by judicial decree. These findings are consistent with other evidence that the great majority of custody cases are settled by negotiation at some stage.

It is widely believed that, regardless of how divorce cases are settled formally, the process of dissolution is attended by high levels of antagonism, resentment, and injury. If disagreements about the location of custody and about capacity to engage in child rearing are significant elements of antagonism during divorce, all the ingredients seemed to exist in the California sample. Mothers and fathers differed greatly in their preferences regarding custody. Eighty-two percent of mothers, but only twenty-nine percent of fathers, preferred sole maternal custody. Parents also diverged widely in their assessments of predivorce participation in child care, which has an obvious bearing on their beliefs about commitments to and capacity for child rearing. While mothers rated fathers' involvement between 4.5 and 4.8 on a 10.0 point scale, fathers rated their own involvement between 7.1 and 7.6 on that scale. Nonetheless, reported hostility was remarkably—perhaps for some unbelievably—low. Maccoby and Mnookin asked parents during their last interviews—two years after the divorce, on average—to rate the level of hostility associated with the divorce on a 10.0-point scale, in which 10.0 was the highest level of hostility. The median ratings were astonishingly low: 2.0 for custody decisions, 2.5 for visitation issues, 2.5 for child support, 1.0 for spousal support, and 3.0 for decisions about the family home. Only about ten percent of the families gave a very high rating—at or above 7.5—for conflict regarding these crucial issues at divorce.

When high levels of *legal* conflict did exist—that is, when the case was settled only by formal mediation, custody evaluation, or court appearance—the reasons did not lie in demographic variables or even in levels of felt hostility. Length of marriage, wealth, and age and race of parents were not associated with conflict. Expressed hostility by a parent had only a slight association with the stage at which the dispute was resolved. The primary determinants of resort to formal methods of dispute resolution had almost entirely to do with perceptions of parenting skills: in descending order of salience, the father's concern about the child's welfare in the mother's home, the mother's concern about the child's welfare in the father's home, and discrepant perceptions of each other's preseparation childrearing roles. Legal conflict over custody resulted, perhaps appropriately, from conflict regarding custodial ability.

In examining patterns of legal conflict, the authors were aware of the widely held hypothesis that mothers purchase favorable resolution of custody questions by forgoing adequate property and alimony awards. Accordingly, they examined the high conflict cases to see whether mothers in those cases received less child support and alimony. No evidence of such trade-offs appeared. Statistical analysis revealed no significant relation between conflict over custody and the level of either child support alone or total support, including alimony. The authors suggest that California's adoption of community-property principles and child-support schedules leaves little room for discretion and therefore makes, and is understood to make, such negotiating strategies futile.

They did find, however, one disturbing pattern among the high conflict cases: a tendency toward using joint physical custody awards to resolve serious disputes. It is not that judges ordered joint custody in these matters; like most cases, these disputes were resolved by negotiation. Rather, the parents themselves appeared to reach a compromise solution to disputed custodial positions. That this was only a compromise to end conflict, and not a genuine solution, may be inferred from the fact that, in many of the instances when joint custody arose from substantial or intense legal conflict, the children in fact resided with the mother.

B. Where Do Children Live?

1. Custodial Arrangements

Maccoby and Mnookin find, with some surprise, that although California law and social opinion favor shared parental responsibility, maternal custody remains the usual arrangement from initial separation through at least the early postdivorce period. Upon separation but before divorce, children resided with their mothers in two-thirds of all cases. Fifteen percent lived in dual residences and ten percent lived primarily with their fathers.

At divorce, the proportion of mothers who received sole physical custody was exactly the same as the proportion of mothers whose children resided primarily with them during the period of separation. Joint physical custody awards were slightly more common (20%) than had been dual residence at the time of separation (15%), and sole physical custody in the father was somewhat less common (8.6% of custody awards). At the latest point when the authors collected data, the distribution of residence arrangements remained the same as at other times, although these nearly identical percentages conceal substantial shifting within the residential groups.

Maccoby and Mnookin's findings are in some respects similar to other data on custodial arrangements and in some respects different. Census figures from 1980 show a similar rate of residence with fathers but also indicate that mothers were the primary custodians in almost ninety percent of divorced families. The prevalence of dual residence and joint custody in the California counties studied plainly accounts for the difference in custody arrangements. It is, as the authors observe, hard to know whether the pattern observed in California reflects some change in custodial behavior because no comparable data from California at an earlier period exist.

2. Dual Residence and Joint Physical Custody

The authors' analysis of dual residence and joint physical custody is particularly interesting in light of the emphasis on continued relationships with both parents at divorce expressed in both California policy and child-development literature. Some determinants of the pattern they found are familiar. For example, some earlier studies based on small samples had suggested that for social and economic reasons, joint custody would be attractive only to the middle class. Such cooperative arrangements were more likely when the parties could relatively easily incur the duplicative costs associated with dual residence and when they held "enlightened" views about divorce and childrearing—particularly, when they accepted termination of their relationship without high levels of anger and resentment and shared strong ideological commitments to co-parenting.

Maccoby and Mnookin's research partly confirms that research, finding that, on average, dual-residence parents were better educated and wealthier than those whose children lived primarily with their mothers. However, their study, drawing on a much larger sample, provides not only greater confidence about previously accepted assumptions but also a sense of nuance that earlier work lacked.

Despite the overrepresentation of wealthier and better-educated parents in dual-residence families, Maccoby and Mnookin found dual living arrangements in a broader range of families than other research might suggest. They also provide some information about determinants of dual physical custody other than wealth.

To begin, parents established dual-residence arrangements even when they did not share a healthy—that is to say, nonhostile—view of their divorces and their partners. Mothers' ratings of the "hostility" of their divorces were only somewhat (although significantly) lower on average in cases of dual residence than when children were living in one home, and fathers' hostility ratings were identical. In addition, while fewer parents who rated their hostility at very high levels settled on dual residence, there were nonetheless many instances of high levels of hostility in the dual-residence families.

Moreover, dual residence was not exclusively reserved for parents with a shared ideological commitment to continuing joint parenthood. While both parents were typically strongly committed to healthy relations with their children, dual-residence families usually occurred when fathers insisted on sharing time more equally than mothers would have wished.

As one might expect, the age of children also played a role in initial living arrangements. Dual residence at the initial stages was most common with children from ages three to eight, and much less common either with infants or with children in the preteen and teen years. Gender was also related to custodial arrangements, with boys more likely to live in dual residence than girls. When mothers initiated the end of the marriage, children were more likely to live in dual or father residence than when fathers initiated the termination.

Employment was related to the residence of children in interesting and very traditional ways. Mothers who were not employed outside the home were, predictably, likely to have the children living with them: indeed, more so than were mothers who did work. Fathers who were not working, however, were significantly less likely than employed fathers to have custody or to share in a dual-residence arrangement.

These predivorce living arrangements often resulted in joint custody decrees when the divorce was complete. Indeed, joint physical custody orders were more common than dual-residence arrangements had been prior to divorce. However, the "compromise" nature of some joint physical custody awards is again evident from the actual living patterns. In more than half of the cases with a joint custody decree, the children did not in fact have dual residence, and, when this was so, the children usually lived with their mothers. Nor does it appear that dual-residence arrangements are themselves stable. While only nineteen percent of children in mother residence at the outset of the study were living with their fathers or in dual residence, by its end, more than one-half of the children who lived initially in dual residence or with their fathers had moved into some different residential arrangement within two years after the divorce.

3. Joint Legal Custody

Dual residence implies, of course, physical care of the child. Joint *legal* custody, by contrast, has no implications of that kind but is concerned with shared responsibility for major decisions affecting the child, wherever he resides. This form of shared responsibility plainly has become the social and legal norm in California. Sixty percent of mothers and seventy-five percent of fathers preferred joint legal custody when interviewed prior to divorce. Moreover, custody petitions echoed these initial prefer-ences. In the majority of cases in which only one parent filed a petition (with the other parent effectively accepting the terms of that petition), the request was usually for joint legal custody. When both parents filed formal requests, both almost always requested joint legal custody. Courts generally followed these requests with some exceptions. Overall, three-quarters of all awards incorporated joint legal custody.

One-fifth of all decrees (20.2%) established both joint physical and joint legal cus-tody. Indeed, joint physical and legal custody were slightly more frequent than were decrees (18.6%) creating the "traditional" pattern of sole physical and legal custody in the mother. Nearly one-half of all decrees (48.6%) gave the mother sole physical cus-tody while awarding joint legal custody. Sole physical custody in the father, combined with joint legal custody, was awarded in about seven percent of all cases, and fathers had sole physical and legal custody in less than two percent of all cases. Four percent of all decrees established other arrangements, such as divided custody.

4. Visitation

If the custodial patterns reported in *Dividing the Child* are somewhat surprising, the findings regarding visitation, at least in comparison with results in other studies, are much more so. Initially—that is, about six months after separation—substantial visi-tation was common. The authors . . . employ a relatively strict notion of what counts as visitation: daytime or overnight visits during typical two-week periods during the school year. Using that definition, they found that children had visitation with their fathers in three-quarters of the mother-residence families. Overnight visitation was the most common arrangement, followed by daytime visits and, least frequently, failure of substantial visitation. In the smaller group of father-residence families, about forty per-cent of the mothers had overnight visitation with their children.

At this early point in the divorce process, then, less than twenty percent of the children had no significant relationship with their fathers. In all other instances, chil-dren were either visiting their fathers in a substantial fashion, living with them part of the time, or making their primary residence with their fathers. Loss of contact with mothers was even more rare, making up only about three percent of the families.

Although these levels of visitation are higher than most would suppose, they might be written off because they were measured so shortly after the parents separated. By the end of the study, one would expect a substantial drop in visitation by fathers. One would, however, be wrong.

When children lived in dual residence, substantial visitation was definitionally the case. But, even when the child lived primarily with one parent, substantial visitation with the nonresidential parent continued to be common. Moreover, visits most com-monly involved overnight stays. The percentage of fathers whose children visited overnight remained relatively constant during the three and one-half years from the beginning to the end of the study, and the same is true of mothers whose children lived primarily with their fathers. There was some decline in daytime visitations by fathers and consequently an increase in families in which children did not visit with their fathers at all. Nonetheless, all of the fathers with sole or dual residence, and more than sixty percent of the fathers whose children lived with their mothers, maintained very substantial relations with their children.

In addition, some of the remaining fathers maintained relationships with their children, although less than *substantial* as we have used that term. Only thirteen percent of the children living with their mothers had not seen their fathers within the past year, and only seven percent of those living with fathers had not seen their mothers during that period.

C. Stability of Living Arrangements

We have already observed several important aspects related to the stability of living arrangements. One is the continued frequency of maternal custody; another is the extensive continued contact by children with both parents. However, there are shifts and nuances within these patterns that are worth noting.

Although the large majority of families maintained their initial residential arrangements, a substantial amount of change did occur. The fact that overall proportions of living arrangements remained stable over the period of the study reveals that change was not in one direction but rather that changes occurred in all directions and, ultimately, compensated for each other.

More than a quarter of the children changed living arrangements during the period of the study. The most stable arrangement was mother custody. Eighty-four percent of the children who lived with their mothers after separation continued to do so at the end of the research period. Father custody was also relatively stable, remaining in place for seventy percent of the families that began with that arrangement at separation. Dual residence was far more unstable; only about one-half of the children in dual residence at the end of the period had been there throughout.

The major reasons for change in living arrangements are diffuse, arising from residential moves, new parental relationships, and, to some extent, children's choices and parental notions of what was best for the children. Perhaps more interesting are factors that did *not* account for change. One might have suspected that the quality of the relationship between the parents would be associated with the likelihood of continued engagement by nonresidential parents, but this did not prove to be the case. One might also expect that, as children grew older, they would prefer to spend more time with parents of the same gender. No such pattern appeared. Inertia, or perhaps continuity, provided the major determinant of residence, and only substantial change— a significant residential move, remarriage (but only of mothers), and the like—altered living or visitation arrangements. . . .

III. THE GENDERING OF DIVORCE AND THE LIMITS OF LAW

The gendering of custodial and financial arrangements is one of the primary concerns of *Dividing the Child*. This focus is closely related to a second central concern: the effect of legal strategies that seek to change long-established social patterns like the distribution of child care responsibilities and economic opportunity. . . .

. . . Professor Mnookin, in a thoughtful series of articles, argues that negotiation takes place "in the shadow of the law"—that is, parties bargain in a context influenced by legal norms and particularly by the knowledge that law creates certain entitlements or "endowments" that will be enforced if the dispute goes before a judge. . . .

All laws may cast such a shadow. California law, as Maccoby and Mnookin describe it, undertook to do so expressly. California lawmakers sought to occupy the cutting edge of gender equality by various strategies, many of which were described at the beginning of this review. . . .

What Maccoby and Mnookin find in their California families seems hard to reconcile with any simple expectation that California law and policy have "ungendered" custody, alimony, and child support and that the bargains struck by parents, usually with the assistance of lawyers, reflect negotiations carried out in the shadow of a gender-neutralizing legal scheme.

The authors find it particularly difficult to explain the inconsistency between the legal context described above and the dominance of maternal custody, which characterized seventy percent of the arrangements at all stages of the divorce process. They also find a continued acceptance by divorcing parties, and particularly mothers, of traditional role assignments.

The primary determinants of child custody in the California sample include predivorce involvement in childrearing and confidence by the parents in their respective interest in, and ability to care for, their children. These phenomena follow conventional patterns. Mothers and fathers generally agreed that mothers had been more involved than fathers in childrearing prior to separation, although they disagreed greatly on the degree of father involvement. The overwhelming majority of mothers, more than four-fifths, said shortly after separation that they wanted to continue to act as the child's primary custodian, and almost all of the mothers who wanted sole custody requested such a decree at the time of divorce. The relation between predivorce responsibilities and custody decrees is reflected in the fact that fathers were likely to receive primary physical custody only in families where mothers rated themselves as less involved in childrearing than was usual.

Maccoby and Mnookin did find that a surprisingly high percentage of fathers interviewed after separation said that they wanted sole or joint custody. One-third of the fathers stated at that time that they preferred primary physical custody of their children, and a slightly larger group (35%) expressed a desire for joint physical custody. However, while almost all of the mothers (82%) followed their initial preferences with formal requests for custody at divorce, only slightly more than one-half of all fathers did so. Of those fathers who petitioned for something other than what they said they preferred, the great majority formally requested *less* physical custody.

The authors also found traditional roles expressed in the effects of parental views of their spouses' childrearing abilities. Children were very unlikely to live with their fathers if their mothers were concerned about the fathers' competence to care for them; indeed, children lived with their fathers in only three percent of the cases in which mothers entertained such doubts. By contrast, when fathers expressed doubts about their ex-wives, the children nonetheless lived with their mothers in fifty-six percent of all cases. . . .

Maccoby and Mnookin conclude that "despite some revolutionary changes in the law to eliminate gender stereotypes and to encourage greater gender equity, the characteristic roles of mothers and fathers remain fundamentally different." This conclusion leads to a pessimistic assessment of the significance of legal reform in the face of "a strong inertial pull—based on social custom rather than law—toward mother residence." They also conclude that "much divorce decision-making takes place outside the law's shadow." Divorcing couples seem to maintain quite traditional values concerning parental roles, which they adopt perhaps without discussion and even without thought. . . .

Although Maccoby and Mnookin are consistently pessimistic about the effects of law on the families they studied, it is possible to read their data quite differently. . . .

Indeed, one can read much of the California sample data as showing real movement toward greater shared responsibility. That a large majority of fathers, some seventy percent, expressed initial interest in either sole or dual *physical* custody itself seems to indicate such movement. While far fewer fathers than mothers formally sought primary or dual physical custody, a substantial number did make such a request. Joint *legal* custody, moreover, has become the norm in California and is so regarded by both mothers and fathers. A majority of both mothers and fathers wanted joint legal custody from the outset. These desires were likely to be reflected in both formal requests and judicial decisions. In two-thirds of the cases in which only one party participated formally, the request was usually for joint legal custody, and, when both parents made the same request, it was almost always for that kind of award. Conflicting requests with regard to legal custody occurred in only eleven percent of all cases.

It might be suggested, although cautiously—because of lack of data from an earlier time—that the very high level of commitment to joint legal custody, the substantial levels of expressed paternal interest in sole or joint physical custody, and the somewhat lower but still substantial level of requests for sole or dual physical custody by fathers do indicate a change in attitudes and behaviors that is influenced by the legal context. The chicken-and-egg problem is, of course, obvious, but there is no compelling basis for saying that law merely followed, rather than participated in shaping, social attitudes.

Moreover, the extraordinarily low levels of both felt hostility and legal conflict may also reflect the effects of divorce reform. This suggestion requires some speculation because, once again, we have no base line from an earlier time against which to compare Maccoby and Mnookin's data. Nonetheless, there is a great deal of popular supposition, supported by genuinely horrible stories, suggesting that divorce generally, and custody matters particularly, are conducted as wars of annihilation. Just that sense accounts in great part for the current enthusiasm for alternative dispute resolution and, indeed, for joint custody.

The remarkably low levels of reported hostility in Maccoby and Mnookin's sample stand at the opposite pole from general assumptions about the experience of divorce. They are so low, indeed, as to call for skepticism, but if one credits the data, they justify a guess that the California sample has internalized the policy of reduced conflict at divorce, at least in what they say about their experiences and perhaps in their behavior as well.

Secondly, Maccoby and Mnookin's critique of the results reached by their sample families and their doubts concerning the importance of the shadow of the law may take too narrow a focus. The authors emphasize heavily one set of values associated with divorce reform in California, and their pessimistic interpretation of their data is measured entirely by success in achieving gender neutrality. However, laws and policies rarely embody a single value. By looking so closely at one set of values, the authors may not have given full weight to other values embodied in the domestic relations law of California and other states.

Perhaps the most important of those other values is continuity in caretaking: a value that is expressly recognized at least in California judicial decisions and, in operation, tends to perpetuate childrearing practices adopted while the family was intact. The usual formula for giving legal effect to the value of continuity within a formally gender neutral scheme is to adopt a preference in favor of the "primary caretaker"—that is, the parent who carried out most childrearing responsibilities prior to separation. . . . In *Burchard v. Garay,* for example, the California Supreme Court reversed a trial court custody award for a father entered for the following reasons:

> William is financially better off—he has greater job stability, owns his own home, and is "better equipped economically . . . to give constant care to the minor child and cope with his continuing needs." . . . William has remarried, and he "and the stepmother can provide constant care for the minor child and keep him on a regular schedule without resorting to other caretakers"; Ana, on the other hand, must rely upon babysitters and day care centers while she works and studies. Finally, the court referred to William providing the mother with visitation, an indirect reference to Ana's unwillingness to permit William visitation.

The trial court also noted that Ana had a history of emotional instability.

Applying the "best interests" standard, the Supreme Court concluded that all of the factors cited by the trial court together "weigh less to our mind than a matter it did not discuss—the importance of continuity and stability in custody arrangements . . . ."

To be sure, *Burchard* establishes no formal presumption and holds only that the trial court erred in giving substantial weight to the father's greater financial capacity and the mother's need to work outside the home. Nonetheless, the court's language and its willingness to reverse the trial court's decision express a strong preference for custody by the primary caretaker, and lawyers could have understood it generally to confirm the value of continuity in custodial decisions. To the extent that mothers more often serve as primary caretakers and that parents and their lawyers assume that maternal claims will be so heavily favored, one would expect just the pattern found by Maccoby and Mnookin. One would, moreover, expect many of the details of that pattern, including the abandonment by fathers of preferences for sole or joint custody, when it is clear that the mother had been and wished to remain the primary caretaker. . . .

It should also be said, however, that the primary caretaker presumption operates to confirm maternal custody because mothers and fathers continue to allocate childrearing responsibilities in "traditional" ways during marriage and themselves value continuity of child care. The presumption only becomes operational after childrearing patterns have existed, in many instances, for a number of years. A divorce decree could only overcome the effects of the maternal preference on those preexisting patterns by *imposing* dual custody.

Although Maccoby and Mnookin believe that result to be consistent with California custody law, both the *Garay* decision and subsequent legislative action cast doubt on that interpretation. Further, as their own data clearly suggest, such a solution carries with it great cost to continuity of child care, considerable initial cost to mothers who wish continuity in their own roles, and substantial risks of hostility and frustration in the subsequent co-parenting relationship—consequences that the parties may have foreseen.

This is not to say that *Dividing the Child* does not reveal gendered patterns in the decisions of both parents and courts. It is to say that the patterns the authors find do not necessarily demonstrate the failure, or irrelevance, of California divorce policy. Those patterns reflect gendered living arrangements established by the spouses long before the divorce. Perhaps it would be better if other patterns existed. However, a body of law that takes effect only after partners have established living patterns and that is rarely contemplated during the marriage cannot be regarded as ineffective because it does not change behavior that occurs prior to the occasion for its use.

Catherine R. Albiston, Eleanor E. Maccoby, & Robert H. Mnookin, *Does Joint Legal Custody Matter?*, 2 STANFORD LAW & POLICY REVIEW 167 (Spring 1990)[*]

Under California law, parents awarded joint legal custody possess equal authority to make decisions about their children, even if one parent has sole physical custody and the children live primarily with that parent. While the distinction between joint legal and joint physical custody was first alluded to in 1979 California legislation, a 1983 amendment explicitly defined joint legal custody to mean "both parents shall share the right and responsibility to make decisions relating to the health, education, and welfare of the child." This was distinct from the legislative definition of joint physical custody as "each of the parents . . . [having] significant periods of physical custody," and the importance of maintaining "frequent and continuing contact with both parents." Since 1979, many other states have enacted statutes concerning joint custody, but most of these do not explicitly distinguish between joint legal or joint physical custody.

Joint legal custody has become very common in California. In data reported elsewhere, 79 percent of families in the study presented in this article had joint legal custody decrees. Joint physical custody decrees, however, were much less common as only about twenty percent of these families had joint physical custody decrees. While joint legal custody has become common, it is unclear whether it has any impact on parents' behavior. It is the purpose of this article to address this question. . . .

CLAIMS ABOUT JOINT LEGAL CUSTODY

Parent-Child Contact

Aside from its ideological attractions, many claims have been made about the benefits of joint legal custody. First, advocates of joint legal custody argue that the formal designation of legal custody strengthens or maintains nonresidential parents' commitment to their children, and that this increased commitment increases nonresidential parents' visitation with their children. Some research has indicated that fathers with joint legal custody have more contact with their children, are more involved in activities with their children, and share parental responsibilities to a greater degree than fathers without legal custody.

Proponents of joint legal custody argue that it increases the nonresidential parents' involvement and influence in the lives of their children and that such involvement is desirable. Prior to the distinction in California law between legal and physical custody, an award of sole custody could mean one parent's loss of control over such decisions as medical care, religious training, and schooling for his or her child. Now an equal role is possible for nonresidential parents in decisions concerning their children. Furthermore, the recognition and exercise of this role may lessen the negative connotations associated with being a noncustodial parent and keep these parents more involved in the major events of their children's lives.

Communication Between Parents

The second argument is that joint legal custody, by requiring communication and cooperation between parents to make decisions concerning the child, encourages parents to develop a positive coparenting relationship. If joint legal custody does promote children's visitation with the nonresidential parent, more cooperation may be required between parents to manage the logistics of this visitation. Luepnitz found that parents with joint custody reported greater cooperation than parents with sole custody, and Ilfeld, Ilfeld, and Alexander found that relitigation rates for joint legal custody families were half those for sole legal custody families, suggesting that joint custody reduces parental conflict. Phear et al., however, found that joint legal custody cases were significantly more likely to relitigate custody than cases with sole legal custody.

Critics of the argument that joint legal custody reduces parental conflict point out that the necessity of communicating and continuing the relationship with a former spouse may be a cause of stress between parents. Joint legal custody may give responsibility for the child to one parent, the physical custodian, and preserve the nonresidential parent's right to meddle in the residential parent's affairs. For example, after a residential custodian remarries, the nonresidential parent may suddenly take an interest in decisions concerning the child, either because of fears of being replaced or a desire to interfere in the new marriage. Additionally, . . . joint legal custody may cause problems when parents bring different values to decisions about their children, for example, deciding whether a pregnant teenage daughter may have an abortion.

Payment of Child Support

A third argument in favor of joint legal custody is that it strengthens the bond between nonresidential fathers and their children, emphasizing fathers' responsibilities and encouraging them to pay more of the child support they owe. In some studies, fathers with joint legal custody show higher compliance with support awards than fathers where the mother has sole legal custody. In addition, if fathers with joint legal custody do in fact spend more time with their children, they may have more opportunities to pay for extra expenses above and beyond the formal child support award. Therefore, joint legal custody may allow fathers greater flexibility in how they support their children. Some caution, however, that a legal preference for joint legal custody may have a negative impact on financial outcomes if, in the negotiation process, mothers give up financial security in the form of child support to keep sole legal custody of their children.

The limitation of most existing research concerning joint legal custody is that it does not control for factors that may be related to choosing joint legal custody and also affect the dependent measures chosen by the researcher. For example, parents who are more cooperative and less hostile at the time of separation may be more likely to choose joint legal custody, and also more likely to have a good coparenting relationship after divorce. Similarly, joint legal custody fathers may be more likely to pay their child support than mother legal custody fathers because they are more affluent and can afford to do so. Finally, some fathers may choose joint legal custody and spend more time with their children after divorce because they were more involved with their children at the time of separation than fathers who choose mother legal custody. Many studies attribute differences in outcomes between the different custodial arrangements to the arrangements themselves, without investigating possible underlying causes related to self-selection in joint legal custody families.

SAMPLE AND METHOD

The Stanford Child Custody Study is a five year longitudinal study involving 1,124 California families who filed for divorce between September 1984 and March 1985. Families were required to meet three eligibility requirements: 1) the petition had to be filed between September 1, 1984 and March 31, 1985 in Santa Clara or San Mateo County; 2) the family had to have at least one child under 16 years of age at the time of the filing; and 3) the couple could have been separated no more than 13 months at the time of the filing. Information was obtained from two sources: 1) court records for families with completed divorces, and 2) three rounds of structured telephone interviews with parents that lasted approximately one hour each. Data from the court record included information about the custody requests of the parents, the final custody outcome for the family, and whether the case had been referred to mediation or evaluation. The parent interviews focused on the decision process of the divorcing couple concerning custody and visitation arrangements, and family functioning following separation. The first parent interview (Time 1) took place on average six months after the parents had separated. The second interview (Time 2) took place one and one-half years after separation, and the third interview (Time 3) took place approximately three and one-half years after separation.

Data are presented for families who received a final divorce decree determining custody of the children by September 1989, and who had an interview with at least one parent at Time 3. To investigate the effects of legal custody separately from the effects of changing de facto residential patterns, the sample was further restricted to families in which the children's de facto residence was with the mother at Time 3. To determine whether joint legal custody made a difference for these families, families with joint legal custody were then compared to those with mother legal custody on a number of dependent measures. The analyses were restricted to families with mother physical custody decrees because the number of families with father physical custody decrees was very small (N = 80) and few residential fathers also had sole legal custody (N = 17). The mother residence sample provided a much better comparison, as 328 of these families had joint legal custody decrees and 121 families had mother legal custody decrees.

Within the sample of mother residential families, those with mother legal custody tended to have lower father incomes than those with joint legal custody. . . . Families were then divided into three income categories: (a) between $0 and $15,000, (b) $15,000 to $30,000, and (c) $30,000 to $70,000. In this way an initial control was provided for the effect of income on our dependent measures, and the two legal custody groups could be compared at all three income levels.

MEASURES

Involvement

There were three primary measures of involvement: overnight visitation, father's contact (including non-overnight visitation), and father's involvement in decision making. Overnight visitation was measured as the number of nights the child spent with the father in a typical two-week period, using information from parent interviews. In addition to overnights, a scale of father's contact ranging from no contact to some overnight visitation was constructed from the interview visitation information.

To examine shared decision making, at Time 3 interview parents were asked how often they talked with each other about such everyday issues as the child's school progress, extracurricular activities, and responsibilities and privileges. Parents also indicated if any major decisions about religious training, schooling, or medical treatment for a serious illness had been made since the separation. Finally, parents rated on a five-point scale the nonresidential parents' involvement in both everyday and major decisions, where one was "the nonresidential parent is usually not informed" and five was "both parents are equally involved in the decision."

Parental Relationship

Maccoby, Depner, and Mnookin, using a larger subsample of the divorced families, constructed a descriptive measure of couples' coparenting abilities. Parents were scored on two dimensions of their coparenting relationship: "Discord" (couples who argue, undermine each other's parenting, and have logistical problems exchanging the children scored high), and "Cooperative Communication" (parents who do not avoid each other, who talk frequently about the children, and coordinate household rules scored high). These two scales were then cross-classified to create four coparenting patterns: "Cooperative" (high cooperative communication and low discord), "Conflicted" (high discord and low cooperative communication), "Disengaged" (low discord and low cooperative communication), and "Mixed" (high cooperative communication and high discord).

As an additional measure of the parental relationship, interviewers rated on a 10-point scale respondents' hostility toward their spouses at both Time 1 and Time 3. A family level hostility score was constructed by taking the mean of the parents' scores. If only one parent was interviewed, that parent's score became the family's score.

Financial Support

The primary measure of financial support was the father's compliance with the court-ordered child support award. Compliance was defined as the percentage of the child support award in the court record that was actually being paid at Time 3. The mother's report of support paid was used unless the father was the only parent interviewed in which case his report of payment was used. Additional information about father's payment behavior was generated using interview information from Time 2 and Time 3. At Time 2, both mothers and fathers were asked if in addition to child support payments, "there was anything else that the nonresidential parent had done to help the child financially this year?" Fathers could help financially in inexpensive, moderately expensive, or very expensive ways, and either occasionally or regularly. Open ended responses indicated that typical extra items were entertainment, school clothes, or summer camp. At Time 3 respondents were asked whether the father paid for extras "like child care, schooling or housing?" At both Time 2 and Time 3 the father was credited with paying for extras if either parent indicated that he did so.

TABLE 2. FATHERS' VISITATION AT TIME 3

Average Number of Overnights per Two Weeks at Time 3							
	$0-15K	$15-30K	$30-70K	Overall Model	Income	Legal Custody	Income x Legal Custody
Joint Legal	0.37	0.88	0.93	4.56***	6.30**	3.57+	0.11
Mother Legal	0.17	0.67	0.61				
Percent of Fathers with High Daytime Contact or Overnight Visitation							
	$0-15K	$15-30K	$30-70K	Overall Model	Income	Legal Custody	Income x Legal Custody
Joint Legal	37%	54%	59%	3.50**	6.62**	2.18	0.42
Mother Legal	17%	48%	54%				

+ $p \leq .10$
** $p \leq .01$
*** $p \leq .001$

RESULTS

Self-Selection Factors

Since we were comparing nonresidential fathers' behavior for those families who did or did not have joint legal custody, it was important to explore how these two groups differed initially (before legal custody awards had been made) on other factors that might be related to the selection of joint legal custody. . . . [T]here were several significant differences between joint legal custody families and mother legal custody families. Fathers who later were awarded joint legal custody spent more overnights with their children at Time 1 (shortly after separation) than mother legal custody fathers. In addition, mothers in joint legal custody families were less hostile at Time 1 than mothers in mother legal custody families, whereas joint legal custody fathers were more hostile than fathers with mother legal custody. Finally, joint legal custody fathers had higher incomes, were more likely to have a college degree, and were more likely to be employed than fathers without legal custody. As these differences could be related to fathers' behavior after divorce, these factors were controlled in the analyses.

Visitation, Contact, and Involvement in Decision Making

Within broad income groups, joint legal custody families were compared to mother legal custody families on the number of overnights the child spent with the father in a typical two-week period at Time 3, at first not controlling for initial differences between the two custody groups. This analysis indicated that fathers with higher incomes spent more overnights with their children. (See Table 2). In addition, there was a trend (p = .06) for fathers to have more overnights if they had joint legal custody than if mother had sole legal custody. Thus, this preliminary examination indicated a small but significant effect for legal custody on fathers' overnight visitation, but it appeared that fathers' time with their children was more strongly related to their income than to the legal custody agreement.

Among fathers who continue to see their children, not all have overnight visitation, especially if they cannot afford housing in which it is suitable for the child to spend the night. To account for this possibility, joint legal custody families were compared to mother legal custody families using a measure of contact that allowed for non-overnight visitation. This scale divided fathers into those with low daytime visitation or no contact, and those with high daytime visitation or overnight visitation. As Table 2 illustrates, fathers' contact with their children at Time 3 was not significantly related to the legal custody decree. Again, contact increased as a function of income. Thus, joint legal custody was not strongly related to children's increased contact with their nonresidential fathers, even when fathers with regular visitation but no overnights were taken into account.

After this initial examination, multiple regression analysis was used to control for the initial differences between the two custody groups. . . . [J]oint legal custody was not related to overnight visitation once other factors were taken into account. Furthermore, father's income was no longer a significant factor. More initial hostility from the mother was related to less overnight visitation, but father's overnight visitation at Time 1 was the strongest predictor of his visitation at Time 3. Findings for father's overall contact were similar, as the strongest predictor of a father's contact at Time 3 was his contact at Time 1 (data not shown). While the preliminary analyses seemed to indicate some differences in visitation between the two custody groups, these subsequent findings clearly indicate that joint legal custody was not significantly related to increased visitation at Time 3 once other factors were taken into account.

Regardless of the amount of time they spent with their children, one would expect joint legal custody fathers to have been more involved in decisions concerning their children. Parents with joint legal custody were significantly more likely than parents with mother legal custody to talk with each other about the child's school progress and extracurricular activities, although there were no significant differences for other everyday decisions. The more frequent discussions of school progress and extracurricular activities, however, may have been related to the need for coordination given their more frequent visitation, as families who chose joint legal custody had more visitation from the outset (Time 1) than mother legal custody families. When we compared fathers' involvement in everyday decisions between custody groups and controlled for initial differences, joint legal custody fathers were no more involved in everyday decisions than mother legal custody fathers, and the only significant relation that emerged was a negative one between mothers' initial hostility and fathers' involvement in such decisions (data not shown).

Joint legal custody fathers also were not more involved than mother legal custody fathers in major decisions concerning their children. Since separation, 25 percent of the families in this sample made a decision concerning the religious training of the child, 45 percent made a decision about which school the child would attend, and 32 percent made a major medical decision concerning the child. . . . [The] father's education and initial overnight visitation were positively related to his involvement in such decisions, whereas mother's initial hostility was negatively related to his involvement. Once again, joint legal custody was not a significant predictor of father's involvement. These data indicate that it is not joint legal custody, but initial hostility within the family as well as characteristics of the father that affect nonresidential fathers' involvement in decision making.

Parental Relationship

To determine whether parents in families with joint legal custody improved their communication and cooperation, joint legal custody families were compared to mother legal custody families on their coparenting styles. If joint legal custody promotes cooperation and communication between divorcing parents, then there should be a greater proportion of "Cooperative" coparenting relationships among families with joint legal custody than among families with mother legal custody. Conversely, if it is the case that joint legal custody gives one parent "meddling rights," a greater proportion of "Conflicted" coparenting relationships should be found among families with joint legal custody than among those with mother legal custody. Regardless of whether the parental involvement was positive or negative, there should be fewer "Disengaged" relationships among the joint legal custody families than among the mother legal custody families. As Table 6 demonstrates, however, families with joint legal custody did not differ significantly from families with mother legal custody in their distribution among "Cooperative," "Conflicted," and "Disengaged" coparenting styles.

TABLE 6. COPARENTING AT TIME 3

Coparenting Style At Time 3[a]	Mother Physical Joint Legal	Mother Physical Mother Legal
(N = 194)	(N = 52)	
Cooperative	30.9%	28.9%
Conflicted	27.8	28.9
Disengaged	41.2	42.3
Total	100%[b]	100%[b]

Chi-Square (2, N =246) = 0.96, ns.
[a] Familes in which the children have contact with both parents.
[b] Percents do not add to 100% due to rounding error

The Cooperative Communication and Discord scales were also considered separately, while controlling for the earlier differences between the two legal custody groups. The strongest predictors of parental cooperation and discord at Time 3 were cooperation and discord at Time 2. Cooperative Communication was marginally higher if the father was employed, but neither joint legal custody nor other factors affected this aspect of coparenting. However, both father's income and joint legal custody were significantly related to Discord. Finally, an analysis of hostility indicated that the only significant predictors of family hostility at Time 3 were parental hostility at Time 1 and a negative relation between father's education and hostility.

The finding concerning decreasing Discord must be interpreted with caution. While joint legal custody families experienced decreasing parental discord, this evidently did not imply increased coordination between the two households. Thus, although open quarreling and active mutual undermining may have diminished, joint legal custody families did not show a parallel increase in cooperative communication. We also emphasize that the analysis of joint legal custody's relation to discord only applied to families in which the children saw both parents. The analysis of parental hostility, however, applied to all families in this sample, and indicated no relation between joint legal custody and decreasing (or increasing) parental hostility.

Financial Support

To investigate the relation between legal custody and financial support three variables were examined: child support awards, fathers' compliance with those awards, and the percentage of fathers who pay for extra items for their children. Not surprisingly, the amount of the support award increased with father's income. The legal custody arrangement, however, was not significantly related to the size of the monthly child support award, suggesting that custodial mothers did not substantially compromise on child support to keep sole legal custody. Similarly, joint legal custody made no difference in father's compliance once income was taken into account and, as one might expect, fathers' compliance increased significantly with their income. Subsequent analysis of compliance, controlling for initial differences, however, revealed that the effect of income disappeared once fathers' education was considered. These analyses suggest two conclusions. First, joint legal custody does not, in fact, improve fathers' compliance with child support awards once their ability to pay is taken into account. Second, the education of the father appears to be more strongly related to his compliance than his level of income (although of course these measures are related).

Although joint legal custody fathers are no better than mother legal custody fathers in their compliance with child support, one could argue that they pay for more extra items, such as clothes, toys, or child care. Our data, however, does not support this hypothesis. At Time 2, neither joint legal custody nor higher father income were related to paying for extras on a regular basis. In addition, only father's income was related to paying for extras on an occasional basis. Although the measure is slightly different at Time 3, the story is the same, as neither joint legal custody nor increases in father's income appeared to increase the percentage of fathers who paid for extras for their children.

CONCLUSIONS

In this paper we explored the possibility that joint legal custody increases nonresidential fathers' involvement in three major areas: contact with their children, relations with their ex-spouse, and financial support of their children. With one exception, all of our evidence suggests that joint legal custody has no significant effect on any of these dependent measures once initial differences between the two custody groups are taken into account. Even the exception, a significant relation between joint legal custody and decreasing discord between the parents, only applied to a subsample of families in which the children visited both parents, and was not accompanied by a parallel increase in parental cooperation.

What are the implications of these findings for policy concerning joint legal custody? Although in aggregate data we found no evidence to support claims for the positive or negative effects of joint legal custody, it is important to emphasize that this does not preclude their occurrence in some families. Nevertheless, it appears that joint legal custody is neither the solution to the problems of divorce nor a catalyst for increasing conflict in divorcing families. Broad legislative policies either advocating or condemning joint legal custody on the basis of such claims thus seem entirely unwarranted. California policy currently encourages joint custody in the interest of "frequent and continuing contact with both parents," with the implicit assumption that joint legal custody will influence the behavior of parents after divorce. Our findings, however, provide no basis for this implicit assumption.

Why is it that joint legal custody has little or no effect on parents' behavior? In data reported elsewhere, we found that in California most joint legal custody decrees were the result of negotiation between parents rather than the exercise of judicial discretion, and few families had disagreements over legal custody. In addition, 79 percent of the families in this study had joint legal custody decrees, making it by far the most common legal custody agreement. Perhaps, during a time when only ten or twenty percent of families had joint legal custody, it did in fact affect parental behavior. Today, however, when this form of legal custody is more widespread, it appears to mean very little in practice. It also is possible that joint legal custody never had a significant effect on parental behavior. Legal custody may be symbolic for most families, whereas the substantive concern of parents is the amount of time they have with their children, not their formal legal authority.

It is also important to recognize the potential impact of joint legal custody on perceptions of gender roles. Perhaps the importance of joint legal custody is that it is a legislative affirmation that fathers, as well as mothers, are responsible for their children after divorce. Behavioral changes related to joint legal custody may best be measured not by comparing sole and joint legal custody families of the same temporal cohort, but by comparing successive cohorts on parental behavior following divorce. For example, nonresidential parents today may be more involved than their counterparts of twenty years ago partially because of a growing expectation in the wake of no-fault reform that they remain involved. Although changes related to joint legal custody are confounded with recent shifts in gender role assumptions as a whole, reflecting these changing assumptions in legal institutions may eventually impact social ideology. Even though our findings indicate that the joint legal custody label alone will not make divorced parents equal partners in the lives of their children, we also find no compelling evidence that joint legal custody generates conflict between parents. Thus, the retention of joint legal custody as an option for its affirmation of the involvement of nonresidential parents and its potential impact on perceptions of gender roles may be warranted. We caution, however, that the absence of harmful effects in families who, for the most part, voluntarily chose joint legal custody cannot be generalized to those who have joint legal custody imposed upon them.

Debate and research concerning joint custody has focused on its most easily observed and popular form, namely joint legal custody. Our data suggest, however, that this focus may be somewhat misplaced, given joint legal custody's apparently marginal effect on family functioning after divorce. By focusing on legal custody or failing to distinguish between legal and physical custody, scholars may be ignoring substantial issues in establishing and maintaining a successful shared physical custody arrangement. More attention should be given to the prevalence and success of joint physical custody agreements, as well as the implications of decrees granting joint physical custody for the actual residential arrangements for children. Insight into the success of joint physical custody decrees, as well as a better understanding of the implications of dual residence for the well-being of children, are essential for the development of policy concerning the custody of children following divorce.

CHAPTER VIII

The Family and Family Law

A. Changing Cultural and Legal Understandings of the Family

In this last chapter, our goal is to look more broadly at the whole field of family law in order to understand what directions it is moving in and should move in, what functions it serves, and how well it serves them. We begin with a series of articles that attempt to understand different cultural constructs that order our understanding of families and the law that governs them. The first of these articles surveys recent developments in family law by looking at the kind of vocabulary that is available to a family law institution and by suggesting that the vocabulary of family law seems to be changing in important ways. In particular, the institutions of family law are decreasingly likely to use moral language and to transfer moral issues to the people the law once regulated. The article also seeks to understand why such a development might occur. To answer that questions it looks at factors both internal and external to family law. That is, it identifies some characteristics of family law that may be shaping it and to intellectual, cultural, and social currents outside the law that may also be affecting it.

Carl E. Schneider, *Moral Discourse and the Transformation of American Family Law*, 83 MICHIGAN LAW REVIEW 1803 (1985)[*]

Four forces in American institutions and culture have shaped modern family law. They are the legal tradition of noninterference in family affairs, the ideology of liberal individualism, American society's changing moral beliefs, and the rise of "psychologic man." These forces have occasioned a crucial change: a diminution of the law's discourse in moral terms about the relations between family members, and the transfer of many moral decisions from the law to the people the law once regulated. I do not mean that this change is complete or will ever be completed. I do not suppose that it is occurring in every aspect of family law, or everywhere in the country with equal speed. I emphasize that there are other trends, and that there is a considered and considerable

---

[*]   Copyright © 1985. Reprinted with permission.

reaction to the trend impelled by a revived conservatism and a politicized fundamentalism. But I do suggest that the change is widespread jurisdictionally, institutionally, and doctrinally; that it is deep-seated; and that it is transforming family law.

Divorce is among the clearest examples of the change I discern. For over a century, divorce law reflected and sought to enforce society's sense of the proper moral relations between husband and wife. Indeed, the law of divorce was virtually the only law that spoke directly or systematically to an ideal of marital relations. That ideal included duties of life-long mutual responsibility and fidelity from which a spouse could be relieved, roughly speaking, only upon the serious breach of a moral duty by the other spouse. In the last two decades, however, every state has statutorily permitted some kind of no-fault divorce. These reforms exemplify the trend I hypothesize because (1) they represent a deliberate decision that the morality of each divorce is too delicate and complex for public, impersonal, and adversarial discussion; (2) they represent a decision that the moral standard of life-long fidelity ought no longer be publicly enforced; and (3) they represent a decision to diminish the extent of mutual spousal responsibility that will be governmentally required.

It is, of course, true that no-fault divorce rests in part on a moral view about the relations of people to each other and about the proper scope of government influence over people's lives. Thus I am far from suggesting that the decision to adopt no-fault divorce was itself amoral or immoral. Rather, my point is that, before no-fault divorce, a court discussed a petition for divorce in moral terms; after no-fault divorce, such a petition did not have to be discussed in moral terms. Before no-fault divorce, the law stated a view of the moral prerequisites to divorce; after no-fault divorce, the law is best seen as stating no view on the subject. Before no-fault divorce, the law retained for itself much of the responsibility for the moral choice whether to divorce; after no-fault, most of that responsibility was transferred to the husband and wife.

I will next examine four features of American life that form yet a broader context of this change in family law—the legal tradition of noninterference in the family, the ideology of liberal individualism, society's changing moral views, and the rise of psychologic man.

A. The Legal Tradition of Noninterference in the Family

Perhaps the oldest impediment to moral discourse in family law is the legal tradition of noninterference in the family. That tradition rests in large measure on the practical difficulties of enforcing family law and the practical consequences of trying to do so. Because of this tradition, the moral problems associated with many kinds of family disputes do not enter legal discourse. The tradition is an old one, has telling rationales, and may be growing in appeal.

The law not only suspects that intervention will do harm; it doubts that intervention will do good: in family law as in few other areas of the law, the enforcement problems are ubiquitous and severe. Consider the frustrations of the law's attempts to prevent divorce; to enforce spousal-support obligations; to compel alimony and child support payments; to deter spouse and child abuse; to enforce fornication, cohabitation, sodomy, and adultery statutes; to regulate the use of contraceptives; to prevent abortions; to supervise neonatal euthanasia; and to enforce visitation rights. Nor is this inefficacy surprising—the very nature of family law suggests that it should be peculiarly and inherently difficult to enforce.

Enforcement difficulties arise first because much of what family law seeks to regulate—from child and spouse abuse to fornication—occurs in private. The distastefulness of investigating private life is sharp enough to have been used to justify the doctrine of constitutional privacy and to have contributed to the rise of no-fault divorce. Family privacy is often hard to breach because the parties all participated in the violation of law, because they wish to protect those who did participate, or because they are ashamed to have people know about the incident in which the state is interested. Families may also seek to maintain their privacy because they disagree with the law's definition of immoral behavior (as the *Rhodes* court suggested), because they dislike the law's meddling in family affairs, or because they feel the common urge of a family to unite against outside criticism.

Family law's second enforcement problem is that the person enforced against is often specially able to injure the very person the law intervened to protect. The spouse who wishes to resist divorce, the abused child or spouse, the pregnant woman, and her fetus are all vulnerable in this way. Legal intervention in these situations thus may be fruitless, or, worse, might provoke the person enforced against to retaliate against the person the law wants to protect. Because the person to be protected often depends on the person enforced against, even legal punishment itself can injure the person to be protected by depriving him or her of the presence or affection of the other.

The third enforcement difficulty arises from the fact that, in many critical areas of family law, the people the law wishes to regulate live in emotional settings and under psychological pressures which make them little susceptible to the law's persuasion or even coercion. None of us is immune "from the frailties of nature," and we are all "sometimes moved by the mysteries of passion," but many of those whom family law most wants to reach lead lives so distressful they can hardly control themselves or their circumstances.

In short, the law has long avoided many of the moral issues facing families under the authority of the tradition of "nonintervention." The bureaucratic and economic capacity of the state to intervene is now greater than ever before, and we now have graphic examples of the state's power to enforce some family laws. Yet the doctrine of nonintervention was probably never stronger. Indeed, the very scope of the state's capacity makes us anxious to cabin its activities, an anxiety that has been increased by the more romantic efforts—Prohibition, for instance—of our own government to enforce its will, as well as by the rise of the modern dictatorship.

The tradition of noninterference persists not only because we fear the state's power, but also because we doubt the state's efficacy. The state's retreat from direct regulation of some areas of family life has reinforced the popular belief that "you can't enforce morality." And that retreat has encouraged people to believe that family law's ultimate goals of permitting, inspiring, and sustaining decent relations between husbands and wives and parents and children can be secured—if society can secure them—only through comprehensive and costly social services and social reform. But the programs such people advocate are so comprehensive and so costly that they are politically absurd. Furthermore, there is now a sense that even comprehensive social reform has proved unsuccessful, and a sense that social science lacks the predictive and analytic power to reverse that failure.

B. The Tradition of Liberal Individualism

The legal tradition of noninterference in the family is in large part based, as we have seen, on practical difficulties encountered in trying to enforce family law. That tradition has been reinforced by an ideological development—the increasing displacement of the old republican ideal and the elevation to legal orthodoxy of that dictum from Mill's *On Liberty* that asserts

> that the sole end for which mankind are warranted, individually or collectively, in interfering with the liberty of action of any of their number, is self-protection. That the only purpose for which power can be rightfully exercised over any member of a civilized community, against his will, is to prevent harm to others.

Family-law thinking has, in places, incorporated this moral preference against social intervention in personal affairs that do not do "harm to others." That moral preference has, for instance, underlain reforms of divorce law, of laws regulating sexual activities between consenting adults, and of laws regulating reproductive matters; indeed, it has probably informed legal attitudes about every aspect of the relationship between the family and the state.

However, Mill's principle applies uneasily to much of family law, for one of the traditional difficulties with that principle—the uncertain meaning of "harm to others"—is particularly acute in family law, which, by definition, deals with one person's relationship with another person and therefore with a situation in which harm is always possible. And, because of the ties of affection (and finance) that bind family members, they are peculiarly vulnerable to each other: One spouse's suit for divorce will harm the other spouse, to say nothing of the distress caused their children and the penury inevitable when the divorcing spouses cannot support two households. (Precisely this vulnerability has, for instance, slowed the law's acceptance of marital contracts.) Not only are there many opportunities within families to harm other members; there are many incentives. The very people to whom the law transfers moral decisions will be "interested parties"—that is why they have been accorded the power to make the decision—and will often have a psychological or even financial interest in a decision adverse to the interests of other family members. That the law has been so greatly influenced by Mill's principle in the face of these difficulties is testimony to the power that principle has acquired in family law.

One explanation of the law's fondness for Mill, and a related cause of the trend toward diminished moral discourse in family law, is the law's increasingly pluralistic view of American society. Pluralism has strengthened the trend by inhibiting society's impulse to impose its moral principles on discrete groups within society and by nurturing a relativistic view of moral principles.

Although pluralism seems to us self-evident among American virtues and implicit in the first amendment, especially in the religion clauses, that amendment did not acquire its modern meaning until well into the twentieth century, long after the country's plural composition had become clear. But the burgeoning political and social power of ethnic groups, the admonitory example of Nazi Germany, the war against poverty, the civil rights movement, and the international passion for regional, ethnic, religious, and national particularism, among other causes, have made us self-conscious, if cautious, pluralists, as is evidenced by the impossibility of reading many late-nineteenth and early-twentieth century family-law opinions without embarrassment. And one way to accommodate diverse views about family morals has been to avoid resolving family law issues in terms of morals.

In principle, the need to accommodate diverse views about the family is diminished by the fact that responsibility for family law is confided to the states: any state is socially less plural than the country as a whole and consequently should be better able to adjust family laws to fit the preferences of its citizens. In practice, however, family law is increasingly subject to national influence. States may, if they choose, reject that influence when it is exerted by scholars or by groups like the American Law Institute and the National Conference of Commissioners on Uniform State Laws. The Supreme Court's contributions to family law, however, are more than precatory, and more than few. The Court's discovery in the fourteenth amendment of the "privacy" doctrine—which, in the Court's open-armed terms, has "some extension to activities relating to marriage, . . . procreation, . . . contraception, . . . and child rearing and education"—has raised constitutional doubts in virtually every area of family law. With that substantive due process provision always in the background, the fourteenth amendment's guarantee of procedural due process and its equal protection clause have further helped nationalize family law. Finally, as the federal government furnishes more social services and continues to be the most convenient means for interest groups to reach their ends, we may expect to see more congressional and administrative participation in family law. Thus, the Department of Health and Human Services has conditioned receipt of federal funds on compliance with its "Baby Doe" regulations, the House of Representatives recently passed its first "sense of Congress" legislation dealing with a family-law issue (visitation rights for grandparents), and the President recently signed legislation making federal funds to states contingent on a state's using wage assignments to collect child-support payments even where the custodial parent receives no federal funds.

The nationalization of family law thus conduces to the trend toward less moral discourse in the law by increasing the number of groups whose moral preferences must be accommodated. Finally, it probably also promotes the trend by accentuating the influence of the relatively elite individuals and institutions who, I have hypothesized, are especially likely to favor the changes that have led to diminished moral discourse, to whom liberal individualism seems natural.

C. Society's Changing Moral Beliefs

Liberal individualism, I have suggested, has increased our national tolerance for heterodox moralities, and has diminished the urge to impose morality profligately. Yet those changes might have altered family law less had not the old family law morality itself lost much of its meaning. As Mill wrote in a related context, so natural to mankind is intolerance in whatever they really care about, that religious freedom has hardly anywhere been practically realized, except where religious indifference, which dislikes to have its peace disturbed by theological quarrels, has added its weight to the scale.

To put it schematically, less is immoral; moral discourse in the law occurs most readily (especially in a law reluctant to be aspirational) when there is something to condemn; because there is less to condemn, there is less moral discourse.

"The sexual revolution" has become the name for that change in moral attitudes toward family and sexual life that has been developing at least since the end of the nineteenth century, when the "'new morality' . . . proclaimed the joys of the body, defended divorce and birth control, raised doubts about monogamy, and condemned interference with sexual life by the state or community." The revolution changed attitudes about every area of sexual morality quite as spectacularly as it changed rates of nonmarital sexual activity and of divorce. Professor Shorter reports, for instance, that "the percent of Americans who believe 'it is wrong for people to have sex relations before marriage' fell from 68 percent in 1969 to 48 percent in 1973 . . . ." So great has the revolution's influence been that, even when it has not changed a person's behavior or his standards for himself, it has commonly softened his standards for other people.

One cause of the sexual revolution has been the waning influence of Christianity among the relatively affluent, educated elite. There are, surely, many believers left among this group. But many of them believe in a liberal Christianity whose moral views on family law matters have long parted from those of traditional Christianity and of conservative churches. And even Catholics and conservative Protestants now give sexual relations—albeit only within marriage—that same unctuous importance given them by psychologized nonbelievers.

These changes in religious beliefs deeply undercut traditional family law, for much of it comes from the law of the English ecclesiastical courts and rests on classic Christian attitudes toward sexual matters. About those attitudes, Professor Rieff writes, "renunciatory controls of sexual opportunity were placed in the Christian culture very near the center of the symbolic that has not held." Quoting von Harnack, Rieff continues,

> At bottom, only a single point was dealt with, abstinence from sexual relationships; everything else was secondary: for he who had renounced these found nothing hard. Renunciation of the servile yoke of sin (*servile peccati iugum discutere*) was the watchword of Christians. . . . Virginity was the specifically Christian virtue, and the essence of all virtues; in this conviction the meaning of the evangelical law was summed up.

Such beliefs are now rejected or even unrecognized by many Christians, and the altered social role of American Christianity has made them virtually incomprehensible to many Americans.

In other words, because religious views are less universally and strongly held, statements of moral aspiration linked to religion have slipped more readily from legal discourse. This change is visible, for example, in the child-custody area, where evidence of concern for the moral welfare of the child—as instanced, for example, by evidence that the parent sends the child to Sunday school—is increasingly thought irrelevant. Because religious views on marital obligations have changed, the move to no-fault divorce was eased, and perhaps even made more necessary. Similarly, because religious views on sexual relations outside of marriage have changed, the law's tolerance, and even encouragement, of such relations has increased, as Marvin et al. indicate. Abortion, neonatal euthanasia, and homosexuality are but a few more examples of areas in which the changing nature and weight of religious views have helped change legal views and language.

D. The Rise of Psychologic Man

Sexual mores are not the only part of the old "family morality" to have lost their meaning; there has also been a larger shift from a "moral" to a "psychological" view of personal affairs. This shift is, of course, a cause (and probably also a consequence) of our changing view of sexual morals, it has sharpened our appreciation of the enforcement problem, and it shapes and is shaped by the tradition of liberal individualism. This shift may not be the most crucial cause of the trend away from moral discourse in family law; indeed, it is pointless to attempt such a distinction at this stage of our knowledge. However, the psychologic view merits particular attention here for several reasons. First, while psychology has, of all the social sciences, contributed most abundantly to family law scholarship, the consequences for family law of the psychologic view have not been sufficiently analyzed. Second, the rise of the psychologic view provokes specially intriguing questions about how ideas from "high" and "popular" culture enter legal thought and about the interplay between modes of popular and of legal thinking. Third, and perhaps most important, because the psychologic view interacts in important ways with each of the other origins of the trend, and because the psychologic view so directly affects the terms of modern discourse, a detailed study of its consequences for the law is an apt way to elaborate a description of the new discourse in family law. I shall therefore devote disproportionate space to it.

a. The complexities of the shift. The shift to psychologism has, of course, been described before, usually in apocalyptic woe or messianic joy. Nevertheless, the shift confounds description because it is intellectually fragmented and complex. Its patriarch and paradigm, surely, is Freud. But no important thought achieves social power undegraded, and Freud's thought has reached its present power in a gaudy array of vulgarizations which have, in the public mind, overwhelmed the sophisticated variants.

The shift further confounds description because it is also sociologically complex. Nevertheless, its scope and significance cannot be doubted. Thus three leading students of the shift announce "the introduction of the 'era of psychology.'" A 1957 study on which those scholars rely "spoke of a psychological orientation, as distinguished from material or moral orientations, and suggested that this way of looking at life experiences and life problems might increase significantly in the future." By 1976, they conclude, "this shift had indeed occurred."

b. From morals to medicine: the role of human happiness. For our purposes, a central feature of the psychologic view is that it replaces moral discourse with medical discourse and moral thought with therapeutic thought. That shift may usefully be understood in terms of the role attributed to human happiness in social life. The old view held that men and women were obligated to lead a good life as that was defined by religious or social convention. Happiness was not the purpose of these conventions, but was expected to be a by-product of performing one's duties. If it did not come, however, one would be consoled by knowing one had led the right kind of life. The psychologic view, at least in its ideal type, denies that there are religious or social conventions that are independently valid. It holds that life's goal is the search for personal well-being, adjustment, and contentment—in short, for "health." Adherence to a religious or social convention may serve that end, but if it does not, other paths to well-being should be tried and used. In short, says Rieff mordantly,

> [E]vil and immorality are disappearing, as Spencer assumed they would, mainly because our culture is changing its definition of human perfection. No longer the Saint, but the instinctual Everyman, twisting his neck uncomfortably inside the starched collar of culture, is the communal ideal, to whom men offer tacit prayers for deliverance from their inherited renuciations.

On the old view, the right life was difficult: one's duties were numerous and onerous (though not necessarily unpleasant); distractions from duty were numerous and dangerous. Thus, codes of family morality were aspirational and ascetic. As Professor Rieff observes:

> Heretofore, the saving arrangements of Western culture have appeared as symbol systems communicating demands by stoning the sensual with deprivations, and were thus operated in a dynamically ambivalent mode. Our culture developed, as its general technique of salvation, assents to moral demands that treated the sensual part of the self as an enemy. From mastery over this enemy-self there developed some triumphant moral feeling; a character ideal was born.

The psychologic view concedes that "stoning the sensual with deprivations" can work, but doubts it will. That view sees the drive of the instincts as crucial to understanding human motivation, believes that confining the drive of the instincts tends to be unhealthy, and, more specifically, sees sexual expression as central to human happiness.

c. Antinomianism, pragmatism, and nonbinding commitments. In his search for health, psychologic man must be skeptical and analytic in method and pragmatic in evaluation. In particular, psychologic man must learn not to judge himself, his relationships, or other people according to moral rules; to do so is dysfunctional, since it asks the wrong question ("Is it right?") and blinds him to the answers to the right question ("Does it work?"). In other words, psychologic man cannot come to rest in any relationship, or any community, or any creed; he must keep asking whether they are working for him. This is the doctrine of "nonbinding commitments." Personal and familial relations, on this view, become "arrangement[s] of convenience designed to advance the personal satisfactions and self-fulfillment of [their] members."

d. The search for self and the psychologic view of human nature. In the psychologic view, happiness comes from discovering and expressing one's unique true self. That self is discovered by peeling off society's false impositions and is expressed by peeling off its false constraints. Among the false impositions and constraints to be peeled off in the search for the "more personalized self-consciousness" are the roles and statuses into which society places people. Thus Veroff, Douvan, and Kulka announce as one of their "central themes" that "[s]ocial organization, social norms, the adaptation to and successful performance of social roles all seem to have lost some of their power to provide people with meaning, identity elements, satisfaction. In fact, role and status designations have become objects of suspicion . . . ."

The psychologic attitude seems to imply an optimistic account of human nature; if its proponents thought people base and vile, they could hardly advocate a Hobbesian world without the Leviathan or be so cheery about man's quest to find and express himself. Much psychologic writing explicitly argues that human nature is benign enough that, freed of socially imposed constraints, men will behave better than they do now. This benignity is buoyed by faith in human malleability: If people behave badly, it is because of environmental factors, which can be manipulated, or because of patterns of thought and behavior, which can (on some therapeutic views) be changed even if they cannot be understood.

Yet psychologic man's view of human nature is profoundly ambivalent. Against the optimism described in the preceding paragraph are pitted a vivid sense of the power and ubiquity of the passions, a dark sense of their cruelty, and a resigned sense that character is irrevocably and inevitably formed by early and universal experiences. Psychologic man's strain of pessimism about individual human nature is matched by a strain of pessimism about the capacity of systematic social activity to enhance human happiness. Professor Allen, in explaining why psychologism has been inimical to penal rehabilitation, notes the movement's frequent anti-intellectualism, its absence of public purpose, and the perverse fact that it "has not generally nourished the autonomy of individuals but has expressed a weariness with self-hood." Even "contemporary expressions of confidence in human malleability are often accompanied by a pervasive pessimism about the effectiveness and integrity of social institutions."

e. The psychologic view of privacy. Psychologic man's ambivalence about human nature extends to his views about privacy. On one hand, searching for one's self and peeling off social constraints seem to require privacy, and "privacy" at least as a slogan has more social (and legal) cachet than it used to. But those most enthralled by the psychologic attitude seem the least interested in privacy, as we may infer from the phrase "let it all hang out," from the techniques of psychotherapy, from the proclivity to use those techniques in ordinary conversation, from the itch of celebrities to discuss the intimacies of their lives on television, from the eagerness of the rest of us to become celebrities by retailing and living the intimacies of our lives on television, from our willingness to tell survey researchers whatever they want to know, from the belief in first names at first sight, and from the compelled contemplation of intimate and ultimate questions imposed on us by the pictures of the dead, the dying, and the *deshabille* which accost us in the daily papers and the monthly magazines. And some sacrifice of privacy seems inherent in the free expression of one's true personality, in the desire to reduce the power of social roles, and in the instant intimacy with family, friends, and colleagues that is also part of the psychologic creed.

The apparent conflict in psychologic man's view of privacy may perhaps be resolved, however, if we recall that privacy has come to have two meanings. The first, conventional, meaning speaks to the secrecy in which one conducts one's affairs. The second, newer, meaning speaks directly to the ability to conduct one's affairs autonomously. It is privacy in the second meaning psychologic man wants, for without autonomy his efforts to find and express himself may be thwarted. And it is privacy in the first meaning that psychologic man does not need, for, to him, secrecy is desired by those who are ashamed of what they do, and psychologic man's moral relativism and his awareness that all men serve unconscious drives make shame shameful. *Honi soit qui mal y pense.*

f. A case study. Perhaps greater concreteness can be given to psychologic man by reporting one version of his rise. Professor Susman suggests that in the nineteenth century, "character" was the word most revelatory of the modal American type, but that in the twentieth century, that word was "personality." The nineteenth century held "that the highest development of self ended in a version of self-control or self-mastery, which often meant fulfilment through sacrifice in the name of a higher law, ideals of duty, honor, integrity. One came to selfhood through obedience to law and ideals." The words "most frequently related to the notion of character" were *"citizenship, duty, democracy, work, building, golden deeds, outdoor life, conquest, honor, reputation, morals, manners, integrity,* and above all, *manhood."* The twentieth century, on the other hand, "stressed self-fulfillment, self-expression, self-gratification . . . ." Its "essentially antinomian . . . vision . . . with its view not of a higher law but of a higher self, was tempered by the suggestion that the self ought to be presented to society in such a way as to make oneself 'well-liked.'" The adjectives most frequently associated with personality "suggest a very different concept from that of character: *fascinating, stunning, attractive, magnetic, glowing, masterful, creative, dominant, forceful."*

Professor Schneider's article on moral discourse in family law analyzes one of the cultural constructs which Americans rely on in understanding families and the work of family law. But there are of course many others. Another approach is represented by our next article. Its starting point is one of the key social conundrums about the family—it seems neither to be an entity nor a collection of distinct individuals. And to say that it is one or the other seems to run the risk of socially undesirable consequences: If we say the family is an entity, we may blind ourselves to the interests of the individuals (particularly the weaker individuals) who make up the family. If we say the family is a collection of discrete individuals, we may blind ourselves to the identity-shaping power of the family and the moral claims families make on their members. In the article that follows, Dean Teitelbaum looks for a way out of these puzzles.

Lee E. Teitelbaum, *The Family as a System: A Preliminary Sketch*, 1996 UTAH LAW REVIEW 537*

IV. THE FAMILY AS A SYSTEM

. . . Thinking of the family as a "system" may not only accommodate, but help define, the relation of individual choice and public power to the family. I do not mean to place too much weight on the term "system." Indeed, the term "community" is in some ways better—at least reminding us that the family provides the paradigm case for "communitarian" values, and the following discussion will talk about the family as an "interpretive community," especially with respect to its internal relations.

However, the term "community" may not as fully capture the importance of relations between families and external agencies and rules as does "system." And the concept of a system surely incorporates a number of aspects of family life. In general, a system is understood as a network that "integrate[s] parts into a whole." This understanding incorporates both the sense of an identifiable, special relationship and the sense of membership by individuals that seem characteristic of families. The concept of a system may also be understood as referring not only to the internal ordering of parts, but to the system's interaction with and response to the environment in which it is situated. This aspect, too, is important in modern family life, having regard to the frequency and significance of the relationship between families and intermediate social systems.

Within this broad conception, systems vary in a number of ways. They may be very general, as in the case of the social system, or they may be devoted to the accomplishment of specific functions. Some systems, such as business organizations, are based on conflict; others, such as schools, on cooperative strategies.

The family is a special case of a social system. It is this in part because, as Niklas Luhmann observes, it is "the most indispensable system of all." The family is also special because of the complexity and variety of its internal relations and its relationship to its environment. These features are worth a moment.

A. The Internal Relations of the Family

Although it is often said that the modern family has lost all but an affective function, that view seems extreme and inaccurate. Families still serve in significant ways as economic, moral, and educational systems; they remain important agencies for the distribution of goods in our society.

Take, for example, the family as an economic system or "unit." Although wealth is no longer produced within the home and the methods of acquiring wealth are largely in the control of public and "private" corporate employers (and hence of even more anonymous "markets"), family members still largely control the consumption of wealth. The importance of these consumptive decisions is, in an odd way, revealed by the literature on divorce, which makes clear the often catastrophic consequences of dissolution for a household. That same literature reveals, by implication, the economic

---

importance of a single household. A family that is "normal" in its composition, income, and role assignments may live adequately together; that same family, dissolved, will suffer greatly. Moreover, a family makes crucial decisions about the generation, consumption, and distribution of its wealth as the family goes along. How many family members will work is ordinarily decided by husband and wife, and that decision defines the level of consumption available to them. When family members generate excess wealth, they typically decide how that wealth will be employed among an almost unlimited range of options.

Families have much to do with social control as well, although they no longer provide the principal mechanism for that purpose. Crime, delinquency, and mental illness are, to a very great extent, social phenomena, and families participate directly in their creation and categorization. A blow by one spouse to another is an act, but the actor will only be treated as a spouse abuser if the victim defines the conduct as intolerable and communicates that view to an official agency. A blow by a parent to a child is an act; whether the act is defined as child abuse rather than reasonable parental discipline depends largely on whether the family (or some other person) so identifies it. What counts as deviance by children within the home is, in very great part, defined within the home. The kinds of conduct that may be defined as disobedient "are virtually infinite because the particular commands that parents may give, and that children may disobey, are virtually infinite."

The family is also a moral and religious system, even though household gods have disappeared. While much of the religious authority rests in corporate churches, families lie at the center of moral choices in several ways. They make initial decisions about religious affiliations. While a child may not be "born into" a religion, parental commitment to that religion will determine at least the child's original religious definition. Moreover, parental conduct and attitudes have much to do with the strength of the child's attachment to a religious organization. This attachment is likely to be stronger if the parents are deeply committed to religious precept and practice and enroll their children in religious activities. Even apart from religion, parental views and conduct seemingly affect a child's moral development and conduct.

And, of course, the family is an emotional system. We generally assume, or perhaps hope, that the family provides a "diffuse, enduring solidarity" and an unconditional acceptance for its members—a place where the crucial question is not, "What have you done for me lately?" This characterization of family values is something of an ideal type; in many families, acceptance is in fact conditional, and solidarity is problematic. As we have seen, households have never been isolated from specific expectations of conduct or from considerations of success outside the household. Nonetheless, the interpretation of those expectations, and the emphasis that will be placed on one rather than another aspect of group life, is largely determined within the home and on highly localized criteria.

This variety of functions itself distinguishes families from specialized or "functions" systems such as business organizations or government agencies. In addition, however, the family is a special system in the sense that it not only performs all of these functions but performs all of them simultaneously. Whereas specialized or functional social systems, such as business organizations and public schools, typically are created to serve particularized purposes and determine their actions by primary reference to those purposes in a more or less formally rational way, the family must accommodate a broad set of purposes, often without a single primary reference.

For example, the decisions of business organizations are expected primarily to advance values of economic productivity. This is true not only of the obviously artificial entity, the corporation, but also of its human owners, the shareholders. While the owners of a corporation may be supposed to hold every imaginable value and goal for their own lives, they are transmuted into anonymous rational maximizers in their capacities as investors.

The specificity of the norm for business decision making differs strikingly from family economic decisions which are not influenced wholly or even largely by economic rationality. Rather, family decisions reflect a wide set of circumstances and values. Whether to save or spend money may depend more on emotional relations within the family than on market conditions. A corporation may or may not be permitted to make gifts to charities; families may do so because of religious or social values. They are, indeed, expected to give gifts and provide services to each other that they are not expected to give or provide to others and are, in some sense, encouraged to do so. The inequality associated with the desire of families to prefer their own members is a well-known source of frustration for ethicists but nonetheless is widely accepted, even among them.

Educational decisions may likewise be driven by religious values, as they were in *Wisconsin v. Yoder,* or by social and political values. Some parents may refuse to send their daughter to college because, in their view, her role is to be a wife and mother. Others may choose not to send a son to a private college for which he is well qualified because they resent its "elitist" attitude or the political tendencies of its faculty. Yet others may elect to send a child to such a college just because the social values the parents hold make doing so seem inevitable. And in doing so, such parents may thereby choose to invest what, if economic rationality were the only consideration, seems a "disproportionate" amount of their earnings in securing "the best" educational opportunity for their children. At least within an intact family, social and legal norms seem to grant families this latitude.

Social control is also diffusely operationalized in the family setting. The rules devised by parents for their children may reflect religious and cultural values. Economic circumstances and historical experience (including the parents' own history, such as an alcoholic relative) may also play a part. Tolerance for disobedience, and hence response to rule violation, are also highly localized. Some parents regard expressions of independence by their children as a normal developmental occurrence; others (again perhaps because of religious or cultural values) regard such demands as disrespectful and inappropriate. Situational factors may play a role as well. Whether a child is referred to court as an incorrigible child or left to "outgrow" his behavior may depend on the attitude of a stepparent and the emotional ties between the mother and her second husband far more than on the severity of the child's misconduct.

One other special aspect of the family system must be mentioned: its dynamism and mutability, both internally and with respect to external authority. The most familiar aspect of the dynamic character of family life is, of course, the parent/child relation.

Spousal relations, however, are also dynamic and mutable, perhaps more so now than previously. Two relatively modern phenomena seem to have contributed to the particularity and dynamic quality of family relationships. One is the prevalence of divorce; the other is the (probably related) increase in the incidence of families where both spouses are employed. These phenomena have created far more complex and changeable relations than we had seen before. The need to maintain two homes may require adjustments in styles of living and will often require, practically and as a matter of current divorce doctrine, a spouse who had been a homemaker to entirely change her occupation. The situation of one partner may be affected in a variety of ways by her own actions and by the actions of her former spouse. The entrance of a stepparent, or a live-in friend, may affect the relation between a custodial parent and her child in a number of ways. The kinds of behavior that are acceptable for the child may change because the custodial parent no longer is available to deal with the child, the conduct is unacceptable to the stepparent, or both.

An understanding of the complexity and dynamism of the family system may help us deal with one of the problems presented by "entity" or contractarian theories of the family: reconciling unity with choice. As we have seen, the notion of the family unit in its "entity" or anthropomorphic form leaves little space for recognizing individual claims—the interests that arise from a wide range of individualized decisions and arrangements—within a family. Respect for the "privacy" of the family unit seemingly requires ignoring other, possibly competing, bearers of rights—the individual family members. So Mr. and Mrs. McGuire are merged into the McGuires, an association whose internal relations are opaque to legal scrutiny. However, a theory of the family as the sum of agreements made by separate individual wills leaves little room for the sense of commitment experienced by and valued in family life.

But if we think of the family as a dynamic system, we need not anthropomorphize the family or decide that respect for unity means ignoring choice by family members. On the contrary, family relations can be seen as a series of choices by which various goals, values, and material conditions are accommodated. Because of their number, interrelatedness, and imbeddedness in everyday life, these choices are made as a matter of course, often without much discussion or even recognition that they are being made. Nonetheless, the success of family arrangements supposes that all parties in the system accept that arrangement on some basis.

At the same time, thinking of the family as an interactive system does not require ignoring the collective character of family life. We can suppose that choices are made, without believing that each choice is a simple expression of individual will. Rather, these choices can be understood in the context of a system that does not expect formal election and negotiation and in which family members at some point cease to think of their wills and choices as radically independent of those of others. Decisions are made as part of a carrying out of collective life and reflect not only individual preference but love, sympathy, and common enterprise. The wishes of each family member are partly defined by the complex histories and relations that characterize the family system, which cannot be reconstructed on an exigently individualistic or rationalistic basis.

B. The Relation of the Family to Other Social Systems

The discussion of internal family relations sought to show that it is possible, by viewing the family as an interactive system, to recognize both unity and choice as aspects of family organization and life. A second problem with both traditional unitary and contractarian views of the family is that of reconciling notions of family privacy with the operation of public power. An entity approach emphasizes distance between families and other institutions and approaches any effort by those institutions to regulate the family as an invasion of domestic sovereignty. A contractarian approach, on the other hand, is largely unconcerned with the effects of these systems and bodies of law on the family as a self-defining group because that approach does not recognize much of a role for the family as a group or institution.

In at least some versions of systems theory, however, systems must be understood in relation to their environment. I have suggested in other places that the family must be understood in this way. It can be imagined as a hub connected by spokes to a variety of other bodies of law, such as tax laws, bankruptcy laws, immigration laws, and medical care laws. The family is also connected to other social systems, including the economy, the insurance market, and the educational system.

At the most general level, family relations exist in a setting that includes legal and social norms that strongly influence the institutional idea of the family, the way families define the arrangements available to them, and the ways family members live their lives together. These norms also say something about what kinds of things require accommodation and something about the ways in which they may be accommodated. Mrs. McGuire's position within the family is defined, in part, because property laws give Mr. McGuire ownership over all wealth he produces and management power over family wealth. His position is further defined by laws that say that Mrs. McGuire can only obtain judicial assistance if she is neglected to the point of serious physical discomfort or if Mr. McGuire (at the age of 86) commits some other marital fault. His position also reflects customary and legal norms creating expectations that Mrs. McGuire would stay at home and help with the farm rather than generate her own income. The Yoder children's position is affected by a legal background that includes rules generally requiring obedience to parents, child-labor laws that do not permit school-age children to seek work outside the home, an economic system that does not remunerate persons with the marginal skills children have at age fourteen, and community religious forces that value being a farmer more than being an astronaut.

That is not to say that formal law and custom universally define intrafamily patterns. Husbands may be given the sole formal power of managing the family wealth, but wives often, and perhaps preponderantly, are practically responsible for managing that wealth. Even when custom and professional opinion together preferred mothers to stay home to care for their children, two-job families existed (and not always because of financial need). However, just as negotiations toward divorce occur "within the shadow of the law," so do the accommodations within the family. Economic power, social custom, and legal schema are qualifications not only on choice, but on the ways in which choice may be perceived and interpreted. An interpretive theory of the family system does not demand that we ignore, or reject as illegitimate, these sources of power. To the extent that we think they improperly constrain choice, the rules expressing that power can be changed.

Thinking of the family as an interactive system may also help us better understand the relationship of the family to other social organizations and systems. We have already seen that standard sociological and social historical interpretations of the family emphasize the positivization of law and the consequent assignment of what were once family responsibilities to a variety of social systems. The foregoing description of the family demonstrates, however, that despite this process of positivization or differentiation, the family continues to play a central role in modern society. Administrative and regulatory systems, such as the educational system and the juvenile court, do not entirely occupy the fields once primarily committed to family authority and, to a considerable extent, these systems' activities still depend on familial decisions. It is more accurate to say that responsibilities for these functions are shared between the family and these intermediate social systems.

In such a setting, it is important to examine these systems and their effects on the family rather than to ignore or reject them. That examination should recognize that choices made by families are influenced by the rules and patterns of systems external to them. Consider, for example, family economic decisions about who will work, where, and in what ways. These decisions are not made as an exercise of simple family autonomy and self-ordering; they are influenced by the employment market, by child-care systems, by tax laws, by public transportation systems, and by educational availability and cost, among other factors. Similarly, family decisions about medical care are influenced by federal and state health-care policy and its preference for an insurance approach that only grudgingly extends benefits to those who did not pay for them. So a person who is ill, and his or her spouse, were at one time expected to exhaust all of their resources as a condition of receiving Medicare assistance. This expectation, in turn, affected a variety of other family choices. Health-care providers, a different system, make price decisions affecting the care available to family members according to their interests in competitive compensation for staff, delivery of what they and their insurance carriers regard as good medical care, and perhaps by considerations of prestige. They also ration care with an eye to the level of payment insurers are willing to pay and thus may shift health-care responsibilities from hospital to family members at the point that hospital care is considered unnecessary by third-party payors. And health-care providers also make pricing and availability decisions that may shift responsibility for patient care from hospital to family members at the election of third-party payors.

Systems outside the family not only make decisions affecting the family, but in some circumstances also define family membership for their own purposes. Zoning ordinances and food stamp regulations may provide certain treatment or benefits for groups defined as "families," even though members of these groups clearly are not related by blood or marriage. The members of these same "families" or "households" would not, of course, be recognized as having a family relationship for other purposes. People who live together or even cohabit but are not related by blood or marriage are ordinarily not eligible for intestate succession, wrongful-death benefits, social security, or workers' compensation benefits. Similarly, a relationship that *would* be recognized as a "family" for domestic relations purposes may not be so treated for other legal purposes. A man and a woman may be validly married, and thus a family for purposes of support, legitimacy of children, and the like, but not be treated as spouses for immigration purposes if their intent does not meet congressional expectations of a marriage relationship.

These circumstances account in part for the temptation to say that the family "is" no one thing but rather a concept with various meanings across various areas of law and even within the brief lives of their human members. However, the existence of varying meanings associated with families in various domains of positive law does not mean that there is no such thing as a family system. It is only to say that the definition of the family is no longer a constant. It also reveals once again the centrality of the family system to other social institutions and the importance of its role in gaining access to, and adapting to the demands of, those social systems.

V. APPLICATIONS OF THE FAMILY SYSTEM APPROACH

There is neither time nor space to review the implications of this view of the family as an interactive system for the many contested aspects of domestic relations and related bodies of law. It might be worthwhile, however, to take a few familiar problems and see what this model of the family might suggest. In some cases, the analysis used here does not imply substantial change from current law, although it may supply a different way of understanding that law. In some cases, it implies significant doctrinal change. In yet others, formal doctrinal change is not required, but modification of what might be called "background rules"—domestic relations or other rules forming the legal and social context within which doctrine operates—seems necessary.

A. Economic Relations During Marriage

Let us return for a moment to the McGuire case. That situation presents what seems to be an insoluble dilemma. On the one hand, it seems quite wrong to leave Mrs. McGuire without the capacity to buy things—linoleum, a new stove, and a new cloth coat—that are surely appropriate to a woman of her age and family wealth. To follow the traditional view of the "family unit" appears to deny her any individual role in the marriage. While she may in principle be able to pledge her husband's credit to purchase necessaries, that remedy is practically uncertain and ethically doubtful. Practically, the availability of credit is up to the seller, and in a small Nebraska town, many merchants may be unwilling to antagonize Mr. McGuire or to risk a lawsuit to collect. Ethically, it seems wrong to treat Mrs. McGuire as if she had, during the course of their marriage, earned nothing and had no call on family resources for expenses associated with family life. The formal equality provided by Married Women's Property Acts is, of course, useless to the many families where, like the McGuires, husbands and wives follow traditional role allocations.

On the other hand, the remedy Mrs. McGuire sought—which seems appropriate if we emphasize a strong notion of individual choice—has real disadvantages. As we have already seen, families may make any number of financial decisions, and these decisions reflect highly contextualized (localized) calculations. For courts to make these decisions—whether savings should be spent on vacation or preserved for retirement, and whether earnings should be spent to purchase homemaking services or saved through the labor of one spouse—seems both inappropriate and unwise, not only for the obvious reasons but because, in many such cases, courts are asked implicitly to decide whether one or both spouses should work. Courts may also be asked to reform the consequences of decisions made, expressly or not, by both parties during the course of the marriage by giving effect to a single preference. In short, the doctrinal basis of the McGuire decision seems defensible.

If, however, the family is regarded as a group that defines and redefines its own values over time, the problem in McGuire may be open to a different analysis. The dilemma we have observed is created by the legal and social background against which this particular aspect of the marital relationship is set. The legal background in question is, of course, a marital property system that regards wealth as earned solely by the spouse in the paid economy. The social background is a cultural understanding that women need not, and even should not, work in the paid economy.

Attention to these background rules may provide a solution that neither denies Mrs. McGuire any access to 'family" wealth nor involves the court in routine supervision of family finances. One possible modification is to define the expectations for wives in a way that takes advantage of Married Women's Property Acts and relieves the need for courts to allocate domestic finances. Wives, it may be said, must behave as if they were unmarried in the economic sphere. They should maintain their own employment throughout marriage and allow their careers to develop as their husbands' careers develop.

Such a solution does not seem, however, to solve the problem of fairness within the family; it rather seeks to avoid the problem by reducing the choices available to women and men. An alternate approach, which recognizes rather than rejects the choices of married couples, is to say that each spouse does not choose his or her own career individually. An interpretive approach would regard the employment, child care, and other decisions within the household as a joint undertaking. Unlike the decisions of formal organizations, whether businesses or clubs, these decisions would inevitably be multivalent. Unlike contracting parties, these decisions might never be the subject of discussion and agreement, and some might never be recognized or articulated in the course of the family's life. They would be made, often enough, *en passant,* without any specification of the time at which minds met or their exact terms. The decisions may also have changed over the course of the marriage, without any conversation that began, "Let's change our agreement regarding employment."

Under this approach, the problem in *McGuire* lies in the relationship of background rules to family decision making. Rules regarding ownership and control of marital wealth should not suppose that married persons will formally decide about paid employment, nor should rules require them to make some particular choice. Rather, those rules should reflect the collective quality of domestic relations and assume that economic decisions are part of the broad range of decisions which will be reached and carried out by both parties within a family. This is, of course, a marital or community property system with joint management of family wealth. Unlike Mr. and Mrs. McGuire, family members within a community property system can work out their relationship under conditions of financial equality, in a setting where "working things out" does not mean implicit deference to the wishes of the spouse who works in the paid economy.

B. Economic Relations at Divorce

The *McGuire* case presents a well-known dilemma concerning economic relations during marriage. Economic relations at divorce present even better-known dilemmas, starting with the question of the basic justification for continuing any economic obligation from one spouse to another. Without any pretense to broad examination of this terribly difficult question, it might be enough to suggest how a view of the family as an interactive system may be helpful.

In his influential article, *The Theory of Alimony,* Ira Ellman argues that alimony has lost its traditional rationale as an expression of a husband's lifelong commitment to support his wife unless she violated her marital responsibilities to him. In a legal system where marriages can easily be terminated and gender roles include economic and social opportunities previously open only to husbands, such a commitment no longer seems intelligible. Nor, Professor Ellman argues, can the theory of alimony be supplied, as modern defenders suggest, by reference to principles of contract or business partnership. Contract analogies are unpersuasive for a variety of reasons. Celebrities perhaps aside, few couples adopt formal premarital or marital agreements, and implied contracts related to marriage are usually vague and therefore unenforceable. Partnership principles are unpersuasive because partnership law does not contemplate any relief resembling alimony and because there is no analogy to the "ordinary business practice" on which courts draw in determining the relief they give in suits for wrongful dissolution or breach of the partnership agreement.

Ultimately, Professor Ellman adopts a very specific application of contract law and argues for a quite restrictive notion of alimony. The relevant contract setting is that of a supplier who will be required to make special capital expenditures to provide some goods to a buyer (IBM, in one example). The supplier would, therefore, insist on a long-term contract to protect against loss of that investment. This, Professor Ellman suggests, resembles the situation of a wife who may make a variety of expenditures to carry out the family relationship: abandonment of a career to keep house or raise children, relinquishment of career opportunities in support of advancement of her husband's career, and the like. Although his reasons are not quite clear, Professor Ellman believes that the wife cannot devise a contract to protect her investment as the supplier could and, therefore, should be entitled to alimony. The measure of that alimony is the "residual loss in earning capacity" resulting from economically rational marital sharing. Professor Ellman then devises a system of rules to recognize the (relatively few) instances in which alimony is due to protect marital investments that do not involve financially irrational decisions.

It is central to Professor Ellman's approach that economically irrational decisions are not protected. His interest in providing incentives to sharing is limited to financially valuable contributions that would go unrecognized without alimony. The result is unfortunate for the classic problem of the wife who follows traditional role assignments and becomes a homemaker, if the marriage is childless. Her decision is described as a "lifestyle preference" made "at her own risk."

In a thoughtful critique of Professor Ellman's approach, Carl Schneider questions the usefulness of seeking economically rational marital sharing or any approach that focuses prospectively. Rather, he suggests, people do not marry with a view toward the consequences of divorce, or toward decisions that will lead to rational marital sharing and create an entitlement to alimony.

The previous discussion concerning family decision making clearly supports much of Professor Schneider's critique. For one thing, the "bargaining" aspect of the spousal relationship seems not as formal and explicit as Professor Ellman apparently contemplates. Perhaps more important, exigently rational decision making concerning financial matters seems to inadequately recognize the complexity of decision making within the family—a complexity that distinguishes the situation of Ms. Smith from the supplier and that of Mr. Smith from IBM, the buyer. The buyer will not be influenced by cultural assumptions of the community in which it grew up. The buyer's values will not include altruism. It will not think about the relationship of IBM's other activities to the welfare of either IBM or itself. In short, the approach to decision making assumed by Professor Ellman seems to ignore the interrelatedness of family decisions described above.

Professor Ellman might respond that the law of alimony cannot take into account all of the conditions that come to pass during a marriage. "[T]he law," he observes, "cannot evaluate every aspect of marital behavior in fixing the divorcing parties' financial obligations." Most particularly, it cannot assign value to what he describes as "lifestyle" preferences. The law can, however, take more than economic rationality into account, and should insofar as we place value on those decisions.

Consider, for example, the situation of the childless homemaker. Assuming conventional role assignments, the husband has a career which is, in the first place, fulfilling and, in the second, well-enough developed that he faces no real risk of struggle or financial discomfort. The wife has no career because the family relationship has led her away from that. It seems a bit glib to say that the wife made the decision not to work on her own and, accordingly, that she made the decision "at her own risk." Concededly, there may well have been no demand by the husband that his wife not work and no agreement that the wife would be cared for if she did not work and the marriage dissolved. That does not mean that both husband and wife did not, for many years, understand and accept such an arrangement.

Moreover, the background social and economic rules to which we have adverted—those dealing with domestic roles and ownership and management of wealth—are part of the setting in which this family functioned. Other background rules, from other systems, are also relevant. Far more than before, individual and family wealth is based on employment. These resources often cannot be divided practically through property distributions at divorce and, in any event, their real value is related to future as well as prior events. For its part, the social security system expects employment in the paid economy as a condition of benefits, and taken together with the health-care system, provides little in the way of a safety net for those who are unemployed or underemployed. The family's daily interactions may well have confirmed the understanding of both that he would work and she would not, and neither would be at risk. If so, it is hard to see why the risk of her lack of marketable skills was one that she, rather than they, assumed. Further, a demand that she now regard herself as "starting over" not only situates her unfairly in comparison to her husband but insufficiently recognizes the circumstances that place her in the position of having to "start over."

Significantly, Professor Ellman recognizes at least one exception to the general rule that a spouse may only recover when the decision is economically rational. That is the obvious situation where one spouse elects to stay home to care for children rather than continue in a position that would provide far more income than child care would cost. While conceding that such a decision is not economically rational, he argues that the decision to have children cannot be analyzed in those terms because having children is never itself an economically rational decision. This is simply a cost, and a shared one.

One may fairly ask whether this situation calls for an "exception" or for a different view of family relations. Child rearing is, after all, not peripheral but central to the institutional idea of marriage. If it is appropriate to abandon the insistence on economically rational decision making in this respect, might that not suggest that economic rationality should not be required for other decisions reached jointly by spouses that we are not prepared to declare inappropriate. Indeed, what Professor Ellman defines as "lifestyle" preferences—decisions about where to live, who will work, who will work part-time, and how resources will be spent—captures as much of family relations as do decisions based on wealth maximization, and often enjoy even greater normative approval. And the variety of factors that are included in such decisions are typical of family decision making, if not of business decisions.

VI. MARITAL DISSOLUTION

A systems view can recognize the relational nature of choice within the family. As we have seen, families generally define their own goals and methods of satisfying those goals. These goals, values, and strategies will generally continue to be accepted and relied on: they characterize the family system even when they are not articulated or even consciously considered. Within some limits, considering the family as an interactive system implies acceptance of the strategies its members choose, as long as a family is successful on its own terms.

These choices also become occasions for conflict and for exploration of exit conditions. Conflict can be defined as the refusal of one member of a system to accept the choices or selections of another, which is communicated. In some settings, such as those that are based solely on interaction (a cocktail party, a date, or the like), conflicts are central to the relationship and therefore cannot be overlooked. If the conflict cannot be ignored, the relationship must either continue as a conflict or end. In such a setting, conflict is a sufficient condition for exiting the relationship.

The entity view of the family denies the significance of all but the most serious kinds of conflict. Traditional grounds for divorce only recognized conflict as justifying exit from marriage when the behavior of one spouse was physically or mentally dangerous to the other. The strongest contractarian view, now followed in many jurisdictions, permits exit whenever one spouse credibly claims that the relationship is irremediably unsatisfactory from his or her point of view.

A systems approach might go at things differently. When a participant in an interactive system refuses to accept the choices or conduct of another, and expresses that rejection in certain ways, the character of the system or community is certainly changed. A spouse like Mrs. McGuire may accept her husband's stinginess for twenty years but, at some point and for some reason, cease to find it tolerable. Similarly, a child may accept his parents' direction and influence for some time, but, at some point, even before majority, begin to determine his or her own path. Of course, the potential for disagreement was always present and is always present in any interactive group, but as long as it does not erupt into crisis, there is little point in piercing the family organization and in regulating its patterns. But when that crisis arises and cannot be managed internally (or through internally selected strategies), individual interests cannot be ignored. Indeed, they have a special claim to be heard just because they are powerful enough to overcome the unifying forces of mutual definition and accommodation.

In this respect, our approach resembles the contractarian view. However, it does not follow that the claim of individual interest is sufficient to justify exit from a marriage. Where both parties wish to end their relationship, it is easy enough to accept their judgment that an unmanageable crisis has occurred. And, unlike traditional divorce law, that seems the right approach where the system has collapsed and both recognize that to be the case.

But suppose that only one spouse wishes to leave the marriage: a situation hardly unknown to our courts and perhaps even more common in fact than case law reflects. The inclination of modern law is to discount that desire. In part, this may be because marriage is viewed as a continuous contract, to which the unwillingness of either party is fatal. Perhaps the desire even seems perverse from an external viewpoint. How, after all, can a wife wish to remain with a husband who no longer cares for her, who insults her by indifference or infidelity, and whose reform cannot be enforced?

A judgment of perversity assumes, however, an external standard of utility or formal rationality, and we have already seen the difficulty of external evaluation of intrafamilial relations. The wife's desire, at least in a relatively long-term marriage, is the product of interactive processes with her husband, her children, and the community. If her reasons for wishing to continue the marriage appear to reflect deep dependency, or an unduly strong concern for community opinion, or a fear of raising her children without even the possibility of assistance from her husband, or simply the circumstance that she cannot now imagine life without a spouse, these conditions cannot fairly be dismissed as individual idiosyncrasies. Their roots may partially lie in individual premarital development, but they also reflect patterns developed (consciously or not) during the marital relationship. Nor are legal and social conventions irrelevant to her decision not to create her own economic base, her own social connections, or indeed her own independence. Whatever weight may be given to these circumstances, they at least suggest that routine acceptance of one spouse's choice is not as easily justified as modern legal rules assume.

Professor Brinig further explores some of the themes Professor Schneider and Dean Teitelbaum investigated. She puts Dean Teitelbaum's conundrum of whether the family is an entity or a collection of individuals in lawyer's terms—in terms of the contrast between contract and status. (Henry Maine's classic formula in *Ancient Law* (1843) was "that the movement of the progressive societies has hitherto been a movement from Status to Contract.") Just as Professor Schneider was concerned to understand how the benefits of moral discourse might be preserved without assuming the burdens, and just as Dean Teitelbaum was concerned to discover how the advantages of the entity view of the family might be secured without sacrificing the advantages of the distinct-individuals view, Professor Brinig is concerned to understand how the virtues of contract might be achieved without abandoning the virtues of status. Professor Brinig looks for a solution to another cultural construct with long and deep roots in American culture (and particularly in the powerful American religious tradition)—the idea of covenant. Her vehicle for pursuing these inquiries is a review of Milton C. Regan, Jr., *Family Law and the Pursuit of Intimacy.*

Margaret F. Brinig, Book Review, *Status, Contract and Covenant,* 79 CORNELL LAW REVIEW 1573 (September 1994)[*]

INTRODUCTION

For many years, I have taught family law from a contracts perspective. Increasingly, this approach has made me uneasy because reducing family law to a nexus of contracts seems to present only a partial picture. Milton Regan illuminates my discomfort in his new book *Family Law and the Pursuit of Intimacy*. He suggests that concentrating on individuality, as we must in studying contracts, causes us to lose sight of the intimacy that makes family relationships worthwhile. Instead, he advocates returning to a world where both contract and a redefined status model coexist. For Regan, status is shorthand for all things of value in a family that are lost in the contractual frame, especially the interdependence that creates a sense of responsibility. In arguing for a return to intimacy, he draws upon an impressive body of social science literature and paints a picture that is sensitive to everyone's feelings and to groups who might object to the use of the venerable term "status."

Like much of the communitarian literature, Regan's book sets a mood rather than providing an agenda. It examines what the family looked like in its "golden age" and how those notions, designed to foster intimacy, have changed in the late twentieth century. Regan is particularly effective in showing how these changes alienate and remove us as people from any real context while simultaneously promoting individuality. Regan's descriptions and attention to details of past and present families make won-

---

derful reading. The book, however, does not provide any real solutions to the lack of intimacy he finds. In the end, though the reader may understand the social criticism and grasp the problems presented, she does not have a clear sense of how to remedy these problems.

Although his criticism of the contract model is effective, Regan's analysis falls short precisely because he strives for fairness and sensitivity. In assuming a defensive posture, he dilutes a powerful analogy to avoid criticism by feminists and gay rights advocates. Regan quickly points out the weakness of status as describing intimacy: historically, status connoted hierarchy, male dominance, and Victorian attitudes. However, Regan assures us that status need not be so encumbered. Regan advocates a refined status by using new default terms for families that would encourage security and intimacy, and discourage inequality. Under this model of status, the American family could then recapture only the golden parts of an earlier era.

Other possible routes for inquiry exist. We could admit the failure of contract and simply return to our grandparents' model for families. Before World War II, the typical American household could be characterized by a husband who earned wages in the labor force, a wife who maintained the home and cared for the couple's children, and the three or four children who lived with them. Despite the attractiveness that this doctrine might possess, however, we would undoubtedly fail to stuff the genies of sexual equality and individual choice back into their bottle.

Alternatively, we could accept Regan's premise that the contract perspective has problems and search for another paradigm. We could, for instance, employ the ancient term "covenant" to describe the bonds between husband and wife, parent and child. The covenant concept lacks the sexist connotations of status, but even more than status it links two individuals unconditionally and permanently. This concept, however, has some problems. Perhaps, like Regan, we ignore covenant because we encounter it in settings that are religious or archaic. Moreover, the covenant traits of faithfulness and permanency might make us uncomfortable in a time when the marriage promise "until death do us part" only works half the time and when even children can divorce their parents.

An example drawn from Regan's book illustrates the difference between contract, status, and covenant. Regan's conclusion features a hypothetical married man who has gradually become more involved with his work and less involved with his wife and daughter. He is contemplating divorce, and Regan notes that modern society promotes the message that "ultimately Dad's involvement with his family is a matter of personal choice." The modern marriage, and even fatherhood, becomes a matter of contract to be honored only if there is no better alternative. Regan suggests that family law should provide an alternative—a vision of a person in context or relationship. This is status, which in this case would, at a minimum, cause the hypothetical man "to think very carefully about the ramifications of what he does" for his wife and daughter. Yet however legally difficult it may be to extricate himself from his family relationships, the man can take this step in Regan's relational or status-based family. A covenant, however, even more than a diamond, is forever. Even if the couple divorces, vestiges of their relationship remain, particularly if there are children. A family covenant, much like a promise "running with the land," cannot ever completely dissolve. The parent remains a parent even when the children have left home and have families of their own.

II

FROM STATUS TO CONTRACT TO COVENANT

One criticism of Regan's book is that he is too apologetic about his use of "status." Few of us would want to eradicate the concept entirely from American usage. Status clearly has value when we speak of children, when we try to describe the basis of jurisdiction for divorce, or when we talk in terms of a "discrete and insular minority" that should be given special protection under the law. While Regan's hesitation is understandable, a different paradigm would alleviate his qualms and still reinvigorate our idea of the family.

Regardless of whether we believe that status evokes sexism or racism, status does remind us of hierarchy. While position may continue to be an important part of the parent-child relationship, hierarchical notions do not fit well with our modern ideal of matrimony as a union of two equals. Covenant, on the other hand, is a concept that is gender and color neutral. The human parties to a covenant may enjoy horizontal equality. However, unlike parties to a contract, they are not interested in fairness, but rather are willing to give beyond what is fair. Like Regan's notion of family in the context of status, the family under the rubric of covenant extends beyond the nuclear arrangement. It includes such close relatives as grandparents and, ultimately, the whole community.

Both status and contract have their roles in Regan's vision of the family. Similarly, I do not believe a concept of covenant always misplaces a contract or law and economics analysis. Some aspects of families make little sense without contractual analysis. For example, the bargaining that takes place at the time of divorce or during antenuptial and separation agreements speaks more to contract than to a status or covenant. Furthermore, unless a private welfare mentality explains alimony, it is difficult to rationalize in a no-fault system without looking at marriage through a contractual or law and economics lens.

Covenant, even better than status, explains why some aspects of marriage and parenthood cannot be varied by contract. For example, spouses cannot contract around marriage's infinite duration, nor can they avoid mutual support during the marriage. Similarly, parents cannot avoid entirely the duty of child support. Even when the minor child marries or moves in with a boyfriend, the parent's duty to support may revive if the child becomes indigent. Even though divorce severs most marital obligations, many states require spouses divorcing insane partners to continue their support obligations.

The strict law and economics view of such terms is that non-contractual obligations are default or off-the-rack provisions, or that they substitute for what parties wanted *ex ante*. However, since both the parties in question may not want these obligations, even *ex ante*, law and economics does not completely answer the objection. Some parts of family life, which I would attribute to covenant, are invariable because they are necessary for the family to meet its historical and present-day societal obligations. They make the family what it is: a set of relationships where intimacy and inter-dependence flourish. Covenant thus explains, at least in part, why moving family law too much toward individuality has large negative consequences.

Anticipating another objection, I also believe that the law is partly aspirational. Although covenant, like contract or status, provides only part of the picture for family law, it can guide our decisionmaking, particularly in the legislative sphere. In other words, before we reform laws, we need to look both at the incentives the new laws will give and at the type of people they will ultimately shape. Before we undertake family law reform on any large scale, we need to take a hard look at the family in this aspirational sense.

Covenant, in the sense I will use it here, describes a relationship characterized by a special kind of love: one that is boundless and undeserved. The person in a covenant relationship expects, with justification, that it will go on forever. The intimacy that Regan seeks flows naturally with this kind of love. Unlike the recent Longines Christmas ads in which the donee always expects something more, the person in covenant is pleased by what the other gets. The emphasis is upon giving rather than receiving, upon enjoying the gifts of others rather than reveling in one's own. Covenant, then, describes altruism in the framework of relationship. This is quite different from economist Gary Becker's definition of altruism, which he derives from a single family member's caring. In addition to requiring only one party, rather than the two or more needed for covenant, Becker's definition of altruism implies that the altruist must have the means to withdraw support from the rest of the family.

In a legal sense, a covenant frequently is an especially solemn type of contract, one that cannot be broken without significant penalties. A covenant, or promise under seal, will support a gift to a third party where a simple contract would not. Covenant implies donative intent and confers a benefit upon another. Each party will always act for the other's good regardless of his or her behavior. Accordingly, once the parties make their initial assents, much of their behavior is constrained by the covenant. Everett suggests, for example, that covenant "had elements of both imposition and voluntarism within the partnership with land and with past and future generations. Covenant formed a web of relationships between the God of history, the people, and the land." In a way, once the covenant is made, more than the two people are involved. The imprimatur of the state (or God) is placed upon the solemn promise.

III

TESTING THE COVENANT MODEL

To test the covenant model in terms of how it comports with practical and aspirational standards, we must reexamine Regan's hard cases involving same sex couples, cohabitants, and natural fathers of children born during the mother's marriage to another. Regan's argument is that the gay or lesbian couple frequently seeks to make a commitment and that their relationships would be more stable if society permitted legal ties.

Covenant would also afford stability in states that do not prohibit the underlying sexual conduct. If the state continues to proscribe sexual expression between non-heterosexual couples, government itself constrains the relationship. The same-sex couple cannot enforce any explicit relationship-related contract because of the illegality of the relationship. However, the couple can make the permanent commitment and exhibit the selfless loving and giving required for a covenant. Some religious groups are now sanctioning such exchanges, and Regan notes that some localities are passing domestic partner legislation.

Similarly, the lens of covenant reveals the same problems with cohabiting couples that Regan demonstrates. Many heterosexual partners that do not marry either deliberately avoid marriage because of its constraints or use cohabitation as a screening function for a later marriage. Although many cohabitation relationships endure successfully for long periods of time, they are clearly less stable than marriage, if only because the parties expect their relationship to last only so long as they "love" each other. Thus, emotional "highs" are even more important than in marriages, and are often a euphemism for infatuation. The couple, even more than the modern married couple, never ends the courtship behavior of looking appraisingly at every potential alternative mate. There is no unequivocal "retirement" from the marriage market. Finally, most (although not all) of these couples refrain from having children, or, as my aunt calls them, little anchors. For the most part, then, cohabitating couples have no permanent commitment to each other or to a lifetime of co-parenting.

Finally, we can look at the situation of the unwed father. He is increasingly litigating his plight by arguing for his lost parental rights. Although there are undoubtedly exceptions to the rule, most unwed fathers are unwilling to make the commitment necessary for fatherhood. This may be simply because the unwed father lacks connection to the child's mother. Particularly if we look in terms of what is best for the child in such situations, the two parent alternative is usually more attractive.

B. The Functions of Family Law

In our work of evaluating the way family law actually works, we may be helped by thinking about what functions family law—and for that matter law of all kinds—actually serves. Some of these functions are well-known and much discussed. We have selected two articles that deal with functions that are less well recognized and probably more controversial. The first of these articles briefly surveys all the functions that family law performs and then discusses in some detail what Professor Schneider calls law's "channelling" function, that is, the way the law helps shape social institutions and expectations and thus behavior. The second article investigates family law's "expressive" function, that is, the way law's ability to articulate and symbolize ideas may be deployed to allow citizens to express themselves and to allow law to influence behavior.

Carl E. Schneider, *The Channelling Function in Family Law,* 20 HOFSTRA LAW REVIEW 495 (Spring 1992)[*]

I. THE THEORY OF THE CHANNELLING FUNCTION

A. What is the Channelling Function?

. . . Family law has, I think, five functions. The first is the protective function. One of law's most basic duties is to protect citizens against harms done them by other citizens. This means protecting people from physical harm, as the law of spouse and child abuse attempts to do, and from non-physical harms, especially economic wrongs and psychological injuries. Law's second function is to help people organize their lives and affairs in the ways they prefer. Family law performs this "facilitative" function by offering people the law's services in entering and enforcing contracts, by giving legal effect to their private arrangements. Family law's third function is to help people resolve disputes. The law of divorce exemplifies family law's "arbitral" function, since today's divorce courts primarily adjudicate conflicting claims to marital property, alimony, and child custody.

Instinct in each of these first three functions of family law lies a relatively commonplace idea: There are people (particularly children) the law is widely expected to protect, contracts it is widely expected to facilitate, and disputes it is widely expected to arbitrate. However, the last two functions of family law are less self-evident and more controversial. The first of these is the expressive function. It works by deploying the law's power to impart ideas through words and symbols. It has two (related) aspects: Law's expressive abilities may be used, first, to provide a voice in which citizens may speak and, second, to alter the behavior of people the law addresses. The ERA exemplifies both aspects. Its proponents had (among other things) two kinds of

---

expressive purposes in mind. They proposed it partly because they wanted the law of their country—their law—to make a symbolic statement about the relationship between men and women. And they also believed that such symbolic statements can promote changes in social sentiment which in turn may promote a reformation of social behavior.

Finally, in the channelling function the law creates or (more often) supports social institutions which are thought to serve desirable ends. "Social institution" I intend broadly: "In its formal sociological definition, an institution is a pattern of expected action of individuals or groups enforced by social sanctions, both positive and negative." Social institutions arise, Berger and Luckmann tell us, "whenever there is a reciprocal typification of habitualized actions by types of actors." Generally, the channelling function does not specifically require people to use these social institutions, although it may offer incentives and disincentives for their use. Primarily, rather, it is their very presence, the social currency they have, and the governmental support they receive which combine to make it seem reasonable and even natural for people to use them. Thus, people can be said to be channelled into them. As Berger and Luckmann write, "Institutions . . ., by the very fact of their existence, control human conduct by setting up predefined patterns of conduct, which channel it in one direction as against the many other directions that would theoretically be possible." Or as James Fitzjames Stephen wrote with characteristic vigor and vividness, "The life of the great mass of men, to a great extent the life of all men, is like a watercourse guided this way or that by a system of dams, sluices, weirs, and embankments. . . . [I]t is by these works—that is to say, by their various customs and institutions—that men's lives are regulated."

Business law offers usefully clear examples of such institutions—the corporation and the partnership. Consider the corporation. People have long united to invest in and run businesses. To encourage such activity, governments give legal recognition to a particular business form—the corporation. They also endow it with special advantages— particularly, limited liability and unlimited life. By now, this form has become familiar, natural, and comfortable. It is habitualized, it is institutionalized.

I have used the example of business institutions because the law's role in forming and supporting them and channelling people into them is particularly evident. In addition, it is probably easier for us to appreciate the channelling function in the relatively uncontroversial context of business life. But how might family law be said to support social institutions and to channel people into them? Here we encounter some difficulty. It must always be hard to define any social institution. "Society" has no voice in which to identify and describe its institutions. Lawmakers do not always speak explicitly and exactly about social institutions, even though they may be much concerned for them. Different people would define the same institution in different ways, and the same institution will affect different people differently. What is more, institutional patterns in a modern society are elaborately complex: Any institution will have both normative and behavioral aspects, and behavior within institutions will rarely live up to the institution's normative aspirations. One institution may take many forms, forms which can, further, vary from place to place and can change over time. A single institution can serve competing functions. Few if any institutions will be unambivalently and unambiguously embraced, and the multiplicity of social goals may interfere with the nurture of the most warmly embraced institution. An institution may encounter competing and even conflicting institutions. And, worse, there is a sense in which institutions do not "exist," but are merely analytic constructs.

None of this, however, makes it pointless to talk about social institutions. Institutions may be analytic constructs, but those constructs can still be useful attempts to describe patterns of attitudes and behavior. That those patterns will always be complex and those attempts will always be imprecise does not mean that the patterns are not there or that the attempts will be pointless.

One other point about the channelling function needs to be made before we explore specific examples of its use in family law. In one important (if limited) sense, the channelling function is normatively neutral: It can be employed to serve all kinds of normative ends. It has been put to many uses, it could be put to many more. Central to any evaluation of a specific example of the channelling function will be an assessment of the particular goals to which it has been put. To illustrate the workings of the function in family law, I have selected two institutions which I think the law can plausibly be said to use in channelling terms. But there are certainly other ways in which the channelling function has been deployed in family law, and there may well be ways in which it would be better deployed.

Having acknowledged the difficulty and asserted the importance of my enterprise, I will now try to describe two broad social institutions which I will use to illustrate the working of family law's channelling function. These two institutions are "marriage" and "parenthood." These are, obviously, quite broadly defined institutions, and my descriptions of them are thus subject to all the difficulties I described above. I have no doubt that both these institutions have somewhat different meanings for different people, that they have changed over time and are still changing, and that they do not monopolize intimate life in modern America. However, a legislator might plausibly identify a core of ideas which have enough social support to justify the term "institution" and which the legislator might conclude the law should try to support, to shape, and to channel people into.

Our legislator might, then, posit a normative model of "marriage" with several fundamental characteristics. It is monogamous, heterosexual, and permanent. It rests on love. Husbands and wives are to treat each other affectionately, considerately, and fairly. They should be animated by mutual concern and willing to sacrifice for each other. In short, they ought to assent to the old question: "Wilt thou love her, comfort her, honour, and keep her in sickness and in health; and, forsaking all others, keep thee only unto her, so long as ye both shall live?"

Of course, as Karl Llewellyn warned, too much can be "thought and written as if we had a pattern of ways that ma[k]e up marriage." Of course, as Llewellyn knew, "The norm is none too uniform." But as he also knew, "major features are observed, are 'recognized,' are made the measure of the 'right.' Right in such matters is most powerfully felt: these are compacted patterns, backed by unreasoning tradition, built around interests that lie deep and close."

In the same way, our legislator might posit an institution of "parenthood" with several key normative characteristics. Parents should be married to each other. They are preferably the biological father and mother of their child. They have authority over their children and can make decisions for them. However, like spouses, parents are expected to love their children and to be affectionate, considerate, and fair. They should support and nurture their children during their minority. They should assure them a stable home, particularly by staying married to each other, so that the child lives with both parents and knows the comforts of security.

Obviously, these two normative models are not and never were descriptions of any universal empirical reality, and I will soon examine recent changes in social practice that might affect them. Nor are they the only models the channelling function might be recruited to serve. Nevertheless, they do describe ideals which have won and retained substantial allegiance in American life. I will thus use these models to illustrate how the channelling function can work. How, then, might our legislator interpret the law as supporting these two institutions and channelling people into them?

Our legislator might see family law as setting a framework of rules, one of whose effects is to shape, sponsor, and sustain the model of marriage I described above: It writes standards for entry into marriage, standards which prohibit polygamous, incestuous, and homosexual unions. It seeks to encourage marital stability by inhibiting divorce (although it pursues this goal much less vigorously than it once did). It tries to improve marital behavior both directly and indirectly: It imposes a few direct obligations during marriage, like the duty of support. Less directly, it has invented special categories of property (like estates by the entirety and rights of dower and curtesy) to reflect and reinforce the special relationship of marriage. It indirectly sets some standards for marital behavior through the law of divorce. Fault-based divorce does so by describing behavior so egregious that it justifies divorce. Marital-property law implicitly sets standards for the financial conduct of spouses. Finally, prohibitions against non-marital sexual activity and discouragements against quasi-marital arrangements in principle confine sexual life to marriage. "What is all this," James Fitzjames Stephen emphatically asked, "except the expression of the strongest possible determination on the part of the Legislature to recognize, maintain, and favour marriage in every possible manner as the foundation of civilized society?"

Similarly, our legislator might see a framework of laws molding and promoting the institution of parenthood. Laws criminalizing fornication, cohabitation, adultery, and bigamy in principle limit parenthood to married couples, and those legal disadvantages that still attach to illegitimacy make it wise to confine parenthood to marriage. Laws restricting divorce make it likelier that a child will be raised by both parents. The law buttresses parents' authority over children. Parents may use reasonable force in disciplining their children. They may decide whether their children should have medical treatment. They may choose their child's school. Parents of "children in need of supervision" can summon up the state's coercive power. However, the law also tries, directly and indirectly, to shape parental behavior. It requires parents to support their children. It penalizes the "abuse" or "neglect" of children and obliges many kinds of people to report evidence of it. It obliges parents to send their children to school. Custody law obliquely sets standards for parental behavior and emphasizes the centrality of children's interests. Finally, some states further elaborate the relationship between parent and child by obliging adult children to support their indigent parents.

These sketches suggest how the law can be seen as performing the first task of the channelling function, namely, to create—or more often, to recruit—social institutions and to mold and sustain them. The function's second task is to channel people into institutions. It can perform these two tasks in several ways. First, it does so simply by recognizing and endorsing institutions, thus giving them some aura of legitimacy and permanence. Recognition may be extended, for instance, through formalized, routinized, and regulated entry and exit to an institution, as with marriage: "By the authority vested in me by the State of Michigan, I now pronounce you man and wife."

A second channelling technique is to reward participation in an institution. Tax law, for instance, may offer advantages—like the marital deduction—to married couples that it denies the unmarried. Similarly, Social Security offers spouses benefits it refuses lovers. These advantages are enhanced if private entities consult the legal institution in allocating benefits, as when private employers offer medical insurance only to "family members" as the law defines that term. In a somewhat different vein, the law of alimony and marital property offers spouses—but generally not "cohabitants"—protections on divorce.

Third, the law can channel by disfavoring competing institutions. Sometimes competitors are flatly outlawed, as by laws prohibiting sodomy, bigamy, adultery, and prostitution. Bans on fornication and cohabitation mean (in principle) that, to have sexual relations, one must marry. Sometimes competing institutions are merely disadvantaged. For instance, the rule making contracts for meretricious consideration unenforceable traditionally denied unmarried couples the law's help in resolving some disputes. Similarly, non-parents are presumptively disadvantaged in custody disputes with parents. Finally, restrictive divorce laws impede re-entry to the alternative institution of singleness.

Fourth, in principle people can be channelled into an institution by directly penalizing its non-use. One might, for instance, say that school taxes penalize childlessness, since non-parents get a good deal less out of those taxes than parents. However, the weakness of this example suggests the difficulty of finding really good instances in American law of direct penalties for not marrying or not having children.

By and large, then, the channelling function does not primarily use direct legal coercion. People are not forced to marry. One can contract out (formally or informally) of many of the rules underlying marriage. One need not have children, and one is not forced to treat them lovingly. Rather, the function forms and reinforces institutions which have significant social support and which, optimally, come to seem so natural that people use them almost unreflectively. It relies centrally but not exclusively on social approval of the institution, on social rewards for its use, and on social disfavor of its alternatives. Some aspects of it may be highly legalized, as divorce is. Some alternatives may, at least formally, be legally prohibited. The law may buttress an institution here and harry its competitors there. But, Berger and Luckmann explain, "the primary social control is given in the existence of an institution as such. . . . Additional control mechanisms are required only insofar as the processes of institutionalization are less than completely successful." They suggest "institutions are *there*, external to [the individual], persistent in their reality. . . . They have coercive power over him, both in themselves, by the sheer force of their facticity, and through the control mechanisms that are usually attached to the most important of them." And as Llewellyn, thinking more particularly about marriage, wrote, "One vital element in the fact-pattern thus made right is (this needs repetition) its recognition by the group. . . . [O]nce conceived, once accepted, the over-simple norm-concept maintains itself stubbornly, despite all changes in conditions; it becomes the socially given, right, ideal-type of 'marriage': the *connubium honestum* of the *vir honestus*." In short, as Philip Rieff observes, "[A] culture survives principally . . . by the power of its institutions to bind and loose men in the conduct of their affairs with reasons which sink so deep into the self that they become common and implicitly understood . . . ." Channelling's reliance on social institutions, then, is both its strength and its weakness, its harshness and its gentleness, its importance and its peril.

B. What Purposes Does the Channelling Function Serve?

The channelling function, I have said, fosters social institutions and channels people into them. But why might the state want to do so? To answer that question, let us revisit the example of the corporation as a "channelling" institution. First, the corporation serves law's three core functions. For example, it serves the protective function by allowing people to invest in enterprises without risking their whole fortunes, by protecting minority shareholders, and by directing economic activity into an institution whose public nature makes it easier to regulate. The corporation serves the facilitative function by giving people a convenient and efficient way of organizing themselves into enterprises. It serves the arbitral function by providing mechanisms for resolving disputes among entrepreneurs and for winding up their affairs.

But the corporate form does more than promote law's core functions. More centrally and obviously, it serves some broad social purposes. Primarily, it promotes the accumulation of large agglomerations of capital and the organization of many people into a single and productive enterprise. In other words, the corporate form makes possible the extensive and complex economic institutions on which rest industrialization, social wealth, and modernity. Less grandly, more specifically, and more subtly, the corporation serves what might be called "efficiency" functions. For instance, it relieves prospective entrepreneurs of the need to figure out *de novo* how to organize their ventures. Much of that work will already have been done by earlier generations and been embodied in the corporate form and in the law, literature, and lore that surround it. Because that form is neither monolithic nor exclusive, entrepreneurs will have important choices to make and considerable flexibility in making them. But the energy they must expend is diminished by the menu of well-developed standard alternatives among which to choose.

In addition, the corporate form makes the world more predictable for everyone. When investors, regulators, employees, creditors, debtors, vendors, and customers encounter a corporation, they essentially know how it is organized and what it can and cannot do. A creditor, for example, realizes that, unlike a partnership, a corporation's liability is limited to its own assets. And so on. Because people have established expectations about corporations they need expend less effort to understand an enterprise. This not only saves them time and trouble, but may make them more willing to join in or deal with the enterprise. In short, both the corporation and those who deal with it benefit from the existence of a well-known, time-tested, socially-accepted, and governmentally-supported economic institution.

Similarly, family law's channelling function is partly a specialized way of performing its protective, facilitative, and arbitral functions. For instance, marriage variously serves the protective function. Law does not just (in conjunction with other social forces) create a shell of an institution; it builds (again with much help) institutions with norms. The institution of marriage which the law recruits and shapes attempts to induce in spouses a sense of an obligation to treat each other well—to love and honor each other. At the elemental level of physical violence, the law has tried to reinforce this socially imposed obligation by making cruelty a ground for divorce, by taking cruelty into account in settling the spouses' economic affairs, and by criminalizing and (increasingly aggressively in some jurisdictions) prosecuting spouse abuse. At the level of economic life, the law has tried to supervise the fairness of antenuptial agreements and the distribution of the spouses' assets on divorce. And marriage protects children by making it likelier that both parents will care for them throughout their minority.

The channelling function also assists the facilitative function. The latter function furnishes people mechanisms that help them organize their lives and affairs as they wish. Family law's institutions offer people models for organizing their lives. These models have been developed over time and have presumably worked for many other people. They become part of a menu of social choice. Further, marriage offers people a kind of relationship with social and legal advantages which are primarily available precisely because the law gives marriage a special status. Finally, marriage serves the dispute-resolution function by providing rules and a forum in which to adjudicate the disputes which flock around divorce like remoras around a shark. In addition, it provides norms of behavior which may help the parties resolve some of their disputes privately.

But the channelling function is more than a specialized means of performing family law's other functions. Like the corporation, marriage and parenthood serve some broad social purposes. These are crucial, but they are also so familiar they hardly need elaboration. Sixty years ago Karl Llewellyn discerned thirteen such purposes in marriage. They included the regulation of sexual behavior, the reduction of sexual conflict, the orderly perpetuation of the species, the "building and reinforcement of an economic unit," the regulation of wealth, and the "development of individual personality." And a large body of writing argues that the present happiness and future well-being of children depend on their growing up in something like the kind of institution I described above.

Less grandly, more specifically, and more interestingly, the institutions of the family also serve what I earlier called "efficiency" functions (but that might in this warmer context be called ways of easing social life). First, channelling's institutions spare people having to invent the forms of family life *de novo*. Imagine two nineteen-year-olds living in a state of nature who find themselves in love. Without established social institutions, they would have to work out afresh how to express that love, how to structure their relationship, and what to expect of each other. The same couple in, say, the United States of the mid-twentieth century would find a set of answers to those questions in the institution of marriage. To be sure, they would see other answers presented by other institutions. They would hear criticisms of marriage. They would not be compelled to marry. But marriage would seem natural to them because most of the adults they knew partook of it, because society and the law supported it, and because they had to some extent internalized its values. As one sociologist remarks, "When people make decisions, they tend to look not to a mathematical formula to determine what is to their best advantage, but to what others do, to what they have traditionally done, or to what they think others think they ought to do." The institution, that is, would be part of a comfortable social vocabulary, a vocabulary that would save our lovers from having to invent their own language.

In short, as Berger and Luckmann observe, "Habitualization carries with it the important psychological gain that choices are narrowed." As Whitehead memorably put it:

> It is a profoundly erroneous truism, repeated by all copybooks and by eminent people when they are making speeches, that we should cultivate the habit of thinking of what we are doing. The precise opposite is the case. Civilization advances by extending the number of important operations which we can perform without thinking about them. Operations of thought are like cavalry charges in a battle—they are strictly limited in number, they require fresh horses, and must only be made at decisive moments.

Of course, this is not to say that cavalry charges are never necessary, that operations of thought are always to be avoided. Quite the contrary. As Berger and Luckman note, habitualization, "by providing a stable background in which human activity may proceed with a minimum of decision-making most of the time . . . frees energy for such decisions as may be necessary on certain occasions. In other words, the background of habitualized activity opens up a foreground for deliberation and innovation."

The channelling function does not just relieve people of the burden of working out afresh how to organize their lives. Even if one could satisfactorily invent modes of living for oneself, they probably could not be lived alone, but would have to be lived with others. People need to understand and predict what other people will think and do so that they can readily and safely deal and cooperate with each other. Social institutions help serve that need. As Martin Krygier writes, "There are many social situations where our decisions are strategically interdependent [with the decisions of other people]. . . . [I]n such situations, *norms* will be generated which provide 'some *anchorage*; some preeminently conspicuous indication as to what action is likely to be taken by (most of) the others . . . .'" Social institutions and the norms they embody, then, help us count on, cope with, and cooperate with other people.

More concretely, for example, the institution of marriage helps people to plan for the future even before becoming engaged and to reach easier understandings with their fiances and spouses about their married lives. People dealing with married couples benefit as well. Mundanely, they know that when they say, "Can you come for dinner on the sixteenth?," the invitation will be taken as including both husband and wife. Less banally and more consequentially, a wedding ring warns anyone attracted to its wearer not to contemplate an intimate relationship.

The kind of "anchorage" of which Krygier speaks may be particularly important to families, for in the complex and long-term intimate relationships that characterize family life, reliance and trust are specially needed. A central source of that reliance and trust is of course a faith in the love and steadfastness of one's family members. But that faith may be more comfortably sustained, and reciprocating love more easily given, where personal feelings are reinforced (and known to be reinforced) by social institutions. As Norval Glenn suggests, even people "who still strongly adhere to the ideal of marital permanence may be afraid to commit strongly to their marriages if they perceive a general weakening of the ideal."

The advantages of institutions in family life are illuminated by situations in which institutions are absent. Andrew Cherlin, for instance, describes the discomfort and even distress of remarried adults and their children whose

> day to day life includes many problems for which there are no insti-
> tutionalized solutions. These problems can range from deciding what
> a stepchild should call his or her stepparent, to resolving the sexual ten-
> sions that can emerge between step-relatives in the absence of a well-
> defined incest taboo, to defining the financial obligations of husbands
> to their spouses and children from current and previous marriages.

Nor are these institutional deficits easily overcome. David Chambers writes that "the relationship between many stepparents and stepchildren remains unclear and uncomfortable well beyond the initial stages." Indeed, Cherlin argues that "the higher divorce rate for remarriages after divorce is a consequence of the incomplete institutionalization of remarriage after divorce in our society." He notes that because institutionalized solutions for the special problems of reconstituted families have not emerged, "there is more opportunity for disagreements and divisions among family members and more strain in many remarriages after divorce."

I have been arguing, then, that social institutions serve what I have wryly called "efficiency" functions. That is, they relieve us of the burden of working out from scratch the forms of family life, and they ease our relations with families, friends, and acquaintances. Social institutions serve at least one more such function—they help integrate members of society over time and place. A crucial problem of living in a large, modern, diverse, industrial society is that we need to be concerned for people we can never know. The reasons for this need can be stated accurately enough in terms of principle. But such abstract statements, however convincing they may logically be, commonly lack the persuasive force to compel people to act. For people to be moved to help each other, they need some sense of commonality with them—some sense that their fellow citizens are people like themselves, whose experiences, concerns, and interests they can at least understand and to some degree share. Social institutions help provide such a sense. Obviously this element of commonality cannot be pushed too far, lest the benefits of living in a modern and diverse society be lost. Yet without some degree of commonality, we lose the practical basis for the private philanthropy and public programs, the commitment to a shared enterprise, the willingness to cooperate in it and to sacrifice for it, that make such a society possible and decent.

Similarly, social institutions link us both to the past and the future. The knowledge that our forebears organized their lives around the social institutions that still shape us and the belief that the lives of our progeny will be made recognizable by their participation in those same institutions add meaning to our lives and help inspire us as individuals and as members of society to cherish the past and our elders and to nurture the future and our children.

We can summarize these workings of the channelling function by imagining two people looking for recreation, who live in a world without tennis, and who are given three balls, two rackets, and one net. They could no doubt find some way of amusing themselves with these toys. But tennis is a good game partly because it developed over many centuries, and our couple could not easily invent as good a game. Further, where tennis is a social institution, the two will readily find people with whom to enjoy their recreation, to improve their game, to relish their successes, and to lament their failures. And part of the pleasure of tennis lies in knowing its past glories and following its current progress. Tennis, in other words, succeeds because it is a shared and well-established social institution. Marriage and parenthood benefit from that same fact.

Let me conclude what I have said in this section and prepare the way for what I will say in the next by calling again on Karl Llewellyn, who wrote:

> Such are the functions of the social institution, in our civilization. Little about the set-up is inevitable. Costs which go here unnoted are bitterly high. In no point is the institution adequate in performance, nor is it always the major factor in such performance as obtains. Any one of the functions could be, at some time or place has been, is now in part, served powerfully in other ways. Few indeed are the cases in which marriage alone is halfway adequate to any of them. . . . But would one for that deny vitality to the work . . . which marriage does?

Carol Weisbrod, *On the Expressive Functions of Family Law,* 22 UNIVERSITY OF CALIFORNIA AT DAVIS LAW REVIEW 991 (1990)[*]

INTRODUCTION

This Essay concerns the suggestion that expressive or symbolic aspects of law should be used in the field of family law to guide people to better behavior.

We are reminded of this ancient theme by Professor Mary Ann Glendon's *Abortion and Divorce in Western Law.* Professor Glendon's argument, in part, is that law has both strong educational functions and significant expressive components. Law is a play, a story, a message, a thing that is shaped by the culture and in turn shapes the culture. To the extent law shapes culture we should use it to send messages.

Stronger versions of the desirability of a message in family law have also been offered. Professor Jan Gorecki writes,

> Those who are unilaterally guilty of disrupting their marriages . . . should be punished . . . . Their punishment conveys a message to the general society:

---

[*]   This work was originally published in 22 U.C. DAVIS L. REV. 991 (1990). Copyright 1990 by The Regents of the University of California. Reprinted with permission.

minimum of responsibility is anyone's family obligation, and so is an effort to avoid inflicting suffering on one's spouse and children, and wrecking their lives. This message, if properly conveyed in the process of instrumental learning, may not but influence general attitudes, and may eventually bring about . . . decline of the total sum of suffering and decrease of the broader social problems generated by widespread family disintegration.

The message that Professor Gorecki envisions is a message to virtue. The message may be enforced if necessary as punishment, as in criminal law. Professor Glendon sees the messages of law in various ways, sometimes the direct communication of a position—as when she speaks of the present message of no-fault-no-responsibility divorce—and sometimes a message in the form of a compromise or a conversation, in which the law contains (or should contain) the voices of different parts of the cultural discussion.

Commentators may concede the uncertainties of the law/behavior interaction. Professor Glendon says, "No one can chart with confidence the ways in which law, customs, new lines of behavior, ideas about law, and ideas about morality reciprocally influence each other." One problem is that "only the most elementary legal information reaches the public, and this almost always in a slightly inaccurate form." Professor Glendon concludes that while there may be problems of communication, "there is no escape from the fact that, willy-nilly, law performs a pedagogical role. It contributes in a modest but not a trivial way to that framework of beliefs and feelings within which even our notions of self-interest are conceived."

Recognition of law as expressive, as a source of symbols and values, has been common in America for some time. This is particularly true in connection with the role of the Supreme Court, where the point is so true that one must work to persuade the public that "constitutional" does not necessarily mean good or wise. This emphasis on expressive functions (linked somehow to instrumental values) has been given new vitality by work in several fields.

Initially, in thinking about this issue we might separate two ideas. First, we look at law because law does in fact express values, and thus teaches. We should know as much as we can about what law teaches as a descriptive matter, despite the complex and contradictory substance of the teaching. It is part of knowing the culture in which we live. Second, we look at law because law can and ought to be used to teach specific things. In brief, the expressive functions of law can and should be used instrumentally. Professor Gorecki quotes Brandeis: "no small part of the law's function is to make men good." Atiyah, describing this aspect of law, referred to the "hortatory" function.

The first position can accommodate, though it does not require, ideas of uncertainty, indeterminacy and even chaos in law. The second idea works best when we assume that in talking about law we deal with a thing that can be known accurately, at least in theory. Clear messages can be sent and received, even when they are complex. This assumption raises the problems reviewed here.

I. MESSAGES SENT

We might compare this idea of a clear legal message with some other ideas about law in general. Thus, Robert Gordon points out that "History helps to teach us that the rule of law 'system' is fundamentally misdescribed, that inspected at close range, it's not really a system at all, but a complex mess of competing and contradictory systems." Grant Gilmore comments that "When we think of our own or of any other legal system, the beginning of wisdom lies in the recognition that the body of the law, at any time or place, is an unstable mass in precarious equilibrium." Gilmore's comments are particularly striking as coming from a scholar who spent his professional life working in fields—contracts and commercial law—in which formalism and theory were dominant ideas and certainty a prime legal value. If these legal contexts could produce and illustrate Gilmore's view, we would expect that this sense of instability and uncertainty would pervade the area of family law where the need for individualization is taken for granted. Indeed, these descriptions of law in general have their analogues in work on family law. Thus, Carl Schneider describes the complexity of the sources of family law, the non-theoretical nature of family law scholarship and the "rarity of attempts" in this field to "go beyond the specific." He writes: "It is hard to produce a systematic view of an unsystematic subject, and perhaps family law must always be ad hoc, responsive to local conditions, sensitive to the day's sensibilities, and willing to compromise irreconcilable differences." Judith Areen describes the relatively "undeveloped state of secular thinking about family life," with particular application to surrogacy questions. Martha Minow discusses the Supreme Court decisions in relation to group conflict, suggesting that the Supreme Court has used debates about family, state and individual to mediate larger social struggles. Thus, "it should not be surprising that constitutional rhetoric about the family is confused and inconsistent."

When we look at the things which law is—things we might legitimately look at in determining a message—we see constitutions, legislation, judicial opinions, official behavior of all sorts. All contribute to the "symbolism" of law or the message that law sends out. This message or symbolism will necessarily not be uniform or consistent since law carries many values. All of this is true in all areas of law, but particularly in family law which is inevitably focused on individuals, and using open standards. It is not merely, as Tennyson had it, that law is a "wilderness of single instances." It is that each single instance can be said to stand for different things. The point is familiar in general. The leading example is probably *Everson v. Board of Education,* in which the holding and rhetoric were so far apart that dissenting Justice Jackson invoked the precedent of Byron's Julia, who "whispering 'I will ne'er consent,'—consented."

In the area of family law, we might consider the messages sent by a single text, *Marvin v. Marvin.* First, the opinion recites the facts of cohabitation as if they matter to the legal system, thus reinforcing the idea that law's function is principally to be responsive to social facts. Then the court opts for a kind of responsibility, by generally recognizing the enforceability of cohabitation contracts, as long as the explicit consideration is something other than meretricious sexual services. The last point is a signal in the direction of traditional moral values and the existing case law. Finally, the court, having gone a long way toward recognizing quasi or alternate marriage, speaks eloquently about marriage:

> The mores of the society have indeed changed so radically in regard to
> cohabitation that we cannot impose a standard based on alleged moral con-

siderations that have apparently been so widely abandoned by so many. Lest we be misunderstood, however, we take this occasion to point out that the structure of society itself largely depends on the institution of marriage, and nothing we have said in this opinion should be taken to derogate from that institution. The joining of the man and woman in marriage is at once the most socially productive and individually fulfilling relationship that one can enjoy in the course of a lifetime.

Considered as a teaching tool, the *Marvin* opinion can be used for many lessons or it can be used for one: expansion of rights of cohabitants. The *Marvin* case, or any case, can be reduced to a proposition or a statement of law, or a holding, or a finite point of view on a problem. However, this approach (which the formal system, integrating its various structural parts and its majority and dissenting opinions, makes possible) is not the approach which those interested in expressive or symbolic functions would take. Even if one did this, the central question of message would remain. Is "expansion of the rights of cohabitants" a symbolic move away from the values of responsibility and cohesion associated with marriage, or a symbolic move towards those values now associated with nonmarital associations?

The problem of "what is the law" is behind one of the criticisms of a well-known 1958 study comparing law and community moral standards on a number of family law issues. As a number of reviewers suggested, the treatment of law was static. The law was taken to mean "law ready to be applied." Said one reviewer, this seems to mean "an application of statutes and judicial precedent without insight or imagination."

The complexity of legal messages suggested here goes beyond what might be viewed as an ordered dialogue or a deliberate attempt to incorporate many voices. The pluralism of law seems to be something that is less planned, less obviously representative of the opinions of identifiable groups. The pluralism of law may not even reflect what we might see as judgments which are surely universal, easy cases. The law of contracts continues to suggest, for example, that a man's feeling for his bull is more important than his feeling for his son.

Assuming there is a law, or rule of law that can be known accurately in principle, we confront the problem of whether it is known in fact. It is suggested that law is known, though somewhat inaccurately, by the public. Even Stanley Kowalski knows that Louisiana is under the Napoleonic Code. The point is made that the message sent is received, but imperfectly.

II. MESSAGES RECEIVED

What do we know about how law is understood?

One approach turns to empirical studies. That material itself is not voluminous. However, a general feeling exists that people do not know much about the law or the legal system. One problem relates to the sources of information about law. Newspapers and broadcast media are listed as prime sources, with informal networks of friends and family following. Lawrence Friedman, reviewing Michael Kammen's book on the Constitution, suggested that people learned what they know from the six o'clock news. Information may be filtered through individuals and groups in a way which is independently worth our attention.

Another response is impressionistic. Thus, Thurman Arnold tells us that: "The trader takes heart by learning that the law ignores the more profitable forms of dishonesty in deference to the principle of individual freedom from governmental restraint. The preacher, however, is glad to learn that all forms of dishonesty which can be curbed without interfering with freedom or with economic law are being curbed."

Still impressionistically, another answer might go to other sources, other understandings, and use those sources as material speaking to this question. At the level of popular material, journalism, or detective fiction, one finds understandings of the law which are not necessarily those of Austinian jurisprudence. For example, in mystery stories, one sometimes finds that multiple legal systems are understood as operating in the world. Ed McBain's *Blood Relatives* tells of a woman wondering whether sexual relations and marriage between cousins are forbidden by the state or only by the church. Arthur Upfield sees two systems, aboriginal and western, tracking the same criminal. Sometimes the issue of the limits of state enforcement in relation to multiple systems of authority is clear. Thus, Philip Mason's *Call the Next Witness* contains a move and counter-move description of a murder trial (based on a case in India in 1931) that centrally involves the relative power of family groups and the Indian legal system. When it deals with the official system, detective fiction may be far from sanguine about its operation. Thus, Austin Freeman comments: "unspeakably dreary and depressing were the brief proceedings that followed, and dreadfully suggestive of the helplessness of even an innocent man on whom the law has laid its hand and in whose behalf its inexorable machinery has been set in motion." These points suggest the possibility of a general knowledge not of legal rules or doctrines but of legal pluralism and the limits of law in the culture.

One also suspects the possibility of vast ignorance of the role of law in general going far beyond ignorance of specific rights or rules in the legal system. Most obviously this may be true of children. Stephen Wizner offered an anecdote relating to a nine-year-old child in a burglary trial:

"Did we win or lose?"
"We won."
"Yeah? What did we win?"

The child was told that "what he had 'won' was a decision that he 'didn't do it . . . .'" The child answered—"but I *didn't* do it." However, ignorance and misunderstanding may also characterize the thinking of adults. Questions might be asked, not about knowledge of rules in the state legal system, but about legal ideas more broadly. A study of knowledge of law might well start with questions devoted to the problem of marriage as a state-created relationship. For example, do people know that two people must participate in an officially structured procedure? *Hewitt v. Hewitt* involved two people who lived together from 1960 until 1975. In that case, the defendant "told her that they were husband and wife and would live as such, no formal ceremony being necessary . . . ." States of knowledge in this case may be suggested as ranging from knowledge of common law marriage via language in the present tense, to knowledge failing to include the idea that both people have to do something to get married. Do people know that they do not have to "ask" for a divorce? That "grounds" are generally no longer necessary?

Will it turn out that the law that people "know" is the law of their childhood? How do people answer or think they should answer the question "were you ever married" when their marriages have been annulled?

Some journalistic discussions of the family in America contain comments about American family law that initially seem to be in the "ignorance" category. Thus, Barbara Ehrenreich, in *The Hearts of Men,* writes: "Men cannot be forced to marry; once married, they cannot be forced to bring home their paychecks, to be reliable jobholders, or of course to remain married." What is meant by the idea that people cannot be forced to do something? Is this about a theory of sanctions, or the limits on physical compulsion? Does she mean that American law does not command men to marry? What is meant by the idea that men do not have to—cannot be forced to—bring home their paychecks? Is there some underlying problem about the idea of the support obligation? Finally, while at the time Ehrenreich wrote people could not be forced to remain married, she presumably knew that the history of the law of divorce is about the problem of forcing reluctant couples to remain married. Yet perhaps these comments by Ehrenreich can be best understood not as a description of actual or possible legal rules, but as a description of effective law or legal results in fact. It may be that people know something about the practical limits of law, as much as about the power and efficacy of law.

CONCLUSION

Family law is a particularly important point at which to examine problems of the expressive function of law. It already contains many examples of messages. Proposals are heard to the effect that it should contain more, despite the acknowledgement that the effectiveness of law is limited. For example, Max Rheinstein concluded that law was not a prime determinant of behavior in relation to marital stability. Mary Ann Glendon notes that the relation between law and behavior are uncertain, and that other factors are critical. Scholars whose concern is law/society issues suggest that law may not be very important in causing particular behavior.

Even if we assume some effectiveness, the problem remains "what message?" One possibility is a message of facilitation of private choice, which may finally lead to the proposition that marriage is not a useful legal idea. Another message would try to invoke the now-gone consensus of the Christian nation.

The fact that the consensus is gone is a point on which we agree. However, that agreement creates a problem, since we want our law of the family to be not merely not evil, but affirmatively good. As Lee Teitelbaum suggests,

> It does not seem enough . . . to content ourselves with saying only that some rule cannot be shown to produce evil. While that may suffice for a commercial contract or the occasional tort, there is some feeling that family relationships should be founded on rules and practices we can call good.

But what we can call "good," and how to justify the description, is precisely the issue that remains unclear. "Like just about every other long-standing institution," Clifford Geertz tells us, "—religion, art, science, the state, the family—law is in the process of learning to survive without the certitudes that launched it." The process is associated in law with the realists and so we return to Grant Gilmore. He wrote in 1951:

> At twenty years distance we may with the prescience of hindsight pass judgment. Llewellyn and his co-conspirators were right in everything they said about the law. They skillfully led us into the swamp. Their mistake was in being sure that they knew the way out of the swamp: they did not, at least we are still there.

Decades later, it is as true in family law as in much else.

But there is something in family law that makes the matter peculiarly difficult. The problem is centrally that we care so much, and that law, finally, can do so little. As to this, it may be that the public is more sensitive to reality than some lawyers. Here is Trollope, particularly acute on the failure of the law to provide anything approaching an adequate remedy in certain situations. In *Kept in the Dark*, involving the concealment of a wife's previous engagement, the wife, rejected by her husband, considers the law's relevance to her situation. The idea of the "limits of law" could not be more clearly set out.

> She could not force him to be her companion. The law would give her only those things which she did not care to claim. He already offered more than the law would exact, and she despised his generosity. As long as he supported her the law could not bring him back and force him to give her to eat of his own loaf, and to drink of his own cup. . . . He had said that he had gone, and would not return, and the law could not bring him back again.

The strength of inquiries into the expressive functions of law is that they focus not only on the formal content of the decision, but also on its effect and tone. They direct attention away from the decision maker, powerful and authoritative, and towards the audiences which the decision both addresses and reflects. While emphasis on rule and decision making gets us to clarification and thus simplification, emphasis on rhetoric gets us to complexity and contradiction. Given the circumstances, while we must somehow still decide things, we might do well to announce our decisions in a less certain voice.

C. The Effectiveness of Family Law

The last question our readings ask is a basic one: How well do the institutions that make and administer family law do their job? How well do they understand the problems of the family? How wisely do they craft laws affecting the family? How ably do they administer those laws? These are questions which can hardly be answered in one reading. In a sense each of the readings in this book has implicitly addressed them. In this last selection, we want to address them explicitly, with particular attention to the work of courts. We do so through the vehicle of a review of a particularly illuminating book—Robert H. Mnookin, et al., IN THE INTEREST OF CHILDREN: ADVOCACY, LAW REFORM, AND PUBLIC POLICY. That book is primarily a detailed study of five cases in which issues involving children became the subject of constitutional litigation.

Carl E. Schneider, *Lawyers and Children: Wisdom and Legitimacy in Family Policy,* 84 MICHIGAN LAW REVIEW 919 (1986)[*]

I. WHAT DOES THE BOOK SAY?

The book's admirable idea is to answer the question whether "test-case litigation [is] a sensible way to promote the welfare of children" (p. ix) by anatomizing five examples of test-case litigation, not just in terms of their doctrinal bases and implications, but also by investigating how they came to be litigated; what tactical, ethical, social, and institutional issues they raised and how they resolved them; and what social and legal consequences they had.

The first case study is of *Smith v. Organization of Foster Families for Equality and Reform (OFFER)* and is by Professor David L. Chambers, of the University of Michigan Law School, and Professor Michael S. Wald, of the Stanford Law School. *OFFER* began with a real client, Madeleine Smith, who had a real problem—that child-welfare authorities in New York City wished to remove her foster children from her home. Ms. Smith persuaded Marcia Lowry, a lawyer with the Children's Rights Project of the New York Civil Liberties Union, to represent her and her foster children. Ms. Lowry's complaint argued that foster parents who have cared for a child for at least a year have a constitutionally protected interest in the child such that he may not be moved (even to be returned to his natural parents) without a prior hearing more complete than those then provided for by New York State and New York City. Louise Gans, a lawyer on the staff of Community Action for Legal Services, intervened on behalf of the class of natural parents with children in foster care; Helen Buttenwieser, a lawyer whose clients included private agencies that handled foster care, was appointed by the three-judge district court to represent the class of foster children. After a one-day trial,

---

[*]   Copyright © 1986. Reprinted with permission.

the court held that foster *children* have a constitutional right to a hearing before a transfer, that the foster parents could not waive the right, and that therefore such a hearing must precede *any* transfer. The Supreme Court reversed, holding that it did not have to decide whether foster parents and children have a constitutionally protected interest in their relationship because New York's procedures already met the standard of due process required where such an interest is governmentally infringed.

Doctrinally, *OFFER* was anti-climactic. Practically, *OFFER* had some immediate effects: Early in the litigation, the authorities decided not to remove Ms. Smith's foster children; later in the litigation New York City (but not New York State) instituted formal hearings for foster children being transferred to another foster home. Ultimately, however, Professors Chambers and Wald conclude that

> the new rules do not appear to have brought substantial change to the system either directly or by inspiring changes elsewhere. . . . Each year since 1975, there have been more than one thousand . . . transfers, but, for only twenty or thirty of them were hearings held. It is nonetheless true that in about 45 percent of the hearings that are held, the agency decision is reversed.

In the Interest of Children's second case study is of *Bellotti v. Baird* and is by Professor Mnookin. In 1974, Massachusetts enacted a law that required any unmarried minor seeking an abortion to have the consent of her parents or, if her parents denied consent, of a judge. Bill Baird, who operated a Boston abortion clinic, filed an action claiming the statute violated the equal protection clause. A group of parents intervened in favor of the statute. A three-judge district court held a three-day hearing and, with one dissent, found the law unconstitutional, but the Supreme Court remanded the case to the Massachusetts Supreme Judicial Court for an "authoritative construction" of the statute. After receiving that construction, the federal district court held a second brief trial and again found the law unconstitutional. During that proceeding, a coalition including the Planned Parenthood League of Massachusetts was allowed to intervene as a plaintiff. The Supreme Court affirmed the district court's result with only one dissent, but it split 4-4 over its reasons. Justice Powell's opinion for one bloc advised states that they may require parental consent to a minor's abortion if the minor can, without notifying her parents, seek a judicial finding that an abortion is in her vest interests or that she is "mature" enough to decide for herself whether to have an abortion. The Massachusetts legislature passed such a statute, and, after nearly seven years of litigation, it went into effect.

Professor Mnookin reports that hearings under the statute are prompt, brief, and informal. But his most striking conclusion is that *"[e]very pregnant minor who has sought judicial authorization for an abortion has secured an abortion"* (p. 239; emphasis in original). In the statute's first two years, some 1300 girls sought such authorization. Ninety percent of them were found mature enough to decide for themselves to have an abortion; an abortion was found to be in the best interests of ten percent; and five girls were originally denied an abortion, of whom four were granted one on appeal and one had her abortion in another state. Whether more teenagers benefit or suffer because of the statute is a question Professor Mnookin discusses searchingly but believes cannot be answered. . . .

The fourth case study is of *Roe v. Norton* and is by Professor Stephen D. Sugarman, of the University of California at Berkeley School of Law. In 1971, responding to its own inclinations and to pressure from the federal government, Connecticut passed a statute threatening with jail for contempt of court any mother receiving Aid to Families with Dependent Children who refused to identify the father of any of her children who were AFDC beneficiaries. Two legal-aid lawyers had clients who wished not to provide that information, and cases they filed were consolidated before a three-judge district court. The court, *sua sponte*, appointed a former legal-aid lawyer to represent the class of children of such mothers. In 1973, after a one-day trial, the court upheld the statute. On appeal, the American Civil Liberties Union, the Children's Defense Fund, and the Welfare Law Center contributed amicus briefs. However, the Supreme Court remanded for reconsideration in light of new federal legislation withholding benefits from uncooperative mothers. In 1975, that legislation was amended to excuse mothers who had "good cause for refusing to cooperate . . . in accordance with standards prescribed by [HEW], which standards shall take into consideration the best interests of the child . . ." (p. 418). HEW's standards were not proposed until August 1976 and were not final until December 1978, after long lobbying and legislative and administrative debate.

Professor Sugarman concludes that "[t]he rules governing coerced maternal cooperation in Connecticut today resemble those before 1969" (p. 429). The class of exceptions is narrow. True, "[t]he exceptions are more clearly spelled out today than in 1968 and only the mother's share of AFDC is at risk." Yet Professor Sugarman believes "these differences are largely irrelevant in practice" (p. 429). He argues that we cannot tell whether more children are helped than hurt by these standards. . . .

The Final Observations

Professor Mnookin concludes *In the Interest of Children* with some brief but probing final observations. He sees the case studies as raising the question of how power over children's lives should be allocated among children, parents, and the various branches of government. More particularly, the cases dealt "primarily with the needs of poor children, minority children, and children with special handicaps" (p. 514). He proposes that "the dilemma of legitimacy . . . is perhaps less troublesome when courts intervene on behalf of children with extraordinary needs" (p. 514), since such children both need more from the state and are less likely to have parents politically able to help them get it. Nevertheless, the prediction and value problems remain, and—exactly because such children and their parents lack power—the problem of the advocate's accountability is intensified.

Turning to the judicial role, Professor Mnookin finds that "the litigation process is not always a deliberative, methodical, rational way of arriving at a decision" (p. 517), and he reminds us that the choice of the judicial forum shapes the way a policy question is framed, the influence of the possible actors, and the nature of the answer. However, he observes that, in these five cases, courts often looked for compromises or for ways of transmuting substantive disputes into due process solutions. "In sum these studies suggest that the courts have been very modest in what they are willing to do" (p. 521). They are neither the imperial judiciary of their critics' fears nor the bold reformers of their enthusiasts' hopes.

III. WHAT CAN WE MAKE OF WHAT THE BOOK SAYS?

In the Interest of Children is about how well and how legitimately family law policy can be made through constitutional "test-case" litigation. As Professor Mnookin observes, both judicial success and judicial legitimacy depend on judicial capacity to identify standards for measuring the "best interests" of children and to apply those standards to particular cases. In constitutional litigation, these questions of capacity depend on the clarity of the constitutional text, on the litigants' ability to identify and articulate their own interests and thereby provide the court information it needs with which to make policy, and on the court's ability to analyze and remedy the problems a case raises. *In the Interest of Children* raises doubts about each of these three factors.

The first factor—the clarity of the constitutional text—is important as one method of resolving what Professor Mnookin calls the "value problem," the problem of deciding what criteria should be used in choosing between policies for children. In this respect, the cases described in *In the Interest of Children* may usefully be compared with *Brown v. Board of Education.* However many complexities the Court may subsequently have encountered in its school-desegregation travails, it was guided in *Brown* by a constitutional provision widely understood to make a basic moral and social statement about government and race. While that statement could be implemented in many ways, its importance, strength, and (relative) simplicity gave unity and direction to the Court's labors. None of the authors of *In the Interest of Children*, on the other hand, really suggests that genuine guidance can be inferred from the various texts that have been thought relevant to children's issues, and even Professor Mnookin's intimation that children might be a "discrete and insular minority" (pp. 41-42) seems halfhearted and perhaps not intended to convince. In any event, since much has been written before about these controversies, little need be said here.

As to the other questions of judicial capacity, however, the book provides evidence from which some generalizations might be inferred, particularly about the interaction of what Professor Mnookin calls the "prediction problem"—the difficulty of predicting the consequences of alternative children's policies—with questions of judicial capacity and legitimacy. Each of the book's authors stresses the complexity of the social problems at issue in each case. Each author demonstrates tellingly what is therefore hardly surprising—that systematic empirical information and skill in analyzing it are needed for understanding the social problems each case concerned. Each author also demonstrates that the complexity of these problems, obvious as it seems, is either unperceived or disregarded by the makers of judicial family policy. What inferences can be drawn, then, from *In the Interest of Children* about the success and legitimacy of test-case litigation in light of the fact that lawyers and judges need this kind of information and skill?

A. *The Independence of the "Child Advocate"*

Judges learn about the social problems a case presents primarily from the lawyers who argue it. Judges depend on lawyers to identify accurately the interests of their clients and to relate fully the information that supports the policies that are in the interests of those clients. Lawyers, in turn, depend on their clients, whom we expect to know their own situations and to bear the consequences of ignorance. And ordinarily lawyers are constrained, if not controlled, by their clients: they need clients before they can bring suit, they are ethically required to serve the client's interest as the client understands it, they learn about the client's problems through the client, and if the client wishes to settle the case, the lawyer is obliged to oblige. But in test-case litigation involving children, it is exactly the problem that children cannot speak for themselves. (Indeed, it is the fact that children lack a voice in government that, in the minds of many of its practitioners, justifies such litigation.) Thus, what is perhaps most striking about the litigation described in *In the Interest of Children* is that, in each case, lawyers were in a meaningful sense not constrained by clients: the hand was the hand of the client, but the voice was the voice of the lawyer.

What is the nature of this independence? How does it affect the choice of interests and policies to be urged on the judge? How does it affect the provision of information to the judge? To these questions we now turn.

The "child advocates'" independence of their clients in test-case litigation has, as *In the Interest of Children* reveals, many sources. The first of these sources is one Professor Mnookin emphasizes: the clients are children and therefore cannot make decisions or speak for themselves. Children's decisions are usually made by their parents, and thus children's lawyers are ordinarily instructed by children's parents. But in cases like *OFFER, Bellotti, Norton,* . . . the question whether the parent was serving the child's interest was itself at issue. Furthermore, even where, as in *OFFER* and *Norton,* lawyers represented adults, those adults often did not control the lawyer: Not only did someone other than the client pay the lawyer, but the named clients in each case . . . dropped out of the case fairly early, their individual problems having been solved. Indeed, some named clients were hardly in the case at all, since, as happened most conspicuously in *OFFER* and most questionably in *Bellotti* (pp. 172-73), they were recruited by the lawyers expressly to allow the lawyers to represent particular points of view.

The lawyers described in *In the Interest of Children* were, then, generally not controlled by named clients. The lawyers' freedom was enhanced by the facts that, in each case, at least some of the lawyers represented either a class or a group of clients and that, in each case, the interests of the members of the class conflicted. . . . The diversity of the class' interests helped free the lawyers to pick for themselves the interests to be urged upon the court. Thus, for instance, one lawyer in *OFFER* declined even to meet her named clients on the ground that "it would be a 'trap' to become embroiled in arguing about the fates of a few children when the real issues at stake were so much broader" (p. 93).

Similar problems with the lawyers' role appear in many, perhaps most, kinds of public interest litigation. Often, however, such litigation is paid for and controlled by organizations whose members are themselves members of the group whose ill treatment the lawyers hope to correct. Those interest groups may have some ability to instruct and supervise their lawyers. Even such groups, of course, can have real difficulties over-seeing lawyers, partly because lawyers sometimes claim exclusive expertise in decid-ing whether and how to litigage. But what is striking about the lawyers described in *In the Interest of Children* is that so many of them initiated suits and conducted litigation quite without genuine supervision from their organizational clients. . . .

If these lawyers are often neither instructed by their clients nor supervised by their employers, how do they decide what the public interest is and what policies to advo-cate for children? *In the Interest of Children* says little about this question, possibly because the lawyers themselves seem hardly to have considered it. One would suppose (and the book sometimes intimates) that lawyers' policy preferences are drawn from their experiences with other clients and opponents, informed by their ideological opinions and their law school training. But given the inexperience of many of these lawyers, given the inescapable narrowness of their training, given the lawyer's neces-sarily limited perspective on a client's problems, and given the prejudice with which lawyers come to view their opponents' positions, the lawyer's experience seems a dis-concerting basis for making policy choices in so complex an area as family law. Nev-ertheless, the lawyers who were asked seemed sanguine about relying on it. One of the NYCLU's lawyers in *OFFER*, for example, thought that children's rights litigation does not "raise such sophisticated issues that you need development experts" (p. 136). And none of the lawyers in that difficult case "saw any need for expert advice for guidance regarding the positions to advance" (p. 133).

The independence of the child's advocate from the child and even from those who hire him raises, then, two kinds of questions. First, how well can the child advocate inform courts? Second, how does the child advocate's independence affect the legiti-macy of judicial decisions that purport to evaluate the constitutional adequacy of a leg-islative policy or to compensate for the child's nonrepresentation in the elected branches of government? The seriousness of these questions will depend in part on the capacity of courts to understand and solve problems of public policy for children, and we will now ask what light *In the Interest of Children* sheds on that capacity.

B. *The Capacity of Courts*

However troubling it is that lawyers who are freed to formulate positions on pub-lic policy seem ill-suited to do so, the adversary process and judicial insight might nev-ertheless flush out all that judges need to know to make wise policy. *In the Interest of Children,* however, suggests reasons to doubt that this happens. We begin with the set of reasons that has to do with a court's ability to collect and interpret information in test-case litigation.

The first kind of problem in this respect was that these proceedings too often lacked the virtues and yet had the faults of an adversary system of justice. For exam-ple, an adversary system depends on a rough equality between the lawyers for each side. But in each of these cases, the government's lawyers seem to have been badly out-matched: The public interest lawyers tended to come from better law schools and to have greater resources—money, time, research services, and the like—than their opponents. Thus, the state's position often seems to have been, relatively, weakly presented. An adversary system, particularly one relied on to formulate social policy in a large and baffling area, also depends on some genuine adverseness between the parties to generate evidence and sharpen argument. In these cases, however, the evidence presented to the courts was limited by the fact that, at some point in each of the cases, the parties had only slight differences. . . .

Not only were some of the adversary system's advantages for collecting information absent in these cases, but some of its impediments were present. In each case, for example, the lawyers seem not to have believed that representing the public interest obliged them to depart from the usual practice of exploiting every ethical litigational advantage. Thus, lawyers for children opposed the appointment of additional lawyers who might have represented more fully the interests of all the children in the class (p. 141), attempted to limit the witnesses and issues presented to courts (p. 141), and used technicalities to prevent a case from being heard on appeal (p. 378).

This brings us to the second kind of limit on the court's ability to collect information in test-case litigation involving children: The hearing in each of the cases was stunningly inadequate. In none of the cases was there a genuine trial of the major issues at stake; . . . hearings lasted from only one to three days. This brevity was sometimes commanded by the court and sometimes caused by the parties. In either event, the court learned little about the named parties, the class, the immediate problem, or the larger social issues. Much of the evidence presented related to the named plaintiffs, partly for tactical reasons and partly, one suspects, because that is what lawyers customarily do. Yet in test-case litigation, anecdotes about a few individuals can rarely be enlightening and are often misleading. And little though the trial judges could have learned from these hearings, the appellate judges who finally decided those cases surely learned even less, since it is unlikely that they read the full trial record.

The third limit on the judicial capacity to collect information is that to ask lawyers in "social policy" cases to be genuinely and thoroughly illuminating is to ask a great deal. Each author of *In the Interest of Children* devastatingly shows the inadequacy of the social information presented in these cases. To some extent, systematic evidence was simply unavailable. To a considerable extent, the lawyers failed to grasp the relevance of what was available or to use experts to inform themselves and the court. Where systematic evidence was available and where lawyers tried to use it, its complexity and ambiguity prevented lawyers from effectively gathering, analyzing, and presenting it, and courts from assimilating it.

Judicial understanding of the social problems presented by test-case litigation for children seems, then, to be hampered by severe problems in acquiring information and ideas. These problems are simultaneously exacerbated and eased (or evaded) by a set of judicial (and lawyer's) attitudes that might be called hyper-rationalism.

Hyper-rationalism is essentially the substitution of reason for information and analysis. It has two components: first, the belief that reason can reliably be used to infer facts where evidence is unavailable or incomplete, and second, the practice of interpreting facts through a set of artificial analytic categories. The first component of hyper-rationalism has three related aspects. In its first aspect, it is the assumption that systematic evidence is generally superfluous to understanding social problems, since the behavior of people and institutions can be logically inferred from a general under-standing of how people and institutions work. In its second aspect, it is the assumption that, in the absence of a general understanding of how people and institutions work, anecdotal evidence is generally sufficient, since the behavior of people and institutions can be logically inferred from a few examples of their actual behavior under the rele-vant circumstances. In its third aspect, it is the assumption that a description of social reality articulated in one case may be taken as demonstrated fact in subsequent cases; it is, in other words, the application of *stare decisis* to evidence about social behavior.

All three attitudes recurred in the cases described in *In the Interest of Children* and are manifest in the evidence presented to and recited by the judges. These attitudes are not, of course, uniquely judicial; they are probably common among public officials, who must formulate policy quickly and who are often temperamentally disinclined to learn about an issue through systematic reading. However, these attitudes are more problematic when held by judges, who lack the general administrative experience and the particular subject-matter expertise that officials can use in interpreting sketchy information and who are ill-situated to revise a policy as experience with it teaches new lessons.

The second component of hyper-rationalism is the practice of analyzing social problems in terms of a small set of legal categories. Legal categories are troublesome and necessary for the same reason—they are a limited set of abstractions from social reality. Legal categories may be specially awkward when the law makes policy for fam-ilies, since many of the values of family life are notoriously nonlegal and extra-ratio-nal. But even aside from this difficulty, drawbacks of analyzing a social problem in terms of the legal categories available abound in *In the Interest of Children*. For instance, judicial policymaking was repeatedly impaired by the fact that each of the . . . cases concerned (and the plaintiffs' lawyers and many of the judges were primar-ily interested in) a perplexing social problem, but the legal issue the cases presented was rarely an apt means of addressing that problem: The legal issue often spoke only indirectly to the social problem; to resolve the legal issue in a way that contributed to resolving the social problem often would have required a remedy far beyond judicial authority; and to define the legal issue so as to give a court scope in solving the social problem often risked creating legal doctrines with unanticipated and unwanted conse-quences. This point is made with particular clarity by Professors Wald and Chambers in their discussion of *OFFER*, but it was or could have been made by each of the authors. *Bellotti* is centrally about the dilemmas of adolescent pregnancy; . . . *Norton* about how the interests of mothers and children receiving welfare can be reconciled and served. . . . Yet the legal issue in each case was defined in terms of (usually procedural, sometimes substantive) due process, and each case was in part resolved by a provision for some kind of hearing.

Due process devices were prominent in these cases not only because due process is the most convenient and plausible category for judicially addressing problems of family policy; due process also allows judges to hope that the social complexity which escapes their immediate understanding and reach will be taken into account in the newly revised process of decision. Yet, on the evidence of these cases, that hope seems unfounded. Few foster parents have used the hearing assured by *OFFER*; virtually every girl who sought judicial authorization for an abortion after *Bellotti* received it; hardly any mothers have fully pursued the procedural rights they secured in the process of which *Norton* was a part, and Professor Sugarman questions whether the fight over the *Norton* regulations "has made any important difference" (p. 429); . . . These results accord with Dean Yudof's conclusion that "[e]xperience with recent federal acts creating procedural rights for parents suggests that few take advantage of these statutory rights" and with Professor Mashaw's observation that "[t]he *Goldberg* requirement of extensive pretermination hearings has not produced a huge, or even very substantial, increase in the number of hearings held."

The difficulties presented by both components of judicial hyper-rationalism can be seen by examining another common feature of these cases. Each case, with the possible exception of *Bellotti*, has centrally to do with a bureaucracy. In each case, a court was asked to make a bureaucracy work "better." Few judges are equipped by training, experience, or temperament to understand bureaucracies. Nevertheless, their hyper-rationalism allows them to believe that their experience with conducting or evaluating trials makes them expert in governmental procedure of all kinds.

The quality of bureaucratic work depends on the characteristics of the particular bureaucracy, of its staff, and of its leaders. But because judges believe they can understand how all bureaucracies work through *a priori* reasoning, they resist inquiring into the individual character of a bureaucracy. Further, because judges are bound to use a limited number of legal categories in dealing with bureaucracies, it is hard for judges to interpret the law in a way that allows for variations between bureaucracies and within a single bureaucracy over time. The upshot of this, as we have just seen, is that judges try to improve bureaucracies by imposing on them procedures that are, at best, *pro forma* or unused. The judicial cure for the ills of bureaucracy is more bureaucracy.

Not only does hyper-rationalism lead courts to impose on bureaucracies and their clients procedures which are, like the hearings described above, unused or meaningless. It also allows courts to underestimate greatly both the difficulties of persuading a bureaucracy to act in the way a court wishes and the resourcefulness of recusant bureaucrats. In other words, because courts substitute anecdote for evidence and legal categories for social analysis, they do not ask why bureaucrats think and act as they do. And because courts do not understand the assumptions of and pressures on bureaucrats, courts are ill-fitted to win their cooperation (and, because of the paucity of judicial remedies and the scarcity of judicial time, ill-equipped to coerce it).

OFFER exemplifies many of these features of the hyper-rational approach to bureaucracies. In that case, the social problem was to ensure that foster children are wisely treated, and thus a central question was whether hearings would improve the bureaucracy's decisions. That question was to be answered for the whole country on the basis of evidence about only two bureaucracies and of a small set of legal assumptions about how hearings generally affect bureaucratic decisions. But it depends on an almost endless number of considerations, many of which will vary from one bureaucracy to another and within a single bureaucracy over time. Will a hearing officer make a better decision than a case worker? Can anything systematic be learned about the comparative sensitivity, training, experience, energy, or judgment of those two bureaucrats? Is the hearing officer a worn-out caseworker or a caseworker whose ability has been rewarded by promotion? Is a caseworker's personal acquaintance with the people involved a help or a hindrance? How important is speed in making a decision? How will hearings affect the morale of caseworkers? Their attitudes toward their clients? Their willingness to take necessary risks? Will the prospect of hearings encourage the caseworker to think more carefully, or merely to avoid making reviewable decisions? To follow rules more faithfully, or to doctor the paper record? Will hearings lead to the formulation of clearer standards for the removal of children? Are clearer standards better standards, or is it preferable to use vaguer standards that preserve a measure of discretion? Is the cost of hearings worth the price? Would the money have been better spent hiring another caseworker? Hiring another supervisor? Improving training programs? Improving record-keeping? Raising salaries to attract abler caseworkers? Does the usefulness of hearings vary with the size of the bureaucracy? Will hearings affect a bureaucracy's ability to recruit and retain foster parents? Its ability to persuade natural parents to put children in foster care? And so on and on.

In these two sections, we have been examining how judicial understanding of public policy affecting children may be limited by judicial problems in acquiring and analyzing evidence. We have seen that for structural and attitudinal reasons, judges are exposed to only a fraction of the information that they need and that they rely on an analytic framework which is often incomplete and ill-fitting. An obvious source of both information and analysis is the social sciences, and these cases often do indicate that the social sciences need to be better used. But I am not arguing that courts should simply shift the burden of decision onto the social sciences. For familiar and understandable reasons, social science evidence is too incomplete, social science theory is too fragile, and social science value choices are too problematic to justify such a tactic.

Nor does my criticism of the incompleteness of the information, analysis, and remedies in these cases imply that the only good policy is a global one, one that tries conclusively to understand and finally to solve the whole problem all at once. On the contrary, there is much to be said for incrementalism, for what Professor Lindblom, in a famous article, called "the science of muddling through." Because incrementalism is a relatively cautious and modest approach to social policy, it seems plausible that courts might be able to make workable contributions to child welfare through incremental changes in policy. But even an incrementalist approach ought to be informed by the best available evidence and the most appropriate analytic framework. It is the apparent failure to achieve that level of understanding that raises questions about whether, even used incrementally, "test-case litigation [is] a sensible way to promote the welfare of children."

Incrementalism is less promising a method of judicial child welfare reform than it might first seem for another reason. Incrementalism requires flexibility and a close and constant attention to the problem being addressed, so that changes can be made as successes and failures emerge. In some ways, courts seem well suited to those requirements. Indeed, the traditional explanation of common law development neatly fits the incrementalist model. That explanation sees courts as deciding a long series of cases each dealing with a small part of a social problem. From the series of holdings courts gradually induce a principle which is itself susceptible to gradual change as further holdings are assimilated.

As a description of how courts actually decide cases, this theory obviously has many deficiencies, but it may help direct us toward two impediments to successful incrementalism in test-case litigation over children's policy. First, such litigation is constitutional, not common law, litigation, and as such it tends to be deductive, not inductive. The Constitution provides not only a text to apply, but embodies principles of importance. This makes it easier for courts to feel they are equipped to deal with whole problems and not just increments of problems (since the text and principles presumably pre-empt many of the aspects of a problem that might otherwise be addressed incrementally) and it makes it harder for courts to respond flexibly (because it is harder to back down over an issue of principle and because of the need to maintain consistent application of a principle over the entire range of assimilable problems). Second, there may simply be too few cases to generate real familiarity with many of the problems children's policy raises and to allow for frequent small adjustments of policy. From this point of view, test-case litigation involving numerous enforcement cases (like *Brown*) ought, *ceteris paribus*, to produce better judicial policy than litigation (like *OFFER*, *Bellotti*, [and] *Norton* . . .) resolved in relatively few cases. Similarly, test-case litigation involving institutions . . . ought to produce better judicial policy than other such reform efforts (again, like *OFFER*, *Bellotti*, [and] *Norton*, . . .), at least to the extent that the intensive interaction between court and institution which is thought to typify institutional litigation forces the court to learn in detail about the particular entity it seeks to change. Yet even these instances of better judicial policy (if such they be) import their own limits: only a greatly expanded judiciary could afford such attention to more than a very few areas of litigation, and it is exactly the intensity of judicial involvement that has provoked criticism of the school desegregation and institutional cases.